P9-BYQ-815

2000

Better Homes and Gardens®

ANNUAL
Recipes
2000

Better Homes and Gardens® Books
Des Moines, Iowa

The question I am most often asked as a food editor is "Where do you get all of your recipes?" Fair question, considering that this *Annual Recipes 2000* cookbook alone includes several hundred recipes from this year's magazine stories plus another hundred or so brand-new ones.

My answer is "anywhere and everywhere." We food editors are always on the lookout for great food ideas. Chocolate Casserole (page 21) is a peanutier, chocolatier rendition of one of my family's favorites, pudding cake. Golden-tailed Cardamom-Orange Bunnies (page 70) made their debut in a 1955 issue of *Better Homes and Gardens*® magazine; the shape's the same, but we updated the flavor by adding cardamom. And with bread salads all the rage in Italian restaurants, we created Three-Bread Salad (page 114); it calls for a combination of sourdough, pita bread, and pumpernickel in place of the traditional Italian bread.

The best and brightest recipes of all come from you. Since the inception of the Prize Tested Recipes (PTRs) contest in 1937, more than a million people have shared their personal recipes with us. I imagine many of you are familiar with the monthly PTRs, as we call them, and may have entered the contest at one time or another. Also this year, to mark the turn of the century and the millennium, we invited you to nominate your family's best for our Century Standouts Recipe contest. The flood of entries for Century Standouts and the touching stories attached to them are proof positive that folks are not turning their backs on home cooking. You'll find the top Century Standouts winners as well as the Prize Tested Recipe winners, including the first-time-published Honor Roll recipes, within these pages.

As always, we've packed much more into this cookbook than there is space for—appealing food photos, menus, and cooking and good-health tips to name a few. Thanks to our Test Kitchen, you'll find that the recipes are thoroughly tested and will deliver everything you expect, the first time and every time you stir them up. We also guarantee they will make your food experiences with family and friends easier, more fun, and more exciting. Enjoy!

Nancy Byal

Nancy Byal
Executive Food Editor
Better Homes and Gardens® Magazine

Better Homes and Gardens® Books
An Imprint of Meredith® Books

Better Homes and Gardens® Annual Recipes 2000

Project Editor: Chuck Smothermon
Contributing Editor: Shelli McConnell
Associate Art Director: Lynda Haupert
Copy Chief: Catherine Hamrick
Copy and Production Editor: Terri Fredrickson
Editorial and Design Assistants: Judy Bailey,
    Mary Lee Gavin, Karen Schirm
Test Kitchen Director: Lynn Blanchard
Electronic Production Coordinator: Paula Forest
Production Director: Douglas M. Johnston
Managers, Book Production: Pam Kvitne,
    Marjorie J. Schenkelberg

Meredith® Books

Editor in Chief: James D. Blume
Design Director: Matt Strelecki
Managing Editor: Gregory H. Kayko
Executive Food Editor: Jennifer Dorland Darling

Vice President, General Manager: Jamie L. Martin

Better Homes and Gardens® Magazine

Editor in Chief: Jean LemMon
Executive Food Editor: Nancy Byal
Senior Food Editor: Nancy Wall Hopkins
Nutrition Editor: Jeanne Ambrose
Associate Editor: Richard Swearinger
Editorial Assistants: Karen Pollock, Anna Anderson

Meredith Publishing Group

President, Publishing Group: Christopher M. Little
Vice President, Finance & Administration:
    Max Runciman

Meredith Corporation

Chairman and Chief Executive Officer:
    William T. Kerr

Chairman of the Executive Committee:
    E. T. Meredith III

Our seal assures you that every recipe in *Better Homes and Gardens® Annual Recipes 2000* has been tested in the Better Homes and Gardens® Test Kitchen. This means that each recipe is practical and reliable, and meets our high standards of taste appeal. We guarantee your satisfaction with this book for as long as you own it.

Cover photograph: Burnt Sugar Candy Bar Cake *(page 15)*
Page 1: Dried Apple Cider Pie *(page 266)*, Caraway Cookies *(page 272)*
Page 2: Cranberry Tarts *(page 268)*
Page 4: Snail's House Cake *(page 270)*

All of us at Better Homes and Gardens® Books are dedicated to providing you with the information and ideas you need to create delicious foods. We welcome your comments and suggestions. Write to us at: Better Homes and Gardens Books, Cookbook Editorial Department, 1716 Locust Street, LN 112, Des Moines, IA 50309-3023.

If you would like to order additional copies of this book, call 800-439-4119.

© Copyright 2000 by Meredith Corporation, Des Moines, Iowa. All Rights Reserved. Printed in the United States of America. First Edition — 00
ISSN: 1083-4451
ISBN: 0-696-21201-3

Contents

30 MINUTE

When this symbol appears with a recipe, rest assured that you can prepare the dish—start to finish—in 30 minutes or less.

LOW FAT

Any recipe that bears this low-fat symbol meets our guideline of having no more than 10 grams of fat per serving (see page 8).

30 MINUTE, LOW FAT

This symbol is assigned to recipes that are both low in fat and can be prepared—start to finish—in 30 minutes or less.

PRIZE WINNER

The recipes that display this blue-ribbon symbol have earned top honors in our monthly Prize Tested Recipes contest.

Nutrition Information

With each recipe, we give you useful nutrition information you easily can apply to your own needs. First read "What You Need" (below) to determine your dietary requirements. Then refer to the Nutrition Facts listed with each recipe. You'll find the calorie count and the amount of fat, saturated fat, cholesterol, sodium, carbohydrates, fiber, and protein for each serving. In most cases, along with the Nutrition Facts per serving, you'll find the amount of vitamin A, vitamin C, calcium, and iron noted as a percentage of the Daily Values. The Daily Values are dietary standards set by the Food and Drug Administration. To stay in line with the nutrition breakdown of each recipe, follow the suggested number of servings.

How We Analyze

The Better Homes and Gardens® Test Kitchen computer analyzes each recipe for the nutritional value of a single serving.
● The analysis does not include optional ingredients.
● We use the first serving size listed when a range is given. For example: If we say a recipe "Makes 4 to 6 servings," the Nutrition Facts are based on 4 servings.
● When ingredient choices (such as margarine or butter) appear in a recipe, we use the first one mentioned for analysis. The ingredient order does not mean we prefer one ingredient over another.
● When milk is a recipe ingredient, the analysis is calculated using 2-percent (reduced-fat) milk.

What You Need

The dietary guidelines below suggest nutrient levels that moderately active adults should strive to eat each day. As your calorie levels change, adjust your fat intake, too. Try to keep the percentage of calories from fat to no more than 30 percent. There's no harm in occasionally going over or under these guidelines, but the key to good health is maintaining a balanced diet *most of the time.*

Calories: About 2,000
Total fat: Less than 65 grams
Saturated fat: Less than 20 grams
Cholesterol: Less than 300 milligrams
Carbohydrates: About 300 grams
Sodium: Less than 2,400 milligrams
Dietary fiber: 20 to 30 grams

Low-Fat Recipes

For recipes that meet our low-fat criteria, a main-dish serving must contain 10 or fewer grams of fat. For side dishes or desserts, the serving must contain 5 or fewer grams of fat. These recipes are flagged with a low-fat symbol.

january

IN THIS CHAPTER

30-minute recipes indicated in COLOR.
Low-fat and no-fat recipes indicated
with a ♥.
Photographs indicated in italics.
*Bonus recipe

- Spinach salad with fresh orange sections, smoked almonds, and a fruit dressing

- Caribbean Seafood Stew (see below)

- Sourdough bread

- Mango sorbet and sugar cookies

Oven Seafood Frittata

Prep: 35 minutes **Bake:** 20 minutes

- 2 Tbsp. margarine or butter
- 1½ cups refrigerated diced potatoes with onions
- 2 cloves garlic, minced
- ½ of a 10-oz. pkg. frozen chopped spinach, thawed and well drained
- 1 6- or 8-oz. pkg. flake-style imitation crabmeat
- 6 beaten eggs
- 1 cup shredded provolone or mozzarella cheese (4 oz.)
- ¼ cup milk
- 1 Tbsp. snipped fresh basil or 1 tsp. dried basil, crushed
- 1 tsp. snipped fresh rosemary or ¼ tsp. dried rosemary, crushed
- ¼ tsp. salt
- ¼ tsp. pepper
- 2 Tbsp. finely shredded Parmesan cheese
- 1 cup bottled spaghetti sauce, heated (optional)

1 Preheat oven to 375°. Melt margarine in a 10-inch oven-going skillet over medium heat. Add potatoes and garlic. Cook, turning vegetables occasionally, until potatoes begin to brown. Remove from heat. Stir spinach into mixture in skillet. Sprinkle with imitation crabmeat.

2 In a medium bowl combine the eggs, provolone or mozzarella cheese, milk, basil, rosemary, salt, and pepper. Pour the egg mixture evenly over crabmeat.

3 Bake for 20 minutes or until eggs are set. Sprinkle with Parmesan cheese. To serve, cut in wedges and, if desired, spoon warmed spaghetti sauce over top. Makes 6 servings.

Nutrition Facts per serving: 275 cal., 16 g total fat (8 g sat. fat), 245 mg chol., 663 mg sodium, 16 g carbo., 2 g fiber, 18 g pro.
Daily Values: 39% vit. A, 17% vit. C, 24% calcium, 11% iron.

PRIZE WINNER

Caribbean Seafood Stew

Gloria Bradley
Naperville, Illinois
$400—Weeknight Fish and Seafood

Start to finish: 30 minutes

- 2 Tbsp. olive oil
- 1 Tbsp. lime juice
- ¼ tsp. salt
- ⅛ tsp. black pepper
- 1 lb. skinless orange roughy or red snapper fillets, cut into 1-inch cubes
- 1 cup chopped onion
- 1 cup chopped green sweet pepper
- 6 cloves garlic, minced (1 Tbsp.)
- 1 fresh jalapeño pepper, seeded and finely chopped*
- 1 14½-oz. can diced tomatoes, undrained
- ½ cup unsweetened coconut milk
- 8 oz. uncooked medium shrimp, peeled and deveined
- ½ cup snipped fresh cilantro
- 2 cups hot cooked rice
- 2 Tbsp. snipped fresh cilantro Bottled hot pepper sauce (optional)

1 In a medium bowl stir together 1 tablespoon of the olive oil, the lime juice, salt, and black pepper. Add fish cubes; toss to coat. Set aside.

2 In a large saucepan heat remaining oil over medium-high heat. Add the onion, sweet pepper, garlic, and jalapeño pepper. Cook and stir about 4 minutes or until onion is tender. Stir in undrained tomatoes and coconut milk. Bring to boiling; reduce heat. Simmer, uncovered, 10 minutes, stirring occasionally. Stir in the fish mixture, shrimp, and the ½ cup cilantro. Return to boiling; reduce heat. Simmer, uncovered, about 5 minutes or until fish flakes easily with a fork and shrimp turn opaque, stirring occasionally.

3 Serve stew over hot cooked rice. Sprinkle with the 2 tablespoons cilantro. If desired, pass hot pepper sauce. Makes 4 to 6 servings.

*Note: Hot peppers contain oils that can burn. Wear plastic gloves to seed and cut pepper. Do not touch eyes or face, and thoroughly wash your hands.

Nutrition Facts per serving: 414 cal., 15 g total fat (6 g sat. fat), 147 mg chol., 576 mg sodium, 35 g carbo., 2 g fiber, 35 g pro.
Daily Values: 13% vit. A, 74% vit. C, 7% calcium, 26% iron.

Linguine with Curried Seafood

Curry lovers will use a full 2 teaspoons in this recipe, but 1½ teaspoons are plenty for a deliciously spicy accent. (See the photograph on page 39.)

Start to finish: 25 minutes

4	oz. fresh or frozen medium shrimp, peeled and deveined
6	oz. dried linguine or spaghetti
⅓	cup apricot nectar
1	Tbsp. soy sauce
1	tsp. cornstarch
¼	tsp. ground ginger
2	Tbsp. cooking oil
1	cup sliced fresh mushrooms
½	cup thinly sliced carrots
3	cups coarsely chopped bok choy
2	green onions, bias sliced into 1-inch pieces
4	oz. sea scallops (halve large scallops)
1½	to 2 tsp. curry powder

1 Thaw shrimp, if frozen. Rinse shrimp and pat dry with paper towels; set aside.

2 Cook pasta according to package directions; drain. Cover and keep warm. Meanwhile, in a small bowl stir together apricot nectar, soy sauce, cornstarch, and ginger; set aside.

3 In a large skillet or wok heat 1 tablespoon of the cooking oil over medium-high heat. Add mushrooms and carrots; stir-fry for 2 minutes. Add bok choy and green onions; stir-fry for 2 minutes more. Remove vegetables with a slotted spoon. Toss shrimp and scallops with curry powder. Add remaining oil and seafood to skillet; cook and stir for 2 to 3 minutes or until seafood is opaque; push from center of skillet.

4 Stir apricot mixture; add to skillet. Cook and stir until thickened and bubbly. Return vegetables to skillet; stir together and heat through.

5 To serve, spoon seafood mixture over hot cooked pasta. Makes 4 servings.

Nutrition Facts per serving: 290 cal., 11 g total fat (2 g sat. fat), 100 mg chol., 451 mg sodium, 33 g carbo., 3 g fiber, 17 g pro.
Daily Values: 63% vit. A, 41% vit. C, 10% calcium, 18% iron.

Hoisin and Citrus Shrimp Sauté

A sprinkling of crushed red pepper will give this mildly sweet, orange-flavored shrimp stir-fry extra kick.

Start to finish: 25 minutes

12	oz. fresh or frozen large shrimp, peeled and deveined
2	Tbsp. cooking oil
2	cloves garlic, minced
1	medium red sweet pepper, cut into thin strips
3	Tbsp. bottled hoisin sauce
⅓	cup orange juice
1½	cups shredded fresh spinach
2	cups hot cooked rice
	Crushed red pepper (optional)

1 Thaw shrimp, if frozen. Rinse shrimp and pat dry with paper towels; set aside.

2 In a large skillet heat 1 tablespoon of the cooking oil over medium-high heat. Add garlic and cook and stir for 15 seconds. Add red sweet pepper; cook and stir about 3 minutes or until pepper is crisp-tender. Remove sweet pepper with a slotted spoon.

3 Add remaining oil to skillet. Add shrimp; stir-fry about 3 minutes or until shrimp turn pink. Remove shrimp with a slotted spoon. Add hoisin sauce and orange juice to the skillet. Bring to boiling. Simmer, uncovered, about 1 minute or until thickened slightly. Return shrimp and sweet pepper to skillet along with spinach; toss just until combined.

4 To serve, spoon shrimp mixture over hot cooked rice. If desired, sprinkle with crushed red pepper. Makes 4 servings.

Nutrition Facts per serving: 306 cal., 9 g total fat (1 g sat. fat), 129 mg chol., 372 mg sodium, 34 g carbo., 1 g fiber, 20 g pro.
Daily Values: 13% vit. A, 48% vit. C, 7% calcium, 18% iron.

CLEVER COOK

Save on Counter Space

With a small kitchen and very little counter space, I've learned to use my refrigerator as a wall. When cooking, I attach my recipe to the side of my refrigerator using a magnet. This allows me to have the recipe at eye level for easy reading. It also keeps food stains off the recipe and eliminates extra clutter on the counter.

Janice Stillman
Norwood, Massachusetts

Shrimp & Vegetable Pasta Toss

Prep: 25 minutes **Cook:** 8 minutes

- 1　lb. fresh or frozen medium shrimp
- ⅓　cup oil-packed dried tomatoes
- 2　Tbsp. butter
- 1　large onion, halved and thinly sliced
- 2　cloves garlic, minced
- 1　medium red sweet pepper, cut into thin strips
- 1　14-oz. can artichoke hearts, drained and quartered
- ½　cup coarsely shredded carrot
- ⅓　cup dry white wine
- ¼　cup finely shredded fresh basil
- 6　oz. dried angel hair pasta
- ½　cup finely shredded Parmesan cheese

1 Thaw shrimp, if frozen. Peel and devein shrimp. Rinse shrimp; pat dry. Drain tomatoes, reserving oil. Cut tomatoes into thin strips; set aside.

2 In a large skillet combine reserved oil and the butter. Add onion and garlic; cook and stir over medium heat for 2 minutes. Add sweet pepper strips and shrimp; cook and stir for 3 to 4 minutes or until shrimp turn pink. Add tomato strips, artichoke hearts, carrot, wine, and basil; heat through.

3 Meanwhile, cook pasta according to package directions; drain. Toss shrimp mixture with hot cooked pasta and half of the cheese. Transfer mixture to a serving bowl; sprinkle with the remaining cheese. Makes 4 servings.

Nutrition Facts per serving: 483 cal., 17 g total fat (7 g sat. fat), 158 mg chol., 621 mg sodium, 49 g carbo., 4 g fiber, 31 g pro.
Daily Values: 71% vit. A, 119% vit. C, 21% calcium, 27% iron.

DINNER MENU

- ■ **Tuna with Fresh Orange Salsa (see below)**
- ■ **Hot cooked couscous**
- ■ **Steamed green beans**
- ■ **Crusty dinner rolls**

30 MINUTE

Tuna with Fresh Orange Salsa

Prep: 20 minutes **Broil:** 8 minutes

- 4　fresh or frozen tuna or sea bass steaks, cut 1 inch thick
- 1　tsp. finely shredded orange peel
- 4　medium oranges, peeled, seeded, sectioned, and coarsely chopped
- 1　large tomato, seeded and chopped
- ¼　cup snipped fresh cilantro
- 2　Tbsp. finely chopped green onion
- 2　Tbsp. chopped toasted walnuts
- 1　Tbsp. lime juice
- ½　tsp. ground cumin
- 1　Tbsp. olive oil

1 Thaw fish, if frozen. Rinse fish and pat dry with paper towels; set aside. In a medium bowl combine the orange peel, orange sections, tomato, cilantro, green onion, walnuts, lime juice, ¼ teaspoon *salt* and ¼ teaspoon *pepper*. Lightly toss mixture to combine; set aside.

2 In a small bowl combine cumin, ¼ teaspoon *salt* and ¼ teaspoon *pepper*. Brush fish with olive oil and sprinkle with cumin mixture.

3 Place fish on the greased unheated rack of a broiler pan. Broil 4 inches from heat for 5 minutes. Using a wide spatula, carefully turn

fish over. Broil 3 to 7 minutes more or until fish flakes easily with a fork. Serve salsa over fish. Makes 4 servings.

Nutrition Facts per serving: 262 cal., 12 g total fat (2 g sat. fat), 43 mg chol., 343 mg sodium, 11 g carbo., 3 g fiber, 28 g pro.
Daily Values: 74% vit. A, 76% vit. C, 5% calcium, 10% iron.

PRIZE WINNER

Tarragon-Pecan Salmon

Wolfgang H.M. Hanau
West Palm Beach, Florida
$200—Weeknight Fish and Seafood

Prep: 20 minutes **Marinate:** 20 minutes
Bake: 12 minutes

- 4　fresh or frozen salmon fillets (6 oz. each)
- 2　tsp. finely shredded orange peel
- ¼　cup orange juice
- 2　Tbsp. olive oil
- 2　tsp. snipped fresh tarragon
- 1　Tbsp. Dijon-style mustard
- 1　Tbsp. margarine or butter, melted
- 1　tsp. honey
- ¼　cup fine dry bread crumbs
- ¼　cup finely chopped pecans
- 2　tsp. snipped fresh parsley
- 2　tsp. snipped fresh tarragon
　　Snipped fresh parsley (optional)
　　Snipped fresh tarragon (optional)

1 Rinse fish; pat dry. Place fish in a plastic bag set in a deep bowl; set aside. Combine orange peel, orange juice, olive oil, and the 2 teaspoons tarragon. Pour mixture over fish, turning to coat. Seal bag and let stand at room temperature for 20 minutes.

2 Meanwhile, preheat oven to 425°. In a small dish combine Dijon-style mustard, melted margarine or butter, and honey; set aside. In another dish combine bread crumbs, pecans, 2 teaspoons parsley, and 2 teaspoons tarragon. Remove fish from marinade; discard marinade.

3 Place fish, skin side down, on a greased shallow baking pan. Brush with mustard mixture; sprinkle with crumb mixture, pressing crumbs gently to coat. Bake, uncovered, for 12 to 16 minutes or just until fish flakes easily with a fork. If desired, sprinkle with additional parsley and tarragon. If desired, garnish with *lemon slices.* Makes 4 servings.

Nutrition Facts per serving: 327 cal., 20 g total fat (4 g sat. fat), 38 mg chol., 272 mg sodium, 9 g carbo., 1 g fiber, 26 g pro.
Daily Values: 6% vit. A, 16% vit. C, 2% calcium, 10% iron.

Mexicali Orange Roughy Salad

See the photograph on page 39.

Prep: 25 minutes **Bake:** 6 minutes

- 4 fresh or frozen orange roughy fillets, ½ inch thick (1 lb. total)
- 2 Tbsp. red jalapeño jelly
- 2 Tbsp. butter or margarine
- ¼ cup yellow cornmeal
- 2 Tbsp. all-purpose flour
- 1 tsp. chili powder
- ½ tsp. salt
- ½ cup dairy sour cream
- ½ tsp. finely shredded lime peel
- 1 Tbsp. lime juice
- ¼ tsp. chili powder
  Boston lettuce leaves
- 1 small cucumber, thinly sliced
- 8 cherry tomatoes, halved
- 2 Tbsp. snipped fresh cilantro

1 Thaw fish, if frozen. Rinse fish and pat dry with paper towels. Preheat oven to 450°.

2 Meanwhile, in a small saucepan melt jelly and butter or margarine. In a shallow dish combine the cornmeal, flour, the 1 teaspoon chili powder, and the salt. Brush jelly-butter mixture on fish; dip fish in cornmeal mixture to coat both sides. Place the coated fish on a greased baking sheet. Bake, uncovered, for 6 to 9 minutes or until fish flakes easily with a fork.

3 For dressing, in a small bowl stir together the sour cream, lime peel, lime juice, the ¼ teaspoon chili powder, and enough *water* (about 2 tablespoons) to make a drizzling consistency.

4 Place several lettuce leaves on each of four serving plates. Top lettuce with a single layer of cucumber slices, a fish fillet, and some of the tomatoes. Drizzle with dressing and sprinkle with cilantro. Makes 4 servings.

Nutrition Facts per serving: 271 cal., 12 g total fat (7 g sat. fat), 50 mg chol., 455 mg sodium, 21 g carbo., 2 g fiber, 19 g pro.
Daily Values: 21% vit. A, 22% vit. C, 8% calcium, 7% iron.

30 MINUTE

Spicy Catfish Po' Boys

Prep: 25 minutes **Cook:** 5 minutes

- 4 fresh or frozen catfish fillets, ½ inch thick (1 lb. total)
- ½ cup buttermilk
- ¼ cup all-purpose flour
- ¼ cup yellow cornmeal
- 4½ tsp. Cajun or Creole seasoning*
- ¼ tsp. ground red pepper
- 1 Tbsp. olive oil or cooking oil
- ¼ cup mayonnaise or salad dressing
- 4 6- to 7-inch loaves French bread, split horizontally and toasted
- ¼ cup bottled roasted red sweet pepper strips
- 4 romaine lettuce leaves

1 Thaw fish, if frozen. Rinse fish and pat dry with paper towels. Cut fillets in half lengthwise; set aside. Pour buttermilk into a shallow dish. In another shallow dish combine flour, cornmeal, 4 teaspoons of the Cajun or Creole seasoning, and ⅛ teaspoon of the ground red pepper. Dip fish in buttermilk and then in flour mixture to coat both sides.

2 In a large skillet heat olive oil or cooking oil over medium heat. Fry fish, half at a time, for 3 to 4 minutes or until golden; turn. Fry 2 to 3 minutes more or until second side is golden and fish flakes easily with a fork. (Add more oil, if necessary, for cooking second batch of fillets.)

3 Meanwhile, combine mayonnaise, remaining Cajun seasoning, and remaining ground red pepper. Spread the top cut sides of bread loaves with mayonnaise mixture. Place two catfish strips on loaf bottoms. Add red pepper strips, a romaine leaf, and bread tops. Makes 4 servings.

*****Note:** If salt-free seasoning is used, add ½ teaspoon salt to flour mixture.

Nutrition Facts per serving: 601 cal., 26 g total fat (5 g sat. fat), 59 mg chol., 895 mg sodium, 61 g carbo., 5 g fiber, 29 g pro.
Daily Values: 24% vit. A, 57% vit. C, 14% calcium, 25% iron.

- **Deep Chocolate Cake with Double-Malt Topping (see below)**
- **Homemade or purchased vanilla ice cream**
- **Fresh strawberries**
- **Punch and/or coffee**

Deep Chocolate Cake With Double-Malt Topping

It's hip to be square, but this stunning cake can be round, too. Use 9×1½-inch round baking pans instead of the 8-inch square pans. (See the photograph on page 43.)

Prep: 25 minutes **Bake:** 17 minutes
Cool: 1 hour **Chill:** 3 hours
Assembly: 15 minutes

    ½ cup unsweetened cocoa powder
    2 cups all-purpose flour
    1 tsp. baking powder
    ½ tsp. baking soda
    ⅔ cup butter, softened
    1¾ cups sugar
    3 eggs
    4 oz. unsweetened chocolate,
         melted and cooled
    2 tsp. vanilla
    1½ cups milk
    1 recipe Chocolate Malt Frosting
    2 cups malted milk balls or
         miniature malted milk balls

1 Grease three 8×8×2-inch baking pans; lightly dust each pan with 1 teaspoon of the cocoa powder.

2 In a medium bowl stir together the flour, remaining cocoa powder, baking powder, and baking soda. Set aside.

3 Preheat oven to 350°. In a large mixing bowl beat butter with an electric mixer on medium-high speed for 30 seconds. Add sugar; beat until combined. Add eggs, one at a time, beating for 30 seconds after each. Beat in chocolate and vanilla. Alternately add flour mixture and milk, beating on low speed until thoroughly combined.

4 Divide batter into prepared pans; spread evenly. Bake for 17 to 20 minutes or until a wooden toothpick inserted near center comes out clean. Cool in pans on wire rack 10 minutes. Remove cakes from pans. Transfer to wire racks; cool completely. Prepare the Chocolate Malt Frosting.

5 To assemble cake, spread ¾ cup of Chocolate Malt Frosting on tops of two of the layers and stack. Add top layer; frost the top and sides of the cake, reserving some frosting for the piping. Place the remaining frosting in a decorating bag fitted with a medium round tip. Starting from the bottom, pipe a zigzag pattern on sides and top edge of cake. If desired, coarsely chop or halve some of the malted milk balls. Decorate the cake with milk balls. Refrigerate. Makes 20 servings.

Chocolate Malt Frosting

1. In a saucepan over medium-high heat bring 2 cups whipping cream just to boiling. Remove from heat. Stir in ⅓ cup malt powder. Add two 11.5-ounce packages milk chocolate pieces (do not stir). Cover; let stand 5 minutes. Stir until smooth. Transfer to a large mixing bowl. Mixture will be thin. Cover and refrigerate 3 hours or until frosting is thoroughly chilled.

2. Set bowl of frosting in a larger bowl of ice water. Beat frosting with an electric mixer on medium speed about 3 minutes or until fluffy and of spreading consistency. (The frosting will turn light brown with beating.)

Before chilling and beating, the frosting will be thin and dark brown in color.

Beat the frosting mixture until it turns light brown with a slight sheen and a fluffy consistency. Set the bowl in a larger bowl of ice to keep the mixture chilled.

Nutrition Facts per serving: 540 cal., 32 g total fat (17 g sat. fat), 83 mg chol., 263 mg sodium, 61 g carbo., 1 g fiber, 8 g pro.
Daily Values: 21% vit. A, 14% calcium, 11% iron.

Burnt Sugar Candy Bar Cake

Cooking the sugar until it's caramelized ("burnt") gives the cake a rich flavor. For the topping, use one or several kinds of candy bars that you love most. (See the photograph on the cover.)

Prep: 40 minutes **Bake:** 25 minutes
Cool: 1 hour **Assembly:** 20 minutes

- ¾ cup granulated sugar
- ¾ cup hot water
- 3 cups all-purpose flour
- 1½ tsp. baking powder
- ¼ tsp. baking soda
- 1½ cups granulated sugar
- ⅔ cup butter, softened
- 2 egg yolks
- 2 tsp. vanilla
- 2 egg whites
- 1 recipe Browned Butter Frosting
- 1½ cups finely chopped assorted candy bars
  Coarsely chopped assorted candy bars, such as Hershey's, Mars, Nestle, or other (optional)

1 Grease and lightly flour three 8×1½-inch round baking pans or two 9×2-inch pans. In a large skillet cook the ¾ cup granulated sugar over medium-high heat until the sugar just begins to melt (do not stir). Reduce heat; cook until sugar is golden brown, about 1 to 3 minutes more, stirring constantly.

2 Carefully stir in hot water (syrup will form lumps). Bring mixture to boiling; reduce heat. Continue stirring until mixture is free of lumps. Remove from heat. Pour syrup into a large glass measuring cup. Add additional water to equal 1¾ cups liquid. Set aside to cool.

3 Preheat oven to 350°. In a large mixing bowl stir together flour, baking powder, and baking soda. In another large mixing bowl beat together the 1½ cups granulated sugar, the ⅔ cup butter, egg yolks, and the vanilla with an electric mixer on medium speed about 1 minute or until the mixture is smooth. Alternately add flour mixture and sugar syrup to egg yolk mixture, beating on low speed after each addition just until combined.

4 Clean beaters thoroughly. In a medium mixing bowl beat egg whites with an electric mixer on high speed until stiff peaks form (tips stand straight). Gently fold whites into batter.

5 Divide batter into prepared pans; spread evenly. Bake for 25 to 30 minutes or until a wooden toothpick inserted near center comes out clean. Cool in pans on wire rack for 10 minutes. Remove cakes from pans. Transfer cakes to wire racks; cool completely. Prepare Browned Butter Frosting.

6 To assemble, spread ½ cup Browned Butter Frosting over bottoms of two of the cake layers. Sprinkle each frosted layer with half of the finely chopped candy. Stack these layers on a cake plate, frosted sides up. Place the third (unfrosted) layer on top, rounded side up.

7 Spread remaining frosting on top and sides of cake. If desired, garnish with the coarsely chopped candy bar pieces. Makes 16 servings.

Browned Butter Frosting

1. In a small saucepan heat and stir ½ cup butter* over low heat until melted. Continue heating until butter turns a nut-brown color. Remove from heat; cool for 5 minutes.

2. In a large mixing bowl beat together two 3-ounce packages of softened cream cheese with 3 tablespoons butter until combined. Beat in about 2 cups sifted powdered sugar. Beat in the browned butter and 1 teaspoon vanilla. Gradually beat in an additional 4½ cups sifted powdered sugar and 2 to 3 teaspoons milk until the frosting is of spreading consistency.

*Note: Use butter only. Margarine or other spreads will not yield the same results and could keep the frosting mixture from setting properly.

Nutrition Facts per serving: 611 cal., 26 g total fat (15 g sat. fat), 80 mg chol., 269 mg sodium, 95 g carbo., 1 g fiber, 5 g pro.
Daily Values: 24% vit. A, 7% calcium, 10% iron.

TEST KITCHEN TIP
Cake Pans

All cake pans are not created equal. For even baking, we suggest sturdy, single-wall aluminum pans. When choosing cake pans, also consider both the pan's depth and surface finish:

Depth: When a recipe calls for 8×1½-inch round pans, make sure the pans you choose are truly 1½ inches deep. Some pans can be as much as ¼ inch shallower than others—cakes may run over these pans.

Surface finish: Bakeware is made in a range of materials that have different effects on a cake. Shiny bakeware, including aluminum, tin, and stainless steel, reflects heat and will result in a thinner cake crust. Dark or dull-finish bakeware, including tin, glass, and many nonstick pans, absorbs more heat, increasing the amount of browning and resulting in a thicker crust.

How Well Are You Eating?

by David Feder, Registered Dietitian

Take the "Healthy People 2000" Quiz

Y2K is here and, as a nation, some promises were made as to how healthy we'd be by now. When it began in 1979, the "Healthy People 2000" campaign (see page 17) targeted reducing our nation's top killers: heart disease, stroke, and cancer. The good news is that, a generation later, there has been progress. Still, the progress has been slower than expected—and there remains a lot of room for improvement. How have you been doing? Take this quiz and find out. Everybody gets 100 points to start.

1. Is your weight proportionate to your height? To figure the ideal weight for women: Allow 100 pounds for the first 5 feet, then add 5 pounds for every inch over 5 feet. Men: Allow 106 pounds for the first 5 feet, then add 6 pounds for every inch over 5 feet. (You are allowed 10 percent plus or minus the total.) After you have your ideal weight, subtract 1 point from your 100-point total for each pound greater or less than the 10 percent range.

2. What's your waist-to-hip ratio? Divide your waist measurement in inches by your hip measurement in inches. A ratio greater than 0.80 in women and 0.95 in men indicates upper-body obesity. Subtract 5 points if you fall above these averages.

3. If you do not know your cholesterol levels, subtract 7 points. If you do, and your total cholesterol is above 200 mg/dl, subtract 10 points. If your LDL cholesterol is above 160 mg/dl, lose 5 more points.

4. Do you smoke? If so, subtract 75 points.

5. If you drink more than two alcoholic drinks per day, take 15 points off for each drink over that two-drink maximum.

6. Is your blood pressure greater than 140/90? Subtract 10 points.

7. Do you engage in moderate exercise? Good for you—add 25 points. (If not, take away 15 points.) At least 30 minutes, three or more days each week, of activities such as biking or walking will do the trick. If you regularly exercise more than this minimum, add a bonus of 15 points.

8. Do you eat at least five servings of fruit and vegetables each day? Add 10 points. No? Subtract 10. For each serving (about one-half cup or one medium-size piece) of fruits and vegetables you eat above five per day, add another 5 points.

9. Are you eating between 6 and 11 servings of grain products per day? Great! Give yourself 5 points. (If not, subtract 3 points.) Grains (especially whole grains) in breads, pastas, rice, and barley act in a number of ways to promote health.

10. Do you know your Body Mass Index (BMI)? An increased BMI puts you at risk for high blood pressure, stroke, osteoarthritis, heart disease, and certain cancers. To calculate, take your height in inches and multiply it by itself. Divide your weight in pounds by the result. Now, take the answer and multiply by 704.5. Any number between 17 and 25 is healthy.

A BMI above 25 to 29.9 is considered overweight, and a BMI of 30 or higher is obese. If you fall into the 17 to 25 category, give yourself 5 points. If you land between 25 and 30, subtract 5 points. If you go above 30, subtract 10 points.

Your Score

100+ = Give yourself a blue ribbon. You've earned it!

80 to 100 = Celebrate 2000 with confidence: You're on the right track for a healthy lifestyle.

70 to 79 = You're almost there; all you need is a little "fine-tuning." Celebrate, but go easy on high-calorie party snacks.

50 to 69 = Add activity to your daily schedule; then plan some New Year's resolutions—you have some work to do.

below 50 = You need to reassess your eating and exercise habits—it could mean your life.

Celebrate 2000

by Constance J. Geiger, Registered Dietitian

The Payoff

Improving your diet today could help prevent heart disease, stroke, and a number of different cancers. It doesn't take a drastic change in lifestyle to help ward off disease; make small changes you can live with. Eating more of protective foods, such as fruits, vegetables, and grains, is easy when you expand your repertoire beyond apples and oranges to include fun, unfamiliar produce.

"Five a day" is just a start. Studies of disease incidence by population suggest that the more fruits and vegetables we eat per day, the better our chances for staving off cancer. According to Ritva Butrum, Ph.D., head of research at the American Institute for Cancer Research, scientists are seeing even greater promise for stopping cancer before it starts. How? By taking advantage of the wide variety of protective substances found only in vegetables, fruits, and grains.

For every decade after age 30, your calorie needs decrease by 2 percent. This means that if you eat the same amount at age 50 as you did at age 30, you'll gain a pound every two months—6 pounds per year. Starving yourself and trying fad diets aren't solutions.

Include more activity in your life instead. Use the stairs, walk more, drive less, and do your own yard work. You'll feel better, think better, and look better. Schedule time for exercise—remember, you only need about 30 minutes a day, three times a week.

Here's a Healthy Tip

Read the Nutrition Facts labels on foods. Focus more on calories, fiber, vitamins, and minerals than on fat. Remember, a food low in fat can still be high in calories. Eat more whole grains from such foods as beans, oatmeal, and other cereals. Use dark leafy greens in salads, and top with toasted wheat berries instead of high-fat croutons.

Healthy People 2000: How America Fared

The Healthy People 2000 campaign by the National Institutes of Health (and other health organizations) set out to drastically reduce the rate of preventable disease in this country. Death rates from heart disease and stroke have decreased, but we haven't accomplished all the objectives. For example, we got high marks for knowing our cholesterol levels. But those of us with cholesterol problems need to further decrease saturated fat in our diets.

We made little progress in adding exercise into our week, and the proportion of overweight people increased dramatically. Obesity, stress, and lack of exercise lead to high blood pressure and other diseases. Research strongly suggests that sodium intake plays little role in lowering blood pressure for most hypertensive people—exercise and weight control is how to win this war.

We need to eat more foods made from whole grains. Few of us eat five or more servings of fruits and vegetables a day (the minimum amount recommended by the 5-A-Day program of the National Cancer Institute). Eating more of these great foods is probably the easiest step to take toward being healthier for the year 2000 and beyond.

–Constance J. Geiger, Ph.D., is assistant professor of Foods and Nutrition at the University of Utah.

TEST KITCHEN TIP

Better Spreader

To melt chocolate for spreading or dipping, there's no need for a double-boiler. Use a deep, heavy saucepan and add one teaspoon shortening for every 3 ounces (½ cup) of chocolate. This will keep the chocolate smooth and keep it from setting up. Melt chocolate and shortening over low heat, stirring constantly. Or, place chocolate and shortening in a microwave-safe measuring cup and melt in a microwave oven on 100 percent power (high) for 60 seconds for each 3 ounces until chocolate is just soft enough to stir smoothly.*

*Note: The chocolate pieces will not appear melted until stirred.

Top-of-the-World Brownies

You can store these fudgy brownies for up to three days. Place them in a tightly covered container to keep them from drying out. (See the photograph on page 42.)

Prep: 20 minutes **Bake:** 1 hour
Cool: 1 hour

- ¾ cup butter
- 3 oz. unsweetened chocolate, coarsely chopped
- 1⅓ cups sugar
- 2 tsp. vanilla
- 3 eggs
- 1 cup all-purpose flour
- 2 Tbsp. unsweetened cocoa powder
- ½ cup coarsely chopped hazelnuts (filberts) or pecans
- 2 egg whites
- ⅔ cup sugar
- 1 Tbsp. unsweetened cocoa powder

1 Preheat oven to 350°. Line the bottom and sides of an 8×8×2-inch baking pan with heavy foil; grease foil and set aside.

2 In a medium saucepan stir the ¾ cup butter and the chocolate over low heat just until melted. Remove from heat. Using a wooden spoon stir in the 1⅓ cups sugar and the vanilla. Cool about 5 minutes.

3 Add eggs, one at a time, beating after each just until combined. Stir in flour and the 2 tablespoons cocoa. Spread batter evenly in prepared pan. Sprinkle with nuts; set aside.

4 In a small mixing bowl beat egg whites with an electric mixer on medium to high speed about 1 minute or until soft peaks form (tips curl). Gradually add the ⅔ cup sugar, beating on high speed until stiff peaks form (tips stand straight) and sugar is almost dissolved. Reduce speed to low; beat in the 1 tablespoon cocoa.

5 Using a tablespoon, carefully spoon the meringue in 16 even mounds on top of the brownie batter, keeping about one-half inch of space between them.

6 Bake for about 1 hour or until a wooden toothpick inserted near the center of the brownie portion comes out clean. Cool brownies in pan on a wire rack for at least 1 hour. To serve, before cutting, lift whole brownie from pan using foil. Cut into 16 pieces.

Nutrition Facts per brownie: 269 cal., 15 g total fat (7 g sat. fat), 63 mg chol., 107 mg sodium, 34 g carbo., 1 g fiber, 4 g pro.
Daily Values: 9% vit. A, 2% calcium, 7% iron.

Chocolaty Cream Cheese Bars

Prep: 15 minutes **Bake:** 25 minutes
Chill: 1 hour

- ⅓ cup butter, softened
- ⅓ cup granulated sugar
- ⅓ cup packed brown sugar
- 1 egg
- 1 egg yolk
- ¾ tsp. baking soda
- 1 tsp. vanilla
- 1½ cups all-purpose flour
- ¾ cup semisweet chocolate pieces
- 1 8-oz. pkg. cream cheese, softened
- ¼ cup granulated sugar
- 1 egg
- ½ tsp. vanilla

1 Preheat oven to 350°. Lightly grease an 8×8×2-inch baking pan and set aside.

2 In a large mixing bowl beat butter on medium to high speed for 30 seconds. Add the ⅓ cup granulated sugar and the brown sugar; beat until well combined. Beat in 1 whole egg, egg yolk, baking soda, and vanilla. By hand stir in the flour and chocolate pieces. Set 1 cup of the dough aside.

3 Press remaining dough into the bottom of the prepared baking pan. Bake for 10 minutes.

4 Meanwhile, in the same mixing bowl beat together the cream cheese and the ¼ cup granulated sugar until combined. Beat in the 1 egg and ½ teaspoon vanilla. Pour mixture over partially baked crust, spreading evenly.

5 Drop the reserved dough by small spoonfuls into mounds over cream cheese mixture. Bake for 15 to

20 minutes more or until filling is set. Transfer to a wire rack and cool completely. Cover and chill at least 1 hour before cutting into pieces. Makes 24 bars.

Nutrition Facts per bar: 143 cal., 8 g total fat (5 g sat. fat), 35 mg chol., 101 mg sodium, 15 g carbo., 1 g fiber, 2 g pro. Daily Values: 7% vit. A, 1% calcium, 3% iron.

Choose-Your-Own Ice-Cream Sandwich

Use a different flavor for each sandwich, or put two different ice creams in one sandwich. It's your delectable choice.

Prep: 10 minutes **Bake:** 7 minutes
Freeze: 2 hours

- ½ cup butter
- ⅓ cup granulated sugar
- ¼ cup packed dark brown sugar
- 1½ tsp. unsweetened cocoa powder
- ¼ tsp. baking powder
- 1 egg
- ½ tsp. vanilla
- 1½ oz. unsweetened chocolate, melted and cooled slightly
- 1 cup plus 2 Tbsp. all-purpose flour
  Miniature chocolate-covered cream-filled mint patties (such as Junior Mints) and/or assorted chocolate pieces
- 1 pint any flavor ice cream

1 Preheat oven to 350°. In a large mixing bowl beat butter with an electric mixer on medium to high speed for 30 seconds. Beat in the granulated sugar, brown sugar, cocoa, and baking powder until just combined. Beat in the egg and vanilla. Stir in the melted chocolate.

2 Beat in as much flour as you can with mixer. Stir in remaining flour by hand. Drop dough by slightly rounded teaspoons, 2 inches apart, onto an ungreased cookie sheet. Spread each dough portion to about 2 inches in diameter.

3 Bake for 7 to 8 minutes or until edges are firm. Immediately (while still warm) top half of the cookies with the chocolate-covered mints or chocolate pieces. Transfer cookies to a wire rack. Cool completely.

4 To assemble, let ice cream stand for 10 minutes to soften slightly. Place about 2 tablespoons ice cream on the flat side of cookies without the candy toppers. Carefully place candy-topped cookies on top of ice cream, flat side down. Press cookie gently in center to slightly flatten sandwich.

5 Wrap each sandwich in plastic wrap and freeze for 2 hours. Let stand at room temperature for 5 minutes before serving. Freeze for up to 1 month. Makes 18 sandwiches.

Nutrition Facts per sandwich: 149 cal., 8 g total fat (5 g sat. fat), 32 mg chol., 74 mg sodium, 18 g carbo., 0 g fiber, 2 g pro. Daily Values: 6% vit. A, 3% calcium, 4% iron.

Chocolate Bread Pudding

Studded with white and dark chocolate and laced with a luscious sauce, this bread pudding has the power to soothe both body and soul.

Prep: 20 minutes **Bake:** 50 minutes

- 3¼ cups milk
- 5 beaten eggs
- 1 16-oz. can chocolate-flavored syrup (1½ cups)
- ¾ cup packed brown sugar
- 2 tsp. vanilla
- 8 to 10 oz. French bread, cut into 1-inch cubes (about 8 cups)
- 3 oz. semisweet chocolate, coarsely chopped
- 3 oz. white chocolate or white baking bar, coarsely chopped
- 1 recipe Bourbon Chocolate Sauce

1 Preheat oven to 350°. In a large bowl stir together milk, eggs, chocolate syrup, brown sugar, and vanilla. Spread bread cubes in an ungreased 3-quart rectangular baking dish. Sprinkle with chopped semisweet and white chocolate. Pour egg mixture evenly over bread.

2 Bake, uncovered, for 50 to 55 minutes or until pudding is puffy and a knife inserted near center comes out clean. Cool slightly (pudding will fall in center). Drizzle with warm Bourbon Chocolate Sauce. Makes 12 servings.

Bourbon Chocolate Sauce

In a heavy saucepan stir 4 ounces chopped semisweet chocolate over low heat just until melted. Stir in ⅔ cup whipping cream and ¼ cup granulated sugar. Cook and stir over medium heat for 5 to 6 minutes or just until mixture begins to boil. Remove from heat; whisk until smooth. If desired, stir in 2 to 3 tablespoons bourbon. Cool slightly before serving.

Nutrition Facts per serving: 424 cal., 17 g total fat (10 g sat. fat), 114 mg chol., 211 mg sodium, 65 g carbo., 1 g fiber, 9 g pro. Daily Values: 13% vit. A, 1% vit. C, 11% calcium, 14% iron.

A Brazilian relative of the cocoa bean, called cupuaçu (koo-poo-AH-soo), has been successfully turned into a twin of chocolate. The resulting product, called an "Amazon Bar," has the look, texture, and flavor of a fine chocolate, with faint notes of fruit and coffee.

Amazon Bars come in dark and milk varieties, plain or with almonds or crisped rice. All are naturally caffeine-free and can be used for baking (although products made with them will be lighter in color than those made with chocolate).

Look for Amazon Bars in specialty supermarkets. Or, order them from the Amazon Origins, Inc., internet site at http://www.amazonorigins.com. Note: A portion of the profits from sales of Amazon Bars benefits preservation of the Brazilian rain forest and endangered species.

Chocolate Buttons

Store these bite-size charmers in an airtight container for up to three days. But they're usually gone in a day! (See the photograph on page 43.)

Prep: 25 minutes **Bake:** 4 minutes

- ¼ **cup butter, softened**
- ½ **cup packed dark brown sugar**
- ¼ **cup unsweetened cocoa powder**
- 1 **Tbsp. milk**
- 1 **tsp. vanilla**
- ¼ **tsp. baking soda**
- ⅔ **cup all-purpose flour**
- 4 **oz. bittersweet chocolate, chopped**
- 1½ **tsp. shortening**
- ½ **tsp. mint extract**
- 4 **oz. white baking bar (optional)**

1 Preheat oven to 375°. In a large mixing bowl beat together the butter, brown sugar, cocoa powder, milk, and vanilla with an electric mixer on medium speed until combined. Beat in baking soda and as much of the flour as you can. By hand, stir in the remaining flour until combined. Shape the dough into a ball.

2 Divide dough in half. On a lightly floured surface roll each half to ¹⁄₁₆-inch thickness. (Rolled dough will be very thin.) Cut with small (1- to 1½-inch) round cookie cutters. Place on ungreased cookie sheets. Bake for 4 to 5 minutes or until edges are firm. Cool on cookie sheet for 1 minute. Transfer cookies to wire racks and cool completely.

3 In a small heavy saucepan melt bittersweet chocolate and shortening over low heat, stirring occasionally. Remove from heat. Stir in mint extract. Let stand until just cool enough to handle. If desired, in a second saucepan melt white baking bar over low heat, stirring occasionally; let stand.

4 Transfer the warm chocolate mixture to a sealable plastic bag. If using, transfer melted white baking bar to a second bag. Snip a ⅛-inch corner from the bag(s). Squeezing gently, drizzle melted chocolate-mint mixture and, if using, melted baking bar over cookies in threads. Let cookies stand until icing hardens. Makes about 12 dozen cookies.

Nutrition Facts per cookie: 15 cal., 1 g total fat (1 g sat. fat), 1 mg chol., 10 mg sodium, 2 g carbo., 0 g fiber, 0 g pro.

Dropped Chocolate Pie

For extra chocolate flavor, use grated bittersweet chocolate for the sprinkles.

Prep: 20 minutes **Bake:** 38 minutes
Cool: 1 hour **Chill:** 2 hours

- 2 **cups all-purpose flour**
- 2 **Tbsp. unsweetened cocoa powder**
- ¼ **tsp. salt**
- ⅓ **cup shortening**
- ⅓ **cup butter**
- 6 **to 7 Tbsp. cold water**
- 4 **oz. semisweet chocolate pieces**
- ¾ **cup sugar**
- ¼ **cup cornstarch**
- 3 **cups milk**
- 4 **oz. unsweetened chocolate, chopped**
- 5 **egg yolks, beaten**
- 1 **Tbsp. butter**
- 2 **tsp. vanilla**
  Sweetened whipped cream (optional)
  Grated chocolate (optional)

1 For crust, in a large bowl stir together the flour, the cocoa, and salt. Using a pastry blender, cut in shortening and ⅓ cup butter until pieces are pea size. Sprinkle 1 tablespoon of the water over the mixture; gently toss with a fork. Push moistened dough to the side of the bowl. Repeat, using 1 tablespoon of water at a time, until all the dough is moistened.

2 Preheat oven to 450°. Divide dough in half. Form each half into a ball. Cover and refrigerate one ball. On a lightly floured surface, flatten remaining ball. Roll from center to edges into a 12-inch circle. Transfer to a 9-inch pie plate; avoid stretching. Gently press into plate. Trim edges. Line with double layer of foil.

3 Bake pastry for 8 minutes. Remove foil; bake about 5 minutes more or until firm and dry. Sprinkle with the semisweet chocolate pieces. Cool completely on a wire rack. Reduce oven temperature to 325°.

4 For filling, in a 2-quart saucepan stir together sugar and cornstarch. Stir in milk and unsweetened chocolate. Cook and stir over medium heat until thickened and bubbly. Cook and stir for 2 minutes more.

5 Slowly stir 1 cup of the hot mixture into the beaten egg yolks. Pour egg yolk mixture into hot filling in pan. Bring just to boiling; reduce heat. Cook and stir for 2 minutes. Remove from heat. Stir in the 1 tablespoon butter and the vanilla. Let cool 10 minutes.

6 Meanwhile, on a lightly floured surface, flatten chilled dough. Roll from center to edges to form a 12-inch circle. Pour warm filling mixture into baked pastry shell. Place pastry top over the filling mixture, pressing into pastry edge to seal. Trim dough to edge of pie plate.

7 Gently prick top of pastry with a fork. Bake about 25 minutes or until crust is firm and dry. Cool for 1 hour on a wire rack. Cover and chill for 2 to 24 hours before serving.

8 To serve, invert a serving platter on top of pie. Turn pie upside down. Remove pie plate. If desired, top with whipped cream and grated chocolate. Makes 10 to 12 servings.

Nutrition Facts per serving: 461 cal., 28 g total fat (13 g sat. fat), 131 mg chol., 169 mg sodium, 50 g carbo., 2 g fiber, 9 g pro.
Daily Values: 27% vit. A, 1% vit. C, 11% calcium, 18% iron.

Fiesta Chocolate Chip Pie

Expect a subtle Mexican flavor from this spice combination of coriander, cloves, and ground red pepper.

Prep: 15 minutes **Bake:** 50 minutes

  2 **eggs, slightly beaten**
  1 **cup sugar**
  ½ **cup all-purpose flour**
  ¼ **cup mild-flavored molasses**
  ½ **tsp. ground coriander**
  ¼ **tsp. salt**
  ⅛ **tsp. ground cloves**
  ⅛ **tsp. ground red pepper**
  1 **cup butter, melted and cooled**
  2 **tsp. vanilla**
  1 **cup semisweet chocolate pieces**
  ¼ **cup white chocolate pieces**
  1 **cup chopped pecans, toasted**
  1 **9-inch unbaked pie shell**
    Whipped cream or cinnamon ice cream (optional)

1 Preheat oven to 325°. In a large bowl stir together eggs, sugar, flour, molasses, coriander, salt, cloves, and ground red pepper. Add melted butter and vanilla; stir to mix well. Stir in both kinds of chocolate pieces and pecans.

2 Pour mixture into the unbaked pie shell. Cover edge of pie with foil. Bake for 25 minutes; remove foil. Bake about 25 minutes more or until filling is set. Transfer pie to a wire rack and let cool. To serve, cut into wedges. If desired, serve with whipped cream or ice cream. Serves 10.

Nutrition Facts per serving: 602 cal., 41 g total fat (18 g sat. fat), 96 mg chol., 331 mg sodium, 50 g carbo., 4 g fiber, 5 g pro.
Daily Values: 20% vit. A, 4% calcium, 10% iron.

Chocolate Casserole

See the photograph on page 43.

Prep: 15 minutes **Bake:** 35 minutes

  ½ **cup all-purpose flour**
  ¾ **cup sugar**
  ¾ **tsp. baking powder**
  ⅓ **cup milk**
  1 **Tbsp. cooking oil**
  1 **tsp. vanilla**
  ¼ **cup peanut butter**
  ⅓ **cup semisweet chocolate pieces**
  ¼ **cup unsweetened cocoa powder**
  ¾ **cup boiling water**
  ⅓ **cup coarsely chopped honey-roasted peanuts**
  2 **Tbsp. crumbled chocolate-flavored graham crackers (optional)**
    Whipped cream (optional)

1 Preheat oven to 350°. In a medium bowl combine flour, ¼ cup of the sugar, and baking powder. Add milk, cooking oil, and vanilla. Using a wire whisk, stir until smooth. Stir in the peanut butter and semisweet chocolate pieces.

2 Pour batter into an ungreased 1-quart casserole; set aside. In the same bowl stir together the remaining sugar and the cocoa. Gradually stir in boiling water. Pour mixture over batter in casserole.

3 Bake, uncovered, for 35 to 40 minutes or until a wooden toothpick inserted into cake portion comes out clean. Remove from oven; top with peanuts and, if desired, graham crackers. If desired, serve warm with whipped cream. Serves 6.

Nutrition Facts per serving: 333 cal., 15 g total fat (3 g sat. fat), 1 mg chol., 170 mg sodium, 42 g carbo., 3 g fiber, 7 g pro.
Daily Values: 9% calcium, 9% iron.

TEST KITCHEN TIP

Cooking Rice

When a recipe calls for cooked rice, keep in mind these proportions: 1 cup of rice (cooked in 2 cups of water) yields about 3 cups cooked rice. Follow package directions, or here's a general guide: Measure water into a saucepan; bring to a full boil. Slowly add rice and return to boiling. Cover; reduce heat. Simmer for time specified on package or until rice is tender and most of the water is absorbed. Remove from heat and let stand, covered, about 5 minutes.

Incredible Rice Pudding

Equal amounts of dark corn syrup or sorghum syrup may be substituted for the molasses in the Molasses-Chocolate Sauce recipe.

Prep: 20 minutes **Bake:** 1 hour

- 4 eggs, slightly beaten
- 2 cups half-and-half, light cream, or whole milk
- ⅓ cup granulated sugar
- ¼ cup unsweetened cocoa powder
- 1 tsp. vanilla
- 1 cup cooked rice, cooled
- 4 oz. semisweet chocolate, chopped
- 1 recipe Molasses-Chocolate Sauce

1 Preheat oven to 325°. In a large mixing bowl beat together eggs, half-and-half, sugar, cocoa, and vanilla with a rotary beater or wire whisk. Stir in cooked rice and chocolate.

2 Pour custard mixture into an ungreased 1½- or 2-quart casserole. Place dish in a 13×9×2-inch baking pan set on the oven rack. Carefully pour 1 inch of boiling water into baking pan.

3 Bake, uncovered, for 60 to 65 minutes or until a knife inserted near center comes out clean. Transfer to a wire rack and cool slightly.

4 To serve, spoon warm pudding into bowls. Pour 1 to 2 tablespoons Molasses-Chocolate Sauce over each serving. Makes 6 to 8 servings.

Molasses-Chocolate Sauce: In a saucepan stir together ¼ cup packed brown sugar and 1 tablespoon cornstarch. Stir in ⅓ cup water, 2 tablespoons chocolate-flavored syrup, and 1 tablespoon molasses. Cook and stir mixture over medium-low heat about 2 minutes more or until thickened and bubbly.

Nutrition Facts per serving: 401 cal., 19 g total fat (11 g sat. fat), 172 mg chol., 84 mg sodium, 52 g carbo., 1 g fiber, 10 g pro.
Daily Values: 16% vit. A, 1% vit. C, 13% calcium, 16% iron.

Chocolate-Mocha Dream

Berries and chocolate are a luscious combination—luckily, fresh berries are now available all year. If you can't find raspberries, strawberries will do. (See the photograph on page 43.)

Prep: 15 minutes **Chill:** 2½ hours

- ⅓ cup sugar
- 4 tsp. instant espresso powder or instant coffee crystals
- 1 envelope unflavored gelatin
- 1 cup milk
- 2 3-oz. pkg. cream cheese, softened
- ½ cup whipping cream
- 4 oz. milk chocolate, chopped
- 2 cups fresh raspberries
- 8 chocolate-flavored rolled sugar ice cream cones

1 In a small saucepan combine sugar, espresso powder or coffee crystals, and gelatin. Stir in milk. Cook and stir over medium-low heat until gelatin is dissolved; set aside.

2 In a medium mixing bowl beat softened cream cheese with an electric mixer on medium speed until fluffy. Gradually beat in milk mixture. Chill 1 hour or until partially set. Cover and chill for 1½ hours more or until firm.

3 In a chilled mixing bowl beat whipping cream with an electric mixer on medium speed about 1 minute or until cream just begins to thicken. Add gelatin mixture; beat 2 to 3 minutes or until smooth. Fold in chopped chocolate. Cover and chill for 15 to 30 minutes or until this mousse mixture mounds when spooned.

4 To serve, fill cones with about ¼ cup raspberries, reserving a few berries for garnish. Scoop about ¼ cup of the mousse into each cone. Serve as a traditional cone or invert into chilled bowls and garnish with remaining berries. Makes 8 servings.

Nutrition Facts per serving: 306 cal., 19 g total fat (11 g sat. fat), 46 mg chol., 132 mg sodium, 31 g carbo., 1 g fiber, 6 g pro.
Daily Values: 19% vit. A, 14% vit. C, 9% calcium, 7% iron.

PRIZE WINNER

Mulled Raspberry Tea

TerryAnn Moore
Oaklyn, New Jersey
$200—Hot Drinks Category

Start to finish: 15 minutes

- 1 cup frozen loose-pack raspberries, slightly thawed
- 2 cups brewed tea
- 2 cups cranberry-raspberry juice
- 1 cup prepared lemonade
- ¼ cup water
- 3 whole allspice
  Sugar (optional)
- 1 lemon, thinly sliced
  Fresh or frozen raspberries (optional)

1 In a medium saucepan slightly mash the 1 cup raspberries with a potato masher. Stir in the tea, cranberry-raspberry juice, lemonade, water, and allspice. Bring to boiling; reduce heat. Simmer, uncovered, for 10 minutes. Strain and discard the fruit pulp and spices.

2 To serve, ladle mixture into heat-proof glass mugs or cups. If desired, sweeten with sugar. Serve with lemon slices and, if desired, additional raspberries. Makes 6 servings.

Nutrition Facts per serving: 104 cal., 0 g total fat, 0 mg chol., 7 mg sodium, 26 g carbo., 3 g fiber, 1 g pro.
Daily Values: 1% vit. A, 80% vit. C, 1% calcium, 3% iron.

TEST KITCHEN TIP

Warming Mugs

Don't let a cold mug put a quick chill on your beverage! Keep hot beverages warm longer by serving them in warm mugs. Before preparing the beverage, pour hot tap water into the mugs. Just before serving, pour the water out.

---

30 MINUTE, NO FAT

Hot Gingered Cider

As soothing as can be, a cupful of this spicy drink just might be the answer during cold and flu season.

Start to finish: 10 minutes

- 2 cups ginger ale
- 2 cups apple cider
- 1 Tbsp. lemon juice
- 2 Tbsp. mulling spices*
- 1 1-inch piece fresh ginger, sliced

1 In a medium saucepan combine ginger ale, apple cider, lemon juice, mulling spices, and fresh ginger. Cover and cook over medium-low heat for 5 to 10 minutes or until heated through (do not boil). Strain and discard the spices.

2 To serve, ladle mixture into heat-proof glass mugs or cups. Makes 4 servings.

Note: If purchased mulling spices are unavailable use a mixture of 1 broken stick cinnamon and 1 tablespoon whole cloves.

Nutrition Facts per serving: 101 cal., 0 g total fat, 0 mg chol., 12 mg sodium, 26 g carbo., 0 g fiber, 0 g pro.
Daily Values: 5% vit. C, 1% calcium, 4% iron.

---

30 MINUTE

Nut-Butter Cocoa

Two nutty spreads combine to give this beverage a wonderfully rich flavor. Look for the chocolate-hazelnut spread near the peanut butter in your local supermarket.

Start to finish: 15 minutes

- ½ cup whipping cream
- 3½ cups milk
- ⅓ cup chocolate-hazelnut spread
- 2 Tbsp. creamy peanut butter
- 3 miniature chocolate-covered peanut butter cups, quartered

1 In a mixing bowl beat whipping cream with an electric mixer on medium to high speed until stiff peaks form (tips stand straight). Cover and chill until needed.

2 In a saucepan combine milk, chocolate-hazelnut spread, and peanut butter. Cook and stir over medium heat until combined and mixture is heated through.

3 To serve, pour mixture into warm mugs. Top each with a spoonful of whipped cream and two pieces of candy. Makes 6 servings.

Nutrition Facts per serving: 310 cal., 21 g total fat (8 g sat. fat), 39 mg chol., 157 mg sodium, 23 g carbo., 1 g fiber, 9 g pro.
Daily Values: 17% vit. A, 2% vit. C, 20% calcium, 2% iron.

TEST KITCHEN TIP

Storing Chocolate

Keep your chocolate in a tightly covered container or sealed plastic bag in a cool, dry place. If stored in a too-warm place (higher than 78 degrees), chocolate may "bloom" or develop a harmless gray film. Keep cocoa powder in a tightly covered container in that same cool, dry place.

PRIZE WINNER

Chocolate Chai

Amy Oldenburg
Bedford, Ohio
$400—Hot Drinks Category

Start to finish: 15 minutes

- 1 black tea bag, such as orange pekoe, English breakfast, Lapsang souchong, or Darjeeling
- ½ cup boiling water
- 3 Tbsp. raw sugar or granulated sugar
- 2 Tbsp. unsweetened Dutch-process cocoa powder
- 2 cups milk
- 1 tsp. vanilla
- ½ tsp. ground cinnamon
- ½ tsp. ground nutmeg
  Whipped cream
  Cinnamon sticks

1 In a small saucepan pour boiling water over tea bag. Cover and let stand 3 to 5 minutes. Remove tea bag.

2 Stir the sugar and cocoa into the tea. Cook and stir over medium heat just until mixture comes to boiling. Stir in milk, vanilla, ground cinnamon, and nutmeg; heat through (do not boil).

3 To serve, pour hot mixture into warm mugs. Top each serving with a spoonful of whipped cream and add a cinnamon stick as a stirrer. Makes 2 or 3 servings.

Nutrition Facts per serving: 279 cal., 11 g total fat (6 g sat. fat), 38 mg chol., 130 mg sodium, 35 g carbo., 0 g fiber, 10 g pro.
Daily Values: 21% vit. A, 4% vit. C, 31% calcium, 7% iron.

30 MINUTE

Hot Chocolate by The Bowlful

With such an enticing array of chocolate choices, it's worth trying different brands each time you make this delightfully decadent cocoa.

Start to finish: 15 minutes

- 4 cups half-and-half, light cream, or whole milk
- 3 to 4 oz. semisweet chocolate, chopped
- 3 to 4 oz. bittersweet chocolate, chopped
- 1 Tbsp. dark-colored corn syrup

1 In a heavy 2-quart saucepan combine half-and-half, semisweet chocolate, and bittersweet chocolate. Stir in dark corn syrup. Cook and stir over medium heat until chocolate melts and mixture is smooth.

2 To serve, pour hot mixture into warm latte bowls or mugs. Makes 8 servings.

Nutrition Facts per serving: 270 cal., 23 g total fat (14 g sat. fat), 45 mg chol., 52 mg sodium, 17 g carbo., 3 g fiber, 6 g pro.
Daily Values: 16% vit. A, 2% vit. C, 12% calcium, 8% iron.

30 MINUTE, LOW FAT

Banana and Caramel Cocoa

Three great flavors—banana, caramel, and chocolate—in one hot drink! Even though the mixture is blended until smooth, there will still be particles of banana adding body to the beverage.

Start to finish: 15 minutes

- 1 cup milk
- 1 large ripe banana, cut up
- ⅓ cup chocolate-flavored syrup
- ¼ cup caramel ice-cream topping
- ¼ teaspoon ground cinnamon
- 2 cups milk
  Whipped cream (optional)
  Cinnamon sticks (optional)

1 Place the 1 cup milk, the banana, chocolate-flavored syrup, caramel ice-cream topping, and ground cinnamon in a blender container or food processor bowl. Cover and blend or process until nearly smooth.

2 Transfer the mixture to a medium saucepan. Add the 2 cups milk. Cook and stir over medium-high heat until heated through.

3 To serve, pour hot mixture into warm mugs. If desired, garnish with whipped cream and a cinnamon stick. Makes 4 servings.

Nutrition Facts per serving: 224 cal., 4 g total fat (2 g sat. fat), 14 mg chol., 187 mg sodium, 44 g carbo., 1 g fiber, 7 g pro.
Daily Values: 11% vit. A, 8% vit. C, 24% calcium, 4% iron.

february

IN THIS CHAPTER

30-minute recipes indicated in COLOR.
Low-fat and no-fat recipes indicated
with a ♥.
Photographs indicated in italics.
*Bonus recipe

PRIZE WINNER

Italian Doughnuts

Mary Ann Marino
West Pittsburg, Pennsylvania
$400—Coffee Cakes and Doughnuts

Prep: 10 minutes **Stand:** 30 minutes
Cook: 2½ minutes per batch

 1 15-oz. container ricotta cheese
 4 eggs
 1 Tbsp. vanilla
 1½ cups all-purpose flour
 ½ cup granulated sugar
 2 Tbsp. baking powder
 ½ tsp. salt
   Cooking oil for deep-fat frying
   Sifted powdered sugar or
     granulated sugar or
     cinnamon/sugar

1 In a large mixing bowl beat ricotta cheese with an electric mixer on medium speed until smooth. Add eggs and vanilla; beat until combined. Add the flour, ½ cup granulated sugar, baking powder, and salt. Beat on low speed just until combined. Let batter stand for 30 minutes.

2 Drop batter by well-rounded teaspoons, four or five at a time, into deep hot oil (365°). Cook for 2½ to 3 minutes or until golden brown, turning once. Remove doughnuts with a slotted spoon and drain on paper towels. Repeat with remaining batter. Cool completely. Shake doughnuts in a bag with desired sugar. Makes 3 dozen.

Nutrition Facts per doughnut: 102 cal., 6 g total fat (2 g sat. fat), 30 mg chol., 107 mg sodium, 9 g carbo., 0 g fiber, 3 g pro.
Daily Values: 2% vit. A, 7% calcium, 2% iron.

Taffy Apple Doughnuts

See the photograph on page 39.
Prep: 15 minutes
Cook: 3 minutes per batch

 2 cups all-purpose flour
 ⅓ cup granulated sugar
 1½ tsp. baking powder
 1 tsp. apple pie spice
 ¼ tsp. baking soda
 1 egg
 3 Tbsp. butter or margarine, melted
 1 cup chopped peeled apple
 ½ cup milk
 ½ cup apple juice
   Cooking oil for deep-fat frying
 1 cup maple-flavored syrup
 ¾ cup packed brown sugar
   Wooden skewers or sticks
 1½ cups finely chopped nuts

1 Stir together flour, granulated sugar, baking powder, spice, soda, and ½ teaspoon *salt*. Combine egg, melted butter, apple, milk, and juice. Stir liquid into flour mixture just until moistened.

2 Drop batter by well-rounded tablespoons, three or four at a time, into deep hot oil (365°). Fry 3 minutes or until brown, turning once. Remove and drain on paper towels. Repeat with remaining batter.

3 In a saucepan combine syrup and brown sugar. Bring just to boiling; remove from heat. Insert a wooden skewer into each doughnut. Dip each doughnut into syrup mixture; sprinkle with nuts. Cool on a wire rack. Makes about 20.

Nutrition Facts per doughnut: 264 cal., 14 g total fat (3 g sat. fat), 16 mg chol., 135 mg sodium, 35 g carbo., 1 g fiber, 3 g pro.
Daily Values: 3% vit. A, 1% vit. C, 6% calcium, 7% iron.

Banana French Toast

Prep: 25 minutes **Chill:** 6 hours
Bake: 25 minutes **Stand:** 10 minutes

 2 medium ripe bananas, sliced
   ¼ inch (1⅓ cups)
 1 Tbsp. lemon juice
 12 ½-inch slices French bread,
   untrimmed
 ½ cup semisweet or milk chocolate
   pieces (3 oz.)
 2 beaten eggs
 ¾ cup milk
 2 Tbsp. honey
 ½ tsp. vanilla
 ¼ tsp. ground cinnamon
 ¼ cup sliced almonds
 1 tsp. sugar
   Maple syrup (optional)

1 In a bowl gently toss bananas with lemon juice. Arrange half the bread slices in the bottom of a greased 2-quart square baking dish. Top with a layer of the bananas, the chocolate pieces, and remaining bread slices.

2 In a medium bowl combine eggs, milk, honey, vanilla, and cinnamon. Pour liquid slowly over bread to coat evenly. Cover and chill for 6 to 24 hours.

3 Preheat oven to 425°. Uncover the baking dish. Sprinkle bread with almonds and sugar. Bake for 5 minutes. Reduce oven temperature to 325°. Bake for 20 to 25 minutes more or until knife inserted near the center comes out clean and top of French toast is light brown. Let stand 10 minutes. If desired, serve with maple syrup. Makes 4 servings.

Nutrition Facts per serving: 403 cal., 15 g total fat (2 g sat. fat), 110 mg chol., 284 mg sodium, 62 g carbo., 2 g fiber, 11 g pro.
Daily Values: 8% vit. A, 15% vit. C, 12% calcium, 19% iron.

Snappy Apple Brunch Cake

Shirley DeSantis
Bethlehem, Pennsylvania
$200—Coffee Cakes and Doughnuts

Prep: 25 minutes **Bake:** 30 minutes
Cool: 1 hour

- 1 cup crushed gingersnap cookies (18 cookies)
- ¼ cup honey crunch wheat germ
- 2 Tbsp. brown sugar
- ⅓ cup butter
- ⅓ cup chopped walnuts
- 1 pkg. 2-layer-size spice cake mix
- 1 pkg. fast-rising active dry yeast
- ¾ cup apple butter
- ½ cup warm water (120° to 130°)
- 2 eggs
- ¼ cup white baking pieces
- 2 tsp. butter
- ⅔ cup sifted powdered sugar
- 1 to 2 Tbsp. apple juice

1 Preheat oven to 350°. Generously grease and flour a 13×9×2-inch baking pan; set aside. In a medium mixing bowl stir together gingersnaps, wheat germ, and brown sugar. Using a pastry blender, cut in butter until crumbly. Stir in walnuts; set aside.

2 In a large mixing bowl stir together cake mix and yeast. Add apple butter, warm water, and eggs. Beat with an electric mixer on low speed until combined. Beat on high speed for 2 minutes. Spread batter evenly into prepared pan. Sprinkle gingersnap mixture evenly over top.

3 Bake about 30 minutes or until a wooden toothpick inserted off-center comes out clean. Place cake in pan on a wire rack; cool slightly. (Some areas of cake will dip slightly.)

4 Meanwhile, in a heavy small saucepan combine white baking pieces and butter. Cook and stir over low heat just until melted. Remove from heat. Stir in powdered sugar and enough apple juice to make a drizzling consistency. Drizzle over coffee cake. Cool at least 1 hour on wire rack. Makes 12 servings.

EDITOR'S TIP

Love You, Honey
by Lisa Kingsley

Isn't it funny how a bear likes honey?
Buzz, buzz, buzz, I wonder why he does?
—Winnie-the-Pooh

As bears of very little brain and smart folks alike are discovering, there are more kinds of honey to love these days than just the sweet stuff that comes from a clover patch. More than 300 varieties of honey are now produced in the United States alone.

Flower power
The flower from which the honey is derived imbues the sweetener with its distinctive aroma and flavor. Common sources include lavender, thyme, orange blossom, apple, cherry, buckwheat, tupelo (a tree that grows in the Southern swamps)—or whatever flourishes in your part of the country. Honey that is lighter in color usually has the mildest flavor, and darker honey, such as buckwheat, will have a more intense flavor. Look for some of the more unusual (and local) varieties at your farmer's market or at gourmet and specialty food shops.

Sweet options
Honey comes in three market forms: comb, liquid, and whipped (also called creme or spun honey). The edible-comb form is just right for those who like their honey in its purest form, while the liquid form is great for cooking, baking, and drizzling. Creme honey is easy to spread and is sometimes flavored with fruits or spices, such as raspberry or cinnamon. If it is stored at room temperature in a dark place, honey has an almost indefinite shelf life. It will, however, crystallize (become solid) and darken with time. To reliquefy it, warm the honey jar slightly in the microwave oven or in a pan of very hot tap water. Honey will occasionally ferment. If it smells or tastes strange, throw it out.

Part of the fun of honey is that it can be enjoyed in many ways—spread, drizzled, scooped, squeezed out of a teddy-bear bottle, and baked into cookies and breads. You can substitute honey for up to one-half of the sugar called for in a recipe. In recipes for baked goods, reduce the liquid by 2 tablespoons for each ½ cup of honey used and add ½ teaspoon baking soda.

Honey of an idea
In addition to stirring a spoonful into your coffee or tea, or topping off warm pancakes or corn bread, here are some other ways to enjoy the sweet stuff:

Sprinkle plain yogurt with coarsely chopped walnuts; drizzle with honey.

Drizzle any blue-veined cheese, such as Roquefort, Gorgonzola, or Stilton, with honey; serve with whole wheat crackers and ripe pears.

Spread hearty slices of toasted bread, bagels, or English muffins with ricotta cheese; sprinkle with almonds and drizzle with honey.

Stir together 2 tablespoons honey with ½ cup of sour cream; use as a topping for fresh berries.

Note: Honey should not be given to children one year or younger. It can contain trace amounts of botulism spores. These spores could trigger a potentially fatal reaction in children with undeveloped immune systems.

Nutrition Facts per serving: 407 cal., 15 g total fat (7 g sat. fat), 52 mg chol., 434 mg sodium, 65 g carbo., 1 g fiber, 4 g pro.
Daily Values: 6% vit. A, 1% vit. C, 9% calcium, 12% iron.

TEST KITCHEN TIP

Coffee Cake 101

How to get even the sleepiest heads up and at 'em? Pop a coffee cake into the oven. There's nothing quite like a piece of warm coffee cake to go with your morning coffee (or tea), as anyone who awakens to the wonderful, homey aroma will heartily agree. Here's how to make a coffee cake just right every time.

If you're baking in a metal pan, be sure it's a shiny one. Shiny pans reflect heat, which produces a golden, delicate, and tender crust.

Most coffee cakes are at their best served warm. Let your coffee cake cool for 20 to 30 minutes before cutting and serving—it will be at its just-right-for-eating stage.

Save leftover coffee cake for a snack or tomorrow's breakfast in a tightly covered container stored at room temperature. If the coffee cake contains cream cheese, store it in the refrigerator.

To reheat coffee cake, wrap it in heavy foil and heat in a 350° oven about 15 minutes or until warm.

Citrus and Cherry Upside-Down Cake

Prep: 30 minutes **Bake:** 40 minutes
Cool: 35 minutes

2 Tbsp. butter or margarine
½ cup packed brown sugar
1 Tbsp. light-colored corn syrup
¼ cup dried tart red cherries
2 oranges, peeled, seeded, and sectioned (⅔ cup)
1 grapefruit, peeled, seeded, and sectioned (⅔ cup)
1½ cups all-purpose flour
2 tsp. baking powder
¼ tsp. baking soda
⅓ cup butter or margarine, softened
¾ cup granulated sugar
1 egg
1½ tsp. vanilla
⅔ cup orange juice

1 Preheat oven to 350°. Melt the 2 tablespoons butter or margarine in a 9×1½-inch round baking pan. Stir in brown sugar and corn syrup; spread evenly in pan. Sprinkle dried cherries and arrange orange and grapefruit segments on top. Set aside.

2 In a bowl combine flour, baking powder, and baking soda; set aside. In a large mixing bowl beat the ⅓ cup butter or margarine with an electric mixer on medium speed for 30 seconds. Gradually beat in the granulated sugar until combined. Beat in egg and vanilla. Add dry mixture and orange juice alternately to butter mixture. Carefully spoon batter over citrus segments, spreading evenly.

3 Bake about 40 minutes or until a wooden toothpick inserted into cake portion comes out clean. Cool cake in pan on a wire rack for 5 minutes. Invert cake onto a serving plate. Cool for 30 to 40 minutes more. Serve warm. Makes 8 servings.

Nutrition Facts per serving: 352 cal., 12 g total fat (7 g sat. fat), 57 mg chol., 270 mg sodium, 58 g carbo., 1 g fiber, 4 g pro.
Daily Values: 148% vit. A, 25% vit. C, 9% calcium, 8% iron.

Pumpkin and Peach Coffee Cake

Prep: 25 minutes **Bake:** 50 minutes
Cool: 2 hours

1 16-oz. pkg. frozen peaches, thawed
½ cup peach preserves
¾ cup broken pecans
3 cups all-purpose flour
2½ tsp. baking powder
1 tsp. pumpkin pie spice
½ tsp. baking soda
½ tsp. salt
½ cup butter, softened
¾ cup granulated sugar
¾ cup packed brown sugar
3 eggs
½ cup canned pumpkin
1 8-oz. carton dairy sour cream
1 recipe Powdered Sugar Icing (optional) (see below)

1 Preheat oven to 350°. Grease a 13×9×2-inch baking pan. In a medium bowl combine peaches, peach preserves, and pecans; set aside. In another bowl combine flour, baking powder, pumpkin pie spice, baking soda, and salt.

2 In a large mixing bowl beat butter with an electric mixer on medium speed for 30 seconds. Beat in sugars until combined. Add eggs, one at a time, beating well after each. Beat in pumpkin. Add dry mixture and sour cream alternately to beaten mixture. Spread about 3 cups batter into the prepared pan. Top with 2 cups of the peach mixture. Spoon on remaining batter and then remaining peaches.

3 Bake for 50 to 60 minutes or until a wooden toothpick inserted into cake portion comes out clean. Cool in pan on a wire rack. If desired, drizzle with Powdered Sugar Icing. Makes 12 servings.

Powdered Sugar Icing

In a small mixing bowl combine 1 cup sifted powdered sugar, ¼ teaspoon pumpkin pie spice, and enough orange juice (2 to 3 teaspoons) to make a drizzling consistency.

Nutrition Facts per serving: 431 cal., 18 g total fat (8 g sat. fat), 83 mg chol., 353 mg sodium, 63 g carbo., 3 g fiber, 6 g pro.
Daily Values: 38% vit. A, 7% vit. C, 11% calcium, 12% iron.

LOW FAT

Indian Paneer Cheese

This creamy white cheese is similar to ricotta, but with a fragrant hint of cumin. Use as a topper for curries, vegetables, or baked potatoes, or as a spread for flat bread.

Prep: 25 minutes **Chill:** 15 hours

- 12 **cups whole milk**
- 2 **tsp. salt**
- ¼ **tsp. cumin seed, crushed**
- ⅓ **cup lemon juice**

1 In a 5-quart Dutch oven bring milk, salt, and cumin seed just to boiling; reduce heat. Simmer, uncovered, for 5 minutes. Remove from heat. Stir in lemon juice. Let stand for 15 minutes.

2 Line a large strainer or colander with several layers of 100-percent cotton cheesecloth. Strain mixture; discard liquid. Gently squeeze the cheesecloth to remove as much liquid from the curds as possible. Wrap cloth around curds. Place wrapped curds in a large strainer or colander and put a weighted bowl on top to help press out any additional liquid. Let stand, covered, in a refrigerator for at least 15 hours.

3 Remove curds. Discard liquid. Form curds into a flat rectangle or press into a large bowl to shape. Refrigerate, covered with plastic wrap, until well chilled. Store in refrigerator, tightly wrapped, for up to 3 weeks. Makes about 1 pound.

Nutrition Facts per ounce: 50 cal., 4 g total fat (2 g sat. fat), 14 mg chol., 290 mg sodium, 1 g carbo., 0 g fiber, 3 g pro.
Daily Values: 4% vit. A, 5% calcium.

LOW FAT

Fresh Yogurt Cheese

Prep: 2 minutes **Chill:** 24 hours

- 1 **16-oz. carton plain yogurt or plain goat's-milk yogurt***
- 2 **tsp. finely snipped fresh herbs (such as basil, oregano, thyme, or marjoram), or ½ tsp. ground spice (such as black, white, or red pepper, or coriander) (optional)**

1 Line a yogurt strainer, sieve, or small colander with three layers of 100-percent cotton cheesecloth or a clean paper coffee filter. Suspend lined strainer, sieve, or colander over a bowl. Spoon in yogurt. Cover with plastic wrap. Refrigerate for at least 24 hours.

2 Remove cheese from refrigerator. Drain and discard liquid. If desired, stir herbs or spices into cheese. Store, covered, in refrigerator for up to 1 week. Makes ¼ to 1 cup.

*Note: Use a brand of yogurt that contains no gums, gelatin, or fillers. These ingredients may prevent whey from separating from curd.

Nutrition Facts per tablespoon (without herbs): 44 cal., 2 g total fat (2 g sat. fat), 10 mg chol., 40 mg sodium, 4 g carbo., 0 g fiber, 2 g pro.
Daily Values: 1% vit. A, 4% calcium.

LOW FAT

Blue Cheese-Walnut Bites

Simplicity is what makes these appetizers so appealing—they are easy to make and don't need a dip or spread to be wonderful.

Prep: 25 minutes **Chill:** 2 hours
Bake: 8 minutes per batch

CLEVER COOK
Hide the Tongs

To store springy kitchen tongs in a kitchen utensil drawer, save the cardboard tube from an empty roll of paper towels. The tongs slide right in, and they're easy to find when you need them.

Billie Foster
Enid, Oklahoma

- 1½ **cups all-purpose flour**
- 2 **to 3 tsp. cracked black pepper**
- 8 **oz. blue cheese**
- ¼ **cup butter**
- 1 **cup chopped walnuts**
- 2 **egg yolks, slightly beaten**

1 In a medium mixing bowl combine flour and pepper. Using a pastry blender, cut in cheese and butter until mixture resembles coarse crumbs. Add walnuts and egg yolks. Stir until combined. Form the mixture into a ball; knead until combined.

2 Divide dough in half. Shape each half into a log about 9 inches long. Wrap logs in plastic wrap; chill at least 2 hours. Preheat oven to 425°.

3 Cut each log into ¼-inch slices. Place slices 1 inch apart on an ungreased baking sheet. Bake for 8 to 10 minutes or until bottoms and edges are golden brown. Transfer to a wire rack. Serve warm or at room temperature. Store, tightly covered, in the refrigerator for up to 1 week. Makes about 6 dozen.

Nutrition Facts per appetizer: 38 cal., 3 g total fat (1 g sat. fat), 11 mg chol., 64 mg sodium, 2 g carbo., 0 g fiber, 1 g pro.
Daily Values: 2% vit. A, 1% calcium, 1% iron.

LOW FAT

Tomato-Onion Spiral Bread

In addition to enjoying this bread hot out of the oven with butter, you can try it as toast or as the foundation for your favorite sandwich. (See the photograph on page 40.)

Prep: 45 minutes **Rise:** 2½ hours
Bake: 30 minutes

    3 Tbsp. dried minced onion
    4 tsp. dried parsley
    1 tsp. poultry seasoning
   ¼ cup boiling water
   ½ cup finely snipped dried tomatoes
       (not oil-packed)
    1 tsp. paprika
   ½ tsp. garlic powder
   ⅓ cup boiling water
    2 pkg. active dry yeast
  1½ cups warm water (105° to 115°)
   ½ cup butter, melted
   ¼ cup sugar
    2 tsp. salt
    1 egg, beaten
  3¼ to 3½ cups all-purpose flour
   ⅓ cup nonfat dry milk powder
    1 cup whole wheat flour
  1¾ to 2 cups all-purpose flour
    1 egg, beaten
    1 Tbsp. water

1 In a small bowl combine dried onion, parsley, and poultry seasoning. Stir in the ¼ cup boiling water; set aside.

2 In another small bowl combine snipped tomatoes, paprika, and garlic powder. Stir in the ⅓ cup boiling water; set aside. Do not drain. In a mixing bowl combine yeast and the 1½ cups warm water. Let stand for 5 minutes to dissolve yeast. Stir in melted butter, sugar, and salt. Divide mixture in half.

3 To one-half of the yeast mixture, stir in 1 egg and the dried onion mixture. Using the 3¼ to 3½ cups all-purpose flour, stir in as much as you can with a wooden spoon. Knead in as much of this remaining flour as necessary to make a moderately stiff dough that is smooth and elastic (6 to 8 minutes). Place in a greased bowl, turning once to grease surface. Cover and let rise in a warm place until double (1 to 1¼ hours).

4 To the remaining half of the yeast mixture, stir in the undrained dried tomato mixture, milk powder, and the whole wheat flour. Using the 1¾ to 2 cups all-purpose flour, stir in as much of it as you can with a wooden spoon. Knead in as much of this remaining flour as necessary to make a moderately stiff dough that is smooth and elastic (6 to 8 minutes). Place in a greased bowl, turning once. Cover and let rise in a warm place until double (1 to 1¼ hours).

5 Punch onion dough down; divide in half. On a lightly floured surface roll one portion of the onion dough to a 12×10-inch rectangle; set aside. Punch tomato dough down and divide in half. On a lightly floured surface roll one portion of tomato dough to a 12×10-inch rectangle. Place tomato dough rectangle on top of onion dough rectangle. Roll up both doughs together from a long side. Moisten seam and ends with *water*, then seal. Place loaf, seam side down, on a baking sheet. Repeat rolling and shaping with remaining halves of doughs. Cover and let loaves rise in a warm place until nearly double (30 to 40 minutes).

6 Preheat oven to 375°. Brush loaves with a mixture of 1 beaten egg and 1 tablespoon water. With a sharp knife gently cut three or four slashes on top of each loaf.

7 Bake for 30 to 40 minutes or until loaves are done. Cover loaves with foil, if necessary, after 20 to 25 minutes to prevent overbrowning. Cool on wire racks. Slice to serve. Makes 2 loaves (32 servings total).

To Make Ahead:
Make and bake bread as directed. Place completely cooled bread in a freezer container or bag. Freeze for up to 3 months. Thaw the wrapped bread at room temperature for 2 hours.

Nutrition Facts per servings: 122 cal., 3 g total fat (2 g sat. fat), 21 mg chol., 189 mg sodium, 20 g carbo., 1 g fiber, 3 g pro.
Daily Values: 4% vit. A, 1% vit. C, 1% calcium, 7% iron.

Doting Husband's Bulgur Salad

Rudolph Nebel, one of 12 Century Standout winners in the magazine's contest, created this salad as a surprise for his wife after an especially busy day. (See the photograph on page 40.)

Start to finish: 40 minutes

    1 cup boiling water
   ½ cup bulgur
   ¼ cup olive oil
    2 Tbsp. balsamic vinegar
    1 Tbsp. brown sugar
    1 Tbsp. finely shredded orange peel
    1 Tbsp. honey
    1 cup finely chopped green or red
       mustard greens
   ½ cup sliced almonds, toasted
   ½ cup thinly sliced green onions
   ½ cup chopped celery
    6 cups torn romaine
   ¼ cup shredded carrot

1 In a medium bowl pour boiling water over bulgur; stir. Cover and let stand 30 minutes or until slightly softened. Drain off any excess liquid.

2 Meanwhile, for dressing, in a small mixing bowl whisk together olive oil, balsamic vinegar, brown sugar, orange peel, honey, and ½ teaspoon *salt*. Set aside.

3 In a large bowl stir together drained bulgur, mustard greens, almonds, green onions, and celery. Pour about ⅓ cup of the dressing over bulgur mixture; toss to coat.

4 To serve, arrange the torn romaine on eight individual serving plates. Spoon bulgur mixture over romaine. Drizzle remaining dressing over bulgur mixture and romaine. Top with shredded carrot. Makes 8 side-dish servings.

Nutrition Facts per serving: 165 cal., 11 g total fat (1 g sat. fat), 0 mg chol., 148 mg sodium, 14 g carbo., 4 g fiber, 4 g pro.
Daily Values: 12% vit. A, 22% vit. C, 4% calcium, 8% iron.

LOW FAT

Risotto

Prep: 10 minutes **Cook:** 35 minutes

- ½ **cup chopped onion**
- 4 **tsp. margarine or butter**
- 1 **cup Arborio rice**
- 3 **cups water**
- ¾ **cup beef broth or vegetable broth**
- ¾ **cup frozen baby peas**
- ¼ **cup grated Parmesan cheese**
- ¼ **cup cubed mozzarella or Muenster cheese (1 oz.)**
- 1 **to 2 Tbsp. snipped fresh thyme, savory, and/or parsley**
  Grated Parmesan cheese

EDITOR'S TIP

Risotto: A Stir-Crazy Adventure

A willing hand, a wooden spoon, and a half-hour later: risotto!

Ingredients for Success:
- ● Patience
- ● Arborio rice
- ● A heavy-bottom saucepan
- ● A flexible attitude since not all risottos cook the same

Patience and the ability to focus on a single task are two things that every cook needs. They'll become second nature when you learn to cook risotto.

One of the many culinary blessings bestowed on us by Italy, risotto (rih-SAW-toh) is a fragrant blend of rice, cheese, and herbs that's worth every ticking second it takes to prepare.

Served as a first course, side dish, or the main event of dinner, risotto packs a meal's worth of taste and texture into every forkful. Firm, separate kernels of rice are bathed in a luxuriously creamy sauce that's infused with the rich flavors of thyme and Parmesan.

Though it tastes wonderful, the dish has a bit of an undeserved reputation for being tricky to make; cook along with us and you'll learn how easy it really is.

The path to perfection is the slow addition of broth and constant stirring. Novices always ask, "Why not add the broth all at once?" The answer itself incorporates the technique for great risotto and reveals the secret to becoming a better cook. Gradual addition of liquid controls the amount of starch that the rice releases—if you get impatient and dump the liquid in all at once, it will wind up as a concretelike mass by the time the rice is cooked. Constant stirring serves the same end, preventing the rice from sticking together.

The rice variety we call for, Arborio, is essential for creating the creaminess that is one of the wonderful qualities in risotto. (Arborio contains a high proportion of the kind of starch that makes the dish so delightful.) Find Arborio rice in the rice or gourmet sections of supermarkets, Italian groceries, and specialty stores.

A few final thoughts: If you need to leave the stove for a few moments (or even an hour), take the risotto off the heat; it will be fine until you return. If you run out of broth and the rice is still too firm for you, substitute water; the flavor will be just as delicious.

1 In a 2-quart saucepan cook onion in hot margarine or butter until onion is tender. Add the uncooked rice. Cook and stir over medium heat about 5 minutes or until the rice is lightly golden.

2 Meanwhile, in another saucepan combine water and broth; bring to boiling. Reduce heat until mixture just simmers. Slowly and carefully add 1 cup of the broth mixture to the rice mixture, stirring constantly. Continue to cook and stir over medium heat until liquid is absorbed. Add another ½ cup of the broth mixture to the rice mixture, stirring constantly. Continue to cook and stir until liquid is

absorbed. Add the remaining liquid, ½ cup at a time, stirring constantly until the liquid is absorbed and rice is just tender. (This will take about 25 minutes total.)

3 Cook and stir until the rice is slightly creamy and kernels are tender. Stir in peas, the ¼ cup Parmesan cheese, mozzarella or Muenster, and herbs; heat through. Serve immediately. Pass additional Parmesan cheese. Makes 4 main-dish or 6 to 8 side-dish servings.

Nutrition Facts per main-dish serving: 276 cal., 9 g total fat (5 g sat. fat), 21 mg chol., 1,015 mg sodium, 45 g carbo., 2 g fiber, 9 g pro.
Daily Values: 9% vit. A, 5% vit. C, 12% calcium, 18% iron.

EDITOR'S TIP

A Peek at Leeks

Leeks may resemble green onions on steroids, but they are not so bold. Rather, leeks are guileless, with a mellow flavor that makes them popular in recipes calling for just a hint of onionlike flavor.

This gentle vegetable is available all year. Shop for leeks with bright green leaves and firm roots. Leeks will store for up to one week when refrigerated loosely covered.

● Leeks are great in soups and sauces.
● Use leeks in place of onions and shallots.
● Leeks have only 16 calories per half-cup serving.
● Minced raw leeks add extra zing to salad dressings.

Leek Casserole Milanese

Serve this rich and creamy leek and mushroom combination alongside roast beef, lamb, or pork.

Prep: 25 minutes **Bake:** 20 minutes

- 5 to 6 leeks (about 1½ lb.)
- 2 tsp. cooking oil
- ½ cup sliced fresh oyster mushrooms or button mushrooms
- ½ cup dry white wine
- ¾ cup whipping cream
- ¼ to ½ tsp. salt
    Dash ground nutmeg
- ¼ cup soft bread crumbs
- ¼ cup shredded Parmesan cheese

1 Trim and discard leek root ends, any tough outer leaves, and several inches from the tops. Clean trimmed leeks thoroughly under cold running water to remove any sand. Bias-cut cleaned leeks into ¼-inch slices. Rinse slices under cold running water to remove any remaining sand. Drain well. Set aside (you should have about 3 cups sliced leeks).

2 Preheat oven to 400°. In a large skillet heat oil over medium heat. Add leeks. Cook and stir for 2 to 3 minutes or just until tender. Remove leeks from skillet; set aside.

3 In the same skillet cook the mushrooms for 3 to 5 minutes or just until tender. Add wine. Bring mixture just to boiling; reduce heat. Cook, uncovered, for 4 to 5 minutes or until most of the liquid has evaporated, stirring occasionally. Add whipping cream, salt, and nutmeg. Return to boiling. Cook and stir about 3 minutes or until slightly thickened (you should have about ¾ cup). Add leeks to mushroom mixture. Pour into a lightly greased, 1-quart casserole. Top with bread crumbs and cheese.

4 Bake for 20 to 25 minutes or until topping is golden and leeks are heated through. Serve at once. Makes 6 side-dish servings.

Nutrition Facts per serving: 187 cal., 14 g total fat (7 g sat. fat), 44 mg chol., 175 mg sodium, 10 g carbo., 3 g fiber, 3 g pro.
Daily Values: 13% vit. A, 8% vit. C, 8% calcium, 8% iron.

PRIZE WINNER

Apple Saucy Pork Roast

Tina Principato
Hampton, New Hampshire
$400—Best Pork and Beef Roasts

Prep: 25 minutes **Roast:** 2 hours
Stand: 10 minutes

- 1 3½- to 4-lb. boneless pork top loin roast (double loin, tied)
- 3 cloves garlic, cut into thin slices
- 1 tsp. coarse salt or regular salt
- 1 tsp. dried rosemary, crushed
- ½ tsp. coarsely ground pepper
- 3 medium apples, cored and cut into wedges (about 3 cups)
- ¼ cup packed brown sugar
- ¼ cup apple juice
- 2 Tbsp. lemon juice
- 2 tsp. dry mustard

1 Preheat oven to 325°. Cut small slits (about ½ inch long and 1 inch deep) in pork roast; insert a piece of garlic in each slit. Combine salt, rosemary, and pepper; rub onto meat surface. Place roast on a rack in a shallow roasting pan. Insert a meat thermometer. Roast, uncovered, for 1½ to 1¾ hours or until the meat thermometer reaches 145°. Spoon off any grease from roasting pan.

2 Combine the apples, brown sugar, apple juice, lemon juice, and dry mustard. Spoon apple mixture around roast. Roast, uncovered, for 30 to 45 minutes longer or until meat thermometer reaches 155° and meat juices are clear.

3 Transfer meat to a platter. Cover and let meat stand for 10 minutes before slicing. (The meat temperature will rise 5° during standing.) Remove the rack from the pan. Stir apple mixture into pan juices. If desired, use a slotted spoon to remove apple wedges, and pass juices. Makes 10 to 12 servings.

Nutrition Facts per serving: 237 cal., 11 g total fat (4 g sat. fat), 72 mg chol., 271 mg sodium, 12 g carbo., 1 g fiber, 23 g pro.
Daily Values: 7% vit. C, 1% calcium, 7% iron.

DINNER MENU

- **Jamaican Jerk Beef Roast (see below)**
- **Cooked jasmine rice**
- **Salad of mixed greens, fresh pineapple chunks, toasted almonds, and a ginger vinaigrette**
- **Ice-cream pie**

Jamaican Jerk Beef Roast

Try a cooked fragrant rice, such as jasmine or basmati, with this fork-tender beef and the slightly sweet, rich brown gravy.

Prep: 25 minutes **Roast:** 1½ hours

- 1 tsp. Jamaican jerk seasoning
- 1 tsp. cracked black pepper
- 1 tsp. bottled minced garlic
- 1 2- to 2½-lb. boneless beef chuck roast
- 1 Tbsp. cooking oil
- ¼ cup steak sauce
- 3 Tbsp. balsamic vinegar
- 2 Tbsp. sugar
- 1 tsp. Jamaican jerk seasoning
- 1 Tbsp. water
- 2 tsp. cornstarch
- ¼ cup raisins

1 Preheat oven to 325°. In a small bowl combine 1 teaspoon Jamaican jerk seasoning, the cracked black pepper, and garlic. With the tip of a knife, randomly cut about 20 small slits in the chuck roast; fill slits with the garlic mixture.

2 In a 4- to 6-quart Dutch oven brown roast on all sides in hot oil. Drain off fat. In a bowl combine steak sauce, balsamic vinegar, sugar, and 1 teaspoon Jamaican jerk seasoning. Pour mixture over roast.

3 Roast, covered, for 1½ to 2 hours or until meat is tender. Transfer meat to a platter; cover to keep warm. Measure 1 cup pan juices and add *water* if necessary to equal 1 cup.

4 In a small saucepan combine the 1 tablespoon water and cornstarch. Add the pan juices and raisins. Cook and stir over medium-high heat until thickened and bubbly. Cook and stir for 2 minutes more. Pass gravy with meat. Makes 8 servings.

Nutrition Facts per serving: 408 cal., 28 g total fat (11 g sat. fat), 96 mg chol., 242 mg sodium, 12 g carbo., 0 g fiber, 27 g pro.
Daily Values: 2% vit. A, 1% vit. C, 2% calcium, 19% iron.

PRIZE WINNER

Dilled Pot Roast

Linda J. Stowers
Tampa, Florida
$200—Best Pork and Beef Roasts

Prep: 20 minutes **Cook:** 5 hours

- 1 2- to 2½-lb. boneless beef chuck roast
- 2 Tbsp. cooking oil
- ½ cup water
- 2 tsp. snipped fresh dillweed or ¾ tsp. dried dillweed
- 1 tsp. coarse salt (kosher) or ¾ tsp. regular salt
- ½ tsp. pepper
- ½ cup plain yogurt
- 2 Tbsp. all-purpose flour
- 1 tsp. snipped fresh dillweed or ¼ tsp. dried dillweed
- 3 cups hot cooked noodles

TEST KITCHEN TIP

What Do We Mean When We Say "Snipped"?

When a recipe calls for snipped fresh herbs, dried fruits, or dried vegetables such as tomatoes, take a tip from our Test Kitchen. Place the food in a cup or small bowl, and use scissors or kitchen shears to cut the food into small, uniform pieces using short, quick strokes. Herbs will pack down slightly when snipped, so start with about one-third more leaves than called for in the recipe.

1 In a large skillet brown roast on all sides in hot oil. Place roast in a 3½- to 4-quart electric crockery cooker, cutting if necessary to fit. Add the water to cooker. Sprinkle the roast with the 2 teaspoons fresh dillweed or the ¾ teaspoon dried dillweed, salt, and pepper. Cover and cook on high-heat setting for 5 to 6 hours or on low-heat setting for 10 to 12 hours, until meat is tender.

2 Remove roast from cooker, reserving liquid; cover roast and keep warm. Measure liquid from cooker; skim any fat. Reserve 1 cup of the juices.

3 For sauce, in a small saucepan stir together the yogurt and flour until combined. Stir in the 1 cup reserved cooking liquid and the 1 teaspoon fresh dillweed or ¼ teaspoon dried dillweed. Cook and stir until thickened and bubbly. Cook and stir for 1 minute more. Serve the meat with the sauce and noodles. Makes 6 to 8 servings.

Nutrition Facts per serving with noodles: 373 cal., 12 g total fat (4 g sat. fat), 136 mg chol., 443 mg sodium, 22 g carbo., 2 g fiber, 41 g pro.
Daily Values: 4% calcium, 33% iron.

EDITOR'S TIP

Carried Away With Caraway

The curious little caraway seed packs so much flavor, yet we tend to meet it only during chance encounters—in rye bread, for example. Slight this pint-size spice no more. Add toasted caraway seeds to soups and salad dressings. Or, use caraway as a key ingredient in dry rubs for poultry, fish, and meat. Caraway seeds lose their power rapidly, so use them within six months of purchasing.

Squash and Caraway Soup

Prep: 20 minutes **Cook:** 35 minutes

1½   lb. yellow squash or zucchini, chopped (6 cups)
  2   Tbsp. cooking oil
  1   medium sweet onion, chopped (½ cup)
  1   Tbsp. caraway seed
  1   serrano pepper or small jalapeño pepper, seeded and chopped
  4   cups reduced-sodium chicken broth
      Caraway seed (optional)

1 Reserve 1 cup of the chopped squash or zucchini; set aside. In a large saucepan heat oil over medium-high heat. Add remaining squash, onion, 1 tablespoon caraway seed, and pepper. Cook, stirring occasionally, for 10 minutes. Add broth. Bring to boiling; reduce heat. Cook, uncovered, for 20 minutes. Remove from heat; cool slightly.

2 Pour one-third of mixture into a blender container or food processor bowl. Cover and blend or process until smooth. Strain into a medium saucepan. Repeat two more times. Add reserved 1 cup squash. Heat just to boiling. Ladle into individual soup bowls. Sprinkle with additional caraway seed, if desired. Makes 4 side-dish servings.

Nutrition Facts per serving: 121 cal., 8 g total fat (1 g sat. fat), 0 mg chol., 482 mg sodium, 9 g carbo., 2 g fiber, 5 g pro.
Daily Values: 4% vit. A, 38% vit. C, 4% calcium, 5% iron.

Caraway-Rubbed Chicken

Prep: 20 minutes **Roast:** 1¼ hours
Stand: 10 minutes

  2   Tbsp. caraway seed
  ¼   tsp. whole black pepper
  1   tsp. finely shredded lemon peel
  ½   tsp. kosher salt or regular salt
  1   3- to 4-lb. whole broiler-fryer chicken
  2   Tbsp. lemon juice
      Lemon slices (optional)

1 Preheat oven to 375°. With a mortar and pestle, slightly crush caraway seed and whole black pepper. Or, in a blender container combine caraway seed with whole pepper; cover and blend on high for 30 seconds. Stir in lemon peel and salt.

2 Rinse chicken; pat dry with paper towels. Skewer neck skin to back; tie legs to tail. Twist wings under back. Rub caraway mixture over entire bird and under skin of breast. Place chicken, breast side up, on a rack in a shallow pan. Insert meat thermometer into center of an inside thigh muscle.

3 Roast, uncovered, for 1¼ to 1¾ hours or until drumsticks move easily and meat is no longer pink or the thermometer registers 180°. Remove chicken from oven. Cover and let stand 10 minutes. Carefully drizzle lemon juice over chicken before carving. Serve with lemon slices, if desired. Makes 6 servings.

Nutrition Facts per serving: 223 cal., 13 g total fat (3 g sat. fat), 79 mg chol., 251 mg sodium, 2 g carbo., 0 g fiber, 25 g pro.
Daily Values: 4% vit. A, 4% vit. C, 2% calcium, 10% iron.

Thai Peanut Meatballs

Total time: 40 minutes

  1   egg, slightly beaten
  2   Tbsp. water
  1   Tbsp. creamy peanut butter
  1   Tbsp. reduced-sodium soy sauce
  ¼   cup fine dry bread crumbs
  ¼   cup finely chopped peanuts
  ¼   tsp. black pepper
  1   lb. lean ground beef
  6   green onions, cut in 1-inch lengths
  2   cloves garlic, minced
  1   Tbsp. cooking oil
  ¼   cup creamy peanut butter
  1   Tbsp. cornstarch
  ⅛   tsp. ground red pepper
1¼   cups chicken broth
  2   Tbsp. reduced-sodium soy sauce
  3   cups hot cooked basmati rice

1 Preheat oven to 350°. In a large mixing bowl combine egg, water, the 1 tablespoon peanut butter, 1 tablespoon soy sauce, the bread crumbs, peanuts, and black pepper. Add ground beef; mix well. Shape into 24 meatballs, about 1½-inches in diameter. Place in ungreased shallow baking pan. Bake, uncovered, for 20 minutes or until no longer pink. Drain on paper towels.

2 Meanwhile in a small saucepan cook green onions and garlic in hot oil for 30 seconds. Stir in the ¼ cup peanut butter until smooth. Add cornstarch and red pepper, stirring until blended. Add broth and the 2 tablespoons soy sauce. Cook and stir until thickened and bubbly. Cook and stir two minutes more.

3 Arrange rice on serving platter. Spoon meatballs over rice. Pour sauce over. Makes 6 servings.

Nutrition Facts per serving: 406 cal., 17 g total fat (4 g sat. fat), 79 mg chol., 601 mg sodium, 38 g carbo., 2 g fiber, 26 g pro.
Daily Values: 2% vit. A, 5% vit. C, 5% calcium, 23% iron.

Artichoke & Olive Boboli Bites

Prep: 15 minutes **Bake:** 8 minutes

- ½ cup finely shredded Parmesan cheese
- ½ cup mayonnaise or salad dressing
- ⅓ cup finely chopped sweet onion
- 4 cloves garlic, minced
- 4 4-oz. individual (6") Italian bread shells (Boboli)
- 1 6-oz. jar marinated artichoke hearts, drained and chopped
- 1 2¼-oz. can sliced pitted ripe olives, drained
- ½ cup slivered fresh basil

1 Preheat oven to 450°. Stir together ¼ cup of the Parmesan cheese, the mayonnaise or salad dressing, onion, and garlic. Spread evenly over individual bread shells. Combine chopped artichoke hearts and olives; divide evenly among the bread shells. Sprinkle with the remaining ¼ cup Parmesan cheese. Place on a large ungreased cookie sheet.

2 Bake for 8 to 10 minutes or until golden and cheese is melted. Remove from oven. Sprinkle with basil. Cut each bread shell into 8 wedges. Makes 32 wedges (16 servings).

Nutrition Facts per serving: 153 cal., 9 g total fat (1 g sat. fat), 8 mg chol., 294 mg sodium, 14 g carbo., 1 g fiber, 4 g pro.
Daily Values: 2% vit. A, 5% vit. C, 7% calcium, 5% iron.

Creamy Lasagna Bake

Prep: 30 minutes **Bake:** 35 minutes
Stand: 10 minutes

- 9 dried lasagna noodles (about 7 ounces)
- 6 slices bacon
- 3 cups sliced fresh mushrooms (8 oz.)
- ½ cup chopped onion (1 medium)
- 1 Tbsp. snipped fresh sage or ½ tsp. dried leaf sage, crushed
- 6 cups torn fresh spinach (8 oz.)
- 2 cups half-and-half or light cream
- 2 Tbsp. cornstarch
- ⅛ tsp. ground nutmeg
- ¾ cup finely shredded Parmesan cheese
- 8 oz. sliced mozzarella cheese
- ¼ cup finely chopped walnuts

1 Preheat oven to 375°. Cook lasagna noodles in lightly salted boiling water according to package directions; drain. Rinse with cold water; drain well.

2 Meanwhile, in a large skillet cook bacon until crisp; drain on paper towels, reserving 2 tablespoons of drippings in skillet. Crumble bacon; set aside. In the same skillet, cook mushrooms, onion, and dried sage, if using, over medium heat about 5 minutes or until the mushrooms are tender. Add spinach; cover and cook for 1 to 2 minutes or just until wilted. Stir in bacon and fresh sage, if using; set aside.

3 For white sauce, in a medium saucepan combine half-and-half, cornstarch, and nutmeg; cook and stir until thickened and bubbly. Remove from heat; stir in ½ cup of the Parmesan cheese.

4 In a 2-quart lightly greased rectangular baking dish layer three noodles, cutting as necessary to fit; ⅓ of the mushroom mixture; ⅓ of the white sauce, and ⅓ of the mozzarella cheese. Repeat layers twice. Sprinkle with remaining ¼ cup Parmesan and the chopped walnuts.

5 Bake, loosely covered, for 25 minutes. Uncover and bake 10 to 15 minutes more or until heated through. Let stand 10 minutes before cutting to serve. Makes 6 to 8 servings.

Nutrition facts per serving: 461 cal., 26 g total fat (14 g sat. fat), 69 mg chol., 484 mg sodium, 33 g carbo., 2 g fiber, 24 g pro.
Daily Values: 40% vit. A, 17% vit. C, 50% calcium, 13% iron.

SUPPER MENU

- **Risotto**
  (see page 31)

- **Salad of torn romaine, tomato wedges, and Caesar ranch or garlic ranch salad dressing**

- **Towering Praline Carrot Cake with Candied Pecans**
  (see page 48)

Polenta Beef Stew

This inviting stew comes from a region of Switzerland near the border of Italy. Swiss cooking is among the heartiest in Europe—and the use of polenta is very traditional. (See the photograph on page 37.)

Prep: 25 minutes **Cook:** 2 hours

¼	cup all-purpose flour
1	tsp. garlic powder
1	tsp. dried thyme, crushed
1	tsp. dried basil, crushed
2	lb. boneless beef chuck steak, cut into 1-inch pieces
2	Tbsp. olive oil
½	cup chopped onion
6	cloves garlic, minced
1	tsp. snipped fresh rosemary or ¼ tsp. dried rosemary, crushed
1	14½-oz. can beef broth
1½	cups dry red wine
8	oz. boiling onions
5	medium carrots, cut into 1-inch chunks
1	recipe Polenta (see right)
½	cup snipped fresh flat-leaf parsley
¼	cup tomato paste

1 In a medium bowl stir together flour, garlic powder, thyme, basil, and ½ teaspoon each *salt* and *pepper*. Coat meat with flour mixture. In a Dutch oven brown half the meat in hot oil over medium-high heat. Remove from Dutch oven. Repeat with remaining meat. Return all meat to pan. Add chopped onion, garlic, and rosemary. Cook and stir until onion is tender but not brown. Add beef broth and red wine. Bring to boiling; reduce heat. Simmer, covered, for 1½ hours.

2 Add boiling onions and carrots to meat. Simmer, covered, about 30 minutes more or until vegetables are tender. Meanwhile, prepare Polenta. Just before serving, stir the parsley and tomato paste into stew. Serve stew in bowls with Polenta. If desired, garnish with additional *parsley*. Makes 8 servings.

Nutrition Facts per serving: 494 cal., 15 g total fat (6 g sat. fat), 97 mg chol., 823 mg sodium, 46 g carbo., 6 g fiber, 36 g pro.
Daily Values: 119% vit. A, 21% vit. C, 14% calcium, 33% iron.

30 MINUTE, LOW FAT

Polenta

Start to finish: 20 minutes

3	cups milk
1	cup cornmeal
2	Tbsp. margarine or butter

1 In a large saucepan bring milk just to a simmer. In a bowl combine cornmeal, 1 cup *water*, and 1 teaspoon *salt*. Stir cornmeal mixture slowly into hot milk. Cook and stir until mixture comes to a boil. Reduce heat to low. Cook for 10 to 15 minutes or until mixture is thick, stirring occasionally. If too thick, stir in additional *milk*. Stir in margarine. Serves 8.

Nutrition Facts per serving: 135 cal., 5 g total fat (3 g sat. fat), 15 mg chol., 371 mg sodium, 18 g carbo., 1 g fiber, 5 g pro.
Daily Values: 9% vit. A, 1% vit. C, 12% calcium, 4% iron.

30 MINUTE, LOW FAT

North Sea Chowder

Serve this quick soup with lefse (a very thin Scandinavian potato bread) or crusty French bread. (See the photograph on page 37.)

Start to finish: 20 minutes

½	cup chopped onion
2	cloves garlic, minced
1	Tbsp. butter or olive oil
4	cups water
2	fish bouillon cubes
1	Tbsp. lemon juice
½	tsp. instant chicken bouillon granules
½	tsp. dried thyme, crushed
¼	tsp. fennel seed
	Dash powdered saffron (optional)
1	bay leaf
1	lb. skinless, boneless sea bass, red snapper, and/or catfish fillets, cut into ¾-inch cubes
4	Roma tomatoes, halved lengthwise and thinly sliced
	Fresh thyme sprigs (optional)

1 In a large saucepan cook onion and garlic in hot butter or olive oil over medium heat until tender. Stir in the water, fish bouillon cubes, lemon juice, chicken bouillon granules, thyme, fennel, saffron (if using), and bay leaf. Cook and stir until boiling.

2 Add fish and tomatoes. Return to boiling; reduce heat. Simmer, covered, for 10 minutes. Remove and discard bay leaf. To serve, ladle soup into bowls. If desired, garnish with fresh thyme sprigs. Makes 4 to 6 servings.

Nutrition Facts per serving: 160 cal., 5 g total fat (2 g sat. fat), 55 mg chol., 683 mg sodium, 6 g carbo., 1 g fiber, 22 g pro.
Daily Values: 12% vit. A, 31% vit. C, 2% calcium, 5% iron.

Left: Polenta Beef Stew
(page 36)
Below: North Sea
Chowder (page 36)

Page 38: Towering Praline
Carrot Cake with Candied
Pecans (page 48)
Left: Linguine with Curried
Seafood (page 11)
Below left: Taffy Apple
Doughnuts (page 26)
Below right: Mexicali Orange
Roughy Salad (page 13)

Above: Tomato-Onion Spiral Bread
(page 30)
Left: Doting Husband's Bulgur Salad
(page 30)
Page 41: Peanut Butter Peanut Brittle
(page 50)

Page 42: Top-of-the-World Brownies (page 18)
Top left: Chocolate-Mocha Dream (page 22)
Bottom left: Chocolate Casserole (page 21)

Top right: Deep Chocolate Cake with Double-Malt Topping (page 14)
Bottom right: Chocolate Buttons (page 20)

Left: Buttermilk Ice Cream (page 45)
Below: Apricot Cornucopias (page 45)

Buttermilk Ice Cream

This smooth treat is delicious alone or when served with a sweet-tart accent such as sour-cherry preserves. (See the photograph on page 44.)

Prep: 10 minutes **Freeze:** 30 minutes
Ripen: 4 hours

- 2 quarts buttermilk
- 2 cups whipping cream
- 2 cups sugar
- 2 Tbsp. vanilla

1 In a large bowl combine buttermilk, cream, sugar, and vanilla. Stir until sugar dissolves. Freeze mixture in a 4- to 6-quart ice-cream freezer according to manufacturer's directions. Ripen about 4 hours. (To ripen ice cream after churning, remove the lid and dasher. Cover top of freezer can with plastic wrap, waxed paper, or foil. Plug hole in lid with a piece of cloth; replace lid. Pack outer freezer bucket with enough ice and rock salt to cover top of freezer can, using 4 cups ice to 1 cup salt.) Makes about 2½ quarts.

To prepare in a no-ice, no-salt ice-cream maker:

Cut ingredients by half, using 1 quart buttermilk, 1 cup whipping cream, 1 cup sugar, and 1 tablespoon vanilla. Freeze according to manufacturer's directions. To ripen ice cream after churning, remove blade; replace lid and cap. Allow to stand 30 minutes. Transfer mixture from ice-cream maker into a covered container; place in freezer compartment of refrigerator for several hours. Makes 1½ quarts.

Nutrition Facts per ½-cup serving: 145 cal., 7 g total fat (4 g sat. fat), 26 mg chol., 80 mg sodium, 18 g carbo., 0 g fiber, 3 g pro.
Daily Values: 8% vit. A, 1% vit. C, 7% calcium.

Apricot Cornucopias

Pinch the dough together firmly when shaping to prevent cornucopias from opening as they bake. (See the photograph on page 44.)

Prep: 55 minutes **Chill:** 1 hour
Bake: 12 minutes per batch

- 1 cup cream-style cottage cheese
- 1 cup butter, softened
- 2 cups all-purpose flour
- ⅔ cup snipped dried apricots
- ¼ cup water
- ⅓ cup granulated sugar
- 1 egg white, beaten
- ¼ cup finely chopped almonds
  Powdered sugar

1 In a strainer drain cottage cheese, reserving liquid. In a large mixing bowl beat the butter with an electric mixer on medium to high speed for 30 seconds. Add the cottage cheese and 2 tablespoons of the reserved liquid (if necessary, add *milk* to equal 2 tablespoons); beat until nearly smooth. On low speed beat in as much of the flour as you can with the mixer. Stir in remaining flour by hand. Divide dough in half. Cover and chill for 1 hour or until dough is firm enough to handle.

2 Meanwhile, for filling, in a small saucepan combine dried apricots and water. Bring just to boiling; reduce heat. Simmer, uncovered, until water is absorbed, stirring occasionally. Remove from heat; stir in granulated sugar. Cover and cool to room temperature. (Mixture will stiffen slightly as it cools.)

PARTY MENU

- **Apple Saucy Pork Roast (see page 32)**

- **Baked sweet potatoes with butter**

- **Steamed green beans**

- **Apricot Cornucopias with Buttermilk Ice Cream (see left)**

3 Preheat oven to 375°. Lightly grease a cookie sheet; set aside. On a lightly floured surface roll half of the dough at a time to ⅛-inch thickness. To shape the cornucopias, using a 2½-inch round cookie cutter, cut out rounds of dough. Place about ½ teaspoon of apricot filling in the center of each round. Fold in sides of dough rounds, overlapping at top and in center to slightly cover the filling. Moisten with *water* and press firmly to seal folded edges. Curve the tip slightly to resemble a cornucopia or a horn of plenty.

4 Place cornucopias about 1 inch apart on the prepared cookie sheet. Brush tops of cornucopias with the beaten egg white. Sprinkle each with almonds.

5 Bake for 12 to 15 minutes or until bottoms are golden brown. Cool on cookie sheet for 1 minute. Transfer cookies to a wire rack to cool. Sprinkle with powdered sugar just before serving. Makes 30 to 36 cookies.

Nutrition Facts per cookie: 94 cal., 6 g total fat (3 g sat. fat), 14 mg chol., 77 mg sodium, 9 g carbo., 0 g fiber, 2 g pro.
Daily Values: 6% vit. A, 3% iron.

Sweet Potato Torte

Cracks in the top are a normal part of cheesecake making, so celebrate them. Those cracks are the badge of honor that tells the world you care enough to make it yourself.

Prep: 70 minutes **Bake:** 65 minutes
Cool: 1 hour 45 minutes **Chill:** 4 hours

Fingers are the best tool for making sure crust adheres firmly to the sides of the springform pan.

potatoes, a portion at a time, in a food processor bowl or covered blender container until smooth.

Nutrition Facts per serving: 417 cal., 25 g total fat (15 g sat. fat), 135 mg chol., 212 mg sodium, 43 g carbo., 1 g fiber, 7 g pro.
Daily Values: 97% vit. A, 14% vit. C, 6% calcium, 8% iron.

1	cup all-purpose flour
¼	cup sugar
1½	tsp. finely shredded lemon peel
1½	tsp. finely shredded orange peel
½	cup cold butter
½	cup flaked coconut
1	egg yolk, beaten
1	Tbsp. water
3	8-oz. pkg. cream cheese, softened
1¾	cups sugar
3	Tbsp. all-purpose flour
1	Tbsp. finely shredded lemon peel
1	Tbsp. finely shredded orange peel
¾	to 1 tsp. ground nutmeg
½	tsp. ground cinnamon
2	cups mashed, cooked sweet potatoes*
4	eggs
¼	cup whipping cream
	Sweetened whipped cream (optional)

1 Preheat oven to 350°. For crust, in a mixing bowl stir together the 1 cup flour, the ¼ cup sugar, and 1½ teaspoons each lemon and orange peels. Cut in cold butter until mixture resembles coarse crumbs. Stir in flaked coconut. Mix the egg yolk with 1 tablespoon water; stir into flour mixture. Form into a ball.

2 Press slightly less than half of the crust mixture onto bottom of a 9×2½-inch springform pan with sides removed. Place on baking sheet. Bake for 14 to 15 minutes or until lightly browned; cool. Attach sides of pan. Press remaining crust mixture all the way up sides of pan (see photo, above). Set aside.

3 In a large mixing bowl beat cream cheese, the 1¾ cups sugar, the 3 tablespoons flour, 1 tablespoon each lemon and orange peels, nutmeg, and cinnamon with an electric mixer on medium speed until smooth. Beat in mashed sweet potatoes. Beat in eggs at low speed just until mixed. Do not overbeat. Stir in ¼ cup cream. Pour into prepared crust. Place springform pan in a shallow baking pan.

4 Bake for 65 to 70 minutes or until a 3-inch circle in the center appears nearly set when gently shaken. Cool in pan on a wire rack for 15 minutes. Using a small spatula or table knife, loosen the crust from sides of pan and cool 30 minutes more. Remove the sides of the pan; cool completely. Cover and chill at least 4 hours before serving. If desired, serve with sweetened whipped cream. Serves 16.

*Note: For 2 cups mashed sweet potatoes, peel and cut up 1 pound, 6 ounces of sweet potatoes. Cook, covered, in boiling water for 25 to 30 minutes or until very tender. Cool slightly. Use a potato masher to mash potatoes. Or, process or blend

Bananas Foster Crème Brûlée

Using a water bath to cook the dessert gently results in the soft, creamy texture that has made Crème Brûlée a favorite for generations.

Prep: 30 minutes **Bake:** 25 minutes
Chill: 1 hour **Stand:** 20 minutes

2½	cups whipping cream
½	cup milk
6	egg yolks
¾	cup sugar
2	tsp. vanilla
2	Tbsp. dark rum (optional)
1	Tbsp. water
1	Tbsp. lemon juice
3	firm, ripe bananas, thinly sliced
⅓	cup sugar

1 Preheat oven to 350°. In a heavy medium saucepan heat cream and milk over medium heat just until bubbly around the edges.

2 Meanwhile, in a large mixing bowl combine egg yolks, the ¾ cup sugar, and vanilla. Beat with a wire whisk or rotary beater just until combined. Slowly whisk the hot cream mixture into the egg mixture. If desired, stir in rum.

3 Place eight ¾-cup ramekins or 6-ounce custard cups in a baking pan. Set pan on an oven rack. Divide

Keep the spoon close to the surface of the dessert; closer is safer because it lessens the chance that the hot caramel will fall where it's not wanted.

custard mixture evenly among ramekins or cups. Pour enough hot water into the baking pan around the ramekins to reach halfway up sides of ramekins.

4 Bake for 25 to 30 minutes or until centers of custards appear set when carefully shaken. Remove custards from water bath; cool on a wire rack. Cover and chill at least 1 hour or up to 8 hours.

5 Before serving, remove custards from the refrigerator; let stand at room temperature for 20 minutes. In a medium bowl stir together the 1 tablespoon water and lemon juice. Add banana slices; toss to coat. Drain. Arrange slices over tops of custards.

6 Meanwhile, to caramelize sugar, place the ⅓ cup sugar in a heavy 8-inch skillet. Heat skillet over medium-high heat until sugar begins to melt, shaking skillet occasionally to heat sugar evenly. Do not stir. Once the sugar starts to melt, reduce heat to low and cook about 3 minutes more or until all of the sugar is melted and very light golden brown, stirring as needed with a wooden spoon.

7 Using a wooden spoon or fork, quickly drizzle the caramelized sugar over custards (see photo, above).

If sugar starts to harden in the skillet, return to heat, stirring until melted. Let custards stand for 2 to 3 minutes before serving to set caramelized sugar slightly. Makes 8 servings.

Nutrition Facts per serving: 456 cal., 32 g total fat (19 g sat. fat), 263 mg chol., 42 mg sodium, 41 g carbo., 1 g fiber, 5 g pro.
Daily Values: 58% vit. A, 8% vit. C, 7% calcium, 4% iron.

Polenta-Pecan Apple Cobbler

Prep: 45 minutes **Bake:** 35 minutes

- ½ **cup all-purpose flour**
- ⅓ **cup quick-cooking polenta mix or yellow cornmeal**
- 2 **Tbsp. granulated sugar**
- 1 **tsp. baking powder**
- 3 **Tbsp. butter**
- ½ **cup chopped pecans**
- 2 **Tbsp. brown sugar**
- ½ **tsp. ground cinnamon**
- 8 **cups peeled, cored, cubed apples**
- ½ **cup dried tart red cherries**
- ⅓ **cup packed brown sugar**
- 1 **Tbsp. lemon juice**
- 1 **Tbsp. cornstarch**
- ⅓ **cup half-and-half or light cream**

1 For topping, in a bowl stir together flour, polenta mix, granulated sugar, baking powder, and ½ teaspoon *salt*. Cut in butter until mixture resembles coarse crumbs; set aside. In another bowl combine pecans, the 2 tablespoons brown sugar, and half of the cinnamon; set aside.

2 Preheat oven to 375°. In a large saucepan combine apples, cherries, the ⅓ cup brown sugar, lemon juice, and the remaining cinnamon. Bring to boiling, stirring constantly; reduce heat. Simmer, covered, about 5 minutes or until fruit is almost

EDITOR'S TIP

What's in a Name?

Cobbler: A distant cousin of the deep-dish pie, cobbler gets its name from its biscuit topping, which resembles cobblestones. For a traditional cobbler, be sure the fruit filling is very hot when you drop the biscuit dough on it or the bottom of the topping might not cook properly. **Betty:** Betties are topped with soft bread cubes, rather than dry cubes as in bread pudding. The bread is easier to cut if it's frozen; use a serrated knife and a sawing motion to cut the bread into ½-inch cubes. **Crisp:** Crisps are topped with a crunchy mixture. The topping keeps well, so try mixing a double batch. Put the extra batch in a freezer bag, seal, label, and freeze it for up to a month. **Pandowdy:** A funny name for a tasty dish, this baked apple or fruit dessert has a pastry-like biscuit topping and is usually served with light cream or a sauce. Traditionally, the topping is broken up with a spoon and stirred into the filling (the "dowdying" of the dish) before it is served.

tender, stirring occasionally. Combine ¼ cup *water* and the cornstarch. Add to saucepan. Cook and stir until thickened and bubbly. Keep hot. Stir ⅓ cup half-and-half into flour mixture, stirring just to moisten.

3 Transfer hot filling to a 2-quart square baking dish. Using a spoon, immediately drop topping into small mounds on top of filling. Sprinkle with pecan mixture. Bake about 35 minutes or until a wooden toothpick inserted into topping comes out clean. If desired, serve with additional *half-and-half*. Serves 6.

Nutrition Facts per serving: 448 cal., 15 g total fat (6 g sat. fat), 24 mg chol., 180 mg sodium, 78 g carbo., 5 g fiber, 4 g pro.
Daily Values: 15% vit. A, 14% vit. C, 9% calcium, 9% iron.

Towering Praline Carrot Cake with Candied Pecans

It's easy to make the cake layers and Candied Pecans a day ahead. Then, prepare frosting and Praline Sauce the morning you plan to serve the dessert. (See the photograph on page 38.)

Prep: 2 hours **Bake:** 35 minutes
Cool: 2 hours

1	lb. carrots, peeled and sliced (3 cups)
3	cups all-purpose flour
2¾	cups sugar
2	tsp. ground cinnamon
1½	tsp. baking powder
1½	tsp. baking soda
1	tsp. salt
1⅓	cups cooking oil
6	eggs
1	8-oz. can crushed pineapple, drained
1	Tbsp. vanilla
1	cup chopped pecans
½	cup flaked coconut
1	recipe Cinnamon-Cream Cheese Frosting (see page 49)
1	recipe Praline Sauce (see page 49)
1	recipe Candied Pecans (see page 49)

1 In a medium saucepan cook carrots, covered, in a moderate amount of boiling water about 20 minutes until very tender. Drain and cool slightly. Chop in a food processor using several on-off turns, or coarsely mash with potato masher (should have about 1½ cups).

2 Grease and lightly flour three 9×1½-inch round cake pans; set aside. (If you only have two pans, prepare two layers and refrigerate remaining third of batter. When the first two are done baking and removed from pans, wash, grease, and lightly flour one pan; bake remaining batter.)

3 Preheat oven to 350°. In a large mixing bowl stir together flour, sugar, cinnamon, baking powder, baking soda, and salt. Make a well in center of dry ingredients. Add cooking oil, eggs, pineapple, and vanilla. Beat with an electric mixer on low speed about 1 minute or until all ingredients are combined. Fold in mashed carrots, the 1 cup pecans, and the coconut.

4 Spread batter evenly into prepared pans. Bake for 35 to 40 minutes or until a wooden toothpick inserted in the center comes out clean. Cool cakes in pans on wire racks for 10 minutes. Using a small spatula or table knife, loosen edges and remove from pans. Bake remaining layer, if necessary. Cool cakes thoroughly on wire racks.

5 While the cakes are cooling, prepare the Cinnamon-Cream Cheese Frosting, Praline Sauce, and Candied Pecans.

6 To assemble, place one of the cooled cake layers, top side up, on a cake plate. Use about 1 cup of the Cinnamon-Cream Cheese Frosting to pipe or spoon a rim about 1 inch wide and ½ inch high around outer edge of cake layer. Spoon about 2 tablespoons frosting in center, leaving an unfrosted ring (see Photo 1, above right).

7 Spoon and spread about half of the Praline Sauce filling into the unfrosted ring (sauce will not fill ring) (see Photo 2, above right). Add a second cake layer, top side up, and repeat frosting and filling steps using Cinnamon-Cream Cheese Frosting and Praline Sauce.

1. The circle of frosting on the outside of the cake keeps the Praline Sauce from dripping out. Frosting in the center prevents the cake from collapsing in the middle.

2. Spoon Praline Sauce into the unfrosted area of the cake. The sauce forms a fairly thin layer.

3. When doing the final frosting step, don't worry about making it look perfect. For this cake, bold strokes with a small spatula or table knife look best.

8 Add final cake layer, top side up. Frost the top and sides of layers with remaining frosting (see Photo 3, above). Garnish top with Candied Pecans. Store cake in the refrigerator. Makes 16 servings.

Nutrition Facts per serving: 789 cal., 41 g total fat (13 g sat. fat), 119 mg chol., 453 mg sodium, 101 g carbo., 2 g fiber, 7 g pro.
Daily Values: 81% vit. A, 4% vit. C, 7% calcium, 15% iron.

30 MINUTE

Cinnamon-Cream Cheese Frosting

Start to finish: 15 minutes

- 1   8-oz. pkg. cream cheese, softened
- ½   cup butter, softened
- 1   tsp. ground cinnamon
- 1   tsp. vanilla
- 5¾   to 6¼ cups sifted powdered sugar

1 In a large mixing bowl beat together cream cheese, butter, cinnamon, and vanilla with an electric mixer on medium speed until light and fluffy. Gradually add about half of the powdered sugar, beating well. Gradually beat in enough of the remaining powdered sugar until spreading consistency. Use as frosting for the Towering Praline Carrot Cake with Candied Pecans. Makes about 4½ cups frosting.

30 MINUTE

Praline Sauce

Start to finish: 10 minutes

- 3   Tbsp. butter
- 3   Tbsp. brown sugar
- 2   Tbsp. whipping cream
- 1   tsp. vanilla

1 In a small saucepan melt butter over medium heat. Stir in brown sugar and cream. Cook and stir until mixture comes to a full boil. Reduce heat. Boil gently for 3 minutes, stirring occasionally. Stir in vanilla. Cool. Use as filling for the Towering

Praline Carrot Cake with Candied Pecans. Makes ⅓ cup sauce.

30 MINUTE

Candied Pecans

Prep: 10 minutes **Bake:** 12 minutes

- ¼   cup packed brown sugar
- 1   Tbsp. orange juice
- ½   cup pecan halves

1 Preheat oven to 350°. Lightly grease an 8×8×2-inch baking pan. In a small bowl combine brown sugar and orange juice. Add pecan halves, stirring to coat. Spread nuts into prepared pan.

2 Bake about 12 minutes or until nuts are browned and syrup is bubbly, stirring once. Pour out onto a lightly greased baking sheet, separating into single nuts. Cool on a wire rack. Use as topping for the Towering Praline Carrot Cake with Candied Pecans. Makes ½ cup nuts.

Caramel-Apple Pudding Cake

Prep: 25 minutes **Bake:** 35 minutes

- 2   cups peeled, cored, and thinly sliced tart cooking apples
- 3   Tbsp. lemon juice
- ½   tsp. ground cinnamon
- ⅛   tsp. ground nutmeg
- ¼   cup raisins
- 1   cup all-purpose flour
- ¾   cup packed brown sugar
- 1   tsp. baking powder
- ¼   tsp. baking soda
- ½   cup milk
- 2   Tbsp. butter, melted
- 1   tsp. vanilla
- ½   cup chopped pecans or walnuts
- ¾   cup caramel ice-cream topping
- ½   cup water

TEST KITCHEN TIP

The Soft Touch

Most recipes that call for cream cheese call for it to be softened. There are two ways to do this.

If you have the time, simply let it stand at room temperature for about 30 minutes. If not, place 3 ounces of cream cheese in a microwave-safe container. Microwave the cheese, uncovered, on 100% power (high) for 15 to 30 seconds or until it is softened. For 8 ounces, heat for 30 to 60 seconds.

- 1   Tbsp. butter or margarine
     Whipped cream or vanilla ice cream (optional)

1 Preheat oven to 350°. Grease a 2-quart square baking dish. Arrange apples in bottom of dish; sprinkle with lemon juice, cinnamon, and nutmeg. Top evenly with raisins.

2 In a large mixing bowl combine flour, brown sugar, baking powder, and soda. Add milk, the 2 tablespoons melted butter, and vanilla; mix well. Stir in nuts. Spread batter evenly over apple mixture. In a small saucepan combine the caramel topping, water, and the 1 tablespoon butter; bring to boiling. Pour mixture over batter.

3 Bake about 35 minutes or until set in center. While warm, cut into squares, inverting each piece onto a dessert plate. Spoon the caramel-apple mixture from bottom of pan over each serving. If desired, serve with whipped cream or vanilla ice cream. Makes 12 servings.

Nutrition Facts per serving: 223 cal., 6 g total fat (1 g sat. fat), 1 mg chol., 173 mg sodium, 42 g carbo., 1 g fiber, 2 g pro.
Daily Values: 4% vit. A, 4% vit. C, 5% calcium, 6% iron.

CLEVER COOK

Safe Storage for a Candy Thermometer

Since a candy thermometer is usually used only a few times a year, it's important to have it carefully stored to avoid breakage. I've found the best place to keep my candy thermometer is inside my turkey baster.

Michell Herman
Murrieta, California

Peanut Butter Peanut Brittle

It is worth your while to search out raw (not roasted) peanuts; they are less likely to burn when stirred into the hot syrup. (See the photograph on page 41.)

Prep: 10 minutes **Cook:** 20 minutes
Cool: 1 hour

2	cups peanut butter
	Butter for greasing pans
1½	cups sugar
1½	cups light-colored corn syrup
¼	cup water
2	Tbsp. butter
2	cups raw peanuts
1	tsp. baking soda, sifted
1	tsp. vanilla

1 In the top of a double boiler warm peanut butter over low heat. (Or, warm peanut butter in a heatproof bowl set over a pan of warm water over low heat.) Meanwhile, butter two large baking sheets. Set aside.

2 Butter sides of a heavy 3-quart saucepan. In pan combine sugar, corn syrup, and water. Cook and stir over medium-high heat until mixture boils. Clip candy thermometer to side of pan. Cook and stir over medium-high heat until thermometer registers 275° (about 15 minutes).

3 Reduce heat to medium. Add the 2 tablespoons butter, stirring until melted. Add peanuts. Cook and stir for 5 minutes more or until candy starts turning brown and thermometer registers 295°. Remove from heat. Remove thermometer.

4 Quickly sprinkle baking soda over mixture, stirring constantly. Stir in vanilla. Gently stir in warm peanut butter until well combined.

5 Immediately pour candy onto prepared baking sheets. Working quickly, spread as thin as possible with a spatula (see photo, below) or stretch using two forks to lift and pull candy as it cools. When cool, break into serving-size pieces. Makes about 3 pounds (48 servings).

Nutrition Facts per 1-ounce serving: 156 cal., 9 g total fat (2 g sat. fat), 1 mg chol., 91 mg sodium, 17 g carbo., 1 g fiber, 4 g pro.
Daily Values: 1% calcium, 5% iron.

Spread hot peanut brittle mixture with a metal spatula, being careful not to burn yourself. The candy remains hot for several minutes after it comes out of the pan.

Sangria for Kids

Don't use red grape juice in this recipe. When combined with the orange juice, it discolors.

Start to finish: 5 minutes

1	quart (4 cups) orange juice, chilled
1½	cups purple or white unsweetened grape juice, chilled
1	1-liter bottle ginger ale, chilled
2	cups ice cubes
2	cups assorted fresh fruit, such as oranges, cut into wedges; thinly sliced and halved lemons and/or limes; pineapple wedges; seedless red or green grapes; peeled, pitted, and sliced peaches; and halved strawberries
	Fresh mint sprigs

1 In a large bowl or pitcher stir together the chilled orange juice and grape juice. Add the ginger ale and stir gently. Add the ice and fruit.

2 To serve, ladle into tall glasses with the fruit. Garnish with fresh mint sprigs. Makes 20 servings.

Nutrition Facts per serving: 57 cal., 0 g total fat, 0 mg chol., 5 mg sodium, 14 g carbo., 0 g fiber, 0 g pro.
Daily Values: 1% vit. A, 35% vit. C, 2% iron.

march

IN THIS CHAPTER

30-minute recipes indicated in COLOR.
Low-fat and no-fat recipes indicated
with a ♥.
Photographs indicated in italics.
*Bonus recipe

PRIZE WINNER

Sesame-Ginger Popcorn

Camilla V. Saulsbury
Bloomington, Indiana
$400—Snacks

Prep: 15 minutes **Bake:** 20 minutes

  6   cups popped popcorn
1½   cups lightly salted cashews
⅔   cup packed brown sugar
  2   Tbsp. butter
  2   Tbsp. light-colored corn syrup
  1   Tbsp. grated fresh ginger
  2   tsp. toasted sesame oil
  2   Tbsp. sesame seed
  1   tsp. vanilla
⅛   tsp. baking soda

1 Preheat oven to 300°. Remove all unpopped kernels from popped popcorn. Put popcorn and cashews in a greased 17×12×2-inch baking pan or roasting pan.

2 In a medium saucepan combine brown sugar, butter, corn syrup, ginger, and sesame oil. Cook and stir over medium heat until mixture boils. Continue boiling at a moderate rate, without stirring, for 5 minutes more. Remove pan from heat. Stir in sesame seed, vanilla, and baking soda. Pour mixture over popcorn and cashews. Stir gently to coat.

3 Bake for 20 to 25 minutes or until golden brown, stirring twice. Spread popcorn mixture on a large piece of buttered foil to cool. Store tightly covered. Makes 8½ cups.

Nutrition Facts per ¾-cup serving: 203 cal., 12 g total fat (3 g sat. fat), 5 mg chol., 49 mg sodium, 23 g carbo., 1 g fiber, 3 g pro. **Daily Values:** 2% vit. A, 3% calcium, 8% iron.

PRIZE WINNER

Red-Hot Pita Chips

Julie Wesson
Hainesville, Illinois
$200—Snacks

Prep: 15 minutes **Bake:** 13 minutes

  1   egg white, slightly beaten
  2   Tbsp. olive oil
  2   tsp. Dijon-style mustard
  2   cloves garlic, minced
  1   tsp. ground cumin
½   tsp. chili powder
½   tsp. paprika
      Dash ground red pepper
  3   white pita bread rounds, split in half horizontally

1 Preheat oven to 350°. In a small bowl whisk together egg white, olive oil, mustard, garlic, cumin, chili powder, paprika, red pepper, and ½ teaspoon *salt*. Brush cut surfaces of pitas with oil mixture. Cut each into 8 wedges. Place wedges, brushed side up, on a baking sheet.

2 Bake for 13 to 15 minutes or until wedges are crisp. Cool on baking sheet on wire rack. Store, tightly covered, at room temperature up to 3 days. Makes 6 servings.

Nutrition Facts per serving: 132 cal., 5 g total fat (1 g sat. fat), 0 mg chol., 376 mg sodium, 18 g carbo., 1 g fiber, 4 g pro. **Daily Values:** 2% vit. A, 1% vit. C, 3% calcium, 5% iron.

Potato-Fennel Au Gratin

See the photograph on page 78.

Prep: 25 minutes **Bake:** 55 minutes

  1   large fennel bulb
½   cup chopped onion

  4   Tbsp. margarine or butter
  2   Tbsp. all-purpose flour
1¼   cups milk
  2   large baking potatoes, thinly sliced
  2   parsnips, peeled and thinly sliced
  2   Tbsp. finely shredded Parmesan cheese
  2   slices rye and pumpernickel swirl bread, cut or torn into 1- to 2-inch pieces (about 1¾ cups)

1 Preheat oven to 350°. Grease a 1½- to 2-quart oval or rectangular baking dish. To prepare fennel, cut off and discard upper stalks. Reserve some feathery fennel tops for garnish, if desired. Remove any wilted outer layers and cut off a thin slice from the fennel base. Wash fennel and cut into quarters. Remove cores. Cut fennel lengthwise into ¼-inch-wide slices (you should have 2 cups).

2 For sauce, in a small saucepan cook onion in 2 tablespoons of the margarine until tender. Stir in the flour, ½ teaspoon *salt*, and ¼ teaspoon *pepper*. Add milk all at once. Cook and stir over medium heat until thickened and bubbly.

3 Place half of the sliced potatoes in the prepared baking dish. Layer half of the parsnips and half of the fennel over potatoes. Cover with half of the sauce. Repeat layers. Bake, covered, for 40 minutes.

4 Meanwhile, in a medium skillet, melt the remaining 2 tablespoons margarine or butter in a medium skillet. Remove from heat; stir in Parmesan cheese. Stir in bread cubes until well combined. Uncover dish and sprinkle with bread cube mixture. Bake, uncovered, for 15 to 20 minutes more or until potatoes and parsnips are tender. If desired, garnish with *fresh dill or fennel tops.* Makes 4 to 6 side-dish servings.

Nutrition Facts per serving: 385 cal., 15 g total fat (3 g sat. fat), 8 mg chol., 621 mg sodium, 56 g carbo., 16 g fiber, 10 g pro.
Daily Values: 19% vit. A, 48% vit. C, 17% calcium, 19% iron.

Kalamata Artichokes

No baby artichokes available at your produce counter? Prepare this recipe with two large 14-ounce artichokes, halved lengthwise. Cook them in boiling water for 15 minutes or until a leaf pulls out easily. Continue recipe as directed below. (See the photograph on page 78.)

Prep: 30 minutes **Cook:** 8 minutes
Bake: 20 minutes

- 16 baby artichokes, halved (about 16 to 20 oz. total)
       Lemon
- 2 Tbsp. olive oil
- 2 Tbsp. snipped fresh Italian parsley
- 2 cloves garlic, minced
- 1 Tbsp. lemon juice
- ¼ tsp. dried marjoram, crushed
- 1½ cups torn ½- to 1-inch pieces sourdough or Italian bread
- ⅓ cup halved pitted kalamata olives or pitted ripe olives (about 18)
- 2 Tbsp. crumbled goat cheese or feta cheese, or shaved Parmesan cheese

1 Wash artichokes. Trim stems and remove any loose, split, or brown outer leaves. Cut off about ½ inch from tops of artichokes. Using kitchen shears, snip off any sharp leaf tips. (To minimize discoloring, use a stainless steel knife or kitchen scissors to trim vegetables.) Halve each artichoke lengthwise. Immediately rub the cut surfaces with a piece of cut lemon.

2 Cook artichoke halves, covered, in a large amount of boiling water for 8 to 10 minutes or until a leaf pulls out easily; drain. When cool enough to handle, use a small spoon to remove purple-tipped leaves and fuzzy choke in the center of each half. (If the interior of baby artichokes is white, the entire artichoke is edible.)

3 Preheat oven to 400°. In a medium saucepan heat olive oil over medium heat for 30 seconds. Add parsley, garlic, and ¼ teaspoon *pepper;* cook 1 minute, stirring occasionally. Remove from heat. Stir in lemon juice and marjoram. Add torn bread and olives, tossing to coat.

4 Place artichokes in a 2-quart square baking dish. Add ¼ cup *water* to baking dish. Bake, covered, for 10 minutes. Uncover; top artichokes with bread mixture and cheese. Bake 10 minutes more or until bread pieces are golden and mixture is heated through. To serve, carefully remove artichokes with a slotted spoon. Makes 4 side-dish servings.

Nutrition Facts per serving: 166 cal., 10 g total fat (1 g sat. fat), 7 mg chol., 295 mg sodium, 16 g carbo., 3 g fiber, 4 g pro.
Daily Values: 3% vit. A, 18% vit. C, 4% calcium, 9% iron.

30 MINUTE LOW FAT

Solid Gold Squash Soup

Winter squash, blessed with a velvety texture, a buttery taste, plus a good amount of dietary fiber, makes a nutrient-packed soup base. Make a meal of squash soup by serving it with corn muffins and a green salad.

Prep: 5 minutes **Cook:** 10 minutes

DINNER MENU

- **Grilled or poached sea bass or mahi mahi**

- **Kalamata Artichokes (see left)**

- **Salad of fresh spinach, grapefruit and/or orange sections, toasted pecans, and a citrus vinaigrette**

- **Sourdough bread and butter**

- **White wine or iced tea**

- 1½ tsp. canola oil or vegetable oil
- ¼ cup finely chopped onion
- 1 to 2 tsp. curry powder
- ½ tsp. ground ginger
- 2 12-oz. pkg. frozen cooked winter squash, thawed
- 1 cup reduced-sodium chicken broth
- 1 cup apple juice or apple cider
- ¼ tsp. salt
- ½ cup plain nonfat yogurt or nonfat dairy sour cream
       Finely chopped pistachio nuts (optional)

1 In a medium saucepan heat oil over medium heat. Add onion, curry powder, and ground ginger. Cook and stir for 2 minutes. Add the squash, chicken broth, apple juice or cider, and salt. Heat through.

2 To serve, ladle into soup bowls. Top each serving with a swirl of yogurt or sour cream. If desired, sprinkle with pistachio nuts. Makes 4 side-dish servings.

Nutrition Facts per serving: 142 cal., 3 g total fat (1 g sat. fat), 1 mg chol., 353 mg sodium, 26 g carbo., 5 g fiber, 5 g pro.
Daily Values: 60% vit. A, 29% vit. C, 7% calcium, 7% iron.

TEST KITCHEN TIP

Max the Knife

A high-quality sharp knife makes cutting up in the kitchen a simple task. When shopping for a knife, look for one made of high-carbon stainless steel that feels balanced and comfortable in your hand. Keep knives from becoming dull by using a wooden or acrylic cutting board. A variety of knives are created with specific purposes in mind. The knives listed below should meet the needs of most home cooks.

Chef's or Cook's Knife: The flat, wide blade of this heavy 8- to 12-inch knife is ideal for crushing garlic and spices. The longer blade length means you can chop large quantities of food more efficiently.

Utility Knife: This knife has a 6-inch-long blade made thin enough to smoothly slice sandwiches and other somewhat softer foods, such as fruit and cheese. It's great for chopping herbs, too.

Paring Knife: With a 3- or 4-inch blade, this knife is comfortable to handle when you're peeling and cutting fruits and vegetables or other small items. It is perfect for mincing just one clove of garlic or peeling an apple.

Bread Knife: Its serrated blade, which is usually about 8 inches long, allows you to easily cut through bread, bagels, tomatoes, cakes, or any other foods with tough exteriors and soft interiors.

Creamy Onion-Rice Casserole

Prep: 45 minutes **Bake:** 30 minutes

- 1½ cups Arborio rice or short-grain rice
- ¼ cup margarine or butter
- 1 cup fresh mushrooms, such as porcini and/or button
- 12 purple or white boiling onions, peeled and halved
- 1 medium Vidalia or other sweet onion, cut into 8 wedges
- 2 cloves garlic, minced
- 1 14½-oz. can vegetable broth
- ¾ cup freshly shredded Romano or Parmesan cheese

1 In a medium saucepan combine 3 cups *water* and ½ teaspoon *salt;* bring to boiling. Remove saucepan from heat; stir in rice. Let stand, covered, 30 minutes. Rinse rice with cold water and drain well. Set aside.

2 Preheat oven to 325°. In a large skillet melt margarine. Cook one-third of the mushrooms in the hot margarine until tender. Remove mushrooms from skillet; set aside. Cook remaining mushrooms, boiling onions, Vidalia onion, and garlic in remaining hot margarine in skillet until tender. Add rice. Cook and stir over medium heat for 4 to 5 minutes more or until rice is golden. Carefully stir broth into rice mixture. Bring to boiling. Transfer rice to a 2-quart soufflé dish or casserole.

3 Bake, covered, for 25 to 30 minutes or until rice is tender and the liquid is absorbed. Fluff with a fork. Stir in ⅔ cup of the Romano cheese. Sprinkle with remaining cheese and reserved mushrooms. Return to oven. Bake, uncovered,

5 minutes or until the cheese melts and turns slightly golden. If desired, garnish with *fresh herb sprigs.* Makes 6 to 8 side-dish servings.

Nutrition Facts per serving: 308 cal., 12 g total fat (7 g sat. fat), 35 mg chol., 712 mg sodium, 43 g carbo., 1 g fiber, 9 g pro.
Daily Values: 9% vit. A, 3% vit. C, 14% calcium, 16% iron.

White Bean and Cumin Chili

See the photograph on page 78.

Prep: 30 minutes **Cook:** 1 hour

- 1 cup chopped onion
- 3 cloves garlic, minced
- 2 Tbsp. cooking oil
- 2 14½-oz. cans tomatoes, undrained and cut up
- 1 12-oz. can beer or nonalcoholic beer
- 1 chipotle chili pepper in adobo sauce, chopped
- 1 Tbsp. cumin seed, toasted*
- 1 tsp. sugar
- 2 19-oz. cans cannellini beans, rinsed and drained
- 1½ cups coarsely chopped, seeded, and peeled Golden Nugget or acorn squash (about 12 oz.)
- ½ cup dairy sour cream
- 2 Tbsp. lime juice
- 1 Tbsp. snipped fresh chives

1 In a 4-quart Dutch oven cook onion and garlic in hot oil until tender. Stir in undrained tomatoes, beer, chipotle pepper, cumin, sugar, and ½ teaspoon *salt.* Stir in beans. Bring to boiling; reduce heat. Stir in squash. Simmer, covered, 1 hour.

2 Meanwhile, combine sour cream, lime juice, and snipped chives. To serve, ladle chili into bowls. Top with sour cream mixture. If desired, garnish with *whole fresh chives* and *small lime wedges*. Makes 4 servings.

*Note: To toast cumin seed, place seeds in a dry skillet over low heat. Cook, stirring often, 8 minutes or until fragrant. Remove from heat; allow to cool before grinding with a food mill or a mortar and pestle.

Nutrition Facts per serving: 365 cal., 15 g total fat (5 g sat. fat), 13 mg chol., 995 mg sodium, 52 g carbo., 13 g fiber, 17 g pro.
Daily Values: 26% vit. A, 67% vit. C, 15% calcium, 33% iron.

Mexican-Style Egg Skillet

See the photograph on page 78.

Start to finish: 25 minutes

4	6-inch corn tortillas, cut into quarters
1	Tbsp. cooking oil
6	oz. chorizo or hot Italian sausage
6	eggs, beaten
1	cup shredded Monterey Jack cheese with jalapeño peppers
¼	cup thinly sliced green onions
1	fresh serrano chili pepper, seeded and finely chopped (optional)
2	Tbsp. snipped fresh cilantro
¼	cup salsa

1 In a large nonstick skillet fry half of the tortillas in half of the oil 2 minutes or until crisp, turning once. Drain on paper towels. Repeat with remaining tortillas and oil; cool. In the same skillet cook chorizo over medium heat until brown; remove from skillet and drain.

2 In a large bowl combine eggs, tortilla wedges, and ¼ teaspoon *salt*. Add egg mixture to skillet. Cook,

TEST KITCHEN TIP
Chopping An Onion

A bit of sharp thinking and a good knife may be all it takes to slice or dice most vegetables. However, chopping a basic onion, with its tricky concentric layers, may leave you weeping in frustration. Our step-by-step guide shows you how to make quick work of dicing that tear-jerking bulb.

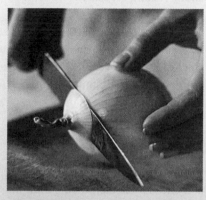

1. A Cut Above
After peeling off the papery outer skin of the onion, place the onion on its side on a cutting board. Slice off the top of the onion.

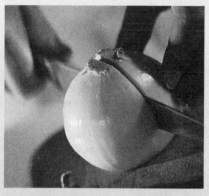

2. Halve It Your Way
Turn the onion so it sits on the newly cut flat surface, and slice the onion in half through the root end.

3. Simple Slicing
Place an onion half, flat side down, on the cutting board. Make ¼-inch slices lengthwise through the onion, cutting up to, but not through, the root end. (This keeps the onion from falling apart.)

4. Dicey Situation
Turn onion and make ¼-inch slices that are perpendicular to previous slices. The onion will fall apart in neat ¼-inch pieces. Repeat steps with remaining onion half.

without stirring, until mixture begins to set on bottom and around edge. Using a spatula, lift and fold partially cooked eggs so uncooked portion flows underneath. Continue cooking 1 to 1½ minutes or until eggs are partially set. Stir in chorizo, ¾ cup of the cheese, onions, and, if desired, serrano. Continue to cook until eggs are set and cheese is melted. Sprinkle with remaining cheese and cilantro. Serve with salsa. Makes 4 servings.

Nutrition Facts per serving: 503 cal., 36 g total fat (14 g sat. fat), 381 mg chol., 994 mg sodium, 15 g carbo., 2 g fiber, 28 g pro.
Daily Values: 19% vit. A, 6% vit. C, 30% calcium, 14% iron.

EDITOR'S TIP

The Skinny on Cutting Fat

Here are three fat-cutting techniques we used in the Smoky Macaroni and Cheese recipe (see below):

● Such full-flavored cheeses as extra-sharp cheddar or pepper cheese provide a big oomph in taste, so you can use less while maintaining flavor. Each ounce of natural cheese (a 1-inch cube) contains 8 to 9 grams of fat and 100 to 115 calories, so even a modest decrease has an impact on healthfulness.

● Fat-free half-and-half boosts creamy richness without increasing fat.

● Cooking onions in broth instead of butter shaves off 10 grams of fat.

LOW FAT

Smoky Macaroni And Cheese

Watch those elbows disappear from the table when served in this yummy favorite. This creamy version has half the fat and calories of the typical homemade combo.

Prep: 20 minutes **Bake:** 20 minutes
Stand: 5 minutes

- 8 oz. large elbow pasta
- 3 oz. smoked cheddar cheese or smoked Gouda
- ½ cup chopped onion
- 1 cup reduced-sodium chicken broth
- ¾ cup fat-free half-and-half
- 1 Tbsp. all-purpose flour
- ½ tsp. dry mustard
- ¼ tsp. pepper
- 1 medium-size tart apple, coarsely chopped (⅔ cup)
- 1 Tbsp. finely shredded Parmesan cheese

1 Cook pasta according to package directions; drain. If desired, use a vegetable peeler to remove any darker outer layer from smoked cheddar cheese. Shred cheese (you should have about ¾ cup); set aside.

2 Preheat oven to 350°. For cheese sauce, in a saucepan cook onion in chicken broth, covered, over medium-high heat about 5 minutes or until tender. In a screw-top jar shake together half-and-half, flour, dry mustard, and pepper; add to broth in pan. Cook and stir over medium heat just until bubbly. Remove from heat; add cheddar cheese, stirring until most of cheese is melted. Pour sauce over pasta, stirring until combined. Turn into a 1½-quart casserole.

3 Bake, covered, for 10 minutes. Uncover and bake about 10 minutes more or until bubbly. Let stand for 5 minutes. Top with chopped apple and Parmesan cheese. Makes 4 main-dish servings.

Nutrition Facts per serving: 376 cal., 8 g total fat (4 g sat. fat), 24 mg chol., 564 mg sodium, 59 g carbo., 3 g fiber, 15 g pro.
Daily Values: 6% vit. A, 3% vit. C, 22% calcium, 16% iron.

Walnut-Crusted Chicken Breasts

Toasting heightens the flavor of the walnuts in the chicken coating. To toast the nuts, place them in a small dry skillet. Cook over medium heat, stirring often, for 5 to 7 minutes or until light golden brown.

Prep: 25 minutes **Bake:** 20 minutes

- 4 skinless, boneless chicken breast halves (1 lb. total)
- ½ of a 5-oz. container semisoft cheese with garlic and herbs
- 1 Tbsp. chopped green onion
- 1 egg
- 2 Tbsp. water
- ½ tsp. salt
- ¼ tsp. pepper
- ¾ cup soft sourdough bread crumbs (about 1 slice)
- ½ cup finely chopped walnuts, toasted
- ¼ cup all-purpose flour
- 1 Tbsp. margarine or butter, melted
- 3 to 4 cups mixed baby greens, such as baby mustard greens, red endive, and Chinese cabbage, or torn mixed greens
- 2 tsp. balsamic vinegar

1 Preheat oven to 400°. Place each chicken breast half between two pieces of plastic wrap. Pound breasts lightly into a rectangle about ⅛ inch thick. Remove plastic wrap. Spread one-fourth of the cheese in center of each breast; sprinkle with green onion.

2 Fold in sides of chicken; roll up from one of the short ends, pressing edges to seal. Secure with wooden toothpicks, if necessary.

3 In a shallow dish combine egg, water, salt, and pepper. Beat with a whisk or fork until well blended; set aside. In another shallow dish combine bread crumbs and walnuts. Coat chicken rolls with flour. Dip chicken in egg mixture, then in walnut mixture to coat all sides. Place chicken, seam side down, in a 2-quart square baking dish. Drizzle with melted margarine or butter.

4 Bake, uncovered, for 20 to 25 minutes or until chicken is tender and no longer pink inside. Top the chicken rolls with mixed baby greens. Return to oven. Bake about

1 minute more or until the greens just begin to wilt. Remove from oven. Sprinkle greens with the balsamic vinegar. Makes 4 servings.

Nutrition Facts per serving: 379 cal., 23 g total fat (7 g sat. fat), 129 mg chol., 414 mg sodium, 14 g carbo., 1 g fiber, 28 g pro.
Daily Values: 11% vit. A, 4% vit. C, 4% calcium, 14% iron.

PRIZE WINNER

Spicy Orange Chicken

Norma J. Keleher
Pacific Grove, California
$200—Mexican Dishes

Prep: 10 minutes Cook: 1¼ hours

- 3 to 3½ lb. meaty chicken pieces (breasts, thighs, and drumsticks)
- 2 Tbsp. olive oil
  Salt and pepper
- 1 large onion, halved and thinly sliced (1 cup)
- 1 large red sweet pepper, cut into bite-size strips (1 cup)
- 4 cloves garlic, minced
- 1 tsp. finely shredded orange peel
- 1 cup orange juice
- ½ cup chicken broth
- ½ cup hot salsa
- 1 15-oz. can black beans, rinsed and drained
  Chopped avocado (optional)

1 Skin chicken. In a 4-quart Dutch oven or a very large skillet cook half of the chicken in hot oil about 15 minutes or until lightly browned, turning to brown evenly. Repeat with remaining half of chicken. Remove all chicken from pan; sprinkle with salt and pepper. Set aside.

2 Add onion, sweet pepper, and garlic to pan. Cook until onion and pepper are just tender. Return chicken to pan. Add orange peel, orange juice, chicken broth, and salsa. Bring to boiling; reduce heat. Simmer, covered, for 35 to 40 minutes or until chicken is tender and no longer pink. Add beans to chicken mixture; heat through. Transfer to a serving dish. If desired, serve with chopped avocado. Makes 8 servings.

Nutrition Facts per serving: 305 cal., 14 g total fat (3 g sat. fat), 78 mg chol., 402 mg sodium, 15 g carbo., 4 g fiber, 29 g pro.
Daily Values: 15% vit. A, 82% vit. C, 5% calcium, 14% iron.

Red Flannel Corned Beef

If you can't find baby beets, go ahead and use the bigger red beets. Cut them into quarters before tossing them into the pot with the corned beef. To serve, drizzle the beef with an easy, make-ahead mustard dressing. (See the photograph on page 82.)

Prep: 20 minutes Cook: 1¾ hours

- 1 2- to 2½-lb. corned beef brisket
- 1¼ lb. red, yellow, and/or candy-stripe baby beets with tops (about 10 oz. after trimming)
- 1 lb. fingerling potatoes or tiny new potatoes, halved or quartered
- 3 cups finely shredded green cabbage
- 1 recipe Spicy Mustard Dressing (see right)

1 Trim excess fat from meat. Place meat in a 4-quart Dutch oven; add any juices and spices from package. Add enough water to cover meat.

SUPPER MENU

- Red Flannel Corned Beef (see left)

- Salad of assorted greens, pear slices, halved red and/or green grapes, and a poppy seed dressing

- Rye bread or rolls and butter

- Warm apple cake

Bring to boiling; reduce heat. Simmer, covered, for 1½ to 2 hours or until almost tender.

2 Meanwhile, trim tops of beets to ½ inch. Trim root ends. Add beets and potatoes to the corned beef. Return to boiling; reduce heat. Simmer, covered, about 15 minutes or until potatoes and beets are tender.

3 Transfer meat to a cutting board. Thinly slice meat across the grain. Arrange meat and cabbage side-by-side on a large serving platter. Using a slotted spoon, remove potatoes and beets, and arrange next to the cabbage. Drizzle with Spicy Mustard Dressing. Makes 6 servings.

Spicy Mustard Dressing

In a small saucepan combine ⅓ cup minced red onion, ⅓ cup vinegar, 3 tablespoons olive oil or salad oil, 2 tablespoons spicy brown mustard, and 1 tablespoon honey; bring to boiling. Remove from heat. Serve warm. Makes about 1 cup.

Nutrition Facts per serving: 449 cal., 28 g total fat (8 g sat. fat), 105 mg chol., 1,321 mg sodium, 29 g carbo., 4 g fiber, 23 g pro.
Daily Values: 86% vit. C, 4% calcium, 27% iron.

No-Guilt Snacking

by Jeanne Ambrose

Let's make it perfectly clear from the start: This is not a snack attack. Instead, we present an ode to snacking. Plus, we'll give you and your busy family plenty of help in making wise choices for those grab-and-go days.

First off, get rid of the guilt. "Snacking is more than OK. It's very important," says registered dietitian Connie Diekman, spokesperson for the American Dietetic Association. "Snacking should be part of your daily routine because most of us cannot eat enough to keep our body fueled for more than three or four hours at a time."

That's especially important to keep in mind for children. Youngsters can't pack enough food into their small tummies to sustain their energy supplies until the next meal. Teens, with rapidly growing bodies, also may need the extra calories and nutrients provided by between-meal munching. The bottom line is: Most people need to snack.

Snacking controls appetite. If you don't overindulge on food high in fat and calories, snacking might even help keep your weight in line. "Most of the research shows that snackers are able to control their weight better than people who go too long between meals," Diekman says. People who skip snacks can be so hungry at mealtime that they overeat and tend to make poor food choices. To avoid those hunger pangs that signal your body has run out of energy, stretch your three daily meals into six mini meals, or nibble a little something between meals.

Reach for foods with complex carbohydrates (whole grains, fruits, vegetables) combined with a protein. For instance, spread a thin layer of peanut butter on a whole-grain cracker. Sample our PB&A Sandwiches or Veggie Roll-ups (see recipes, page 59). Try fat-free bean dip with baked tortilla chips. Nibble on pear slices sprinkled with shredded cheddar cheese.

(Go easy on the cheese: a 1-inch square of cheddar contains 115 calories and 9 grams of fat.) The combination of carbs and protein keeps your fuel reservoir topped off.

It's even OK to occasionally snack on a cookie or other treat. "You don't have to deprive yourself," says Cyndi Thomson, Ph.D., R.D., of the Arizona Prevention Center in Tucson. She suggests putting miniature candy bars in the freezer for a now-and-then snack. The size provides portion control. Tucking them in the freezer helps you avoid compulsive eating. The secret to successful snacking is in making nutritious choices most of the time.

Snack in the box. Prepare and package individual portions of healthy tidbits to tuck into a box or drawer at the office. "It's just a matter of thinking ahead in the morning so you're not eating out of a vending machine in the middle of your workday," says Linda Nebeling, Ph.D., a National Cancer Institute nutritionist. "I keep the equivalent of a snack drawer in my office with dried fruits, boxed juices, and fresh fruit that I bring in." Check the calorie content of reduced-fat snacks. Just because they're touted as fat-free or low fat doesn't mean they're low in calories. Sweeteners, often added to boost the flavor, also may boost the calorie count.

For a quick fix, munch on fortified dry cereal. Look for cereals with 3 grams or less of sugar per serving. Each serving should have at least 3 grams of fiber, too.

Put fruit on a pedestal. As soon as you get fresh fruit home from the market, wash it and display it. You and your family are more likely to eat fruit if it's in plain sight. A study published in the Journal of the American Medical Association reported that people who ate five servings of fruits and vegetables daily lowered their stroke risk. The National Cancer Institute also suggests eating "five a day" to prevent cancer.

If your daily meals don't include five servings of fruits and vegetables, it makes sense to fill in the blanks with snacks, Nebeling says. Some nutrient-rich fruits include oranges, nectarines, and kiwi fruit, as well as dried fruit, such as cranberries, cherries, and mangoes. Vegetables to tote include carrots, sweet peppers, and cherry tomatoes.

Confused about serving size? A serving of fruits or vegetables is equivalent to one of the following:

1 medium fruit (apple, banana, pear)

½ cup berries or cut-up fruit

¼ cup dried fruit

¾ cup (6 ounces) fruit or vegetable juice

½ cup non-leafy raw or cooked vegetables

1 cup leafy, raw vegetables (spinach, lettuce)

Sandwich with a Smile

Take a look at the photo below and you'll see why we call this a lip-smacking treat. These lip look-alikes are a mouthful of crunchy flavor with a good-for-you bonus. Each finished PB&A Sandwich (a.k.a. Peanut Butter and Apple) has 2 grams of fat, a bit of protein and fiber, and just 54 calories.

All you need is an apple, some peanut butter, a little lemon juice, and your favorite wheat or bran cereal flakes. (We like Total cereal because it's especially loaded with vitamins and minerals, or Special K Plus, which has plenty of calcium. Most cereals are fortified. Read nutrition labels.)

First step: Core the apple; cut it into 16 slices.

Next, stir together 3 tablespoons of creamy peanut butter and 3 tablespoons of crushed cereal flakes. Make a "sandwich" by spreading some of the peanut butter mixture between two slices of apple. Lightly brush outsides of apple sandwich with lemon juice. Wrap in plastic wrap. Repeat until you have 8 sandwiches. Chill up to 6 hours.

Veggie Roll-ups

You'll be well on your way to a "high five" with this two-fisted salad snugged tightly in a rolled-up tortilla. This super snack—held together with protein-packed hummus (pureéd chickpeas and garlic)—makes it easy for you to reach toward the "five-a-day" fruit and vegetable goals (see story, page 58). It only takes about 5 minutes to make, too.

Here's how: On one side of an 8-inch wheat-flour tortilla, spread about 3 tablespoons of hummus or bean dip. Top it with a lettuce leaf. Add about ½ cup of your favorite raw veggies that are cut into matchstick-size pieces. Try radishes, carrots, zucchini, and plum tomatoes. Crisp mint leaves add an incredibly fresh taste.

Tightly roll up tortilla. Cut in half. Wrap each half in plastic wrap and chill up to 6 hours. Makes 2 snack servings, each with only 92 calories and 3 grams of fat.

SUPPER MENU

■ Spiced Pot Roast with Garbanzo Beans (see below)

■ Indian pappadams or flour tortillas, toasted and rolled

■ Chocolate pudding topped with a dollop of whipped cream and a sprinkling of cinnamon

Spiced Pot Roast With Garbanzo Beans

Soak: 1 hour or overnight
Prep: 30 minutes **Cook:** 2 hours

1	cup dry garbanzo beans
1	3-lb. boneless beef chuck pot roast
3½	tsp. Garam Masala (see right) or purchased garam masala
2	Tbsp. cooking oil
1	14½-oz. can beef broth
16	tiny whole carrots or packaged, peeled baby carrots
4	small onions, cut into wedges, or pearl onions
2	Tbsp. cornstarch
1	8-oz. carton plain low-fat yogurt Indian pappadams or flour tortillas, toasted and rolled (optional)

1 Rinse beans. In a 4- to 6-quart Dutch oven combine beans and 8 cups *water*. Bring to boiling; reduce heat. Simmer, uncovered, 2 minutes. Remove from heat. Cover; let stand 1 hour. (Or, do not precook beans. Soak them in water overnight in a covered pan.) Drain beans and rinse.

2 Trim excess fat from meat. Combine 2½ teaspoons of the Garam Masala and ½ teaspoon *salt*; rub the mixture onto meat. In the same Dutch oven brown meat on all sides in hot oil. Drain off fat.

3 Pour broth over roast. Add soaked beans. Bring to boiling; reduce heat. Simmer, covered, 1¼ hours. Add carrots and onions. Return to boiling; reduce heat. Simmer, covered, 45 to 60 minutes more or until meat and vegetables are tender. Transfer meat and vegetables to a platter.

4 Pour drippings into a large measuring cup, scraping out the crusty brown bits from the pan. Measure 1 cup for sauce (cover and refrigerate remainder for another use or discard). For sauce, return the 1 cup reserved cooking liquid to the Dutch oven. Stir in the remaining 1 teaspoon Garam Masala. Bring to boiling. In a screw-top jar shake together cornstarch and 2 tablespoons *cold water*; add to the Dutch oven. Cook and stir until thickened and bubbly. Cook and stir for 2 minutes more. Remove from heat; stir in yogurt until well combined. (Do not return to heat.) Serve sauce with meat and vegetables. If desired, accompany with Indian pappadams or tortillas. Makes 10 to 12 servings.

Nutrition Facts per serving: 419 cal., 19 g total fat (7 g sat. fat), 102 mg chol., 378 mg sodium, 25 g carbo., 5 g fiber, 36 g pro.
Daily Values: 154% vit. A, 5% vit. C, 10% calcium, 37% iron.

30 MINUTE

Garam Masala

For this mix use cardamom seeds from the pod or from a spice bottle. If using pods, remove seeds by gently crushing outer shell. Discard pods before measuring seeds.

Prep: 5 minutes **Cook:** 3 minutes

1	Tbsp. cardamom seeds
1	Tbsp. cumin seeds
1	Tbsp. black peppercorns
12	whole cloves
1	3-inch piece stick cinnamon

1 In a medium skillet cook the cardamom seeds, cumin seeds, peppercorns, cloves, and cinnamon over medium-low heat for 3 to 4 minutes or until aromatic, stirring constantly. Remove from heat. Cool.

2 Place cinnamon in a self-sealing plastic bag; seal. Using a rolling pin or mallet, crush cinnamon. In a spice grinder or blender container combine spices. Cover and grind or blend to a fine powder. Store spice blend in a tightly sealed container in a cool, dry place up to 6 months. Makes about ¼ cup.

Spicy Sausage Potpie

Remove any casings from the sausage before crumbling meat into the skillet for browning.

Prep: 40 minutes **Bake:** 40 minutes

6	oz. chorizo or hot Italian sausage, crumbled
1½	cups coarsely chopped, peeled rutabaga or turnip
1	cup mild or medium salsa
¾	cup cooked ham, cut into ½-inch cubes
½	cup reduced-sodium chicken broth
1	14½- or 15-oz. can golden hominy, rinsed and drained
1	recipe Cornmeal Pastry (see page 61)
	Fresh cilantro sprigs (optional)

1 In a large skillet cook chorizo for 8 to 10 minutes or until brown. Drain fat. Stir in rutabaga, salsa, ham, and broth. Bring to boiling; reduce heat. Cover and simmer for 8 to 10 minutes or until rutabaga is crisp-tender. Stir in hominy. Spoon the sausage mixture into an ungreased 1½-quart casserole.

2 Preheat oven to 375°. Prepare Cornmeal Pastry. Measure diameter of top of casserole; roll pastry about 1 inch larger than top of casserole. Place pastry on top of casserole. Turn edges under and flute. Cut slits in top for steam to escape.

3 Bake for 40 to 45 minutes or until pastry is golden brown. If desired, garnish with cilantro sprigs. Serves 4.

Cornmeal Pastry In a medium mixing bowl combine ¾ cup all-purpose flour, ½ cup yellow cornmeal, and ¼ teaspoon salt. Using a pastry blender, cut in ⅓ cup shortening until pieces are pea-size. Stir in 2 tablespoons snipped fresh cilantro or Italian parsley. Sprinkle 3 to 5 tablespoons cold water, 1 tablespoon at a time, over mixture, tossing with a fork after each addition until moistened. Form dough into a ball. Use pastry to prepare Spicy Sausage Potpie (see recipe, page 60).

Nutrition Facts per serving: 422 cal., 38 g total fat (11 g sat. fat), 14 mg chol., 909 mg sodium, 48 g carbo., 3 g fiber, 22 g pro.
Daily Values: 8% vit. A, 58% vit. C, 3% calcium, 22% iron.

30 MINUTE LOW FAT

Simmering Seafood

Check food mail-order catalogs for the special smoked paprika. (See the photograph on page 79.)

Start to finish: 20 minutes

- 1 lb. fresh or frozen sea bass steaks or red snapper fillets, ½ to 1 inch thick
- 2 tsp. smoked sweet paprika or regular sweet paprika
  Cooking oil or shortening for deep-fat frying
- 2 to 4 leeks, very thinly sliced
- 1 Tbsp. cooking oil
- 1 recipe Sweet Pepper Broth (see right)
  Lime and lemon peel (optional)

1 Thaw fish, if frozen. Remove and discard skin, if present. Rinse fish; pat dry. Cut fish into 4 serving-size pieces, if necessary. Measure thickness of fish. In a small bowl combine paprika, ½ teaspoon *salt*, and ½ teaspoon *pepper*; rub onto all sides of the fish.

2 In a large saucepan heat 1½ inches of oil to 365°. Fry sliced leeks, a few slices at a time, 30 seconds to 1 minute or until crisp and golden. Using a slotted spoon, remove leeks from hot oil. Drain on paper towels.

3 Heat the 1 tablespoon cooking oil in a large nonstick skillet over medium heat. Add fish fillets in a single layer. Fry fish on one side until golden, allowing 3 to 4 minutes per side for ½-inch-thick fish fillet and 4 to 6 minutes per side for 1-inch-thick fish fillet. Turn carefully. Fry until second side is golden and fish just flakes easily when tested with a fork. Drain the fish on paper towels.

4 To serve, place one fish piece in each of four shallow bowls. Ladle Sweet Pepper Broth over fish. Garnish with fried leeks and, if desired, citrus peel. Makes 4 servings.

Nutrition Facts per serving (fish and broth): 253 cal., 10 g total fat (2 g sat. fat), 47 mg chol., 774 mg sodium, 17 g carbo., 5 g fiber, 23 g pro.
Daily Values: 13% vit. A, 134% vit. C, 7% calcium, 19% iron.

Sweet Pepper Broth

Prep: 20 minutes **Cook:** 65 minutes

  Nonstick cooking spray
- 1 large yellow sweet pepper, seeded and chopped (1 cup)
- 3 medium leeks, thinly sliced (about 1 cup)
- 6 cloves garlic, minced
- 5¼ cups water
- 1 bay leaf
- ¾ tsp. salt
- ¾ tsp. cracked black pepper
- ⅓ cup dry white wine or chicken broth
- ⅓ cup snipped fresh parsley
- 1½ tsp. finely shredded lime peel or lemon peel

1 Coat a large nonstick saucepan with nonstick cooking spray. Cook sweet pepper, leeks, and garlic over medium heat for 5 to 7 minutes or until tender, stirring frequently. Stir in water, bay leaf, salt, and pepper. Bring to boiling; reduce heat. Cover and simmer for 1 hour.

2 Stir in wine or broth, parsley, and shredded lime peel. Heat through. Remove bay leaf and discard. Use to make Simmering Seafood (see recipe, left). Makes 5½ cups.

PRIZE WINNER

Tequila-Lime Shrimp

Lynn Moretti
Oconomowoc, Wisconsin
$400—Mexican Dishes

Prep: 30 minutes **Chill:** 2 hours
Cook: 10 minutes

- 1 lb. fresh or frozen medium shrimp in shells
- 8 oz. fresh or frozen sea scallops
- ¼ cup lime juice
- ¼ cup snipped fresh cilantro
- 2 Tbsp. cooking oil
- 2 Tbsp. tequila
- 2 cloves garlic, minced
- 1 to 2 tsp. bottled hot pepper sauce
- ½ tsp. dried oregano, crushed
- ½ tsp. ground cumin
- ½ tsp. black pepper
- 1 large onion, cut into thin wedges
- 1 large green sweet pepper, cut into bite-size strips
- 1 large red sweet pepper, cut into bite-size strips
- 1½ cups sliced fresh mushrooms
- 6 9- to 10-inch warmed flour tortillas
- 1½ cups shredded Monterey Jack cheese or Chihuahua cheese (6 oz.)
  Lime wedges

1 Thaw shrimp and scallops, if frozen. Peel and devein shrimp. Rinse shrimp and scallops. Cut scallops in half; set aside.

2 In a mixing bowl stir together lime juice, cilantro, 1 tablespoon of the oil, the tequila, garlic, pepper sauce, oregano, cumin, and black pepper. Add shrimp and scallops. Cover and chill for 2 hours, stirring occasionally.

3 Meanwhile, in a large skillet cook onion and peppers over medium-high heat in the remaining oil for 2 minutes. Add mushrooms; cook and stir 2 minutes more. Add shrimp mixture to skillet; bring to boiling. Cook and stir for 3 minutes or until shrimp are pink and scallops are opaque.

4 To serve, using a slotted spoon, fill each tortilla with about ¾ cup shrimp mixture. Top with cheese and roll up. Spoon a small amount of remaining shrimp mixture with some of the juices over rolls. Serve with lime wedges. Makes 6 servings.

Nutrition Facts per serving: 354 cal., 14 g total fat (5 g sat. fat), 115 mg chol., 396 mg sodium, 27 g carbo., 3 g fiber, 27 g pro.
Daily Values: 25% vit. A, 112% vit. C, 24% calcium, 18% iron.

Chocolate-Prune Accordion Bread

If you've ever seen an accordion in action—or made a paper fan—you'll have no trouble folding and shaping the dough for this fun breakfast or dessert bread. Mix and knead the dough by hand in the conventional manner, or let your bread machine do the work before you do the shaping and filling. (See the photograph on page 83.)

Conventional Prep: 40 minutes
Conventional Total Rise: 1¼ minutes
Bread Machine Prep: 30 minutes
(plus rise time in machine)
Final Rise (bread machine): 30 minutes
Bake: 35 minutes

- 4 cups bread flour
- ¼ tsp. active dry yeast or bread machine yeast
- 1 cup milk
- 3 Tbsp. water
- 3 Tbsp. sugar
- 1 Tbsp. margarine or butter
- 1 tsp. salt
- 1 tsp. ground cinnamon
- 1 egg
- 1⅓ cups pitted prunes, snipped
- ¾ cup chopped bittersweet or semisweet chocolate (about 4 oz.)
  Long wooden skewers

Conventional Dough Preparation:

1 In a large mixing bowl combine 2 cups of the flour and the yeast; set aside. In a small saucepan heat and stir milk, water, sugar, margarine or butter, salt, and cinnamon just until warm (120° to 130°) and the margarine almost melts.

2 Add milk mixture to flour mixture along with the egg. Beat with an electric mixer on low to medium speed for 30 seconds, scraping sides of bowl constantly. Beat on high speed for 3 minutes.

3 Using a wooden spoon, stir in as much of the remaining flour as you can. (Dough should be just stiff enough to knead.)

4 Turn dough out onto a lightly floured surface. Knead in enough of the remaining flour (you may not need entire 4 cups) to make a moderately soft dough that is smooth and elastic (3 to 5 minutes total).

5 Shape dough into a ball. Place in a lightly greased bowl, turning once to grease surface of the dough. Cover and let rise in a warm place until double in size (45 to 60 minutes).

Bread Machine Preparation:
Add all ingredients except the prunes and chocolate to the pan of a 2-pound bread machine. Select dough cycle.

Shaping and Baking:
6 After first rise of conventional method (or when bread-machine dough cycle is complete), remove dough. Punch dough down. Cover and let rest for 10 minutes.

7 Meanwhile, lightly grease a baking sheet; set aside. In a small mixing bowl combine the prunes and chocolate; set aside.

8 On a lightly floured surface, roll dough to a 15×10-inch rectangle. Sprinkle about one-fourth of the prune-chocolate mixture crosswise over 3 inches of dough along the 10-inch side (see Photo 1, right). Fold dough over filling, allowing long edge of dough to extend beyond topped dough. Add another one-fourth of the prune-chocolate mixture on top of the filled layer (see Photo 2, right), pressing filling lightly. Fold dough back over topping. Repeat topping and folding dough and filling, accordion-style, twice more (see Photo 3, right). Fold remaining dough on top, pressing lightly. It is very important to measure dough carefully during shaping. Gently pat sides of the loaf to form a rectangle.

1. After the dough is rolled out, sprinkle some of the prune-chocolate mixture along one side.

2. Gently fold dough over the mixture, then add another prune-chocolate layer.

3. Fold the dough back over the prune-chocolate mix.

9 Place the shaped dough on the prepared baking sheet. Cover and let rise in a warm place until nearly double in size (about 30 minutes).

CLEVER COOK

Removing Sticky Agitator from Bread Machine

Sometimes the agitator sticks to the inside bottom of my bread machine. I use a wooden stick from a frozen dessert pop to help easily pry out the stubborn agitator without marring the surface of the container.

Jerry Wing
Oak Ridge, Tennessee

10 Preheat the oven to 350°. Using a sharp knife, score the top layer of the loaf once lengthwise down the center and then crosswise at 1-inch intervals, creating a large checkerboard pattern. Insert two long wooden skewers (one close to each end of loaf) completely through the loaf to keep the bread layers from slipping while baking.

11 Bake about 35 minutes or until bread sounds hollow when lightly tapped the top with your fingers (cover with foil the last 20 minutes of baking to prevent overbrowning). Transfer bread to a wire rack; cool completely. Remove the wooden skewers. Slice to serve. Makes 1 large loaf (12 to 16 servings).

Nutrition Facts per serving: 297 cal., 6 g total fat (3 g sat. fat), 19 mg chol., 206 mg sodium, 55 g carbo., 3 g fiber, 8 g pro.
Daily Values: 6% vit. A, 1% vit. C, 4% calcium, 18% iron.

Whether you're making biscuits or Sunday supper, you need a clear head and a good plan to cook with kids. Here are a few tips to make you smile:

Get out the goods. Kids—especially young ones—have limited attention spans. They want to cook, not wait around while you search high and low for the baking powder. Gather the ingredients, find the utensils, and grab the baking sheet before you say, "Let's make biscuits!" Kids like to stay focused on the destination. Side trips only distract.

Do a dry run. If your destination is something good to eat, the recipe is your map. Review the recipe before you set out. Are the directions clear? Visualize the steps. Tune in to age-appropriate tasks you can assign.

Show and tell. Even if a child can read, you're still the mouthpiece that makes a recipe come to life. Your words are the barometer for how things are going. So keep up the chatter. Demonstrate steps as you work. Be positive—"You did a good job measuring the flour"—and bite your tongue when little mistakes happen. That's how all cooks, both young and old, learn.

Put safety first. Kitchens are safe places with some potentially unsafe tools and situations. Let common sense prevail. Young children should never stand in front of an open oven. Kids 12 and over, on the other hand, can usually slide a tray of biscuits into a hot oven—as long as they wear oven mitts and you're close by to supervise.

By Ken Haedrich

Basic Anytime Biscuits

A plain biscuit is swell; a biscuit that's been "topped" has a tasty touch that youngsters can brag about. Grab 'em while they're hot.

Prep: 20 minutes **Bake:** 12 minutes

2	cups all-purpose flour
1½ tsp.	baking powder
½ tsp.	baking soda
½ tsp.	salt
¼ cup	cold butter
½ cup	milk
½ cup	dairy sour cream

1 Preheat oven to 400°. In a large mixing bowl stir together the flour, baking powder, baking soda, and salt. Using a pastry blender, cut the butter into dry ingredients until the mixture resembles coarse crumbs. (Or, crumble the butter into the dry ingredients with your fingers.)

2 In a small bowl stir together the milk and sour cream until mixture is almost smooth. Make a well in the center of the flour mixture. Add the milk mixture all at once. Using a wooden spoon, stir just until the dough sticks together.

3 Using hands or a wooden spoon, turn dough onto a lightly floured surface. Sprinkle a little flour on hands. Gently knead 8 or 10 times or just until dough holds together.

When making homemade biscuits, I've found an easy way to clean up the mess that's left on the work surface. Use two pieces of waxed paper on the work surface, one on top of the other, making an X. Sprinkle flour on the waxed paper and roll out the dough on this surface. When you finish cutting biscuits, simply roll up the waxed paper and discard it.

Erika J. Holmes
Mebane, North Carolina

4 Pat dough to ½-inch thickness. (Or, roll dough with a floured rolling pin.) Using the edge of a clean, floured ruler, cut dough into large diamonds or squares, approximately 3 inches. Place on an ungreased baking sheet, leaving about 1 inch space between each biscuit.

5 Bake for 12 to 15 minutes or until golden brown. Using a wide spatula, carefully remove biscuits from baking sheet. Serve immediately. Makes 10 biscuits.

Biscuit Toppers: Before baking, you may brush tops of homemade or purchased ready-to-bake biscuits with melted butter. Add toppers such as mini chocolate chips, chopped nuts, cinnamon-sugar, or shredded cheddar cheese and pepperoni slices.

Nutrition Facts per biscuit: 154 cal., 7 g total fat (4 g sat. fat), 18 mg chol., 300 mg sodium, 19 g carbo., 1 g fiber, 3 g pro.
Daily Values: 7% vit. A, 7% calcium, 6% iron.

april

IN THIS CHAPTER

30-minute recipes indicated in COLOR.
Low-fat and no-fat recipes indicated
with a ♥.
Photographs indicated in italics.
*Bonus recipe

Cappuccino Chip Muffins

See the photograph on page 83.

Prep: 15 minutes **Bake:** 18 minutes

    2   cups all-purpose flour
    ⅔   cup sugar
    3   Tbsp. unsweetened cocoa powder
  1½   tsp. baking powder
  1½   tsp. instant espresso powder or
            2 tsp. instant coffee crystals
    ½   tsp. ground cinnamon
    ¼   tsp. baking soda
  1⅓   cups buttermilk or sour milk
    1   egg
    ½   cup cooking oil
    ¾   cup miniature semisweet
            chocolate pieces
    ¼   cup chopped hazelnuts (filberts)
            or pecans

1 Preheat oven to 400°. Lightly grease eighteen 2½-inch muffin cups or line with paper bake cups. In a large bowl stir together flour, sugar, cocoa, baking powder, espresso powder, cinnamon, baking soda, and ⅛ teaspoon *salt*. Make a well in center of dry mixture; set aside.

2 In another bowl combine the buttermilk, egg, and oil; add all at once to dry mixture. Stir just until moistened. Stir in chocolate pieces and nuts. Spoon batter into prepared muffin cups, filling each three-fourths full. Bake about 18 minutes or until wooden toothpick inserted in centers comes out clean. Cool on wire rack for 5 minutes. Remove from muffin pans. Serve warm. Makes 18 muffins.

Nutrition Facts per muffin: 190 cal., 10 g total fat (2 g sat. fat), 12 mg chol., 90 mg sodium, 21 g carbo., 1 g fiber, 3 g pro.
Daily Values: 1% vit. A, 6% calcium, 5% iron.

LOW FAT
Coffee Cake Show-Off

Prep: 20 minutes **Rise:** 1½ hours
Bake: 35 minutes

    2   to 2¼ cups all-purpose flour
    1   pkg. active dry yeast
    ⅓   cup fat-free evaporated milk
    1   Tbsp. granulated sugar
    1   Tbsp. butter
    1   egg
    6   oz. reduced-fat cream cheese
            (¾ of an 8-oz. pkg.), softened
    2   Tbsp. powdered sugar
    1   tsp. vanilla
    ½   cup spreadable fruit, any flavor
            Sifted powdered sugar

1 In a large bowl mix 1 cup of the flour and yeast; set aside. In a pan heat and stir milk, 3 tablespoons *water*, granulated sugar, butter, and ¼ teaspoon *salt* until warm (120° to 130°) and butter almost melts. Add to flour mixture along with egg. Beat with an electric mixer on low speed for 30 seconds, scraping bowl. Beat on high speed 3 minutes. Stir in as much remaining flour as you can.

2 Turn dough onto a floured surface. Knead in enough remaining flour to make a moderately stiff dough that is smooth and elastic (4 to 6 minutes). Shape into a ball. Put in a greased bowl; turn once. Cover and let rise in a warm place until double (1 hour). Punch down; turn onto floured surface. Divide into two portions, with three-fourths of dough in larger portion. Cover and let rest 10 minutes. Preheat oven to 350°.

3 Grease a 10-inch springform pan or 10-inch cake pan with removable bottom. In a small bowl

EASY LUNCH

- **Asparagus Quiche** (see page 67)

- **Kitchen Garden Bouquets** (see page 71)

- **Spring Fling Icebox Dessert** (see page 86)

- **Iced tea or sparkling water**

combine cream cheese, powdered sugar, and vanilla until smooth. Roll larger dough ball to an 11-inch circle. Fit into pan, covering bottom and ½ inch up sides. Layer with cream cheese mixture and spreadable fruit; spread each evenly.

4 Roll remaining dough into a 9×5-inch rectangle. Cut into five 1-inch-wide strips. Twist each strip four times. Lay three strips on spreadable fruit at 2-inch intervals, stretching strips slightly, if necessary. Place remaining strips horizontally across strips already in place. Press ends into crust rim, trimming if necessary. Cover and let rise until almost double (about 30 minutes).

5 Bake 35 minutes or until crust is golden brown. (If necessary, loosely cover with foil for the last 10 minutes of baking to prevent overbrowning.) Cool on rack about 45 minutes. Sprinkle with sifted powdered sugar. Makes 10 servings.

Nutrition Facts per serving: 185 cal., 5 g total fat (3 g sat. fat), 34 mg chol., 143 mg sodium, 30 g carbo., 1 g fiber, 6 g pro.
Daily Values: 7% vit. A, 6% calcium, 8% iron.

Asparagus Quiche

Prep: 30 minutes **Bake:** 48 minutes
Stand: 10 minutes

  8 oz. asparagus spears, trimmed
       and halved crosswise
  ½ cup grated Parmesan cheese
  2 tsp. dried basil, crushed
  1 10-oz. pkg. refrigerated pizza
       dough
  3 slices bacon
  ½ cup chopped onion
  5 eggs, beaten
  ½ cup milk
       Dash ground nutmeg
1½ cups shredded Swiss cheese
  1 Tbsp. all-purpose flour
  2 tsp. cooking oil

1 Preheat oven to 425°. Coat a 9-inch springform pan with *nonstick cooking spray;* set aside. In a medium saucepan cook asparagus, covered, in a small amount of boiling water for 2 minutes. Drain; set aside.

2 In a bowl combine the Parmesan and basil. Sprinkle work surface with half of the mixture; roll out dough on surface to a 12-inch square. Sprinkle with remaining Parmesan mixture. Using a rolling pin, gently press mixture into dough by rolling over top (see Photo 1, above).

3 Turn dough into prepared pan. Press dough up sides of pan, folding under edges as needed, to form sides that are 2 inches high (see Photo 2, above). Line dough in pan with a double thickness of foil. Bake for 8 minutes. Remove foil; bake for 5 minutes more. Remove from oven. Reduce oven temperature to 350°.

4 In a skillet cook bacon until crisp. Drain, reserving 1 tablespoon drippings. Crumble bacon; set aside.

1. Using a rolling pin, gently press mixture into dough by rolling over top.

2. Fold crust edges under to form sides about 2 inches high; pat to form a firm edge.

Cook onion in reserved drippings over medium heat until tender but not brown; drain. In a bowl combine eggs, milk, nutmeg, and ⅛ teaspoon *salt.* Stir in bacon and onion. Toss together Swiss cheese and flour. Add to egg mixture, mix well, then pour into the dough-lined pan. Toss asparagus with oil. Arrange asparagus in spoke-like pattern on top of egg mixture.

5 Bake 35 to 40 minutes or until a knife inserted near the center comes out clean. Let stand 10 minutes before serving. Remove sides of pan to serve. If desired, top with shaved *Parmesan cheese.* Makes 6 servings.

Nutrition Facts per serving: 386 cal., 20 g total fat (9 g sat. fat), 214 mg chol., 649 mg sodium, 28 g carbo., 1 g fiber, 23 g pro.
Daily Values: 20% vit. A, 15% vit. C, 37% calcium, 14% iron.

30 MINUTE, LOW FAT

The Casual Omelet

Prep: 10 minutes **Cook:** 8 minutes

  8 oz. refrigerated or frozen egg
       product, thawed, or 4 eggs
  1 Tbsp. snipped fresh chives, Italian
       parsley, or chervil
  ¼ cup shredded, reduced-fat sharp
       cheddar cheese (1 oz.)
  1 cup spinach leaves
  1 recipe Red Pepper Relish (see
       below)

1 Coat a cold 8-inch nonstick skillet with flared sides or a crepe pan with *nonstick cooking spray.* Heat skillet over medium heat.

2 In a large bowl combine egg product, chives, a dash of *salt,* and a dash of *ground red pepper* with an electric mixer on medium speed until frothy. Pour into prepared skillet. Cook over medium heat until eggs begin to set. As eggs set, run a spatula around edge of skillet, lifting eggs so uncooked portion flows underneath. When eggs are set but still shiny, sprinkle with cheese. Top with ¾ cup of the spinach and 2 tablespoons Red Pepper Relish. Fold one side of omelet partially over filling. Top with remaining spinach and 1 tablespoon relish. Reserve remaining relish for another use. Makes 2 servings.

Red Pepper Relish Combine ⅔ cup chopped red sweet pepper, 2 tablespoons finely chopped onion, 1 tablespoon cider vinegar, and ¼ teaspoon black pepper.

Nutrition Facts per serving: 121 cal., 3 g total fat (2 g sat. fat), 10 mg chol., 380 mg sodium, 7 g carbo., 3 g fiber, 16 g pro.
Daily Values: 51% vit. A, 166% vit. C, 16% calcium, 19% iron.

Poaching an Egg

Some folks shy away from poaching an egg, thinking it's a complicated operation. These step-by-step directions make the process effortless. Fill a 2-quart, stainless steel or glass saucepan (don't use cast iron) with 6 cups water. Add ½ teaspoon salt, if desired. Bring the water just to boiling (rapid bubbles), then reduce to a low simmer (small bubbles just breaking the surface of the water). If the water is boiling too briskly, the egg may toughen and could break up from the agitation. If the water temperature is too low, the egg will not hold together, leaving a murky mess. Two eggs may be poached at once in a 2-quart saucepan.

1. Give 'em a Break
Break the egg onto a shallow plate or into a shallow bowl. With the edge of the plate just touching the water, let the egg slip gently into the simmering water. Cook for 3 to 5 minutes or until the white is firm and the yolk begins to thicken but is not hard.

2. Spoon and Drain
Using a slotted spoon, remove the poached egg from the water. Drain well. A properly poached egg should be firm, shiny, and round, with a warm, soft yolk. (Use kitchen shears to trim the edges of the egg, if desired.)

Three to Get Ready
● To poach more than two eggs, use a large skillet instead of a saucepan.
● Use the freshest eggs—they'll keep their shape better during poaching.
● Watch the time! Overcooking makes the white tough and the yolk mealy.

PRIZE WINNER

Stuffed Sweet Potatoes

Jenni and Joe Dise
Phoenix, Arizona
$200—Micro Meals

Prep: 20 minutes **Micro-cook:** 12 minutes

 2 large sweet potatoes (8 oz. each)
¼ of an 8-oz. pkg. reduced-fat cream cheese (Neufchâtel), softened
 2 tsp. balsamic vinegar
 1 tsp. dried minced onion
 1 tsp. soy sauce
¼ tsp. garlic powder
½ cup diced cooked ham
    Snipped fresh chives

1 Scrub potatoes. Prick several times with a fork. Place in a microwave-safe shallow dish. Micro-cook on 100% power (high) for 8 to 10 minutes, or until tender, rearranging once. Cool slightly. Cut a lengthwise slice 2 inches wide from top of each potato. Discard skin from slice; place pulp in a bowl. Scoop pulp out of each potato, leaving a ¼-inch shell. Add pulp to same bowl. Mash pulp with a potato masher or an electric mixer on low speed. Add cream cheese, vinegar, onion, soy sauce, garlic powder, and ⅛ teaspoon *pepper*. Stir or beat until smooth. Stir in ham. If desired, stir in a little *milk* to make of desired consistency.

2 Spoon mashed potato mixture into potato shells. Return to baking dish. Micro-cook, uncovered, on 100% power (high) 4 to 5 minutes or until heated through. Sprinkle with chives. Makes 2 servings.

Nutrition Facts per serving: 401 cal., 11 g total fat (6 g sat. fat), 46 mg chol., 934 mg sodium, 59 g carbo., 7 g fiber, 17 g pro.
Daily Values: 441% vit. A, 66% vit. C, 8% calcium, 12% iron.

LOW FAT

Easter Egg Potatoes

We give you a choice. You can bake these potatoes at a temperature compatible with the other food in the oven. (See the photograph on page 77.)

Prep: 40 minutes
Bake: 40 minutes plus 20 minutes

 8 small baking potatoes (about 4 oz. each) or 4 large baking potatoes (about 8 oz. each)
½ cup light dairy sour cream or plain yogurt
½ cup shredded Gouda cheese
 2 Tbsp. snipped fresh chives
 2 tsp. Dijon-style mustard
 2 hard-cooked eggs, peeled and coarsely chopped

1 Preheat oven to 425° or 350°. Scrub potatoes; pat dry. Prick potatoes with a fork. (If desired, for softer skins, rub potatoes with *shortening* or wrap in foil.)

1. Cut enough off the potato to allow it to stand without wobbling.

2. When hollowing out the cooked potatoes, leave a ¼-inch-thick shell.

2 Place potatoes in a shallow baking pan. Bake in a 425° oven for 40 to 50 minutes for smaller potatoes or 60 to 70 minutes for larger potatoes (or in a 350° oven 60 to 70 minutes for smaller potatoes or for 80 to 90 minutes for larger potatoes) or until tender. Cool slightly.

3 For small potatoes, cut a thin crosswise slice off both ends of each (see Photo 1, above). (For large potatoes, cut them in half crosswise. Cut a thin crosswise slice from the round ends of the potatoes.) Scoop pulp from slices (see Photo 2, above); discard skin. Place pulp in a bowl. Carefully scoop pulp from each potato, leaving a ¼-inch-thick shell. Add pulp to bowl; set shells aside. Mash potato pulp. Stir in sour cream, cheese, chives, mustard, ½ teaspoon

salt, and ¼ teaspoon *pepper*. If necessary, add a little *milk* to make of desired consistency. Stir in hard-cooked eggs. Carefully spoon mixture into shells. Stand potato "eggs" upright in a 2-quart rectangular or square baking dish.

4 Bake, uncovered, in a 425° oven for about 20 minutes or in a 350° oven about 30 minutes or until heated through and tops are lightly browned. If desired, top with whole fresh *chives*. Makes 8 servings.

Nutrition Facts per serving: 185 cal., 5 g total fat (2 g sat. fat), 64 mg chol., 266 mg sodium, 29 g carbo., 1 g fiber, 7 g pro.
Daily Values: 5% vit. A, 29% vit. C, 7% calcium, 10% iron.

PRIZE WINNER

Veggies & Couscous

Nancy Blumenthaler
Copley, Ohio
$400—Micro Meals

Prep: 10 minutes **Micro-cook:** 3 minutes

½	cup reduced-sodium chicken broth
1	small carrot, thinly sliced (¼ cup)
¼	cup chopped green sweet pepper
½	tsp. onion powder
¼	tsp. garlic powder
	Dash bottled hot pepper sauce
½	cup spinach, coarsely chopped
⅓	cup quick-cooking couscous
1	tsp. lemon juice
6	cherry tomatoes, quartered
2	Tbsp. finely shredded Parmesan cheese
1	Tbsp. snipped fresh cilantro
¼	cup shredded reduced-fat or regular mozzarella cheese (1 oz.)

1 In a 1-quart microwave-safe casserole stir together the first six ingredients. Micro-cook, covered, on 100% power (high) for 2 to 3 minutes or until carrots are just tender, stirring once. Stir in spinach, couscous, and lemon juice. Cook, covered, on high for 1 to 1½ minutes more or until spinach is just wilted and couscous has absorbed liquid. Stir in tomatoes, Parmesan, and cilantro; sprinkle with mozzarella. Let stand, covered, until cheese is melted. Makes 2 main-dish or 4 side-dish servings.

Nutrition Facts per main-dish serving: 204 cal., 4 g total fat (2 g sat. fat), 12 mg chol., 299 mg sodium, 30 g carbo., 4 g fiber, 11 g pro.
Daily Values: 58% vit. A, 51% vit. C, 18% calcium, 7% iron.

EDITOR'S TIP

Purple Carrots?

Back in the 10th century, nobody knew what an orange carrot was. They were either white or purple. Today, with the help of scientists, carrots are getting back to their purple roots.

Leonard Pike, Ph.D., director of the Vegetable and Fruit Improvement Center at Texas A&M University, first bred a maroon carrot in 1989 as a novelty (Texas A&M's colors are maroon and white). He later learned that the color had more implications.

Anthocyanin, the substance that makes the carrots purple, is an antioxidant that scientists believe may help fight cancer and heart disease. The carrots are orange on the inside, so they still contain high levels of beta-carotene. Our bodies convert beta-carotene to vitamin A, another antioxidant.

Dr. Pike says color doesn't drastically change flavor. His carrot, the BetaSweet, is a bit sweeter than an orange carrot and has the texture of celery without the fibers. BetaSweet carrots are sold in A&P, Kroger, Giant, and HEB grocery stores. Or, you can buy seeds for Dragon carrots—another purple carrot variety—from Garden City Seeds in Hamilton, Montana. To request a catalog, call 406/961-4837.

Cardamom-Orange Bunnies

See the photograph on page 81.

Prep: 45 minutes **Rise:** 1½ hours
Bake: 11 to 13 minutes

- 5¼ to 5¾ cups all-purpose flour
- 1 pkg. active dry yeast
- ¾ tsp. ground cardamom
- 1¼ cups milk
- ½ cup butter or margarine
- ⅓ cup sugar
- 2 eggs
- 2 Tbsp. finely shredded orange peel or 1 Tbsp. finely shredded lime peel
- ¼ cup orange juice or 2 Tbsp. lime juice and 2 Tbsp. water
- 1 recipe Orange or Lime Icing (see right) (optional)

1 In bowl combine 2 cups of the flour, the yeast, and cardamom. Set aside. In saucepan heat and stir milk, butter, sugar, and ½ teaspoon *salt* just until warm (120° to 130°) and butter almost melts. Add milk mixture to dry mixture along with eggs. Beat on low to medium speed 30 seconds, scraping bowl. Beat on high speed 3 minutes. Stir in peel and juice, and as much remaining flour as you can.

2 Turn dough onto a floured surface. Knead in enough remaining flour to make a moderately soft dough that is smooth and elastic (3 to 5 minutes total). Shape into a ball. Place in a lightly greased bowl; turn once. Cover; let rise in a warm place until double (about 1 hour).

3 Punch dough down. Turn out onto a lightly floured surface. Divide in half. Cover and let dough rest 10 minutes. Lightly grease two

A double twist turns the ropes of dough into bunny-shape rolls.

baking sheets. (Large bunnies will go on one sheet; the small bunnies will go on the other.)

4 For small bunnies, divide one half of dough into 4 portions; roll each portion into a 16-inch long rope. On one of the prepared baking sheets lap one end of a rope over the other to form a loop; bring the end that's underneath over the top, letting one end extend on each side to make ears (see photo, above). Pat tips of ears to shape into a point. Repeat with remaining ropes.

5 For small bunnies, divide remaining half of dough into 12 portions. Roll 10 of the portions into 12-inch ropes. Shape 10 small bunnies as above, using the second baking sheet. With remaining 2 pieces of dough, shape 4 large balls and 10 small balls for the tails. Moisten balls and place atop dough at the bottom of the loops. Press tails onto dough.

6 After shaping, cover and let rise until nearly double (30 to 45 minutes). Meanwhile, preheat oven to 375°. Bake small bunnies 11 to 12 minutes or until golden. Bake large

bunnies 13 to 15 minutes or until golden. Remove from baking sheets; cool on racks. If desired, frost while warm with Orange or Lime Icing. Makes 4 large and 10 small bunnies.

Orange or Lime Icing Combine 1½ cups sifted powdered sugar and 1 teaspoon finely shredded orange or lime peel. For Orange Icing, stir in enough orange juice (2 to 3 tablespoons) to make easy to drizzle. For Lime Icing, stir in enough milk (2 to 3 tablespoons) to make easy to drizzle.

Nutrition Facts per small bunny: 214 cal., 6 g total fat (3 g sat. fat), 36 mg chol., 125 mg sodium, 36 g carbo., 1 g fiber, 5 g pro.
Daily Values: 6% vit. A, 6% vit. C, 3% calcium, 8% iron.

Country Spoon Bread

Prep: 20 minutes **Bake:** 55 minutes

- 3 egg whites
- 2 cups milk
- 1½ cups yellow cornmeal
- 3 egg yolks, beaten
- 1 cup cream-style cottage cheese with chives
- ¾ cup shredded Havarti cheese with dill (3 oz.)
- 1 8½-oz. can cream-style corn

1 Allow egg whites to stand at room temperature 20 minutes. Preheat oven to 350°. In saucepan combine milk and cornmeal. Cook and stir over medium heat 5 minutes or until the mixture is very thick and pulls away from the sides. Remove from heat.

2 In a mixing bowl combine egg yolks, cottage cheese, Havarti, corn, and ½ teaspoon *salt*. Stir into cornmeal mixture in saucepan.

3 Beat egg whites on high until stiff peaks form (tips stand straight). Fold into cornmeal mixture. Spoon into a greased 2-quart casserole. Bake, uncovered, for 55 to 60 minutes or until a knife inserted near the center comes out clean. Serve immediately. Makes 8 side-dish servings.

Nutrition Facts per serving: 249 cal., 9 g total fat (2 g sat. fat), 101 mg chol., 438 mg sodium, 30 g carbo., 2 g fiber, 13 g pro.
Daily Values: 20% vit. A, 3% vit. C, 13% calcium, 9% iron.

30 MINUTE, LOW FAT

Kitchen Garden Bouquets

Start to finish: 25 minutes

- 1 cup torn watercress, tough stems removed
- 1 cup baby mustard greens or baby spinach
- 1 cup edible flowers
- 3 medium cucumbers
- ¼ cup tarragon vinegar or white wine vinegar
- 2 Tbsp. olive oil or salad oil

1 Combine greens and edible flowers. Remove lengthwise strips of peel from cucumber. Cut cucumbers into 2½-inch lengths. Using a peeler-corer, remove core, leaving a ¼-inch shell. Tuck some greens mixture into an end of each of the cucumber shells. Stand filled cucumbers, greens end up, on a serving platter. Arrange the remaining greens mixture on platter, if desired.

2 In a screw-top jar combine vinegar, oil, ¼ teaspoon *salt*, and ¼ teaspoon coarsely ground *pepper*. Cover; shake well. Drizzle some of the dressing over cucumber bouquets; pass remainder. Makes 6 to 8 servings.

Nutrition Facts per serving: 55 cal., 5 g total fat (1 g sat. fat), 0 mg chol., 101 mg sodium, 4 g carbo., 1 g fiber, 1 g pro.
Daily Values: 11% vit. A, 17% vit. C, 2% calcium, 4% iron.

Pick-of-the-Patch Salad

See the photograph on page 80.

Prep: 30 minutes **Cook:** 3 minutes

- 2 cups fresh shelled peas
- 1 cup 3- to 4-inch strips green onions
- 6 cups arugula or baby spinach
- 4 cups baby Swiss chard, torn red-tip leaf lettuce, or torn romaine
- ¼ cup Strawberry Vinegar (see recipe, below) or purchased raspberry vinegar
- ¼ cup salad oil
- ½ cup borage flowers or other edible flowers

1 In a medium saucepan cook peas, covered, in a small amount of boiling salted *water* for 3 minutes. Drain and cool. Arrange peas, green onions, arugula, and baby Swiss chard in rows on a large platter or in a serving bowl.

2 In a screw-top jar combine Strawberry Vinegar and oil. Cover and shake well. Drizzle over salad. Garnish with edible flowers. Store remaining dressing in refrigerator. Makes 8 to 10 servings.

Strawberry Vinegar In a medium stainless steel saucepan combine 1 cup chopped fresh strawberries and 1 cup cider vinegar. Bring to boiling; reduce heat. Simmer, uncovered, 3 minutes.

EDITOR'S TIP

Tender Greens Are Tough to Beat

Quick. Beat those bunnies to your garden and snip a bowl full of tiny, tender spring greens. (Or pick some from your grocer's produce shelves.)

Then take the advice of Alice Waters, chef-owner of Chez Panisse in Berkeley, California, and dress those greens in next to nothing. At her organic food restaurant, a splash of extra virgin olive oil, a squeeze of fresh lemon juice, and a sprinkling of salt allows salads to flaunt their flavors.

Waters fancies baby greens because of their subtle, fresh taste and their visual interest. Wander into her restaurant and you're bound to be served a salad that looks like a miniature nature still life. Her edible art may begin with baby blush-pink radishes, newly sprouted green onions, and tiny arugula leaves, picked by area farmers. She sometimes includes a scattering of vivid red nasturtium petals.

Waters' latest book, *Chez Panisse Café Cookbook*, shares recipes that encourage creativity in the kitchen.

Restaurant: Chez Panisse Café and Restaurant

Address: 1517 Shattuck Ave., Berkeley, California

Telephone: 510/548-5525

Remove from heat. Pour the vinegar-berry mixture through a fine-mesh strainer; let liquid drain into a bowl. Discard berries. Transfer vinegar to a jar or bottle. Cover tightly with a nonmetallic lid (or cover with plastic wrap and tightly seal with a metal lid). Store in refrigerator up to 6 months. Makes about 1¼ cups.

Nutrition Facts per serving: 97 cal., 7 g total fat (1 g sat. fat), 0 mg chol., 38 mg sodium, 7 g carbo., 2 g fiber, 3 g pro.
Daily Values: 13% vit. A, 20% vit. C, 3% calcium, 7% iron.

Soy, the magic bean

by Bev Bennett

Soybeans are the Cinderella of the food world. They're a workhorse, used for everything from cooking oil to livestock feed. And soybeans are touted today as the closest thing we have to a miracle ingredient.

Scientists are delving into the many possible roles soy foods could play in bettering our health, such as reducing the risk of developing heart disease and certain cancers, and lowering chances of developing osteoporosis.

What's Inside

Isoflavones, estrogenlike plant compounds thought to be soy's main cancer-fighting component, are abundant in the little legumes. Studies indicate that people who eat at least two servings of soy products per day—for example, a 3-ounce portion of tofu and 8 ounces of soy milk—show a reduction in cancers of the breast, colon, and prostate. The data are especially encouraging with prostate cancer, according to Mark Messina, Ph.D., a nutrition researcher on soy. "One study found that one to two servings of soy milk a day is associated with a 70-percent reduction in prostate cancer risk," says Messina. One type of soy isoflavone, called genistein, has been shown in lab studies to halt development of the blood vessels that tumors need to thrive.

The Heart Helper

Soy's cholesterol-lowering qualities are well documented. People with elevated cholesterol levels who eat about an ounce of soy protein a day may see up to a 10-percent drop in their total cholesterol levels. What's more, it's the level of undesirable, heart-disease-associated cholesterols—LDLs and triglycerides—that declines. And, as an added bonus, there is a slight elevation in desirable (HDL) cholesterol.

"The largest improvement is seen in people with high cholesterol levels," says Dr. Gregory Burke, of the Wake Forest University School of Medicine, Winston-Salem, North Carolina. "For people with normal cholesterol, the difference may not be significant." Although scientists believe that isoflavones are soy's cholesterol-lowering factor, the compound doesn't seem to work in supplement form. "It's possible that a combination of isoflavones and soy protein is necessary," Burke says.

Soy and Women

Women have reason to be encouraged about soy's health potential: Strong evidence exists that soy can help fight osteoporosis. In a recent six-month study of 24 subjects, those who ate 40 grams daily of soy protein (with isoflavones) had no significant bone loss. In contrast, a group who ate soy with the isoflavones removed had a measured bone density loss of 0.66 percent. The control group, who ate no soy or isoflavones, suffered a 1.28-percent loss.

Soy may offer some of the same heart- and bone-protecting advantages as estrogen-replacement therapy, but without the increased breast or uterine cancer risk thought to be associated with the therapy. (Estrogen can trigger cells in the uterus and breast to turn cancerous.) Soy's phytoestrogens block regular estrogen from attaching to those cells, thus decreasing their potential to turn cancerous, explains Dr. Tom Clarkson, professor of comparative medicine at Wake Forest.

Although soy foods have been extolled for relieving such menopause symptoms as hot flashes, night sweats, and vaginal dryness, the science is still iffy. In some experiments women experienced no change with a high-soy diet; other tests showed modest relief.

Soy Bang for Your Buck

Considering all the evidence, eating about two ounces of soy foods or drinking two glasses of enriched soy beverages daily will provide most of the health benefits that the bean has to offer. It's easy to find foods high in soy that you'll enjoy incorporating into your menu. There are more choices than ever, from soy-enriched breads to energy bars. Look for new soy-containing cereals, too.

The United Soybean Board lists the following popular soy foods and their protein content.

Food	Protein content
¼ cup roasted soy nuts	17 g
½ cup tempeh	16 g
½ cup cooked soybeans	14 g
1 soy-protein bar	14 g
1 soy burger	10 to 12 g
½ cup firm tofu	10 g
½ cup soft tofu	9 g
1 cup plain soy milk	7 g
¼ cup shelled green soybeans (edamame)	5 g

Soy-Snack Fix-ups

Dry-roasted soybeans are now readily available. You can turn them into a great crunchy snack in less than 10 minutes: Preheat oven to 350°. Spread 8 ounces dry roasted soybeans (2 cups) in an even layer on a baking sheet. Sprinkle the beans with your choice of the following spice mixtures:

1½ tsp. dried thyme, crushed;
¼ tsp. garlic salt; and
⅛ to ¼ tsp. ground red pepper.

2 tsp. brown sugar,
1½ tsp. chili powder, and
½ tsp. garlic salt.

2 tsp. toasted sesame oil,
¾ tsp. ground ginger, and
½ tsp. onion salt.

1½ tsp. garam masala,
¼ tsp. salt, and
⅛ to ¼ tsp. ground red pepper.

1 Bake for 5 minutes or until just heated through, shaking pan once. Remove from oven. Cool.

2 Store for up to a week in an airtight container. Eat plain, toss in soups or salads, add to hot baked potatoes, or mix with popcorn or other party mixes. Makes 2 cups.

Nutrition Facts per 2-tablespoon serving: 75 cal., 3 g fat (1 g sat. fat), 0 mg chol., 27 mg sodium, 4 g carbo., 2 g fiber, 7 g pro.
Daily Values: 1% vit. A, 0% vit. C, 3% calcium, 5% iron.

EDITOR'S TIP

What Age, What Tool?

It's easy to feel clueless when it comes to determining whether your child is ready to start using kitchen cutters and peelers. Desire, dexterity, and your child's ability to focus must all be considered. When in doubt, start slow and follow the tips below.

Children 7 to 10 can handle peeling tasks. The more often they hear "always peel away from your other hand, not toward it" the better. Guide small hands with your own hand at first.

Children 11 and older are generally ready to begin using a paring knife. Start out with vegetables that offer little resistance such as zucchini and peeled cucumbers, for example. For lessons in peeling, vegetables with sufficient length (carrots and parsnips) help keep the hands and the peeler farther apart.

Kids 13 and older are more adept than their younger counterparts. They can, perhaps, use larger knives and tackle more challenging cutting jobs. Be watchful that increased confidence doesn't breed carelessness. A gentle reminder to slow down is often the best way to keep a young cook on track.

Chicken à la Spring

Roast chicken is a traditional Passover main course. This version is basted with a lemony blend of oil and garlic. (See the photograph on page 81.)

Prep: 15 minutes **Stand:** 30 minutes
Roast: 1 hour plus 10 minutes standing time

- 3 Tbsp. cooking oil
- 2 cloves garlic, minced
- 1 Tbsp. finely shredded lemon peel
- 6 to 8 leaves fresh sorrel (optional)
- 1 lemon, cut into wedges

- 1 3- to 3½-lb. whole broiler-fryer chicken
- ⅔ cup reduced-sodium chicken broth
- 1½ tsp. potato starch (or cornstarch, if not observing Passover)
- 1 Tbsp. lemon juice
- 2 Tbsp. coarsely shredded fresh sorrel or spinach leaves
   Red Russian kale or other kale variety (optional)
   Chamomile flowers or other edible flowers (optional)

1 In a small saucepan cook and stir oil and garlic over low heat for 2 minutes. Remove from heat. Stir in lemon peel; set oil mixture aside.

2 Place sorrel leaves, if using, and lemon wedges in the cavity of the bird. Tie legs to tail. Twist wing tips under back. Loosen and lift skin above breast. Brush a little of the garlic-oil mixture under the breast skin; skewer neck skin to back. Brush a little more of the oil mixture over the skin of the bird. Cover and chill remaining oil mixture. Cover chicken; let stand at room temperature for 30 minutes, or refrigerate up to 24 hours.

3 Preheat oven to 375°. Uncover chicken; place, breast side up, on a rack in a shallow roasting pan. If desired, insert a meat thermometer into center of an inside thigh muscle. Do not allow thermometer tip to touch bone. Roast, uncovered, for 1 to 1¼ hours or until drumsticks move easily in their sockets, chicken is no longer pink, and meat thermometer registers 180°. Baste with remaining oil mixture about halfway through cooking time. Remove sorrel leaves, if using, and lemon wedges from cavity. Cover chicken loosely with foil; let stand 10 minutes.

4 Meanwhile, pour juices and browned bits from roasting pan into a small glass measure. Skim off and discard fat, reserving pan juices (1 to 2 tablespoons total). In a small saucepan gradually stir broth into potato starch. Add pan juices. Cook and stir over medium heat until slightly thickened and bubbly. Stir in lemon juice. Season to taste with *salt* and *pepper*. Transfer chicken to a serving platter. Pour sauce into a bowl; top with shredded sorrel or spinach. If desired, top chicken with kale and edible flowers. Serves 6.

Nutrition Facts per serving: 285 cal., 19 g total fat (4 g sat. fat), 79 mg chol., 136 mg sodium, 3 g carbo., 1 g fiber, 25 g pro.
Daily Values: 4% vit. A, 28% vit. C, 3% calcium, 8% iron.

LOW FAT

Four-Veggie Roast

Here's a recipe to have kids assist with. Be sure to supervise when they're using kitchen scissors or peelers.

Prep: 20 minutes **Roast:** 20 minutes

- 2 large carrots
- 1½ cups fresh green beans (6 oz.)
- 5 to 6 small new potatoes (8 oz.)
- 1 small onion
- 1 Tbsp. olive oil
- 2 tsp. soy sauce
- 2 cloves garlic, minced
- 1 tsp. grated fresh ginger

1 Preheat oven to 425°. Thoroughly wash vegetables. To trim and peel carrots, have child steady each carrot on a cutting board with one hand. Starting at about halfway, peel carrot, using swivel vegetable peeler, with sweeping movements away from the hand holding the carrot. Turn carrot around; peel other half. Cut carrots,

on the bias, if desired, into slices not quite ½ inch thick.

2 Using kitchen scissors or a small paring knife, snip the tiny ends off green beans. Using hands, snap beans into pieces about 2 inches long. Using a small paring knife, cut new potatoes in half. Peel onion; cut into wedges.

3 In a large bowl combine olive oil, soy sauce, garlic, and ginger. Add all the vegetables. Stir gently to coat with seasonings. Spread coated vegetables evenly in a 9×9×2- or 8×8×2-inch baking pan. Sprinkle with freshly ground *black pepper*.

4 Roast vegetables, uncovered, 20 to 25 minutes, or until just tender, stirring vegetables once or twice with a long-handled wooden spoon. (Be careful when opening oven door as hot steam from pan may escape.) Test the vegetables with a fork to check doneness. Makes 3 or 4 servings.

Nutrition Facts per serving: 157 cal., 5 g total fat (1 g sat. fat), 0 mg chol., 238 mg sodium, 26 g carbo., 6 g fiber, 4 g pro.
Daily Values: 195% vit. A, 43% vit. C, 6% calcium, 10% iron.

French-Style Short Ribs

Plain red beets will turn the sauce a deep red. To make a lighter color sauce, cook red beets separately, or use pink or golden varieties.

Prep: 20 minutes **Cook:** 1½ hours

2	lb. boneless beef short ribs
1	Tbsp. cooking oil
¾	cup chicken broth
½	tsp. dried rosemary, crushed
½	tsp. dried thyme, crushed

8	oz. fresh morel mushrooms or other fresh mushrooms
16	baby pink or golden beets, or 4 medium carrots cut into 1-inch pieces
4	medium leeks
2	tsp. finely shredded lemon peel
⅓	cup dairy sour cream
1	Tbsp. all-purpose flour

1 Cut meat into 8 serving-size pieces. In a heavy, large saucepan or Dutch oven brown ribs in hot oil over medium-high heat. Drain off fat. Add broth, rosemary, thyme, ½ teaspoon *pepper*, and ¼ teaspoon *salt*. Bring to boiling; reduce heat. Cover and simmer for 1 hour.

2 Meanwhile, clean mushrooms. If using morel mushrooms, soak in a bowl of cold, lightly salted water for 15 minutes. Drain, rinse, and drain well. Wash other mushrooms by wiping with a damp towel. Halve mushrooms. For beets, remove roots and all but 1 inch of stems; wash beets well. Do not peel. Cut in half lengthwise. For leeks, remove tough outer leaves. Trim roots and cut away tops leaving white portion. Slit lengthwise; wash well. Cut crosswise into 2-inch slices.

3 Add beets or carrots and lemon peel to meat mixture; simmer, covered, 20 minutes. Add mushrooms and leeks; simmer, covered, about 10 minutes more or until vegetables and meat are tender. Use a slotted spoon to transfer meat and vegetables to serving dish; cover to keep warm.

4 Measure 1 cup cooking liquid; if necessary, add more chicken broth to make 1 cup. Return to large saucepan. In a small bowl stir together sour cream and flour. Stir into the cooking liquid. Cook and stir until

slightly thickened and bubbly; cook and stir for 1 minute more. Spoon meat and vegetables into serving bowls. Ladle sauce over meat and vegetables. Makes 8 servings.

Nutrition Facts per serving: 256 cal., 13 g total fat (5 g sat. fat), 55 mg chol., 271 mg sodium, 8 g carbo., 2 g fiber, 25 g pro.
Daily Values: 2% vit. A, 6% vit. C, 5% calcium, 16% iron.

TEST KITCHEN TIP

Kitchen Tools and Kid Safety

No one can guarantee that accidents won't happen between kids and kitchen tools, but a little caution goes a long way in preventing mishaps. Here are a few safety points to ponder:

Sharp Tools Rule
Contrary to common belief, sharp tools are safer than dull ones. A sharp knife blade is easier for a child to control; a dull one is more likely to slide off a vegetable with potentially harmful results.

Handle with Care
A slip-resistant rubber handle makes for a sure grip. Many manufacturers offer complete lines of such kitchen tools, including a number of peelers, small knives, and kitchen shears. Check your local kitchen and housewares shops and large supermarkets.

Steady, Ready, Go
Safe cutting and peeling requires a stable surface. A cutting board is the proper resting place for the business at hand. Mom or Dad can halve a vegetable and place it securely on its flat surface before cutting and peeling.

Wash 'em and Stow 'em
Tossing sharp kitchen tools into a sink full of sudsy water where someone might reach is an accident waiting to happen. Clean and store kitchen tools right away.

Choucroute Garni: What Is It?

Familiar. It's meat and potatoes, French bistro-style satisfying. A satisfying entrée for stoking cold-weather appetites. *Portable.* A one-pot supper that knows how to travel to a potluck. *Trendy.* Even fancy chefs are serving up the likes of this casual dish.

Choucroute Garni

Prep: 25 minutes **Bake:** 1 hour

- 4 slices bacon, chopped
- 1 large onion, thinly sliced and separated into rings
- 4 cloves garlic, minced
- 1 Tbsp. cooking oil
- 6 pork loin rib chops, cut ¾ inch thick (about 2½ lb.)
- 1 2-lb. pkg. refrigerated sauerkraut
- 4 medium potatoes, peeled and cut into 1- to 2-inch pieces
- 12 oz. smoked sausage, cut in 1-inch pieces
- ¾ cup dry white wine or chicken broth
- ¾ cup chicken broth
- 1 tsp. juniper berries
- 2 bay leaves
  Fresh rosemary sprigs

1 Preheat oven to 375°. In an 8-quart Dutch oven cook bacon over medium heat until crisp. Add onion; cook 8 minutes, stirring often. Add garlic; cook 1 minute. Drain fat.

2 Meanwhile, in a heavy 12-inch skillet heat cooking oil over medium-high heat. Season chops with *salt* and *pepper*. Brown chops in hot oil for 3 minutes per side.

3 Drain sauerkraut and rinse well. Squeeze excess liquid; add to onion mixture. Stir in the potatoes,

smoked sausage, wine, broth, juniper berries, and bay leaves. Bring to boiling. Remove from heat. Place chops on top of sauerkraut.

4 Cover and bake 1 hour or until no pink remains in the chops and potatoes are tender. To serve, discard bay leaves. Arrange sauerkraut mixture on dinner plates and top with chops. Garnish with fresh rosemary sprigs. Makes 6 servings.

Nutrition Facts per serving: 565 cal., 30 g total fat (10 g sat. fat), 104 mg chol., 1,865 mg sodium, 24 g carbo., 6 g fiber, 42 g pro.
Daily Values: 1% vit. A, 53% vit. C, 5% calcium, 15% iron.

LOW FAT

Brown-Sugar-Glazed Ham

The glaze also works wonderfully when brushed on chicken as meat comes off the barbecue grill. (See the photograph on page 77.)

Prep: 10 minutes **Bake:** 1 hour 35 minutes
Stand: 15 minutes

- 1 5- to 6-lb. cooked bone-in ham (rump half or shank portion)
- 1½ cups packed brown sugar
- 1½ cups red wine vinegar
- 4 sprigs fresh mint (each sprig about 2 inches)
- ½ tsp. cracked black pepper
  Green onions and leeks (optional)

1 Preheat oven to 325°. If desired, score ham by making diagonal cuts 1 inch apart in fat in a diamond pattern. Place on a rack in a shallow roasting pan. Insert meat thermometer not touching bone. Bake until the thermometer registers 125°. For rump, allow 1¼ to 1½ hours; for shank, allow 1¾ to 2 hours.

- Brown-Sugar-Glazed Ham (see below)
- Cardamom-Orange Bunnies (see page 70)
- Easter Egg Potatoes (see page 68)
- Pick-of-the-Patch Salad (see page 71)
- Frozen Eggstravagance (see page 85)

2 Meanwhile, for glaze, in a medium saucepan stir together brown sugar, vinegar, and mint sprigs. Bring to boiling; reduce heat. Boil gently, uncovered, about 30 minutes or until reduced to 1 cup. Remove from heat. Remove and discard mint. Brush ham with some of the glaze.

3 Bake ham 20 to 30 minutes more or until thermometer registers 135°, brushing three more times with additional glaze. Sprinkle with the ½ teaspoon pepper. Let stand for 15 minutes before carving. (The meat temperature will rise 5° during standing to the safe temperature of 140°.)

4 If desired, serve meat on a platter layered with green tops of uncooked leeks and uncooked green onions. If desired, sprinkle ham with additional *pepper*. Bring any remaining glaze to boiling and serve with ham. Serves 16 to 20.

Nutrition Facts per serving: 232 cal., 8 g total fat (3 g sat. fat), 51 mg chol., 1,305 mg sodium, 22 g carbo., 0 g fiber, 20 g pro.
Daily Values: 33% vit. C, 2% calcium, 12% iron.

Top: Easter Egg Potatoes (page 68)
Above: Brown-Sugar-Glazed Ham (page 76)

Top left: Mexican-Style Egg Skillet (page 55)
Bottom left: Kalamata Artichokes (page 53)

Top right: White Bean and Cumin Chili (page 54)
Bottom right: Potato-Fennel Au Gratin (page 52)
Page 79: Simmering Seafood (page 61)

Above: Chicken à la Spring
(page 74)
Left: Cardamom-Orange
Bunnies (page 70)
Page 80: Pick-of-the-Patch
Salad (page 71)

Top left: Upside-Down Chip Cake (page 88)
Bottom left: Chocolate-Prune Accordion Bread (page 62)
Page 82: Red Flannel Corned Beef (page 57)

Top right: Fruit Chip Cookies (page 88)
Bottom right: Cappuccino Chip Muffins (page 66)

Left: Spring Fling Icebox Dessert (page 86)
Below: Frozen Eggstravagance (page 85)

Frozen Eggstravagance

Frozen sorbets come in all kinds of fruity flavors. Use your favorites! (See the photograph on page 84.)

Prep: 35 minutes **Stand/Freeze:** 2 hours
Final Freeze: 2¼ hours

- 3 cups vanilla ice cream
- 2 cups raspberry sorbet
- 1½ cups mango sorbet
- 1 cup lemon sorbet
- 1 recipe Raspberry Sauce or Beaujolais Sauce (see recipes, right)

1 Place vanilla ice cream in a large bowl; allow to stand in the refrigerator about 30 minutes. When ice cream is softened, quickly spread it about ½ inch thick over the bottom and sides of a 6½- to 8-cup ice cream mold or bowl (see Photo 1, right). Place bowl in freezer.

2 Place raspberry sorbet in a large bowl; allow to stand in the refrigerator about 30 minutes. When sorbet is softened, quickly spread it about ¾ inch thick over vanilla ice cream in mold (see Photo 2, right). Immediately return mold or bowl to freezer.

3 Repeat with mango and lemon sorbets, filling entire mold with sorbet. Return to freezer 2 hours or until frozen hard.

4 To unmold, dip mold or bowl in a larger bowl or sink filled with warm water for several seconds or until the edges appear to separate from the mold. Immediately invert mold onto serving platter. Carefully remove mold. Return ice cream to freezer for 15 minutes.

5 To serve, cut into slices with a knife dipped in hot water. Serve with the Raspberry Sauce or the Beaujolais Sauce. Makes 8 servings.

Nutrition Facts per serving with 2½ tablespoons Raspberry Sauce: 358 cal., 8 g total fat (5 g sat. fat), 27 mg chol., 78 mg sodium, 73 g carbo., 1 g fiber, 3 g pro.
Daily Values: 7% vit. A, 11% vit. C, 10% calcium, 3% iron.

1. Spread ice cream in mold using the back of a spoon (above). The first layer may be slightly slippery. If that occurs, place in freezer for a minute or two and spread again.

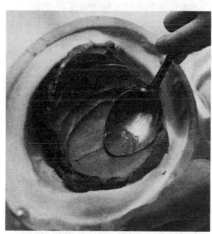

2. Build up remaining ice cream and sorbets in even layers, allowing plenty of time for ice cream to harden (above).

30 MINUTE, NO FAT
Raspberry Sauce
Start to finish: 2 to 3 minutes

- 1 cup raspberry pourable fruit
- ¼ cup fresh raspberries

1 In a small bowl stir together pourable fruit and fresh raspberries. Serve with Frozen Eggstravagance (see recipe, left). Makes 1¼ cups sauce.

Nutrition Facts per tablespoon: 42 cal., 0 g total fat, 0 mg chol., 0 mg sodium, 11 g carbo., 0 g fiber, 0 g pro.
Daily Values: 1% vit. C.

NO FAT
Beaujolais Sauce

This slightly spiced wine sauce is a sweet sensation when drizzled over poached fruit such as pears.

Prep: 20 minutes **Chill:** 1 hour

- 2 cups Beaujolais wine
- ¾ cup sugar
- 2 tsp. lemon juice
- ⅛ tsp. ground cinnamon

1 In a large saucepan stir together wine and sugar. Bring mixture to boiling over medium-high heat; reduce heat. Continue boiling gently, uncovered, about 15 minutes or until mixture is reduced to about 1 cup, stirring occasionally. Stir in lemon juice and cinnamon; cook and stir for 2 minutes more. Remove from heat; cover and chill. Serve with Frozen Eggstravagance (see recipe, left). Makes 1 cup.

Nutrition Facts per tablespoon: 55 cal., 0 g total fat (0 g sat. fat), 0 mg chol., 2 mg sodium, 9 g carbo., 0 g fiber, 0 g pro.
Daily Values: 1% iron.

Spring Fling Icebox Dessert

Here's a wild and wiggly way to end holiday dinners as well as weeknight meals. To prevent the top of the dessert from looking monotonous, we decorated it with varying sizes of strawberries and mint leaves. (See the photograph on page 84.)

Prep: 1½ hours **Chill:** 8 hours

1½   cups coarsely crushed crisp
        chocolate chip cookies
  3   Tbsp. butter, melted
  1   8-oz. pkg. or two 4-serving-size
        pkg. sparkling wild
        berry-flavored gelatin
1⅓   cups boiling water
  2   cups chilled white grape juice or
        lemonade
  1   8-oz. pkg. cream cheese, softened
  ½   cup whipping cream
        Fresh strawberries with leaves
        (optional)
        Mint sprigs (optional)

1 In a medium bowl stir together crushed cookies and butter. Line an 8×8×2-inch baking pan with heavy foil. Press crumbs into bottom of foil-lined pan; set aside.

2 In a large bowl combine gelatin and boiling water; stir until gelatin dissolves. Stir in chilled grape juice or lemonade. Chill until mixture is partially set (the consistency of unbeaten egg whites).

3 Meanwhile, in a large mixing bowl beat cream cheese with an electric mixer on medium speed until fluffy. With mixer running on low speed, gradually beat in partially set gelatin.

4 In a chilled small mixing bowl beat whipping cream until soft peaks form. Fold the whipped cream into gelatin mixture. Chill again until mixture mounds when spooned.

5 Turn the gelatin mixture into the crumb-lined pan. Cover and chill for 8 to 24 hours or until firm.

6 Using foil, carefully lift dessert from pan. To serve, cut dessert into squares. If desired, top with strawberries and mint sprigs. Makes 9 servings.

Nutrition Facts per serving: 329 cal., 20 g total fat (12 g sat. fat), 58 mg chol., 205 mg sodium, 35 g carbo., 1 g fiber, 5 g pro.
Daily Values: 20% vit. A, 5% vit. C, 3% calcium, 4% iron.

Rhubarb Hand Tarts

Flavor magic happens when rhubarb and apples are combined. The sweetness of the apples mellows the rhubarb, while the tartness of the rhubarb helps perk up the apple flavor.

Prep: 50 minutes **Bake:** 30 minutes
Cool: 30 minutes

  1   cup granulated sugar
  2   Tbsp. quick-cooking tapioca
  1   tsp. grated fresh ginger
        Dash ground nutmeg
  3   cups ½-inch slices fresh rhubarb
        or frozen sliced rhubarb
  1   cup sliced, peeled tart apples
  1   recipe Pastry for Double-Crust
        Pie (see page 87)
        Milk
        Coarse sugar

1 Line a large baking sheet with foil; grease foil and set aside.

2 In a large saucepan stir together granulated sugar, tapioca, fresh ginger, and nutmeg. Stir in rhubarb and apples until coated; let stand about 15 minutes or until a syrup begins to form, stirring occasionally. Cover and cook over medium heat about 15 minutes or just until fruit is softened, stirring occasionally. Remove from heat. Let cool for 30 minutes.

3 Meanwhile, preheat oven to 375°. Prepare Pastry for Double-Crust Pie; divide in half. On a lightly floured surface roll out each portion of pastry to a 12-inch square. Cut each portion into four 6-inch squares.

4 Spoon about ¼ cup of the cooked rhubarb mixture onto half of one pastry square, leaving a 1-inch border around edge of pastry. Brush edges of square with water. Fold pastry over filling, forming a rectangle. Press edges gently to seal. Brush edges lightly with water again. Fold edges up and over about ¼ inch. Press edges with tines of a fork to seal again.

5 Place tart on prepared baking sheet. Repeat with remaining squares of pastry and rhubarb filling. Prick tops 2 or 3 times with the tines of a fork to let steam escape. Gently pat down top to get rid of excess air around filling. Brush tops with milk and sprinkle with coarse sugar.

6 Bake for 30 to 35 minutes or until golden brown. Remove tarts from baking sheet and cool on a wire rack about 30 minutes. Serve warm. Makes 8 tarts.

Pastry for Double-Crust Pie

In a large mixing bowl combine 2 cups all-purpose flour and ½ teaspoon salt. Using a pastry blender, cut in ½ cup shortening until pieces are pea-size. Sprinkle 1 tablespoon of water over part of the mixture; gently toss with a fork. Push the moistened mixture to side of bowl. Repeat, using 1 tablespoon of water at a time, until all the dough is moistened (about 7 to 9 tablespoons of water total).

Nutrition Facts per tart: 344 cal., 13 g total fat (3 g sat. fat), 0 mg chol., 149 mg sodium, 54 g carbo., 2 g fiber, 3 g pro.
Daily Values: 1% vit. A, 7% vit. C, 5% calcium, 8% iron.

Holiday Tortes

If you plan to serve these desserts on Passover, check with your rabbi to make sure the use of matzoh meal is part of your temple's tradition. Because there is no leavening, the tops of the cakes stay fairly flat.

Prep: 45 minutes **Bake:** 15 minutes

4	**eggs**
	Nonstick cooking spray
2	**Tbsp. sugar**
⅛	**tsp. salt**
⅓	**cup matzoh meal**
⅓	**cup ground walnuts**
½	**tsp. finely shredded orange peel**
2	**Tbsp. orange juice**
2	**Tbsp. sugar**
¼	**cup honey**
¼	**tsp. finely shredded orange peel**
¼	**cup sliced toasted almonds**
	Shredded orange peel (optional)

1 Separate eggs; let stand, covered, at room temperature for 30 minutes. Preheat oven to 325°.

2 Coat the cups of six 3¼-inch muffin pans or twelve 2½-inch muffin pans with nonstick cooking spray. Set prepared pans aside.

3 In a mixing bowl beat egg yolks, 2 tablespoons sugar, and the salt with an electric mixer on medium to high speed about 4 minutes until thick and lemon-colored. Stir in the matzoh meal, walnuts, the ½ teaspoon orange peel, and the orange juice. Set aside. Wash beaters thoroughly.

4 In a large mixing bowl beat egg whites with an electric mixer on medium speed about 1 minute or until soft peaks form (tips curl). Increase the speed to high and beat in 2 tablespoons sugar, beating until stiff, glossy peaks form (tips stand straight).

5 Gently fold the egg yolk mixture into egg whites. Divide batter evenly among prepared pans, filling smaller cups to the top. Bake about 15 minutes for small pans or 30 minutes for large pans or until golden and a wooden toothpick inserted near center comes out clean. Cool in pans on a wire rack for 5 minutes. Loosen sides. Remove from pans. Place, top sides up, on the wire rack or serving platter.

Before tying on a decorative ribbon, secure the paper collars with a paper clip, then remove clip before serving.

CLEVER COOK

Bridal Shower Recipe Book

Add a blank recipe card to bridal shower invitations for guests to fill out with their favorite recipe. The new couple gets to start out with a personal cookbook of known hits.

Barbara Franzetti
Manasquan, New Jersey

6 To make paper collars: If making small cakes cut 12 pieces of heavyweight stiff pink paper 8½×2 inches. Fold in half lengthwise and cut half-inch deep snips along the folded edge every quarter inch (see photo, below left). Form into a circle around cake and secure with a paper clip or transparent tape. Tie with ½-inch ribbon and remove paper clip. Repeat with remaining tortes. If baking large cakes, cut six 11×2½-inch pieces of heavyweight stiff pink paper.

7 In a small bowl combine honey and ¼ teaspoon orange peel. Drizzle over tops of cakes. Sprinkle with almonds and, if desired, additional shredded orange peel. Serve warm. Makes 6 large or 12 small cakes.

Nutrition Facts per large cake: 231 cal., 10 g total fat (2 g sat. fat), 142 mg chol., 89 mg sodium, 29 g carbo., 1 g fiber, 7 g pro.
Daily Values: 7% vit. A, 5% vit. C, 3% calcium, 7% iron.

Drop cookies are so easy to make, the time they take out of your day is a drop in the bucket. These tips will make homemade cookies a staple at your house:

● If a recipe calls for greased cookie sheets, use only a very light coating or your cookies may spread too far when baking. If a recipe specifies ungreased cookie sheets, use either regular or nonstick sheets—and don't grease them.

● If your electric mixer begins to strain while mixing heavy cookie dough, stir in the last bit of flour with a wooden spoon.

● Drop the dough using flatware spoons—not measuring spoons—to get the right number of cookies from each batch. Make sure the mounds are rounded and about the same size so they'll bake evenly.

● Let cookie sheets cool between batches so the dough doesn't spread too much.

● Bake on only one oven rack at a time for even browning.

● Drop cookies are done when the dough looks set and the edges and bottoms of the baked cookies are lightly brown.

PRIZE WINNER

Upside-Down Chip Cake

Lisa J. Hill
Sulphur, Louisiana
$400—Chocolate Chip Creations
(See the photograph on page 83.)

Prep: 20 minutes **Bake:** 40 minutes
Stand: 30 minutes

  3 Tbsp. butter
  ½ cup packed brown sugar
  4 tsp. water
  ½ cup coconut
  ½ cup coarsely chopped pecans
  1 cup all-purpose flour
  ⅔ cup granulated sugar
  ½ cup unsweetened cocoa powder
  ¼ cup packed brown sugar
  2 tsp. baking powder
  ½ cup milk
  ¼ cup butter, softened
  2 eggs
  1 tsp. vanilla
  ¾ cup miniature semisweet
      chocolate pieces

1 Preheat oven to 350°. Melt the 3 tablespoons butter in a 9×1½-inch round baking pan. Stir in the ½ cup brown sugar and the water. Sprinkle coconut and pecans in the pan. Set pan aside.

2 In a medium mixing bowl stir together flour, granulated sugar, cocoa powder, the ¼ cup brown sugar, and the baking powder. Add milk, the ¼ cup butter, the eggs, and vanilla. Beat with an electric mixer on low speed until combined. Beat on medium speed for 1 minute. By hand, stir in ½ cup of the chocolate pieces. Spread batter into the prepared pan.

3 Bake for 40 to 45 minutes or until cake feels firm in center when lightly touched. Cool on a wire rack for 5 minutes. Loosen sides; invert onto a plate. Immediately sprinkle remaining miniature chocolate pieces over the topping. Let stand about 30 minutes before slicing. Serve warm. Makes 8 servings.

Nutrition Facts per serving: 456 cal., 24 g total fat (11 g sat. fat), 83 mg chol., 239 mg sodium, 52 g carbo., 3 g fiber, 6 g pro.
Daily Values: 13% vit. A, 16% calcium, 11% iron.

PRIZE WINNER

Fruit Chip Cookies

Lisa Goodfellow
Iowa City, Iowa
$200—Chocolate Chip Creations
(See the photograph on page 83.)

Prep: 25 minutes **Bake:** 11 minutes per batch

  1 cup butter, softened
  ¾ cup packed brown sugar
  ½ cup granulated sugar
  1 tsp. baking soda
  2 eggs
  1 tsp. vanilla
  1⅔ cups all-purpose flour
  2 cups granola cereal
  1 6-oz. pkg. mixed dried fruit bits
  1 cup chopped hazelnuts (filberts)
      or walnuts
  1 cup white baking pieces

1 Preheat oven to 325°. In a large mixing bowl beat butter with electric mixer on medium speed for 30 seconds. Add brown sugar, granulated sugar, and baking soda; beat until combined. Beat in eggs and vanilla until combined. On low speed beat in as much of the flour as you can with the mixer. By hand, stir in remaining flour and granola. Stir in fruit bits, nuts, and baking pieces.

2 Drop dough by slightly rounded tablespoonfuls 2 inches apart on an ungreased baking sheet. Flatten slightly. Bake 11 to 13 minutes or until edges are browned. Cool on baking sheet for 1 minute. Transfer to wire racks. Cool completely. Makes about 48 cookies.

Nutrition Facts per cookie: 137 cal., 7 g total fat (4 g sat. fat), 21 mg chol., 86 mg sodium, 17 g carbo., 1 g fiber, 2 g pro.
Daily Values: 6% vit. A, 1% vit. C, 2% calcium, 3% iron.

may

IN THIS CHAPTER

30-minute recipes indicated in COLOR.
Low-fat and no-fat recipes indicated
with a ♥.
Photographs indicated in italics.
*Bonus recipe

Pancakes for Mom

Hey Mom, close your eyes and imagine a yummy Mother's Day breakfast of hot-from-the-griddle pancakes. Complete the scene with raspberries, fresh-squeezed orange juice, and a cup of your favorite tea—all served up by a good-looking chef and his cute assistant.

Breakfast in a dream cafe? Actually, you're at home and that's Dad and your young one at the stove. So go ahead and bask in the experience of your family preparing a delicious—and slightly decadent—breakfast just for you. You deserve it.

Even better, they deserve the unexpected pleasures of cooking together, an experience kids and dads don't often share. Kids learn that dad has a place in the kitchen. He gets to flaunt his cooking prowess and see the kitchen through his child's eyes. All this in a scheme to feed the one they care for most.

Best of all, pancakes are so easy to prepare. The most advanced skill needed to make these pancakes is the ability to use a whisk. Cleanup is minimal. Who knows? If you lavish your team with praise, you might get a repeat performance before next Mother's Day.

Teamwork Counts

Listen up, Dad. Whether you have one child or four, these guidelines will help you keep the troops busy.

● "I-can-do-it-by-myself" independence and simple scooping, spooning, and stirring—that's what you can expect from 3- to 5-year-olds.

● Six- to 8-year-olds can easily measure ingredients, such as flour and milk. You'll have to help them with the sour cream, though. Give them a hand when cracking eggs, too.

● With a supportive captain, 9- to 10-year-olds can make the batter entirely by themselves. Leave heating the griddle to older kids.

Chocolate Chip Pancakes with Raspberry Sauce

Kids will love this chocolate-raspberry combination, and for more pancake options, see the tip on page 91.

Prep: 25 minutes
Cook: 3 to 4 minutes per batch

1	recipe Raspberry Sauce (see page 91)
1½	cups all-purpose flour
3	Tbsp. sugar
1	tsp. baking powder
½	tsp. baking soda
¼	tsp. salt
2	eggs
1	8-oz. carton dairy sour cream
1	cup milk
¼	cup margarine or butter, melted
½	cup miniature or regular semisweet chocolate pieces
1	tsp. cooking oil
	Pressurized whipped cream
	Fresh raspberries
	Miniature or regular semisweet chocolate pieces (optional)

1 Prepare the Raspberry Sauce. Set sauce aside.

2 In a large mixing bowl combine the flour, sugar, baking powder, baking soda, and salt. Stir together using a whisk.

3 In a medium bowl whisk eggs until the whites and the yolks are combined. Add sour cream. Whisk until smooth. Stir in milk and melted margarine or butter. Add egg mixture to dry ingredients. Whisk or stir gently just until dry ingredients are wet. (Do not try to remove all the small lumps. The batter should be a little lumpy, not smooth.) Gently fold in the ½ cup chocolate pieces. Set batter aside.

4 Heat griddle or large heavy skillet over medium heat for 3 to 4 minutes or until a few drops of water sizzle when carefully sprinkled on griddle. Pour the teaspoon of cooking oil onto griddle and spread around with a heat-safe pastry brush. Stir batter again to distribute chocolate pieces.

5 For larger pancakes, ladle about ⅓ cup batter per pancake onto hot griddle. For smaller pancakes, ladle a slightly rounded tablespoon of batter per pancake onto hot griddle. Cook for 1 to 2 minutes on the first side or until the pancakes have bubbly surfaces and the edges look slightly dry. Using a wide pancake turner, carefully flip the pancakes. Cook 1 to 1½ minutes more on the second side or until golden brown. Remove from the griddle with pancake turner. (Add additional oil to griddle as necessary to keep later batches of pancakes from sticking.) Repeat with the remaining batter.

6 Serve pancakes immediately. Drizzle them with Raspberry Sauce. Top with whipped cream, fresh raspberries, and, if desired, additional chocolate pieces. Makes about 12 (4-inch) pancakes or 48 (2-inch) pancakes.

Nutrition Facts per 4-inch pancake: 230 cal., 12 g total fat (7 g sat. fat), 56 mg chol., 207 mg sodium, 25 g carbo., 3 g fiber, 4 g pro.
Daily Values: 11% vit. A, 20% vit. C, 8% calcium, 5% iron.

Raspberry Sauce

This bright berry sauce takes the place of traditional pancake syrup. If you are lucky enough to have any sauce left over, try it served over ice cream or frozen yogurt.

Start to finish: 5 minutes

- 1 12-oz. pkg. frozen lightly sweetened red raspberries, thawed
- 3 Tbsp. sugar
- 3 Tbsp. lemon juice
- ¼ cup orange juice

1 In a food processor bowl or blender container combine thawed raspberries, sugar, lemon juice, and orange juice. Cover and process or blend until smooth. Using a rubber spatula press sauce through a sieve; discard seeds. Stir before serving. Makes 1½ cups.

LOW FAT

Fruit-Filled Oven Pancake

Doubly delicious. You'll find spiced apples and raspberries hidden in the center of this light and fluffy breakfast treat.

Prep: 15 minutes **Bake:** 20 minutes

- 1 Tbsp. margarine or butter
- 2 medium cooking apples, such as Jonathan or Granny Smith, peeled, cored, and thinly sliced
- 1 Tbsp. brown sugar
- ½ tsp. ground cinnamon
- ½ cup fresh raspberries, blueberries, or other fresh berries
- ⅓ cup all-purpose flour
- ½ tsp. baking powder
- ⅛ tsp. salt
- 4 egg whites
- ⅓ cup granulated sugar
- 4 egg yolks
- ⅓ cup milk
  Powdered sugar
  Fresh raspberries or other fresh fruit (optional)
  Maple or fruit-flavored syrup (optional)

1 Preheat oven to 400°. In a large skillet melt margarine or butter. Add the apple slices, brown sugar, and cinnamon. Cook, covered, over medium heat about 6 minutes or until the apples are just tender, stirring occasionally. Gently stir in the ½ cup raspberries. Set aside.

2 In a small mixing bowl stir together the flour, baking powder, and salt; set aside. In a medium mixing bowl beat the egg whites with an electric mixer on medium to high speed until soft peaks form (tips curl). Gradually beat in the granulated sugar, 1 tablespoon at a time, until stiff peaks form (tips stand straight). In a large mixing bowl beat the egg yolks until combined. Alternately stir flour mixture and milk into beaten egg yolks. Gently fold in the egg whites, leaving a few fluffs of egg white in the batter.

3 Preheat a greased, 10-inch, ovenproof skillet by placing it in the hot oven for 10 minutes. Pour half the batter into the preheated skillet. Spoon the cooked fruit over the first layer of batter; carefully pour remaining batter over fruit.

TEST KITCHEN TIP

Batter Up!

Can't picture your crew making pancakes from scratch? That's fine; maybe a pancake mix is a better way to launch their cooking careers. The point is that they should have fun. To help matters along, here are additional pancake possibilities:

● **Go candy crazy.** Instead of chocolate chips, add chunks of your favorite candies. Candy-coated milk chocolates, white chocolate chunks, and other types of candy work well.

● **Shape 'em when you make 'em.** Simply spoon batter into a self-sealing plastic bag. Snip off one corner and gently squeeze batter onto hot griddle in any shape you like. Make bunnies with tall ears or butterflies with big wings.

● **Serve breakfast in bed.** Line a tray with a pretty napkin and make a card. Include a favorite magazine and a bouquet.

4 Bake for 20 to 25 minutes or until a knife inserted near the center comes out clean. Sprinkle with powdered sugar and, if desired, fresh raspberries or other fruit. Cut into 6 wedges to serve. If desired, serve with maple or fruit-flavored syrup. Makes 6 servings.

Nutrition Facts per serving: 171 cal., 6 g total fat (2 g sat. fat), 143 mg chol., 144 mg sodium, 25 g carbo., 2 g fiber, 6 g pro.
Daily Values: 24% vit. A, 4% vit. C, 5% calcium, 6% iron.

A cup of java awakens you with a jolt; a strip of bacon starts you with a sizzle. But a warm, crumbly scone for breakfast gently nudges you into the beginning of your day.

No time for breakfast? The quintessentially British scone is also a welcome break in the middle of the day. Falling somewhere between muffins and biscuits in texture, scones are heavenly when slathered with butter and jam. They're usually made into rounds or wedges, but the recipe below treats them to a more casual drop-style preparation.

30 MINUTE, LOW FAT

Date-Maple Drop Scones

For a special treat, beat heavy whipping cream past the stiff peak stage—but not quite to the butter stage—and spread on a scone fresh from the oven.

Prep: 10 minutes **Bake:** 12 minutes

2	cups all-purpose flour
1	Tbsp. baking powder
½	tsp. crushed or ground cardamom
⅓	cup butter or margarine
1	egg, beaten
⅓	cup maple syrup or maple-flavored syrup
⅓	cup half-and-half or light cream
½	cup snipped, pitted dates

1 Preheat oven to 400°. Grease a baking sheet; set aside. In a large mixing bowl combine flour, baking powder, and cardamom. Using a pastry blender, cut in butter or margarine until mixture resembles coarse crumbs.

2 In a small bowl combine egg, maple syrup, and half-and-half or light cream. Stir in dates. Add the liquid mixture all at once to the dry ingredients. Stir just until the mixture clings together. Drop scone batter from a rounded tablespoon onto the prepared baking sheet.

3 Bake for 12 to 15 minutes or until golden. Serve warm. Makes 16 scones.

Nutrition Facts per scone: 129 cal., 5 g total fat (3 g sat. fat), 25 mg chol., 114 mg sodium, 20 g carbo., 1 g fiber, 2 g pro.
Daily Values: 4% vit. A, 6% calcium, 6% iron.

Make-Ahead Directions:

Prepare scones as directed. Tightly wrap individual scones in plastic wrap; seal in an airtight container. Store in freezer for up to 2 months. To reheat, unwrap scones and rewrap in foil. Heat in a 300° oven for 15 to 18 minutes or until heated through. Or, rewrap scones in a paper towel and microwave on 100% power (high) for 30 seconds per scone or until heated through.

LOW FAT

Egg Cakes with Sweet-and-Sour Plum Sauce

Make these brunch-size egg cakes Mexican-style by omitting the Sweet-and-Sour Plum Sauce. Instead, sprinkle with shredded cheddar cheese and serve with salsa and sour cream.

Prep: 20 minutes **Bake:** 12 minutes

	Nonstick cooking spray
¾	cup cooked rice
⅔	cup chopped cooked ham
⅓	cup thinly sliced green onions
1	tsp. cooking oil
8	eggs, slightly beaten
½	tsp. salt
1	recipe Sweet-and-Sour Plum Sauce (see below)

1 Preheat oven to 375°. Lightly coat twelve 2½-inch muffin cups with nonstick cooking spray. Press about 1 tablespoon cooked rice into bottom of each muffin cup; set aside.

2 In a medium nonstick skillet cook ham and green onions in hot oil until onion is tender but not brown; remove from heat. Spoon ham and onion mixture evenly over rice in muffin cups. In a medium mixing bowl combine eggs and salt. Divide egg mixture among muffin cups.

3 Bake for 12 to 15 minutes or until egg mixture is slightly puffed and golden brown. Allow to stand for 2 minutes. Run a knife around edge of muffin cups to loosen; remove from cups. Drizzle with Sweet-and-Sour Plum Sauce. Makes 6 servings.

Sweet-and-Sour Plum Sauce:

In a small saucepan combine ¼ cup plum jam or preserves, ¼ cup chicken broth, 2 tablespoons red wine vinegar, 2 teaspoons soy sauce, and 1 teaspoon cornstarch. Cook and stir until thickened and bubbly. Cook and stir for 2 minutes more. Makes about ½ cup.

Nutrition Facts per serving: 202 cal., 9 g total fat (3 g sat. fat), 293 mg chol., 637 mg sodium, 16 g carbo., 0 g fiber, 12 g pro.
Daily Values: 13% vit. A, 4% vit. C, 4% calcium, 9% iron.

PRIZE WINNER

Ham and Egg Pie

Denise M. Rowtham
East Hartford, Connecticut
$400—Eggs-traordinary Ideas Category

Prep: 20 minutes **Bake:** 50 minutes
Stand: 10 minutes

    2   cups all-purpose flour
    1   Tbsp. baking powder
    ½   tsp. salt
    ½   cup milk
    ⅓   cup cooking oil
    6   eggs, slightly beaten
    1   cup cream-style cottage cheese
    ½   cup shredded sharp cheddar
        cheese (2 oz.)
    ½   cup shredded mozzarella cheese
        (2 oz.)
    2   oz. cooked ham, chopped
    2   oz. salami, chopped
    2   Tbsp. sliced green onion
    2   Tbsp. snipped fresh Italian parsley

1 Preheat oven to 350°. In a medium bowl stir together flour, baking powder, and salt. Make a well in center of dry ingredients. In a small bowl combine milk and cooking oil. Add liquid ingredients all at once to dry mixture; stir until moistened.

2 Turn dough out onto a lightly floured surface. Quickly knead dough by gently folding and pressing dough 10 to 12 strokes or until nearly smooth. On a lightly floured surface roll dough to a 12-inch circle. Line a 9-inch pie plate with dough. Fold under the extra pastry and crimp edge as desired.

3 For filling, in a medium bowl stir together eggs, cottage cheese, cheddar cheese, mozzarella cheese, ham, salami, green onion, and parsley. Pour into unbaked crust.

SIMPLE BREAKFAST

■ **Ham and Egg Pie (see left)**

■ **Cantaloupe wedges and small bunches of green grapes**

■ **Orange or grapefruit juice and/or coffee**

---

4 Bake for 50 to 55 minutes or until a knife inserted near the center comes out clean. If necessary, cover edge of crust with foil during baking to prevent overbrowning. Let stand 10 minutes before serving. Makes 8 servings.

Nutrition Facts per serving: 369 cal., 22 g total fat (7 g sat. fat), 185 mg chol., 763 mg sodium, 25 g carbo., 1 g fiber, 18 g pro.
Daily Values: 13% vit. A, 3% vit. C, 25% calcium, 12% iron.

Mushroom, Blue Cheese, and Walnut Scramble

The occasion doesn't need to be breakfast when serving this creamy scrambled-egg dish. It's rich and wonderful enough to stand up to the best of lunches or dinners.

Prep: 20 minutes **Cook:** 15 minutes

    6   eggs, beaten
    ¼   cup milk
    ¼   tsp. salt
    ⅛   tsp. pepper
    2   Tbsp. margarine or butter
    1   cup sliced fresh mushrooms
    4   tsp. all-purpose flour
    ½   tsp. dry mustard
    ¼   tsp. salt
    ⅛   tsp. pepper
    ¾   cup milk
    1   tsp. Worcestershire sauce
    ⅓   cup crumbled blue cheese or
        shredded Swiss cheese
        (about 1½ oz.)
        Toast points or toasted English
        muffin halves
    2   Tbsp. finely chopped toasted
        walnuts

1 In a medium bowl combine eggs, ¼ cup milk, ¼ teaspoon salt, and ⅛ teaspoon pepper. Melt 1 tablespoon of the margarine in a large skillet. Add egg mixture. Cook without stirring until mixture begins to set. Using a large spoon lift and fold partially cooked eggs so uncooked portion flows underneath. Continue cooking just until set. Remove eggs from skillet.

2 Add the remaining margarine to the skillet; add mushrooms. Cook and stir until tender. Stir in flour, mustard, ¼ teaspoon salt, and ⅛ teaspoon pepper. Stir in the ¾ cup milk and the Worcestershire all at once. Cook and stir until thickened and bubbly. Cook and stir for 1 minute more. Set aside 1 tablespoon of the blue cheese. Add remaining blue cheese and the scrambled eggs to the sauce; heat through.

3 To serve, spoon eggs on top of toast points or toasted English muffin halves. Sprinkle reserved blue cheese and walnuts on top of each serving. Makes 4 servings.

Nutrition Facts per serving: 341 cal., 22 g total fat (9 g sat. fat), 348 mg chol., 777 mg sodium, 20 g carbo., 1 g fiber, 17 g pro.
Daily Values: 26% vit. A, 2% vit. C, 20% calcium, 13% iron.

Great egg dishes depend on eggs that are in top condition. Here are some egg-handling pointers to remember:

● Select clean, fresh eggs from refrigerated display cases. Don't use dirty, cracked, or leaking eggs. They may have become contaminated with harmful bacteria.

● When you come home from the grocery store, promptly refrigerate the eggs with the large ends up. Store them in their cartons because eggs easily absorb refrigerator odors. Fresh eggs can be refrigerated for up to 5 weeks after the packing date (a number stamped on the carton from 1 to 365, with 1 representing January 1 and 365 representing December 31).

● To store raw egg whites, refrigerate them in a tightly covered container for up to 4 days. Cover raw yolks with water and refrigerate them, tightly covered, for up to 2 days. Refrigerate hard-cooked eggs in their shells for up to 7 days.

● When cracking eggs, avoid getting shells in the raw eggs. When separating eggs, don't pass the yolk from shell half to shell half. Instead, use an egg separator, so if bacteria are present on the shell, they won't contaminate the yolk or the white.

● Be sure to wash your hands, utensils, and countertop before and after working with eggs.

● Serve hot egg dishes as soon as they're cooked. Refrigerate cold egg dishes immediately. Chill leftovers promptly and reheat thoroughly before serving.

● Eating uncooked or slightly cooked eggs may be harmful because of possible bacterial contamination. Most susceptible are the elderly, infants, pregnant women, and those who are already ill. Check with your doctor to see if you are at risk. If you are, avoid eating foods that contain raw or partially cooked eggs. Healthy people should use discretion when eating raw eggs.

For more information on handling eggs safely, call the U.S. Department of Agriculture Meat and Poultry Hotline at 800/535-4555.

Egg and Potato Skillet

Prep: 20 minutes **Cook:** 27 minutes
Stand: 2 minutes

- 3 Tbsp. margarine or butter
- 1 24-oz. pkg. frozen loose-pack diced hash brown potatoes with onions and peppers
- 2 Tbsp. finely chopped, seeded jalapeño pepper (optional)*
- 6 eggs
- 1 cup shredded cheddar cheese or shredded Mexican cheese blend (4 oz.)
- ½ cup milk
- ¾ tsp. salt
- ¾ tsp. dried oregano, crushed
- ½ tsp. chili powder
- 1 6-oz. carton frozen avocado dip, thawed
- 1 large tomato, chopped

1 Melt margarine or butter in a large skillet over medium heat. Add potatoes; cover and cook 10 minutes, stirring occasionally. Uncover; add jalapeño pepper, if using. Cook, uncovered, about 10 minutes more or until potatoes are light brown, turning occasionally with a spatula.

2 Meanwhile combine eggs, cheese, milk, salt, oregano, chili powder, and ¼ teaspoon *black pepper*; pour over mixture in skillet. Cook, uncovered, over medium heat for 4 minutes. As eggs set, run a spatula around the edge of the skillet, lifting eggs so uncooked portion flows underneath. Cover and cook for 3 to 4 minutes more or until center is set. Let stand 2 minutes.

3 To serve, cut into wedges. Top each wedge with avocado dip and tomato. Makes 6 servings.

*Note: Hot chili peppers contain oils that can burn eyes, lips, and sensitive skin. Wear plastic gloves while preparing them and be sure to wash your hands thoroughly afterward.

Nutrition Facts per serving: 357 cal., 24 g total fat (7 g sat. fat), 234 mg chol., 670 mg sodium, 23 g carbo., 3 g fiber, 15 g pro.
Daily Values: 27% vit. A, 20% vit. C, 20% calcium, 11% iron.

PRIZE WINNER, 30 MINUTE

Grilled Egg Sandwich

Ruth Leaf
Bloomington, Minnesota
$200—Eggs-traordinary Ideas Category

Start to finish: 20 minutes

- 2 Tbsp. mayonnaise or salad dressing
- 1 Tbsp. Dijon-style mustard or brown mustard
- 4 slices English muffin bread or firm white bread
- 2 Tbsp. margarine or butter
- 4 eggs, divided
- 4 to 6 spinach leaves
- 1 small tomato, halved and sliced
- 2 slices Swiss cheese or American cheese
- 2 Tbsp. milk

1 In a small bowl stir together mayonnaise and mustard. Spread mixture on one side of each slice of bread. Set aside.

2 In a large skillet melt 1 tablespoon of the margarine or butter over medium heat; break 2 eggs into a measuring cup and slide into the skillet. Stir each egg gently with a fork to break up yolk. Cook eggs for 3 to 4 minutes or to desired doneness, turning once.

3 Place each egg on the spread side of two bread slices. Layer 2 to 3 spinach leaves, half of the tomato slices, and 1 slice of cheese on each egg. Top with remaining bread slices, spread-side down.

4 In a shallow dish beat together the remaining eggs and the milk. Carefully dip sandwiches into egg mixture, coating both sides. Melt remaining margarine in same skillet over medium heat. Cook sandwiches about 4 minutes or until golden brown, turning once. To serve, cut in half. Makes 2 sandwiches.

Nutrition Facts per sandwich: 748 cal., 45 g total fat (19 g sat. fat), 490 mg chol., 1,021 mg sodium, 56 g carbo., 3 g fiber, 30 g pro.
Daily Values: 45% vit. A, 17% vit. C, 48% calcium, 34% iron.

LOW FAT

Dilled Celery Root Spread

Look for small, firm celery root (celeriac). Celery root may be kept in the refrigerator, wrapped in plastic wrap, for up to 1 week. (See the photograph on page 118.)

Prep: 15 minutes **Chill:** 1 hour

  1 **small celery root (about 1 lb.)**
  ¼ **cup light mayonnaise dressing**
  2 **Tbsp. white vinegar**
  2 **tsp. snipped fresh dillweed**

Celery grown for its root has pungent leaves that are often removed before sale. If your celery root has leaves, save them for use in soups and stews.

  ½ **tsp. sugar**
  ¼ **tsp. coarsely ground white pepper (optional)**
Assorted crackers

1 Scrub celery root under cold running water. Using a peeler or paring knife, peel root. Shred into a bowl. Stir in mayonnaise dressing, vinegar, 2 teaspoons snipped dillweed (reserve additional for garnish), sugar, ¼ teaspoon *salt*, and, if desired, ¼ teaspoon white pepper. Cover and chill 1 to 24 hours.

2 Stir before serving. Transfer to a chilled serving bowl or individual ramekins. Top with additional dill. Serve with crackers. Makes 1½ cups.

Nutrition Facts per tablespoon: 12 cal., 1 g total fat (0 g sat. fat), 1 mg chol., 47 mg sodium, 1 g carbo., 0 g fiber, 0 g pro.
Daily Values: 1% vit. C.

30 MINUTE, LOW FAT

Sugar Pea and Jerusalem Artichoke Sauté

See the photograph on page 121.

Prep: 15 minutes **Cook:** 3 minutes

 12 **oz. fresh sugar snap pea pods (with pea shoots, optional)**
  8 **oz. Jerusalem artichokes or one 8-oz. can sliced water chestnuts, drained**
  2 **tsp. margarine or butter**

1 Remove and discard strings from pea pods. Rinse pods under cold running water. Drain. Set aside.

2 Remove peel from Jerusalem artichokes. Cut into ¼-inch pieces. In a large skillet heat the margarine or butter over medium-high heat. Cook and stir Jerusalem artichokes, uncovered, for 2 minutes. Add ⅛ teaspoon *salt* and ⅛ teaspoon *pepper*. Stir in pea pods.

3 Cook mixture, covered, for 1 to 1½ minutes or until the pea pods are just heated through but still crunchy. Transfer to a serving bowl or individual bowls. Top with pea shoots, if desired. Serve immediately. Makes 4 side-dish servings.

Nutrition Facts per serving: 108 cal., 2 g total fat (1 g sat. fat), 5 mg chol., 184 mg sodium, 19 g carbo., 4 g fiber, 4 g pro.
Daily Values: 2% vit. A, 13% vit. C, 6% calcium, 14% iron.

Jerusalem artichokes (also called sunchokes) are not artichokes—they're the root of the sunflower. They can be enjoyed raw or lightly cooked.

Tossed Crisp Vegetable Salad

The fresher and firmer the vegetables, the better the salad. Choose those in the recipe (below) or any desired vegetable combination.

Start to finish: 25 minutes

- 4 thin asparagus spears
- 1 small beet
- 1 small carrot
- 1 small parsnip or parsley root
- 1 small celery root
- 1 small fennel bulb
  Salt
  Freshly ground pepper
- ¼ to ⅓ cup bottled low-fat Italian, sesame, or poppy seed salad dressing

1 Snap off and discard woody bases from asparagus. Wash asparagus and drain. Using a sharp knife, cut spears lengthwise into very thin strips. Wash beet; trim ends. Using a mechanical slicer or sharp peeler, peel thin strips of beet. Rinse under cold water; set aside. Trim carrot, parsnip or parsley root, celery root, and fennel bulb. Using a mechanical slicer or sharp peeler, cut vegetables into wide, thin strips.

2 In a large salad bowl combine vegetables. Season to taste with salt and freshly ground pepper. Serve and pass choice of bottled dressing. Makes 6 side-dish servings.

Nutrition Facts per serving with 1 tablespoon dressing: 79 cal., 6 g total fat (1 g sat. fat), 4 mg chol., 159 mg sodium, 6 g carbo., 2 g fiber, 1 g pro.
Daily Values: 2% vit. A, 15% vit. C, 1% calcium, 3% iron.

Pan-Fried Baby Bok Choy

Baby bok choy—a mild vegetable with pale-green stalks and leaves—is becoming more available. Look for it in Asian specialty markets or larger supermarkets throughout the spring and summer.

Start to finish: 10 minutes

- 12 oz. baby bok choy (4 to 8 pieces) or 1 small bunch regular bok choy, quartered lengthwise
- 2 Tbsp. peanut oil or cooking oil
- ½ cup coarse soft sourdough bread crumbs
- 1 clove garlic, minced
- 1 Tbsp. soy sauce
- 2 tsp. toasted sesame seed

1 Cut any large pieces of baby bok choy in half lengthwise. Rinse bok choy under cold running water. Shake gently to remove water. Drain well.

2 In a large skillet heat oil. Cook bread crumbs in hot oil about 1 minute or until just beginning to brown. Add garlic. Cook and stir about 1 minute more or until crumbs are golden brown. Using a slotted spoon, remove crumb mixture from skillet. Set aside. Add bok choy to hot skillet. Cook, uncovered, for 3 to 5 minutes or until stalks are heated through and leaves are wilted, turning often. Transfer to a serving dish. Toss with crumbs, drizzle with soy sauce and sprinkle with sesame seed. Makes 4 side-dish servings.

Nutrition Facts per serving: 96 cal., 8 g total fat (1 g sat. fat), 0 mg chol., 314 mg sodium, 4 g carbo., 1 g fiber, 3 g pro.
Daily Values: 26% vit. A, 64% vit. C, 10% calcium, 4% iron.

Avocado Rings with Radish "Fireworks"

Seasoned rice vinegar can be found in most large supermarkets. If not available, stir 2 teaspoons sugar into plain rice vinegar or distilled white vinegar until dissolved. (See the photograph on page 118.)

Start to finish: 15 minutes

- ½ cup shredded red radishes
- ½ cup shredded daikon
- 2 Tbsp. lime juice
- 1 Tbsp. seasoned rice vinegar
- ⅛ tsp. salt
- 2 medium ripe avocados
  Fresh red and/or green serrano peppers (optional)*

1 In a medium bowl stir together red radishes, daikon, lime juice, vinegar, and salt. Cover radish mixture. If desired, chill for 2 hours.

2 Cut avocados crosswise around pit into ¼- to ½-inch-thick rings. Gently twist off each ring (see photo, page 97). Carefully remove and discard the peel from each ring. Discard the pit.

3 If using serrano peppers, split peppers lengthwise. Remove and discard stem and seeds. Cut peppers into matchstick-size strips. Finely mince several of the matchsticks. Set peppers aside.

4 To serve, stack three or four avocado rings on each of four chilled salad plates. Fill the center of each avocado stack with a spray of

Using a sharp knife, make a series of crosswise, circular cuts ¼ to ½ inch apart around the avocado, down to the pit. Gently twist off each ring. Use the flat of the blade to pry the ring off the pit.

radish slaw and, if desired, fresh serrano pepper matchsticks. Drizzle with any remaining dressing from the slaw. If desired, sprinkle plate with minced serrano pepper. Makes 4 side-dish servings.

*Note: Hot chili peppers contain oils that can burn eyes, lips, and sensitive skin. Wear plastic gloves while preparing them and be sure to wash your hands thoroughly afterward.

Nutrition Facts per serving: 162 cal., 14 g total fat (2 g sat. fat), 0 mg chol., 91 mg sodium, 8 g carbo., 5 g fiber, 2 g pro.
Daily Values: 10% vit. A, 25% vit. C, 2% calcium, 6% iron.

LOW FAT

Minted French Green Beans

Haricots verts ('ah-ree-co VARE)—thin, sweet green beans—are available from April through July. This variety will store for several days, refrigerated, in a plastic bag.

Prep: 15 minutes **Cook:** 2 minutes
Chill: 2 hours

- 8 oz. haricots vert or other small, thin green beans (2 cups)
- 1 Tbsp. minced shallot
- 2 tsp. olive oil
- 2 tsp. snipped fresh mint
  Salt
  Freshly ground pepper

1 Rinse beans. If desired, trim tips off beans; drain.

2 Place a steamer basket in a large skillet. Add water to just below the bottom of basket. Bring water to boiling. Place beans in steamer basket. Cover and steam for 2 minutes. Drain. Rinse with cold water. (Or, plunge into ice water.) Drain well.

3 In a medium mixing bowl lightly toss together beans, shallot, olive oil, and mint. Season to taste with salt and pepper. Cover and chill for 2 hours. Serve as a salad or side dish. Makes 4 servings.

Nutrition Facts per serving: 40 cal., 2 g total fat (0 g sat. fat), 0 mg chol., 39 mg sodium, 5 g carbo., 2 g fiber, 1 g pro.
Daily Values: 4% vit. A, 14% vit. C, 2% calcium, 4% iron.

30 MINUTE

Asparagus with Fresh Mozzarella

Thick asparagus halved lengthwise can be used instead of thin spears.

Start to finish: 10 minutes

- 1 lb. thin asparagus spears
- 4 oz. fresh mozzarella cheese, cut or torn into pieces
  Salt
  Freshly ground pepper
  Fresh lemon verbena leaves or
  ½ tsp. grated lemon peel

1 Snap off and discard woody bases from asparagus. Rinse asparagus and drain.

2 Place a steamer basket in a large skillet. Add enough water to come just below the bottom of the basket. Bring water to boiling. Place asparagus evenly in steamer basket. Cover and steam for 2 minutes.

3 Transfer asparagus to an 8×8×2-inch baking pan. Top with fresh mozzarella cheese. Season to taste with salt and pepper. Broil 4 inches from heat about 1 minute or until cheese melts. Top with verbena or lemon peel. Makes 4 side-dish servings.

Nutrition Facts per serving: 99 cal., 7 g total fat (4 g sat. fat), 22 mg chol., 150 mg sodium, 2 g carbo., 1 g fiber, 8 g pro.
Daily Values: 8% vit. A, 31% vit. C, 16% calcium, 3% iron.

EDITOR'S TIP

Wild for Walnut Oil

Anyone who's crazy about walnuts will love the nutty aroma and taste of walnut oil. Extracted from the meat of walnuts, this oil costs more than regular cooking oils, but the investment offers a handsome return in taste. Look for it in gourmet food stores or the specialty food section of your supermarket. To store walnut oil, keep it tightly capped in a cool, dark place for up to three months. For longer storage, refrigerate it for up to four months. Don't be alarmed if it turns cloudy. Just bring it to room temperature and it should clear up nicely.

Try these ideas for using walnut oil:

● Drizzle it over steamed vegetables.

● Substitute walnut oil for vegetable oil in baked goods (such as muffins or quick breads) and delicately flavored cookies (such as sugar cookies).

● Cook shrimp, fish, or chicken in a little walnut oil.

● Brush it lightly over slices of French bread instead of using butter.

● Toss some walnut oil with hot pasta, grated Parmesan cheese, snipped fresh chives, and toasted walnuts for a satisfying side dish.

● Make Walnut Oil Vinaigrette to splash over a fresh salad of your favorite greens, sliced mushrooms, strawberries, and toasted walnuts.

Walnut Oil Vinaigrette: In a screw-top jar combine ¼ cup walnut oil, 3 tablespoons vinegar, 2 teaspoons sugar, 2 teaspoons sliced green onion, 2 teaspoons Dijon-style mustard, ⅛ teaspoon pepper, and dash salt. Cover; shake well. Chill. Store in the refrigerator up to 2 weeks. Makes ½ cup dressing.

Nutrition Facts per tablespoon: 66 cal., 7 g total fat (1 g sat. fat), 0 mg chol., 16 mg sodium, 2 g carbo., 0 g fiber, 0 g pro.

Italian Bean and Artichoke Salad

Prep: 15 minutes **Cook:** 15 minutes
Chill: 6 hours

- 1 9-oz. pkg. frozen Italian or cut green beans, cooked and drained
- 1 8- or 9-oz. package frozen artichoke hearts, cooked and drained
- 1 medium red sweet pepper, cut into thin bite-size strips
- 3 Tbsp. walnut oil or salad oil
- 3 Tbsp. white wine vinegar
- 1 Tbsp. honey mustard
- ¼ tsp. salt
- ⅛ tsp. ground red pepper
- 4 cups torn romaine
- ¼ cup chopped walnuts or pecans, toasted

1 In a large bowl combine the drained beans, drained artichoke hearts, and sweet pepper strips. Set aside.

2 For dressing, in a screw-top jar combine walnut oil or salad oil, white wine vinegar, honey mustard, salt, and ground red pepper. Cover and shake well. Pour dressing over bean mixture. Stir gently to coat. Cover and chill for 6 to 24 hours, stirring once or twice.

3 To serve, spoon vegetables and marinade over romaine; sprinkle with walnuts or pecans. Makes 6 side-dish servings.

Nutrition Facts per serving: 141 cal., 10 g total fat (1 g sat. fat), 0 mg chol., 143 mg sodium, 11 g carbo., 5 g fiber, 3 g pro.
Daily Values: 23% vit. A, 83% vit. C, 6% calcium, 8% iron.

30 MINUTE

Broken Pasta with Italian Parsley

This uncomplicated pasta tossed with tiny sweet tomatoes is popular in the sunny farming region of Apulia, Italy. If the small tomatoes aren't available, use any fresh tomato, cut into wedges.

Start to finish: 15 minutes

- 2 Tbsp. olive oil
- ½ tsp. snipped fresh rosemary*
- 6 oz. dried lasagna noodles (about 7 noodles)
- ⅔ cup red and/or gold grape tomatoes, teardrop tomatoes, or cherry tomatoes, halved lengthwise
- ¼ cup fresh Italian parsley leaves
   Salt
   Coarsely ground black pepper
   Parmesan or other hard cheese, crumbled

1 In a small container stir together the olive oil and the snipped rosemary. Cover and set aside.

2 Break lasagna noodles into irregular pieces (about 2 to 3 inches long). In a Dutch oven or large saucepan bring 3 quarts salted water to boiling. Cook pasta, uncovered, for 8 to 10 minutes or until tender but still firm (al dente). Drain and rinse the pasta.

3 Toss the cooked pasta with the olive oil-rosemary mixture, tomatoes, and parsley. Season to taste with salt and pepper.

4 To serve, divide the pasta mixture among four hot pasta bowls or other shallow bowls. Sprinkle with cheese. Makes 4 side-dish servings.

*Note: If desired, you may substitute purchased rosemary-flavored oil for the oil and rosemary mixture.

Nutrition Facts per serving: 251 cal., 10 g total fat (2 g sat. fat), 6 mg chol., 77 mg sodium, 33 g carbo., 1 g fiber, 7 g pro.
Daily Values: 9% vit. A, 18% vit. C, 6% calcium, 10% iron.

PRIZE WINNER

Salmon Pinwheel Salad

Jane Stennen Gaither
Nashville, Tennessee
$400—Salad Suppers Category
(See the photograph on page 120.)

Prep: 20 minutes Cook: 6 minutes
Chill: 2 hours

1½ lb. fresh or frozen skinless salmon fillet, ½ to ¾ inch thick
½ cup dry white wine or water
¼ tsp. salt
¼ tsp. pepper
1 bay leaf
4 cups torn curly endive
4 cups torn red-tip leaf lettuce
2 medium oranges, peeled and sectioned
1 cup thinly sliced cucumber
¼ cup sliced almonds, toasted
1 recipe Fresh Orange Dressing (see right)

1 Cut fillet lengthwise into six even strips. Lightly season with *salt* and *pepper*. Starting with the thick end of each strip, roll into pinwheels. Secure each pinwheel with a wooden toothpick or wooden skewer.

2 In a medium skillet combine white wine or water, the ¼ teaspoon salt, ¼ teaspoon pepper, and bay leaf; bring to boiling. Add salmon. Return

to boiling; reduce heat. Simmer, covered, for 6 to 8 minutes, turning once, or until fish just flakes easily with a fork. Using a slotted spoon, remove salmon from cooking liquid. Discard cooking liquid. Cover and chill salmon for 2 to 12 hours.

3 To serve, arrange endive, leaf lettuce, orange sections, cucumber slices, and almonds in six salad bowls. Spoon some of the Fresh Orange Dressing over salad mixture. Top each with a salmon roll. Makes 6 servings.

Fresh Orange Dressing:

In a small bowl stir together ½ cup light dairy sour cream, ½ teaspoon finely shredded orange peel, 2 tablespoons orange juice, 2 teaspoons sugar, and ½ teaspoon poppy seed. Add additional orange juice, 1 teaspoon at a time, to desired consistency. Makes about ½ cup.

Nutrition Facts per serving: 229 cal., 10 g total fat (2 g sat. fat), 66 mg chol., 144 mg sodium, 9 g carbo., 3 g fiber, 26 g pro.
Daily Values: 21% vit. A, 39% vit. C, 11% calcium, 11% iron.

30 MINUTE

Island-Style Seafood Slaw

Start to finish: 20 minutes

1 12-oz. pkg. frozen peeled, cooked shrimp
6 cups packaged shredded cabbage with carrot (coleslaw mix)
2 medium red and/or yellow sweet peppers, cut into thin, bite-size strips
⅓ cup thinly sliced green onions
¼ cup snipped fresh cilantro
¾ cup light mayonnaise dressing or salad dressing

SUNNY LUNCH

- Island-Style Seafood Slaw (see below left)

- Rye or whole wheat rolls

- Iced tea

- Fresh pineapple wedges, sprinkled with brown sugar, broiled until warm, and topped with vanilla ice cream

1 tsp. finely shredded lime peel
3 Tbsp. lime juice
¼ tsp. salt
⅛ tsp. ground red pepper
¼ cup honey roasted peanuts (optional)

1 Thaw and rinse shrimp. In a very large bowl toss together shrimp, cabbage mix, sweet peppers, green onions, and cilantro.

2 For dressing, in a small bowl stir together mayonnaise dressing or salad dressing, lime peel, lime juice, salt, and ground red pepper. Pour dressing over salad, tossing to coat. Serve at once. Sprinkle with peanuts, if desired. Makes 4 main-dish servings.

Make-Ahead Directions: Prepare salad as directed, except cover and chill for up to 2 hours. Just before serving, stir the salad and sprinkle with peanuts.

Nutrition Facts per serving: 327 cal., 17 g total fat (3 g sat. fat), 185 mg chol., 613 mg sodium, 21 g carbo., 5 g fiber, 25 g pro.
Daily Values: 128% vit. A, 245% vit. C, 13% calcium, 22% iron.

Ginger Aid

by David Feder, Registered Dietitian

There's real science behind the legends and myths that are associated with ginger.

Decades of research have revealed the wealth of health locked inside fresh ginger. In addition to containing nutritional pluses such as vitamin A, vitamin C, and phytochemicals, this robust rhizome can soothe an upset tummy, kill harmful microbes, and help clear toxins from the blood. Best of all, you don't need to eat ginger by the pound to get the effects and benefits. Most studies have found that as little as a gram a day—less than a teaspoon of freshly grated ginger—gets right to work helping to protect your system from a number of diseases.

An All-Around Good Guy

The concentrated antioxidants in ginger guard against cancer before it starts by halting cell damage by rogue oxygen molecules. Other powerful compounds in ginger show the ability to stop existing tumors from reproducing, and even kill some pre- and early-stage cancer cells. Scientists have found other attributes to ginger, including evidence that ginger can:

● prevent blood clots from forming.

● reduce blood cholesterol.

● kill harmful microorganisms that contaminate food.

● protect against unwanted microbes that pass into the digestive system.

● soothe the symptoms associated with colds (and even be toxic to the types of viruses believed to cause the common cold).

● work topically as an antibacterial ointment, provide relief of arthritis pain and swelling, and inhibit development of precancerous skin growths.

● act as an effective antinausea remedy, especially for the nausea associated with motion sickness or pregnancy.

Feed a Cold...Ginger

To use ginger to relieve cold symptoms or nausea, steep 2 tablespoons of thinly sliced fresh ginger (peeled, if desired) in a large mug of boiling water for several minutes. This herbal tea is also effective at alleviating some of those unwanted menopause symptoms, such as hot flashes and headaches.

Any Way You Like It

Although many of the ginger studies relied on the whole root or extracts, some showed that dried ginger may be helpful too. Also, the juice from fresh ginger is effective. Use a clean garlic crusher to extract the juice. Then, add ginger juice to iced desserts, stir it into hot or cold beverages, or incorporate it in salad dressings. See the tips (page 101) for more ideas. Look for foods that already contain ginger, such as herbal teas, crystallized ginger candies, and gingersnaps made with real ginger.

Ginger On My Mind

Ginger boasts attributes above and beyond its versatile flavor and its natural compounds that promote physical health. Ginger has a pleasant aroma that could soothe the savage beast within. In a study on depression, the smell of fresh ginger was considered by subjects to be so pleasant that they ranked it as one of the most calming fragrances among the choices tested. In one study of migraine sufferers, ginger was reviewed for its qualities as an analgesic when eaten and as a provider of comfort via its aroma. In both aspects, ginger was able to provide at least some temporary relief from the debilitating headaches.

Ginger Scallion Fish

Look for fish sauce in the Asian cooking section of your supermarket or at an Asian food store.

Prep: 10 minutes **Microwave:** 6 minutes

1½ lb. fresh or frozen skinless sea
     bass or other firm-fleshed
     white fish fillets (¾ to 1 inch
     thick)
1   cup thinly sliced scallions or
     green onions
2   Tbsp. lemon juice or dry sherry
4   tsp. grated fresh ginger
2   cloves garlic, minced
1   Tbsp. bottled fish sauce or
     reduced-sodium soy sauce
1   fresh jalapeño pepper, seeded
     and finely chopped*

1 Thaw fish, if frozen. Rinse fish and pat dry with paper towels. In a small bowl stir together scallions or green onions, 1 tablespoon of the lemon juice or dry sherry, ginger, and garlic.

2 Arrange fish fillets in a single layer in an ungreased 2-quart rectangular baking dish, tucking under any thin edges. Spoon scallion mixture over fish. Cover dish with vented clear plastic wrap. Micro-cook on 100% power (high) for 6 to 10 minutes (depending on wattage of your microwave oven) or until fish flakes easily with a fork. To ensure even cooking, give dish a half-turn and rotate fillets halfway through cooking time.

3 To serve, transfer fish to a serving platter using a slotted spatula. Stir together remaining lemon juice or sherry, the fish sauce, and chopped jalapeño; drizzle over fish. Makes 6 servings.

EDITOR'S TIP
Putting Ginger To Work

Adding small amounts of ginger to your regular diet may also add big amounts of protection. Here are eight ways a little bit of ginger can work its magic for you:

● Stir a few teaspoons of grated fresh ginger into nut bread, muffin, or banana bread batter.

● Include a half teaspoonful of dried ginger in rice pudding or bread pudding recipes.

● Simmer matchsticks of fresh ginger with fruit for a snazzy compote.

● Cook rice with minced fresh ginger and raisins for a piquant, healthful pilaf.

● Add finely chopped pieces of peeled ginger to fruit pie fillings.

● Heat a few pieces of candied ginger in a quarter cup of maple syrup; pour over waffles or pancakes.

● Toss a teaspoon of minced ginger in the steamer basket when preparing fresh vegetables.

● Grate peeled fresh ginger over vanilla ice cream.

*Note: Hot chili peppers contain oils that can burn eyes, lips, and sensitive skin. Wear plastic gloves while preparing them and be sure to wash your hands thoroughly afterward.

Nutrition Facts per serving: 122 cal., 2 g total fat (1 g sat. fat), 46 mg chol., 312 mg sodium, 3 g carbo., 1 g fiber, 22 g pro.
Daily Values: 6% vit. A, 13% vit. C, 3% calcium, 4% iron.

Sea Bass with Fruited Tomatillo Salsa

Prep: 25 minutes **Bake:** 15 minutes

4   fresh or frozen sea bass steaks,
     1 inch thick
1   cup chopped pineapple
½   cup chopped, peeled peaches or
     nectarines
½   cup chopped tomatillos
2   Tbsp. snipped fresh cilantro
1   Tbsp. finely chopped green onion
1   serrano pepper, seeded and
     chopped*
1   tsp. finely shredded lime peel
1   Tbsp. lime juice
2   tsp. honey
1   cup quick-cooking couscous

1 Preheat oven to 450°. Thaw fish, if frozen. Rinse fish; pat dry with paper towels. Set aside. For salsa, combine pineapple, peaches, tomatillos, cilantro, onion, and serrano. Stir in lime peel and juice and honey; set aside. Combine the couscous, ¼ cup *boiling water*, and ¼ teaspoon *salt*.

2 Spread couscous evenly in a greased 2-quart rectangular baking dish. Arrange fish over couscous. Spoon salsa over fish. Bake, uncovered, 15 to 18 minutes or until fish flakes with a fork. Serves 4.

*Note: Hot chili peppers contain oils that can burn eyes, lips, and sensitive skin. Wear plastic gloves while preparing them and be sure to wash your hands thoroughly afterward.

Nutrition Facts per serving: 357 cal., 5 g total fat (1 g sat. fat), 77 mg chol., 233 mg sodium, 50 g carbo., 4 g fiber, 28 g pro.
Daily Values: 7% vit. A, 27% vit. C, 11% calcium, 14% iron.

Trout with Mushrooms

Whether you pull them from a stream or from the nearest supermarket, fresh trout need few seasonings to complement their delicate flavor.

Prep: 15 minutes **Broil:** 8 minutes

- 4 8-oz. fresh or frozen dressed whole trout (heads removed, if desired)
- 1 large lemon, halved
- ¼ cup olive oil
- 4 tsp. snipped fresh thyme or
     1 tsp. dried thyme, crushed
- ¼ tsp. salt
- ¼ tsp. crushed red pepper
- 1½ cups sliced jumbo button mushrooms
- 1 bunch green onions (8 to 10)
- 4 sprigs fresh thyme

1 Thaw fish, if frozen. Rinse fish and pat dry with paper towels. Strain juice from half of lemon into small bowl. Set aside. Thinly slice remaining lemon half. Cut the slices in halves. Set aside.

2 In a small bowl stir together the lemon juice, olive oil, snipped thyme, salt, and crushed red pepper. Set aside ¼ cup of the mixture. Toss the sliced mushrooms with the remaining mixture; cover and set aside.

3 Trim the root end plus first inch of the green tops off of the green onions. Cut onions crosswise into 2½-inch pieces. (If grilling, leave onions whole.) Place onion pieces in one layer on the unheated rack of a broiler pan (or arrange whole onions

SUMMER SUPPER

- ■ **Trout with Mushrooms (see left)**

- ■ **Salad of mesclun greens tossed with cooked, halved new potatoes; halved grape or cherry tomatoes; and a balsamic vinaigrette**

- ■ **French rolls with butter**

- ■ **Fruit-Filled Nachos (see page 108)**

in a grill basket). Brush the onion pieces with some of the reserved lemon juice mixture.

4 Arrange trout on top of onions. Tuck two halved lemon slices and a thyme sprig inside the cavity of each trout. Brush skin and inside flesh of trout with lemon juice mixture.

5 Broil 4 inches from the heat for 8 to 12 minutes or until fish flakes easily when tested with a fork, turning fish once. (Or, grill fish in grill basket on the rack of an uncovered grill over medium coals for 8 to 12 minutes or until fish just flakes easily with a fork, turning once.) Grill whole onions separately, cooking for 2 to 3 minutes per side.

6 To serve, arrange onions over four dinner plates. Top each with a broiled or grilled fish. Spoon the marinated mushroom slices across the top. Makes 4 servings.

Nutrition Facts per serving: 454 cal., 26 g total fat (5 g sat. fat), 133 mg chol., 231 mg sodium, 4 g carbo., 1 g fiber, 49 g pro.
Daily Values: 19% vit. A, 26% vit. C, 18% calcium, 8% iron.

Pulled Chicken-Peanut Salad

Store watercress, stems down, in one-half inch of clean water. Loosely cover and refrigerate for up to one week.

Start to finish: 20 minutes

- 2 Tbsp. frozen orange-tangerine or orange juice concentrate
- 1 Tbsp. water
- 2 tsp. toasted sesame oil
- ¼ tsp. salt
- ⅛ tsp. coarsely ground black pepper
- 12 oz. skinless, boneless chicken breast halves
- 3 cups watercress sprigs
- ¼ cup cocktail peanuts

1 In a small bowl combine juice concentrate, water, sesame oil, salt, and pepper. Reserve 1 tablespoon of orange juice concentrate mixture. Cover remaining mixture. Set aside.

2 Place a steamer basket in a large skillet. Add water to just below the bottom of basket. Bring to boiling. Reduce heat to simmer. Carefully arrange chicken in a single layer in basket. Brush chicken with the reserved 1 tablespoon juice mixture. Cover and steam chicken for 10 to 12 minutes or until tender and no longer pink.

3 Remove chicken. Transfer to a cutting board. Cool slightly (about 5 minutes). Using a pair of forks, pull chicken into bite-size pieces about 1½ inches long (see photo, page 103).

To make finger-size shreds, hold the cooled, cooked chicken to cutting board with one fork. Use second fork to gently pull the meat.

4 To serve, in a large salad bowl combine watercress, chicken, and peanuts. Pour remaining juice mixture over salad and toss to coat. Makes 4 main-dish servings.

Nutrition Facts per serving: 186 cal., 8 g total fat (1 g sat. fat), 49 mg chol., 241 mg sodium, 5 g carbo., 1 g fiber, 23 g pro.
Daily Values: 13% vit. A, 42% vit. C, 5% calcium, 5% iron.

30 MINUTE

Grain Pilaf, Turkey, and Pear Salad

Start to finish: 20 minutes

- ⅔ cup pear nectar or apple juice
- ⅓ cup white wine vinegar
- 3 Tbsp. walnut oil or salad oil
- 1½ cups cooked seven grain and sesame breakfast pilaf
- ¾ cup dried cranberries
- 2 Tbsp. sliced green onion
  Leaf lettuce
- 12 oz. sliced, smoked turkey breast
- 2 pears, cored and thinly sliced

- ⅓ cup crumbled feta cheese
- ⅓ cup chopped toasted walnuts

1 For dressing, in a small bowl whisk together pear nectar or apple juice, white wine vinegar, and walnut or salad oil. Set aside.

2 In a medium bowl toss together the cooked pilaf, dried cranberries, and green onion.

3 To serve, line six dinner plates with leaf lettuce. Arrange pilaf mixture, turkey breast slices, and pear slices on top of the lettuce. Drizzle dressing over salads and sprinkle with crumbled feta and walnuts. Makes 6 main-dish servings.

Nutrition Facts per serving: 340 cal., 14 g total fat (2 g sat. fat), 32 mg chol., 694 mg sodium, 39 g carbo., 4 g fiber, 17 g pro.
Daily Values: 2% vit. A, 7% vit. C, 6% calcium, 8% iron.

30 MINUTE

Lamb Chops and Lima Beans

This recipe also works well with medallions of turkey tenderloin or pork, instead of the lamb chops. (See the photograph on page 119.)

Prep: 10 minutes **Cook:** 14 minutes

- ⅓ cup fine dry bread crumbs
- 4 tsp. mustard seed, crushed
- ¼ tsp. salt
- ¼ tsp. black pepper
- 8 2- to 3-oz. lamb chops, cut ½ inch thick
- ¼ cup chicken broth
- 12 oz. shelled fresh or frozen baby lima beans (2¼ cups)
- ⅓ cup diced red sweet pepper
- 1 Tbsp. butter

- 1 Tbsp. snipped fresh thyme
  Several dashes bottled green hot pepper sauce
- 1 Tbsp. cooking oil
  Fresh thyme sprigs (optional)

1 In a small bowl combine bread crumbs, mustard seed, salt, and black pepper. Trim and discard fat from chops. Coat chops with bread-crumb mixture, pressing firmly to coat evenly. Cover. Set aside.

2 In a medium saucepan bring broth to boiling; reduce heat. Add beans and sweet pepper. Cover. Cook mixture over medium-low heat for 8 to 10 minutes or until just tender for fresh lima beans, or according to package directions for frozen lima beans. Remove from heat. Drain. Stir in butter, snipped thyme, and hot pepper sauce. Set aside; keep warm.

3 Meanwhile, in a large skillet heat oil over medium-high heat. Cook chops, uncovered, for 6 to 9 minutes, turning once. Reduce heat to prevent overbrowning, if needed. (An instant-read meat thermometer inserted into the thickest portion of the chop should register 145° for medium-rare doneness or 155° for medium doneness.) Drain on paper towels.

4 To serve, spoon cooked beans onto 4 serving plates. Serve 2 chops on each plate alongside beans. Top with thyme sprigs, if desired. Makes 4 main-dish servings.

Nutrition Facts per serving: 452 cal., 30 g total fat (12 g sat. fat), 70 mg chol., 448 mg sodium, 24 g carbo., 5 g fiber, 22 g pro.
Daily Values: 12% vit. A, 57% vit. C, 8% calcium, 24% iron.

PRIZE WINNER

Piquant Pork Salad

Liz Barclay
Annapolis, Maryland
$200—Salad Suppers Category

Prep: 25 minutes **Marinate:** 30 minutes
Grill: 30 minutes **Stand:** 10 minutes

- 1 **12-oz. pork tenderloin**
- ⅔ **cup bottled balsamic vinaigrette salad dressing**
- 1 **cup pecan halves**
- 2 **Tbsp. purchased basil pesto**
- 4 **cups mesclun salad mix**
- 1 **small zucchini, thinly sliced**
- 1 **medium red sweet pepper, cut into thin strips**
- ½ **small red onion, thinly sliced**
- ½ **cup peeled baby carrots, halved lengthwise**
- ¼ **cup finely shredded Parmesan cheese**

1 Preheat oven to 350°. Place pork in a plastic bag; add ⅓ cup of the salad dressing. Seal bag; let stand at room temperature 30 minutes, turning bag over occasionally. Meanwhile, place pecans in a shallow baking pan; add pesto, tossing to coat. Bake for 15 minutes, stirring every 5 minutes. Remove from oven; cool in pan.

2 Lift pork from marinade, reserving marinade. In a grill with a cover, arrange preheated coals around a drip pan. Test for medium heat above the pan. Place meat on grill rack above the drip pan. Insert a meat thermometer in pork. Grill, covered, for 30 to 40 minutes or until meat thermometer registers 160°. Brush occasionally with reserved marinade until the last 5 minutes of cooking. Remove pork from grill. Discard any remaining marinade. Let pork stand 10 minutes. Thinly slice pork.

3 In a large salad bowl combine mesclun mix, zucchini, sweet pepper, onion, and carrots. Add pecans and sliced pork. Toss with remaining salad dressing. Sprinkle with Parmesan cheese. Makes 4 main-dish servings.

Nutrition Facts per serving: 478 cal., 35 g total fat (5 g sat. fat), 57 mg chol., 541 mg sodium, 16 g carbo., 4 g fiber, 27 g pro.
Daily Values: 36% vit. A, 122% vit. C, 15% calcium, 16% iron.

30 MINUTE

Garlic-Thyme Pork Chops

Take advantage of one of the growing number of wonderful rice side dishes available on supermarket shelves as an easy go-with for the glazed chops.

Prep: 10 minutes **Broil:** 18 minutes

- 4 **pork loin or rib chops, cut 1¼ to 1½ inches thick (about 3 lb.)**
- 3 **medium red onions, quartered**
- 1 **cup apple juice or dry vermouth**
- 1 **tsp. cornstarch**
- 1 **tsp. cold water**
- 1 **Tbsp. olive oil**
- 3 **cloves garlic, minced**
- 3 **Tbsp. snipped fresh thyme or 1½ tsp. dried thyme, crushed**
- ½ **tsp. coarsely ground black pepper Fresh thyme sprigs (optional)**

1 Place pork chops on the unheated rack of a broiler pan. Arrange onions around pork chops. Broil 4 to 5 inches from heat, without turning, for 9 minutes.

2 Meanwhile, for glaze, in a medium saucepan bring apple juice or vermouth to boiling; boil, uncovered,

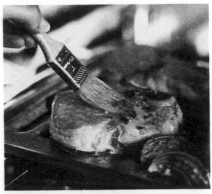

To glaze the chops, brush lightly during the last 5 minutes of broiling. Brushing earlier will cause the glaze to burn.

over high heat for 5 to 6 minutes or until reduced to ½ cup.

3 Meanwhile, combine cornstarch with cold water; stir into apple juice or vermouth. Cook and stir until slightly thickened and bubbly. Cook and stir for 2 minutes more. Remove from heat. Stir in olive oil, garlic, 2 tablespoons of the fresh thyme or 1 teaspoon of the dried thyme, the pepper, and ¼ teaspoon *salt*. Remove 2 tablespoons of the glaze; set aside.

4 Turn pork chops; broil for 9 to 13 minutes more or until juices run clear. Using a pastry brush, coat the pork chops and onions with glaze during the last 5 minutes of cooking (see photo, above).

5 Remove onions to a small serving bowl. Remove pork chops to serving platter or dish. Stir the reserved glaze and remaining thyme into onions. Pass with pork chops. If desired, garnish with fresh thyme sprigs. Makes 4 servings.

Nutrition Facts per serving: 387 cal., 18 g total fat (6 g sat. fat), 102 mg chol., 216 mg sodium, 7 g carbo., 1 g fiber, 33 g pro.
Daily Values: 6% vit. C, 2% calcium, 13% iron.

LOW FAT

Wrap-and-Roll Cabbage

Prep: 40 minutes **Steam:** 5 minutes

    8 large Napa, savoy, or head
       cabbage leaves
    1 small carrot, coarsely shredded
  ¼ cup sliced fresh shiitake or button
       mushrooms
    2 tsp. peanut oil or cooking oil
1½ to 2 cups shredded cooked pork
       or ground pork, cooked and
       drained
    1 Tbsp. grated fresh ginger
  ½ tsp. five-spice powder*
  ½ cup bean sprouts
  ¼ cup red sweet pepper, cut into
       thin strips
    2 green onions, bias-sliced
  ½ cup bottled hoisin sauce

1 In a 2-quart saucepan bring 6 cups water to boiling. Immerse whole cabbage leaves 2 to 3 minutes or until leaves are limp. Drain well; set aside on paper towels. Remove center rib from leaves if it is too thick.

2 For filling, in a large skillet cook carrot and mushrooms in hot oil for 2 to 3 minutes or until just tender. Stir in pork, ginger, and five-spice powder. Cook 2 minutes more or until heated through. Remove from heat. Stir in sprouts, pepper strips, onions, and half of the hoisin sauce.

3 To assemble, place about ¼ cup filling on each cabbage leaf. Fold in sides. Starting at unfolded edge, carefully roll up each leaf, making sure the folded sides are caught in the roll. Place in a steamer basket.

4 Steam cabbage rolls, covered, over a small amount of boiling water for 5 minutes or until just heated

through. Thin the remaining hoisin sauce with a little water; serve with cabbage rolls for dipping. Makes 4 main-dish servings.

*Note: Look for five-spice powder with the other seasonings in your supermarket or Asian specialty store.

Nutrition Facts per serving (2 rolls): 241 cal., 6 g total fat (2 g sat. fat), 52 mg chol., 676 mg sodium, 24 g carbo., 2 g fiber, 21 g pro.
Daily Values: 44% vit. A, 64% vit. C, 6% calcium, 9% iron.

30 MINUTE, LOW FAT

Incredible Quesadillas

Prep: 20 minutes **Cook:** 3 minutes each

  ½ cup shredded, reduced-fat
       Mexican-cheese blend
    4 8-inch fat-free flour tortillas
    4 low-fat brown-and-serve sausage
       links, cooked and coarsely
       chopped
    2 Tbsp. well-drained pineapple
       salsa or regular salsa
    1 small red onion, sliced and
       separated into rings
    2 Tbsp. finely snipped fresh cilantro
  ½ cup pineapple salsa or regular salsa

1 Preheat a waffle baker to a medium-high heat setting.* Sprinkle 2 tablespoons of the cheese over half of each tortilla. Top with sausage, the 2 tablespoons salsa, onion, and cilantro. Fold tortillas in half, pressing gently.

2 Place one quesadilla on preheated waffle baker. Close lid, pressing slightly. Bake for 3 to 6 minutes or until tortilla is lightly browned and cheese is melted. Remove from waffle baker. Cut quesadilla in half. Repeat with remaining quesadillas.

EDITOR'S TIP

Quesadillas

These Mexican treats are like thin-crust grilled cheese sandwiches with a south-of-the-border attitude. We've heightened the taste—and slashed the calories and fat—from this marvelous snack of cheese and tortillas. A typical quesadilla, oozing cheese, sausage, and refried beans, often is cooked in oil. As a result, it can tally 15 grams of fat and 350 calories. Our version shaves off about 3 grams of fat per tortilla merely by using fat-free tortillas.

Smart Touches

● Add extra flavor, but not extra fat, by using reduced-fat cheese blends.

● Substitute low-fat pork and turkey sausage for traditional chorizo, which has twice the calories and four times the fat.

● Tuck salsa into the filling for a fat-free jolt of taste.

● Skip the cooking oil (120 calories; 13 fat grams per tablespoon) by using a nonstick skillet or waffle baker.

3 To serve, place the ½ cup salsa on a plate. Top with quesadilla pieces. If desired, serve with *tomatillos*. Makes 8 appetizer servings.

*Note: Or use a 10-inch nonstick skillet to cook each quesadilla over medium heat for 3 to 4 minutes or until golden brown. Using a spatula, turn quesadilla over. Cook for 2 to 3 minutes more or until golden brown. Remove the quesadilla from the skillet.

Nutrition Facts per serving: 104 cal., 2 g total fat (1 g sat. fat), 8 mg chol., 362 mg sodium, 17 g carbo., 2 g fiber, 5 g pro.
Daily Values: 2% vit. A, 1% vit. C, 4% calcium, 2% iron.

LOW FAT

Stirred Custard

Prep: 15 minutes **Chill:** 2 hours

5	egg yolks, beaten
1½	cups milk
¼	cup sugar
1½	tsp. vanilla
	Fresh fruit, such as blueberries or strawberries (optional)

1 In a heavy medium saucepan use a wooden spoon to stir together egg yolks, milk, and sugar.

2 Cook and stir continuously with a wooden spoon over medium heat until mixture just coats the back of a clean metal spoon. Remove pan from heat. Stir in vanilla.

3 Quickly cool the custard by placing the saucepan in a large bowl of ice water for 1 to 2 minutes, stirring constantly.

4 Pour custard mixture into a bowl. Cover the surface with plastic wrap to prevent a skin from forming. Chill at least 2 hours or until serving time. Do not stir. If desired, serve custard over fresh fruit. Makes about 2 cups (8 servings).

Nutrition Facts per ¼-cup serving:
85 cal., 4 g total fat (2 g sat. fat),
136 mg chol., 27 mg sodium, 8 g carbo.,
0 g fiber, 3 g pro.
Daily Values: 9% vit. A, 1% vit. C,
7% calcium, 2% iron.

TEST KITCHEN TIP

Stirred Custard: The Any-Occasion Treat

Invest about a dollar for ingredients, and in return you'll create a velvety delight and get the recognition you deserve as a great cook. Though slightly tricky to make, the rich, pale-yellow sauce transforms plain fruit or cake into an any-occasion treat. Preparing it will teach you the basics of working with eggs over heat, a skill that will open up a world of comforting custard-based desserts, including cream pies and old-fashioned puddings.

1. For the smoothest sauce, stir the ingredients together thoroughly before putting the pan on the stove.

2. Continuous stirring is key; a few seconds of inattention can overcook the eggs and allow lumps to form.

3. When you draw your finger down the back of a metal spoon and the custard edges hold their shape, it's ready to remove from the heat.

4. Set out a bowl of ice and water before you begin. Then you're ready to cool the mixture quickly, which will prevent curdling.

Whipped Cream

Nothing quite matches the chiffonlike texture of real whipped cream. One billowy cloud turns plain pie into a peak experience, while a single dollop moves fresh fruit from simple to sublime. And where would banana splits or hot fudge sundaes be without such indulgences? That's why it's worth digging out the mixer to whip up a batch.

Start to finish: 12 minutes

- 1 **cup light or heavy whipping cream**
- 2 **Tbsp. sugar**
- ½ **tsp. vanilla**

1 Read the carton to be sure you have pure (either light or heavy) whipping cream. Light whipping cream contains between 30 and 36 percent milk fat. Heavy whipping cream, also called heavy cream, contains not less than 36 percent milk fat. Either type will work when making whipped cream.

2 Do not use plain light cream (without the word whipping on the carton) or half-and-half—they contain less than 30 percent milk fat and will not whip.

3 You'll also need the right utensils. Choose a mixing bowl—preferably metal—that's deep enough to allow the cream to double in volume, since each cup of whipping cream yields 2 cups of whipped cream. Bowls and beaters should be perfectly clean. Impurities can affect the ability of the cream to reach desired volume.

4 Chill the mixing bowl and the beaters, rotary beater, or wire whisk about 10 minutes in the freezer. Whipping cream whips faster and to a greater volume when it's very cold.

5 In the chilled mixing bowl combine whipping cream, sugar, and vanilla. Beat on medium speed to keep the cream in the bowl, and to keep from overbeating. The cream should turn slightly foamy at first and slowly increase in volume.

6 As the cream mixture thickens, check for soft peaks and scrape the sides of the bowl with a rubber spatula. Stop beating when cream reaches soft-peak stage. At this point, the thickened cream will form peaks that curl as you lift the beaters. (Beating past this point causes the cream to stiffen and separate into butter and water.) To serve, pipe or spoon whipped cream onto your favorite dessert or dollop in coffee or hot cocoa. Makes 2 cups (8 servings).

Nutrition Facts per ¼-cup serving:
103 cal., 11 g total fat (7 g sat. fat),
41 mg chol., 11 mg sodium, 1 g carbo.,
0 g fiber, 1 g pro.
Daily Values: 13% vit. A, 1% calcium.

Chocolate Whipped Cream:

Prepare cream as directed above, except add 2 tablespoons unsweetened cocoa powder and 1 tablespoon additional sugar with the vanilla.

TEST KITCHEN TIP
Storing Cream

Most of the whipping cream you buy today is ultrapasteurized, meaning it can be stored for longer than the fresh cream of days gone by. You may have several weeks after buying it to whip it—even a few days beyond the sell-by date.

Once you whip cream, expect it to stay fluffy for an hour in the refrigerator. You may want to wait until just before dessert to prepare it.

Even though whipped cream won't hold long in the refrigerator, you can freeze it for 2 to 3 days. Spoon the whipped cream to be frozen into mounds on a baking sheet lined with waxed paper, then freeze until firm. Transfer the mounds to a freezer container. To serve, let the frozen cream stand for 5 minutes, then place it on the dessert. Or, if topping hot beverages, use mounds directly from the freezer.

Spirited Whipped Cream:

Prepare cream as directed at left, except slowly add 2 tablespoons Amaretto or other liqueur, such as coffee, hazelnut, orange, or praline, during the whipping stage.

Whipped Cream Amandine:

Prepare cream as directed at left, except add ½ teaspoon almond extract with the vanilla.

Citrus Whipped Cream:

Prepare cream as directed at left, except add ½ teaspoon grated lemon, orange, or lime peel with the vanilla.

Fruit-Filled Nachos

Follow this versatile recipe to the letter, or get creative—mix and match the combination of fresh seasonal berries and fruits you enjoy most.

Start to finish: 25 minutes

- 8   oz. fresh apricots (about 5)
- ¼   cup apricot nectar
- 2   tsp. sugar
- ½   cup sliced fresh strawberries
- ½   tsp. ground cinnamon
- 1   tsp. margarine or butter, melted
- 2   6- to 8-inch flour tortillas
- 1   cup vanilla ice cream
- ¼   cup fresh golden or red raspberries

1 Halve apricots, discarding pits. In a medium skillet cook apricots and nectar with 1 teaspoon of the sugar, uncovered, over low heat about 8 minutes or until apricots are cooked through. Stir in strawberries. Cover and set aside. Stir together the remaining 1 teaspoon sugar and the cinnamon. Set aside.

2 Brush a clean skillet with some of the melted margarine or butter. Heat over medium heat. Cook a tortilla for 1 to 1½ minutes or until lightly browned. Turn; sprinkle with half of the sugar-cinnamon mixture. Cook for 1 minute longer or until lightly brown but still pliable (not crisp). Repeat with second tortilla.

3 Place a cooked tortilla, cinnamon-side down, on a clean cutting surface. Spoon apricot mixture onto the tortilla. Top with second tortilla, cinnamon-side up. Cut into 4 wedges.

4 To serve, scoop about ¼ cup of ice cream into each of 4 dessert dishes. Place a fruit nacho in each dish. Garnish with fresh raspberries. Serve immediately. Makes 4 servings.

Nutrition Facts per serving: 339 cal., 12 g total fat (6 g sat. fat), 31 mg chol., 207 mg sodium, 55 g carbo., 7 g fiber, 6 g pro.
Daily Values: 44% vit. A, 67% vit. C, 12% calcium, 13% iron.

Angel Food Cake with Tropical Fruits

For a faster version of this luscious dessert, skip preparing the lime custard and instead serve the cake and fruit with a scoop of lime sherbet. (See the photograph on page 122.)

Prep: 20 minutes   **Chill:** 3 hours

- ⅓   cup sugar
- 1   Tbsp. cornstarch
- ¾   cup milk
- 1   egg
- 1   egg yolk
- 3   Tbsp. lime juice
- 1   Tbsp. butter
- 1   drop green food coloring
- ⅔   cup plain yogurt
- ½   of a 16-oz. purchased angel food cake or one 10-oz. frozen pound cake, thawed
- 2   small red and/or gold papayas, sliced
- 2   medium kiwi fruit, peeled and sliced
- 1   guava, cut into wedges (optional)

1 In a small saucepan combine sugar and cornstarch. Stir in milk. Cook and stir milk mixture over medium heat until thickened and bubbly.

Reduce heat. Cook and stir milk mixture for 2 minutes more. In a small mixing bowl beat the egg and egg yolk. Gradually stir about ½ cup of the hot milk mixture into the beaten egg mixture.

2 Return milk and egg mixture to saucepan. Cook and stir until nearly bubbly. Do not boil. Cook and stir mixture for 2 minutes more. Remove from heat.

3 Stir in lime juice, butter, and food coloring. Cover surface of custard with plastic wrap. Cool completely in the refrigerator. Fold the custard into yogurt. Cover and chill.

4 To serve, cut angel food cake or pound cake into 8 slices. Place one slice on each of eight dessert plates. Spoon lime custard onto each piece. Top with sliced fruits. Serve with guava wedges, if desired. Makes 8 servings.

Nutrition Facts per serving: 188 cal., 4 g total fat (2 g sat. fat), 113 mg chol., 266 mg sodium, 34 g carbo., 2 g fiber, 5 g pro.
Daily Values: 7% vit. A, 87% vit. C, 12% calcium, 3% iron.

CLEVER COOK

Spice Bottle Shaker

Recycle empty spice bottles (the kind that have holes in the caps). Clean and dry well. Refill them with flour for dusting cake pans, powdered sugar for decorating desserts, or a mixture of cinnamon and sugar for making cinnamon toast.

Maxine Salomonsky
Virginia Beach, Virginia

june

IN THIS CHAPTER

30-minute recipes indicated in COLOR.
Low-fat and no-fat recipes indicated
with a ♥.
Photographs indicated in italics.
*Bonus recipe

Sweet Zinfandel Granita

For an alcohol-free version, combine 4 cups chilled white grape juice and ⅓ cup sugar. Pour into a 2-quart square baking dish. Cover and freeze at least 8 hours. Remove from freezer for 15 minutes. Use a metal spoon to scrape granita into bowls.

Prep: 5 minutes **Freeze:** 6 hours

    1   cup water
    ½   cup sugar
    1   750 ml bottle white Zinfandel
        wine (about 3¼ cups), chilled
    2   cups assorted fresh whole berries,
        sliced nectarines, and halved
        kumquats

1 In a small bowl stir together water and sugar until sugar dissolves.

2 In a 2-quart square baking dish combine sugar mixture and wine. Cover and freeze about 6 hours or until firm, stirring once or twice.

3 Use a large metal spoon or ice cream scoop to scrape mixture into small bowls. To serve, place each bowl into a slightly larger bowl. Surround small bowl with fresh fruit. Makes about 8 to 10 servings.

Nutrition Facts per serving: 134 cal., 0 g total fat, 0 mg chol., 6 mg sodium, 19 g carbo., 2 g fiber, 0 g pro. Daily Values: 1% vit. A, 11% vit. C, 1% calcium, 2% iron.

EDITOR'S TIP

Kiwi Facts

● Kiwis are an excellent source of vitamin C, fiber, and cancer-fighting phytochemicals. They also offer good amounts of vitamin E, calcium, magnesium, iron, and potassium.

● Buy firm (but not hard) fruits that have a sweet, floral aroma. Size doesn't matter—small kiwis taste the same as the larger fruit.

● Ripe kiwis will keep for several days at room temperature. Unripe kiwi fruit can be held for 2 weeks or more in the fruit or vegetable drawer of your refrigerator. Once fully ripe, use kiwis within a few days or they will wrinkle.

30 MINUTE, LOW FAT
Fuzzy Kiwi Lemonade

One of America's most popular fruits, the kiwi fruit has a taste that combines strawberry, pineapple, and nectarine. When used in the favorite summertime drink, lemonade, each sip bursts with fruit flavor.

Start to finish: 20 minutes

    6   kiwi fruit
    1   cup sugar
    ¾   cup lemon juice
    1   liter carbonated water, chilled
    1   recipe Kiwi Ice Cubes (see above
        right) (optional)

1 Peel kiwi. Place peeled fruit in a blender container. Cover and puree until smooth. Strain mixture through a fine-mesh wire strainer placed over a bowl. Discard seeds (some may remain).

2 In a large pitcher combine sugar and lemon juice. Stir until sugar is dissolved. Stir in strained kiwi. Cover and chill.

3 Slowly add the chilled carbonated water just before serving. Stir. Fill six tall glasses with Kiwi Ice Cubes, if desired, or with plain ice cubes. Pour the kiwi lemonade over the ice. Makes 6 servings.

Kiwi Ice Cubes
Peel 4 additional kiwi fruit; cut into 8 pieces each. Fill two ice-cube trays with cut fruit. Add cold water; freeze.

Nutrition Facts per serving: 196 cal., 1 g total fat (0 g sat. fat), 0 mg chol., 36 mg sodium, 48 g carbo., 0 g fiber, 1 g pro. Daily Values: 167% vit. C, 3% calcium, 3% iron.

Gold Kiwi Starter

Green kiwi works in this skewered appetizer, but go for the gold if you find it. This newly introduced variety is available in markets during the summer. For information about kiwi fruit, or to find the location of the nearest retailer, check out www.zespri.com or call 604/435-1386.

Start to finish: 20 minutes

    4   gold or green kiwi fruit
    4   oz. semi-soft goat cheese
        (log form)

Fresh basil

2 Tbsp. rice vinegar

1 Tbsp. olive oil

¼ tsp. coarsely ground pepper

⅛ tsp. salt

1 Tbsp. toasted pistachio nuts or walnuts,* chopped

1 Peel and cut the kiwi fruit into ½-inch slices. Cut the goat cheese into ¼-inch slices. On short metal skewers alternately thread slices of kiwi fruit, goat cheese, and basil.

2 For dressing, in a screw-top jar combine the rice vinegar, olive oil, pepper, and salt. Cover and shake until mixed.

3 To serve, arrange skewers on a platter; drizzle dressing over skewers. Sprinkle with toasted nuts. Makes 4 appetizer servings.

*Note: To toast nuts, place nuts in a small ungreased skillet. Cook over medium-low heat, stirring or shaking skillet often, for 7 to 10 minutes or until nuts are golden brown. Watch carefully to avoid overbrowning.

Nutrition Facts per serving: 195 cal., 13 g total fat (6 g sat. fat), 22 mg chol., 223 mg sodium, 13 g carbo., 3 g fiber, 7 g pro.
Daily Values: 6% vit. A, 125% vit. C, 11% calcium, 6% iron.

TEST KITCHEN TIP

How to Peel a Kiwi

The skin of the kiwi fruit is edible, but many people prefer to peel the fruit first. To peel a kiwi, first cut the ends off the fruit with a sharp knife. Run a teaspoon—bowl facing inward—under the skin and halfway down the length of the fruit to separate it (below). Turn fruit over and repeat from other end. Gently push the fruit through the loosened skin. Or, you can slice the kiwi fruit in half and scoop the pulp out with a teaspoon.

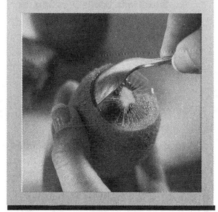

LOW FAT

Crab and Vegetable Roll-Ups

This sort-of sushi without the rice and seaweed uses zucchini ribbons to wrap up a crab-filled package of flavor. Creating an assembly line with the ingredients lets you wrap and roll with ease. (See the photograph on page 124.)

Start to finish: 40 minutes

2 medium zucchini or yellow summer squash

½ cup cooked lump crabmeat (cleaned)

1 Tbsp. mayonnaise or salad dressing

1 tsp. wasabi paste

⅛ tsp. salt

½ of a medium avocado, seeded and peeled

2 Tbsp. coarsely shredded carrot

16 small fresh basil leaves

1 Trim ends of zucchini. Using a sharp vegetable peeler, slice zucchini lengthwise into wide, flat "ribbons." Discard first and last slices, and the seedy portion in the middle. (You will need 32 ribbons.) Set ribbons aside.

2 Drain crabmeat well in a colander, pressing with the back of a spoon to remove most of the liquid. Pat dry with paper towels.

3 In a small bowl stir together the drained crabmeat, mayonnaise or salad dressing, wasabi paste, and salt. Cut the avocado half into thin strips.

4 For each roll-up, on a clean work surface, place a zucchini ribbon on top of another. Place 1 slightly rounded teaspoon of crab mixture at one end of a doubled zucchini ribbon. Top with avocado strips, a few shreds of carrot, and a basil leaf. Roll up; secure with toothpick.

5 To serve, arrange roll-ups on a platter. Serve immediately or cover and chill up to 30 minutes. Makes 16 appetizer roll-ups.

Nutrition Facts per roll-up: 23 cal., 2 g total fat (0 g sat. fat), 4 mg chol., 37 mg sodium, 1 g carbo., 1 g fiber, 1 g pro.
Daily Values: 4% vit. A, 5% vit. C, 1% calcium, 1% iron.

Cheesy Spinach Quesadillas

Oozing with cheese and studded with spinach, dried tomatoes, and nuts, these appetizer triangles are best served just out of the oven. (See the photograph on page 122.)

Prep: 15 minutes **Bake:** 6 minutes

- ½ of a 10-oz. pkg. frozen chopped spinach, thawed and well drained
- ¼ cup purchased basil pesto
- 2 Tbsp. seasoned fine dry bread crumbs
- 2 tsp. snipped, drained oil-pack dried tomatoes
- 1½ cups shredded Colby and Monterey Jack cheese or cheddar cheese (6 oz.)
- ⅓ cup finely chopped toasted pine nuts or pecans
- 6 8-inch flour tortillas

1 Preheat oven to 450°. In a small bowl stir together spinach, pesto, bread crumbs, dried tomatoes, 1 cup of the Colby and Monterey Jack or cheddar cheese, and half of the pine nuts or pecans.

2 Spread mixture evenly over three of the tortillas. Top each with a remaining tortilla. Place on a very large baking sheet. Sprinkle remaining cheese and pine nuts or pecans on top of tortillas. Bake for 6 to 8 minutes or until tortillas are lightly browned and crisp. Cut each into 8 wedges. Makes 24 appetizers.

Nutrition Facts per appetizer: 78 cal., 5 g total fat (2 g sat. fat), 8 mg chol., 109 mg sodium, 5 g carbo., 0 g fiber, 3 g pro.
Daily Values: 7% vit. A, 2% vit. C, 8% calcium, 3% iron.

Dad's Best-Dressed Pasta Salad

Here's a salad designed for mom and the kids to make especially for dad.

Start to finish: 30 minutes

- 12 oz. packaged dried wagon wheel, bow tie, or other specialty-shaped pasta
- 1 recipe Creamy French Dressing, Buttermilk Garlic Dressing, or Italian Dressing (see right and page 113)
- 6 small green onions
- 1 15½-oz. can red kidney beans, rinsed and drained
- 2 large stalks celery, thinly sliced (about 1 cup)
- 1 medium red sweet pepper, seeded and cut into ½-inch cubes

1 Cook pasta according to package directions. Meanwhile, prepare the dressing of your choice; set aside. Drain pasta in a colander and rinse under cold water until cool; set aside.

2 Using kitchen scissors, snip off the root ends from green onions and about 2 inches of green tops; leave some of the green tops attached. Snip trimmed onions crosswise into thin slices. (Or, an adult can slice trimmed green onions using a sharp knife.)

3 In a large bowl gently toss together cooked pasta, green onions, kidney beans, celery, and red pepper. Add dressing and toss until pasta is well coated. Serves 8 to 10.

Nutrition Facts per serving: 349 cal., 15 g total fat (2 g sat. fat), 4 mg chol., 301 mg sodium, 46 g carbo., 5 g fiber, 10 g pro.
Daily Values: 21% vit. A, 51% vit. C, 4% calcium, 13% iron.

Creamy French Dressing

Start to finish: 10 minutes

- ⅓ cup salad oil
- ¼ cup catsup
- ¼ cup mayonnaise or salad dressing
- 3 Tbsp. cider vinegar
- 1 tsp. sugar
- ½ tsp. paprika
- ¼ tsp. salt
- ¼ tsp. pepper

1 Place ingredients in a plastic container with a tight-fitting lid. Cover; shake until smooth. Pour over Dad's Best-Dressed Pasta Salad (see recipe, left) or serve over your favorite mixed green salad. Store any leftover dressing in the refrigerator up to 2 weeks. Shake before serving. Makes 1 cup.

Buttermilk Garlic Dressing

Start to finish: 10 minutes

- ½ cup mayonnaise or salad dressing
- ½ cup buttermilk
- 1 Tbsp. cider vinegar
- 1 Tbsp. snipped parsley
- 1 Tbsp. snipped green onions with tops
- 1 small clove garlic, minced
- 1 tsp. Dijon-style mustard
- ½ tsp. onion powder

1 Place mayonnaise and buttermilk in a plastic container with a tight-fitting lid. Cover and shake until smooth. Add vinegar, parsley, green onions, garlic, Dijon-style mustard, onion powder, and ¼ teaspoon *salt*. Cover and shake until well combined.

Pour over Dad's Best-Dressed Pasta Salad (see recipe, page 112) or serve over your favorite mixed green salad. Store any leftover dressing in the refrigerator up to 2 weeks. Shake before serving. Makes 1 cup.

(see recipe, page 112)

30 MINUTE

Italian Dressing

Start to finish: 10 minutes

½ cup salad oil
⅓ cup cider vinegar
3 cloves garlic, crushed
1 Tbsp. snipped fresh basil and
   1 Tbsp. snipped fresh oregano
   or 2 tsp. dried Italian
   seasoning, crushed
1 tsp. sugar

1 Place salad oil, vinegar, garlic, basil and oregano, sugar, ½ teaspoon *salt*, and ¼ teaspoon *pepper* in a plastic container with a tight-fitting lid. Cover and shake until smooth. Pour over Dad's Best-Dressed Pasta Salad (see recipe, page 112) or serve over your favorite mixed green salad. Store any leftover dressing in the refrigerator up to 2 weeks. Shake before serving. Makes 1 cup.

(see recipe, page 112)

NO FAT

Sweet & Sour Radishes

In place of the fresh dill, you may substitute ½ teaspoon dried dill.

Prep: 15 minutes **Chill:** 6 hours

⅓ cup vinegar
3 Tbsp. water
4 tsp. sugar
1 Tbsp. snipped fresh dillweed
3 cloves garlic, minced
¼ tsp. salt
1 small fresh red chili pepper,
   such as serrano or Thai
   chili pepper, seeded and sliced
   (optional)*
2 cups whole small or halved
   radishes, such as red, icicle,
   Easter egg, and/or French
   breakfast

1 In a glass measure or small mixing bowl combine vinegar, water, sugar, dill, garlic, salt, and, if desired, chili pepper. Place radishes in a self-sealing plastic bag; pour vinegar mixture over vegetables; seal bag, turning to coat. Chill 6 to 8 hours before serving, turning bag occasionally.

2 To serve, transfer radish mixture to a serving bowl. Serve with a slotted spoon. Makes 6 servings.

*Note: Hot peppers contain oils that can burn eyes, lips, and sensitive skin. Wear plastic gloves while preparing them and be sure to wash your hands thoroughly afterward.

Nutrition Facts per serving: 24 cal., 0 g total fat (0 g sat. fat), 0 mg chol., 107 mg sodium, 6 g carbo., 1 g fiber, 0 g pro.
Daily Values: 6% vit. A, 38% vit. C, 1% calcium, 2% iron.

EDITOR'S TIP

Salad Day Tips For Mom

Say, mom, when you plan to gather the kids in the kitchen to prepare the Dad's Best-Dressed Pasta Salad (see recipe, page 112), here are a few hints to help things run smoothly:

● **Get a head start.** Cook, drain, and rinse the pasta, and cut up the celery and sweet pepper before getting your kids into the kitchen. Lightly toss cooked pasta with a little oil to keep it from sticking.

● **Watch out for slippery fingers.** Make sure little hands are completely dry before snipping the onions or shaking the dressing.

● **Keep a clean scene.** If one of the ingredients spills or drops on the floor, even if it's just a little, stop and wipe up the spill immediately.

● **Share silly Dad stories:** Tell your children funny stories about things their dad did when they were just babies.

● **Play the kitchen math quiz:** For example, when does 1+1+1=1? Simple. When you talk teaspoons. Three teaspoons equal one tablespoon. Or, when does 4x1=¼? When you talk tablespoons. Four tablespoons equal one-quarter cup. To prove it, carefully measure four tablespoons of water into a measuring cup and show how they add up to ¼ cup. Or, count the pieces of green pepper as you add them to the salad. When little ones can't count any higher, toss in the remaining pieces.

● **Stage a tasting** with a red and a green sweet pepper. Chat about how the red pepper started out green. Explain that when you leave green peppers on the vine, they change to red and become sweeter as they ripen. Then have the children shut their eyes, and don't let them see what color the pepper is. Can they tell which it is just by tasting?

Cabbage Makes the Cut

The trick to a great, freshly made coleslaw—the kind that snaps with bright flavor—is all in the wrist. Using the right technique to cut and core a round, dense cabbage into long, thin shreds will bring out the best of the flavor. Follow the three steps shown here to keep your coleslaw a cut above the rest.

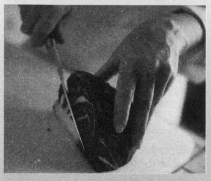

1. Remove and discard any wilted or brown-edged leaves from the outside of the cabbage. Place the cutting board on a damp towel on a level work surface to keep the board from slipping. Using a large, sharp knife, carefully quarter the cabbage lengthwise. Place a flat side of the cabbage against the cutting board. Hold firmly. With the tip of the knife at the point of the core, cut away the core and discard (above).

2. To keep red cabbage from staining coleslaw blue, place the cabbage in a large colander (above). Rinse cabbage, before and after cutting into shreds, under cold running water until the water runs clear.

3. Keeping a flat side of the cabbage quarter to the cutting board (above), use the whole length of the knife blade to cut cabbage into long, lengthwise shreds. Cut the shreds as thinly as possible (about ⅛ of an inch or less).

Coleslaw with A Twist

The lemon and dill highlights make this crunchy salad perfect to pair with grilled fish or seafood kabobs.

Prep: 20 minutes **Chill:** 2 hours

- 1 cup finely cut red cabbage (¼ of a 1-lb. head)
- 6 cups finely cut green cabbage (1¼-lb. head)
- ½ cup shredded carrot (1 medium)
- ½ small red sweet pepper, cut into small matchsticks
- ⅓ cup light mayonnaise or salad dressing
- 2 Tbsp. lime juice or lemon juice
- 1 Tbsp. snipped fresh dillweed or 1 tsp. dried dillweed (optional)
- 1 tsp. sugar
- ¼ tsp. salt
- ¼ tsp. black pepper

1 Rinse the cut red cabbage; pat dry. In a large bowl combine cut red cabbage, green cabbage, carrot, and red sweet pepper.

2 For dressing, in a small bowl stir together the mayonnaise or salad dressing, lime juice or lemon juice, dillweed (if desired), sugar, salt, and black pepper.

3 Pour dressing over cabbage mixture. Toss to coat. (Mixture may appear dry at first, but will moisten as it chills.) Cover and chill for 2 to 24 hours. Stir before serving. Makes 8 to 10 servings.

Nutrition Facts per serving: 57 cal., 4 g total fat (1 g sat. fat), 3 mg chol., 146 mg sodium, 7 g carbo., 2 g fiber, 1 g pro.
Daily Values: 49% vit. A, 63% vit. C, 3% calcium, 2% iron.

30 MINUTE

Three-Bread Salad

Try this Italian classic with romaine lettuce and fun toppers, such as crumbled bacon or dry-roasted sunflower seeds. (See the photograph on page 123.)

Start to finish: 25 minutes

- 1 recipe Dried Yellow Tomato Vinaigrette (see page 115)
- 6 cups mixed salad greens

- 2 1-inch-thick slices crusty sourdough bread, cut into irregular pieces
- 1 8-inch whole wheat pita bread round, cut into 12 wedges
- 2 slices pumpernickel bread, torn into pieces
- 1 small sweet onion, very thinly sliced and separated into rings
- 1 cup yellow and/or red pear-shaped tomatoes or cherry tomatoes
- 2 oz. shaved dry Monterey Jack cheese or other hard grating cheese

1 Prepare Dried Yellow Tomato Vinaigrette. Transfer to a storage container. Cover and chill.

2 In a large salad bowl combine mixed greens, sourdough pieces, pita wedges, torn pumpernickel, sliced onion, and tomatoes. Drizzle with the Dried Yellow Tomato Vinaigrette; toss gently to coat. Top with cheese. Makes 6 side-dish servings.

Dried Yellow Tomato Vinaigrette

1. Place ¼ cup snipped dried yellow or red tomatoes (not oil-packed) in a small bowl. Add 1 cup boiling water; cover and let stand 10 minutes. Drain tomatoes, reserving ½ cup of the liquid.

2. In a blender container or food processor bowl combine tomatoes and their reserved liquid; ¼ cup red wine vinegar; 1 tablespoon Dijon-style mustard; 2 teaspoons snipped fresh thyme or ½ teaspoon dried thyme, crushed; ¼ teaspoon *salt*; and ⅛ teaspoon coarsely ground *pepper*.

3. Cover and blend or process until nearly smooth. Gradually add ⅓ cup olive oil, processing until combined and slightly thickened.

Nutrition Facts per serving: 269 cal., 16 g total fat (4 g sat. fat), 7 mg chol., 599 mg sodium, 24 g carbo., 3 g fiber, 9 g pro.
Daily Values: 14% vit. A, 28% vit. C, 16% calcium, 11% iron.

PRIZE WINNER

Pasta with Prosciutto

Margaret N. Tanimoto
Honolulu, Hawaii
$200—Great Pasta Plates

Start to finish: 20 minutes

- 6 oz. dried angel hair pasta
- 4 cloves garlic, minced
- 2 Tbsp. olive oil
- 1 Tbsp. margarine or butter
- 8 oz. fresh mushrooms, sliced (3 cups)
- 1 medium red onion, thinly sliced
- 3 oz. thinly sliced prosciutto, cut into ¾-inch strips
- 3 cups loosely packed torn fresh spinach (about 4 oz.)
- ⅓ cup finely shredded Parmesan cheese
- ¼ tsp. salt
- ¼ tsp. freshly ground pepper Parmesan cheese curls or finely shredded Parmesan cheese (optional)

1 Cook the pasta according to package directions; drain. Cover and keep warm.

2 Meanwhile, in a 12-inch skillet cook garlic in hot olive oil and margarine or butter for 30 seconds. Add mushroom slices, red onion slices, and prosciutto strips. Cook over medium-high heat for 4 to 5 minutes or until mushrooms and red onion are tender, stirring occasionally.

3 Add spinach to skillet; remove from heat. Add cooked pasta, the ⅓ cup shredded Parmesan cheese, salt, and pepper. Toss well.

4 To serve, turn pasta mixture out onto four serving plates or a large platter. If desired, sprinkle with additional Parmesan cheese before serving. Makes 4 main-dish servings.

Nutrition Facts per serving: 382 cal., 19 g total fat (5 g sat. fat), 17 mg chol., 676 mg sodium, 37 g carbo., 2 g fiber, 17 g pro.
Daily Values: 21% vit. A, 14% vit. C, 13% calcium, 13% iron.

TEST KITCHEN TIP

Cabbage Know-How

To make a perfect coleslaw, use these simple hints:

● Start with chilled cabbages. Chilled cabbages stay crisp and the strands separate more easily.

● Use only a stainless-steel knife, or chemicals naturally occurring in the cabbage will react with the metal and turn both the knife and the cabbage black.

● Try different varieties of cabbages for your coleslaw. Savoy and Napa cabbages are milder in flavor than green cabbage, and closer to lettuce in texture. These cabbages have softer cores than green and red cabbages, and should only be chilled about 2 hours after preparing or they'll begin to lose their crispness.

- Ham and Pear Melt (see below)

- Salad of torn fresh spinach, tomato wedges, sliced fresh mushrooms, and a vinaigrette

- Shortbread cookies and fruit sorbet

- Sparkling water with strawberries and lemon wedges

PRIZE WINNER

Ham and Pear Melt

Karna Hess
Fortuna, California
$200—Wrap It Up

Start to finish: 10 minutes

- 2   7- to 8-inch whole wheat flour tortillas
- 6   oz. thinly sliced ham (deli sliced)
- 2   small ripe pears, cored and thinly sliced
- 1   cup finely shredded Swiss, Colby-Monterey Jack, or mozzarella cheese (4 oz.)

1 Place tortillas on a cookie sheet or broiler pan. Broil tortillas 4 to 5 inches from the heat until just warm. Layer half of the ham, the sliced pears, and the shredded cheese on each warm tortilla. Broil layered tortillas about 2 minutes or until cheese is melted and bubbly. Fold tortillas in half or roll up into a spiral. Cut each in half. Makes 2 main-dish servings.

Nutrition Facts per serving: 474 cal., 25 g total fat (13 g sat. fat), 100 mg chol., 1,446 mg sodium, 29 g carbo., 11 g fiber, 33 g pro.
Daily Values: 14% vit. A, 6% vit. C, 57% calcium, 6% iron.

Cool Antipasto Kabobs

Here's a no-cook kabob with lots of crunch and bursts of flavor. Follow the recipe or put out a batch of similar ingredients and let everyone make a skewer of favorites to nibble. (See the photograph on page 117.)

Prep: 30 minutes **Marinate:** 1 hour

- 2   cups assorted vegetables, such as baby carrots with tops; radishes; 1-inch red sweet pepper squares, halved; or small pattypan squash
- 4   oz. firm cheese, such as peppercorn cheese, smoked gouda, or kasseri, cut into ½-inch chunks
- 4   oz. summer sausage, cut into ¾-inch slices and quartered
- 2   Tbsp. refrigerated basil pesto
- 1   Tbsp. white wine vinegar
- 1   cup lightly packed fresh spinach leaves

1 Place vegetables, cheese, and summer sausage in a plastic bag set in a bowl. For the marinade, stir together pesto sauce and vinegar. Pour over vegetable mixture in plastic bag. Close bag. Marinate in the refrigerator for 1 to 24 hours.

2 Remove vegetable mixture from refrigerator. Alternately thread vegetables, cheese, summer sausage, and spinach (accordion-pleat style) onto eight 10-inch bamboo skewers. Makes 4 main-dish servings.

Nutrition Facts per serving: 242 cal., 19 g total fat (9 g sat. fat), 39 mg chol., 733 mg sodium, 7 g carbo., 2 g fiber, 11 g pro.
Daily Values: 115% vit. A, 60% vit. C, 22% calcium, 5% iron.

30 MINUTE

Tri-Tip Salad Plate

For a snazzier mushroom relish, use an assortment of different mushroom varieties. (See the photograph on page 117.)

Start to finish: 20 minutes

- 1   cup finely chopped fresh button mushrooms
- ¼   cup minced green onions
- 2   Tbsp. white wine Worcestershire sauce
- 1   Tbsp. hazelnut oil, walnut oil, or salad oil
- ¼   tsp. freshly ground white pepper
- 3   cups beet greens or other leafy greens, rinsed, drained, and patted dry
- 1   lb. packaged cooked beef tri-tip roast, thinly sliced
- 4   red and/or yellow Roma, cherry, or teardrop tomatoes, cut up
- ½   of a small red onion, thinly sliced
      Snipped fresh rosemary (optional)
- 12 crisp breadsticks (optional)

1 In a bowl stir together mushrooms, green onions, Worcestershire sauce, oil, and pepper. If desired, cover and chill 2 to 24 hours.

2 To serve arrange greens on chilled plates along with beef, tomatoes, and red onion. Spoon mushroom relish onto plates. If desired, sprinkle tomatoes and onion with rosemary and serve with breadsticks. Serves 4.

Nutrition Facts per serving: 296 cal., 19 g total fat (6 g sat. fat), 80 mg chol., 377 mg sodium, 6 g carbo., 2 g fiber, 28 g pro.
Daily Values: 37% vit. A, 23% vit. C, 5% calcium, 21% iron.

Left: Cool Antipasto Kabobs
(page 116)
Below: Tri-Tip Salad Plate
(page 116)

Top: Avocado Rings with Radish "Fireworks" (page 96)
Above: Dilled Celery Root Spread (page 95)
Right: Lamb Chops and Lima Beans (page 103)

Top: Pulled Chicken-Peanut Salad (page 102)

Above left: Piquant Pork Salad (page 104)

Above Right: Salmon Pinwheel Salad (page 99)

Page 120: Sugar Pea and Jerusalem Artichoke Sauté (page 95)

Top left: Cheesy Spinach Quesadillas (page 112)
Top right: Fizzy Mint-Chocolate Soda (page 133)
Above left: Smoked Salmon Club (page 129)
Above Right: Angel Food Cake with Tropical Fruits (page 108)
Page 123: Three-Bread Salad (page 114)

Top: Ginger-Lime Chicken Salad (page 125)
Above: Cobb Salad Wraps (page 125)
Right: Crab and Vegetable Roll-Ups (page 111)

Ginger-Lime Chicken Salad

Purchased roasted chicken saves time and keeps your kitchen cool. Use it as the basis for a breezy chicken salad with a taste of the tropics. (See the photograph on page 124.)

Start to finish: 25 minutes

- ½ cup light mayonnaise dressing or salad dressing
- 2 Tbsp. lime juice
- 1 Tbsp. chopped red onion
- 2 tsp. grated fresh ginger
- 1 small clove garlic, minced
- 2 cups coarsely chopped roasted chicken breast
- 2 stalks celery, cut into thin strips (1 cup)
- ¼ cup salted pumpkin seeds

1 In a blender container combine mayonnaise dressing or salad dressing, lime juice, red onion, ginger, and garlic. Cover container and blend until smooth.

2 In a medium bowl combine mayonnaise mixture and chicken. Toss to coat chicken. Serve immediately. Or, cover and chill up to 4 hours.

3 To serve, divide celery strips among four salad bowls. Top with the chicken mixture. Sprinkle chicken with the salted pumpkin seeds. Makes 4 main-dish servings.

Nutrition Facts per serving: 270 cal., 17 g total fat (3 g sat. fat), 70 mg chol., 251 mg sodium, 7 g carbo., 1 g fiber, 24 g pro.
Daily Values: 1% vit. A, 7% vit. C, 2% calcium, 9% iron.

Cobb Salad Wraps

Megan Murphy
Austin, Texas
$400—Wrap It Up
(See the photograph on page 124.)

Start to finish: 10 minutes

- ½ cup bottled blue cheese salad dressing
- 4 8- to 10-inch whole wheat or Southwest-flavored flour tortillas
- 4 romaine lettuce leaves, ribs removed
- 4 strips bacon, crisp-cooked and drained
- 2 green onions, cut into thin strips
- 2 medium plum tomatoes, seeded and cut into thin wedges
- ½ cup shredded mozzarella cheese (2 oz.)
- 8 oz. cooked chicken, shredded (1½ cups)

1 Spread salad dressing over one side of each tortilla. Top each with the lettuce leaves, bacon strips, green onions, tomato wedges, mozzarella cheese, and shredded chicken. Fold in sides and roll up tightly. Serve immediately. Makes 4 servings.

To Make-Ahead:

Prepare wraps as directed. Wrap in plastic wrap and chill up to 4 hours.

Nutrition Facts per serving: 404 cal., 26 g total fat (7 g sat. fat), 69 mg chol., 734 mg sodium, 17 g carbo., 10 g fiber, 26 g pro.
Daily Values: 11% vit. A, 18% vit. C, 16% calcium, 7% iron.

Dried Tomato and Basil Chicken Wraps

Start to finish: 20 minutes

- ½ of a 3-oz. pkg. dried tomatoes (not oil-packed) (about ¾ cup)
- 3 cups shredded roasted or grilled chicken (about 1 pound)
- 1 cup shredded mozzarella or Monterey Jack cheese (4 oz.)
- ½ cup chopped pecans, toasted
- ⅓ cup bottled creamy Italian or ranch salad dressing
- 6 10-inch dried tomato, spinach, and/or plain flour tortillas*
- 1 cup large fresh basil leaves

1 Soak dried tomatoes in hot water to cover for 10 minutes. Drain and chop tomatoes.

2 In a large bowl combine the chopped dried tomatoes, chicken, mozzarella or Monterey Jack cheese, pecans, and salad dressing.

3 Line each tortilla with some of the basil leaves. Divide chicken mixture evenly among the tortillas. Fold in sides and roll up tightly; cut each diagonally in half to serve. Makes 6 servings.

*Note: If tortillas do not roll up easily, place the stack between layers of microwave-safe white paper towels and heat in microwave oven for 30 to 60 seconds on 100% power (high).

Nutrition Facts per serving: 449 cal., 24 g total fat (6 g sat. fat), 73 mg chol., 701 mg sodium, 29 g carbo., 3 g fiber, 30 g pro.
Daily Values: 8% vit. A, 7% vit. C, 20% calcium, 19% iron.

Southwest Chicken Wraps

Save time by not having to cook your own chicken. Use a great convenience product—thawed, frozen cooked chicken strips.

Prep: 15 minutes   **Bake:** 25 minutes

    1   3-oz. pkg. cream cheese,
          softened
   ¼   cup snipped dried tomatoes
    1   Tbsp. snipped fresh cilantro
    6   7- to 8-inch flour tortillas
    1   4-oz. can whole green chili
          peppers, drained
  1½   cups cooked chicken strips
   ½   cup shredded Monterey Jack
          cheese (2 ounces)
        Bottled salsa

1 Preheat oven to 350°. In a small bowl stir together the cream cheese, dried tomatoes, and cilantro. Spread over tortillas. Cut chilies lengthwise into 6 strips; place a strip on top of cream cheese mixture. Top with chicken and cheese. Roll up tortillas over filling.

2 Place wraps in a 3-quart rectangular baking dish. Cover and bake for 25 to 30 minutes or until heated through. Serve with salsa. Makes 6 servings.

Nutrition Facts per serving: 252 cal., 13 g total fat (6 g sat. fat), 55 mg chol., 377 mg sodium, 17 g carbo., 1 g fiber, 16 g pro.
Daily Values: 10% vit. A, 14% vit. C, 15% calcium, 11% iron.

Chicken Cordon Bleu Wraps

An all-time favorite gets revisited. This time the fixin's for chicken *cordon bleu* get all wrapped up in tortillas.

Prep: 20 minutes   **Bake:** 12 minutes

    6   8-inch flour tortillas
    1   cup sliced fresh mushrooms
    2   Tbsp. chopped shallots
   ½   tsp. dried rosemary, crushed
    1   Tbsp. margarine or butter
    1   6-oz. pkg. sliced cooked
          chicken breast
    3   oz. thinly sliced prosciutto or
          cooked smoked ham
    4   oz. Swiss or Gruyère cheese, cut
          into 6 sticks
    1   Tbsp. margarine or butter, melted
   ⅓   cup dairy sour cream
    2   Tbsp. milk
    1   Tbsp. snipped fresh chives
    1   Tbsp. Dijon-style mustard

1 Preheat oven to 375°. Wrap tortillas in foil and heat in the hot oven for 15 minutes.

2 Meanwhile, in a medium skillet cook mushrooms, shallots, and rosemary in 1 tablespoon margarine or butter until tender and most of the liquid is absorbed. Set aside.

3 Working with one tortilla at a time, arrange sliced chicken and proscuitto on top. Add a stick of cheese and some mushroom mixture. Fold in sides; roll up over filling. Place on a 15×10×1-inch baking pan. Brush lightly with melted margarine. Repeat with remaining tortillas.

4 Bake, uncovered, for 12 to 15 minutes or until light brown and heated through.

5 Meanwhile, in a small bowl stir together sour cream, milk, chives, and Dijon-style mustard. Use as a dipping sauce for wraps. Makes 6 servings.

Nutrition Facts per serving: 320 cal., 19 g total fat (6 g sat. fat), 46 mg chol., 508 mg sodium, 17 g carbo., 1 g fiber, 21 g pro.
Daily Values: 12% vit. A, 1% vit. C, 24% calcium, 8% iron.

<u>**LOW FAT**</u>

Crispy Chicken and Orange Finger Wraps

Baking these bundles in a hot oven turns the tortillas into crispy shells.

Prep: 30 minutes   **Bake:** 10 minutes

    2   Tbsp. chopped onion
    2   cloves garlic, minced
    1   tsp. olive oil
    3   Tbsp. dairy sour cream
    1   Tbsp. seeded and finely chopped
          fresh hot pepper (such as
          habañero, serrano,
          or jalapeño)*
    1   Tbsp. snipped fresh cilantro
    1   Tbsp. honey
    2   medium skinless, boneless
          chicken breast halves (8 oz.)
    1   Tbsp. olive oil
    6   6- to 8-inch flour tortillas
    2   medium oranges, peeled, seeded,
          and sectioned

1 For sauce, in a small skillet cook onion and garlic in 1 teaspoon hot olive oil for 3 to 4 minutes or until tender but not brown. Transfer mixture to a small bowl. Stir in sour cream, hot pepper, cilantro, and honey; set aside.

2 Preheat oven to 350°. In a medium skillet cook chicken in 1 tablespoon hot olive oil over medium heat for 10 to 12 minutes or until tender and no longer pink, turning once halfway through cooking time. Remove chicken to a cutting board and cool slightly. Cut chicken into bite-size strips.

3 Spread each tortilla with a scant 1 tablespoon of the sauce. Divide chicken strips and orange sections among tortillas. Fold in sides and roll up tortillas. Place tortillas, seam sides down, on a baking sheet. Bake about 10 minutes or until heated through. Serve immediately. Makes 6 servings.

*Note: Hot chili peppers contain oils that can burn eyes, lips, and sensitive skin. Wear plastic gloves while preparing them and be sure to wash your hands thoroughly afterward.

Nutrition Facts per serving: 196 cal., 7 g total fat (2 g sat. fat), 25 mg chol., 115 mg sodium, 21 g carbo., 1 g fiber, 11 g pro.
Daily Values: 2% vit. A, 23% vit. C, 6% calcium, 7% iron.

Cajun-Style Burritos

For a one-plate meal, top this spicy bundle with shredded lettuce and tomato, and serve with a side of hot cooked rice.

Prep: 15 minutes **Bake:** 20 minutes

 1 **cup fresh or frozen peeled, cooked crawfish tail meat or peeled, cooked small shrimp**
 1 **15-oz. can black beans, rinsed and drained**
 ¾ **cup chopped roasted red sweet peppers***

 1 **cup shredded Monterey Jack cheese with jalapeño peppers**
 2 **Tbsp. snipped fresh cilantro**
 1½ **tsp. chili powder**
 ¼ **tsp. ground cumin**
   Dash ground red pepper
 4 **10-inch flour tortillas**

1 Thaw crawfish or shrimp, if frozen.

2 Preheat oven to 350°. In a large mixing bowl stir together the crawfish or shrimp, black beans, roasted red sweet peppers, Monterey Jack cheese, cilantro, chili powder, cumin, and ground red pepper.

3 Divide mixture among the tortillas, spooning the mixture down the center of each tortilla. Fold in sides. Roll up tightly from bottom. Place on a foil-lined baking sheet. Bake, uncovered, about 20 minutes or until golden and heated through. Makes 4 servings.

*Note: You can use jarred roasted red sweet peppers, or you can roast your own. To roast your own, halve the peppers; remove and discard stems, seeds, and membranes. Cut each pepper half in half again. Place pepper, cut sides down, on a foil-lined baking sheet. Bake in a 425° oven for 20 to 25 minutes or until pepper skins are blistered and dark. Remove from oven and immediately wrap foil up around peppers. Let stand about 30 minutes to steam so the skins peel away more easily. Remove skin from peppers; discard. Use as directed in recipe.

Nutrition Facts per serving: 348 cal., 13 g total fat (6 g sat. fat), 73 mg chol., 638 mg sodium, 39 g carbo., 7 g fiber, 23 g pro.
Daily Values: 26% vit. A, 130% vit. C, 32% calcium, 20% iron.

TEST KITCHEN TIP
Storing It Smart

Improper food storage lets uninvited guests find their way into even the cleanest and best-kept kitchens. Welcome family and friends, but don't show any hospitality to insects or other pesky undesirables. Remember: An ounce of prevention is worth a pound of cure.

Here are some household strategies to effectively bar the door to insects, or evict them if the little monsters get a wing across your threshold, despite your best efforts.

● For prolonged storage of a month or more, move susceptible foods from easily attacked containers (such as paper or cardboard packages) into sealed plastic or glass containers.

● Store all packaged dry goods in a cool, dark place and away from the stove, sink, or floor.

● Keep in mind FIFO (First In, First Out): Rotate your stock to use older cereals, snacks, or other treats before opening the new ones.

● Buy staples in small quantities that you can use quickly. Once the packages have been opened, little pests love to worm their way into such foods as grains, flours, cereals, cornmeal, chocolate, nuts, dried soups, and seasonings.

● Wrap infested food in plastic; then seal it. Throw the food away in an outside trash container, or if you bought the food item recently, return it for a refund.

● Inspect other products in your cupboard for evidence of pests; seal infested food in plastic and discard if necessary.

● Empty and clean pantry and cupboard shelves with a vacuum cleaner (especially in cracks and corners). Empty or throw away the vacuum cleaner bag to prevent reinfestation.

● Clean cupboards with warm, sudsy water or equal parts vinegar and water, and let dry.

● Never use insect sprays on, or even near, your family's food.

Picking Pockets

Pita is a 2,000-year-old staple made new. This Middle Eastern bread with a pocket is the darling of American fast-food restaurants everywhere. And no wonder: Pita sandwiches are convenient, packing well for school or the office. The taste of pita bread adds an Old World emphasis to any filling you choose.

---

30 MINUTE

Smoked Turkey in The Corner Pocket

Although we chose tomato and red onion slices as toppers for this quick barbecue sandwich, you can use any fresh vegetables.

Start to finish: 5 minutes

- 1 large wheat or white pita bread round
- 2 to 3 oz. sliced smoked turkey
- 1 oz. sliced Havarti or Swiss cheese
- 1 Tbsp. bottled barbecue sauce
- 1 small tomato, thinly sliced
- ½ of a small red onion, thinly sliced

1 Cut pita round in half crosswise. Fill pita halves with turkey and Havarti or Swiss cheese. Drizzle barbecue sauce over turkey and cheese and top with tomato and red onion. Makes 1 sandwich.

Nutrition Facts per sandwich: 394 cal., 15 g total fat (1 g sat. fat), 64 mg chol., 1,188 mg sodium, 44 g carbo., 2 g fiber, 25 g pro.
Daily Values: 11% vit. A, 31% vit. C, 15% calcium, 5% iron.

---

30 MINUTE, LOW FAT

Chicken-in-a-Pita

Any kind of cooked chicken tastes delicious in this salad-style filled pita, but grilled chicken adds a hint of summertime flavor.

Start to finish: 5 minutes

- 1 8-inch white or wheat pita bread round
- ½ cup chopped cooked chicken
- ½ cup prepared deli coleslaw
- 1 Tbsp. snipped, drained, oil-packed dried tomatoes

1 Cut pita round in half crosswise. Fill pita halves with chicken, coleslaw, and dried tomatoes. Makes 1 sandwich.

Nutrition Facts per sandwich: 367 cal., 9 g total fat (2 g sat. fat), 76 mg chol., 420 mg sodium, 43 g carbo., 2 g fiber, 28 g pro.
Daily Values: 7% vit. A, 46% vit. C, 7% calcium, 19% iron.

---

30 MINUTE

Pronto Egg Salad Pita

Simplify lunch and pick up egg salad at your neighborhood deli. Make your trip count by purchasing enough salad for a couple of sandwiches. Date the lid of the salad with a marker, as egg salad should only be stored for up to 2 days.

Start to finish: 5 minutes

- 1 large wheat or white pita bread round
- ½ cup prepared egg salad
  Pepper to taste

- 2 Tbsp. alfalfa or radish sprouts, rinsed and drained
- 6 slices bread-and-butter pickles
- 1 radish, thinly sliced

1 Cut pita round in half crosswise. Fill pita halves with egg salad and sprinkle with pepper. Arrange sprouts, pickles, and radish on top of salad. Makes 1 sandwich.

Nutrition Facts per sandwich: 371 cal., 18 g total fat (4 g sat. fat), 221 mg chol., 644 mg sodium, 42 g carbo., 0 g fiber, 13 g pro.
Daily Values: 10% vit. A, 5% vit. C, 3% calcium, 7% iron.

---

30 MINUTE

Very Veggie Pita

You can purchase fresh marinated vegetable salad at the deli counter, or you can find jars of marinated salad in the condiment section of your supermarket. Since this sandwich has some Italian accents, be sure to select a salad that will blend in flavor.

Start to finish: 5 minutes

- 1 large white or wheat pita bread round
- ¼ cup marinated vegetable salad or marinated eggplant salad, drained (chop any large pieces)
- ¼ cup roasted red sweet peppers, cut into strips
- 1 oz. fresh mozzarella or provolone cheese, sliced
- ½ cup shredded romaine lettuce
- 2 Tbsp. snipped fresh basil
  Freshly ground black pepper

1 Cut pita round in half crosswise. Fill pita halves with marinated vegetable salad, roasted red sweet

---

peppers, mozzarella or provolone cheese, romaine, and basil. Sprinkle with pepper. Makes 1 sandwich.

Nutrition Facts per sandwich: 306 cal., 12 g total fat (4 g sat. fat), 22 mg chol., 568 mg sodium, 39 g carbo., 1 g fiber, 12 g pro.
Daily Values: 32% vit. A, 186% vit. C, 18% calcium, 16% iron.

30 MINUTE
Smoked Salmon Club

Need to save a little time? Prepare the Veggie Confetti Spread the day before. Cover tightly with plastic wrap, and refrigerate until needed. (See the photograph on page 122.)

Start to finish: 30 minutes

- 1 recipe Veggie Confetti Spread (see right)
- 12 slices sesame sourdough bread
- 2 Tbsp. dairy sour cream
- 6 to 8 oz. thinly sliced smoked salmon (lox-style)
- 1½ cups lightly packed sorrel or spinach leaves
- 1 medium cucumber, thinly bias-sliced

1 Prepare Veggie Confetti Spread. Cover and chill until needed.

2 Spread 4 slices of bread with half of the sour cream. Arrange salmon on sour cream. Add sorrel or spinach. Spread 4 more bread slices with Veggie Confetti Spread. Set on top of sorrel layer, spread-side up. Arrange cucumber on top.

3 Spread 4 more bread slices with remaining sour cream. Stack on cucumber layer, sour cream-side

---

QUICK LUNCH

- Smoked Salmon Club (see left)

- Salad of chilled cooked green beans, diced tomato, chopped shallots, and a white wine vinaigrette

- Sparkling water

- Super Mango Smoothie (see page 131) or Fizzy Mint-Chocolate Soda (see page 133)

down. Secure each sandwich with toothpicks. Cut into quarters. Makes 4 sandwiches.

Veggie Confetti Spread

In a small bowl stir together one 3-ounce package cream cheese, softened; 1 small zucchini, seeded and very finely chopped (about ⅔ cup); 1 small carrot, very finely chopped (about ⅓ cup); 1 small red sweet pepper, seeded and very finely chopped (about ⅓ cup); and 2 Tbsp. snipped fresh chives. Cover and chill.

Nutrition Facts per sandwich: 388 cal., 12 g total fat (6 g sat. fat), 36 mg chol., 1,380 mg sodium, 52 g carbo., 4 g fiber, 19 g pro.
Daily Values: 32% vit. A, 38% vit. C, 12% calcium, 21% iron.

LOW FAT
Garden Vegetable Tortilla Grabs

Tailor the flavor of these fresh vegetable wraps to your liking by using a flavored hummus. Choose from roasted garlic, cucumber and dill, roasted red pepper, and chile-lime to name a few.

Prep: 10 minutes Chill: 1 hour

- 1 7-ounce container hummus
- 4 8-inch flour tortillas*
- 2½ cups assorted vegetables (zucchini, yellow summer squash, sweet peppers, cucumbers, carrots), cut into thin strips, and/or sliced mushrooms

1 Evenly spread the hummus to within 1 inch of edges of each of the flour tortillas.

2 Divide vegetables among the tortillas and place in a row on one edge. Roll up tortilla tightly around vegetables. Wrap in clear plastic wrap and chill up to 1 hour before serving.

3 To serve, unwrap tortilla rolls. Using a sharp knife, cut rolls diagonally in half. Makes 4 servings.

*Note: If tortillas do not roll up easily, place the stack between layers of microwave-safe white paper towels and heat in microwave oven on 100% power (high) for 30 to 60 seconds.

Nutrition Facts per serving: 195 cal., 7 g total fat (1 g sat. fat), 0 mg chol., 250 mg sodium, 29 g carbo., 5 g fiber, 5 g pro.
Daily Values: 60% vit. A, 44% vit. C, 7% calcium, 12% iron.

The Best and the Brightest

Instead of squeezing, pinching, and thumping fruits and vegetables, here are better ways to choose fresh produce:

Greens. Fresh leafy greens—such as lettuces, escarole, chard, spinach, and herbs—should be crisp. Pick greens that are bright in color and have no yellowing or decomposed leaves. Check bulk salad mixes leaf by leaf. For bagged salad mixes, inspect the front and back of packages thoroughly. There may be decomposed bits that not only taste bad but indicate spoiled greens.

Summer squash. Yellow crookneck and zucchini are best when they're small and slender. They should be free of soft, discolored spots. Summer squash should be firm and tender—but not soft. Don't buy them if they bend.

Green beans and peas. Sugar snap peas and snow peas should have small, crisp pods. Green beans should be stiff and slender. Choose pods with a brilliant and uniform green color, and no mottling.

Sweet and hot peppers. All fresh peppers should be free of spots. To test a pepper's crispness, press down lightly on the stem end. It should not yield to gentle pressure.

Berries. Buy in season—that is, early spring through late summer—and look for small berries with a vivid hue. Berries should smell richly of the fruit. Look for any fuzz of mold, as berries are especially prone to it.

Peaches, plums, and nectarines. Stone fruits are best when purchased through the summer months. Their colors may be deceiving, so look for firm, unblemished flesh with little or no green. The aroma should be rich and floral.

Pears. These fruits should be plump and free of cuts or bruises. They can be bought underripe (firm). Ripen in a brown paper bag on the counter for a few days.

Melons, mangoes, and papayas. There are two ways to assess when these fruits are ripe and sweet. First, they should smell strongly of the fruit itself. Then, gently press the stem end of the fruit with your thumb. The end should yield only slightly.

---

30 MINUTE, LOW FAT

Summer Chicken and Mushroom Pasta

Light, fresh, and perfect for a summertime supper.

Start to finish: 30 minutes

- 8 oz. packaged dried penne pasta
- 12 oz. skinless, boneless chicken breast halves, cut into bite-size strips
- ¼ tsp. salt
- ⅛ tsp. freshly ground black pepper
- 2 Tbsp. olive oil or cooking oil, divided
- 3 large cloves garlic, minced
- 3 cups sliced fresh mushrooms
- 1 medium onion, thinly sliced
- ½ cup chicken broth
- ¼ cup dry white wine
- 1 cup cherry tomatoes, halved
- ¼ cup shredded basil leaves
- 3 Tbsp. snipped fresh oregano
- ¼ cup shaved Parmesan cheese
- ⅛ tsp. freshly ground black pepper

1 Cook pasta in lightly salted boiling water according to package directions. Drain and return to saucepan; keep warm.

2 Meanwhile, season chicken with salt and pepper. Heat 1 tablespoon of the oil in a large skillet over medium-high heat. Add chicken and garlic; cook and stir about 5 minutes or until chicken is tender and no longer pink. Remove from skillet; keep warm.

3 Add remaining olive oil to skillet. Cook mushrooms and onion in hot olive oil until just tender, stirring occasionally. Carefully add chicken broth and white wine. Bring to boiling; reduce heat. Boil gently, uncovered, about 2 minutes or until liquid is reduced by half. Remove skillet from heat.

4 Add cooked pasta, chicken, cherry tomatoes, basil, and oregano to mushroom mixture; toss to coat. Transfer to a serving dish; sprinkle with shaved Parmesan cheese and freshly ground pepper. Serve immediately. Makes 6 servings.

Nutrition Facts per serving: 299 cal., 8 g total fat (2 g sat. fat), 37 mg chol., 249 mg sodium, 33 g carbo., 2 g fiber, 22 g pro.
Daily Values: 5% vit. A, 14% vit. C, 7% calcium, 11% iron.

PRIZE WINNER

Ravioli and Snap Peas

Sally A. Heller
West Valley, New York
$400—Great Pasta Plates

Start to finish: 20 minutes

- 1 lb. refrigerated or frozen cheese ravioli
- 4 cups sugar snap pea pods (1 lb.)
- ½ cup chopped onion
- 1 Tbsp. margarine or butter
- 1 cup whipping cream
- ¼ cup snipped fresh dillweed
- 2 Tbsp. snipped fresh parsley
- 1 tsp. lemon-pepper seasoning
- ½ tsp. finely shredded lemon peel
- ⅓ cup finely shredded Parmesan cheese
  Additional snipped fresh dillweed (optional)

1 Cook ravioli according to package directions, adding the sugar snap peas during the last 2 minutes of cooking. Drain; transfer to a serving platter and keep warm.

2 Meanwhile, in a large skillet cook onion in hot margarine or butter over medium heat for 4 minutes. Stir in whipping cream, the ¼ cup dillweed, parsley, lemon-pepper seasoning, and lemon peel. Bring to boiling; reduce heat. Boil gently, uncovered, about 2 minutes or until slightly thickened.

3 To serve, spoon cream sauce over pasta and pea pods. Toss gently. Sprinkle Parmesan cheese over all. If desired, sprinkle with additional snipped dillweed. Makes 4 to 6 servings.

Nutrition Facts per serving: 682 cal., 42 g total fat (25 g sat. fat), 199 mg chol., 921 mg sodium, 54 g carbo., 3 g fiber, 25 g pro.
Daily Values: 56% vit. A, 42% vit. C, 48% calcium, 18% iron.

Oven-Roasted Vegetable Penne

Turn this terrific vegetarian main dish into a family-favorite chicken dish by adding some shredded grilled chicken just before serving.

Prep: 15 minutes **Roast:** 30 minutes

- **9** medium plum tomatoes, cored and sliced ¼ inch thick
- **2** medium zucchini, halved lengthwise and sliced ½ inch thick
- **2** Tbsp. olive oil
- **4** cloves garlic, minced
- **½** tsp. salt
- **¼** tsp. pepper
- **6** oz. packaged dried penne or rotini pasta

- **3** Tbsp. Italian-style tomato paste
- **½** cup finely shredded Parmesan cheese (2 oz.)
- **¼** cup slivered fresh basil

1 Preheat oven to 400°. Place tomatoes and zucchini in a 3-quart rectangular baking dish. In a small bowl combine olive oil, garlic, salt, and pepper; drizzle over tomato mixture. Roast vegetables, uncovered, for 20 minutes, stirring once.

2 Meanwhile, cook pasta according to package directions; drain. Stir pasta into the roasted vegetable mixture along with the tomato paste. Bake, uncovered, for 10 minutes more.

3 To serve, stir pasta and vegetable mixture. Divide mixture evenly among four dinner plates. Sprinkle each with Parmesan cheese and basil. Makes 4 servings.

Nutrition Facts per serving: 344 cal., 13 g total fat (4 g sat. fat), 11 mg chol., 682 mg sodium, 46 g carbo., 5 g fiber, 14 g pro.
Daily Values: 17% vit. A, 66% vit. C, 23% calcium, 16% iron.

30 MINUTE, LOW FAT

Super Mango Smoothie

Cardamom should be used at its freshest. When cardamom develops a camphor-like aroma and flavor, that means the spice is old and should be thrown away.

Start to finish: 5 minutes

- **10** cardamom pods
- **3** cups mango nectar (about two 11.5- to 12.5-oz. cans), chilled
- **2** 8-oz. cartons plain yogurt

CLEVER COOK

Strawberry Smoothies

Freeze fresh summer strawberries by putting them in a single layer on a baking pan. Once frozen, place berries in an airtight container or plastic bag and seal. The frozen berries keep well for 12 months. They're great to use in smoothies.

Chris Cummings
Sacramento, California

- **1** Tbsp. honey
- **2** tsp. ground pistachio nuts
  Fresh mango and cantaloupe or honeydew melon pieces (optional)

1 Open cardamom pods by crushing with a blunt instrument, such as a knife handle. Remove seeds; discard pods. Use a mortar and pestle to crush seeds to make ⅛ to ¼ teaspoon.

2 In a blender container combine chilled nectar, plain yogurt, honey, and cardamom. Cover and blend until smooth.

3 To serve, pour mixture into glasses. Sprinkle with ground pistachio nuts. If desired, garnish glasses with fresh mango and melon pieces threaded on skewers. Makes 5 servings.

Nutrition Facts per serving: 169 cal., 3 g total fat (2 g sat. fat), 12 mg chol., 45 mg sodium, 30 g carbo., 23 g fiber, 3 g pro.
Daily Values: 4% vit. A, 32% vit. C, 12% calcium, 1% iron.

CLEVER COOK

No-Mess Frosted Cupcakes

When wrapping frosted cake for lunches, I've found a way to ensure mess-free unwrapping. Slice the cake through the middle; then turn the frosted parts into the center. Icing won't stick to the plastic wrap anymore.

Marilyn V. Cooper
O'Fallon, Missouri

Icy Orange-Filled Cupcakes

Slice a purchased cupcake in half and insert citrusy frozen yogurt between each half.

Prep: 20 minutes **Freeze:** 3 hours

- 1 pint frozen vanilla yogurt
- ¼ cup frozen orange juice concentrate
- 6 purchased frosted yellow cupcakes

1 Line a 9-inch pie plate with foil; set aside. Soften half of the frozen yogurt in a chilled bowl by pressing it against the sides of the bowl with a wooden spoon. Spread the softened frozen yogurt in prepared pie plate. Cover with plastic wrap and freeze about 1 hour or until firm.

2 In a chilled bowl combine the remaining half of the frozen yogurt and the orange juice concentrate. Stir with a wooden spoon until frozen yogurt is softened and mixture is smooth. Remove plastic wrap from yogurt layer in pie plate. Spread orange mixture over plain vanilla yogurt layer. Cover with plastic wrap and freeze 2 hours or until yogurt layers are firm.

3 Remove paper liners from cupcakes, if present; set aside. Slice cupcakes in half horizontally. Remove plastic wrap from layered frozen yogurt. Lift the layered frozen yogurt from plate using the foil. With a 2- to 2½-inch round scalloped cutter (depending on size of cupcakes), cut out 6 rounds from layered frozen yogurt. (Return remaining frozen yogurt to freezer for another use.)

4 To serve, place a round of frozen yogurt between cupcake halves. Return to reserved paper liners, if using. Makes 6 cupcakes.

Nutrition Facts per cupcake: 232 cal., 6 g total fat (2 g sat. fat), 6 mg chol., 138 mg sodium, 41 g carbo., 0 g fiber, 3 g pro.
Daily Values: 4% vit. A, 30% vit. C, 26% calcium, 2% iron.

Kiwi Peach Cobbler

For a true golden cobbler, use golden kiwi fruit instead of the more common green fruit. The golden fruit will add a hint of mango flavor to this yummy peachy dessert.

Prep: 30 minutes **Bake:** 20 minutes

- 1 cup all-purpose flour
- 2 Tbsp. sugar
- 1 tsp. baking powder
- ½ tsp. ground cinnamon
- ¼ tsp. ground cloves
- ¼ cup butter
- ¾ cup sugar
- 1 Tbsp. cornstarch
- 2 cups sliced, peeled, pitted fresh peaches or sliced loose-pack frozen peaches, thawed
- ¼ cup water
- 3 cups kiwi fruit, peeled and sliced (about 9)
- 1 egg
- ¼ cup milk

1 Preheat oven to 400°. In a large mixing bowl stir together the flour, the 2 tablespoons sugar, baking powder, cinnamon, and cloves. Using a pastry blender, cut in butter until the mixture resembles coarse crumbs; set aside.

2 In a large saucepan combine the ¾ cup sugar and cornstarch (if using frozen peaches, add 2 extra teaspoons cornstarch). Add peaches and water. Cook and stir until thickened and bubbly. Add the sliced kiwi fruit. Heat through. Remove pan from heat; keep warm.

3 In a small bowl beat together egg and milk. Add to flour mixture, stirring just enough to moisten. Transfer hot fruit filling to an ungreased 2-quart square baking dish. Spoon topping over the filling in mounds. Bake, uncovered, about 20 minutes or until a wooden toothpick inserted in topping comes out clean. Makes 8 servings.

Nutrition Facts per serving: 291 cal., 7 g total fat (4 g sat. fat), 43 mg chol., 118 mg sodium, 53 g carbo., 1 g fiber, 4 g pro.
Daily Values: 10% vit. A, 166% vit. C, 8% calcium, 9% iron.

30 MINUTE

Thick Shake Starter

Watch those soaring summer temperatures melt away when you shake up a little action with your blender and some ice cream. You'll need a spoon to slurp these super-thick concoctions. They're loaded with stir-in surprises.

Start to finish: 5 minutes

- 1 pint vanilla or chocolate ice cream
- ¼ cup milk

1 In a blender container combine the ice cream and milk. Cover and blend until smooth. Continue as directed in the recipes below, stirring in desired ingredients. Shakes may be made 20 to 30 minutes before serving if kept in freezer. Makes 2 servings.

Go-Bananas Caramel Shake

1. Prepare the Thick Shake Starter as directed on page 132 using the vanilla ice cream. Stir in ½ cup coarsely chopped bananas, 2 tablespoons chopped pecans, 1 tablespoon chocolate-flavored syrup, and 1 tablespoon caramel ice-cream topping.

2. To serve, spoon into glasses. If desired, reserve some of the chopped bananas, chopped pecans, and chocolate-flavored syrup or caramel ice-cream topping to garnish the top of each shake.

Nutrition Facts per serving: 285 cal., 13 g total fat (5 g sat. fat), 24 mg chol., 106 mg sodium, 43 g carbo., 2 g fiber, 5 g pro.
Daily Values: 10% vit. A, 7% vit. C, 10% calcium, 7% iron.

Cherries 'n' Chocolate Shake

1. Prepare the Thick Shake Starter as directed on page 132 using the chocolate ice cream. Stir in ⅓ cup chopped, drained maraschino cherries and ¼ teaspoon almond extract.

2. To serve, spoon into glasses. Drizzle each shake with 1 tablespoon chocolate-flavored syrup.

Nutrition Facts per serving: 246 cal., 8 g total fat (5 g sat. fat), 24 mg chol., 76 mg sodium, 43 g carbo., 1 g fiber, 4 g pro.
Daily Values: 10% vit. A, 3% vit. C, 9% calcium, 7% iron.

Confetti Rainbow Shake*

1. Prepare the Thick Shake Starter as directed on page 132 using the vanilla ice cream and adding 2 to 3 drops desired food coloring with the milk. Cover and blend until smooth. Stir in 2 tablespoons candy-coated gum pieces.

2. To serve, spoon into glasses. If desired, reserve some of the candy-coated gum to top each shake.

*Note: Because gum may pose a choking hazard, this shake is not intended for children under the age of 3.

Nutrition Facts per serving: 383 cal., 15 g total fat (9 g sat. fat), 60 mg chol., 124 mg sodium, 66 g carbo., 0 g fiber, 6 g pro.
Daily Values: 17% vit. A, 1% vit. C, 17% calcium.

30 MINUTE

Fizzy Mint-Chocolate Soda

Sitting in your yard sipping one of these ice-cream quenchers makes a summer day just about perfect. These old-fashioned favorites are bound to lure the neighbors. (See the photograph on page 122.)

Start to finish: 10 minutes

- 4 **Milk Chocolate Curls (see right)**
- ¼ **cup chocolate-flavored syrup**
- 1 **pint mint-chocolate chip ice cream**
- 2 **cups carbonated water or cream soda, chilled**

1 Prepare the milk chocolate curls. Set aside.

2 Pour 1 teaspoon of the chocolate syrup into the bottom of each of four tall glasses. Add 1 scoop (¼ cup)

of mint-chocolate chip ice cream to each glass. Add 2 more teaspoons of chocolate syrup to each glass. Top with another scoop of mint-chocolate chip ice cream.

3 Slowly pour ½ cup carbonated water or cream soda into each glass. Place a chocolate curl over the rim of each glass. Makes 4 servings.

Milk Chocolate Curls

Let a 7-ounce bar of milk chocolate stand until at room temperature. Cut off about one-eighth of the chocolate bar, forming a piece about 4 inches long and 1 inch wide. Carefully draw a vegetable peeler across the broad, flat surface of the chocolate bar, making 4 wide chocolate curls. Use a toothpick to transfer curls to the rim of each soda glass so the heat from your hand doesn't melt curls.

Nutrition Facts per serving: 245 cal., 11 g total fat (6 g sat. fat), 26 mg chol., 84 mg sodium, 33 g carbo., 0 g fiber, 4 g pro.
Daily Values: 6% vit. A, 10% calcium, 3% iron.

Frosty Glasses

Put an extra chill on your favorite summer beverage or ice cream drink by serving it in a frosty beverage glass. To frost the glasses:

● Be sure the glasses are made of glass. Plastic cups won't frost.

● Place them on a shelf in the freezer for at least one hour.

● Remove them from the freezer just before filling with an icy cold drink.

Eat well, Feel great, Lose weight!

Stop banning bread from your breakfast table and counting all those carbohydrates. Fad diets won't keep the weight off. The smartest way to a healthy lifestyle is to adopt a healthy eating plan tailored to your own body. You'll lose weight and feel great.

We'll get you started with a step-by-step guide and tips from Dr. Lawrence Cheskin, director of the Johns Hopkins Weight Management Center, and his staff who created a plan just for Better Homes and Gardens® readers.

"We tell you how many calories you need to live, to lose weight, and then transition into a maintenance plan you can really stick with," Dr. Cheskin says. You'll lose about one pound a week.

It's simple. **Step One:** Check the weight chart (below). **Step Two:** Find the standard calorie count based on activity levels (see page 135). The information from those two steps helps determine your specific daily calorie needs, which you'll need when you move on to **Step Three:** Follow the plan (see page 135). Try the flavor-packed, nutrient-rich recipes developed in the Better Homes and Gardens® Test Kitchen (recipes begin on page 136).

Check your weight

To find out if you're overweight or obese, find your height in the left-hand column and move across to find your weight. Then look at the top of the column to find the weight category you fall into. This information will help you tailor the BH&G® eating plan to your needs. Obesity can lead to heart disease, high blood pressure, and diabetes. Be sure to check with your doctor before embarking on a weight-loss plan or dietary change.

Weight in Pounds

	HEALTHY						OVERWEIGHT					OBESE		
4'10"	91	96	100	105	110	115	119	124	129	134	138	143	167	191
4'11"	94	99	104	109	114	119	124	128	133	138	143	148	173	198
5'0"	97	102	107	112	118	123	128	133	138	143	148	153	179	204
5'1"	100	106	111	116	122	127	132	137	143	148	153	158	185	211
5'2"	104	109	115	120	126	131	136	142	147	153	158	164	191	218
5'3"	107	113	118	124	130	135	141	146	152	158	163	169	197	225
5'4"	110	116	122	128	134	140	145	151	157	163	169	174	204	232
5'5"	114	120	126	132	138	144	150	156	162	168	174	180	210	240
5'6"	118	124	130	136	142	148	155	161	167	173	179	186	216	247
5'7"	121	127	134	140	146	153	159	166	172	178	185	191	223	255
5'8"	125	131	138	144	151	158	164	171	177	184	190	197	230	262
5'9"	128	135	142	149	155	162	169	176	182	189	196	203	236	270
5'10"	132	139	146	153	160	167	174	181	188	195	202	207	243	278
5'11"	136	143	150	157	165	172	179	186	193	200	208	215	250	286
6'0"	140	147	154	162	169	177	184	191	199	206	213	221	258	294
6'1"	144	151	159	166	174	182	189	197	204	212	219	227	265	302
6'2"	148	155	163	171	179	186	194	202	210	218	225	233	272	311
6'3"	152	160	168	176	184	192	200	208	216	224	232	240	279	319
6'4"	156	164	172	180	189	197	205	213	221	230	238	246	287	328

What you need to live

To find out how many calories your body needs, match your weight in the left column with the activity level that best describes your lifestyle. Write down that number. Then refer to your results from Step One and get ready to do a little math. Use the resulting number to begin your eating program as recommended below.

- If you are overweight, subtract 500 calories from your daily needs.
- If you are obese, subtract 750 calories.
- If your weight falls within the healthy weight range, congratulations. No math for you. Just use the number from the chart below.

Couch Spud—Mainly sitting all day, standing, reading, or typing.
Go-Lightly—Walking is main exercise, but no more than two hours a day.
Fairly Brisk—Heavy housework, gardening, and brisk walking (about a 15-minute mile).
Very Active—Labor-intensive job or rigorous daily exercise, such as running.

WOMEN'S DAILY CALORIE NEEDS

Weight	Couch Spud	Go-Lightly	Fairly Brisk	Very Active
100	1300	1400	1500	1600
110	1430	1540	1650	1760
120	1560	1680	1800	1920
130	1690	1820	1950	2080
140	1820	1960	2100	2240
150	1950	2100	2250	2400
160	2080	2240	2400	2560
170	2210	2380	2550	2720
180	2340	2520	2700	2880
190	2470	2660	2850	3040
200	2600	2800	3000	3200
210	2730	2940	3150	3360
220	2860	3080	3300	3520

MEN'S DAILY CALORIE NEEDS

Weight	Couch Spud	Go-Lightly	Fairly Brisk	Very Active
150	2145	2310	2475	2640
160	2288	2464	2640	2816
170	2431	2618	2805	2992
180	2574	2772	2970	3168
190	2717	2926	3135	3344
200	2860	3080	3300	3520
210	3003	3234	3465	3696
220	3146	3388	3630	3872
230	3289	3542	3795	4048
240	3432	3696	3960	4224
250	3575	3850	4125	4400
260	3718	4004	4290	4576

Your daily eating plan

After you find your daily calorie goal based on the charts on page 134 and above, find the correct plan below to help you lose weight or maintain a healthy diet. Then use the food list on page 136 and our recipes, which begin on page 136, to guide you to success.

1200-1500 Calories

Food group	Number of servings	Calories per serving	Fat per serving (grams)
Bread/Cereal/Rice/Pasta	5	80	0-3
Vegetables	4	25	0
Fruits	2	60	0
Milk/Milk products	3	100	0-5
Meat/Meat Substitutes	2	110	0-6
Fats, Oils, & Sweets	2	50	0-5

1500-1800 Calories

Food group	Number of servings	Calories per serving	Fat per serving (grams)
Bread/Cereal/Rice/Pasta	6	80	0-3
Vegetables	4	25	0
Fruits	3	60	0
Milk/Milk products	3	100	0-5
Meat/Meat Substitutes	3	110	0-6
Fats, Oils, & Sweets	3	50	0-5

1800-2100 Calories

Food group	Number of servings	Calories per serving	Fat per serving (grams)
Bread/Cereal/Rice/Pasta	9	80	0-3
Vegetables	4	25	0
Fruits	3	60	0
Milk/Milk products	3	100	0-5
Meat/Meat Substitutes	3	110	0-6
Fats, Oils, & Sweets	4	50	0-5

2100-2400 Calories

Food group	Number of servings	Calories per serving	Fat per serving (grams)
Bread/Cereal/Rice/Pasta	10	80	0-3
Vegetables	5	25	0
Fruits	4	60	0
Milk/Milk products	3	100	0-5
Meat/Meat Substitutes	4	110	0-6
Fats, Oils, & Sweets	4	50	0-5

FOOD LIST

Bread/Cereal/Pasta

1 cup dry cereal
  (high fiber)
½ whole wheat pita
½ English muffin
½ cup cooked beans, peas,
  or lentils
½ cup cooked cereal
¾ oz. pretzels
1 slice whole-grain bread
5 whole wheat crackers
2 slices reduced-calorie
  bread
½ cup cooked pasta
6-inch flour or corn tortilla
3 graham crackers
15-20 fat-free snack chips
⅓ cup couscous

Starchy vegetables

½ cup sweet potato
⅓ cup baked beans
½ cup corn
1 small baked potato or
  ½ large baked potato

Vegetables

1 cup leafy greens:
  lettuce, endive, escarole,
  romaine, spinach, kale,
  collard, or turnip greens
1 cup raw vegetables:
  carrots, celery, bean
  sprouts, onions, pea
  pods, tomato, water
  chestnuts, or cucumber
½ cup cooked vegetables:
  broccoli, carrots,
  asparagus, green beans,
  squash, red peppers,
  spinach, artichoke
  hearts, eggplant, or
  Brussels sprouts

Fruit

6 oz. 100% fruit juice
1 mango
¾ cup blueberries
1 medium banana
1 papaya
1 medium apple
1 cup strawberries
12 fresh cherries
¼ of a medium cantaloupe
½ cup honeydew melon
1 cup raspberries
1 medium orange
¾ cup fresh pineapple
1 medium grapefruit
2 Tbsp. raisins
1 kiwi fruit
1 peach
2 small plums
1¼ cups watermelon

Meat/Meat Substitute

2 oz. turkey or chicken
  (skinless, white meat)
½ to ¾ oz. egg substitute
2 eggs
3 oz. crab, tuna, or broiled
  fish
2 oz. lean red meat
  (at least 90% lean)
1 protein-fortified
  nutritional shake
2 oz. lean pork (Canadian
  bacon, tenderloin, fresh
  ham)
2 oz. duck or pheasant
  (without skin)
2 oz. roasted lamb
½ cup cottage cheese
4 oz. (½ cup) tofu

Milk/Milk Products

1 cup fat-free, low-fat, or
  reduced-fat milk
1 cup soy milk

1½ to 2 oz. fat-free or
  reduced-fat cheese
1 cup unsweetened or
  artificially sweetened
  yogurt

Fat, Oils, and Sweets (FOS)

1 tsp. oil (canola, olive,
  or peanut)
2 Tbsp. jelly or preserves
1 Tbsp. margarine
2 Tbsp. reduced-calorie
  salad dressing
1 Tbsp. regular dressing
1 Tbsp. sesame seeds
2 Tbsp. half-and-half
3 Tbsp. reduced-fat
  sour cream
1 Tbsp. reduced-fat butter
2 tsp. peanut butter
2 Tbsp. reduced-fat
  cream cheese
1 Tbsp. reduced-fat
  mayonnaise
8 black olives
6 almonds or cashews
10 peanuts

Free Food (negligible calories)

Bouillon
Sugar-free gum
Club soda
Coffee and tea
Diet soft drinks
Sugar-free tonic water
Sugar-free drink mixes
Lemon or lime juice
Mustard
Salsa
Soy sauce

MONDAY MENU

Menu=1,302 Calories
Breakfast: ½ cup Summertime
  Granola*, 8 oz. skim milk, 4 oz.
  orange juice
Lunch: Turkey pita sandwich,
  1 cup raw broccoli florets,
  2 figs
Snack: Strawberries and low-fat
  yogurt
Dinner: 4 oz. seared tuna steak,
  1 cup halved pattypan squash,
  ½ cup cooked rice, 1 cracked
  wheat roll
* *Recipe shown below*

LOW FAT

Summertime Granola

Prep: 15 minutes **Bake:** 38 minutes

Nonstick cooking spray
2½ cups regular rolled oats
1 cup whole bran cereal
½ cup toasted wheat germ
¼ cup sliced almonds
½ cup raspberry applesauce
⅓ cup honey
¼ tsp. ground cinnamon
⅓ cup dried berries and cherries
Vanilla low-fat yogurt (optional)
Fresh apricot halves (optional)

1 Preheat oven to 325°. Spray a
15×10×1-inch baking pan with
nonstick cooking spray; set aside. In a
large bowl stir together oats, bran,
wheat germ, and almonds. In a small
bowl stir together applesauce, honey,
and cinnamon. Pour applesauce
mixture over cereal mixture. Use a
wooden spoon to mix well.

2 Spread granola evenly onto
prepared pan. Bake for 35 minutes,
stirring occasionally. Carefully stir in
dried berries and cherries. Bake

3 to 5 minutes more or until golden brown. Spread on foil to cool. Store in an airtight container for up to 2 weeks. If desired, serve with vanilla low-fat yogurt and fresh apricots. Makes 5 cups.

Nutrition Facts per 1 cup: 216 cal., 4 g total fat (1 g sat. fat), 0 mg chol., 18 mg sodium, 41 g carbo., 6 g fiber, 7 g pro.
Daily Values: 4% vit. A, 6% vit. C, 6% calcium, 14% iron.

LOW FAT

Fish Cakes with Green Goddess Sauce

Prep: 30 minutes
Cook: 4 minutes per batch

- 12 oz. skinless fresh or frozen white fish fillets (such as haddock or cod)
- 1 egg, beaten
- ¼ cup fine dry bread crumbs
- 2 Tbsp. finely chopped onion
- 4 tsp. light mayonnaise or salad dressing
- 1 Tbsp. Dijon-style mustard
- 1 Tbsp. snipped fresh Italian parsley
- 1 tsp. finely shredded lime peel
- ¼ tsp. salt
- 2 Tbsp. cornmeal
- 1 Tbsp. cooking oil
- 1 recipe Green Goddess Sauce (see right)

1 Thaw fish, if frozen. Cut into ½-inch pieces. Set aside. In a medium bowl combine egg, bread crumbs, onion, mayonnaise dressing, mustard, parsley, lime peel, and salt. Add fish; mix well. Form mixture into twelve ½-inch-thick patties, about 2½ inches in diameter. Coat patties with cornmeal.

TUESDAY MENU

Menu=982 Calories

Breakfast: 2 multigrain waffles, 1 orange

Lunch: Salad of 2 oz. roasted chicken chunks, 2 cups fresh fruit, 1 cup lettuce with low-fat vinaigrette

Snack: ½ oz. soy nuts, 1 oz. low-fat cheese

Dinner: Fish Cakes with Green Goddess Sauce*, 6 steamed baby carrots, 1 cup fresh spinach, 1 slice corn bread, 8 oz. skim milk

* *Recipe shown at left*

2 In a large nonstick skillet or on griddle, heat oil. Add half of the fish cakes. Cook over medium heat for 2 to 3 minutes per side or until fish just flakes when tested with a fork and patties are gold. Repeat with the remaining cakes. For each serving, place three fish cakes on a plate along with 2 tablespoons Green Goddess Sauce. Makes 4 servings.

Green Goddess Sauce

In a blender container or food processor bowl combine ¼ cup nonfat plain yogurt, ¼ cup light dairy sour cream, and 3 tablespoons snipped fresh tarragon. Cover and process or blend until smooth. Transfer to bowl. Stir in ¼ cup light dairy sour cream, 2 tablespoons snipped fresh chives, 2 teaspoons lime juice, and 1 clove minced garlic. Serve with fish cakes. Cover and refrigerate remaining sauce to use over salad greens. Makes ¾ cup.

Nutrition Facts per serving: 217 cal., 9 g total fat (2 g sat. fat), 109 mg chol., 337 mg sodium, 12 g carbo., 1 g fiber, 20 g pro.
Daily Values: 7% vit. A, 7% vit. C, 9% calcium, 10% iron.

EDITOR'S TIP

Exercise Can Help Melt Pounds

You will lose weight by following this eating plan, but you'll see faster results and feel better if you combine the plan with regular daily exercise.

If you're a typical American, you're not getting nearly enough exercise. In fact, only 22 percent of Americans exercise often enough to reap the health benefits of working up a good sweat.

Try to get 30 minutes of cardiovascular exercise, such as walking, swimming, or jogging, every day. Walk or swim fast enough that you get your heart pumping, but not so hard that you can't carry on a conversation.

A 150-pound person can burn 200 calories swimming laps for 22 minutes. The same person can burn 200 calories walking briskly for 39 minutes or planting flowers for 44 minutes. If you can't work in exercise every day, get in at least three days each week.

Besides making you look better in your swimsuit, exercise reduces cholesterol levels, lowers your blood pressure, and strengthens your heart and bones. Exercise is also an inexpensive, non-habit-forming stress reliever. Many people who exercise regularly report feeling more relaxed, especially one to two hours after a workout.

Menu=1,305 Calories

Breakfast: 1 cup high-fiber cereal with ½ of a papaya, 1 slice wheat bread with jam

Lunch: 2 slices toasted French bread topped with 1.5 oz. soft goat cheese, 1 oz. prosciutto, ½ cup steamed Swiss chard, 1 sliced tomato, 1 cup red grapes

Snack: 1 cup blueberries, low-fat frozen yogurt

Dinner: Spicy Chicken Breasts with Fruit*, ½ cup rice, 6 oz. asparagus, 1 wheat roll

* Recipe shown below

30 MINUTE, LOW FAT

Spicy Chicken Breasts with Fruit

Prep: 15 minutes **Cook:** 14 minutes

- 2 tsp. Jamaican jerk seasoning
- 2 fresh serrano peppers, seeded and finely chopped*
- 4 skinless, boneless chicken breast halves
  Nonstick cooking spray
- ½ cup peach nectar
- 3 green onions, cut into 1-inch pieces
- 2 cups sliced, peeled peaches
- 1 cup sliced, pitted plums
- 1 Tbsp. brown sugar
- ½ cup pitted dark sweet cherries
  Hot cooked rice (optional)

1 Combine jerk seasoning and one of the chopped serrano peppers. Rub mixture onto both sides of chicken breasts. Lightly coat an unheated large skillet with nonstick cooking spray. Preheat skillet over medium heat. Add chicken. Cook for 8 to 10 minutes or until tender and no longer pink, turning once. Transfer to a platter; keep warm.

2 Add 2 tablespoons peach nectar and onions to skillet. Cook and stir over medium heat 4 to 5 minutes or until onions are just tender.

3 In a bowl combine remaining nectar, half of the peaches, half of the plums, remaining serrano, brown sugar, and ⅛ teaspoon *salt*; add to skillet. Cook and stir over medium heat about 2 minutes or until slightly thickened and bubbly. Remove from heat. Stir in cherries and remaining peaches and plums. Spoon over chicken. If desired, serve with cooked rice. Serves 4.

*Note: Hot chili peppers contain oils that can burn eyes, lips, and sensitive skin. Wear plastic gloves while preparing them and be sure to wash your hands thoroughly afterward.

Nutrition Facts per serving: 270 cal., 2 g total fat (0 g sat. fat), 66 mg chol., 227 mg sodium, 36 g carbo., 5 g fiber, 28 g pro.
Daily Values: 17% vit. A, 42% vit. C, 4% calcium, 9% iron.

Steak Salad with Cilantro Oil

Prep: 25 minutes **Marinate:** 2 hours
Grill: 12 minutes

- 12 oz. beef flank steak or boneless sirloin steak, cut 1 inch thick
- ¼ cup lime juice
- 1 recipe Cilantro Oil (see right)
- 6 cups small romaine lettuce leaves
- 5 oz. jicama, peeled and cut into 2-inch sticks (1 cup)
- 1 medium mango, sliced
- 1 small red onion, cut in thin wedges
- 2 tsp. honey

1 Season steak with ⅛ teaspoon each *salt* and *pepper*. Place in a self-sealing plastic bag set in a shallow bowl. In a small bowl combine lime juice and Cilantro Oil. Pour half the juice mixture over meat. Seal bag. Marinate in refrigerator for 2 to 24 hours, turning bag occasionally. Cover and chill remaining lime-cilantro mixture for dressing.

2 Drain meat. Discard marinade. Grill meat on the rack of an uncovered grill directly over medium coals for 12 to 14 minutes for medium doneness, turning once. Remove from grill. Thinly slice across grain.

3 To serve, divide romaine leaves among four individual salad bowls. Top with steak slices, jicama, mango, and onion. In a bowl combine reserved lime-cilantro mixture and honey. Drizzle over salad. Serves 4.

Cilantro Oil

Combine ⅓ cup packed fresh cilantro; 2 tablespoons olive oil; ½ clove garlic, minced; and ⅛ teaspoon bottled hot pepper sauce.

Nutrition Facts per serving: 274 cal., 13 g total fat (3 g sat. fat), 34 mg chol., 131 mg sodium, 20 g carbo., 3 g fiber, 21 g pro.
Daily Values: 46% vit. A, 82% vit. C, 5% calcium, 16% iron.

Menu=1,184 Calories

Breakfast: 1 bagel with light cream cheese, 1 cup cubed cantaloupe

Lunch: ¼ cup hummus, 1 cup veggies for dipping, 10 crackers

Snack: Blend 8 oz. chocolate-flavored soy milk with 1 banana, ½ oz. candy-coated milk-chocolate pieces

Dinner: Steak Salad with Cilantro Oil*, 2 slices crusty sourdough bread

* Recipe shown at left

Breakfast: ¼ cup Summertime Granola,** 6 oz. nonfat yogurt, 1 banana

Lunch: Gazpacho Sandwich to Go,* 1 cup honeydew melon cubes, ¼ cup pretzels, 2 shortbread cookies

Snack: 1 oz. reduced-fat cheese, 3 fresh apricots

Dinner: 4 oz. roasted pork tenderloin, 1½ cups zucchini and greens, low-fat dressing, ⅓ cup herbed couscous, ½ cup peach ice cream

** *Recipe shown on page 136*
* *Recipe shown below*

Menu=1,117 Calories

Breakfast: Two 4-inch pancakes, 2 Tbsp. raspberry syrup, 1 sliced peach

Lunch: Grilled Vegetable Salad*

Snack: 1 cinnamon granola bar, ¾ cup cherries

Dinner: 4 oz. broiled turkey tenderloin, 3 oz. steamed green beans, ½ cup roasted new potatoes, 1 ear sweet corn, 1 Tbsp. melted canola oil margarine and ½ tsp. snipped thyme

* *Recipe shown at left*

LOW FAT

Gazpacho Sandwich To Go

Prep: 20 minutes **Chill:** 4 hours

½ of an 8-oz. loaf baguette-style French bread
¾ cup yellow pear, cherry, and/or grape tomatoes, quartered
¼ cup coarsely chopped cucumber
2 thin slices of a red onion, separated into rings
2 oz. fresh mozzarella, cubed
1 Tbsp. snipped fresh mint
1 Tbsp. red wine vinegar
1 tsp. olive oil
½ cup fresh basil leaves

1 Slice the half baguette vertically through center, leaving two mini baguettes. Cut a thin horizontal slice from top of each portion. Remove bread from center of baguettes, leaving ¼-inch shells. Set aside. Reserve center pieces of baguette for another use.

2 In a medium bowl combine tomatoes, cucumber, red onion, mozzarella, mint, vinegar, oil,

¼ teaspoon *salt*, and ⅛ teaspoon *white pepper*. Line bottoms of baguettes with basil; fill with tomato mixture. Replace tops. Wrap sandwiches and chill 4 to 6 hours. Makes 2 servings.

Nutrition Facts per serving: 237 cal., 8 g total fat (3 g sat. fat), 16 mg chol., 691 mg sodium, 29 g carbo., 3 g fiber, 12 g pro.
Daily Values: 17% vit. A, 42% vit. C, 24% calcium, 14% iron.

LOW FAT

Grilled Vegetable Salad

Prep: 20 minutes **Marinate:** 4 hours
Grill: 10 minutes

1 lb. reduced-fat firm tofu, drained
¾ cup bottled reduced-fat Italian salad dressing
12 oz. yellow summer squash, halved lengthwise and cut into 2-inch pieces
4 large orange and/or red sweet peppers, quartered and seeded
½ cup quinoa, rinsed and drained*
½ cup quick-cooking barley
¼ cup shredded sorrel or spinach

1 Cut tofu lengthwise into 8 slices, about ¼ to ½ inch thick. Place tofu in a shallow baking dish. Pour ¼ cup of the dressing over tofu; cover. Place vegetables in a large self-sealing plastic bag set in a deep bowl. Pour 3 tablespoons of the remaining dressing over vegetables. Close bag, turning to coat. Chill tofu and vegetables 4 to 24 hours, turning occasionally. Chill remaining dressing.

2 Remove tofu from dressing; discard dressing. Drain vegetables; reserve dressing. Grill vegetables on rack of an uncovered grill directly over medium heat 6 to 8 minutes or until vegetables are crisp-tender, turning

occasionally. Grill tofu on grill rack directly over medium heat 4 to 6 minutes or until lightly browned, turning once. Cut tofu into triangles; keep warm. In a large mixing bowl combine grilled vegetables. Add reserved dressing; toss to coat.

3 Meanwhile, in a 2-quart saucepan bring 2 cups water to boiling. Add quinoa and barley. Return to boiling; reduce heat. Simmer, covered, 15 minutes or until water is nearly absorbed and grains are tender. Drain.

4 In a large bowl gently toss quinoa and barley mixture with shredded sorrel and remaining chilled dressing. Serve warm grains with vegetables and tofu. If desired, add additional sorrel leaves. Makes 6 servings.

*Note: Look for quinoa (KEEN-wah) near the grains at your supermarket or health-food store. Rinse the tiny grain in a fine sieve before using.

Nutrition Facts per serving: 202 cal., 5 g total fat (1 g sat. fat), 2 mg chol., 306 mg sodium, 31 g carbo., 5 g fiber, 9 g pro.
Daily Values: 16% vit. A, 154% vit. C, 4% calcium, 16% iron.

Menu=1,065 Calories

Light Breakfast: 1 whole-grain bagel, 2 tsp. apple butter, 1 cup fresh berries

Brunch: Baked Brie Strata,* 3 oz. poached salmon, 1 cup cubed cantaloupe, 8 oz. orange-mango juice blend

Light Dinner: 5 oz. grilled portobello mushroom on a roll with 1 tomato slice and lettuce, 1 diced mango, ½ cup broccoli slaw

* Recipe shown below

LOW FAT

Baked Brie Strata

Prep: 25 minutes **Chill:** 4 hours
Bake: 55 minutes

- 2 small zucchini, cut crosswise into ¼-inch slices (about 2 cups)
  Nonstick cooking spray
- 6 ½-inch-thick slices crusty sourdough bread (6 oz.)
- 8 oz. Brie cheese, cut into ½-inch cubes
- 2 Roma tomatoes, cut lengthwise into ¼-inch slices
- 6 to 8 cherry tomatoes
- 1 cup refrigerated or frozen egg product, thawed
- ⅔ cup evaporated skim milk
- ⅓ cup finely chopped onion
- 3 Tbsp. snipped fresh dillweed
- ½ tsp. salt
- ⅛ tsp. pepper

1 Cook zucchini, covered, in a small amount of boiling lightly salted water for 2 to 3 minutes or until just tender. Drain zucchini and set aside.

2 Meanwhile, coat a 2-quart rectangular baking dish with nonstick cooking spray. Arrange bread slices in the prepared baking dish, cutting as necessary to fit. Sprinkle half of the Brie evenly on top. Arrange zucchini and tomatoes on top of bread. Sprinkle with remaining cheese.

3 In a medium bowl combine egg product, evaporated skim milk, onion, dill, salt, and pepper. Pour evenly over vegetables and cheese. Lightly press vegetables down with back of spoon to be sure everything is saturated with egg mixture. Cover with plastic wrap and chill for 4 to 24 hours.

4 Preheat oven to 325°. Remove plastic wrap from strata; cover with foil. Bake 30 minutes. Uncover and bake 25 to 30 minutes more or until a knife inserted near center comes out clean. Let stand 10 minutes before serving. Makes 8 servings.

Nutrition Facts per serving: 198 cal., 8 g total fat (5 g sat. fat), 29 mg chol., 525 mg sodium, 18 g carbo., 1 g fiber, 13 g pro.
Daily Values: 13% vit. A, 13% vit. C, 13% calcium, 9% iron.

LOW FAT

Make-Your-Own Energy Bar

If you thought energy bars were fairly recent concoctions created for athletes, think again. Legend has it that medieval Italian crusaders toted a version, called panforte, to sustain themselves on their journeys. Modern-day crusaders on a quest for fitness can make their own fruit-and-nut bar.

Prep: 15 minutes **Bake:** 30 minutes

- Nonstick cooking spray
- 1 cup quick-cooking rolled oats
- ½ cup all-purpose flour
- ½ cup Grape Nuts cereal
- ½ tsp. ground ginger
- 1 egg, beaten

EDITOR'S TIP

Snack on This

Go ahead and nibble, but aim for only one snack a day. Here are some healthful suggestions.

- Combine whole-grain, bite-size cereal; toasted soy nuts; and candy-coated milk-chocolate pieces.
- Splash low-calorie lime-flavored sparkling water over a serving of fresh fruit.
- Drizzle a banana or wedges of nectarine with apricot-flavored honey, and roll in toasted chopped pecans.

- ⅓ cup applesauce
- ¼ cup honey
- ¼ cup packed brown sugar
- 2 Tbsp. cooking oil
- 1 6-oz. pkg. mixed dried fruit bits
- ¼ cup sunflower seeds
- ¼ cup chopped walnuts

1 Preheat oven to 325°. Line an 8×8×2-inch baking pan with aluminum foil. Coat foil with nonstick cooking spray. Set pan aside.

2 In a large bowl combine rolled oats, flour, Grape Nuts cereal, and ginger. Add egg, applesauce, honey, brown sugar, and oil; mix well. Stir in fruit bits, sunflower seeds, and walnuts. Spread the mixture evenly in the prepared pan.

3 Bake for 30 to 35 minutes or until lightly browned around the edges. Cool on a wire rack. Use edges of foil to lift from pan. Cut into bars. Makes 24 bars.

Nutrition Facts per bar: 104 cal., 3 g total fat (0 g sat. fat), 9 mg chol., 24 mg sodium, 18 g carbo., 1 g fiber, 2 g pro.
Daily Values: 3% vit. A, 1% calcium, 5% iron.

july

IN THIS CHAPTER

30-minute recipes indicated in COLOR.
Low-fat and no-fat recipes indicated
with a ♥.
Photographs indicated in italics.
*Bonus recipe

Fresh Onion Dip

Go wild with dippers! We started with chips: potato, sweet potato, beet, and corn; piled on lavosh and home-baked tortilla chips; then added vegetables, such as wax beans, daikon, and carrots.

Prep: 20 minutes **Chill:** 1 hour

1½ cups chopped sweet onion
      (such as Vidalia or Walla Walla)
2 Tbsp. margarine or butter
1 8-oz. carton dairy sour cream
¼ tsp. salt
¼ tsp. coarsely ground black pepper
⅛ tsp. ground red pepper
4 tsp. snipped fresh chives
   Milk (optional)
   Dippers

1 In a medium skillet cook onion in margarine or butter about 5 minutes or until tender. Cool.

2 In a blender container or food processor bowl combine cooked onion, sour cream, salt, black pepper, and red pepper. Cover and blend or process until nearly smooth.

3 Transfer to a small bowl. Stir in chives. Cover and chill for 1 to 24 hours.

4 Before serving, stir in milk, a teaspoon at a time, if necessary, to make of dipping consistency. Serve with a variety of dippers, such as chips and sliced raw vegetables. Makes about 1½ cups.

Nutrition Facts per tablespoon: 33 cal., 3 g total fat (1 g sat. fat), 4 mg chol., 41 mg sodium, 1 g carbo., 0 g fiber, 0 g pro.
Daily Values: 3% vit. A, 1% vit. C, 1% calcium.

LOW FAT

Watermelon Steaks With Melon Salsa

To determine if a watermelon is ripe, turn it over. The underside should have a creamy, pale yellow hue, and the entire rind should have a healthy sheen and be free of dents or bruises. (See the photograph on page 161.)

Prep: 15 minutes **Chill:** 2 hours

2 cups melon, such as cantaloupe, honeydew, or seedless yellow or red watermelon, cut into ¼- to ½-inch cubes
¼ cup bottled Sangría or sparkling white grape juice
2 Tbsp. seeded and finely chopped fresh jalapeño peppers (optional)*
4 2-inch-thick slices cut from half of a seedless red watermelon, chilled
1 Tbsp. lemon juice

1 For salsa, in a medium bowl combine cubed melon, Sangría or juice, and, if desired, jalapeño. Toss gently. Cover and chill for 2 to 6 hours.

2 Cut each watermelon slice in half. Place two chilled watermelon steaks on each serving plate. Sprinkle with lemon juice. Spoon some of the salsa over each. Makes 4 servings.

*Note: Hot peppers contain oils that can burn eyes, lips, and sensitive skin, so wear plastic gloves while preparing them and be sure to wash your hands thoroughly afterward.

Nutrition Facts per serving: 114 cal., 1 g total fat (0 g sat. fat), 0 mg chol., 8 mg sodium, 25 g carbo., 2 g fiber, 2 g pro.
Daily Values: 12% vit. A, 56% vit. C, 3% calcium, 3% iron.

LOW FAT

Blueberry-Corn Relish

Pick blueberries that are smooth-skinned, plump, and firm. Color, not size, indicates ripeness. Ripe berries are deep purple-blue to blue-black.

Prep: 12 minutes **Cook:** 4 minutes
Chill: 2 hours

2 ears fresh corn on the cob or ½ of a 10-oz. pkg. frozen whole kernel corn (1 cup)
¼ cup chopped onion
¼ cup vinegar
2 Tbsp. honey
2 tsp. seeded and finely chopped fresh serrano pepper* (See note, below left.)
¼ tsp. salt
¼ tsp. ground cardamom
½ cup chopped jicama
1 cup fresh blueberries

1 If using fresh ears of corn, remove husks and silks; rinse corn. Cut kernels from cob. (You should have 1 cup of kernels.)

2 In a medium saucepan combine fresh or frozen corn kernels, onion, vinegar, honey, serrano, salt, and cardamom. Bring mixture to boiling; reduce heat. Cook, uncovered, over medium-low heat about 4 minutes or until corn is just tender. Remove from heat; cool slightly. Stir in the jicama. Cover and refrigerate until chilled.

3 Just before serving, gently stir in blueberries. Serve with a slotted spoon. Makes 2 cups.

To Make Ahead:

Prepare corn mixture as directed. Transfer to a nonmetal container with a lid. Store in the refrigerator for up to 1 month. Stir in the blueberries and serve.

Nutrition Facts per ½-cup serving: 111 cal., 1 g total fat, (0 g sat. fat), 0 mg chol., 247 mg sodium, 28 g carbo., 2 g fiber, 2 g pro. Daily Values: 1% vit. A, 21% vit. C, 1% calcium, 4% iron.

Three-Bean Salad

This version is more emphatic and uses different beans than the usual bean salad, but it still induces cravings. (See the photograph on page 160.)

Prep: 20 minutes **Marinate:** 2 hours

- ⅔ cup cider vinegar
- ¼ cup salad oil
- 1 Tbsp. dark brown sugar
- ½ tsp. salt
- ¼ tsp. black pepper
- 1 15-oz. can chickpeas (garbanzo beans), rinsed and drained
- 1 15-oz. can small white beans, rinsed and drained
- 1 10-oz. pkg. frozen lima beans, thawed
- 2 medium carrots, thinly bias-sliced (1 cup)
- 2 small fresh jalapeño or serrano peppers, seeded and finely chopped* (See note, page 142.)
- ⅓ cup snipped fresh cilantro
  Lime wedges (optional)
  Chopped jalapeño pepper (optional)
  Kosher salt, sea salt, or regular salt (optional)
  Bottled hot pepper sauce (optional)
  Fresh cilantro sprigs (optional)

EDITOR'S TIP

Go Blue

A big handful of blueberries each day may help maintain brain power as you age. Well, it works for rats, anyway, according to studies at Tufts University Human Nutrition Research Center on Aging. Scientists discovered that when the rodents were fed a diet supplemented with blueberry extract, the critters showed amazing improvement in memory as well as in balance and coordination.

Researchers believe that anthocyanin–the pigment that gives blueberries their deep color–is responsible for the results. Anthocyanin is a plant chemical that scavenges for free radicals in the body in order to keep them from attacking and damaging cells.

That may sound like scientific mumbo jumbo, but it comes down to this: Blueberries hold the potential for holding off age-related memory loss. Human trials to test that theory are under way, but in the meantime it's not such a bad idea to add a serving of blueberries to your five-a-day fruit and veggie quota. How much is a serving? About half a cup of berries.

Eat the little gems like candy or toss them into a Blueberry-Corn Relish (see recipe, page 142) for a colorful accompaniment to poultry or pork.

QUICK...No pitting, no peeling, no chopping. With blueberries, all you need to do is wash them and eat them.

EASY...Store unwashed berries in their original container in the fridge for up to 10 days after buying. Or freeze for up to a year. To freeze: Put dry berries in a single layer on a baking sheet. Freeze. Transfer berries to freezer bags.

HEALTHY...Like cranberries, blueberries contain compounds that may prevent urinary tract infections. These compounds keep bacteria from sticking to the walls of the urinary tract.

Treating the Blues

These sweet blue gems need little embellishment. But you're in for even more of a treat if you gussy them up just a bit.

● Toss ½ teaspoon of finely shredded lemon peel over a cup of blueberries. Dust with powdered sugar just before serving. The combo is outstanding over lemon or mango sorbet.

● Stir ⅓ cup of fresh berries into 1 cup of blueberry preserves with a pinch of cinnamon or cardamom. Serve it over waffles, pancakes, or angel food cake.

● Combine a big splash of orange juice with a little honey and candied ginger. Stir in blueberries. Spoon into half a seeded papaya.

1 For dressing, in a small bowl whisk together the vinegar, oil, brown sugar, salt, and black pepper; set aside.

2 In a large plastic bag set in a deep bowl combine chickpeas, white beans, lima beans, carrots, jalapeño or serrano peppers, and cilantro. Pour dressing over bean mixture. Close bag. Marinate in the refrigerator 2 to 24 hours, turning bag occasionally.

3 Transfer to a serving bowl. Serve with lime wedges, chopped jalapeño, coarse salt, bottled hot pepper sauce, and cilantro sprigs, if desired. Makes 8 servings.

Nutrition Facts per serving before extra lime, peppers, or salt added: 221 cal., 8 g total fat (1 g sat. fat), 0 mg chol., 576 mg sodium, 30 g carbo., 8 g fiber, 9 g pro. Daily Values: 45% vit. A, 14% vit. C, 6% calcium, 13% iron.

Pea and Macaroni Salad

It's not necessary to allow the macaroni to cool before mixing with the dressing. Once it's chilled, you can stir in additional milk to moisten the salad. (See the photograph on page 159.)

Prep: 20 minutes **Chill:** 4 hours

- 1 **cup fresh pea pods**
- 8 **oz. dried elbow macaroni**
- 1 **cup frozen peas, thawed**
- ½ **cup mayonnaise or salad dressing**
- ½ **cup dairy sour cream**
- ⅓ **cup milk**
- ¼ **cup horseradish mustard**
- 2 **cloves garlic, minced**
- ¼ **tsp. salt**
- ¼ **tsp. pepper**
- ¾ **cup thinly sliced celery**
- 2 **Tbsp. chopped onion**
    Milk (optional)
    Pea pods (optional)

1 Remove tips and strings from pea pods. Cook macaroni according to package directions in lightly salted boiling water, adding pea pods and peas during the last 1 minute of cooking. Drain and rinse. Halve pea pods diagonally; set macaroni, pea pods, and peas aside.

2 In a small bowl stir together mayonnaise or salad dressing, sour cream, milk, mustard, minced garlic, salt, and pepper; set aside.

3 In a large bowl combine cooked macaroni mixture, celery, and onion. Pour mayonnaise mixture over the macaroni mixture. Stir gently to combine.

4 Cover and chill 4 to 24 hours. Stir mixture before serving. If necessary, add additional milk (1 to 2 tablespoons) to moisten. If desired, top with additional pea pods. Makes 12 to 16 side-dish servings.

Nutrition Facts per serving: 178 cal., 10 g total fat (2 g sat. fat), 7 mg chol., 169 mg sodium, 18 g carbo., 2 g fiber, 4 g pro.
Daily Values: 3% vit. A, 11% vit. C, 3% calcium, 5% iron.

Skillet-Roasted Potato Salad

Though the potatoes are cooked in a skillet, the fat content is about the same as other marinated potato salads. (See the photograph on page 162.)

Prep: 30 minutes **Chill:** 4 hours

- 1 **lb. potatoes, cut into 1-inch pieces (do not peel potatoes)**
- 2 **Tbsp. cooking oil or olive oil**
- ¼ **tsp. salt**
- ⅛ **tsp. black pepper**
- 2 **medium summer squash, cut into 1½-inch pieces (8 oz. total)**
- ⅓ **cup bottled white wine, olive oil, or Italian vinaigrette, or other oil-and-vinegar salad dressing**
- 1 **small red sweet pepper, cut into ½- to ¾-inch squares**
- 6 **cherry tomatoes, halved**
- ¼ **cup snipped fresh parsley**
- 1 **tsp. snipped fresh thyme**
    Sprigs of fresh thyme (optional)

1 In a large skillet cook potatoes in hot oil over medium heat about 15 minutes or until tender and brown on all sides, turning occasionally. Spoon potatoes into a serving bowl. Sprinkle with the salt and black pepper.

2 To same skillet add summer squash. Cook and stir over medium heat for 3 to 5 minutes or until just tender. Add to the potatoes in the serving bowl.

3 Pour vinaigrette dressing over potatoes and summer squash. Add sweet pepper, cherry tomatoes, parsley, and snipped thyme. Toss gently to mix. Cool.

4 Cover and chill for 4 to 24 hours, stirring salad occasionally. If desired, top with thyme sprigs. Makes 6 side-dish servings.

Nutrition Facts per serving: 172 cal., 12 g total fat (2 g sat. fat), 0 mg chol., 103 mg sodium, 15 g carbo., 3 g fiber, 3 g pro.
Daily Values: 11% vit. A, 72% vit. C, 2% calcium, 6% iron.

NO FAT

Tomatillo Salsa

Say ¡Si! to this fresh and spicy salsa. Serve with tortilla chips or use as a condiment for enchiladas, burritos, or other Tex-Mex favorites.

Prep: 20 minutes **Chill:** 1 hour

10	tomatillos (about 8 oz.)
1	small tomato, chopped (½ cup)
¼	cup chopped red onion
¼	cup snipped fresh cilantro
6	cloves garlic, minced
2	to 4 fresh jalapeño peppers, seeded and finely chopped*
1	to 2 Tbsp. lime juice
⅛	tsp. salt

1 Remove and discard the tomatillos' papery husks. Rinse and finely chop tomatillos with a sharp knife.

2 In a medium bowl stir together the chopped tomatillos, tomato, red onion, cilantro, garlic, jalapeño peppers, lime juice, and salt. Cover and chill the salsa about 1 hour before serving. Serve with tortilla chips, if desired. Store salsa in an airtight container in the refrigerator for several days. Makes about 2 cups.

*Note: Hot peppers contain oils that can burn eyes, lips, and sensitive skin, so wear plastic gloves while preparing them and be sure to wash your hands thoroughly afterward.

To Make Ahead:
Prepare salsa as directed. Transfer to a covered nonmetal container and store in the refrigerator for up to 1 week.

Nutrition Facts per ¼ cup: 17 cal., 0 g total fat, 0 mg chol., 36 mg sodium, 4 g carbo., 0 g fiber, 1 g pro.
Daily Values: 1% vit. A, 25% vit. C, 1% iron.

Roasted Garlic and Tomatillo Soup

Exploding with flavor, this "green soup" is a fun starter for a meal of enchiladas or fajitas. (See the photograph on page 159.)

Prep: 25 minutes **Bake:** 20 minutes
Cook: 10 minutes

1	head garlic
2	tsp. olive oil or cooking oil
1	lb. tomatillos
3	14½-oz. cans chicken broth
¼	tsp. black pepper
2	large tomatoes, cored and chopped
1	avocado, halved, seeded, peeled, and chopped
½	cup snipped fresh cilantro
1	cup coarsely crushed tortilla chips
4	oz. Chihuahua, queso quesadilla, or Monterey Jack cheese

1 Preheat oven to 425°. Peel away outer skin from head of garlic. Cut off the pointed top portion with a knife, leaving the bulb intact but exposing the individual cloves. Place garlic head in a custard cup; drizzle with oil. Cover with foil.

2 Remove husks, stems, and cores from tomatillos. Cut tomatillos in half. Place cut side down on a foil-lined 15×10×1-inch baking pan. Bake the tomatillos and garlic for 20 minutes. Remove from oven and cool slightly.

3 Using your fingers, press garlic to remove paste from individual cloves. In a blender container combine half of the tomatillos, the garlic paste, and 1 cup of the chicken broth. Cover and blend until nearly smooth.

4 Transfer blended mixture to a large saucepan; add remaining chicken broth and black pepper. Chop remaining tomatillos and add to pan along with the chopped tomatoes. Heat through.

5 To serve, ladle soup into bowls. Top each with avocado, cilantro, tortilla chips, and cheese. Makes 8 side-dish servings.

Nutrition Facts per serving: 169 cal., 12 g total fat (4 g sat. fat), 15 mg chol., 758 mg sodium, 11 g carbo., 3 g fiber, 6 g pro.
Daily Values: 8% vit. A, 28% vit. C, 12% calcium, 6% iron.

EDITOR'S TIP

Meet the Tomatillo

Tomatillos, those emerald-green curiosities winking from their papery husks in the produce section of your supermarket, lend an authentic flavor to Tex-Mex foods. Despite the name, tomatillos (toe-muh-TEE-os) are not related to tomatoes. But you'll love how their green tomato and lime flavor complements tomatoes in sauces and salsas.

Buying Tomatillos

Tomatillos begin to appear in supermarkets in the spring and continue through the summer and fall. The best ones are evenly colored and firm (but not rock-hard) with clean husks. Leave them in their husks until ready to use. Store at room temperature if you plan to use them within a few days, or in the refrigerator, loosely wrapped, for up to a week.

When you're ready to use fresh tomatillos, remove the husks and rinse them to remove the sticky coating on the skin. Consider using canned tomatillos to make sauces if fresh ones are not available.

CLEVER COOK

Better Buttered Toast

I once struggled with getting everyone's toast buttered and served while still warm. Then, one morning while cooking for houseguests, I discovered that if I melted the butter in a bowl and used a pastry brush to spread it on, the process was faster and the toast was served warm. An added bonus—I used less butter.

Lori Kroll
Holly Springs, North Carolina

Surf-Side Tuna Sandwiches

All the ingredients you love in the lunch-box version of this classic are here, but with the added smoky charm of barbecued tuna. Soaking the onions briefly in water and lemon juice reduces their harshness without diminishing flavor.

Prep: 20 minutes **Chill:** 2 hours
Grill: 4 minutes per ½-inch thickness

- 1 lb. fresh or frozen tuna steaks
- 2 to 3 Tbsp. olive oil or cooking oil
- ½ tsp. salt
- ¼ tsp. pepper
- 1 Tbsp. lemon juice
- 1 small red onion, very thinly sliced
- ⅓ to ½ cup mayonnaise
- 3 Tbsp. dill pickle relish
- 1 tsp. finely shredded lemon peel
- 1 Tbsp. lemon juice
- 1 tsp. minced garlic
- ½ tsp. yellow mustard
- 4 6-inch-long Italian-style or French-style rolls, halved lengthwise
  Sliced hard-cooked eggs, dill pickle slices, and/or tomato slices (optional)
  Sprigs of fresh dillweed (optional)

1 Thaw tuna, if frozen. Rinse tuna and pat dry. Brush tuna generously with oil; sprinkle with salt and pepper. Cover and chill 2 hours.

2 In a medium bowl combine the 1 tablespoon lemon juice with 2 cups *water*. Add onion and allow to soak for 15 minutes. Drain.

3 Remove tuna from refrigerator. Place tuna on the greased rack of an uncovered grill. Grill directly over medium coals for 4 to 6 minutes per ½-inch thickness or until fish begins to flake easily when tested with a fork, turning once. Remove from grill; break tuna into chunks with two forks.

4 In a small bowl stir together the mayonnaise, pickle relish, lemon peel, 1 tablespoon lemon juice, garlic, and mustard.

5 In a medium bowl combine tuna and mayonnaise mixture. Stir gently to mix.

6 Spoon mixture onto bottoms of rolls. Top with some of the onions and, if desired, sliced hard-cooked eggs, dill pickle slices, and/or tomato slices. If desired, add a few sprigs of dill. Top with remaining halves of the rolls. Makes 4 sandwiches.

Nutrition Facts per sandwich: 539 cal., 31 g total fat (6 g sat. fat), 155 mg chol., 1,218 mg sodium, 29 g carbo., 2 g fiber, 34 g pro.
Daily Values: 75% vit. A, 25% vit. C, 7% calcium, 17% iron.

PRIZE WINNER

Ginger Tuna Kabobs

Phyllis M. Durrant
Rochester, New York
$200—Short-Order Kabobs

Prep: 20 minutes **Marinate:** 20 minutes
Grill: 6 minutes

- 12 oz. fresh or frozen skinless tuna steaks
- 3 Tbsp. reduced-sodium soy sauce
- 3 Tbsp. water
- 1 Tbsp. snipped green onion tops or snipped fresh chives
- 2 tsp. grated fresh ginger
- ½ of a medium pineapple, peeled, cored, and cut into 1-inch cubes
- 1 medium red or green sweet pepper, cubed
- 6 green onions, cut into 2-inch pieces
- ¼ cup honey

1 Thaw tuna, if frozen. Rinse tuna and pat dry. Cut tuna into 1-inch cubes. Place in a large plastic bag set in a deep bowl. Add soy sauce, water, snipped green onion tops or chives, and ginger. Seal bag and turn gently to coat cubes. Let stand at room temperature for 20 minutes. Drain, reserving marinade.

2 Alternately thread tuna, pineapple, sweet pepper, and green onion pieces onto skewers. Grill kabobs on the greased rack of an uncovered grill directly over medium coals for 6 to 9 minutes or until tuna just flakes easily with a fork, turning once.

3 Meanwhile, bring the reserved marinade to boiling; strain. Discard any solids. Stir honey into hot

marinade. Brush tuna, fruit, and vegetables generously with honey-soy mixture just before serving. Serves 4.

Nutrition Facts per serving: 251 cal., 5 g total fat (1 g sat. fat), 32 mg chol., 446 mg sodium, 32 g carbo., 2 g fiber, 22 g pro.
Daily Values: 53% vit. A, 69% vit. C, 4% calcium, 10% iron.

High-and-Dry Clambake

Nori, a Japanese form of seaweed that's dried in sheets, adds a hint of ocean flavor. Find nori in Asian markets or the Asian section of supermarkets. If you can't find it, use parsley. (See the photograph on page 163.)

Prep: 30 minutes **Grill:** 15 minutes

20	littleneck, Manila, or cherrystone clams in shells
1	cup salt
¾	cup butter, melted
1	tsp. finely shredded lemon peel
2	Tbsp. lemon juice
2	Tbsp. snipped fresh basil or 3 Tbsp. snipped fresh dillweed
4	small fresh ears of corn in husks
8	sheets nori or 1 large bunch fresh parsley
2	7- to 8-oz. fresh or frozen lobster tails, thawed and halved lengthwise
8	oz. cooked kielbasa or other smoked sausage, cut into 8 slices
12	to 16 sprigs of fresh basil and/or dillweed
	Salt and pepper

1 Thoroughly wash clams in shells. In a large pot or kettle combine 4 quarts cold water and ⅓ cup of the salt. Place clams in the salt water

mixture; let stand 15 minutes. Drain and rinse well. Repeat soaking and rinsing twice more, using new water and salt each time.

2 In a small bowl stir together butter, lemon peel, lemon juice, and the 2 to 3 tablespoons snipped fresh herbs; set aside. Remove corn husks; clean several husks and set aside. Use hands or a stiff brush to remove silk from corn. Brush corn with about 2 tablespoons of the butter mixture. Lay the clean corn husks back in place around ears of corn.

3 Tear off four 24×18-inch pieces of heavy foil. Lay 2 sheets of nori or 3 or 4 large sprigs of fresh parsley in the center of each piece of foil. Cut four 12-inch squares of 100-percent cotton cheesecloth; place 1 square over nori or parsley on each piece of foil.

4 For each packet, arrange the following on cheesecloth: 5 clams in shells, 1 ear of corn, ½ of a lobster tail, and 2 slices of kielbasa (see photo 1, right). Brush about 2 tablespoons butter mixture over cut sides of lobsters. Drizzle about 1 tablespoon of remaining butter over each packet. (Reserve remaining butter mixture until serving time.) Top with a few sprigs of basil or dillweed. Sprinkle lightly with salt and pepper. Bring ends of cheesecloth together in center. Seal foil packets, allowing room for steam to build (see photo 2, right).

5 In a grill with a cover, place foil packets, seam side up, on grill rack directly over medium coals. Cover and grill for 15 to 20 minutes or until clams are open, lobster is opaque, and corn is tender, carefully opening packets to check doneness.

1. Arrange ingredients in a single layer in packet to ensure even cooking.

2. When sealing packet, leave room for expansion caused by steam, and be sure to roll foil tightly.

6 To serve, open packets. Discard any clams that have not opened, the nori, if using, and herb sprigs. (If desired, replace with fresh herb sprigs.) Pass remaining lemon-butter mixture. Makes 4 servings.

Nutrition Facts per serving: 667 cal., 54 g total fat (29 g sat. fat), 203 mg chol., 1,177 mg sodium, 21 g carbo., 3 g fiber, 28 g pro.
Daily Values: 46% vit. A, 32% vit. C, 10% calcium, 49% iron.

Spicy Fish Kabobs with Couscous

Here's a super supper recipe that's quick enough for weekday cooking, yet special enough for last-minute entertaining.

Prep: 20 minutes **Broil:** 6 minutes

1½	lb. fresh or frozen halibut or sea bass steaks
1	tsp. ground cumin
1	tsp. ground coriander
¾	tsp. salt
½	tsp. ground black pepper
⅛	tsp. ground red pepper
3	Tbsp. butter or margarine
¼	cup orange juice
1	10-oz. pkg. quick-cooking couscous (1½ cups)
1	14½-oz. can reduced-sodium chicken broth or vegetable broth
½	cup orange juice
2	medium zucchini, cut into ½-inch slices
1	medium yellow summer squash, cut into ½-inch slices

1 Thaw fish, if frozen. Rinse fish and pat dry. Cut fish into 1-inch cubes. Set aside.

2 In a small bowl combine cumin, coriander, salt, ground black pepper, and ground red pepper. In a medium saucepan melt butter or margarine; add spice mixture and cook 1 minute. Transfer 2 tablespoons of the mixture to a small bowl. Stir the ¼ cup orange juice into mixture in bowl. Stir couscous into remaining mixture in saucepan. Cook 1 minute more. Stir in broth and the ½ cup orange juice. Bring to boiling. Cover and remove from heat. Set aside.

SUPPER MENU

- **Spicy Fish Kabobs with Couscous (see left)**
- **Salad of fresh spinach greens, assorted berries, and poppy seed dressing**
- **Chilled white wine**

3 Alternately thread fish, zucchini, and yellow summer squash onto 6 long skewers. Brush with the reserved butter and spice mixture.

4 Place kabobs on the greased rack of an unheated broiler pan. Broil 3 to 4 inches from heat for 6 to 10 minutes or until fish flakes easily with a fork, turning once. Serve fish with couscous. Makes 6 servings.

Nutrition Facts per serving: 391 cal., 10 g total fat (4 g sat. fat), 52 mg chol., 640 mg sodium, 42 g carbo., 4 g fiber, 32 g pro.
Daily Values: 14% vit. A, 21% vit. C, 9% calcium, 12% iron.

Grilled Peanut Shrimp Skewers

The cardamom, coriander, cumin, turmeric, and ground red pepper make up a curry powderlike mixture. So, if you wish, omit those spices and instead use 1 teaspoon curry powder.

Prep: 20 minutes **Marinate:** 30 minutes
Grill: 10 minutes

1	lb. fresh or frozen large shrimp in shells
⅓	cup orange marmalade
2	Tbsp. lime juice
2	Tbsp. peanut butter
1	Tbsp. cooking oil
1	tsp. grated fresh ginger
½	tsp. ground cardamom
½	tsp. ground coriander
½	tsp. ground cumin
¼	tsp. ground turmeric
⅛	tsp. ground red pepper
1	clove garlic, minced
2	Tbsp. coconut, toasted
	Hot cooked rice (optional)

1 Thaw shrimp, if frozen. Peel and devein shrimp. Rinse shrimp and pat dry with paper towels.

2 For marinade, in a large bowl use a wire whisk to combine orange marmalade, lime juice, peanut butter, cooking oil, ginger, cardamom, coriander, cumin, turmeric, ground red pepper, and garlic. Remove ¼ cup of the marinade; set aside. Add shrimp to remaining marinade, tossing to coat. Cover and let stand at room temperature 30 minutes, stirring shrimp occasionally.

3 Thread shrimp onto 4 long metal skewers. Grill kabobs on the rack of an uncovered grill directly over medium coals for 10 to 12 minutes or until shrimp turn opaque, turning once. Or, to broil, place kabobs on the unheated rack of a broiler pan. Broil kabobs 4 inches from the heat for 10 to 12 minutes or until the shrimp turn opaque.

4 Heat the reserved ¼ cup marinade to boiling; spoon over shrimp and sprinkle with toasted coconut. If desired, serve over hot cooked rice. Makes 4 servings.

Nutrition Facts per serving: 248 cal., 10 g total fat (2 g sat. fat), 129 mg chol., 180 mg sodium, 22 g carbo., 2 g fiber, 20 g pro.
Daily Values: 5% vit. A, 9% vit. C, 6% calcium, 13% iron.

PRIZE WINNER

Jambalaya on a Stick

Helen D. Conwell
Fairhope, Alabama
$400—Short-Order Kabobs

Prep: 20 minutes **Marinate:** 1 hour
Grill: 12 minutes

18	fresh or frozen large shrimp in shells (about 12 oz.)
12	oz. cooked smoked sausage, cut into 12 pieces
8	oz. skinless, boneless chicken breast halves, cut in twelve 1-inch pieces
1	medium green sweet pepper, seeded and cut in 1-inch pieces
1	medium onion, cut in 1-inch wedges
⅓	cup white wine vinegar
⅓	cup tomato sauce
2	Tbsp. olive oil
2	tsp. dried thyme, crushed
2	tsp. bottled hot pepper sauce* (See note, below right)
¾	tsp. dried minced garlic
3	cups hot cooked rice
2	Tbsp. snipped fresh parsley
6	cherry tomatoes

1 Thaw shrimp, if frozen. Peel and devein shrimp. Rinse shrimp and pat dry with paper towels. In a large plastic bag set in a large bowl combine shrimp, sausage, chicken, sweet pepper, and onion. Set aside.

2 In a small bowl combine vinegar, tomato sauce, olive oil, thyme, bottled hot pepper sauce, and garlic. Pour half the mixture over the meat and vegetables. Seal bag. Chill 1 to 2 hours, turning bag occasionally. Cover and chill the remaining tomato sauce mixture.

3 Drain meat and vegetables; discard marinade. Alternately thread the meat and vegetables on twenty-four 8-inch wooden skewers** (use two skewers per kabob). Grill kabobs on the rack of an uncovered grill directly over medium coals for 12 to 14 minutes or until shrimp are opaque and chicken is no longer pink, turning occasionally.

4 Meanwhile, in a small saucepan heat remaining tomato sauce mixture. Combine cooked rice and parsley. Garnish with cherry tomatoes. Serve rice mixture alongside kabobs and pass tomato sauce. Serves 6.

**Note: Soak skewers in water for 30 minutes before using to prevent burning and scorching.

Nutrition Facts per serving: 451 cal., 23 g total fat (9 g sat. fat), 112 mg chol., 632 mg sodium, 30 g carbo., 2 g fiber, 27 g pro.
Daily Values: 8% vit. A, 45% vit. C, 5% calcium, 18% iron.

Firecracker Fried Chicken

Whether you're serving tender-tongued tots or fire-hardened chileheads, our chicken recipe lets you adjust the heat level to whatever suits your family. The longer the chicken chills in the hot pepper sauce, the hotter it gets. (See the photograph on page 158.)

Prep: 10 minutes **Marinate:** 1 hour
Cook: 25 minutes

8	chicken drumsticks (about 2 lb. total)
1	2-oz. bottle hot pepper sauce (¼ cup)*
⅓	cup all-purpose flour
2	Tbsp. yellow cornmeal Cooking oil (about 3 cups)

1 If desired, remove and discard skin from drumsticks. Place chicken in a plastic bag set in a shallow dish (see photo, below). Pour hot pepper sauce over chicken. Seal bag. Marinate in the refrigerator for 1 to 24 hours, turning bag occasionally.

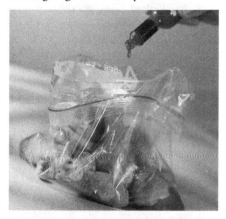

Using a plastic bag makes simple work out of turning chicken as it marinates.

2 Drain chicken, discarding marinade. In another plastic bag combine the flour, cornmeal, and ½ teaspoon *salt*. Add chicken, a few pieces at a time, shaking to coat.

3 In a 12-inch skillet heat ½ inch oil over medium heat until a bread cube dropped into oil sizzles. Carefully add chicken to skillet. Cook, uncovered, over medium heat for 25 to 30 minutes, turning occasionally to brown evenly, until chicken is tender and no longer pink. Drain on paper towels; transfer to a serving platter. Makes 8 drumsticks.

*Note: Hot pepper sauce contains oils that can burn eyes, lips, and sensitive skin, so wear plastic gloves when using and be sure to wash your hands thoroughly afterward.

Nutrition Facts per drumstick with skin removed: 164 cal., 11 g total fat (2 g sat. fat), 38 mg chol., 203 mg sodium, 5 g carbo., 0 g fiber, 11 g pro.
Daily Values: 2% vit. A, 3% vit. C, 5% iron.

LOW FAT

Zesty Curried-Lime Chicken Kabobs

Prep: 20 minutes **Marinate:** 4 hours
Grill: 18 minutes

- 1 **lb. skinless, boneless chicken breast halves, cut into 1½-inch pieces**
- ½ **cup plain yogurt**
- ¼ **cup snipped fresh cilantro**
- 1 **tsp. finely shredded lime peel**
- 2 **Tbsp. lime juice**
- 2 **Tbsp. olive oil or cooking oil**
- 1 **Tbsp. honey**
- 1 **Tbsp. Dijon-style mustard**
- 2 **cloves garlic, minced**
- ½ **tsp. curry powder**
- ¼ **tsp. salt**
- ¼ **tsp. black pepper**
- 2 **medium green and/or red sweet peppers, cut into 1-inch pieces**
- 1 **medium zucchini, sliced ½-inch thick**
- 8 **cherry tomatoes**

1 Place chicken in a plastic bag set in a large bowl; set aside. For marinade, in a small bowl stir together the yogurt, cilantro, lime peel, lime juice, olive oil or cooking oil, honey, Dijon-style mustard, garlic, curry powder, salt, and black pepper. Pour over chicken; seal bag. Turn to coat chicken. Chill for 4 to 24 hours, turning bag occasionally. Drain chicken, reserving marinade.

2 Alternately thread chicken, sweet peppers, and zucchini on eight metal skewers, leaving ¼-inch space between pieces. Brush vegetables with reserved marinade.

3 In a grill with a cover arrange preheated coals for indirect grilling. Test for medium heat where the kabobs will cook. Place kabobs on the grill rack. Cover and grill for 18 to 20 minutes or until chicken is tender and no longer pink, turning once. Place a cherry tomato on the end of each skewer during the last 1 minute of grilling. Makes 4 servings.

Nutrition Facts per serving: 261 cal., 9 g total fat (2 g sat. fat), 68 mg chol., 256 mg sodium, 15 g carbo., 2 g fiber, 30 g pro.
Daily Values: 11% vit. A, 103% vit. C, 97% calcium, 10% iron.

LOW FAT

Skewered Five-Spice Pork and Vegetables

Prep: 30 minutes **Marinate:** 2 hours
Grill: 10 minutes

- 1 **lb. boneless pork loin, cut into bite-size strips**
- ¼ **cup bottled salsa**
- 2 **Tbsp. soy sauce**
- 2 **Tbsp. bottled oyster sauce**
- 1 **Tbsp. sugar**
- 1 **tsp. five-spice powder**
- ¼ **tsp. ground red pepper**
- 1 **medium red sweet pepper, cut into 1-inch pieces**
- 4 **green onions, cut diagonally into 1½-inch pieces**
- 8 **large fresh mushrooms**
- 1 **Tbsp. cooking oil**

1 Place pork in a plastic bag set in a large bowl. In a small bowl stir together the salsa, soy sauce, oyster sauce, sugar, five-spice powder, and ground red pepper. Pour over meat in bag; seal bag. Turn to coat meat. Chill 2 to 4 hours, turning bag occasionally. Drain meat, reserving marinade.

2 Brush vegetables lightly with cooking oil. Alternately thread pork, sweet pepper, green onions, and mushrooms onto four 12- to 14-inch metal skewers.

3 Grill kabobs on the rack of an uncovered grill directly over medium coals for 10 to 12 minutes or until meat is tender and juices run clear and vegetables are tender, turning and brushing with marinade halfway through grilling. Makes 4 servings.

Nutrition Facts per serving: 237 cal., 10 g total fat (3 g sat. fat), 66 mg chol., 710 mg sodium, 9 g carbo., 2 g fiber, 27 g pro.
Daily Values: 18% vit. A, 87% vit. C, 4% calcium, 11% iron.

30 MINUTE

Picnic Hot Dog Platter

Setting out a platter loaded with a variety of hot dogs and sausages will please everyone at your gathering.

Prep: 10 minutes **Grill:** 20 minutes (fresh) or 10 minutes (cooked)

- 12 **frankfurters, uncooked bratwurst, smoked pork sausages, veal sausages, turkey sausages, vegetarian frankfurters, or other favorites**
- 1 **dozen frankfurter or bratwurst buns or French-style rolls, split**
- 1 **recipe Tart Apple Mustard (see page 151)**
- 1 **recipe Bacon Brown-Sugar Mustard (see page 151)**
- 1 **recipe Early Girl Tomato Mustard (see page 151)**
  Other condiments, such as chopped pickled peppers, sliced tomatoes, pickle relish, and crumbled cooked bacon (optional)

1 Pierce uncooked sausages all over with a fork or cut several shallow crosswise slits in each uncooked sausage.

2 In a grill with a cover arrange preheated coals around a drip pan. Test for medium heat above the pan. Grill the uncooked sausages on grill rack above the drip pan, turning once, for 20 to 25 minutes or until brown and a thermometer registers 170°. Grill the frankfurters and cooked sausages on grill rack above the drip pan about 10 minutes or until brown and a thermometer registers 165°, turning once.

3 To serve, place sausages in buns and top with desired mustards and condiments. Makes 12 servings.

Nutrition Facts per frankfurter, bun, and about 1 tablespoon Tart Apple Mustard: 281 cal., 16 g total fat (6 g sat. fat), 24 mg chol., 757 mg sodium, 24 g carbo., 1 g fiber, 9 g pro. Daily Values: 6% calcium, 10% iron.

NO FAT

Tart Apple Mustard

Shreds of fresh apple combine with honey mustard for a spread that balances sweetness and bite.

Prep: 5 minutes **Chill:** 2 hours

- ½ cup honey mustard
- 2 Tbsp. shredded, unpeeled tart green apple
- ½ tsp. ground black pepper

1 In a small bowl stir together honey mustard, apple, and pepper. Cover and refrigerate 2 hours to blend flavors before serving.

2 Serve with Picnic Hot Dog Platter (see recipe, page 150). Store any remaining mustard in the refrigerator up to 24 hours. Makes about ⅔ cup.

Nutrition Facts per tablespoon: 23 cal., 0 g total fat, 0 mg chol., 11 mg sodium, 5 g carbo., 0 g fiber, 0 g pro.

LOW FAT

Bacon Brown-Sugar Mustard

Every kind of sausage tastes better when bacon, mustard, and brown sugar join forces.

Prep: 10 minutes **Chill:** Overnight

- ¾ cup yellow mustard
- 3 slices bacon, crisp-cooked, drained, and finely crumbled
- 4 tsp. brown sugar

1 In a small bowl stir together yellow mustard, bacon, and brown sugar. Cover and refrigerate overnight to blend flavors before serving.

2 Serve with Picnic Hot Dog Platter (see recipe, page 150). Store any remaining mustard in the refrigerator up to 2 days. Makes 1 cup.

Nutrition Facts per tablespoon: 22 cal., 1 g total fat (0 g sat. fat), 1 mg chol., 161 mg sodium, 1 g carbo., 0 g fiber, 1 g pro. Daily Values: 1% calcium, 1% iron.

30 MINUTE, LOW FAT

Early Girl Tomato Mustard

Take advantage of early-ripening tomato types, such as Early Girl, with this topper. To peel tomatoes easily: Using kitchen tongs or a fork, gently lower tomato into boiling water for 30 seconds or until skins split. Dip in cold water or rinse under a running faucet. Remove skin.

Start to finish: 15 minutes

- ⅓ cup creamy Dijon-style mustard blend
- ½ tsp. dry mustard

EDITOR'S TIP

Picnic Safety Guidelines

Keep food safe when out of doors by following these rules:

● Allow food to stand out at room temperature no more than 2 hours. When temperatures are 80° or above, allow to stand no more than 1 hour. After that, it's safest to discard the food because bacteria can multiply to dangerous levels.

● For longer storage outdoors, keep food in a cooler with plenty of ice. (The Better Homes and Gardens® Test Kitchen recommends using at least one 10-pound bag of ice in a 54-quart cooler.)

● Try to keep hot foods hot, though this is more difficult under picnic or backyard conditions. In the case of ribs, burgers, and hot dogs, food-safety experts say that if meats have been sitting out long enough to cool off, return them to the grill until they're heated through.

- ½ cup peeled, seeded, and chopped tomatoes

1 In a small bowl stir together Dijon-style mustard blend and dry mustard until well combined. Gently stir in tomatoes.

2 Serve mustard with Picnic Hot Dog Platter (see recipe, page 150). Or, cover and refrigerate mustard up to 24 hours before serving. Makes about ⅔ cup.

Nutrition Facts per tablespoon: 20 cal., 2 g total fat (0 g sat. fat), 0 mg chol., 102 mg sodium, 2 g carbo., 0 g fiber, 0 g pro. Daily Values: 1% vit. A, 3% vit. C.

Iced Tea Gets Hot

A frosty glass of iced tea on a sultry day is one of summer's coolest pleasures—especially when you brew this amber thirst-quencher in a way that brings out its best of flavors.

The secret: Fresh tea, careful measurement, and close attention to timing. So grab your measuring cup, a timer, and get ready to make iced tea that stands up to the pickiest palates and the hottest days.

Iced Tea

Prep: 5 minutes Steep: 3 to 5 minutes

6 tea bags
1 quart boiling water

Place tea bags in a heatproof pitcher or glass measure. Add boiling water. Let steep 3 to 5 minutes; remove tea bags. Use immediately, or cool at room temperature. (Don't chill quickly or tea will cloud.) Serve over ice. Sweeten as desired. (For tips, see right.) Makes 5 servings.

Tea-Making Tips

● Place tea bags into a heatproof glass measure. Boiling water can crack plain glass vessels, so save Grandma's best pitcher for serving tea after it has cooled.
● Ever burn your fingers fishing for the tea bags? Tie strings of tea bags to the handle of the glass measure, and bags won't fall in when the boiling water is added.

● Dressed up or down, iced tea is enjoyed everywhere. In addition to the traditional lemon or mint garnishes, try topping off your glasses with lavender sprigs, lemon verbena, fresh pineapple spears, or edible flowers.

Sweet Touch

If you prefer your tea sweetened, take a tip from folks in the South where lunch and dinner would be unthinkable for many without a pitcher of "sweet tea" on the table. Just stirring sugar into a glass won't satisfy the finicky taste buds of those below the Mason-Dixon line. Spooned into cold tea, sugar dissolves very slowly, if at all. Many folks get around this by stirring their sugar in while the tea is still hot. But if you have a mix of sweet tea and plain tea drinkers among those you're serving, here's a tip that will let you please them all. Alongside the tea, offer them a pitcher of Simple Syrup (recipe below) made of water and sugar. Using this syrup makes it easy to bring tea to a just-right level of sweetness. The syrup has other uses as well, such as poaching fruit and making mint juleps.

Simple Syrup: In a small saucepan combine 1 cup of water and 1 cup of sugar. Bring to boiling over medium heat, stirring until sugar dissolves. (The syrup is done when it is completely clear and the surface is covered with bubbles.) Remove from heat; allow to cool. Transfer syrup to a covered glass pitcher or jar. Pass with tea. Store remaining syrup, tightly covered, in the refrigerator up to two weeks.

LOW FAT

Pork and Wild Mushroom Kabobs

Use as little olive oil as possible when coating vegetables by using a pump spray to apply instead of a pastry brush.

Prep: 15 minutes **Marinate:** 1 hour
Grill: 12 to 14 minutes

12 oz. pork tenderloin, cut into
     1-inch cubes
2   shallots, finely chopped
2   Tbsp. lime juice
1   Tbsp. olive oil
1   tsp. chili powder
1   tsp. curry powder
1   tsp. lemon grass, finely chopped
¼   tsp. black pepper

6   oz. fresh shiitake, crimini, or
     button mushrooms, stems
     removed
1   medium green sweet pepper, cut
     into 1-inch pieces
1   small red onion, cut into 1-inch
     wedges
4   teaspoons olive oil
     Hot cooked rice

1 Place pork cubes in a plastic bag set in a large bowl; set aside. In a small bowl combine the shallots, lime juice, 1 tablespoon olive oil, chili powder, curry powder, lemon grass, and black pepper. Pour mixture over meat; seal bag. Turn bag to coat meat. Marinate in refrigerator for 1 to 4 hours, turning bag occasionally. Drain pork, discarding marinade.

2 Alternately thread the pork, mushrooms, sweet pepper, and onion on eight 8- to 10-inch metal skewers, leaving ¼-inch space between pieces. Lightly brush vegetables with olive oil.

3 Grill on the rack of an uncovered grill directly over medium heat for 12 to 14 minutes or until meat is tender and juices run clear and vegetables are tender. Serve with hot cooked rice. Makes 4 servings.

Nutrition Facts per serving: 321 cal., 10 g total fat (2 g sat. fat), 50 mg chol., 45 mg sodium, 33 g carbo., 2 g fiber, 24 g pro.
Daily Values: 5% vit. A, 45% vit. C, 3% calcium, 15% iron.

LOW FAT

Summer Breeze Ribs

A coating of yellow mustard—a trick borrowed from barbecue champions— helps the spice rub stay on and gives the meat a distinctive flavor. Well-chilled coleslaw makes a palate-reviving accompaniment, whether the slaw is purchased or homemade. (See the photograph on page 161.)

Prep: 20 minutes **Chill:** 6 hours
Grill: 1 hour 20 minutes

- ¼ cup packed brown sugar
- 2 tsp. seasoned salt
- 2 tsp. chili powder
- 4 lb. pork loin back ribs or pork spareribs
- ¼ cup yellow mustard
- 4 cups hickory or fruitwood chips
- ¼ cup bottled barbecue sauce
  Bottled barbecue sauce

1 In a small bowl combine brown sugar, seasoned salt, and chili powder. Brush ribs with mustard. Sprinkle brown sugar mixture onto ribs. Cover and refrigerate for 6 to 24 hours.

2 At least 1 hour before grilling, soak wood chips in enough water to cover. Drain.

3 In a grill with a cover arrange preheated coals around a drip pan. Test for medium heat above the pan. Sprinkle some of the drained wood chips over the coals. Pour 1 inch of water into the drip pan. Place ribs, meaty side up, on grill rack over drip pan but not over coals, or use a rib rack placed over the drip pan. Cover and grill for 1¼ to 1½ hours or until ribs are tender, adding more coals and wood chips as necessary.

4 Brush with the ¼ cup barbecue sauce. Grill ribs for 5 minutes more. Serve with additional bottled barbecue sauce. Makes 6 servings.

Nutrition Facts per serving: 244 cal., 9 g total fat (3 g sat. fat), 57 mg chol., 810 mg sodium, 11 g carbo., 1 g fiber, 27 g pro.
Daily Values: 4% vit. A, 3% vit. C, 3% calcium, 7% iron.

Rhubarb and Raisin Cobbler

This dessert—sugar-coated spiced biscuits over bubbly sweet, yet tart, rhubarb filling—demands a scoop of rich and creamy vanilla ice cream.

Prep: 25 minutes **Bake:** 20 minutes
Stand: 45 minutes

- 1 cup all-purpose flour
- 3 Tbsp. brown sugar
- 1 tsp. baking powder
- 1 tsp. ground cinnamon
- ¼ tsp. baking soda
- ¼ tsp. ground nutmeg
- ¼ cup cold butter
- 1⅓ cups granulated sugar
- 3 Tbsp. cornstarch
- ⅓ cup water
- 8 cups sliced fresh or frozen rhubarb
- ½ cup raisins
- 1 egg, slightly beaten
- ¼ cup milk
- 1 Tbsp. coarse sugar
  Vanilla ice cream (optional)

1 For topping, in a medium bowl stir together flour, brown sugar, baking powder, cinnamon, baking soda, and nutmeg. Using a pastry blender cut in butter until mixture resembles coarse crumbs. Set aside. Preheat oven to 400°.

BARBECUE MENU

- **Summer Breeze Ribs (see left)**

- **Purchased or homemade coleslaw**

- **Hot-cooked corn on the cob with herb butter**

- **Hard rolls or French-style rolls**

- **Fresh-squeezed lemonade, iced tea, or cold beer**

- **Home Run Pie (see page 165)**

2 For filling, in a large saucepan stir together the granulated sugar and cornstarch. Add the water. Stir in rhubarb and raisins. Cook and stir until thickened and bubbly. Remove from heat. Keep filling hot.

3 In a small bowl stir together the egg and milk. Add the egg-milk mixture to the flour mixture, stirring just to moisten.

4 Transfer hot filling to ungreased 2-quart casserole. Immediately spoon biscuit topping in eight mounds on top of filling. Sprinkle the coarse sugar over biscuits.

5 Bake about 20 minutes or until a wooden toothpick inserted into a biscuit comes out clean. Cool on wire rack at least 45 minutes. Serve warm. If desired, serve with vanilla ice cream. Makes 8 servings.

Nutrition Facts per serving: 327 cal., 7 g total fat (4 g sat. fat), 44 mg chol., 171 mg sodium, 64 g carbo., 3 g fiber, 4 g pro.
Daily Values: 8% vit. A, 14% vit. C, 16% calcium, 8% iron.

Dip It!

With the right tool, a bit of parental guidance, and a go-for-it-attitude, dipping ice cream is a cinch. Here's the scoop on scooping:

● **Choose a sturdy ice cream scoop with an easy-grip, nonslip handle.**

● **Slightly softened ice cream is the easiest to dip. Allow the container of ice cream to sit out on the counter for 10 to 15 minutes before scooping. If the outside temperature is super-hot, let ice cream soften in the refrigerator, instead.**

● **For an effortless release, first dip a scoop into warm water, shake it off, then dip it into ice cream. Dip into water between scoops.**

Strawberry Ice Cream Tart

Prep: 30 minutes **Bake:** 20 minutes
Cool: 1 hour

> **Strawberry and/or vanilla ice cream (about 2 pints)**
> **Nonstick cooking spray**
> 1 **roll (18 oz.) refrigerated sugar cookie dough**
> ⅓ **cup sliced almonds**
> 1 **Tbsp. sugar**
> ¼ **tsp. ground cinnamon**
> 4 **cups fresh strawberries**
> ¼ **cup strawberry ice cream topping**
> **Toasted coconut (optional)**

1 Use an ice cream scoop to form 12 balls of ice cream. Place the ice cream balls on a large, cold plate; store in the freezer.

2 Preheat oven to 350°. Line an 11×7×1½-inch baking pan with foil. Coat foil lightly with nonstick cooking spray. With fingers, press the cookie dough evenly into the foil-lined pan. Sprinkle almonds over the dough and press lightly into dough.

3 In a bowl stir together sugar and cinnamon. Sprinkle mixture over dough. Bake about 20 minutes or until top is golden brown. Cool completely in pan before gently lifting out.

4 Meanwhile, wash strawberries and remove green caps. Slice large strawberries in half. Place strawberries in a bowl. Cover and chill.

5 To assemble tart, stir ice cream topping into strawberries. Gently peel foil from crust. Carefully place crust on serving tray. Quickly transfer ice cream scoops from freezer to crust, alternating strawberry and vanilla, if using both kinds of ice cream. Spoon some of the strawberry mixture on top. If desired, sprinkle with coconut. Cut tart into 12 pieces. Serve immediately. Pass remaining strawberry mixture to spoon on top of each serving. Makes 12 servings.

Nutrition Facts per serving: 282 cal., 12 g total fat (4 g sat. fat), 19 mg chol., 193 mg sodium, 41 g carbo., 2 g fiber, 3 g pro.
Daily Values: 2% vit. A, 48% vit. C, 8% calcium, 6% iron.

Banana Split Ice Cream Tart

Prepare tart as directed, except use vanilla, chocolate, and strawberry ice creams. Substitute a sliced banana for half of the strawberries. Top each serving with bananas and strawberries, your favorite fudge sauce, whipped cream, and maraschino cherries.

Individual Ice Cream Tarts

Bake the refrigerated cookies as directed on the package, topping each one with some sliced almonds and sugar-cinnamon mixture before baking. To serve, top each cookie with a scoop of strawberry or vanilla ice cream, the strawberries, and a spoon or two of whipped cream.

Apple and Cranberry Maple Crisp

A drizzle of pure maple syrup makes this traditional crisp something special.

Prep: 25 minutes **Bake:** 45 minutes
Cool: 30 minutes

> 3 **Tbsp. granulated sugar**
> 2 **Tbsp. all-purpose flour**
> 5 **cups peeled, sliced apples**
> 1 **cup cranberries**
> ⅔ **cup pure maple or maple-flavored syrup**
> ½ **cup quick-cooking rolled oats**
> ½ **cup packed brown sugar**
> ¼ **cup all-purpose flour**
> ¼ **cup chopped walnuts**
> ½ **tsp. ground mace**
> ½ **tsp. ground cinnamon**
> ¼ **cup butter**
> ½ **cup whipping cream**
> 1 **Tbsp. brown sugar**

1 Preheat oven to 350°. In a large bowl stir together the granulated sugar and 2 tablespoons flour. Add apples and cranberries, tossing gently to coat. Transfer fruit mixture to a 2-quart rectangular baking dish. Drizzle the maple syrup over fruit.

2 In a medium bowl combine oats, the ½ cup brown sugar, the ¼ cup flour, walnuts, mace, and cinnamon. Cut in the butter until crumbly. Sprinkle over apple mixture.

3 Bake, uncovered, 45 minutes or until apples are tender. Cool on a wire rack for 30 minutes.

4 Meanwhile, in a chilled mixing bowl beat whipping cream and the 1 tablespoon brown sugar with an electric mixer on medium speed until soft peaks form. Serve crisp warm with whipped cream. Makes 8 servings.

Nutrition Facts per serving: 369 cal., 15 g total fat (8 g sat. fat), 37 mg chol., 80 mg sodium, 60 g carbo., 3 g fiber, 3 g pro.
Daily Values: 14% vit. A, 8% vit. C, 6% calcium, 8% iron.

Peach Melba Crisp

Summer fresh flavors can be savored in the winter with this simple crisp that can be made using frozen fruit.

Prep: 10 minutes **Bake:** 40 minutes

 5 ripe peaches, peeled, pitted, and sliced, or 5 cups frozen unsweetened peach slices, thawed but not drained
2½ tsp. cornstarch
 1 10-oz. pkg. frozen red raspberries in syrup, thawed
1½ cups plain granola
 ⅔ cup flaked or shredded coconut
 3 Tbsp. butter, melted
    Vanilla or cinnamon-flavored ice cream (optional)

1 Preheat oven to 350°. Place peaches in a 2-quart square baking dish. Sprinkle with cornstarch and toss gently to coat.

2 If desired, press the undrained raspberries through a sieve; discard seeds. Spoon the whole or sieved raspberries over the peaches. Bake, uncovered, for 20 minutes.

3 Meanwhile, in a medium bowl combine granola, coconut, and melted butter. Stir peach mixture gently. Sprinkle granola mixture over peaches. Bake for 20 to 25 minutes more or until topping is golden and sauce is bubbly. Serve warm. If desired, serve with ice cream. Makes 6 servings.

Nutrition Facts per serving: 462 cal., 16 g total fat (7 g sat. fat), 16 mg chol., 81 mg sodium, 80 g carbo., 10 g fiber, 5 g pro.
Daily Values: 22% vit. A, 39% vit. C, 5% calcium, 11% iron.

Two-Tone Lemonade Mousse

Make sure all the gelatin is dissolved before you take it off the heat or the dessert will turn out heavy. The gelatin mixture should be crystal-clear, and there should be no granules in the bottom of the pan. (See the photograph on page 164.)

Prep: 25 minutes
Chill: 1¼ hours plus 2 hours

 1 envelope unflavored gelatin
 ⅓ cup sugar
 ⅔ cup frozen lemonade concentrate, thawed
 4 drops red food coloring
 1 cup whipping cream
 ½ cup fresh blueberries
 3 thin lemon slices, halved, or pink grapefruit slices, halved (optional)
    Lemon peel curls (optional)

1 In a small saucepan combine gelatin and sugar; add ⅔ cup *water*. Cook and stir over medium heat until dissolved. Remove from heat. Stir in ⅓ cup *water* and lemonade concentrate. Divide mixture in half, transferring each to a medium bowl. Stir red food coloring into one portion of the mixture. Cover and chill about 1¼ to 1½ hours or until mixtures mound.

2 In a chilled mixing bowl beat whipping cream with an electric mixer on medium speed until soft peaks form (tips curl); set aside.

EDITOR'S TIP
Prickly, But Delicious

Spice up your summer fruit bowl by slipping a horned melon into the usual mix of apples, bananas, and oranges.

The spiky skin of this tropical fruit ranges from golden yellow to bright orange. The skin isn't edible, but the lime-green pulp flecked with soft white seeds is, and it tastes like a cross between a melon and a cucumber. Cut the fruit open, scoop out the pulp, and enjoy. Or you can spoon it over ice cream. For fun, try using the hollowed-out melon halves as whimsical dessert bowls. Besides being fun to look at, horned melons contain vitamins A and C, iron, and potassium.

3 Wash beaters. Beat plain lemonade mixture with electric mixer on medium speed about 30 seconds or until light and foamy. Beat pink mixture until light and foamy. Fold half the whipped cream into each lemonade mixture.

4 Carefully layer plain mixture and pink mixture into six small glasses or dessert dishes, dividing evenly.

5 Cover and chill at least 2 hours before serving. Garnish with fresh berries and, if desired, citrus slices and lemon peel curls. Makes 6 servings.

Nutrition Facts per serving: 249 cal., 15 g total fat (9 g sat. fat), 55 mg chol., 21 mg sodium, 29 g carbo., 0 g fiber, 2 g pro.
Daily Values: 17% vit. A, 13% vit. C, 3% calcium, 2% iron.

Peaches 'n' Cream Ice Cream

Cream cheese creates a smooth ice cream with a slight tang that helps to balance the sweetness of the peaches. (See the photograph on page 157.)

Prep: 20 minutes **Chill:** 2 hours
Freeze: 30 minutes **Ripen:** 4 hours

2½	cups half-and-half or light cream
¾	cup granulated sugar
½	cup packed brown sugar
2	eggs, beaten
1	8-oz. pkg. cream cheese or reduced-fat cream cheese (Neufchâtel), softened
2	cups fresh or frozen (thawed), unsweetened peaches
½	tsp. finely shredded lemon peel
1	Tbsp. lemon juice
1	tsp. vanilla
2	rolled sugar ice cream cones
¼	cup sliced almonds, toasted
	Peach slices (optional)

1 In a large saucepan combine 1½ cups of the half-and-half or light cream, the granulated sugar, brown sugar, and eggs. Cook and stir over medium heat just until boiling; remove from heat. (Mixture will appear curdled.) Set aside.

2 In a large mixing bowl beat cream cheese with an electric mixer on medium speed until smooth. Gradually beat in the hot mixture. Cover and chill mixture in the refrigerator for 2 hours.

3 In a blender container or food processor bowl place half of the peaches. Cover and blend or process until nearly smooth. Coarsely chop remaining peaches and set aside.

4 Stir remaining half-and-half, pureed peaches, lemon peel, lemon juice, and vanilla into chilled mixture. Freeze in a 4- or 5-quart ice cream freezer according to manufacturer's directions (see photo 1, below).

5 Remove dasher from freezer. Stir in chopped peaches (see photo 2, below). Ripen ice cream 4 hours (see "What's Ripening?", right).

1. Add rock salt with ice cream maker running. If canister sticks, pour about a half-cup of water around perimeter of ice.

2. Remove dasher before trying to stir in peaches. If you try to stir them in with the machine running, they'll get smashed.

TEST KITCHEN TIP
What's Ripening?

"Ripening" means allowing newly made ice cream to firm up, undisturbed, in the ice cream maker. The result is ice cream that is better tasting and smoother.

To ripen, drain off excess liquid from the freezer bucket. Remove the dasher from the canister; cover canister with waxed paper, plastic wrap, or foil; and replace the lid. Plug the hole in the lid with a cork. Push the can back down into the ice.

Using 4 parts ice to 1 part rock salt, pack additional layers of ice and rock salt into the freezer to cover the top of the can. Cover the freezer with newspaper or a heavy cloth to keep it cold. Allow to stand, in the shade, at least 4 hours, repacking with additional ice and rock salt as ice melts away, about every hour or so in hot weather.

6 Meanwhile, for topping: In a plastic bag crush ice cream cones with a rolling pin, reserving bottom tips, if desired, for garnish. Combine crushed ice cream cones and almonds.

7 To serve, scoop ice cream into individual serving mugs or bowls and sprinkle with topping. If desired, garnish with ice cream cone tips and peach slices. Makes 14 (½-cup) servings.

Nutrition Facts per serving: 241 cal., 12 g total fat (7 g sat. fat), 64 mg chol., 78 mg sodium, 29 g carbo., 1 g fiber, 4 g pro.
Daily Values: 15% vit. A, 7% vit. C, 8% calcium, 4% iron.

Peaches 'n' Cream Ice Cream (page 156)

Left: Roasted Garlic and Tomatillo Soup (page 145)
Below: Pea and Macaroni Salad (page 144)
Page 158: Firecracker Fried Chicken (page 149)

Right: Many-Splendored Tomato-Crab Salad (page 176)
Below: Three-Bean Salad (page 143)
Page 161, top: Watermelon Steaks with Melon Salsa (page 142)
Page 161, bottom: Summer Breeze Ribs (page 153)

Right: Fruit Salsa in a Big Way
(page 170)
Below: Skillet-Roasted Potato Salad
(page 144)
Page 163: High-and-Dry Clambake
(page 147)

Top: Home Run Pie (page 165)
Above: Pear and Blueberry Crisp
(page 165)
Right: Two-Tone Lemonade
Mousse (page 155)

Home Run Pie

Make sure the piecrust extends all the way to the lip of the pie pan so that no filling can leak underneath. Leaks cause pie to stick to the pan, making it impossible to remove. If you don't have individual metal pie pans, foil ones from the supermarket work well. (See the photograph on page 164.)

Prep: 25 minutes **Bake:** 38 minutes

- 1 recipe Pastry for Single-Crust Pie (see right)
- 2 eggs, slightly beaten
- ⅔ cup light-colored corn syrup
- ½ cup sugar
- ¼ cup margarine or butter, melted
- 1 tsp. vanilla
- ¾ cup lightly salted dry-roasted peanuts
- 1½ to 2 cups caramel-coated popcorn and peanuts

1 Preheat oven to 350°. Prepare Pastry for Single-Crust Pie. Divide pastry into 4 portions. On a lightly floured surface roll each portion of pastry into a 6-inch circle. Ease each pastry round into a 5-inch individual pie pan. Trim pastry, if necessary, to within ¼ inch of the edge of pie pan. Snip star-shaped points around edges with kitchen shears (see photo, below).

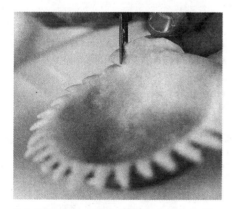

Snip edges into points using scissors; hold the uncut piecrust to avoid tearing.

2 For filling, in a medium bowl combine eggs, corn syrup, sugar, margarine, and vanilla. Mix well. Stir in dry-roasted peanuts. Place pans on a 15×10×1-inch baking pan. Divide filling evenly among the pastry shells.

3 Bake for 35 to 40 minutes or until a knife inserted near the center comes out clean. Remove pans from oven. Divide caramel-coated popcorn and peanuts over the 4 pies. Return to oven; bake 3 minutes more. Cool on a wire rack. Refrigerate within 2 hours of cooling. Cover for longer storage. Makes 4 tart-size pies (8 servings).

Pastry for Single-Crust Pie

Stir together 1¼ cups all-purpose flour and ¼ teaspoon salt. Cut in ⅓ cup shortening until pieces are the size of small peas. Using a total of 4 to 5 tablespoons cold water, sprinkle 1 tablespoon water at a time over part of the mixture. Gently toss with a fork. Push to side of bowl. Repeat until all is moistened. Form into a ball.

Food Processor Directions for Pastry

Prepare as above, except use steel blade in bowl of food processor. Add flour, shortening, and salt. Cover; process with on/off turns until most of mixture resembles cornmeal, but with a few larger pieces. With food processor running, quickly add ¼ cup water through feed tube. Stop processor when all water is added; scrape down sides. Process with two on/off turns (mixture may not all be moistened). Remove dough from bowl. Shape into a ball.

Nutrition Facts per serving: 504 cal., 24 g total fat (4 g sat. fat), 50 mg chol., 346 mg sodium, 67 g carbo., 1 g fiber, 8 g pro.
Daily Values: 8% vit. A, 2% calcium, 10% iron.

PRIZE WINNER

Pear and Blueberry Crisp

Janice M. Herron
Evergreen, Colorado
$200—Summer Cobblers and Crisps
(See the photograph on page 164.)

Prep: 20 minutes **Bake:** 30 minutes
Stand: 40 minutes

- ¾ cup granulated sugar
- 1 Tbsp. cornstarch
- 8 ripe medium pears, peeled, cored, and cut into large chunks
- 2 cups fresh or frozen blueberries, thawed
- 4 tsp. lemon juice
- 1¼ cups all-purpose flour
- ½ cup packed brown sugar
- ½ cup cold butter, cut up
- 2 Tbsp. cognac or brandy (optional)
- 1 cup whipping cream
- 2 Tbsp. powdered sugar

1 Preheat oven to 400°. Combine ¼ cup of the granulated sugar and the cornstarch. Add fruit and lemon juice, stirring to combine. Transfer to a 3-quart rectangular baking dish.

2 Combine flour, remaining ½ cup granulated sugar, and brown sugar. Cut in butter until mixture is crumbly; sprinkle over fruit. Bake 30 to 35 minutes or until lightly browned. Remove from oven. If desired, drizzle with cognac. Let stand 40 minutes.

3 In a chilled small mixing bowl beat whipping cream and powdered sugar together until soft peaks form. Serve with warm crisp. Serves 10.

Nutrition Facts per serving: 421 cal., 19 g total fat (12 g sat. fat), 59 mg chol., 115 mg sodium, 63 g carbo., 4 g fiber, 3 g pro.
Daily Values: 20% vit. A, 17% vit. C, 5% calcium, 7% iron.

PRIZE WINNER

Rhubarb Surprise Crisp

Barbara M. Wolcott
San Luis Obispo, California
$400—Summer Cobblers and Crisps

Prep: 20 minutes **Bake:** 30 minutes

⅔ cup granulated sugar
2 or 3 tsp. cornstarch
¼ tsp. ground cinnamon
2 cups sliced fresh rhubarb or
     frozen unsweetened sliced
     rhubarb, thawed
2 cups coarsely chopped
     strawberries
2 Tbsp. snipped fresh basil
½ cup all-purpose flour
½ cup quick-cooking rolled oats
⅓ cup packed brown sugar
¼ tsp. salt
3 Tbsp. margarine or butter, melted

1 Preheat oven to 375°. In a medium bowl combine the granulated sugar, the cornstarch, and cinnamon. (For fresh rhubarb, use 2 teaspoons cornstarch. For frozen, use 3 teaspoons cornstarch.) Stir in rhubarb, strawberries, and basil. Transfer fruit mixture to a 2-quart square baking dish, spreading evenly. Set aside.

2 For topping, in another medium bowl stir together flour, oats, brown sugar, and salt. Stir in melted margarine or butter. Sprinkle topping evenly over fruit.

3 Bake for 30 to 35 minutes or until fruit is tender and topping is golden brown. Serve warm. Makes 6 servings.

Nutrition Facts per serving: 276 cal., 7 g total fat (4 g sat. fat), 16 mg chol., 167 mg sodium, 52 g carbo., 3 g fiber, 3 g pro.
Daily Values: 7% vit. A, 51% vit. C, 6% calcium, 7% iron.

Blackberry Crisp

When the bushes are loaded with plump, ripe berries, pick a bowl for this classic crisp. Frozen berries won't do, as the topping gets too soggy and won't "crisp."

Prep: 20 minutes **Bake:** 40 minutes

¼ cup granulated sugar
3 Tbsp. all-purpose flour
1 tsp. ground cinnamon
5 cups fresh blackberries
¼ cup honey
⅔ cup regular rolled oats
⅔ cup packed brown sugar
⅓ cup all-purpose flour
¼ tsp. ground cinnamon
⅓ cup butter
     Vanilla ice cream

1 Preheat oven to 375°. For filling, in a large bowl stir together the granulated sugar, 3 tablespoons flour, and 1 teaspoon cinnamon. Add berries and toss to coat. Transfer berry mixture to a 2-quart square baking dish, spreading evenly. Drizzle honey over berry mixture. Set aside.

2 For topping, in a medium bowl stir together the oats, brown sugar, ⅓ cup flour, and cinnamon. Using a pastry blender, cut in the butter until mixture resembles coarse crumbs. Sprinkle topping evenly over berry mixture.

3 Bake about 40 minutes or until topping is golden. Serve warm with ice cream. Makes 8 servings.

Nutrition Facts per serving: 302 cal., 9 g total fat (5 g sat. fat), 22 mg chol., 91 mg sodium, 56 g carbo., 6 g fiber, 3 g pro.
Daily Values: 9% vit. A, 32% vit. C, 6% calcium, 9% iron.

TEST KITCHEN TIP
The Best of Crisps And Cobblers

True to their homey nature, crisps and cobblers bake well in either metal baking pans or casseroles of any kind: glass, pottery, or ceramic baking dishes. Remember these tips:

Size is more important than shape. Always use the size dish called for in the recipe. The dish needs to be deep enough to allow for the fruit filling to bubble up during baking. It's best to place a baking sheet beneath the dish to catch any spills.

If the fruit filling is acidic (pineapple, citrus fruits, and cranberries contain acid, for instance), the cobbler or crisp can be baked in a metal pan but shouldn't be stored in one because the acid can react with the metal. Any leftovers should be stored in a glass baking dish.

A few helpful gadgets to keep on hand when preparing cobblers and crisps include:

● An apple corer for removing core and seeds from apples and pears.

● A vegetable peeler for removing cores and peeling fruits.

● A pastry blender for easily cutting in cold butter for biscuit toppings and crumbly crisp toppings.

august

IN THIS CHAPTER

30-minute recipes indicated in COLOR.
Low-fat and no-fat recipes indicated
with a ♥.
Photographs indicated in italics.
*Bonus recipe

Just Say "Oui" to Brie

Give Brie a boost by glamorizing the subtle cheese with sublime toppings and fillings. Let your taste buds and the ideas *below* be your guide to creating impressive appetizers. No need to cut off the snowy-white rind before serving. It's edible and has a nice earthy taste.

● **Add a spice coating** to the creamy, mellow cheese with a generous sprinkling of a Cajun seasoning blend. First brush the rind with 1 to 2 teaspoons olive oil; then top with the peppery-hot seasoning blend. Place cheese on an ovenproof platter; bake in a 350° oven until cheese is warm and soft, but not runny (about 10 minutes for a 4½-ounce wheel or 15 minutes for a 15- to 17-ounce wheel). Remove from oven; serve with slices of crusty bread and salsa.

● **Top Brie** with apricot preserves and sprinkle with chopped almonds and pecans, if desired. Place the Brie on an ovenproof platter and bake as directed in previous example.

● **Slice a 4½-ounce wheel** of Brie in half horizontally (freeze cheese for 30 minutes to make it easier to slice or use unflavored dental floss to cut). Pick a filling, such as those *below,* to put on bottom half; replace top half and heat Brie on an ovenproof platter in a 350° oven for 7 to 8 minutes. Try these combinations for the filling: thinly sliced prosciutto and snipped fresh basil; smoked salmon, snipped dill, and capers; or ¼ to ⅓ cup chopped hazelnuts or walnuts tossed with ¼ to ½ teaspoon nutmeg. Serve with crusty bread and grapes for an elegant touch.

LOW FAT

Chicken Liver and Mushroom Pâté

Pâté may be a rich and luxurious appetizer, but you don't have to be rich to enjoy it. Chicken liver pâté tastes sinfully expensive, yet costs pennies a serving. This creamy and mellow-flavored spread offers just the right introduction for pâté novices. Serve it with crusty baguette slices, on melba rounds or toast points, or even with plain crackers or bagel chips.

Prep: 15 minutes **Cook:** 15 minutes
Chill: 6 hours

1 lb. chicken livers
2 Tbsp. olive oil
1 cup chopped fresh portobello or button mushrooms
1 small tart apple, chopped (¾ cup)
½ cup chopped onion
6 cloves garlic, chopped
1 tsp. dried thyme, crushed
½ tsp. salt
¼ to ½ tsp. coarsely ground black pepper
⅔ cup hard apple cider or apple juice
¼ cup milk

1 Rinse chicken livers under cold running water; remove fat and connective tissue. In a skillet heat olive oil. Cook livers with mushrooms, apple, onion, garlic, thyme, salt, and pepper in oil until livers are browned with only slightly pink centers, stirring often. Add cider or juice; reduce heat. Simmer, uncovered, until liquid is nearly evaporated. Add milk. Cook, uncovered, for 3 minutes or until slightly thickened.

2 Transfer liver mixture to a food processor bowl. Cover and process until smooth. Press mixture through a strainer. Spoon into a serving dish or individual ramekins. Cover and chill for at least 6 hours or for up to 3 days. Makes about 1¾ cups.

Nutrition Facts per tablespoon: 33 cal., 2 g total fat (0 g sat. fat), 63 mg chol., 45 mg sodium, 2 g carbo., 0 g fiber, 3 g pro.
Daily Values: 49% vit. A, 3% vit. C, 6% iron.

---

30 MINUTE, LOW FAT

Quick Focaccia Breadsticks

Refrigerated pizza dough takes the time and labor out of making homemade breadsticks. Easy to make, these soft and tender delicacies are loaded with traditional focaccia flavors of tomatoes, rosemary, and cheese.

Prep: 15 minutes **Bake:** 12 minutes

¼ cup oil-packed dried tomatoes
¼ cup grated Romano cheese
1½ tsp. snipped fresh rosemary or ½ tsp. dried rosemary, crushed
⅛ tsp. cracked black pepper
2 tsp. water
1 10-oz. pkg. refrigerated pizza dough

1 Preheat oven to 350°. Lightly grease a baking sheet; set aside. Drain dried tomatoes, reserving 2 teaspoons of the oil. Finely snip tomatoes. In a bowl combine tomatoes, cheese, rosemary, pepper, the reserved oil, and the water. Set aside.

2 Unroll pizza dough. On a lightly floured surface roll the dough into a 10×8-inch rectangle. Spread the tomato mixture crosswise over half of the dough.

3 Fold plain half of dough over filling; press lightly to seal edges. Cut folded dough lengthwise into ten ½-inch strips. Fold each strip in half and twist two or three times. Place 1 inch apart on the prepared baking sheet.

4 Bake for 12 to 15 minutes or until golden brown. Cool on a wire rack. Makes about 10 breadsticks.

Nutrition Facts per breadstick: 113 cal., 3 g total fat (1 g sat. fat), 3 mg chol., 263 mg sodium, 18 g carbo., 1 g fiber, 5 g pro.
Daily Values: 1% vit. A, 5% vit. C, 3% calcium, 5% iron.

LOW FAT
Sausage Calzone Bites

For more of a "bite," use bulk hot Italian sausage.

Prep: 30 minutes **Bake:** 12 minutes

- **2 oz. bulk sweet Italian sausage**
- **⅓ cup chopped green sweet pepper (1 small)**
- **¼ cup shredded provolone or mozzarella cheese**
- **½ of an 8-oz. can pizza sauce (about ½ cup)**
- **½ tsp. dried Italian seasoning, crushed**
- **1 10-oz. pkg. refrigerated pizza dough**
- **2 tsp. milk**
- **2 Tbsp. finely shredded Parmesan or Romano cheese**

1 Preheat oven to 350°. Lightly grease baking sheets; set aside. In a medium skillet cook sausage and sweet pepper until sausage is no longer pink; drain off fat. Stir in the provolone or mozzarella cheese, half of the pizza sauce, and the Italian seasoning.

2 Unroll pizza dough. On a lightly floured surface, roll or stretch dough to a 12-inch square. Cut into sixteen 3-inch squares.

3 Spoon a rounded teaspoonful of sausage mixture onto half of each square. Moisten edges of dough with water and fold over, forming a rectangle. Pinch or press with a fork to seal edges. Place on prepared baking sheets. Prick tops of calzones with a fork; brush lightly with milk and sprinkle with Parmesan or Romano cheese.

4 Bake for 12 to 15 minutes or until golden brown. Warm remaining pizza sauce to serve with calzones for dipping. Makes 16 mini calzones.

Nutrition Facts per mini calzone: 60 cal., 2 g total fat (1 g sat. fat), 4 mg chol., 148 mg sodium, 4 g carbo., 1 g fiber, 2 g pro.
Daily Values: 2% vit. A, 13% vit. C, 2% calcium, 4% iron.

Beet Biscuits

Wear plastic gloves when shredding the red beets, and you'll protect your hands from staining.

Prep: 25 minutes **Bake:** 13 minutes

- **¾ cup coarsely shredded, peeled, fresh red beets (3 oz.)**
- **4 cups all-purpose flour**
- **5 tsp. baking powder**
- **⅔ cup shortening**
- **1½ cups milk**

1 Preheat oven to 450°. Place shredded beets between several pieces of paper towels; press to remove excess moisture. Set aside.

2 In a large bowl stir together flour, baking powder, and 1 teaspoon *salt*. Using a pastry blender, cut in shortening until mixture resembles coarse crumbs. Make a well in center of dry mixture. Add milk all at once. Using a fork, stir just until moistened.

3 Turn dough out onto a lightly floured surface. Knead dough by gently folding and pressing dough 10 to 12 strokes or until nearly smooth. Pat or lightly roll dough to an 8×6-inch rectangle. Cut dough into twelve 2-inch squares.

4 Place biscuit squares 2 inches apart on a large ungreased baking sheet. Press a deep indentation into center of each with your thumb. Bake for 13 to 15 minutes or until golden brown. Remove biscuits from cookie sheet; cool slightly. Generously pile about 1 tablespoon shredded beets into each depression; serve warm. Makes 12 biscuits.

Nutrition Facts per biscuit: 260 cal., 12 g total fat (3 g sat. fat), 2 mg chol., 380 mg sodium, 32 g carbo., 1 g fiber, 5 g pro.
Daily Values: 2% vit. A, 1% vit. C, 7% calcium, 10% iron.

Mellow Roasted Garlic

Imagine eating a whole head of garlic. You likely conjure up an unpleasant experience—that is, if you have raw garlic in mind. But, when roasted in the oven, garlic cloves soften to a buttery consistency and a mild garlicky flavor. Even those who dislike garlic will be smitten with the roasted flavor.

To add this delicious, mellow ingredient to food, follow the simple roasting directions; then try our suggestions on page 171 for using it. Nothing else comes close to its rich taste.

How to Roast Garlic

Peel away the dry outer layers of skin from the desired number of heads of garlic (1 medium head yields about 1 tablespoon of garlic paste). Leave skins of cloves intact. Cut off the pointed top portion (about ¼ inch) with a sharp knife, leaving the bulb intact but exposing the individual cloves of garlic.

Place the head(s) of garlic, cut side up, in a small baking dish. Drizzle with olive oil (allowing about 2 teaspoons oil for each head). Bake, covered, in a 400° oven for 25 to 35 minutes or until cloves feel soft when pressed.

Allow head(s) to cool slightly before handling to prevent burning yourself. Use the paste warm or cooled. If serving it warm, such as when serving as a spread for bread, use the tip of a small knife to remove the soft garlic paste from each head. If using the paste as a seasoning in cooking, remove the cooled garlic paste from the head by cutting off its stem end. Then, use your fingers to squeeze the paste from each clove into a small bowl; discard the skins. Mash the garlic paste with a fork or back of a spoon until smooth. Use paste as desired.

It might be a good idea to roast several bulbs at a time to have the paste on hand for seasoning. Freeze the paste in ice cube trays or wrap small portions in heavy plastic wrap; put into freezer bags. Thaw to use. Or, refrigerate the paste in an airtight container or wrapped in heavy plastic for up to one week.

NO FAT

Fruit Salsa in a Big Way

Here is an easy way to peel peaches: Plunge a few at a time into boiling water for 20 seconds. Remove peaches and plunge them into cold water. Peel off skin, working from the stem end to the bottom. (See the photograph on page 162.)

Prep: 15 minutes **Chill:** 30 minutes

    3   medium peaches, peeled, pitted,
          and cut into ¼- to ½-inch-thick
          slices
    3   small apricots, halved and pitted
    8   oz. dark or light sweet cherries,
          such as Bing or Rainier
          cherries, halved and pitted
    4   oz. yellow pear-shaped tomatoes,
          halved, or 1 medium yellow
          tomato, cut into 1-inch pieces
    2   to 3 fresh serrano peppers,
          seeded and finely minced*
    ¼   cup lime juice
    2   Tbsp. snipped fresh cilantro
    1   to 2 Tbsp. sugar

1 In a bowl combine peaches, apricots, cherries, tomatoes, peppers, lime juice, cilantro, and sugar. Cover and chill for 30 minutes before serving. If desired, serve with thin *lime wedges*. Store, covered, in the refrigerator up to 12 hours. Makes 10 servings.

*Note: Hot peppers contain oils that can burn eyes, lips, and sensitive skin, so wear plastic gloves while preparing them and be sure to wash your hands thoroughly afterward.

Nutrition Facts per serving: 75 cal., 0 g total fat, 0 mg chol., 2 mg sodium, 19 g carbo., 3 g fiber, 1 g pro.
Daily Values: 10% vit. A, 24% vit. C, 1% calcium, 2% iron.

NO FAT

Spunky Watermelon Relish

You only need the peeled rind—the green and white part—of the watermelon for this treat that's especially good on grilled hot dogs.

Prep: 30 minutes **Cook:** 25 minutes
Chill: 12 hours plus 24 hours

    ½   of a 12- to 14-lb. watermelon
    1   Tbsp. pickling salt
    ½   tsp. pickling spice
    1   cup vinegar
    ½   cup sugar
    1   tsp. crushed red pepper
    1½ cups chopped assorted red,
          yellow, and green sweet
          peppers
    1   cup chopped onion
    1   fresh small jalapeño pepper,
          seeded, if desired, and thinly
          sliced* (see note, below left)

1 Cut pink flesh from watermelon. Refrigerate and save for another use. Using a vegetable peeler, remove green peel from rind; discard peel. Dice rind. Measure 2 cups rind; place in a bowl.

2 Combine 1 cup *water* and pickling salt; pour over rind. Cover bowl and refrigerate overnight. Pour the rind into a colander set in a sink; rinse under cold running water. Drain.

3 Place pickling spice on a double-thick, 6-inch-square piece of 100-percent cotton cheesecloth. Bring corners together and tie with a clean string.

4 In a 4-quart Dutch oven or kettle combine pickling spice bag, vinegar, sugar, and crushed red pepper. Bring to boiling, stirring to dissolve sugar. Stir in diced

---

watermelon rind, sweet peppers, onion, and jalapeño. Return mixture to boiling; reduce heat. Simmer, covered, over medium-low heat about 25 minutes or until rind is clear. Discard spice bag.

5 Pack relish and syrup into three hot, clean half-pint jars. Cover jars loosely with flat lids. Allow to cool 30 minutes. Screw bands tightly and refrigerate relish at least 24 hours before serving. Store relish in the refrigerator up to 1 month. Makes 3 half-pints.

Nutrition Facts per 2 tablespoons: 26 cal., 0 g total fat, 0 mg chol., 25 mg sodium, 7 g carbo., 0 g fiber, 0 g pro.
Daily Values: 5% vit. A, 27% vit. C, 1% iron.

NO FAT

Chili-Pepper Splash

Splash this "pepper water" over foods as you might hot pepper sauce.

Prep: 10 minutes **Cool:** 30 minutes **Chill:** 48 hours

½ cup white vinegar
3 cloves garlic, cut into eighths
2 red Thai chili peppers or red pequín peppers, thinly bias-sliced* (see note, left)
2 or 3 whole red Thai chili peppers or 6 to 8 whole red pequín peppers

1 In a small saucepan combine 1¼ cups *water*, vinegar, garlic, sliced peppers, and ¼ teaspoon *salt*. Heat to boiling. Remove from heat.

2 Place whole peppers into a hot, clean pint jar or divide among decorative bottles. Pour hot liquid over whole peppers, dividing remaining solids among bottles. Loosely cover and cool 30 minutes. Tightly cover and refrigerate at least 48 hours before serving. Store in the refrigerator up to 1 month. Makes 1¾ cups.

Nutrition Facts per teaspoon: 0 cal., 0 g total fat, 0 mg chol., 7 mg sodium, 0 g carbo., 0 g fiber, 0 g pro.
Daily Values: 1% vit. C.

NO FAT

Chive-Onion Vinegar

Drizzle this flavored vinegar over salad greens or use as an ingredient to prepare salad dressings.

Prep: 10 minutes **Stand:** 1 week

2 cups white wine vinegar or rice vinegar
1 Tbsp. snipped fresh chives
1 green onion, chopped
2 3- to 4-inch strips of lemon peel
1 whole green onion

1 In a clean 1-quart glass jar combine vinegar, chives, chopped onion, and lemon peel. Cover with plastic wrap; refrigerate for 1 week, stirring once a day. Pour vinegar-chive mixture through a fine-mesh strainer; drain into a bowl. Discard solids.

2 Transfer strained vinegar to a clean 1-quart jar or bottle. Add whole green onion to jar. Cover tightly with a nonmetallic lid (or cover with plastic wrap and tightly seal with a metal lid). Store in refrigerator up to 6 months. Makes about 2 cups.

Nutrition Facts per tablespoon: 5 cal., 0 g total fat, 0 mg chol., 1 mg sodium, 0 g carbo., 0 g fiber, 0 g pro.

EDITOR'S TIP

16 Ways to Use Roasted Garlic

1. Serve whole roasted garlic heads warm as an appetizer spread for French or Italian bread.

2. Mix with a little olive oil and toss with hot cooked pasta and Parmesan cheese.

3. Add a tablespoon or two to hot potatoes when mashing.

4. Stir into mayonnaise or salad dressing and use in dressings for meat salads, such as chicken, or vegetable salads, such as potato.

5. Add to cream soups, such as potato or onion, seasoning to taste.

6. Stir into plain soft-style cream cheese along with some Italian seasoning or lemon-pepper seasoning to spread on crackers.

7. Combine with softened margarine or butter and use for basting chicken.

8. Stir into cooked rice pilaf or lentils.

9. Add to your favorite white sauce and serve over steamed vegetables or broiled fish.

10. Combine with sour cream to serve over baked potatoes.

11. Stir into melted margarine or butter and drizzle over baked fish or serve as a dipping sauce for lobster.

12. Blend into oil and vinegar for a dressing for tossed salad.

13. Stir into margarine or butter and brush over corn on the cob.

14. Mix a spoonful into prepared biscuit dough or yeast bread dough and bake as usual.

15. Roll up a teaspoon in refrigerated crescent roll dough before baking.

16. Stir into the sauce for your pizza.

Help with Herbs

In supermarkets and home gardens alike, fresh herbs are at their peak of flavor and variety in mid-summer. But fresh herbs require a little pampering if they're going to be at their best. Here's what to do with herbs when they reach your kitchen:

Selection and Storage

• In the market, reject herbs with drooping or brown leaves or, if packaged, slime or excess water. In your garden, harvest only tender, leafy tops and flower clusters.

• Keep herbs fresh up to a week by cutting ½ inch from the stems and storing them, stems submerged, in a jar of water in your refrigerator. Cover tops with a loosely fitting plastic bag. Pinch off wilting, dried out, or brown leaves as they appear.

Drying and Freezing

• When preserving herbs, keep in mind that light and heat will rob them of their flavor. For air-drying tie six to eight herb branches together by their stems. Hang from stems in a dark, warm (but not hot), dry, airy room or attic until leaves become brittle. This should take one to two weeks. To store, pick off leaves and discard stems. The herbs will keep, tightly covered and away from light, up to one year.

• To freeze: Wash herbs and dry well, removing stems from herbs such as basil, sage, mint, oregano, and parsley. Place herbs in plastic freezer containers or bags. The herbs will darken, but it won't affect flavor. There's no need to thaw frozen herbs before cooking. They will keep, frozen, up to one year.

---

30 MINUTE, LOW FAT

Summer Fruit with Sesame Dressing

A simple three-ingredient dressing livens up a bowl of fresh fruit. We used peaches, papaya, strawberries, and raspberries, but you can create your own fruit combination.

Start to finish: 25 minutes

- 2 cups sliced, peeled peaches or sliced nectarines
- 1 cup sliced, peeled papaya or mango
- ½ cup sliced strawberries
- ½ cup fresh raspberries
- ¼ cup rice vinegar
- 1 tsp. honey
- ½ tsp. toasted sesame oil
- 6 cups fresh spinach leaves
- 2 Tbsp. snipped fresh mint

1 In a large bowl combine the peaches or nectarines, papaya or mango, strawberries, and raspberries. Set aside.

2 For vinaigrette, in a small bowl combine the vinegar, honey, and sesame oil using a fork or wire whisk. Pour vinaigrette over fruit, tossing gently to coat.

3 Serve fruit mixture over fresh spinach leaves. Sprinkle with fresh mint. Makes 6 servings.

Nutrition Facts per serving: 80 cal., 1 g total fat (0 g sat. fat), 0 mg chol., 40 mg sodium, 18 g carbo., 7 g fiber, 2 g pro.
Daily Values: 24% vit. A, 68% vit. C, 4% calcium, 15% iron.

NO FAT

Herb-Salt Sprinkle

Sea salt is available fine-grained, but choose the coarse-grained crystals or coarse kosher salt to prepare this seasoning mixture.

Prep: 5 minutes **Stand:** 24 hours

- ¼ cup coarse-grained sea salt or kosher salt
- ¼ cup snipped fresh herbs, such as basil, tarragon, thyme, dillweed, savory, or rosemary
  Radishes or other raw or fresh vegetables (optional)

1 Place 1 tablespoon salt in a 1-pint screw-top jar. Sprinkle about half of the herbs over the salt. Sprinkle 1 tablespoon salt over herbs. Sprinkle remaining herbs over salt and top with remaining salt. Screw on the lid. Let stand for 24 hours or up to 6 months.

2 If desired, serve the salt with radishes or other raw or fresh vegetables. Also use it wherever you need a seasoning boost, such as on grilled steak. Makes about ½ cup.

Nutrition Facts per ¼ teaspoon: 0 cal., 0 g total fat, 0 mg chol., 241 mg sodium, 0 g carbo., 0 g fiber, 0 g pro.

---

30 MINUTE

Parsley-Thyme Vinaigrette

Champagne vinegar, found in gourmet food shops, is an alternative to the homemade Chive-Onion Vinegar (see recipe, page 171).

Start to finish: 5 minutes

- ½ cup Chive-Onion Vinegar (see recipe, page 171) or champagne vinegar
- ¼ cup olive oil or salad oil

1 Tbsp. sugar
1 Tbsp. snipped fresh parsley
1 Tbsp. snipped fresh thyme or
   ½ tsp. dried thyme, crushed

1 In a screw-top jar combine the vinegar, olive oil or salad oil, sugar, parsley, thyme, ¼ teaspoon *salt*, and ¼ teaspoon *pepper*. Cover; shake well.

2 To serve, pour over Two-Bean Salad (see below), over a summer salad, or steamed veggies. Cover and store any remaining vinaigrette in the refrigerator up to 2 weeks. Makes about ¾ cup.

Nutrition Facts per tablespoon: 47 cal., 5 g total fat (1 g sat. fat), 0 mg chol., 1 mg sodium, 1 g carbo., 0 g fiber, 0 g pro.
Daily Values: 1% vit. A, 1% vit. C, 1% iron.

Two-Bean Salad

The brighter and bolder the red skin of the cranberry bean, the fresher it is. Leave the outer shells on until you're ready to cook. Store unwashed beans in a perforated plastic bag in the fridge up to five days. For a shortcut, use a purchased vinaigrette instead of the vinaigrette in this recipe.

Prep: 25 minutes **Cook:** 30 minutes
Chill: 4 hours

1½ lb. fresh cranberry and/or lima beans, shelled (1½ cups shelled)
8 oz. haricot verts (French green beans) or small green beans
1 fennel bulb
¼ cup minced sweet onion
1 recipe Parsley-Thyme Vinaigrette (see recipe, page 172)

1 In a large saucepan cook fresh cranberry or lima beans, covered, in a small amount of boiling salted water until tender. Allow 30 to 40 minutes for cranberry beans and 20 to 30 minutes for lima beans. Add haricot verts or green beans and cook for 1 to 2 minutes more or until they are crisp-tender. Drain well.

2 Meanwhile, prepare fennel (see tip, above right), reserving 2 tablespoons of the feathery leaves. (You should have 1¼ cups sliced fennel.) In a large bowl combine beans, haricot verts, fennel slices, and onion. Drizzle with Parsley-Thyme Vinaigrette. Toss to combine. Cover and chill in the refrigerator 4 hours or up to 3 days. Before serving, top with reserved feathery leaves. Serve with a slotted spoon. Makes 8 to 10 servings.

Nutrition Facts per serving: 136 cal., 7 g total fat (1 g sat. fat), 0 mg chol., 84 mg sodium, 14 g carbo., 5 g fiber, 4 g pro.
Daily Values: 2% vit. A, 13% vit. C, 4% calcium, 7% iron.

30 MINUTE

Summer Herbed Beans

As an option to the tomato wedges, use a cup of bite-size red or yellow baby pear tomatoes in this fresh and colorful sauté.

Start to finish: 20 minutes

8 oz. yellow wax beans, cut into 1-inch pieces (1½ cups)
4 oz. green beans, cut into 1-inch pieces (¾ cup)
2 Tbsp. snipped fresh basil or 2 tsp. dried basil, crushed
1 Tbsp. snipped fresh dillweed or 1 tsp. dried dillweed
1 Tbsp. melted margarine or butter

TEST KITCHEN TIP
To Prepare Fennel

Cut off upper stalks of fennel bulb, including feathery leaves. Reserve 2 tablespoons feathery leaves for the Two-Bean Salad (see recipe, left). Refrigerate leaves in a sealed plastic bag up to 3 days. Discard upper stalks and remaining feathery leaves. Remove any wilted outer layer of stalks; cut off and discard a thin slice from base. Wash fennel. Cut lengthwise into quarters; cut into thin slices.

¼ tsp. pepper
   Dash salt
1 Tbsp. olive oil or cooking oil
1 large tomato, cut into wedges
½ cup crumbled feta cheese (2 oz.)

1 Precook wax beans and green beans, covered, in a small amount of boiling salted water for 4 minutes; drain well.

2 Meanwhile, for sauce, in a small mixing bowl combine basil, dill, melted margarine or butter, pepper, and salt. Set sauce aside.

3 Pour the olive oil or cooking oil into a wok or large skillet. (Add more oil as necessary during cooking.) Preheat over medium heat. Add the partially cooked beans to the wok or skillet; stir-fry about 3 minutes or until beans are crisp-tender. Add tomato wedges, feta cheese, and sauce to wok or skillet. Stir all ingredients together to coat with sauce. Heat through. Serve immediately. Makes 4 servings.

Nutrition Facts per serving: 120 cal., 9 g total fat (3 g sat. fat), 12 mg chol., 233 mg sodium, 7 g carbo., 3 g fiber, 4 g pro.
Daily Values: 17% vit. A, 25% vit. C, 10% calcium, 5% iron.

LUNCH MENU

■ **Grilled turkey breast tenderloins**

■ **Asian Chopped Salad (see right)**

■ **Grilled pita bread wedges or hard white rolls**

■ **Sparkling water with lime wedges**

Italian Vegetable Salad

A bag of frozen mixed vegetables promises a garden of color without all the cleaning and cooking. These ready-to-go vegetables are the secret to this step-saving salad.

Prep: 10 minutes **Chill:** 8 hours

- 1 **16-oz. pkg. loose-pack frozen zucchini, carrots, cauliflower, lima beans, and Italian beans**
- ½ **cup cubed provolone or mozzarella cheese (2 oz.)**
- ¼ **cup sliced pitted ripe olives**
- 2 **green onions, sliced**
- ⅓ **cup bottled clear Italian salad dressing**
- 2 **Tbsp. grated Parmesan cheese**

1 In a medium bowl combine frozen vegetables, cubed cheese, olives, and onions. Add dressing; toss to coat. Cover and chill for 8 to 24 hours.

2 To serve, sprinkle Parmesan cheese over salad; toss to coat. Makes 5 or 6 servings.

Nutrition Facts per serving: 156 cal., 12 g total fat (4 g sat. fat), 10 mg chol., 319 mg sodium, 7 g carbo., 6 g pro., 2 g fiber.
Daily Values: 86% vit. A, 49% vit. C, 17% calcium, 4% iron.

Asian Chopped Salad

Keep the crunch in this fresh veggie salad by serving it immediately after tossing with the dressing.

Start to finish: 40 minutes

- 1 **cup trimmed and coarsely chopped fresh pea pods**
- 3 **cups coarsely chopped Chinese cabbage or green cabbage**
- 1 **cup coarsely chopped radicchio or red cabbage**
- 1 **8-oz. jar baby corn, rinsed, drained, and coarsely chopped**
- ⅓ **cup coarsely chopped red onion**
- ½ **cup cubed daikon or red radish**
- 2 **to 3 Tbsp. chopped pickled ginger or 1 to 1½ tsp. grated fresh ginger**
- 1 **recipe Asian Dressing (see below)**
- ½ **cup fresh enoki mushrooms (optional)**

1 In a small saucepan cook chopped pea pods, uncovered, in a small amount of boiling water for 1 minute. Drain and cool.

2 In a large salad bowl toss together pea pods, cabbage, radicchio, baby corn, red onion, daikon or radish, and ginger. Shake dressing. Drizzle over salad; toss to coat. If desired, top with enoki mushrooms. Makes 6 servings.

Asian Dressing

In a screw-top jar combine ¼ cup rice vinegar, 2 tablespoons salad oil, 1½ teaspoons chili oil, and 1 teaspoon sugar. Cover and shake well.

Nutrition Facts per serving: 86 cal., 6 g total fat (1 g sat. fat), 0 mg chol., 20 mg sodium, 8 g carbo., 2 g fiber, 2 g pro.
Daily Values: 7% vit. A, 76% vit. C, 4% calcium, 7% iron.

Chopped Salmon Salad

You don't have to be a trained chef to pull off the spectacular presentation of this layered salad. The secrets are 6-ounce coffee cups and a steady hand when unmolding.

Start to finish: 35 minutes

- Nonstick cooking spray
- ¾ **cup flaked smoked salmon**
- ¼ **cup thinly sliced green onions**
- ½ **cup coarsely chopped yellow sweet pepper**
- 1⅓ **cups chopped, seeded tomatoes**
- ¼ **cup chopped onion**
- 1 **medium cucumber, coarsely chopped (2 cups)**
- 2 **tsp. small capers, drained**
- 1 **recipe Lemon Vinaigrette (see below)**

1 Coat four 6-ounce coffee cups with nonstick cooking spray. Equally divide and layer ingredients in each cup in the following order: salmon, green onions, sweet pepper, tomatoes, onion, and cucumber. Cover tops with plastic wrap and firmly press mixture into cups with a soup can or similar object slightly smaller than diameter of cup.

2 To serve, invert salads onto individual plates; carefully lift off cups. Sprinkle salads with capers and drizzle with Lemon Vinaigrette. Makes 4 servings.

Lemon Vinaigrette

In a screw-top jar combine 2 tablespoons olive oil or salad oil, 2 teaspoons finely shredded lemon peel, 2 tablespoons lemon juice, ½ teaspoon sugar, ¼ teaspoon salt, and several dashes bottled hot pepper sauce. Let stand at room temperature for 30 minutes before using. Shake well before drizzling over salad.

Nutrition facts per serving: 137 cal., 9 g total fat (1 g sat. fat), 8 mg chol., 445 mg sodium, 8 g carbo., 2 g fiber, 8 g pro.
Daily Values: 8% vit. A, 77% vit. C, 1% calcium, 5% iron.

30 MINUTE

Chicken, Cherry, and Melon Salad

Here's an intriguing flavor combo—chutney dressing over cooked chicken, dark sweet cherries, and juicy honeydew chunks. For a simple summer lunch, add a lemon-poppy seed muffin alongside.

Start to finish: 25 minutes

¼	cup chutney
2	Tbsp. salad oil
2	Tbsp. vinegar
2	tsp. Dijon-style mustard
2	tsp. soy sauce
¼	tsp. toasted sesame oil
⅛	tsp. crushed red pepper
1	small clove garlic, halved
2½	cups cooked chicken or turkey, cut into bite-size strips (about 12 oz.)
2	cups honeydew melon or cantaloupe chunks
½	cup canned sliced water chestnuts, drained and halved
½	cup halved pitted dark, sweet cherries or halved seedless red grapes
⅓	cup cashew halves
1	green onion, sliced
	Red or white salad savoy leaves or savoy cabbage leaves
1	Tbsp. snipped fresh chives

1 For dressing, in a blender container or food processor bowl combine chutney, salad oil, vinegar, Dijon-style mustard, soy sauce, toasted sesame oil, red pepper, and garlic. Cover and blend or process until pureed. Set dressing aside.

2 In a large salad bowl combine chicken or turkey strips, melon chunks, water chestnuts, cherry or grape halves, cashews, and green onion. Pour dressing over salad. Toss gently to coat.

3 Line plates with salad savoy or savoy cabbage leaves. Arrange chicken mixture among the plates. Sprinkle with the snipped chives. Makes 4 main-dish servings.

Nutrition Facts per serving: 387 cal., 19 g total fat (4 g sat. fat), 78 mg chol., 358 mg sodium, 27 g carbo., 4 g fiber, 29 g pro.
Daily Values: 6% vit. A, 72% vit. C, 6% calcium, 14% iron.

Kohlrabi and Pear Salad

If available, choose a red pear, like red Bartlett, for this salad.

Prep: 25 minutes **Marinate:** 4 hours

4	small kohlrabies (about 1 pound), peeled and cut into thin strips (3 cups)
1	medium pear, cored and thinly sliced (1 cup)
3	Tbsp. salad oil
3	Tbsp. white wine vinegar
1	Tbsp. snipped fresh chives
1	Tbsp. honey
¼	tsp. pepper
⅛	tsp. ground nutmeg
	Red-tipped leaf lettuce
¼	cup chopped pecans, toasted

EDITOR'S TIP

Crunchy Kohlrabi

Kohlrabi is a globe-shaped vegetable that grows above the ground and is topped with dark green leaves. Although purple varieties may be found, the pale green variety is the most common.

This sweet, mild turniplike-flavored vegetable is available mid-spring through mid-fall, with its peak season being June and July. When shopping for kohlrabi, look for those that are small, young bulbs with healthy-looking stems and leaves. Kohlrabi will store in a plastic bag in the refrigerator for up to one week.

1 Cook kohlrabi, covered, in a small amount of boiling salted water for 6 to 8 minutes or until crisp-tender. Drain well. In a medium bowl combine cooked kohlrabi and pear slices.

2 Meanwhile, for marinade, in a screw-top jar combine salad oil, white wine vinegar, chives, honey, pepper, and ground nutmeg. Cover and shake well. Pour marinade over kohlrabi and pear slices. Toss lightly to coat. Cover and chill for 4 to 24 hours, stirring occasionally.

3 Line salad plates with lettuce leaves. Arrange kohlrabi and pear slices among the plates. Sprinkle with pecans. Makes 4 servings.

Nutrition Facts per serving: 216 cal., 15 g total fat (2 g sat. fat), 0 mg chol., 24 mg sodium, 19 g carbo., 6 g fiber, 3 g pro.
Daily Values: 9% vit. A, 86% vit. C, 5% calcium, 6% iron.

TEST KITCHEN TIP

How to Ripen Tomatoes Indoors

When tomatoes fall before their time or the first frost spurs you to pick them earlier than their prime, store them at room temperature in a brown paper bag or in a fruit-ripening bowl with other fruits. Keep tomatoes in the refrigerator only after they have turned ripe. Don't stand them in the sun or they'll turn mushy. When ripe, tomatoes feel slightly soft.

Cauliflower-Cilantro Salad

If you're taking this fresh, crisp-flavored salad to a picnic, pack the tomatoes and bacon separately and sprinkle on just before serving.

Prep: 20 minutes **Chill:** 4 hours

- 1 head cauliflower (about 1½ lb.)
- 1 small red onion, thinly sliced and separated into rings
- 3 Tbsp. salad oil
- 3 Tbsp. white wine vinegar or vinegar
- 2 Tbsp. snipped fresh cilantro or parsley
- ½ tsp. sugar
- 1 clove garlic, minced
- 1 medium tomato, cut into wedges
- 4 slices bacon, crisp-cooked, drained, and crumbled

1 Wash cauliflower and remove leaves and woody stem. Break into florets. (You should have about 4 cups.) In a medium saucepan cook cauliflower, covered, in a small amount of boiling salted water for 2 minutes. Drain. In a large salad bowl combine cooked cauliflower and onion rings. Set aside.

2 For dressing, in a screw-top jar combine salad oil, vinegar, cilantro or parsley, sugar, and garlic. Cover and shake well. Pour dressing over cauliflower mixture, tossing gently to coat. Cover and chill in the refrigerator for 4 to 24 hours.

3 Before serving, add tomato wedges; toss lightly. Sprinkle with crumbled bacon. Makes 6 to 8 servings.

Nutrition Facts per serving: 114 cal., 9 g total fat (2 g sat. fat), 4 mg chol., 103 mg sodium, 5 g carbo., 3 g fiber, 4 g pro.
Daily Values: 5% vit. A, 103% vit. C, 3% calcium, 4% iron.

30 MINUTE

Herbed Summer Salad

Halved cherry tomatoes may be substituted for the small tomato wedges called for in this recipe.

Start to finish: 25 minutes

- ¼ cup salad oil
- 3 Tbsp. white wine vinegar
- 2 Tbsp. thinly sliced green onion
- 2 Tbsp. snipped fresh parsley
- 2 Tbsp. mayonnaise or salad dressing
- 1 Tbsp. snipped fresh basil or ½ tsp. dried basil, crushed
- 1 Tbsp. snipped fresh dillweed or ½ tsp. dried dillweed
- 1 tsp. snipped fresh oregano or ¼ tsp. dried oregano, crushed
- ¼ tsp. salt
- ⅛ tsp. pepper
- 1 clove garlic, minced

- 2 medium yellow summer squash or zucchini, cut into ¼-inch-thick slices (2½ cups)
- 2 small tomatoes, cut into wedges
- 1 cup sliced fresh mushrooms
   Lettuce leaves

1 For dressing, in a screw-top jar combine salad oil, vinegar, green onion, parsley, mayonnaise or salad dressing, basil, dill, oregano, salt, pepper, and garlic. Cover and shake well. Set dressing aside.

2 In a large bowl combine yellow summer squash or zucchini, tomato wedges, and mushrooms. Pour dressing over all, stirring gently to coat. Transfer to a lettuce-lined salad bowl. Makes 6 servings.

Nutrition Facts per serving: 142 cal., 13 g total fat (2 g sat. fat), 3 mg chol., 131 mg sodium, 5 g carbo., 2 g fiber, 2 g pro.
Daily Values: 11% vit. A, 28% vit. C, 2% calcium, 4% iron.

Many-Splendored Tomato-Crab Salad

Use a variety of tomatoes—colors and shapes—to create an eye-catching mixture. Cut larger tomatoes into slices or wedges; halve cherry or pear-shaped varieties. (See the photograph on page 160.)

Prep: 15 minutes **Chill:** up to 8 hours

- 2 lb. ripe tomatoes, such as Brandywine, Green Zebra, and/or yellow cherry
- 3 Tbsp. tarragon vinegar or cider vinegar
- 2 Tbsp. extra-virgin olive oil
- ¼ cup snipped fresh tarragon

¾ tsp. Herb-Salt Sprinkle (see
    recipe, page 172) or salt
½ tsp. cracked black pepper
½ cup cooked lump crabmeat
    (about 3 oz.)
    Fresh tarragon sprigs (optional)

1 Arrange tomatoes on a platter. For dressing, in a screw-top jar combine tarragon or cider vinegar, olive oil, and 3 tablespoons of the snipped tarragon. Cover and shake well. Drizzle dressing over salad. Sprinkle with remaining snipped tarragon. Cover and chill in the refrigerator up to 8 hours.

2 Just before serving, sprinkle Herb-Salt Sprinkle and the cracked pepper over salad. Top with crabmeat. If desired, garnish with tarragon sprigs. Makes 6 side-dish servings.

Nutrition Facts per serving: 89 cal., 5 g total fat (1 g sat. fat), 8 mg chol., 166 mg sodium, 7 g carbo., 2 g fiber, 4 g pro.
Daily Values: 10% vit. A, 50% vit. C, 2% calcium, 5% iron.

Couscous-Stuffed Tomato Tulips

Sear fish steaks, such as tuna or swordfish, on the grill to serve with these tangy salad-filled tomatoes.

Prep: 25 minutes **Chill:** 2 hours

½ cup water
¼ cup quick-cooking couscous
2 Tbsp. olive oil or salad oil
1 Tbsp. finely chopped shallot
    or onion
1 Tbsp. lemon juice
1 tsp. Dijon-style mustard

⅛ tsp. salt
⅛ tsp. black pepper
¼ cup chopped peeled kohlrabi or
    jicama
¼ cup chopped yellow or green
    sweet pepper
4 medium tomatoes
    Leaf lettuce (optional)

1 In a small saucepan bring water to boiling. Stir in couscous. Cover and let stand about 5 minutes or until liquid is absorbed.

2 Meanwhile, for marinade, in a screw-top jar combine olive oil or salad oil, chopped shallot or onion, lemon juice, Dijon-style mustard, salt, and black pepper. Cover and shake well.

3 In a small bowl combine couscous, kohlrabi or jicama, and yellow or green sweet pepper. Shake marinade; pour over couscous mixture. Cover and chill in the refrigerator for 2 to 24 hours.

4 To serve, cut out ½ inch of the core from each tomato at the stem end. Invert tomatoes. Cutting from the top to, but not through, the stem end, cut each tomato into 6 wedges. Place tomatoes on lettuce-lined plates, if desired. Spread tomato wedges apart slightly; fill with the couscous mixture. Makes 4 servings.

Nutrition Facts per serving: 138 cal., 7 g total fat (1 g sat. fat), 0 mg chol., 95 mg sodium, 17 g carbo., 2 g fiber, 3 g pro.
Daily Values: 16% vit. A, 94% vit. C, 2% calcium, 5% iron.

TEST KITCHEN TIP
Peeling Tomatoes

Ever struggle with peeling a tomato? Here's a trick to make it easier: Spear the tomato in the stem end with a fork, or hold in a slotted spoon, and plunge the tomato into boiling water for 30 seconds or just until the skin splits. Immediately dip the tomato into cold water. Using a sharp paring knife, pull the skin off the tomato. (HINT: Peel apricots and peaches the same way.)

30 MINUTE, LOW FAT
Tomato-Sage Pasta

Start to finish: 20 minutes

2 cloves garlic, minced
1 Tbsp. olive oil or cooking oil
1½ lb. plum tomatoes, peeled and
    quartered
1 small green or yellow sweet
    pepper, cut into thin strips
1 Tbsp. snipped fresh sage or
    1 tsp. dried sage, crushed
4 oz. packaged dried linguine or
    fettuccine

1 For sauce, in a medium saucepan cook the garlic in hot oil for 30 seconds. Stir in the tomatoes, ¼ teaspoon *salt*, and ¼ teaspoon *black pepper*. Bring to boiling; reduce heat. Simmer, uncovered, 12 minutes. Stir in sweet pepper and sage; cook 5 minutes or to desired consistency.

2 Meanwhile, cook pasta according to package directions. Drain well. Toss pasta with sauce. Serve immediately. Makes 4 servings.

Nutrition Facts per serving: 179 cal., 4 g total fat (1 g sat. fat), 0 mg chol., 162 mg sodium, 31 g carbo., 3 g fiber, 5 g pro.
Daily Values: 24% vit. A, 98% vit. C, 2% calcium, 10% iron.

Aw, Shucks!

You'll have to remove the husks from ears of fresh corn to keep the kernels plump and juicy. Wrap the ears in plastic wrap and refrigerate. Although fresh-picked corn is a special treat, supersweet varieties found at farm stands and in markets maintain their sugar content up to a week.

Apricot-Corn Pudding

A water bath surrounding the pudding during baking helps protect the outside edges from overcooking before the center is done.

Prep: 25 minutes **Bake:** 45 minutes
Stand: 10 minutes

Nonstick cooking spray
8 fresh ears of corn
1 cup whipping cream
4 eggs
½ tsp. salt
¼ tsp. pepper
⅔ cup thinly sliced, pitted fresh apricots
3 Tbsp. snipped fresh basil and/or lemon thyme
Fresh basil leaves

1 Preheat oven to 350°. Lightly coat a 2-quart square baking dish with nonstick cooking spray; set aside.

2 Using a sharp knife, cut corn kernels from cobs (do not scrape cobs). Measure 4 cups corn. In a food processor bowl or blender container process or blend 2 cups of the corn kernels and about ¼ cup of the cream until nearly smooth. Set aside.

3 In a large mixing bowl use a fork or wire whisk to combine eggs, remaining cream, salt, and pepper.

4 Add the pureed corn, the remaining corn kernels, apricots, and the snipped basil to the egg mixture. Stir to combine. Pour mixture into prepared baking dish.

5 Set dish in a 13×9×2-inch baking pan on oven rack. Pour hot water around the dish to a depth of 1 inch. Bake for 45 to 50 minutes or until center is set. Let stand 10 minutes before serving. Top with fresh basil leaves. Makes 8 servings.

Nutrition Facts per serving: 235 cal., 15 g total fat (8 g sat. fat), 147 mg chol., 387 mg sodium, 23 g carbo., 3 g fiber, 7 g pro.
Daily Values: 23% vit. A, 11% vit. C, 4% calcium, 5% iron.

NO FAT

Corn and Cucumber Relish

Pair this out-of-the-ordinary relish with overtones from ginger, sesame oil, and red pepper with grilled poultry or fish.

Prep: 25 minutes **Chill:** 8 hours

1¾ cups seeded and chopped cucumber
2 tsp. salt
1 cup cut fresh corn kernels
½ cup sugar
½ cup white wine vinegar
2 green onions, thinly sliced
1 tsp. grated fresh ginger
2 Tbsp. diced pimiento
½ tsp. toasted sesame oil
⅛ tsp. ground red pepper

1 In a medium bowl sprinkle the chopped cucumber with salt. Let stand for 20 minutes. Rinse the cucumber; drain well, pressing out the excess liquid.

2 Meanwhile, in a medium saucepan combine corn, sugar, vinegar, green onion, and ginger. Bring to boiling, stirring occasionally. Reduce heat. Simmer, uncovered, for 4 minutes. Remove from heat. Stir in the drained cucumber, diced pimiento, toasted sesame oil, and red pepper.

3 Transfer mixture to a nonmetallic container. Cover and chill in the refrigerator at least 8 hours before serving. Refrigerate any leftovers, covered, for up to 1 week. Drain mixture before serving. Makes 2 cups (sixteen 2-tablespoon servings).

Nutrition Facts per serving: 41 cal., 0 g total fat, 0 mg chol., 317 mg sodium, 9 g carbo., 0 g fiber, 0 g pro.
Daily Values: 2% vit. A, 5% vit. C, 1% iron.

30 MINUTE

Skillet Okra and Vegetables

When cooked, okra develops a slippery quality called ropy. This is what helps to thicken the mixture in which the okra is cooked.

Start to finish: 30 minutes

¾ cup chopped green sweet pepper
½ cup chopped onion
2 cloves garlic, minced
2 Tbsp. margarine or butter
2 large tomatoes, peeled and chopped (2½ cups)

8 oz. whole okra, cut into ½-inch-
thick pieces (2 cups)
1 cup cut fresh corn
¼ tsp. salt
⅛ tsp. paprika
⅛ tsp. ground red pepper
3 slices bacon, crisp-cooked,
drained, and crumbled

1 In a large skillet cook green
pepper, onion, and garlic in
margarine or butter until onion is
tender but not brown. Stir in the
tomatoes, okra, corn, salt, paprika, and
red pepper. Cook, covered, over
medium-low heat about 20 minutes or
until okra is tender. Sprinkle with
crumbled bacon. Makes 4 servings.

Nutrition Facts per serving: 165 cal.,
9 g total fat (2 g sat. fat), 4 mg chol.,
306 mg sodium, 20 g carbo., 5 g fiber,
5 g pro.
Daily Values: 29% vit. A, 93% vit. C,
6% calcium, 7% iron.

Horseradish-Sauced Garden Vegetables

The tang this dish gets from the
horseradish makes it just right to serve
with a thick and juicy grilled steak.

Prep: 20 minutes **Bake:** 15 minutes

1½ cups cauliflower florets
3 medium carrots, sliced ½ inch
thick (1½ cups)
8 oz. broccoli, cut into 1-inch pieces
(1¾ cups)
½ cup mayonnaise or salad dressing
2 Tbsp. finely chopped onion
4 tsp. prepared horseradish
⅛ tsp. salt
Dash pepper
¼ cup fine dry bread crumbs
1 Tbsp. margarine or butter, melted
Dash paprika

1 Preheat oven to 350°. In a
2-quart saucepan cook cauliflower
and carrots, covered, in a small
amount of boiling water for 5 minutes.
Add broccoli and cook 5 minutes
more or until vegetables are crisp-
tender. Drain.

2 Meanwhile, in a small bowl
combine mayonnaise or salad
dressing, onion, horseradish, salt, and
pepper. In a 1½-quart casserole
combine cooked vegetables and
mayonnaise mixture.

3 In a small bowl combine bread
crumbs, melted margarine or
butter, and paprika. Sprinkle over
vegetable mixture.

4 Bake, uncovered, about 15 minutes
or until heated through and
topping is golden. Makes 4 or
5 servings.

Nutrition Facts per serving: 294 cal.,
25 g total fat (4 g sat. fat), 16 mg chol.,
364 mg sodium, 15 g carbo., 4 g fiber,
4 g pro.
Daily Values: 273% vit. A, 126% vit. C,
6% calcium, 8% iron.

30 MINUTE, NO FAT

Royal Purple Mashed Potatoes

If you can't find purple potatoes in
your supermarket, substitute Yukon
gold potatoes for a golden dish.

Start to finish: 20 minutes

1½ lb. purple potatoes
¼ tsp. dried thyme, crushed
¼ tsp. salt
⅛ tsp. fresh ground black pepper
3 Tbsp. milk

EDITOR'S TIP

Pretty in Purple

When you see purple potatoes in
your supermarket, don't think, "How
odd!" Think instead, "How royal!"
History tells us the first potatoes
cultivated were purple, grown high
in the Peruvian Andes for Inca kings.

Purple potatoes have an appealing
look but are small (the size of a large
new potato) and thin-skinned. Their
brilliant violet color is also a mark of
one of their health advantages: They
contain powerful cancer-fighting
compounds called anthocyanins.

This variety is becoming more
readily available each year. Many
supermarkets stock them during a
long August-through-May season. If
you can't find these potatoes, ask
your grocer to order them.

The natural buttery flavor of
purple potatoes invites you to enjoy
them without added butter or
margarine. The Royal Purple Mashed
Potatoes recipe (see bottom left)
passes taste tests with flying colors.

1 Peel potatoes, if desired, and
quarter. Cook, covered, in a small
amount of boiling water about
15 minutes or until tender; drain.

2 Mash the potatoes with a potato
masher or fork. Add thyme, salt,
and black pepper. Gradually beat in
milk to make potatoes light and fluffy,
adding an extra tablespoon or two of
milk, if necessary. Makes 4 to 6 side-
dish servings.

Nutrition Facts per serving: 113 cal.,
0 g total fat (0 g sat. fat), 0 mg chol.,
101 mg sodium, 25 g carbo., 1 g fiber,
3 g pro.
Daily Values: 24% vit. C, 2% calcium,
13% iron.

Vegetarian Sandwich Stacks

The key to even vegetable layers and even cooking is to slice the vegetables thinly and evenly. Use a sharp knife or a mandolin for perfect slicing.

Prep: 20 minutes
Cook: 4 minutes per sandwich

- ¼ cup mayonnaise or salad dressing
- 1 Tbsp. snipped fresh basil or
  - ½ tsp. dried basil, crushed
- 1 clove garlic, minced
- ¼ tsp. pepper
- 12 slices rye bread
- 1 3- to 4-inch fresh portobello mushroom cap, thinly sliced
- 1 medium red onion, thinly sliced
- 1 cup thinly sliced zucchini
- 4 thin slices peeled eggplant
- 4 slices Swiss cheese
- 1 Tbsp. butter or margarine

1 For spread, in a small bowl stir together the mayonnaise or salad dressing, basil, garlic, and pepper.

2 Spread one side of all bread slices lightly with mayonnaise mixture. Top four of the slices with mushroom and onion slices. Top each with another bread slice, spread side up. Top with zucchini, eggplant, and Swiss cheese. Top with remaining bread slices, spread side down.

3 Heat butter or margarine in a large skillet or griddle over medium heat until melted. Add two sandwich stacks. Cook about 2 minutes per side or until golden and sandwiches are heated through.

Repeat with remaining stacks, adding more butter if necessary. Secure stacks with decorative wooden toothpicks before cutting in half diagonally to serve. Makes 4 servings.

Nutrition Facts per serving: 511 cal., 25 g total fat (9 g sat. fat), 42 mg chol., 821 mg sodium, 54 g carbo., 8 g fiber, 18 g pro.
Daily Values: 13% vit. A, 8% vit. C, 37% calcium, 18% iron.

Mushroom and Pepper Pitas

Alter the flavor of this cheesy vegetable sandwich by substituting assorted wild mushrooms and Gouda or Havarti cheese.

Prep: 20 minutes **Bake:** 5 minutes

- 3 cups sliced fresh mushrooms
- 2 medium yellow, red, and/or green sweet peppers, cut into bite-size strips
- 1 medium onion, sliced
- 2 Tbsp. olive oil
- 1 Tbsp. balsamic vinegar
- 4 large pita bread rounds
- 1½ cups shredded mozzarella cheese (6 oz.)

1 Preheat oven to 400°. In a very large skillet cook mushrooms, peppers, and onion in hot olive oil for 6 to 8 minutes or until vegetables are tender and most of the liquid has evaporated. Stir in balsamic vinegar, ½ teaspoon *salt*, and ¼ teaspoon *coarsely ground black pepper*; set aside and keep warm.

2 Meanwhile, place pita rounds on a baking sheet. Sprinkle evenly with cheese. Bake about 5 minutes or until cheese melts. Spoon mushroom mixture over pitas. Fold in half to serve. Makes 4 servings.

Nutrition Facts per serving: 380 cal., 16 g total fat (5 g sat. fat), 24 mg chol., 813 mg sodium, 43 g carbo., 3 g fiber, 19 g pro.
Daily Values: 9% vit. A, 150% vit. C, 34% calcium, 14% iron.

Taco Turkey Sandwiches

Lisa Pregent
East Swanzey, New Hampshire
$200—Family Favorite Sandwiches

Prep: 15 minutes **Bake:** 15 minutes

- ½ cup chopped pitted ripe olives
- ½ tsp. chili powder
- ½ tsp. ground cumin
- ¼ tsp. salt
- ¼ cup sliced green onions
- 2 Tbsp. dairy sour cream
- 2 Tbsp. mayonnaise or salad dressing
- 4 kaiser rolls or hoagie buns, split
- 8 oz. thinly sliced cooked turkey breast
- ½ cup shredded cheddar cheese (2 oz.)
- ½ cup shredded Monterey Jack cheese with jalapeño peppers (2 oz.)
- 4 thin tomato slices, halved (about ½ of a large tomato)
  - Sliced jalapeño peppers* (optional)

1 Preheat oven to 350°. In a small bowl stir together the olives, chili powder, cumin, and salt. Remove 2 tablespoons of the mixture; set aside. Stir green onions, sour cream, and mayonnaise or salad dressing into the remaining olive mixture.

2 Spread sour cream mixture over cut side of roll bottoms. Place on a large baking sheet, cut side up. Top with the sliced turkey. Place roll tops on baking sheet, cut side up. Sprinkle tops with cheeses and reserved olive mixture; top with the tomato slices. Cover loosely with foil. Bake for 15 to 20 minutes or until heated through.

3 To serve, combine sandwich halves. If desired, serve with sliced jalapeño peppers. Makes 4 servings.

*Note: Hot peppers contain oils that can burn eyes, lips, and sensitive skin, so wear plastic gloves while preparing them and be sure to wash your hands thoroughly afterward.

Nutrition Facts per serving: 420 cal., 20 g total fat (8 g sat. fat), 57 mg chol., 1,454 mg sodium, 35 g carbo., 2 g fiber, 24 g pro.
Daily Values: 13% vit. A, 10% vit. C, 29% calcium, 20% iron.

30 MINUTE

Chicken and Pesto Focaccia Wedges

Use a long serrated knife to evenly cut the bread horizontally in half.

Prep: 20 minutes **Cook:** 6 minutes

- 1   1-lb. focaccia round
- 4   medium skinless, boneless chicken breast halves (1 lb.)
- ½   tsp. salt
- ¼   tsp. garlic powder
- ¼   tsp. black pepper
- 1   Tbsp. olive oil
- ¼   cup purchased basil pesto
- 4   lettuce leaves
- 4   slices provolone or mozzarella cheese

- ½   cup roasted red sweet peppers, cut into bite-size strips
- ½   cup packed fresh basil leaves

1 Cut focaccia in half horizontally. Set bread aside.

2 Place each chicken breast half between two pieces of plastic wrap. Using the flat side of a meat mallet and working from the center to the edges, lightly pound chicken to ¼-inch thickness. Remove plastic wrap. Season chicken with salt, garlic powder, and black pepper.

3 In a large skillet cook chicken in hot oil over medium heat for 6 to 8 minutes or until no pink remains, turning halfway through cooking. Remove from skillet. Spread each chicken breast half with 1 tablespoon of the pesto.

4 To assemble sandwich, layer lettuce on the bottom of the focaccia. Top with cheese slices, chicken, roasted peppers, and basil leaves. Top with focaccia top. Cut into 6 wedges. Makes 6 servings.

Nutrition Facts per serving: 413 cal., 17 g total fat (4 g sat. fat), 64 mg chol., 770 mg sodium, 36 g carbo., 1 g fiber, 30 g pro.
Daily Values: 13% vit. A, 59% vit. C, 26% calcium, 7% iron.

PRIZE WINNER

Italian Sandwiches

Penny A. Eller
Lemont, Illinois
$400—Family Favorite Sandwiches

Prep: 15 minutes **Bake:** 12 minutes

SUPPER MENU

- **Italian Sandwiches (see bottom left)**

- **Romaine hearts drizzled with bottled Caesar dressing and sprinkled with freshly shredded Parmesan cheese**

- **Berry-Chocolate Frozen Yogurt (see page 190)**

- **Sparkling water**

- 6   ½-inch bias slices Italian bread (about ⅓ of a 1-lb. loaf)
- ⅓   cup purchased basil pesto
- 3   oz. thinly sliced prosciutto
- 1   14-oz. can artichoke hearts, drained and thinly sliced
- 1   7-oz. jar roasted red sweet peppers, drained and cut into strips
- 12   oz. cooked chicken or turkey, cut into bite-size strips (about 2¼ cups)
- 4   to 6 oz. shredded provolone cheese (1 to 1½ cups)

1 Preheat oven to 450°. Spread one side of bread slices lightly with pesto. Top with the prosciutto, artichoke slices, red pepper strips, and chicken strips. Place sandwiches on a large foil-lined baking sheet. Cover loosely with foil.

2 Bake about 8 minutes or until nearly heated through. Uncover and sprinkle with provolone cheese. Bake for 4 to 5 minutes more or until cheese melts. Makes 6 servings.

Nutrition Facts per serving: 387 cal., 20 g total fat (6 g sat. fat), 67 mg chol., 855 mg sodium, 20 g carbo., 1 g fiber, 31 g pro.
Daily Values: 19% vit. A, 118% vit. C, 23% calcium, 17% iron.

Aw, Nuts!

Recent studies have suggested that eating nuts—almonds in particular—might help lower blood cholesterol levels. Armed with this evidence, The Almond Board of California challenged two *Better Homes and Gardens®* staff members to eat a rounded half-cup of raw almonds every day for a month and see how their cholesterol levels were affected. We drew the volunteers' blood before they ate the almonds, after the month-long almond feast, and one month after they stopped eating almonds. Here's what we found:

MAN: 42, 6' 2", 167 lbs., lightly active

Before
Total cholesterol: 253 HDL: 48

After
Total cholesterol: 223 HDL: 45

One month later
Total cholesterol: 219 HDL: 42

WOMAN: 52, 5' ½", 113 lbs., moderately active

Before
Total cholesterol: 307 HDL: 67

After
Total cholesterol: 268 HDL: 68

One month later
Total cholesterol: 274 HDL: 60

Note: Total cholesterol levels should be 200 or lower. HDL should be over 35.

Although our experiment was far from scientific, the results were pretty impressive, especially considering our staffers didn't change their diets or exercise habits during the experiment. We reviewed our findings with Dr. Gene Spiller, the director of the Health Research and Studies Center in Los Altos, California, and the principal researcher on two almond studies sponsored by the Almond Board.

He says that many nuts seem to be effective in lowering cholesterol levels. This is primarily due to their high unsaturated fat content, which doesn't raise cholesterol like artery-clogging saturated fat. Almonds, and some other nuts, also contain other vitamins and minerals that have been linked to healthy hearts, such as vitamin E, folate, magnesium, and copper. A study of more than 30,000 women found that women who ate nuts two or more times each week reduced their risk of dying from heart disease by 40 percent.

Spiller recommends eating a handful of nuts three or four times a week, but that doesn't mean you can gorge yourself on steaks and sit on the couch. To keep cholesterol low, eat a diet rich in fruits, vegetables, and whole grains, and exercise for 30 minutes at least three times a week. "You can never rely on just one thing to reduce your cholesterol," Spiller says.

Chocolate Chip Peanut Brittle Bites

A sprinkling of peanut brittle turns a somewhat traditional chocolate chip cookie into a rich and chewy bit of goodness. (See the photograph on page 197.)

Prep: 30 minutes
Bake: 9 minutes per batch

½ cup butter, softened
⅓ cup shortening
1 cup packed brown sugar
½ cup granulated sugar
1 tsp. baking soda
½ tsp. salt
2 eggs
2 tsp. vanilla
2¼ cups all-purpose flour
1 12-oz. pkg. semisweet chocolate pieces
¾ cup chopped peanuts
½ cup crushed peanut brittle

1 Preheat oven to 350°. In an extra-large mixing bowl beat together the butter and shortening with an electric mixer on medium speed for 30 seconds. Add brown sugar, granulated sugar, baking soda, and salt. Beat mixture until combined, scraping sides of bowl occasionally. Beat in eggs and vanilla. Using a wooden spoon, stir in the flour until combined. Stir in chocolate pieces and peanuts.

2 Drop dough by rounded teaspoons 2 inches apart on ungreased cookie sheets. Flatten slightly with back of spoon. Sprinkle ½ teaspoon of crushed peanut brittle in center of each cookie.

3 Bake for 9 to 11 minutes or until centers appear set. Cool on cookie sheet for 1 minute. Transfer cookies to a wire rack and let cool. Makes about 48 cookies.

Nutrition Facts per cookie: 133 cal., 7 g total fat (3 g sat. fat), 14 mg chol., 81 mg sodium, 14 g carbo., 1 g fiber, 2 g pro.
Daily Values: 2% vit. A, 1% calcium, 2% iron.

Cranberry-Oatmeal Cookies

Hazelnuts by the heap guarantee a tasty crunch in every bite of these tempting treasures shimmering with gems of dried cranberries.

Prep: 20 minutes
Bake: 9 minutes per batch

1½ cups all-purpose flour
1 tsp. baking powder
¼ tsp. baking soda
½ cup butter
¼ cup shortening

- 1 cup packed brown sugar
- ½ cup granulated sugar
- 2 eggs
- 1 tsp. vanilla
- 2 cups rolled oats
- 1½ cups dried cranberries
- 1 cup coarsely chopped toasted hazelnuts (filberts)

1 Preheat oven to 375°. In a medium bowl combine flour, baking powder, and baking soda; set aside.

2 In a large mixing bowl beat butter and shortening with an electric mixer on medium to high speed for 30 seconds. Add brown sugar and granulated sugar. Beat mixture until combined, scraping sides of bowl occasionally. Beat in eggs and vanilla until combined. Beat as much of the flour mixture into the sugar mixture as you can with the mixer. Stir in remaining flour mixture. Stir in rolled oats, dried cranberries, and hazelnuts.

3 Drop dough by rounded teaspoons 2 inches apart on an ungreased cookie sheet. Bake for 9 to 11 minutes or until edges of cookies are golden. Transfer cookies to a wire rack and let cool. Makes about 54 cookies.

To Make Ahead:

Bake cookies as directed; then cool completely. Place in a freezer container or bag and freeze up to 1 month. Thaw at room temperature before serving.

Nutrition Facts per cookie: 95 cal., 4 g total fat (2 g sat. fat), 13 mg chol., 34 mg sodium, 13 g carbo., 1 g fiber, 1 g pro.
Daily Values: 1% vit. A, 1% calcium, 3% iron.

Apricot Shortbread Squares

You can serve these tart squares, a cross between a layered bar cookie and a homey fruit dessert, with a dollop of whipped cream.

Prep: 30 minutes **Bake:** 50 minutes

- Nonstick cooking spray
- 1½ cups all-purpose flour
- ½ cup ground almonds
- ⅓ cup sugar
- 1 tsp. baking powder
- ½ tsp. salt
- ¾ cup butter
- 2 egg yolks
- 1 8-oz. pkg. cream cheese, softened
- ⅓ cup sugar
- 2 egg whites
- Few drops of almond extract
- 1¾ lb. apricots, pitted and sliced (12 to 15 small)
- ½ cup apricot preserves
- Whipped cream (optional)

1 Preheat oven to 350°. Lightly coat a 13×9×2-inch baking pan with nonstick cooking spray; set aside.

2 In a large bowl stir together the flour, ground almonds, ⅓ cup sugar, baking powder, and salt. Using a pastry blender cut in butter until mixture resembles coarse crumbs. Beat egg yolks slightly; add to dry mixture and toss with a fork until moistened (mixture will be crumbly). Pat dough into prepared pan. Bake for 20 minutes.

TEST KITCHEN TIP

Heavenly Hazelnuts

Hazelnuts, which add a rich flavor to cookies and other baked goods, are available throughout the year. You'll likely see a greater supply of them in the winter months when more are distributed. These mild, sweet nuts—also called filberts—are great keepers, too. You can store them in airtight containers or plastic freezer bags for up to one year in the refrigerator or up to two years in the freezer.

3 Meanwhile, in a medium mixing bowl beat the cream cheese and ⅓ cup sugar with an electric mixer on medium speed until fluffy. Beat in egg whites and almond extract just until combined. Spread cream cheese mixture over partially baked crust. Arrange apricot slices in even rows on top of cream cheese mixture to cover. Bake for 30 minutes more.

4 Finely snip any large pieces of apricots in preserves. In a small saucepan, cook and stir preserves over low heat until melted. Brush over warm bars. Cool completely in pan on a wire rack. Cut into squares. If desired, serve with whipped cream. Store in an airtight container in the refrigerator for up to 3 days. Makes 20 squares.

Nutrition Facts per square: 228 cal., 14 g total fat (7 g sat. fat), 53 mg chol., 195 mg sodium, 24 g carbo., 2 g fiber, 4 g pro.
Daily Values: 22% vit. A, 8% vit. C, 4% calcium, 5% iron.

SUMMER MENU

- **Rotisserie or grilled chicken**

- **Two-Bean Salad (see page 173)**

- **Fresh tomato platter**

- **Assorted breads with herb butter**

- **Black-and-Blueberry Cobbler Supreme (see right)**

Two-Berry Tarts

Pile the berry filling into individual baked tart shells for easy serving, or into one large piecrust.

Prep: 1½ hours **Chill:** 2 hours

¼	cup water
3	Tbsp. cornstarch
⅛	tsp. salt
3½	cups fresh blueberries
2½	cups fresh blackberries
⅔	cup sugar
¼	cup water
2	tsp. finely shredded lemon peel
1	recipe Pastry for Baked Tart Shells or Piecrust (see recipe, right)

1 In a bowl stir together ¼ cup water, the cornstarch, and salt to make a smooth paste; set aside.

2 In a small bowl gently combine 1 cup of the blueberries and 1 cup of the blackberries. Set aside.

3 In a saucepan combine 1 cup of the blueberries, the sugar, and ¼ cup water. Bring to boiling. Add cornstarch mixture; cook and stir over medium heat until thickened and bubbly. Cook and stir for 2 minutes

more. Remove from heat. Cool for 30 minutes.

4 Stir in remaining 1½ cups blueberries, remaining 1½ cups blackberries, and the lemon peel. Divide mixture among the Baked Tart Shells, using about ¼ cup for each tart. Pile the reserved berries onto center of each tart. Or, pour mixture into baked piecrust and top with the reserved berries. Chill at least 2 hours before serving. Cover for longer storage. Makes 10 servings.

Nutrition Facts per serving (one individual tart): 219 cal., 7 g total fat (2 g sat. fat), 0 mg chol., 87 mg sodium, 38 g carbo., 4 g fiber, 2 g pro. Daily Values: 1% vit. A, 24% vit. C, 2% calcium, 5% iron.

30 MINUTE

Pastry for Baked Tart Shells or Piecrust

Measure your ingredients carefully: Too much flour makes a tough pastry; too much shortening makes it crumbly; too much water makes it tough.

Prep: 15 minutes **Bake:** 10 minutes

1¼	cups all-purpose flour
⅓	cup shortening
4	to 5 Tbsp. cold water

1 Preheat oven to 450°. In a bowl stir together flour and ¼ teaspoon *salt*. Cut in shortening until pieces are pea-size. Sprinkle 1 tablespoon of the water over part of the mixture; gently toss with a fork. Push moistened dough to side of bowl. Repeat, using 1 tablespoon water at a time, until all the dough is moistened. Form dough into a ball. On a lightly floured surface, slightly flatten dough.

For Baked Tart Shells: Roll dough from center to edges into a 20×12-inch rectangle. Cut pastry rectangle into ten 6×4-inch rectangles. Ease pastry rectangles into ten 4×2×¾-inch rectangular tart pans with removable bottoms, being careful not to stretch pastry. Trim edges of pastry. Generously prick bottom and sides of pastry with a fork. Bake for 10 to 12 minutes or until golden brown. Cool on a wire rack. Makes 10 individual tart shells.

For Baked Piecrust: Roll dough from center to edges into a 12-inch circle. Transfer pastry to a 9-inch pie plate, easing pastry into pie plate and being careful not to stretch it. Trim pastry to ½ inch beyond edge of pie plate. Fold under extra pastry. Crimp edge as desired. Generously prick bottom and sides of pastry with a fork. Line pastry with a double thickness of foil. Bake for 8 minutes. Remove foil. Bake 5 to 6 minutes more or until golden brown. Cool on a wire rack. Makes 1 piecrust.

Black-and-Blueberry Cobbler Supreme

If you've got frozen blackberries and blueberries, you can use them to make this fabulous cobbler. Just thaw the fruit, reserving the liquid. Then add enough grape juice or water to the fruit liquid to equal 2 cups. Use this liquid to pour over the fruit before baking the cobbler.

Prep: 20 minutes **Bake:** 40 minutes

1	cup all-purpose flour
1	cup whole wheat flour
2	tsp. baking powder
¼	tsp. salt

- ½ cup butter or margarine, softened
- 1 cup granulated sugar
- ¾ cup milk
- 2 cups fresh blackberries
- 1 cup fresh blueberries
- ½ to ¾ cup granulated sugar
- 2 cups grape juice or water
  Powdered sugar (optional)
  Ice cream or light cream

1 Preheat oven to 350°. Grease a 13×9×2-inch baking pan or a 3-quart baking dish; set aside. In a medium bowl stir together all-purpose flour, whole wheat flour, baking powder, and salt; set aside.

2 In a large mixing bowl beat butter or margarine and the 1 cup granulated sugar with an electric mixer on medium to high speed until fluffy. Add dry mixture alternately with milk. Beat until smooth. Spread batter evenly over the bottom of the prepared baking pan.

3 Sprinkle blackberries and blueberries over batter. Sprinkle with the ½ to ¾ cup granulated sugar, depending on the sweetness of fruit. Pour grape juice or water over fruit.

4 Bake for 40 to 45 minutes or until a wooden toothpick inserted in cake comes out clean. (Some of the fruit should sink toward the bottom as the cake rises to top.) Cool in pan on a wire rack. If desired, sprinkle lightly with powdered sugar. Serve warm with ice cream or cream. Makes 12 servings.

Nutrition Facts per serving (with ⅓ cup ice cream): 404 cal., 17 g total fat (10 g sat. fat), 53 mg chol., 236 mg sodium, 61 g carbo., 3 g fiber, 5 g pro.
Daily Values: 18% vit. A, 12% vit. C, 14% calcium, 6% iron.

PRIZE WINNER

Triple Fruit Pie

.Louise Piper
Rolfe, Iowa
$400—Peaches, Plums, Apricots, and Nectarines

Prep: 30 minutes **Bake:** 50 minutes

- ¾ to 1 cup granulated sugar
- 2 Tbsp. quick-cooking tapioca
- ⅛ tsp. salt
- 2 cups sliced, pitted apricots
- 1 cup sliced, pitted nectarines
- 1 cup sliced, pitted plums
- 2 Tbsp. honey
- 1 recipe Pastry for Double-Crust Pie (see bottom right)
- 1 Tbsp. milk
- 1 Tbsp. coarse sugar or granulated sugar

1 In a large bowl combine the ¾ to 1 cup granulated sugar (depending on the tartness of the fruit), tapioca, and salt. Add apricots, nectarines, plums, and honey, tossing gently until coated. Let stand 15 minutes.

2 Meanwhile, preheat oven to 375°. Prepare Pastry for Double-Crust Pie and roll out half. Line a 9-inch pie plate with rolled-out pastry. Transfer filling to pastry-lined pie plate. Trim pastry to edge of pie plate. Roll out remaining pastry. Cut slits; place on filling and seal. Crimp edge as desired.

3 Brush top of pie with milk; sprinkle with coarse or granulated sugar. To prevent overbrowning, cover edge of pie with foil. Bake for 25 minutes. Remove foil. Bake for 25 to 30 minutes more or until top is golden brown and filling is bubbly. Cool on a wire rack. Makes 8 servings.

EDITOR'S TIP

In Praise of Prunes

Prunes, the ugly duckling of the dried-fruit world, are an antioxidant powerhouse. Of the foods scoring highest for their Oxygen Radical Absorbance Capacity (ORAC)—a test measuring antioxidant ability—prunes top the list.

Eating plenty of prunes and other high-ORAC fruits and vegetables may reduce the risk of age-related diseases and senility, says the U.S. Department of Agriculture. Other foods that scored high on the ORAC list include raisins, blueberries, strawberries, kale, and spinach.

In tests, women who ate large servings of spinach or strawberries increased their blood antioxidant scores by 25 percent. Don't expect these results from an antioxidant vitamin pill, says the USDA.

—by Bev Bennett

Pastry for Double-Crust Pie

1. In a medium bowl stir together 2 cups all-purpose flour and ½ teaspoon salt. Using a pastry blender, cut in ⅔ cup shortening until pieces are pea-size.

2. Using 6 to 7 tablespoons cold water, sprinkle 1 tablespoon water at a time over part of the mixture; gently toss with a fork. Push moistened dough to side of bowl. Repeat until all is moistened. Divide dough in half. Form each half into a ball. Use immediately, or cover and chill until needed.

Nutrition Facts per serving: 397 cal., 18 g total fat (4 g sat. fat), 0 mg chol., 172 mg sodium, 57 g carbo., 2 g fiber, 4 g pro.
Daily Values: 12% vit. A, 11% vit. C, 2% calcium, 9% iron.

PRIZE WINNER

Peach-Nectarine Torte

Marci Niemi
Sheboygan, Wisconsin
$200—Peaches, Plums, Apricots, and Nectarines

Prep: 30 minutes **Bake:** 35 minutes

1½	cups all-purpose flour
½	cup sugar
1½	tsp. baking powder
⅓	cup butter
1	egg
1	to 3 Tbsp. milk
½	cup sugar
½	cup chopped nuts
½	cup raisins
½	tsp. ground cinnamon
¼	tsp. ground nutmeg
5½	cups cut-up, peeled peaches
⅔	cups cut-up, peeled nectarines
1	Tbsp. sugar

1 For dough, in a medium bowl stir together the flour, ½ cup sugar, and the baking powder. Using a pastry blender, cut in butter until mixture resembles coarse crumbs. Combine egg and 1 tablespoon of the milk; add to flour mixture, stirring to moisten. Add enough of remaining milk to moisten all the flour.

2 Turn dough out onto a lightly floured surface. Gently knead 10 to 12 strokes or until nearly smooth. (Dough will be soft.) Roll dough to a 14×7½-inch rectangle; cut lengthwise into ten ¾-inch-wide strips. Cut five of the strips in half crosswise. (You will have ten short strips and five long strips.) Cover with plastic wrap; set aside. Preheat oven to 350°.

3 For filling, in a Dutch oven combine ½ cup sugar, nuts, raisins, cinnamon, and nutmeg. Stir in peaches and nectarines. Cook over medium heat about 5 minutes or until bubbly, stirring occasionally.

4 Spoon fruit filling into a 3-quart rectangular baking dish. Gently place dough strips over filling in a mock-lattice pattern, trimming ends as necessary. Short dough strips won't reach completely across dish, but spread as they bake. Sprinkle with 1 tablespoon sugar. Place dish on a baking sheet. Bake for 35 to 40 minutes or until top is golden brown. Serve warm. Makes 12 servings.

Nutrition Facts per serving: 304 cal., 9 g total fat (4 g sat. fat), 32 mg chol., 112 mg sodium, 55 g carbo., 5 g fiber, 4 g pro.
Daily Values: 17% vit. A, 21% vit. C, 5% calcium, 7% iron.

Plum Strudel

Prep: 30 minutes **Bake:** 35 minutes

2½	cups chopped, pitted plums
½	cup snipped, dried apricots
½	cup chopped almonds, toasted
¼	cup raisins
¾	cup granulated sugar
1	tsp. ground cinnamon
10	to 12 sheets frozen phyllo dough (17×12-inch rectangles), thawed
⅓	cup butter or margarine, melted
1	egg white, slightly beaten
2	Tbsp. powdered sugar

1 For filling, in a medium bowl combine fruits, nuts, and raisins. Add granulated sugar and cinnamon; toss until mixed. Set filling aside. Lightly grease a 15×10×1-inch baking pan; set aside. Preheat oven to 350°.

2 Cover a large surface with a cloth; flour cloth. Unfold phyllo dough. Stack two sheets of phyllo on the floured cloth. (Do not brush butter or margarine between sheets.) Arrange another stack of two sheets on the cloth, overlapping the stacks 2 inches. Add three or four more stacks, forming a rectangle about 40×20 inches (stagger stacks so all seams are not down the middle). Trim to a 40×20-inch rectangle. Brush with melted butter or margarine.

3 To assemble strudel, beginning 4 inches from a short side of the dough, spoon the plum filling in a 4-inch-wide band across the dough. Using the cloth underneath the dough as a guide, gently lift the 4-inch piece of dough and lay it over the plum filling. Slowly and evenly lift cloth and continue to roll up the dough and plum filling into a tight roll. If necessary, cut off excess dough from ends to within 1 inch of the plum filling. Fold ends under to seal.

4 Carefully transfer the strudel roll to the prepared baking pan. Slightly curve the roll to form a crescent shape. In a small mixing bowl stir together the egg white and 1 tablespoon *water*. Brush top of the strudel with the egg white mixture.

5 Bake for 35 to 40 minutes or until golden. Carefully remove strudel from pan. Cool. Sprinkle powdered sugar over strudel before serving. Makes 12 to 16 servings.

Nutrition Facts per servings: 222 cal., 9 g total fat (4 g sat. fat), 15 mg chol., 137 mg sodium, 33 g carbo., 2 g fiber, 3 g pro.
Daily Values: 14% vit. A, 6% vit. C, 2% calcium, 7% iron.

Cherry Turnovers

Prep: 30 minutes **Chill:** 2 hours
Bake: 30 minutes

- 3 cups fresh or frozen unsweetened pitted tart red cherries, thawed
- ¾ cup granulated sugar
- 2 Tbsp. cornstarch
- ½ tsp. finely shredded orange peel
- ¼ cup slivered almonds
- 1 recipe Pastry for Double-Crust Pie (see recipe, page 185)
- 1 Tbsp. milk
- 1 Tbsp. coarse sugar or granulated sugar

1 For filling, in a saucepan combine undrained cherries, the ¾ cup sugar, cornstarch, and orange peel. Cook and stir over medium heat until thickened and bubbly; add almonds. Cover and chill, without stirring, 2 hours or until completely cool.

2 Preheat oven to 375°. Divide pastry in half. On a lightly floured surface roll out each portion of pastry to a 10-inch square. Cut each pastry into four 5-inch squares. Spoon about ¼ cup of cherry mixture in center of one pastry square. Brush edges of square with water. Pull up corners to form a turnover. Press edges together to form a tight seal. Place in a 15×10×1-inch baking pan. Repeat with remaining pastry squares and cherry filling. Brush tops with milk; sprinkle with sugar.

3 Bake for 30 to 35 minutes or until golden. Cool on a wire rack about 30 minutes; serve warm. Serves 8.

Nutrition Facts per serving: 394 cal., 20 g total fat (5 g sat. fat), 0 mg chol., 137 mg sodium, 51 g carbo., 2 g fiber, 4 g pro.
Daily Values: 5% vit. A, 2% vit. C, 2% calcium, 12% iron.

Cherry Pastry Fingers

Fresh cherries are meant to be enjoyed as soon as possible. You can cover and refrigerate them up to 4 days.

Prep: 30 minutes **Chill:** 1 hour
Bake: 12 minutes

- 1 cup butter or margarine
- 1 8-oz. pkg. cream cheese, softened
- 2 cups all-purpose flour
- 2 Tbsp. granulated sugar
- ¼ tsp. salt
- 3 Tbsp. granulated sugar
- 4 tsp. cornstarch
- 1 Tbsp. water
- 4 cups pitted fresh tart red cherries
- 1 tsp. finely shredded lemon peel
- 1 cup sifted powdered sugar
- ¼ tsp. almond extract
  Milk

1 For pastry, in a large mixing bowl beat butter or margarine and cream cheese with an electric mixer on medium to high speed until fluffy. Stir in flour, the 2 tablespoons granulated sugar, and salt. Divide dough in half. Cover and chill dough for 1 hour or until easy to handle. (Dough may be chilled overnight.)

2 For filling, in a large saucepan stir together the 3 tablespoons granulated sugar, cornstarch, and water. Add cherries. Cook and stir over medium heat until thickened and bubbly. Cook and stir for 2 minutes more. Stir in lemon peel. Remove filling from heat. Cover and chill until completely cool.

3 Preheat oven to 375°. On a lightly floured surface, roll each portion of dough into a 15×10½-inch rectangle. With a sharp knife, cut each rectangle into nine 5×3½-inch

EDITOR'S TIP

Deep Freeze Delight

Satisfaction is as close as the freezer section of your supermarket when you're looking for a low-fuss, fruity dessert. There you'll find an orchard's worth of frozen fruit that's perfect for sweet treats. And, because frozen fruit is processed shortly after picking, it can be as fresh tasting (or fresher) as what you find in the produce aisles. Take, for example, fresh tart red cherries. They don't ship well, so the frozen version may be the closest you'll get to the intense flavor of fresh cherries, especially once the July-through-August harvest ends. Unlike fresh, frozen cherries come already pitted. In general, frozen fruit can be substituted on a cup-for-cup basis for fresh.

rectangles. Spoon about 2 tablespoons of the cherry filling lengthwise down the center of each small rectangle to within ½ inch of each end. Starting from one of the long sides, lift dough up and over cherries, then lift dough from other long side over center; seal. Press ends with the tines of a fork to seal. Place pastry fingers, seam side down, on a foil-lined baking sheet.

4 Bake about 12 minutes or until lightly brown. Transfer pastries to a wire rack and let cool.

5 Meanwhile, for icing, in a small bowl stir together powdered sugar, almond extract, and enough milk (1 to 2 tablespoons) to make an icing of drizzling consistency. Drizzle icing over pastry fingers. Makes 18 pastries.

Nutrition Facts per pastry: 241 cal., 15 g total fat (10 g sat. fat), 43 mg chol., 182 mg sodium, 24 g carbo., 1 g fiber, 3 g pro.
Daily Values: 21% vit. A, 6% vit. C, 2% calcium, 5% iron.

CLEVER COOK

Favorite Flavored Frosting

Use your favorite flavored instant coffee powder or cocoa mix to make a unique frosting. In a medium bowl whisk together 2 tablespoons melted butter, 2 tablespoons milk, and 2 tablespoons of the beverage powder. Beat in about 2½ cups sifted powdered sugar or enough to make a pourable glaze or a thicker spreadable frosting. This is enough to glaze or frost a two-layer cake.

Lewy Olfson
Madison, Wisconsin

Strawberry-Banana Cream Pie

Prep: 35 minutes **Bake:** 12 minutes
Chill: 1 hour

- 1 recipe Toasted Almond Pastry (see bottom right)
- ½ cup sugar
- 2 Tbsp. cornstarch
- 1¾ cups milk
- 2 egg yolks, beaten
- 1 Tbsp. margarine or butter
- ½ tsp. vanilla
- 2 medium bananas
- 2 tsp. lemon juice
- 2 cups sliced strawberries
- ½ cup whipping cream
- 1 Tbsp. sugar
- ¼ tsp. almond extract

1 Preheat oven to 450°. Prepare Toasted Almond Pastry. On a floured surface, roll pastry to a 12-inch circle. Wrap pastry around rolling pin. Unroll onto a 9-inch pie plate. Ease pastry into pie plate. Trim pastry to ½ inch beyond edge of plate. Fold under extra pastry; crimp edge. Do not prick pastry. Line pastry shell with a double thickness of foil. Bake 8 minutes. Remove foil. Bake 4 to 5 minutes more or until set. Cool.

2 For filling, in a medium saucepan mix the ½ cup sugar and cornstarch. Gradually stir in milk. Cook and stir until bubbly. Cook and stir 2 minutes more. Remove from heat. Stir about 1 cup of the hot mixture into the beaten egg yolks. Return all to saucepan. Bring to a gentle boil. Cook and stir 2 minutes more. Remove from heat. Stir in margarine or butter and vanilla. Cover surface with plastic wrap.

3 Slice bananas ¼ inch thick; toss with lemon juice. (You should have about 1¼ cups.) Spread half the hot filling evenly into pastry shell. Arrange half of the bananas and strawberries on top. Top with remaining filling, bananas, and strawberries. Cover and chill in the refrigerator for 1 to 6 hours.

4 Just before serving, in a medium mixing bowl beat the whipping cream, 1 tablespoon sugar, and almond extract with an electric mixer on medium speed until stiff peaks form (tips stand straight up). Pipe or dollop whipped cream onto pie. Makes 8 servings.

Toasted Almond Pastry

Mix 1¼ cups all-purpose flour, ¼ cup finely chopped toasted almonds, and ¼ teaspoon salt. Using a pastry blender, cut in ⅓ cup shortening or lard until pieces are pea-size. Sprinkle 3 to 4 tablespoons cold water, 1 tablespoon at a time, over mixture, tossing with a fork after each addition until all is moistened. Form dough into a ball.

Nutrition Facts per serving: 368 cal., 20 g total fat (7 g sat. fat), 78 mg chol., 119 mg sodium, 42 g carbo., 3 g fiber, 6 g pro.
Daily Values: 10% vit. A, 46% vit. C, 10% calcium, 8% iron.

Sundae-Style Pastries

Build an elegant sundae with vanilla ice cream and a reduced balsamic fruit sauce over a flaky pastry shell.

Start to finish: 45 minutes

- 1 10-oz. pkg. frozen puff pastry shells (6 shells)
- ¾ cup white grape juice
- ½ cup dried apricot halves, cut into thin strips
- ¼ cup balsamic vinegar
- 2 Tbsp. light-colored corn syrup
- 2 tsp. cornstarch
- ⅛ tsp. ground ginger
- ⅛ tsp. ground cinnamon
- 2 medium peaches, peeled, pitted, and sliced, and/or nectarines, pitted and sliced
- 1 pint vanilla or cinnamon-flavored ice cream

1 Bake the puff pastry shells according to package directions. Set aside to cool.

2 In a small saucepan heat grape juice just until boiling. Remove from heat. Place apricots in a small bowl. Pour hot grape juice over apricots. Cover and let stand for 10 minutes.

3 Meanwhile, in the same saucepan bring balsamic vinegar to boiling. Boil gently for 2 to 3 minutes or until reduced to 2 tablespoons. In a small bowl stir together corn syrup, cornstarch, ginger, and cinnamon until combined. Add to vinegar in saucepan, stirring to combine. Stir in apricot mixture. Cook and stir until thickened and bubbly. Cook and stir

2 minutes more. Remove from heat. Cool slightly. Stir peaches or nectarines into thickened mixture.

4 To serve, place a scoop of ice cream in each baked puff pastry shell. Spoon warm sauce over. Makes 6 servings.

Nutrition Facts per serving: 461 cal., 23 g total fat (5 g sat. fat), 30 mg chol., 221 mg sodium, 61 g carbo., 3 g fiber, 5 g pro.
Daily Values: 23% vit. A, 29% vit. C, 7% calcium, 4% iron.

30 MINUTE

Raspberry-Lemon Dessert Biscuits

Prep: 20 minutes **Bake:** 10 minutes

- 2 cups all-purpose flour
- 2 Tbsp. granulated sugar
- 1 Tbsp. baking powder
- 1 Tbsp. finely shredded lemon peel
- ½ tsp. cream of tartar
- ¼ tsp. salt
- ¼ tsp. baking soda
- ½ cup butter or margarine
- 1 cup buttermilk or sour milk
- 1 cup fresh red raspberries
- 1 recipe Lemon Butter Frosting (see right)

1 Preheat oven to 450°. Grease a baking sheet; set aside. In a medium bowl stir together flour, granulated sugar, baking powder, lemon peel, cream of tartar, salt, and baking soda. Using a pastry blender, cut in butter or margarine until mixture resembles coarse crumbs. Make a well in center of dry mixture; add buttermilk or sour milk all at once. Using a fork, stir just until moistened. Gently fold in raspberries.

2 Drop dough from a tablespoon 1 inch apart on the prepared baking sheet. Bake for 10 to 12 minutes or until the biscuits are golden. Transfer biscuits to a wire rack and let cool while preparing frosting. Frost tops of biscuits with Lemon Butter Frosting. Serve warm. Makes 12 biscuits.

Lemon Butter Frosting

In a small bowl stir together 1 cup sifted powdered sugar and 1 tablespoon softened margarine or butter. Stir in ¼ teaspoon finely shredded lemon peel and enough water or lemon juice to make of spreading consistency.

Nutrition Facts per biscuit: 204 cal., 9 g total fat (5 g sat. fat), 23 mg chol., 290 mg sodium, 27 g carbo., 1 g fiber, 3 g pro.
Daily Values: 7% vit. A, 6% vit. C, 9% calcium, 5% iron.

30 MINUTE

Rosy Plum Sauce

Start to finish: 10 minutes

- ¼ cup sugar
- 1 tsp. cornstarch
- 5 or 6 medium plums, pitted and sliced (2½ cups)
- 2 Tbsp. water
   Vanilla ice cream
   Plum wedges

1 In a medium saucepan combine the sugar and cornstarch. Stir in the sliced plums and water. Bring to boiling, stirring occasionally. Reduce heat. Simmer sauce, covered, for 6 to 8 minutes or until desired consistency. Cool sauce slightly.

2 Serve warm sauce over vanilla ice cream and top with fresh plum wedges. Makes 6 to 8 servings.

Nutrition Facts per serving (with ⅓ cup ice cream): 195 cal., 8 g total fat (5 g sat. fat), 30 mg chol., 28 mg sodium, 30 g carbo., 1 g fiber, 2 g pro.
Daily Values: 11% vit. A, 13% vit. C, 6% calcium, 1% iron.

30 MINUTE, NO FAT

Fruit Blast Refresher

When you're using very juicy melons and mangoes, you may not need quite as much orange juice in this vitamin-rich drink.

Start to finish: 25 minutes

- 1 cup thinly sliced carrots (2 medium)
- 1 cup cantaloupe chunks
- 1 cup chopped, peeled mango
- ½ to ⅔ cup orange juice
- 3 cups ice cubes
   Whole baby carrots (optional)

1 In a saucepan cook the sliced carrots, covered, in a small amount of boiling water for 8 to 10 minutes or until very tender. Drain carrots in a colander. Plunge the colander into ice water to cool carrots completely. Drain.

2 In a blender container combine cooked carrots, cantaloupe, mango, and orange juice. Cover and blend until smooth. Add ice; cover and blend until cubes are just chopped. Pour into glasses. If desired, garnish each with a baby carrot. Makes 5 or 6 servings.

Nutrition Facts per serving: 63 cal., 0 g total fat, 0 mg chol., 25 mg sodium, 16 g carbo., 2 g fiber, 1 g pro.
Daily Values: 106% vit. A, 79% vit. C, 2% calcium, 2% iron.

The Benefits of Bacteria

Bacteria is usually seen as an enemy. But if you're nagged by yeast infections, it might be your friend.

Almost everybody has hundreds of different species of bacteria in their system, but it's just when bad bacteria outnumber good that things run amok. Some doctors think that adding good bacteria to your diet can help turn the balance in your favor.

A study published in *The Annals of Internal Medicine* found women with recurrent yeast infections reduced their infections by eating 1 to 1½ cups of yogurt every day. The bacteria Lactobacillus, which is found in some yogurt, was credited for restoring bacterial balance. "For most women, yogurt is helpful for fighting yeast infections," says Dr. Mark Martens, a professor of obstetrics and gynecology at the University of Minnesota. He recommends eating ½ cup to 1½ cups every day, but benefits come only from yogurt labeled with the phrase "made from live, active cultures." He also suggests buying the freshest yogurt you can because the amount of bacteria seems to be highest then. Dr. Martens says to skip Lactobacillus supplements because you can never tell how much good bacteria you're getting.

LOW FAT

Berry-Chocolate Frozen Yogurt

The loganberry, a cross between a blackberry and a raspberry, is typically red in color. Because of their tart nature, loganberries are great in pies, jams, and jellies.

Prep: 15 minutes **Freeze:** 40 minutes
Ripen: 4 hours

- 2 16-oz. cartons vanilla low-fat yogurt

- 2½ cups fresh loganberries or raspberries
- ½ cup light-colored corn syrup
- ¼ cup sugar
- ½ cup coarsely chopped semisweet chocolate (3 oz.)

1 In a blender container or food processor bowl combine half of the yogurt, ½ cup of the berries, half of the corn syrup, and half of the sugar. Cover and blend or process until almost smooth. Pour mixture into ice cream freezer container. Repeat.

2 Freeze mixture in an electric ice cream freezer according to manufacturer's directions. Remove dasher from freezer. Add remaining 1½ cups berries and the chopped chocolate; stir to distribute. Ripen.* Makes 1½ quarts.

*Note: To ripen frozen yogurt or ice cream, after stirring in berries and chocolate, cover top of freezer can with waxed paper or foil. Plug hole in lid and replace lid. Pack outer freezer bucket with enough ice and rock salt to cover top of freezer can, using about 4 cups ice and 1 cup salt. (When using an ice cream freezer with an insulated can, after churning, remove dasher; replace lid. Cover lid with ice and cover with a towel.) Ripen about 4 hours.

Nutrition Facts per ½-cup serving: 175 cal., 3 g total fat (2 g sat. fat), 5 mg chol., 70 mg sodium, 32 g carbo., 3 g fiber, 4 g pro.
Daily Values: 1% vit. A, 9% vit. C, 14% calcium, 1% iron.

LOW FAT

Plum-Citrus Frozen Yogurt

For a dessert with a pink-blush color, choose red-skinned plums.

Prep: 20 minutes **Freeze:** 7 hours

- ⅔ cup sugar
- 1 envelope unflavored gelatin
- 1½ cups milk
- 1 8-oz. carton orange low-fat yogurt
- 1 tsp. vanilla
- 5 or 6 medium plums, pitted and quartered (about 3 cups)

1 In a small saucepan stir together the sugar and gelatin; stir in milk. Cook and stir over low heat until gelatin is dissolved. Remove from heat; stir in yogurt and vanilla.

2 In a blender container combine plum pieces and gelatin mixture. Cover and blend until nearly smooth. Pour plum mixture into a 9×9×2-inch pan. Cover and freeze about 4 hours or until almost firm.

3 Break the frozen plum mixture into chunks. Transfer the chunks to a large, chilled mixer bowl. Beat with an electric mixer on medium speed until smooth but not melted. Return quickly to the cold pan. Cover and freeze about 3 hours more or until firm.

4 Before serving, let frozen yogurt stand at room temperature 10 to 15 minutes to soften. Serves 6 to 8.

Nutrition Facts per servings: 205 cal., 2 g total fat (1 g sat. fat), 7 mg chol., 55 mg sodium, 43 g carbo., 1 g fiber, 5 g pro.
Daily Values: 8% vit. A, 18% vit. C, 14% calcium, 1% iron.

september

IN THIS CHAPTER

30-minute recipes indicated in COLOR.
Low-fat and no-fat recipes indicated with a ♥.
Photographs indicated in italics.
*Bonus recipe

EDITOR'S TIP

Dick and Jane Eat Their Grains

Sit up straight, kids, and take note. You need to eat at least six servings of breads, cereals, pasta, and grains each day for good health. Kids over age 6 and teenage girls need about nine servings to fuel their growing bodies. Teenage boys need even more—as many as 11 servings from this food group. Reach for one or more of these high-carb servings every time you eat:

First thing in the morning:
1 slice of toast or ½ of an English muffin or bagel
½ cup cooked cereal, such as oatmeal
½ cup flaked cereal
1 small bran muffin
2 small pancakes
1 small waffle

At lunch or dinner:
½ cup cooked pasta, such as macaroni or spaghetti
½ cup chow mein noodles
1 small flour or corn tortilla
½ of a hamburger or hot dog bun
⅛ of a small pizza
2 breadsticks
1 biscuit
¼ cup bread stuffing
⅓ cup cooked rice

When you're starving for a snack:
2 to 3 cups popcorn
3 graham cracker squares
6 saltine crackers
8 animal crackers
3 gingersnap cookies
6 vanilla wafers
1 plain granola bar
10 pretzels
3 rice or popcorn cakes

PRIZE WINNER

Apple Breakfast Bars

Bobbie Harms
Erie, Colorado
$400—Breakfast on the Run

Prep: 15 minutes **Chill:** 1 hour

½   cup dried apples, snipped
⅓   cup honey
¼   cup raisins
1   Tbsp. brown sugar
⅓   cup peanut butter
¼   cup apple butter
½   tsp. ground cinnamon
½   cup rolled oats
½   cup chopped walnuts or pecans
⅓   cup toasted wheat germ
¼   cup roasted sunflower seeds
2   cups cornflakes and/or wheat flakes

1 In a Dutch oven combine dried apples, honey, raisins, and brown sugar. Heat and stir until mixture boils; reduce heat slightly. Cook, uncovered, for 1 minute, stirring constantly. Remove from heat. Stir in peanut butter until melted. Stir in apple butter and cinnamon. Stir in rolled oats, walnuts or pecans, wheat germ, and sunflower seeds until well combined. Add cereal, stirring to coat.

2 Press mixture very firmly (or bars will crumble) and evenly into an ungreased 8×8×2-inch pan. Chill to set. Cut into 8 bars. Store in an airtight container in the refrigerator up to 2 days. Makes 8 bars.

Nutrition Facts per bar: 327 cal., 14 g total fat (2 g sat. fat), 0 mg chol., 118 mg sodium, 48 g carbo., 4 g fiber, 8 g pro.
Daily Values: 1% vit. A, 2% vit. C, 3% calcium, 11% iron.

Chocolate-Peanut Butter Granola Bars

These chewy chocolaty bars can be stored in an airtight container at room temperature up to 2 days.

Prep: 20 minutes **Stand:** 1 hour

2   cups chocolate-flavored crisp rice cereal
1   cup granola
½   cup finely crushed chocolate graham crackers (6 squares)
½   cup honey-roasted peanuts or peanuts, chopped
⅓   cup butter
½   cup peanut butter
½   cup semisweet chocolate pieces
1   10½-oz. pkg. tiny marshmallows (6 cups)

1 Lightly grease an 8×8×2-inch baking pan. In a large bowl combine rice cereal, granola, graham cracker crumbs, and peanuts; set aside.

2 In a large saucepan stir butter, peanut butter, and chocolate pieces over medium-low heat until mixture is melted and smooth. Add marshmallows; heat and stir just until melted. Pour over cereal mixture. Stir with a wooden spoon until combined.

3 Working quickly, with a wide metal spatula, press mixture firmly (or bars will crumble) and evenly into prepared pan. Let stand at room temperature until firm.* Makes 24 bars.

*Note: To firm bars faster, place in refrigerator for 30 minutes or in the freezer for 10 minutes.

Nutrition Facts per bar: 185 cal., 10 g total fat (4 g sat. fat), 7 mg chol., 112 mg sodium, 22 g carbo., 1 g fiber, 3 g pro.
Daily Values: 4% vit. A, 3% vit. C.

Bananas Foster Oatmeal

Kids will love a bowl of this warm oatmeal because of the banana, nuts, and caramel toppings. Moms will love it because of the few minutes it takes to make.

Start to finish: 10 minutes

- 2   1-oz. envelopes instant oatmeal (plain)
- 1   medium banana, peeled and sliced
- 2   Tbsp. chopped toasted pecans
- 2   to 3 tsp. caramel-flavored ice cream topping
       Half-and-half, light cream, or milk (optional)

1 In two microwave-safe bowls prepare oatmeal according to package directions. Top each serving with bananas and pecans; drizzle with ice cream topping. If desired, heat in microwave on 100% power (high) for 30 seconds. If desired, serve with half-and-half or milk. Serves 2.

Nutrition Facts per serving: 230 cal., 7 g total fat (1 g sat. fat), 0 mg chol., 17 mg sodium, 38 g carbo., 5 g fiber, 6 g pro.
Daily Values: 1% vit. A, 9% vit. C, 3% calcium, 9% iron.

Oatmeal 'n' Raisins

If you have dried tart red cherries or dried cranberries on hand, you can substitute them for the raisins.

Start to finish: 25 minutes

- ½   cup steel-cut oats
- 2   Tbsp. frozen apple juice concentrate, thawed
- ⅓   cup milk
- 3   Tbsp. raisins
- 3   Tbsp. brown sugar

1 In a medium saucepan bring 2 cups *water* and ⅛ teaspoon *salt* to boiling. Stir in oats. Cover and simmer about 15 minutes or until oats are just tender and liquid is nearly absorbed. Stir in thawed apple juice concentrate.

2 Serve with milk. Sprinkle with raisins or, if desired, *dried cherries or cranberries*, and brown sugar. Serve immediately. Makes 3 servings.

Nutrition Facts per serving: 206 cal., 1 g total fat (1 g sat. fat), 2 mg chol., 128 mg sodium, 47 g carbo., 3 g fiber, 4 g pro.
Daily Values: 2% vit. A, 1% vit. C, 6% calcium, 7% iron.

Crumb-Topped Dried Cherry Coffee Cake

A subtle hint of cardamom flavors the tender, fruit-studded cake that hides beneath a layer of crumb topping.

Prep: 30 minutes   **Bake:** 40 minutes
Cool: 30 minutes

- ⅓   cup butter, softened
- ⅓   cup packed brown sugar
- ⅓   cup granulated sugar
- 2   eggs
- 2   cups all-purpose flour
- 1½   tsp. baking powder
- ½   tsp. ground cardamom
- ¼   tsp. baking soda
- ¼   tsp. salt
- ¾   cup buttermilk or sour milk
- 1   cup dried tart red cherries
- 1   recipe Crumb Topping (see right)

1 Preheat oven to 350°. Grease an 8×8×2-inch baking pan. In a large mixing bowl beat butter with an

BREAKFAST MENU

- **Scrambled eggs topped with strips of roasted red sweet peppers and feta cheese crumbles**

- **Chicken and apple breakfast sausages or other sausages**

- **Assorted fresh fruits**

- **Crumb-Topped Dried Cherry Coffee Cake (see below)**

electric mixer on medium speed for 30 seconds. Add sugars and beat until light and fluffy. Add eggs, one at a time, beating well after each.

2 Combine flour, baking powder, cardamom, baking soda, and salt. Add alternately with buttermilk or sour milk to beaten mixture, beating on low speed after each addition just until combined. Fold in dried cherries. Spread evenly in prepared baking pan. Sprinkle with Crumb Topping.

3 Bake 40 minutes or until a wooden toothpick inserted near the center comes out clean. Cool in pan on wire rack at least 30 minutes. Serve warm or at room temperature. Serves 9.

Crumb Topping

In a bowl combine ½ cup all-purpose flour, ½ cup packed brown sugar, and ¼ cup softened butter. Stir with a fork until mixture is crumbly.

Nutrition Facts per serving: 402 cal., 14 g total fat (8 g sat. fat), 82 mg chol., 339 mg sodium, 63 g carbo., 2 g fiber, 6 g pro.
Daily Values: 22% vit. A, 10% calcium, 11% iron.

Pancakes and muffins are breakfast naturals when adorned with creamy butter. But whip honey or maple syrup into that butter and these customary breakfast items turn positively transcendent. You can even stir in some finely chopped hazelnuts, walnuts, or almonds to add some crunch along with the extra flavor. For a decorative touch when you're entertaining, press the butter mixtures into a mold and chill until firm.

When sweetened butters gild pancakes, waffles, or raisin toast, simple breakfast fare shines. Use sweetened butters immediately or store them, tightly covered, in the refrigerator for up to 2 weeks. They also can be frozen for up to 2 months if tightly wrapped and sealed in an airtight container.

• Honey Butter: Honeys differ in flavors depending on which flowers the bees pollinated. This results in variations in the tastes of honey butters, too. For example, clover honey has a mild flavor and a light golden color, while the flavor of orange blossom honey has a stronger, floral hint and a darker golden color. Buckwheat renders the honey a deep brown color while giving it an intense, earthy flavor.

To make honey butter, soften a stick of butter. Beat it together with a few tablespoons of the honey of your choice until thoroughly combined. Add a few pinches of ground cinnamon, cloves, or cardamom, if desired.

• Maple Butter: Different brands of maple syrup also have individual flavors, though they are more subtle. Pure maple syrup, instead of maple-flavored syrup, endows the butter with the ultimate maple taste. To make maple butter, soften a stick of butter. Beat in several tablespoons of maple syrup to taste, adding ground cinnamon, if desired.

• Orange Butter: Citrus adds a little more briskness to sweetened butters. For orange butter, soften a stick of butter. Beat in several teaspoons of finely shredded orange peel, adding a tablespoon of powdered sugar, if desired.

Oatmeal Carrot Bread

For an on-the-run breakfast or for a simple snack, slather some softened cream cheese between two thin slices of this wholesome bread.

Prep: 20 minutes **Bake:** 55 minutes

    1½ cups all-purpose flour
    ⅔ cup packed brown sugar
    ½ cup quick-cooking oats
    2 tsp. baking powder
    1 tsp. ground cinnamon
    ¼ tsp. baking soda
    1 cup finely shredded carrot
    2 eggs, beaten
    ¾ cup milk
    ⅓ cup cooking oil
    ½ cup raisins
    ½ cup chopped walnuts

1 Preheat oven to 350°. Grease the bottom and ½ inch up the sides of an 8×4×2-inch loaf pan; set aside.

2 In a bowl combine flour, sugar, oats, baking powder, cinnamon, baking soda, and ¼ teaspoon *salt*. In another bowl combine carrot, eggs, milk, and oil. Add carrot mixture to flour mixture, stirring just until moistened. Stir in raisins and walnuts.

3 Spoon batter into the prepared pan. Bake for 55 to 60 minutes or until a wooden toothpick inserted near center comes out clean. Cool on wire rack 10 minutes. Remove from pan. Cool completely on the rack. Wrap and store overnight before serving. Makes 1 loaf (16 servings).

Nutrition Facts per serving: 180 cal., 8 g total fat (1 g sat. fat), 27 mg chol., 126 mg sodium, 24 g carbo., 1 g fiber, 3 g pro.
Daily Values: 19% vit. A, 1% vit. C, 7% calcium, 6% iron.

Havarti & Mushroom Breakfast Rounds

Mushrooms, cheese, and eggs top English muffin halves for these open-faced, breakfast-style sandwiches.

Prep: 25 minutes **Bake:** 10 minutes

    3 English muffins, split and toasted
    1½ cups sliced fresh mushrooms
    ½ cup finely chopped onion
    1 Tbsp. butter or margarine
    2 eggs, lightly beaten
    1½ cups shredded Havarti or Swiss
        cheese (6 oz.)
    ¼ tsp. seasoned salt
    ⅛ tsp. pepper

1 Preheat oven to 400°. Arrange toasted English muffin halves, cut side up, on a baking sheet. Set aside.

2 In a large skillet cook mushrooms and onion in hot butter or margarine until tender. Remove from skillet with a slotted spoon. Drain in a colander and divide evenly among the muffin halves.

3 Stir together eggs, Havarti or Swiss cheese, seasoned salt, and pepper. Spoon mixture over mushrooms on muffin halves.

4 Bake for 10 to 12 minutes or until cheese is melted and bubbly. Serve immediately. Makes 6 servings.

Nutrition Facts per serving: 240 cal., 16 g total fat (2 g sat. fat), 111 mg chol., 391 mg sodium, 15 g carbo., 1 g fiber, 11 g pro.
Daily Values: 10% vit. A, 1% vit. C, 25% calcium, 6% iron.

Spiced Berry-Carrot Cheese Spread

You can prepare this perfect-for-toast spread the night before, then cover and chill it until everyone is bright-eyed and ready for breakfast.

Start to finish: 10 minutes

- 1 8-oz. tub apple-cinnamon cream cheese
- 1 tsp. finely shredded orange peel
- 1 Tbsp. orange juice
- ½ cup dried cranberries, chopped
- ⅓ cup finely shredded carrot
- ¼ cup chopped toasted pecans or walnuts

1 In a small bowl combine cream cheese, orange peel, and orange juice. Using a wooden spoon, stir until well mixed. Stir in the chopped dried cranberries, shredded carrot, and chopped pecans or walnuts. Serve immediately or cover and refrigerate up to 24 hours.

2 Serve as a spread for *toasted bagel halves, English muffin halves, or slices of quick bread.* Makes 1¼ cups.

Nutrition Facts per 2 tablespoons: 117 cal., 8 g total fat (4 g sat. fat), 18 mg chol., 73 mg sodium, 9 g carbo., 1 g fiber, 1 g pro.
Daily Values: 15% vit. A, 2% vit. C, 3% calcium, 1% iron.

PRIZE WINNER

Piña Colada Plus

Kimberly Tomblinson-Ramm
Lansing, Michigan
$200—Breakfast on the Run

Start to finish: 10 minutes

- 1 8-oz. can crushed pineapple (juice pack), chilled
- 1 medium banana, cut up
- ¾ cup soy milk
- ½ cup orange juice
- 2 Tbsp. bottled or canned piña colada mix, chilled
  Ice cubes (optional)

1 In a blender container combine the undrained pineapple, banana, soy milk, orange juice, and piña colada mix. Cover and blend until nearly smooth. If desired, serve over ice. Makes 2 servings.

Nutrition Facts per serving: 203 cal., 3 g total fat (0 g sat. fat), 0 mg chol., 15 mg sodium, 44 g carbo., 4 g fiber, 4 g pro.
Daily Values: 2% vit. A, 79% vit. C, 3% calcium, 7% iron.

Garden-Patch Fish Dinner

Soybeans are marketed as "sweet beans" and are found in the frozen food section of the market. They're also available occasionally in the pod—buy about 3 pounds unshelled. (See the photograph on page 203.)

Prep: 15 minutes **Bake:** 25 minutes

- 1½ lb. fresh or frozen skinless salmon fillets, cut into 6 serving-size portions
- 1 20-oz. pkg. refrigerated mashed potatoes
- ¼ cup plain yogurt
- ¼ tsp. salt
- ¼ tsp. pepper
- 3 Tbsp. olive oil
- ½ cup snipped fresh basil
- 3 cups frozen shelled soybeans (sweet beans) or peas, thawed
- 1 cup grape tomatoes or small cherry tomatoes
- ¼ tsp. salt
- ¼ tsp. pepper

CLEVER COOK

Blender Cappuccino

Instead of purchasing an expensive cappuccino machine, I use a blender. Simply use traditional cappuccino proportions of hot water, instant coffee, milk, and sugar, then blend together until foamy. Pour the mixture into cups and sprinkle with ground cinnamon.

Beth Garcia
San Jose, California

1 Thaw fish, if frozen. Preheat oven to 350°. In a medium bowl stir together potatoes, yogurt, ¼ teaspoon salt, and ¼ teaspoon pepper. Set aside.

2 In a large skillet heat olive oil over medium-low heat. Add basil. Cook and stir 3 minutes. Add soybeans to skillet; cook and stir 5 minutes more or until almost tender (if using peas, cook only 1 minute).

3 With a slotted spoon, remove soybeans from skillet and divide among six 12- to 16-ounce individual casseroles or au gratin dishes. Divide tomatoes among the casseroles. Place fish on top of bean-tomato mixture. Sprinkle fish with ¼ teaspoon salt and ¼ teaspoon pepper. Brush with some of the basil oil from the skillet. Divide the potato mixture among the casseroles, spooning into a mound on one side of the fish.

4 Bake, uncovered, about 25 minutes or until fish is opaque and just begins to flake easily with a fork. Makes 6 servings.

Nutrition Facts per serving: 470 cal., 21 g total fat (3 g sat. fat), 59 mg chol., 439 mg sodium, 30 g carbo., 7 g fiber, 42 g pro.
Daily Values: 9% vit. A, 80% vit. C, 27% calcium, 31% iron.

- Salmon with Pesto Mayo (see right) served over steamed baby bok choy

- Creamy risotto topped with ribbons of summer squash and snipped fresh herbs

- Italian-style whole wheat or multigrain bread

- Cranberry-Apple Dumplings (see page 214)

Red Seafood Chowder

If puff pastry toppers aren't in your schedule, use croutons or crackers. (See the photograph on page 197.)

Start to finish: 45 minutes

- ½ cup chopped onion (1 medium)
- ½ cup chopped fennel (half of a medium fennel bulb); reserve leafy tops for garnish, if desired
- 1 Tbsp. olive oil or cooking oil
- 4 medium tomatoes, peeled, seeded, and cut up
- 2 14½-oz. cans reduced-sodium chicken broth
- ¼ tsp. curry powder
- ¼ tsp. pepper
- 12 oz. fresh bay scallops and/or peeled and deveined medium shrimp, and/or skinless fish fillets, such as red snapper or halibut, cut into bite-size pieces

- ½ of a 17¼-oz. pkg. frozen puff pastry (1 sheet), thawed
  Fennel tops (optional)

1 Preheat oven to 400°. In a large saucepan cook onion and fennel in hot olive oil or cooking oil until tender but not brown. Stir in the tomatoes, chicken broth, curry powder, and pepper. Bring to boiling; reduce heat. Simmer, covered, for 15 minutes.

2 Add scallops and/or shrimp, and/or fish to saucepan. Return to boiling; reduce heat. Simmer, uncovered, for 2 to 3 minutes more or until scallops and/or shrimp are opaque, and fish just begins to flake easily.

3 Meanwhile, unfold pastry onto a floured surface. Cut into 8 squares, triangles, rounds, and/or other shapes with a sharp knife or cookie cutter. Place pieces on an ungreased baking sheet. Bake about 10 minutes or until golden brown and puffed.

4 To serve, ladle hot chowder into bowls. Top each with a piece of baked puff pastry. If desired, add fennel tops. Makes 4 servings.

Nutrition Facts per serving: 431 cal., 24 g total fat (1 g sat. fat), 28 mg chol., 861 mg sodium, 34 g carbo., 5 g fiber, 21 g pro.
Daily Values: 11% vit. A, 58% vit. C, 6% calcium, 9% iron.

PRIZE WINNER

Salmon with Pesto Mayo

Gloria Pleasants
Williamsburg, Virginia
$400—Five-Ingredient Main Dishes

Start to finish: 20 minutes

- 4 5- to 6-oz. skinless, boneless fresh or frozen salmon fillets
- 2 Tbsp. crumbled firm-textured bread
- ¼ cup mayonnaise or salad dressing
- 3 Tbsp. purchased basil pesto
- 1 Tbsp. grated Parmesan cheese

1 Thaw fish, if frozen. Preheat broiler. Place the bread crumbs in a shallow baking pan. Broil 4 inches from heat for 1 to 2 minutes or until lightly toasted, stirring once. Set bread crumbs aside.

2 Measure thickness of fish. Place fish on the greased unheated rack of broiler pan, tucking under any thin edges. Broil 4 inches from heat for 4 to 6 minutes per ½-inch thickness or until fish just begins to flake easily with a fork. Turn over 1-inch-thick fillets halfway through broiling.

3 Meanwhile, in a small bowl stir together mayonnaise and pesto; set aside. Combine toasted bread crumbs and cheese. Spoon mayonnaise mixture over fillets. Sprinkle with crumb mixture. Broil 1 to 2 minutes more or until crumbs are lightly browned. Makes 4 servings.

Nutrition Facts per serving: 363 cal., 24 g total fat (3 g sat. fat), 84 mg chol., 309 mg sodium, 5 g carbo., 0 g fiber, 31 g pro.
Daily Values: 6% vit. A, 4% calcium, 7% iron.

Above: Red Seafood Chowder (page 196)
Right: Chocolate Chip Peanut Brittle Bites (page 182)

Left: Wednesday Night Pork
Chops (page 208)
Above: Cranberry-Apple
Dumplings (page 214)
Right: No-Drip Chocolate
Dip (page 215) served with
Cutout Cookies (page 216)

Top: Figgy Cheese Conserve (page 213)
Above: Vegetarian Shepherd's Pie (page 206)
Right: Easy Pot Roast (page 210)

Above: Top Sirloin with Onions and Carrots (page 209)
Left: Garden-Patch Fish Dinner (page 195)
Page 202: Citrus Chicken (page 207)

Above: Skillet Pasta Supper
(page 205)
Right: Spicy Tex-Mex Pizza
(page 205)
Far Right: Chocolate-Dipped
Orange Biscotti (page 216)

Skillet Pasta Supper

Use your favorite combination of frozen vegetables. The cooking time is about the same for all varieties. (See the photograph on page 204.)

Start to finish: 50 minutes

- 2 Tbsp. olive oil
- 2 cloves garlic, minced
- 8 ½-inch-thick slices baguette-style French bread
- 2¼ cups water
- 1 14-oz. jar chunky-style spaghetti sauce with mushrooms (about 1½ cups)
- 8 oz. wagon wheel macaroni (about 2½ cups)
- 3 cups loose-pack frozen vegetables, such as white boiling onions, sugar-snap peas, and cauliflower
- 2 tsp. olive oil
- ½ cup ricotta cheese
- 2 Tbsp. milk
- ½ tsp. dried oregano, crushed
- ½ cup shredded mozzarella cheese (2 oz.)
- ¼ cup grated Parmesan cheese
- ¼ cup shredded mozzarella cheese (1 oz.)
   Fresh oregano sprigs (optional)

1 Preheat oven to 400°. Combine the 2 tablespoons olive oil and garlic. Brush both sides of bread slices with olive oil mixture. Place on a baking sheet and bake for 4 minutes. Turn and bake for 4 to 5 minutes more or until toasted. Set aside.

2 In a 10-inch skillet bring water and spaghetti sauce to boiling; stir in macaroni (see photo, above right). Return to boiling; reduce heat. Cover and simmer 12 minutes, stirring pasta occasionally.

To avoid splashing when pouring the uncooked pasta into the skillet, keep bag close to the surface of the pan.

3 Meanwhile, place vegetables in a colander; run cool water over the vegetables to thaw. Press with rubber spatula to remove excess liquid. Transfer vegetables to a large bowl. Add the 2 teaspoons olive oil, ¼ teaspoon *salt*, and ⅛ teaspoon *pepper*; toss mixture gently to coat. Set aside.

4 In a small bowl stir together ricotta cheese, milk, dried oregano, and ¼ teaspoon *pepper*. Stir in the ½ cup mozzarella cheese and the Parmesan cheese.

5 Spoon cheese mixture into center of skillet over pasta mixture, spreading slightly to make a 4- or 5-inch circle. Spoon vegetables evenly around edge of skillet over pasta mixture (do not cover cheese in center). Simmer, covered, 10 minutes or until vegetables are crisp-tender.

6 Just before serving, sprinkle the ¼ cup mozzarella over vegetables and cheese mixture, and arrange bread slices on top of cheese mixture. If desired, garnish with fresh oregano sprigs. Makes 6 servings.

Nutrition Facts per serving: 483 cal., 17 g total fat (6 g sat. fat), 22 mg chol., 845 mg sodium, 65 g carbo., 5 g fiber, 18 g pro.
Daily Values: 24% vit. A, 35% vit. C, 28% calcium, 18% iron.

PRIZE WINNER

Spicy Tex-Mex Pizza

Cathy Minich
Scituate, Massachusetts
$200—Five-Ingredient Main Dishes
(See the photograph on page 204.)

Prep: 10 minutes **Bake:** 20 minutes
Stand: 5 minutes

- 1 12-inch thin-crust Italian bread shell (10-oz. Boboli) or Italian flat bread (12½-oz. focaccia)
- 2 cups shredded Monterey Jack cheese with jalapeño peppers or Monterey Jack cheese (8 oz.)
- 1 15-oz. can black beans, rinsed and drained
- 1 11-oz. can whole kernel corn with red and green peppers, drained
- 2 to 4 Tbsp. chopped pickled jalapeño peppers (optional)*

1 Preheat oven to 425°. Place crust on an ungreased pizza pan or baking sheet. Sprinkle with half of the Monterey Jack cheese, all of the black beans, the drained corn, and, if desired, jalapeño peppers. Top with remaining cheese.

2 Bake about 20 minutes or until heated through and cheese is melted. Let stand 5 minutes. Cut into wedges to serve. Makes 6 servings.

Nutrition Facts per serving: 413 cal., 17 g total fat (8 g sat. fat), 46 mg chol., 971 mg sodium, 48 g carbo., 4 g fiber, 24 g pro.
Daily Values: 12% vit. A, 2% vit. C, 40% calcium, 7% iron.

*Note: Hot peppers contain oils that can burn eyes, lips, and sensitive skin, so wear plastic gloves while preparing them and be sure to wash your hands thoroughly afterward.

Vegetarian Shepherd's Pie

To cook as one dish rather than as individual portions, spoon mixture into a greased 2-quart casserole and bake for 15 to 20 minutes or until bubbly. (See the photograph on page 200.)

Prep: 20 minutes **Cook:** 30 minutes
Bake: 15 minutes **Stand:** 10 minutes

1	14½-oz. can vegetable broth or chicken broth
¼	cup water
1	cup dry lentils, rinsed and drained
6	purple boiling onions, halved, or 2 medium red onions, quartered
3	cloves garlic, minced
1½	lb. parsnips, peeled and cut into 1-inch slices (about 4 cups)
1	14½-oz. can diced tomatoes with Italian herbs
2	Tbsp. tomato paste
3	cups water
1	cup quick-cooking polenta mix
1	Tbsp. snipped fresh thyme or ½ tsp. dried thyme, crushed
½	tsp. salt
1	cup shredded Monterey Jack cheese with jalapeño peppers or Monterey Jack cheese (4 oz.)

When ready, the polenta will be slightly thicker than cooked oatmeal.

EDITOR'S TIP

Celery Solutions

Sometimes you find it in your salad or stew. It's a must-show in bread stuffing. Heavens, what would a Bloody Mary be without a long stalk for stirring? But as commonplace as celery may seem, in the 1800s it was considered trendy, only appearing at the most prestigious food occasions.

Today you'll find celery in every supermarket produce section, any time of year. Buying celery, however, is one thing; using it is another. All too often the stalk wilts away in the refrigerator drawer, with only a rib or two used. Here's help to avoid waste.

Storage Sense
● Before you store celery, trim a thin slice from the root end. Rinse the stalks thoroughly, drain well, and dry.

● Refrigerate celery as soon as you get home from the store. Celery on the stalk keeps up to two weeks if you place the whole stalk in a sealed plastic bag in the vegetable drawer of your refrigerator.

● Cut-up celery stays crisp about three days if refrigerated in an airtight container or sealed plastic bag.

● To freshen limp celery, trim off the base and tops. Place in ice water in the sink for several minutes (time depends on extent of wilting).

Fresh Ways with Celery
● Stir chopped celery into bottled salsa for added crunch.

● Serve thinly sliced celery with sliced fresh tomatoes and your favorite salad dressing.

● Stir chopped celery and sliced cucumber into plain yogurt or sour cream. Use as a topper for baked potatoes.

● Stir-fry sliced celery and mushrooms in a little oil and soy sauce. Serve as a side dish over rice.

● Boil chopped celery along with potatoes in water; drain and mash as usual.

● Use cut-up celery stalks and apple wedges to stuff the cavity of a chicken before roasting. Remove and discard before serving. The celery imparts flavor to the meat.

● Finely chop celery and use as a low-calorie garnish for creamed soups, such as potato or tomato.

● Substitute chopped celery for nuts in main dishes and side dishes to cut the fat.

● Try sliced celery instead of water chestnuts in recipes.

● Don't overcook celery; add it to soups and stews during the last 20 minutes of cooking.

1 In a large saucepan combine vegetable broth, the ¼ cup water, lentils, onions, and garlic. Bring to boiling; reduce heat. Simmer, covered, for 20 minutes. Add parsnips. Return to boiling; reduce heat. Cover and simmer for 10 to 15 minutes more or until vegetables and lentils are just tender. Remove from heat. Stir in tomatoes and tomato paste.

2 Meanwhile, preheat oven to 350°. In a 2-quart saucepan bring the 3 cups water to boiling. Stir in polenta mix, thyme, and salt. Cook and stir over low heat about 5 minutes or until thick (see photo, left). Remove from heat. Stir in ¾ cup of the cheese until melted.

3 Spoon lentil mixture into six 12- to 15-ounce individual au gratin dishes. Spoon polenta mixture over lentil mixture. Sprinkle with remaining cheese. Place on a large, shallow baking pan. Bake, uncovered, 15 to 20 minutes or until bubbly. Let stand 10 minutes. Makes 6 servings.

Nutrition Facts per serving: 460 cal., 7 g total fat (4 g sat. fat), 20 mg chol., 790 mg sodium, 80 g carbo., 20 g fiber, 21 g pro.
Daily Values: 10% vit. A, 40% vit. C, 22% calcium, 22% iron.

30 MINUTE
Quick Lentil Cassoulet

Start to finish: 15 minutes

- 2 19-oz. cans ready-to-serve lentil soup
- 1 14-oz. can chunky tomatoes with garlic and spices or one 14½-oz. can chunky pasta-style tomatoes
- 3 medium carrots, coarsely chopped
- 4 5- to 6-inch round bread loaves, about 4 inches high
- 4 oz. fully cooked smoked sausage, thinly sliced
- 4 tsp. grated Parmesan cheese

1 In a large saucepan combine the soup, undrained tomatoes, and carrots. Bring to boiling; reduce heat. Simmer, uncovered, about 10 minutes or until the carrots are just tender.

2 Meanwhile, to make bread bowls, cut a ½-inch slice from the top of each round loaf. Hollow out center, leaving a ½-inch shell. Set bread bowls aside. Reserve the hollowed-out bread to make bread crumbs or for another use.

3 Using a potato masher, slightly mash soup mixture. Stir in sausage. Simmer, uncovered, about 10 minutes more or to desired consistency, stirring occasionally.

4 To serve, spoon soup mixture into bread bowls. Sprinkle with Parmesan cheese. Makes 4 servings.

Nutrition Facts per serving: 725 cal., 18 g total fat (5 g sat. fat), 21 mg chol., 2,631 mg sodium, 110 g carbo., 14 g fiber, 31 g pro.
Daily Values: 139% vit. A, 26% vit. C, 24% calcium, 48% iron.

Citrus Chicken

Keep it easy: It's not necessary to peel the ginger before grating. (See the photograph on page 202.)

Prep: 20 minutes **Cook:** 43 minutes

- 2 to 2½ lb. meaty chicken pieces (breasts, thighs, and drumsticks)
- ¼ cup all-purpose flour
- ¾ tsp. salt
- ¼ tsp. pepper
- 2 Tbsp. cooking oil
- 1 cup chopped onion
- ½ cup chopped celery
- 2 cups water
- 1 cup uncooked long grain rice
- 1 Tbsp. grated fresh ginger or 1 tsp. ground ginger
- ½ tsp. salt
- ¼ tsp. ground allspice
- ¼ tsp. ground turmeric
- 1 lemon, cut into thick slices
- 3 Tbsp. snipped fresh flat-leaf parsley

1 Remove skin from chicken. In a shallow dish combine flour, the ¾ teaspoon salt, and the pepper. Coat chicken with flour mixture. Discard any remaining flour mixture.

DINNER MENU

- Salad of mixed greens, dried cranberries, toasted almonds, and a poppy seed dressing

- Citrus Chicken (see below, left)

- Warm pita bread wedges

- Double Chocolate Lava Baby Cakes (see page 214)

2 In a 12-inch skillet brown chicken in hot oil over medium heat for 20 minutes, turning occasionally. Remove from skillet, reserving drippings. Set chicken aside. Add onion and celery to drippings in skillet. Cook and stir 3 to 4 minutes or until vegetables are just tender.

3 Carefully stir water, rice, ginger, the ½ teaspoon salt, allspice, and turmeric into vegetables in skillet. Bring to boiling; add chicken pieces. Reduce heat. Simmer, covered, for 20 to 25 minutes or until rice is tender and chicken is no longer pink. Top with lemon slices the last 5 minutes of cooking.

4 Just before serving, sprinkle parsley over chicken mixture. Squeeze warm lemon juice from the slices in pan over the chicken for additional citrus flavor. Makes 4 servings.

Nutrition Facts per serving: 470 cal., 15 g total fat (3 g sat. fat), 92 mg chol., 832 mg sodium, 48 g carbo., 2 g fiber, 34 g pro.
Daily Values: 3% vit. A, 18% vit. C, 5% calcium, 21% iron.

LOW FAT

Roasted Chicken With Citrus Salsa

Ease into dinnertime by making the salsa ahead and chilling up to 4 hours.

Prep: 25 minutes **Roast:** 1¼ hours
Stand: 15 minutes

1	3-lb. whole broiler-fryer chicken
2	cloves garlic, minced
1	Tbsp. cooking oil
2	tsp. ground cinnamon
½	tsp. salt
½	tsp. ground nutmeg
¼	tsp. black pepper
3	Tbsp. honey
⅓	cup dried tart red cherries
1⅓	cups orange sections, halved (about 4 oranges)
2	nectarines, pitted and chopped*
2	Tbsp. snipped fresh cilantro
1	fresh jalapeño pepper, seeded and chopped**
1	Tbsp. lime juice

1 Preheat oven to 375°. Remove skin from chicken (except for wings). Rub garlic over chicken. Tie legs to tail. Twist wing tips under back. Place breast side up on a rack in a roasting pan. Brush chicken with the cooking oil. In a small bowl combine cinnamon, salt, nutmeg, and black pepper. Sprinkle spice mixture all over chicken. Insert a meat thermometer into center of an inside thigh muscle.

2 Roast, uncovered, for 1 hour. Remove string from legs. Brush honey over chicken. Roast about 15 minutes more or until chicken is no longer pink and meat thermometer registers 180°. Let stand, covered, for 15 minutes before carving.

3 Meanwhile, for salsa, place cherries in a small saucepan; cover with water. Bring to boiling; remove from heat. Cover and let stand 5 minutes. Drain excess water. Combine drained cherries, orange sections, nectarines, cilantro, jalapeño, and lime juice. Cover and chill until ready to serve. Serve salsa with roasted chicken. Makes 6 servings.

*Note: If nectarines are out of season, substitute 1½ cups frozen peach slices, thawed and coarsely chopped.

**Note: Hot peppers contain oils that can burn eyes, lips, and sensitive skin, so wear plastic gloves while preparing them and be sure to wash your hands thoroughly afterward.

Nutrition Facts per serving: 314 cal., 10 g total fat (2 g sat. fat), 92 mg chol., 279 mg sodium, 26 g carbo., 3 g fiber, 31 g pro.
Daily Values: 11% vit. A, 45% vit. C, 5% calcium, 10% iron.

Wednesday Night Pork Chops

This pair of chops is ideal for dinner when the kids are away; double the recipe and you'll be ready to impress the hungriest quartet. (See the photograph on page 198.)

Prep: 10 minutes **Cook:** 23 minutes

1	Tbsp. cooking oil
2	pork loin or rib chops, cut 1¼ to 1½ inches thick (about 1½ lb.)
¼	tsp. coarsely ground black pepper
⅛	tsp. salt
1	cup baby summer squash, such as green or yellow pattypan and zucchini
¾	cup half-and-half or light cream
½	tsp. coriander seed, coarsely crushed

1 In a large skillet heat oil over medium heat. Season pork chops with pepper and salt. Add pork chops to skillet. Cook chops, uncovered, for 18 to 20 minutes or until juices run clear, turning once. If necessary, cut larger squash pieces into slices or halves. Add squash to skillet during the last 5 minutes of cooking. Remove chops and squash; keep warm.

2 Pour off drippings from skillet. Add half-and-half or light cream and coriander to skillet, stirring to scrape up brown bits. Bring to boiling; reduce heat. Simmer, uncovered, for 5 to 7 minutes or until sauce is slightly thickened and reduced to about ¼ cup. Spoon sauce over pork chops. Makes 2 servings.

Nutrition Facts per serving: 758 cal., 44 g total fat (17 g sat. fat), 254 mg chol., 388 mg sodium, 8 g carbo., 2 g fiber, 76 g pro.
Daily Values: 13% vit. A, 13% vit. C, 18% calcium, 18% iron.

30 MINUTE

Currant-Mustard-Glazed Sausage

Similar to the sweet-glazed smoked sausages offered as an appetizer, these spunky sausage pieces served over French bread slices are sure to become one of the family favorites.

Start to finish: 20 minutes

½	cup currant jelly
¼	cup yellow mustard
¼	tsp. dry mustard
⅛	tsp. ground nutmeg
1	lb. fully cooked smoked sausage, bias sliced into 1-inch pieces
4	½-inch-thick slices French bread, toasted

1 In a large skillet over medium heat stir together the currant jelly, yellow mustard, dry mustard, and nutmeg using a wire whisk until bubbly and smooth.

2 Add sausage pieces. Simmer, covered, about 5 minutes or until heated through.

3 Spoon sausage mixture over toasted bread slices. Makes 4 servings.

Nutrition Facts per serving: 572 cal., 35 g total fat (16 g sat. fat), 50 mg chol., 1,272 mg sodium, 44 g carbo., 1 g fiber, 17 g pro.
Daily Values: 5% vit. C, 3% calcium, 10% iron.

LOW FAT

Top Sirloin with Onions and Carrots

If you don't have a 12-inch skillet, brown the onions in two batches in a 9- or 10-inch skillet. (See the photograph on page 203.)

Start to finish: 1 hour

4	slices bacon
4	small onions, peeled and cut into 1-inch slices
8	small white or orange carrots, halved lengthwise
4	small red potatoes, cut up (1 lb. total)
½	cup beef broth
¼	cup beer, dark beer, or beef broth
1	Tbsp. brown sugar
1	tsp. dried thyme, crushed
1¼	lb. boneless beef top sirloin steak, cut 1½ to 2 inches thick
¼	tsp. salt
¼	tsp. pepper
	Snipped fresh thyme (optional)

1 In a 12-inch skillet cook bacon over medium heat until crisp. Remove from skillet; set bacon on paper towels to dry. Drain all but about 1 tablespoon of the drippings from the skillet.

2 In skillet brown onions on both sides, about 3 minutes per side. Remove onions; set aside. Add carrots to skillet; cook about 5 minutes or until light brown, turning occasionally. Remove skillet from heat. Carefully add potatoes, broth, beer or broth, brown sugar, and half of the dried thyme. Return onions to skillet. Return skillet to stovetop. Bring to boiling; reduce heat. Simmer, covered, for 30 to 35 minutes or until vegetables are tender.

3 Meanwhile, season beef with remaining dried thyme, salt, and pepper. Place on unheated rack of broiler pan. Broil 4 to 5 inches from heat for 16 to 22 minutes for medium-rare or 22 to 28 minutes for medium, turning once halfway through broiling. Cut into 4 pieces.

4 Remove vegetables from pan with a slotted spoon. Gently boil juices, uncovered, for 1 to 2 minutes or until slightly thickened. Divide steak, vegetables, and bacon among four dinner plates. Spoon juices over. If desired, sprinkle with fresh thyme. Makes 4 servings.

Nutrition Facts per serving: 384 cal., 10 g total fat (4 g sat. fat), 87 mg chol., 455 mg sodium, 37 g carbo., 7 g fiber, 35 g pro.
Daily Values: 288% vit. A, 44% vit. C, 7% calcium, 28% iron.

TEST KITCHEN TIP
Claim Your Steak

Beef became leaner to satisfy our demand for a healthier product. But if beef seems tougher, too, it may be because you need to adjust your cooking techniques to account for the change. Don't give up on steaks yet: The following information pairs the right grade of steak with the way to cook it, helping you serve A+ steak every time.

Beef cuts are given grades based on the age of the animal and the amount of fat in the meat (marbling). Marbling is one of the qualities that makes a steak tender. The three major grades of beef (usually noted on the package label) are Prime, Choice, and Select.

Prime steaks are considered the best grade for flavor and tenderness. They have a high amount of marbling, so by definition a prime steak won't be the leanest. They also will be more expensive than choice or select. Prime beef is available from specialty butchers, or your supermarket butcher can order it for you. These steaks are the best you can grill, so save 'em for the big splurge.

Choice steaks have less marbling than prime. Since choice steaks are lower in fat, they can be the preferred cut for those who eat red meat often. Choice steaks are also good grilling steaks, but cook them to medium doneness (160°) or less for optimum tenderness. A seasoned rub can maximize the flavor.

Choice steaks can be broiled or panfried, too. To broil, place on the unheated rack of the broiler pan 3 to 4 inches from the heat. Broil each steak to medium-rare—about 10 minutes for a 1-inch-thick steak—turning once. To panfry steaks, rub with coarse-ground pepper or other seasonings. Heat a lightly greased skillet on medium-high heat, place steaks an inch or so apart, then cook for 3 to 4 minutes per side for medium-rare.

Select steaks have the least amount of marbling. Provided you don't overcook it, a select steak can be almost as juicy or flavorful as a choice steak. For best results, marinate a select steak overnight in the refrigerator, then cook it to medium (160°) or medium-rare (145°) doneness.

SUPPER MENU

- **Meat Loaf Supper Salad (see right)**

- **Country-style Italian bread**

- **Dry red wine or iced tea**

- **Apple tart or apple crisp drizzled with light cream or topped with a scoop of vanilla ice cream**

30 MINUTE

Easy Pot Roast

Any noodle will complement this dish, but consider spaetzle—sold packaged in the pasta or baking goods section of supermarkets. (See the photograph on page 201.)

Start to finish: 25 minutes

1	17-oz. heat-and-serve beef pot roast
2	Tbsp. minced shallots
1	Tbsp. margarine or butter
2	Tbsp. tarragon vinegar
2	cups fresh, pitted fruit cut into wedges, such as peaches, green plums, and red plums
	Hot cooked spaetzle (optional)
1	tsp. snipped fresh tarragon

1 Remove meat from package, reserving juices. In a large skillet cook shallots in hot margarine or butter over medium heat for 1 minute. Add pot roast; reduce heat. Cover and simmer about 10 minutes or until pot roast is heated through.

2 In a small bowl stir together reserved meat juices and tarragon vinegar. Pour over meat. Toss fruit over top. Cover; heat for 2 minutes more. If desired, serve with cooked spaetzle. Top with snipped tarragon. Makes 4 servings.

Nutrition Facts per serving: 259 cal., 12 g total fat (5 g sat. fat), 64 mg chol., 459 mg sodium, 19 g carbo., 2 g fiber, 24 g pro.
Daily Values: 9% vit. A, 17% vit. C, 1% calcium, 12% iron.

Meat Loaf Supper Salad

A meat loaf fortified with just a hint of pungent horseradish and red sweet pepper is served in rounds on a bed of greens made lustrous by a splash of balsamic vinaigrette.

Prep: 25 minutes **Bake:** 35 minutes
Stand: 5 minutes

1	egg, beaten
¾	cup soft bread crumbs (1 slice)
3	Tbsp. sliced green onions
2	Tbsp. finely chopped red sweet pepper or snipped dehydrated red sweet pepper strips
2	tsp. prepared horseradish
¼	tsp. salt
⅛	tsp. black pepper
12	oz. lean ground beef
⅔	cup coarsely crushed herb-seasoned stuffing mix
6	cups torn baby spinach, baby kale, or romaine
1	cup thinly bias-sliced carrots
1	cup sliced fresh shiitake mushrooms
1	large tomato, seeded and cut into wedges (about 1 cup)
2	Tbsp. sliced green onion
¾	cup bottled balsamic vinaigrette salad dressing
	Dehydrated red sweet pepper strips (optional)

1 Preheat oven to 350°. In a large bowl combine egg, soft bread crumbs, the 3 tablespoons sliced green onions, the 2 tablespoons fresh or dehydrated sweet pepper, horseradish, salt, and black pepper. Add ground beef; mix well. Shape meat mixture into a log about 10 inches long. Roll log in the crushed stuffing mix to coat well. Carefully transfer the meat log to a shallow baking pan.

2 Bake, uncovered, about 35 minutes or until an instant-read thermometer registers 160° and meat juices run clear. Cover and let stand 5 minutes for easier slicing.

3 To serve, slice meat log into "medallions" 2 to 3 inches thick. On six individual serving plates arrange baby spinach, baby kale, or romaine; carrot slices; mushroom slices; tomato wedges; and the 2 tablespoons sliced green onion. Arrange beef rounds on top of greens. Drizzle dressing over top. If desired, top meat rounds with additional dehydrated red pepper strips. Makes 6 servings.

Nutrition Facts per serving: 278 cal., 16 g total fat (4 g sat. fat), 72 mg chol., 646 mg sodium, 20 g carbo., 6 g fiber, 15 g pro.
Daily Values: 100% vit. A, 113% vit. C, 6% calcium, 24% iron.

Grilled Corn On the Cob

Corn comes to the table like a gift. Pull off the charred string, peel back the toasty husks, and there it is—row after row of buttery golden kernels cooked creamy and tender.

We're going to show you a simple way to grill corn. You will see that adding flavor at the very beginning can make a big difference later on where it counts: at the table.

In this case, we put the butter and herbs on the corn, resealed it in nature's own tinfoil—the husk—and let the heat from the fire drive flavor deep into the kernels.

Some recipes tell you to soak the ears of corn before cooking to prevent the husks from burning. We've tried it wet and dry, but found that distance from the heat is what really matters. When corn is placed right over coals or gas flame, it chars more than when grilled indirectly.

Which leads to the final point: This recipe was tested specifically to make sure that you can make your corn while other food is on the grill. The timing is the same—about 25 minutes—whether the cobs are set directly over the coals or off to one side.

Peel back the husks, being careful not to tear them (see Photo 1). To remove silk, start at the tip of the cob and work downward, pulling silk off with your fingers. You also can gently scrub with a vegetable brush. After removing silk, gently rinse the corn.

Spread room-temperature butter over the entire surface of the corn (see Photo 2). If butter is melted, it's harder to make herbs stick.

Space herbs evenly around the ear (see Photo 3). In tests with a variety of herbs, our tasters liked cilantro and basil best.

Carefully fold husks back over herb-and-butter-coated corn; tie top closed with kitchen string (see Photo 4).

Because husks are sturdy, the corn can be grilled indirectly or directly over coals. For both methods, keep the grill lid on to make sure the ears of corn cook evenly.

Grilled Corn On the Cob

Prep: 20 minutes **Grill:** 25 minutes

- 6 fresh ears yellow and/or white sweet corn (with husks)
- 6 Tbsp. butter or margarine, softened
- 36 sprigs or leaves of cilantro or basil
100-percent cotton kitchen string
Lime or lemon wedges (optional)

1 Carefully peel back corn husks, but do not remove. Remove and discard the silk. Gently rinse corn. Pat dry. Spread softened butter or margarine evenly over each ear of corn. Space six herb sprigs or leaves evenly around cob, gently pressing herbs into butter. Carefully fold husks back around tops of cobs. Tie husk tops with kitchen string.

2 Grill corn on the rack of a covered grill directly over medium coals for 25 to 30 minutes, turning and rearranging with long-handled tongs three times, until kernels are tender. Or, grill corn indirectly on the rack of a covered grill, arranging coals around the edge of the grill. Place corn on the rack above the center of the grill, and cook 25 to 30 minutes, turning and rearranging three times, until kernels are tender.

3 To serve, remove the string from corn. Peel back husks. If desired, squeeze lime juice over cilantro corn or lemon juice over basil corn. Makes 6 servings.

Nutrition Facts per serving: 185 cal., 13 g total fat (8 g sat. fat), 33 mg chol., 137 mg sodium, 17 g carbo., 2 g fiber, 3 g pro.
Daily Values: 14% vit. A, 9% vit. C, 1% calcium, 3% iron.

1. Carefully peel back husks and remove silk.

2. After washing spread with softened butter.

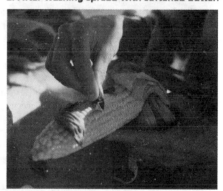

3. Place herbs or leaves around corn.

4. Fold husks back and tie with string.

EDITOR'S TIP

Eating Like an Olympian

You don't need to mimic the diet of the first Olympians who believed strength and speed came from eating raw meat. But what you eat and drink before, during, and after a workout has a big impact on how you perform and feel the rest of the day.

Running a four-minute mile or performing a perfect tuck and land off the balance beam may not be in your immediate fitness plans, but eating like an Olympic athlete should be. Good nutrition can help energize you during those morning walks and marathon yard-work sessions.

While in motion, your body needs energy. Walking 2 miles or gardening for 40 minutes, for example, burns about 200 calories. This fuel comes from a combination of stored fat (in fat cells and muscle) and stored carbohydrates called glycogen (in muscles). As you burn off this energy throughout your workout, you sweat, which is the body's way of getting rid of the heat your muscles generate. At the same time, your brain needs carbohydrates to stay alert and focused during your workout.

All of this means that your body needs some properly timed nourishment for you to feel energized, even if weight loss is your only exercise goal.

● **Pre-workout meal:** Eating a meal two to four hours before a workout gives your brain and muscles carbohydrate energy to sustain you through your session. Select high carbohydrate foods, such as whole grain cereals and breads, or bagels with a light spread of peanut butter and jam. Leftover rice or pasta drizzled with honey and topped with raisins also works well. Aim for 400 to 600 calories.

Also, drink at least 12 to 16 ounces of fluid two hours before exercise. This helps top off your fluid levels and allows you enough time to eliminate any excess before your workout.

● **Fueling during exercise:** Since most of us work out for 30 to 60 minutes, the primary concern is staying hydrated. Drink about 4 ounces of water (more if temperatures and humidity are high) every 15 minutes. If you work out more than one hour at a time, you should drink 5 to 12 ounces of fluid (starting early on in your exercise session) every 20 minutes. Adjust the amount depending upon your size and sweat rate. Consume about 30 grams of an easily digested carbohydrate each hour. Sport drinks supply about 15 grams of carbs per cup, so 2 cups along with water will take you through your long workouts. You also can eat foods such as dried fruit, fresh fruit (apples or bananas), or an energy bar.

● **Post-workout recovery eating:** Within 15 minutes of completing your workout, drink 2 to 4 cups of water or a sport drink. Drink beyond the feeling of thirst because your body needs replacement fluids. Within an hour of working out, eat a meal that contains both carbohydrates and protein. A tuna sandwich or a bean salad served with a piece of fresh fruit is a refreshing recovery meal. Finally, avoid caffeinated drinks, such as coffee, soft drinks, and tea, which decrease fluid by increasing urine volume.

The secret to eating like an athlete is balancing the right carbohydrate-packed foods with adequate protein for muscle repair. Along with the carbs and protein, your body needs a wealth of nutrients: B vitamins for energy metabolism; iron and zinc for healthy blood circulation; and antioxidant nutrients, such as vitamins C and E along with carotenes, which protect your body from damage that can cause muscle soreness.

Active women need about 55 to 60 percent of their calories from carbohydrates. That tallies to about 300 grams daily for a 2,000-calorie intake. Aim for at least 3 to 4 servings of fruit and 4 servings of vegetables daily.

Make at least four of your daily grain servings whole grain. For example, oatmeal, whole-grain ready-to-eat breakfast cereals, whole-grain bread (check the label for 100-percent whole grain), brown rice, and barley are packed with energizing carbohydrates along with fiber and B vitamins. These foods are a must for active people.

Feeding Your Teen Machine

If you have teen athletes at home, you know how crazy their schedules (and yours) are. Where do eating and sleeping fit in? Too often teen athletes fall into a performance slump as a result of poor nutrition and too little sleep. This often leads them into a season of sickness or poor recovery from injuries. Here are a few tips on getting the right foods into your young athletes:

● **Insist on breakfast.** Even if it's eaten while going out the door, breakfast should supply a good dose of protein along with fresh fruit and energizing carbohydrates. Some suggestions: a breakfast bar, milk, and a banana; a breakfast burrito of scrambled eggs and cheese wrapped in a whole wheat tortilla, plus a glass of calcium-fortified orange juice; or even leftovers work well—two slices of pizza and a yogurt smoothie made with fresh or frozen berries.

● **Make snacking healthful.** Active teens need to eat every three hours or so, and foods like soda and chips go nowhere toward fueling their bodies. Trail mix (nuts, dried fruit, and soy nuts) is a great protein source that can be eaten on the run. Energy bars work well as snack alternatives to less-healthy candy bars. Buy bars with at least 10 to 15 grams of protein and 5 grams of fiber.

● **Eat before practice or a game.** Like adults, a teen's body needs carbohydrate-rich foods before exercise. Offer one or two sandwiches with a light filling (a few slices of turkey or peanut butter and jam) along with juice or fresh fruit to eat.

● **Make hydration part of the game.** Teens lose large amounts of liquids and need to drink a hefty 10 to 14 cups of fluids daily to replace sweat losses. Carrying around a sport bottle filled with water or taking along a chilled bottle of sport drink to guzzle before or during practice or a game works well.

Figgy Cheese Conserve

As an appetizer or snack, you can spoon this sizzling glazed fig and onion combo onto crisp crackers with a creamy exclamation point of goat cheese. Or, you can break the goat cheese into pieces and strew cheese, figs, and onions on top of your favorite salad greens. (See the photograph on page 200.)

Start to finish: 30 minutes

- 8 dried figs (about 4 oz.), halved or quartered*
- 1 Tbsp. margarine or butter
- 1 cup thinly sliced onions
- 1 tsp. snipped fresh thyme
- 1 Tbsp. balsamic vinegar
- 6 oz. soft goat cheese
  Assorted crackers, such as water crackers, pepper-flavored crackers, or stone-ground wheat crackers

1 Remove stems from figs, if desired. Place figs in a medium saucepan and cover with water. Bring to boiling; reduce heat. Cover and simmer for 5 minutes. Drain well; cool slightly.

2 In a medium skillet melt margarine or butter over medium heat. Add sliced onions. Cook and stir about 5 minutes or until brown. Stir in drained figs and thyme. Cook, stirring gently, about 2 minutes or until slightly softened. Add balsamic vinegar. Cook for 2 to 3 minutes more or until glazed.

3 To serve, place the goat cheese in a serving bowl. Spoon the fig mixture over cheese. Serve with assorted crackers. Makes 8 servings.

*Note: Find dried figs in the produce or baking-products section of your supermarket.

Nutrition Facts per serving (without crackers): 137 cal., 8 g total fat (5 g sat. fat), 21 mg chol., 128 mg sodium, 12 g carbo., 2 g fiber, 5 g pro.
Daily Values: 10% vit. A, 2% vit. C, 9% calcium, 4% iron.

Italian-Style Snack Mix

There is no magic—but a bowl of this tasty, crispy snack is sure to disappear.

Prep: 10 minutes **Bake:** 30 minutes

- 6 cups crispy corn and rice cereal
- 1 1.7-oz. can shoestring potatoes
- 2 cups crisp cheese breadsticks, broken into 2-inch pieces
- 1 5-oz. can smoky-flavored whole almonds
- ¼ cup butter or margarine
- 3 Tbsp. bottled clear Italian salad dressing
- ¼ cup grated Parmesan cheese
- ¼ tsp. garlic powder

1 Preheat oven to 300°. In a 17×11×2-inch baking pan combine cereal, shoestring potatoes, broken breadsticks, and smoked almonds.

2 In a small saucepan heat butter or margarine and salad dressing over low heat until butter is melted. Stir in 2 tablespoons of the Parmesan cheese. Drizzle butter mixture over cereal mixture, tossing to coat. Sprinkle with remaining cheese and garlic powder.

3 Bake, uncovered, for 30 minutes, stirring twice. Spread mixture out onto a large piece of foil to cool. Store mixture in an airtight container. Makes 10 cups.

Nutrition Facts per ½-cup serving: 166 cal., 11 g total fat (3 g sat. fat), 8 mg chol., 260 mg sodium, 14 g carbo., 1 g fiber, 4 g pro.
Daily Values: 3% vit. A, 1% vit. C, 7% calcium, 10% iron.

Strawberry and Apricot Shake

Because this summertime-flavored treat is made with frozen strawberries and apricot nectar, you can enjoy it in the wintertime, too.

Prep: 10 minutes **Stand:** 30 minutes

- 1½ cups frozen unsweetened whole strawberries
- 2 cups vanilla ice cream
- 2 5½-oz. cans apricot nectar, chilled
- 2 tsp. vanilla
  Fresh strawberries (optional)

1 Let strawberries stand at room temperature for 30 minutes to thaw slightly.

2 In a blender container combine the partially thawed strawberries, ice cream, apricot nectar, and vanilla. Cover and blend until smooth.

3 Pour shake into four chilled tall glasses. If desired, garnish with a fresh strawberry. Makes 4 servings.

Nutrition Facts per serving: 207 cal., 7 g total fat (4 g sat. fat), 29 mg chol., 57 mg sodium, 33 g carbo., 2 g fiber, 3 g pro.
Daily Values: 19% vit. A, 40% vit. C, 10% calcium, 4% iron.

Double-Chocolate Lava Baby Cakes

Praline sauce gushes out of each little cake just like the lava of a volcano.

Prep: 20 minutes **Bake:** 15 minutes

- ¾ cup butter
- 6 oz. semisweet chocolate pieces (1 cup)
- 1 recipe Praline Sauce (see recipe, right)
- 3 eggs
- 3 egg yolks
- ⅓ cup granulated sugar
- 1½ tsp. vanilla
- ⅓ cup all-purpose flour
- 3 Tbsp. unsweetened cocoa powder
- ⅓ cup pecan halves, toasted

1 Preheat oven to 400°. Lightly grease and flour six 1- to 1¼-cup soufflé dishes or six 10-ounce custard cups. Place soufflé dishes or custard cups in a shallow baking pan and set pan aside. In a heavy small saucepan melt butter and semisweet chocolate over low heat, stirring constantly. Remove from heat; cool.

2 Meanwhile, prepare Praline Sauce; cover and keep warm until needed.

3 In a large mixing bowl beat eggs, egg yolks, granulated sugar, and vanilla with an electric mixer on high speed about 5 minutes or until thick and lemon-colored. Beat in cooled chocolate mixture on medium speed. Sift flour and cocoa powder over chocolate mixture; beat on low speed just until combined. Divide batter evenly into prepared dishes or cups.

4 Bake 10 minutes. Remove cakes from oven. Using a small spatula or table knife, puncture top of each partially baked cake and gently enlarge to make a dime-size hole. Slowly spoon about 1 tablespoon Praline Sauce into center of each cake. Return to oven. Bake 5 minutes more or until cakes feel firm at the edges.

5 Cool cakes in soufflé dishes or custard cups on a wire rack for 3 minutes. Using a small spatula or knife, loosen cake edges from sides of dish or cup and slip cake out upright onto individual dessert plates.

6 Stir the pecan halves into the remaining Praline Sauce. If necessary, stir 1 to 2 teaspoons of hot water into remaining sauce to thin. Spoon warm Praline Sauce on top of cakes. Serve immediately. Makes 6 servings.

Praline Sauce

In a heavy medium saucepan combine ½ cup granulated sugar, ⅓ cup packed brown sugar, and 2 tablespoons dark-colored corn syrup. Stir in ½ cup whipping cream. Cook over medium-high heat until mixture boils, stirring constantly to dissolve sugar. Reduce heat. Cook, uncovered, about 10 minutes or until thickened, stirring occasionally. Makes about 1 cup sauce.

Nutrition Facts per serving with 2½ tablespoons sauce: 700 cal., 48 g total fat (21 g sat. fat), 302 mg chol., 281 mg sodium, 67 g carbo., 1 g fiber, 8 g pro.
Daily Values: 51% vit. A, 7% calcium, 17% iron.

Cranberry-Apple Dumplings

For the most tender crust, knead the dough just until it holds together—no more. (See the photograph on page 199.)

Prep: 35 minutes **Bake:** 45 minutes

- 6 medium (3-inch diameter) apples (such as Braeburn, Fuji, Granny Smith, or Golden Delicious apples), cored
- ½ cup packed brown sugar
- 1 Tbsp. cornstarch
- 1 cup cranberry juice
- 1 cup all-purpose flour
- 2 Tbsp. granulated sugar
- ⅛ tsp. salt
- ⅓ cup butter
- 3 to 4 Tbsp. cold water
  Milk
- 2 Tbsp. coarse sugar

1 Preheat oven to 350°. Using a vegetable peeler partially peel apples, leaving vertical strips of skin intact (see photo 1, page 215). Place apples in six 10-ounce custard cups or 10-ounce au gratin dishes; set aside.

2 In a bowl stir together brown sugar and cornstarch. Add cranberry juice. Stir until sugar dissolves. Divide syrup evenly among the dishes. Place dishes in a large shallow baking pan.

3 For pastry, in a medium bowl stir together flour, granulated sugar, and salt. Using a pastry blender, cut in butter until pieces are pea-size. Sprinkle 1 tablespoon of the water over part of the mixture. Toss with a

1. Retaining part of the apple skin keeps the fruit attractive; vertical peeling makes the dessert easier to eat.

2. Lay strips of dough gently across the top of the apple, tucking about ½ inch of dough into the apple core.

fork. Push moistened dough to one side of the bowl. Repeat, using 1 tablespoon of water at a time, until all the dough is moistened. If necessary, gently knead the dough just until a ball forms.

4 On a lightly floured surface roll dough into a 10-inch square. Cut square in half. Cut each half crosswise into three rectangles. (You will have six rectangles total.) Set aside one rectangle of pastry.

5 Cut the remaining five rectangles into ¼- to ½-inch-wide strips. Randomly arrange strips vertically over apples in dishes, tucking one end

of each pastry strip into the center of the apple and pressing the rest of the strip onto the surface of the apple (see photo 2, left). Using a leaf cookie cutter or a knife, cut remaining rectangle of pastry into 6 leaf shapes. Brush all of the pastry pieces with milk. Sprinkle with coarse sugar.

6 Place the leaves on an ungreased cookie sheet. Bake for 5 to 7 minutes or until golden brown. Transfer to a wire rack to cool.

7 Bake apples, uncovered, for 40 to 45 minutes or until pastry is golden brown and apples are tender. Stand prebaked leaves in the centers of baked apples before serving. Serve warm. Makes 6 servings.

Nutrition Facts per serving: 373 cal., 12 g total fat (7 g sat. fat), 29 mg chol., 168 mg sodium, 68 g carbo., 4 g fiber, 2 g pro.
Daily Values: 11% vit. A, 35% vit. C, 4% calcium, 9% iron.

<u>30 MINUTE</u>

No-Drip Chocolate Dip

Purchased cookies or fresh fruit, such as grapes or pears, may be served instead of Cutout Cookies. (See the photograph on page 199.)

Start to finish: 15 minutes

- 1 recipe Cutout Cookies (see recipe, page 216) or cut-up fresh fruit
- 8 oz. unsweetened chocolate, chopped
- 1 14-oz. can (1¼ cups) sweetened condensed milk
- 2 Tbsp. light-colored corn syrup
- ½ cup milk
- 1 tsp. vanilla
- ½ tsp. ground cinnamon Milk

1 Prepare Cutout Cookies or cut-up fruit as desired. Set aside.

2 In a heavy medium saucepan melt chocolate over low heat, stirring constantly. Stir in the sweetened condensed milk and corn syrup until combined. Gradually stir in the ½ cup milk until combined. Stir in vanilla and cinnamon. Stir in additional milk as necessary until dipping consistency.

3 Serve dip warm, using cookies and fruit as dippers. Cover and store any leftover dip in the refrigerator up to 3 weeks. Makes 2 cups.

To Make Ahead:

1. Prepare dip as directed; cool slightly. Cover and refrigerate up to 3 weeks.

2. To reheat, transfer chocolate mixture to a medium saucepan. Cook and stir over low heat until smooth and heated through. Or, transfer to a microwave-safe dish. Micro-cook, uncovered, on 100% power (high) for 35 to 60 seconds or until smooth and heated through, stirring halfway through cooking time. Serve warm, stirring in additional milk as necessary to reach dipping consistency.

Nutrition Facts per 1 tablespoon dip: 83 cal., 5 g total fat (3 g sat. fat), 4 mg chol., 20 mg sodium, 10 g carbo., 1 g fiber, 2 g pro.
Daily Values: 1% vit. A, 1% vit. C, 5% calcium, 3% iron.

Cutout Cookies

Dunk these sweet shapes in No-Drip Chocolate Dip (see recipe, page 215) or adorn them with your favorite frosting and decorative candies. (See the photograph on page 199.)

Prep: 10 minutes **Bake:** 7 minutes per batch

½ cup all-purpose flour
1 18-oz. roll refrigerated sugar
    cookie dough

1 Knead flour, ¼ cup at a time, into refrigerated sugar cookie dough. On a lightly floured surface, roll out dough to ⅛-inch thickness. Cut into desired shapes, such as alphabet letters. (Re-roll dough as necessary to make desired number of cookies.) Place cookies 1 inch apart on an ungreased cookie sheet. Bake according to package directions. Makes about 26 (3-inch) cookies.

Nutrition Facts per cookie: 94 cal., 4 g total fat (1 g sat. fat), 6 mg chol., 83 mg sodium, 13 g carbo., 0 g fiber, 1 g pro.
Daily Values: 2% calcium, 2% iron.

Chocolate-Dipped Orange Biscotti

See the photograph on page 204.

Prep: 30 minutes **Bake:** 45 minutes
Cool: 30 minutes

⅓ cup butter, softened
½ cup sugar
¼ cup orange marmalade
1 tsp. finely shredded orange peel
½ tsp. almond extract
2 eggs
1½ tsp. baking powder
2½ cups all-purpose flour
1⅔ cups miniature semisweet
    chocolate pieces
½ cup chopped toasted almonds
2 tsp. shortening

1 Preheat oven to 325°. In a large mixing bowl beat butter with an electric mixer on medium speed for 30 seconds. Beat in sugar, marmalade, orange peel, and almond extract until fluffy. Beat in eggs, one at a time, until combined. Beat in baking powder and ¼ teaspoon *salt.* Using a wooden spoon, stir in flour, ⅔ cup of the chocolate pieces, and the almonds. Divide dough in half.

2 On waxed paper, shape each dough half into a 10×1½-inch log. Transfer logs to a large ungreased cookie sheet, placing them about 4 inches apart. Flatten logs slightly.

3 Bake for 25 minutes. Cool on cookie sheet on a wire rack for 30 minutes. Reduce oven temperature to 300°.

4 With a serrated knife, cut each log crosswise into ½-inch-thick slices. Place slices, cut side down, on an ungreased cookie sheet. Bake for 10 minutes. Turn slices over; bake for 10 minutes more. Transfer cookies to a wire rack and let cool.

5 In a heavy small saucepan heat remaining 1 cup chocolate pieces and shortening over low heat until melted, stirring occasionally. Dip one end of each cookie into chocolate mixture, letting excess chocolate drip off. Place cookies on waxed paper until chocolate is set. Makes 36.

Nutrition Facts per cookie: 117 cal., 6 g total fat (2 g sat. fat), 17 mg chol., 56 mg sodium, 13 g carbo., 2 g fiber, 2 g pro.
Daily Values: 2% vit. A, 2% calcium, 3% iron.

EDITOR'S TIP

Fresh Life for Leftovers

The frugal cooks of yesteryear found a use for every morsel of food, turning past-prime ingredients into new, delicious dishes. Now you can do the same, following these ideas. You'll save money and feel good about reducing food waste.

Stale cake doughnuts: Cut into cubes for bread puddings or trifles.

Dry bread: Cut into cubes and sauté in seasoned butter for croutons, crumble for bread crumbs, or use slices whole for grilled cheese sandwiches or French toast.

Dry tortillas: Make tortilla chips by cutting them into wedges, brushing with butter, and oven toasting. For a sweet snack, sprinkle with cinnamon and sugar before toasting.

Stale crackers: Crush and use as a binder in meat loaves or hamburgers.

Broken cookies: Crumble and stir into ice cream. Use crushed wafer-type cookies in crumb crusts for pies and tarts.

Leftover cooked rice: Use for rice puddings, casseroles, soups, or stuffings. Or, freeze until needed.

Cooked pasta: Toss with cut-up vegetables, cubed cheese, and Italian dressing for a quick salad.

Overripe bananas: Mash and stir into yogurt or use in banana breads, cakes, or muffins.

Overripe strawberries: Whirl in the blender with orange juice, a pinch of sugar, and ice for a fruit drink. This also works with sliced peaches and bananas.

Bruised apples: Peel and use in applesauce or apple crisp.

Mushy or bruised avocados: Make guacamole.

Wilted or limp vegetables: Add to soups, stews, and casseroles.

october

IN THIS CHAPTER

30-minute recipes indicated in COLOR.
Low-fat and no-fat recipes indicated
with a ♥.
Photographs indicated in italics.
*Bonus recipe

Citrus Salad with Glazed Pecans

Start to finish: 20 minutes

- 3 Tbsp. red wine vinegar
- 3 Tbsp. olive oil
- 2 Tbsp. Dijon-style mustard
- 1 Tbsp. pure maple syrup or maple-flavored syrup
- ⅓ cup coarsely chopped pecans
- 2 Tbsp. pure maple syrup or maple-flavored syrup
- 2 slices bacon, cut up
- ½ of a medium red onion, cut into thin wedges
- 6 oz. fresh baby spinach, washed and stems removed
- 4 blood oranges or oranges, peeled, seeded, and thinly sliced

1 In a screw-top jar combine vinegar, olive oil, Dijon-style mustard, and the 1 tablespoon maple syrup. Cover and shake well. Set aside.

2 In a medium skillet cook pecans in the 2 tablespoons maple syrup over medium heat for 3 to 4 minutes or until lightly toasted. Spread nuts on foil; cool. Break nuts into clusters.

3 Meanwhile, in a small saucepan cook bacon and red onion wedges until bacon is crisp, stirring occasionally. Remove from heat.

4 To serve, divide spinach and oranges among four salad plates. Top with bacon-onion mixture and pecans; drizzle with dressing. Makes 4 side-dish servings.

Nutrition Facts per serving: 254 cal., 19 g total fat (3 g sat. fat), 3 mg chol., 142 mg sodium, 20 g carbo., 6 g fiber, 14 g pro.
Daily Values: 23% vit. A, 64% vit. C, 8% calcium, 19% iron.

Spinach-Apricot Salad

Marie Rizzio
Traverse City, Michigan
$200—Swift Side Dishes

Start to finish: 20 minutes

- 8 cups torn fresh prewashed baby spinach
- ⅓ cup dried apricots, snipped
- 1 Tbsp. olive oil
- 1 clove garlic, thinly sliced or minced
- 4 tsp. balsamic vinegar
  Salt
  Freshly ground black pepper
- 2 Tbsp. slivered almonds, toasted

1 Remove stems from spinach, if desired. In a large bowl combine spinach and apricots; set aside.

2 In a 12-inch skillet heat oil over medium heat. Cook and stir garlic in hot oil until golden. Stir in the balsamic vinegar. Bring to boiling; remove from heat.

3 Add the spinach-apricot mixture to skillet. Return to heat and toss mixture in skillet about 1 minute or until spinach is just wilted.

4 Transfer mixture to a serving dish. Season to taste with salt and pepper. Sprinkle with almonds. Serve salad immediately. Makes 4 side-dish servings.

Nutrition Facts per serving: 91 cal., 6 g total fat (1 g sat. fat), 0 mg chol., 146 mg sodium, 9 g carbo., 7 g fiber, 3 g pro.
Daily Values: 40% vit. A, 16% vit. C, 6% calcium, 27% iron.

DINNER MENU

- **Spinach-Apricot Salad (see left)**
- **Roasted pork loin**
- **Oven-roasted new potatoes with garlic and fresh thyme**
- **Glazed Carrots (see below)**
- **Multigrain rolls with butter**
- **Apple Cake with Caramel-Raisin Sauce (see page 248)**

Glazed Carrots

Ann Christine Tabaka
Hockessin, Delaware
$400—Swift Side Dishes

Start to finish: 15 minutes

- 2½ cups ½-inch-thick crinkle-cut and/or plain sliced carrots
- 1 Tbsp. margarine or butter
- 3 Tbsp. ginger preserves or orange marmalade plus 1 tsp. grated fresh ginger
- 2 Tbsp. frozen orange juice concentrate, thawed

1 In a medium saucepan cook carrots, covered, in a small amount of lightly salted boiling water for 3 minutes. Drain and set aside.

2 In the same saucepan over medium heat combine margarine or butter, ginger preserves or orange marmalade and ginger, and orange juice concentrate. Return carrots to saucepan. Cook, uncovered, over medium heat for 5 to 6 minutes or until carrots are just tender and glazed, stirring occasionally. Makes 4 servings.

Nutrition Facts per serving: 108 cal., 3 g total fat (0 g sat. fat), 0 mg chol., 65 mg sodium, 21 g carbo., 3 g fiber, 1 g pro.
Daily Values: 195% vit. A, 31% vit. C, 3% calcium, 3% iron.

Squash, Pear, and Onion Au Gratin

Prep: 25 minutes **Bake:** 1 hour

1½ lb. butternut, buttercup, or banana squash
  1 large onion, sliced and separated into rings (1 cup)
  1 Tbsp. margarine or butter
  1 medium pear, peeled, cored, and thinly sliced (1 cup)
     Salt
  3 Tbsp. fine dry bread crumbs
  3 slices bacon, crisp-cooked, drained, and crumbled
  2 Tbsp. chopped walnuts
  1 Tbsp. grated Romano cheese
  1 Tbsp. melted margarine or butter
  2 Tbsp. snipped parsley

1 Preheat oven to 350°. If using butternut squash, cut the squash in half lengthwise. Peel and slice squash crosswise into ½-inch-thick slices. Remove seeds from butternut, buttercup, or banana squash. Set aside.

2 Cook onion rings in 1 tablespoon hot margarine or butter for 5 to 10 minutes or until tender.

3 Arrange half of the squash slices in the bottom an 8×8×2-inch baking dish. Top with half of the pear slices. Repeat layers. Sprinkle lightly with salt. Cover with cooked onions.

4 Bake, covered, about 45 minutes or until nearly tender. Meanwhile, in a small bowl combine bread crumbs, bacon, walnuts, Romano cheese, and melted margarine or butter. Sprinkle over vegetables. Bake, uncovered, about 15 minutes more or until squash is tender. Garnish with parsley. Makes 6 servings.

Nutrition Facts per serving: 144 cal., 8 g total fat (1 g sat. fat), 4 mg chol., 184 mg sodium, 18 g carbo., 3 g fiber, 3 g pro.
Daily Values: 110% vit. A, 28% vit. C, 6% calcium, 6% iron.

Steamed Leeks in Orange Vinaigrette

This simple yet sophisticated side dish pairs well with grilled steaks and crusty Italian bread.

Prep: 5 minutes **Cook:** 5 minutes
Stand: 2 hours

  6 medium leeks (1½ lb.)
  2 Tbsp. salad oil
  ½ tsp. finely shredded orange peel
  2 Tbsp. orange juice
1½ tsp. Dijon-style mustard
  ⅛ tsp. pepper
  1 Tbsp. snipped parsley

1 Rinse leeks several times with cold water. Remove any tough outer leaves. Trim roots from base. Cut into ½-inch-thick slices, cutting 1 inch into green portion (you should have 2 cups).

2 To steam leek slices, place a steamer basket in a saucepan. Add water to just below the bottom of the steamer basket. Bring to boiling. Add leeks. Cover and reduce heat. Steam about 5 minutes or until tender.

3 Meanwhile, for orange vinaigrette, in a screw-top jar combine salad

oil, orange peel, orange juice, Dijon-style mustard, and pepper. Cover and shake well.

4 Pat leeks dry. Arrange in a shallow dish. Shake vinaigrette; pour over warm leeks. Cover; let stand at room temperature 2 to 4 hours. Sprinkle with parsley. Serves 4.

Nutrition Facts per serving: 94 cal., 7 g total fat (1 g sat. fat), 0 mg chol., 20 mg sodium, 7 g carbo., 1 g fiber, 1 g pro.
Daily Values: 2% vit. A, 17% vit. C, 3% calcium, 6% iron.

30 MINUTE, LOW FAT

Snow Peas and Tomatoes

Start to finish: 10 minutes

  1 large shallot, peeled and sliced
  2 tsp. peanut oil
  ¼ tsp. toasted sesame oil
  6 cups fresh snow pea pods, strings removed (about 1 lb.)
  1 Tbsp. bottled teriyaki sauce
  ½ cup grape tomatoes or cherry tomatoes, halved
  2 tsp. toasted sesame seeds

1 In a 12-inch skillet over medium heat cook shallot in hot oils until tender. Add pea pods and teriyaki sauce. Cook and stir 2 to 3 minutes or until pea pods are crisp-tender. Add tomatoes; cook 1 minute more.

2 Transfer mixture to a serving bowl. Sprinkle with sesame seeds. Makes 6 servings.

Nutrition Facts per serving: 63 cal., 2 g total fat (0 g sat. fat), 0 mg chol., 120 mg sodium, 8 g carbo., 2 g fiber, 3 g pro.
Daily Values: 3% vit. A, 41% vit. C, 5% calcium, 11% iron.

Greek-Style Mashed Potatoes

Greek-inspired ingredients such as feta cheese, fresh oregano, and walnuts turn ordinary mashed potatoes into something special.

Prep: 30 minutes **Bake:** 12 minutes

- 6 medium baking potatoes (2 lb.)
- 2 Tbsp. butter or margarine
- ½ tsp. salt
- ¼ tsp. pepper
- ¼ to ½ cup milk
- 1 cup crumbled feta cheese (4 oz.)
- 1 Tbsp. snipped fresh oregano or
  ½ tsp. dried oregano, crushed
- ⅓ cup chopped walnuts

1 Preheat oven to 400°. Grease a 1½-quart casserole; set aside.

2 Peel and quarter potatoes. Cook, covered, in a small amount of lightly salted, boiling water for 20 to 25 minutes or until tender; drain. Mash with a potato masher or beat with an electric mixer on low speed. Add butter, salt, and pepper. Gradually beat in enough milk to moisten.

3 Fold in half of the feta and all of the oregano. Spoon into prepared casserole. Sprinkle with remaining cheese and the walnuts.

4 Bake, uncovered, for 12 to 15 minutes or until nuts are lightly toasted and mixture is heated through. Makes 6 servings.

Nutrition Facts per serving: 244 cal., 13 g total fat (6 g sat. fat), 28 mg chol., 453 mg sodium, 26 g carbo., 3 g fiber, 8 g pro.
Daily Values: 7% vit. A, 35% vit. C, 13% calcium, 9% iron.

Wild Rice and Cranberry Pilaf

Flavors of the autumn season come together in this fruited rice dish. Serve it alongside roasted pork or poultry.

Prep: 20 minutes **Bake:** 55 minutes

- ¾ cup wild rice
- 3 cups chicken broth
- ½ cup pearl barley
- ¼ cup snipped dried cranberries, apricots, or tart red cherries
- ¼ cup dried currants
- 1 Tbsp. margarine or butter
- ⅓ cup sliced almonds, toasted

1 Preheat oven to 325°. Rinse wild rice with cold water; drain. In a saucepan combine rice and chicken broth. Bring to boiling; reduce heat. Cover and simmer for 10 minutes. Remove from heat.

2 Stir barley; cranberries, apricots, or cherries; currants; and margarine or butter into rice in saucepan. Spoon into a 1½-quart casserole.

3 Bake, covered, for 55 to 60 minutes or until rice and barley are tender and liquid is absorbed, stirring once. Fluff rice mixture with a fork. Stir in the almonds. Makes 6 servings.

Nutrition Facts per serving: 242 cal., 7 g total fat (1 g sat. fat), 0 mg chol., 528 mg sodium, 38 g carbo., 6 g fiber, 8 g pro.
Daily Values: 2% vit. A, 4% calcium, 8% iron.

EDITOR'S TIP

Wild Rice

Wild rice grows wild in Minnesota lakes, so if you live in the "Land of 10,000 Lakes," you probably can go to a local farmer's market and buy wild rice that's been harvested by hand.

Wild rice is the long, dark brown or black, nutty-flavored seed of an annual marsh grass. Though early explorers dubbed it "rice" because it grows in water, it is not a rice at all and is the only cereal grain native to North America.

Uncooked wild rice keeps indefinitely stored in a cool, dry place or in the refrigerator. If cooked with no added ingredients, you can freeze it for several months. It's often combined with brown or white rice and used in cold salads, pilafs, or stuffings.

30 MINUTE, NO FAT

Tutti-Frutti Spiced Fruit Soup

Make up your own dried fruit mix to suit your preferences. Want something a little stronger? Stir in a splash of brandy or rum before serving.

Start to finish: 25 minutes

- 4 cups apple cider or apple juice
- 1½ cups apricot nectar
- 4 bags cranberry-flavored tea
- 7 oz. mixed dried fruits, such as apples, pears, apricots, plums, and/or persimmons
- 3 medium cooking apples (such as Granny Smith, Jonathan, or Braeburn), cored and cut into large chunks

1 In a saucepan combine apple cider or juice and apricot nectar. Bring to boiling; remove from heat. Add tea bags. Steep for 3 minutes. Remove tea bags; discard.

2 Meanwhile, cut up any large pieces of dried fruit. Add dried fruit and apple chunks to saucepan. Return to boiling; reduce heat. Simmer, uncovered, about 5 minutes or until dried fruit is tender and the fresh apple chunks are just cooked. Don't overcook the fresh apples.

3 To serve, ladle the fruit and liquid into bowls. Makes 8 side-dish servings.

Nutrition Facts per serving: 165 cal., 0 g total fat (0 g sat. fat), 0 mg chol., 6 mg sodium, 32 g carbo., 2 g fiber, 1 g pro.
Daily Values: 12% vit. A, 7% vit. C, 2% calcium, 8% iron.

PRIZE WINNER

Walnut-Apple Pizza

Jennifer Noble
Elk Grove, California
$400—Pizzas—Breakfast, Lunch, and Dinner

Prep: 25 minutes **Rise:** 45 minutes
Bake: 20 minutes

- ½ **of a pkg. active dry yeast (1¼ tsp.)**
- ¾ **cup warm water (105° to 115°)**
- 1 **cup all-purpose flour**
- ⅔ **cup whole wheat flour**
- 1 **tsp. sugar**
- 1 **tsp. salt**
- 1 **Tbsp. cooking oil**
- ¾ **cup Stilton or blue cheese, crumbled (3 oz.)**
- 1 **large tart apple, cored and thinly sliced (about 1⅓ cups)**
- ½ **cup shredded Monterey Jack cheese (2 oz.)**
- ½ **cup chopped walnuts**
- 1½ **tsp. snipped fresh rosemary**

1 Stir yeast into warm water. Let stand 5 minutes to dissolve. In a large bowl stir together all-purpose flour, whole wheat flour, sugar, and salt. Make a well in the center of the dry ingredients. Add the yeast mixture and oil. Stir until combined.

2 Turn dough out onto a lightly floured surface. Knead gently about 20 times. Place dough in a greased bowl. Cover and let rise in a warm place until doubled in size (this will take about 45 minutes). Punch down dough.

3 Preheat oven to 450°. Grease a 12-inch pizza pan. On a lightly floured surface roll dough to a 13-inch circle. Transfer to prepared pizza pan. Build up edges slightly.

4 Bake crust about 10 minutes or until just beginning to brown. Remove from oven. Sprinkle dough with Stilton or blue cheese. Top with apple slices. Sprinkle with Monterey Jack cheese, walnuts, and rosemary.

5 Bake for 10 to 12 minutes more or until edges are lightly browned. Cut into wedges. Makes 12 appetizer servings or 8 main-dish servings.

Nutrition Facts per appetizer serving: 152 cal., 8 g total fat (3 g sat. fat), 9 mg chol., 319 mg sodium, 15 g carbo., 2 g fiber, 5 g pro.
Daily Values: 3% vit. A, 1% vit. C, 8% calcium, 5% iron.

Polenta Pie

Prep: 20 minutes **Bake:** 20 minutes

-    **Nonstick cooking spray**
- 2½ **cups milk**
- 1 **cup quick-cooking polenta**
- 1 **Tbsp. instant chicken bouillon granules**
- 1 **tsp. dried Italian seasoning, crushed**
-    **Dash bottled hot pepper sauce**
- 1½ **cups shredded Monterey Jack cheese (6 oz.)**
- 1 **16-oz. pkg. loose-pack frozen broccoli, corn, and red peppers, thawed**
- 3 **roma tomatoes, thinly sliced**
- 1 **Tbsp. snipped fresh basil**

1 Preheat oven to 350°. Coat a 2-quart square baking dish with nonstick cooking spray; set aside. In a medium saucepan bring milk to boiling. Stir in polenta, chicken bouillon granules, Italian seasoning, and bottled hot pepper sauce. Cook and stir over low heat for 3 to 5 minutes or until thickened.

2 Spread polenta mixture into prepared baking dish. Sprinkle a third of the cheese over top. Top with thawed vegetables and another third of the cheese. Arrange sliced tomatoes in a single layer over cheese; sprinkle with remaining cheese.

3 Bake, uncovered, about 20 minutes or until heated through and cheese is melted. Sprinkle with snipped basil. Cut into rectangles. Makes 6 main-dish servings.

Nutrition Facts per serving: 360 cal., 11 g total fat (7 g sat. fat), 33 mg chol., 851 mg sodium, 50 g carbo., 7 g fiber, 16 g pro.
Daily Values: 60% vit. A, 36% vit. C, 37% calcium, 8% iron.

SUPPER MENU

- **Picadillo Chicken Pizza (see below)**

- **Salad of mixed greens, sliced avocado, thinly sliced onion, and orange vinaigrette**

- **Margaritas, Mexican beer, or sparkling water**

- **Brownies with ice cream**

PRIZE WINNER

Picadillo Chicken Pizza

Patricia Schroedl
Jefferson, Wisconsin
$200—Pizzas—Breakfast, Lunch, and Dinner

Prep: 10 minutes **Bake:** 15 minutes

1 **12-inch Italian bread shell (Boboli)**
1 **cup bottled salsa**
¼ **tsp. ground cinnamon**
¼ **tsp. ground cumin**
2 **cups chopped cooked chicken or turkey**
½ **cup dried cranberries or raisins**
½ **cup pitted green olives, coarsely chopped**
¼ **cup chopped red onion**
1 **Tbsp. sliced almonds**
1 **cup shredded manchego or Monterey Jack cheese (4 oz.)**
1 **Tbsp. snipped fresh cilantro**

1 Preheat oven to 400°. Place bread shell on a baking sheet. In a small bowl combine salsa, cinnamon, and cumin. Spread evenly over bread shell. Top with chicken or turkey, cranberries or raisins, olives, red onion, and almonds.

2 Bake for 10 minutes. Sprinkle with manchego or Monterey Jack cheese. Bake for 5 to 7 minutes more or until pizza is heated through and cheese is melted. Sprinkle with cilantro. Cut into wedges to serve. Makes 6 main-dish servings.

Nutrition Facts per serving: 424 cal., 15 g total fat (5 g sat. fat), 65 mg chol., 930 mg sodium, 44 g carbo., 1 g fiber, 30 g pro.
Daily Values: 8% vit. A, 6% vit. C, 30% calcium, 8% iron.

LOW FAT

Chicken and Artichoke Pizza

Prep: 20 minutes **Bake:** 22 minutes

1 **10-oz. pkg. refrigerated pizza dough**
8 **oz. skinless, boneless chicken breast or thigh, chopped**
½ **tsp. garlic salt**
1 **Tbsp. cooking oil**
½ **cup thinly sliced celery**
⅓ **cup pizza sauce**
½ **cup chopped green sweet pepper**
1 **6-oz. jar marinated artichoke hearts, drained and quartered**
¼ **cup sliced green onions**
1 **cup shredded mozzarella cheese**
½ **cup crumbled blue cheese (optional)**

1 Preheat oven to 375°. Grease a 12-inch pizza pan. Unroll pizza dough and press into prepared pan, building up edges slightly. Bake for 12 minutes or until lightly browned. Set aside.

2 Toss together chicken and ¼ teaspoon of the garlic salt. Pour cooking oil into a large skillet. Preheat over medium-high heat. Stir-fry chicken and celery about 3 minutes or until chicken is no longer pink.

3 Combine pizza sauce and remaining ¼ teaspoon garlic salt; spread over crust. Top with chicken mixture, green pepper, artichoke hearts, and green onions. Sprinkle mozzarella and, if desired, blue cheese over pizza.

4 Bake for 10 to 15 minutes more or until cheese is melted and bubbly. Cut into wedges to serve. Makes 6 main-dish or 10 appetizer servings.

Nutrition Facts per main-dish serving: 242 cal., 9 g total fat (3 g sat. fat), 33 mg chol., 442 mg sodium, 23 g carbo., 2 g fiber, 17 g pro.
Daily Values: 8% vit. A, 34% vit. C, 15% calcium, 11% iron.

Garlic Veggie Pizza

Prep: 20 minutes **Bake:** 12 minutes

1 **12-inch Italian bread shell (Boboli)**
1 **Tbsp. cooking oil**
1 **medium sweet onion, cut in thin wedges (½ cup)**
1 **medium zucchini, thinly sliced (1¼ cups)**
1 **small red sweet pepper, cut into thin strips (½ cup)**
⅓ **cup bottled creamy garlic or creamy roasted garlic salad dressing**
¾ **cup shredded mozzarella cheese (3 oz.)**
½ **cup crumbled basil and tomato feta cheese (2 oz.)**

1 Preheat oven to 450°. Place bread shell on a cookie sheet; set aside.

2 In a large skillet heat oil over medium-high heat. Add onion. Cook and stir until onion is tender. Add zucchini and sweet pepper; cook 2 minutes more. Remove from heat.

3 Spread salad dressing over bread shell; spoon on vegetable mixture. Combine mozzarella cheese and feta cheese. Sprinkle cheeses over vegetables.

4 Bake, uncovered, about 12 minutes or until cheese is melted and just beginning to brown. Cut into wedges to serve. Makes 6 main-dish servings.

Nutrition Facts per serving: 336 cal., 16 g total fat (4 g sat. fat), 20 mg chol., 735 mg sodium, 37 g carbo., 2 g fiber, 14 g pro.
Daily Values: 11% vit. A, 38% vit. C, 22% calcium, 10% iron.

30 MINUTE

Caesar Salmon Pizzas

If you like chicken tossed in your Caesar salad, try shredded chicken on top of these salad-style pizzas in place of the salmon.

Prep: 15 minutes **Bake:** 10 minutes

2 6-inch Italian bread shells (Boboli)
¼ cup bottled creamy Caesar salad dressing
2 cups torn fresh spinach
2 Tbsp. thinly sliced green onion
2 oz. smoked salmon, flaked, with skin and bones removed
¼ cup walnut pieces, toasted
¼ cup finely shredded Parmesan cheese
1 tsp. capers

1 Preheat oven to 400°. Spread bread shells lightly with some of the salad dressing; place bread shells on a baking sheet.

2 In a bowl toss together spinach, green onion, salmon, walnuts, half of the Parmesan cheese, the capers,

and remaining dressing. Pile mixture over the two bread shells. Sprinkle with remaining Parmesan cheese.

3 Bake about 10 minutes or until just heated through. Makes 2 servings.

Nutrition Facts per serving: 652 cal., 39 g total fat (6 g sat. fat), 19 mg chol., 1,480 mg sodium, 54 g carbo., 4 g fiber, 26 g pro.
Daily Values: 20% vit. A, 15% vit. C, 33% calcium, 32% iron.

Two-Tomato Soup

For the fresh tomatoes in this recipe, use the ripest available. If homegrown or farm-fresh tomatoes are available, they'll make the best soup. (See the photograph on page 241.)

Prep: 45 minutes **Cook:** 65 minutes

1 3-oz. pkg. dried tomatoes (not oil-packed)
1 Tbsp. olive oil or cooking oil
½ cup chopped onion
¼ tsp. coarsely ground black pepper
8 medium fresh tomatoes, chopped (about 2½ lb.)
4 cups water
1 tsp. salt
1 cup whipping cream
Olive oil (optional)
8 yellow teardrop or dried yellow tomato halves (optional)

1 Place the dried tomatoes in a small bowl. Add enough boiling water to cover. Soak them for 30 minutes. Drain and rinse. Coarsely chop rehydrated tomatoes.

2 In a Dutch oven heat the 1 tablespoon olive oil or cooking oil. Cook and stir onion, rehydrated tomatoes, and pepper in hot oil about 5 minutes or until onion is tender.

3 Reserve ¾ cup chopped fresh tomatoes; set aside. Add remaining fresh tomatoes to rehydrated tomato mixture. Cook, covered, over low heat about 20 minutes or until tomatoes are soft. Add water and salt. Cook, uncovered, over low heat for 40 minutes more, stirring often.

4 Transfer one-fourth of mixture at a time to a blender container or food processor bowl. (See tip, page 224.) Cover and carefully blend or process until smooth. Return mixture to Dutch oven. Heat to simmering. Stir in cream. Return just to simmering. Remove from heat.

5 To serve, ladle soup into bowls. Spoon some of the reserved fresh chopped tomatoes into each bowl. If desired, drizzle each serving with some olive oil and top with a yellow teardrop or dried yellow tomato half. Makes 8 side-dish servings.

To Make Ahead:

1. Prepare soup as directed up to stirring in the cream. Cool soup. Transfer to an airtight container. Seal, label, and freeze up to 2 months.

2. To reheat, transfer frozen soup to a saucepan. Cook, covered, over medium heat for 15 to 20 minutes, stirring occasionally. Stir in cream. Cook and stir 5 to 10 minutes more or until heated through.

Nutrition Facts per serving: 176 cal., 14 g total fat (7 g sat. fat), 41 mg chol., 540 mg sodium, 13 g carbo., 3 g fiber, 3 g pro.
Daily Values: 21% vit. A, 47% vit. C, 4% calcium, 9% iron.

TEST KITCHEN TIP

A Careful Blend

When blending or processing heated mixtures, use caution to avoid being splashed by the scalding liquid. Do not fill the blender or food processor bowl completely. Cover the container tightly. Slightly open the center of the lid to vent the hot air. Cover the blender or processor lid with a clean dish towel while operating.

30 MINUTE

Butternut Squash Soup with Ravioli

This soup freezes well, so make an extra batch. (See the photograph on page 240.)

Start to finish: 30 minutes

- 2 lb. butternut squash
- 2 14½-oz. cans vegetable broth
- ½ cup water
- ⅛ tsp. ground red pepper
- 1 Tbsp. margarine or butter
- 1 9-oz. pkg. refrigerated cheese ravioli
- 1 Tbsp. molasses

1 Peel squash. Halve lengthwise. Remove seeds and discard. Cut squash into ¾-inch pieces.

2 In a large saucepan combine squash, broth, water, and pepper. Cook, covered, over medium heat for 20 minutes or until squash is tender.

3 Transfer one-fourth of the squash and broth mixture to a blender container. Carefully blend, covered, until smooth (see tip, above). Repeat until all of the mixture is blended.

4 Return blended mixture to large saucepan. Bring just to boiling. Immediately reduce heat. Simmer, uncovered, 5 minutes. Add the margarine or butter, stirring until just melted.

5 Meanwhile, prepare the ravioli according to package directions. Drain. Ladle hot soup mixture into bowls. Divide cooked ravioli among bowls. Drizzle with molasses. Makes 5 side-dish servings.

To Make Ahead:

1. Prepare soup as directed, except do not add ravioli. Cool soup. Transfer to an airtight container. Store in the refrigerator up to 2 days or label and freeze for up to 2 months.

2. To reheat, transfer frozen soup to a large saucepan. Cook, covered, over medium-low heat for 15 to 20 minutes or until heated through, stirring often. Cook ravioli as directed and serve with soup.

Nutrition Facts per serving: 259 cal., 10 g total fat (5 g sat. fat), 52 mg chol., 933 mg sodium, 36 g carbo., 2 g fiber, 10 g pro.
Daily Values: 95% vit. A, 40% vit. C, 18% calcium, 10% iron.

Roasted Garlic Potato Soup

To make this soup ahead of time, prepare as directed and refrigerate, covered, for up to 24 hours. Reheat slowly over medium-low heat, stirring frequently to avoid scorching.

Prep: 15 minutes **Bake:** 45 minutes
Cook: 30 minutes

- 6 medium baking potatoes (about 2 lb.), peeled and cut into 1-inch pieces
- 2 Tbsp. olive oil
- ½ tsp. pepper
- 6 cloves garlic, peeled
- 1 medium onion, chopped
- 3 cups chicken broth
- 1 cup water
- 1 cup whole milk
  Salt
- 1 cup thinly sliced Colby, cheddar, or desired cheese (4 oz.)

1 Preheat oven to 425°. Place potatoes in a shallow roasting pan. Drizzle with 1 tablespoon of the olive oil. Sprinkle with pepper. Stir to coat.

2 Bake, uncovered, for 25 minutes. Turn potatoes with a metal spatula. Toss in garlic cloves. Bake about 20 minutes or until potatoes are browned. Set aside 1 cup of roasted potatoes and garlic.

3 In a 3-quart saucepan heat remaining oil. Cook and stir onion over medium-high heat 5 minutes. Add remaining roasted potatoes and garlic to onions in saucepan. Stir in chicken broth and water. Bring just to boiling; reduce heat. Simmer, covered, about 20 minutes or until potatoes are very tender.

4 Spoon about half of potato mixture into a blender container. Cover and blend until nearly smooth. Repeat with remaining mixture. Return all to saucepan. Stir in milk. Season to taste with salt. Heat through.

5 To serve, ladle soup into bowls. Top each serving with some of the reserved roasted potatoes and sliced cheese. Makes 6 main-dish servings.

Nutrition Facts per serving: 266 cal., 12 g total fat (5 g sat. fat), 23 mg chol., 449 mg sodium, 28 g carbo., 3 g fiber, 11 g pro.
Daily Values: 6% vit. A, 38% vit. C, 20% calcium, 8% iron.

NO FAT

Beet Borscht

Depending on the sugar content of the beets used, you may want to adjust the amount of sugar to taste. Favorite traditional borscht stir-ins are a drizzle of half-and-half or a dollop of plain yogurt or sour cream. (See the photograph on page 238.)

Prep: 20 minutes **Cook:** 30 minutes

- 1½ lb. beets, tops removed
- 2 small onions, halved lengthwise (about 8 oz.)
- 1 tsp. salt
- 5 cups water
- 2 Tbsp. sugar
- 2 Tbsp. lemon juice
- ¾ cup finely shredded green cabbage

1 Cut off all but 1 inch of beet stems and roots; wash. Do not peel.

2 In a Dutch oven combine beets, onions, and salt. Add water. Bring to boiling; reduce heat to medium-low. Cover and simmer for 20 minutes. Cool slightly. Slip skins off beets; discard. Cut beets into large pieces.

3 Stir in sugar and lemon juice. Return to boiling; reduce heat. Simmer, uncovered, for 10 minutes. Cover and chill, if desired.

4 To serve, ladle soup into bowls, using one onion half per serving. Sprinkle cabbage over soup. Makes 4 side-dish servings.

Nutrition Facts per serving: 107 cal., 0 g total fat (0 g sat. fat), 0 mg chol., 700 mg sodium, 25 g carbo., 5 g fiber, 3 g pro.
Daily Values: 5% vit. A, 34% vit. C, 7% calcium, 7% iron.

30 MINUTE

Fresh Mushroom Soup

Homemade soup made of fresh mushrooms is no longer a lost art. This one uses shiitake or white button and oyster mushrooms.

Prep: 10 minutes **Cook:** 10 minutes

- 8 oz. shiitake or button mushrooms
- 6 oz. small oyster mushrooms
- ⅓ cup chopped shallots
- 2 Tbsp. butter, melted
- 2 Tbsp. all-purpose flour
- ½ tsp. salt
- ¼ tsp. coarsely ground black pepper
- 1 14½-oz. can vegetable broth or chicken broth (1¾ cups)
- 2 cups half-and-half or light cream
- ⅛ tsp. ground saffron or saffron threads
    Saffron threads (optional)

1 Remove any tough or woody stems from mushrooms. Cut large shiitake mushrooms in half; set aside. Chop the remaining shiitake mushrooms. Cut oyster mushrooms into large pieces.

2 In a large saucepan cook mushrooms and shallots in melted butter, uncovered, over medium-high heat for 4 to 5 minutes or until tender, stirring occasionally. Stir in flour, salt,

AUTUMN MENU

- **Roasted Garlic Potato Soup (see page 224)**

- **Sourdough Breadsticks (see page 246) or Toasted Caraway & Rye Skillet Bread (see page 245)**

- **Salad of romaine with chopped fresh tomatoes and cucumber and a balsamic vinaigrette**

- **Apple tart or apple dumplings with ice cream or fresh whipped cream**

and pepper. Add broth. Cook and stir over medium heat until slightly thickened and bubbly. Cook and stir 1 minute more. Stir in half-and-half and saffron; heat through.

3 To serve, ladle soup into bowls. If desired, top with saffron threads. Makes 6 side-dish servings.

To Make Ahead:

1. Prepare soup as directed. Cool soup. Transfer to an airtight container. Store in the refrigerator up to 2 days or seal, label, and freeze up to 2 months.

2. To reheat, transfer frozen soup to a large saucepan. Cook, covered, over medium heat 20 minutes or until heated through, stirring occasionally.

Nutrition Facts per serving: 193 cal., 14 g total fat (8 g sat. fat), 40 mg chol., 565 mg sodium, 15 g carbo., 2 g fiber, 5 g pro.
Daily Values: 15% vit. A, 3% vit. C, 9% calcium, 5% iron.

Roasted Mushroom Stock

Clear enough for consommé, bold enough for broth: Mushroom stock contributes rich flavor subtleties different from those of meat stocks.

Prep: 20 minutes **Roast:** 30 minutes
Cook: 2 hours

- 4 medium onions, quartered
- 4 stalks celery with tops, cut up
- 2 medium carrots, cut up
- 6 cloves garlic
- 1 tsp. salt
- ¼ tsp. whole black peppercorns
- 2 lb. button or other mushrooms, cleaned and trimmed
- 2 sprigs fresh thyme
- 2 sprigs fresh marjoram
- 2 sprigs fresh parsley

1 Preheat oven to 450°. Place onions, celery, carrots, and garlic in a shallow roasting pan. Sprinkle with salt and peppercorns. Roast, uncovered, for 15 minutes. Add mushrooms; stir vegetables and roast 15 minutes more. Remove from oven. Add 1 cup cold *water* to roasting pan.

2 In a 6- to 8-quart Dutch oven place roasted vegetable mixture and 6 cups additional cold *water*. Bring mixture just to boiling; reduce heat. Simmer, uncovered, for 1½ hours. Add thyme, marjoram, and parsley.

3 Simmer, uncovered, 30 minutes more. Strain reduced stock through a double thickness of 100-percent cotton cheesecloth; discard solids.

4 To serve, ladle into bowls and serve as consommé with garnishes of thinly sliced, sautéed *mushrooms*

TEST KITCHEN TIP
Hot Stock Tips

As with other stocks, use cold water to avoid clouding. Bring stock gently to boiling, then simmer it slowly to draw out the flavors. Let the stock gradually cook down to condense all of its richness. Stirring or covering a stock also makes it cloudy. Since mushroom stock is virtually fat-free, it needs no skimming.

and *green onion curls*. Makes 4 side-dish servings.

To Make Ahead:

1. Prepare stock as directed. Cool stock. Transfer to an airtight container. Store in the refrigerator up to 1 week or seal, label, and freeze up to 6 months.

2. To reheat, transfer frozen stock to a large saucepan. Cook, covered, over medium heat 20 minutes or until heated through, stirring occasionally.

Nutrition Facts per serving: 50 cal., 1 g total fat (0 g sat. fat), 0 mg chol., 561 mg sodium, 11 g carbo., 0 g fiber, 3 g pro.
Daily Values: 42% vit. A, 19% vit. C, 3% calcium, 14% iron.

Farmer's Vegetable Broth

Many different root vegetables will work in this versatile, homey soup. Use an equivalent amount of potato or fennel in place of one of the vegetables we've chosen. (See the photograph on page 237.)

Start to finish: 45 minutes

- 2 medium leeks, trimmed and bias-cut into 1- to 2-inch slices
- 1 medium rutabaga, peeled and cut into 1-inch pieces
- 1 medium turnip, peeled and cut into 1-inch pieces
- 1 small parsnip, peeled and cut up
- 1 small carrot, peeled and cut up
- 3 cups beef broth
- 3 cups water
- ½ cup dry sherry or beef broth
- 1 4-inch sprig fresh rosemary or ½ tsp. dried rosemary, crushed

1 In a Dutch oven combine leeks, rutabaga, turnip, parsnip, carrot, broth, water, sherry or broth, and the 4-inch sprig of rosemary or ½ teaspoon dried rosemary. Bring to boiling; reduce heat. Simmer, uncovered, 25 to 30 minutes or until turnip and rutabaga are tender. Remove rosemary sprig.

2 To serve, ladle into bowls. If desired, top with additional rosemary sprigs. Serves 4 to 6.

Nutrition Facts per serving: 123 cal., 0 g total fat (0 g sat. fat), 0 mg chol., 678 mg sodium, 18 g carbo., 4 g fiber, 3 g pro.
Daily Values: 28% vit. A, 42% vit. C, 7% calcium, 7% iron.

Herb and Pepper Lentil Stew

Look for pappadams, which are wafer-thin East India breads made with lentil flour, in Indian specialty markets or in large supermarkets. To toast, preheat oven to 375°. Place pappadams directly on oven rack. Bake about 1 minute or until lightly browned. Set aside to crisp. (See the photograph on page 244.)

Prep: 10 minutes **Cook:** 28 minutes

1 Tbsp. cooking oil
2 medium onions, quartered
1 medium green sweet pepper, cut into ½-inch rings
1 Tbsp. snipped fresh thyme or 1 tsp. dried thyme, crushed
¼ tsp. crushed red pepper
5 cups water
1¼ cups dry red (Egyptian) lentils*, rinsed and drained
1½ tsp. salt
4 sprigs fresh thyme (optional)
 Pappadams (optional)

1 In a Dutch oven heat oil over medium-high heat 30 seconds. Add onion quarters. Cook about 8 minutes or until browned, stirring occasionally.

2 Add green pepper, thyme, and crushed red pepper. Cook and stir 2 minutes. Remove from heat. Add water, 1 cup of lentils, and salt. Return to heat. Bring to boiling; reduce heat. Simmer, uncovered, for 15 minutes.

3 Add remaining lentils. Cook, uncovered, for 3 to 5 minutes more or until lentils are tender.

4 To serve, ladle stew into bowls. If desired, top with fresh thyme sprigs and serve with pappadams. Makes 4 main-dish servings.

***Note:** Brown or green lentils may be substituted for the red lentils. Prepare recipe as directed, except add all the lentils with water and salt. Bring to boiling; reduce heat. Simmer, covered, 25 minutes. Uncover. Simmer for 5 minutes more.

Nutrition Facts per serving: 246 cal., 4 g total fat (1 g sat. fat), 0 mg chol., 902 mg sodium, 39 g carbo., 10 g fiber, 15 g pro.
Daily Values: 3% vit. A, 41% vit. C, 6% calcium, 18% iron.

LOW FAT

No-Prep Lentil Stew

Here's a dry-mix version of the Herb and Pepper Lentil Stew (see recipe, page 226) to keep on hand to accommodate spur-of-the-moment cravings for homemade soup.

Prep: 2 minutes **Cook:** 35 minutes

1¼ cups dry green or brown lentils
¼ cup dried minced onion
¼ cup dried green sweet pepper
1 tsp. salt
1 tsp. dried thyme, crushed
½ tsp. fennel seed, crushed
¼ tsp. crushed red pepper

1 Combine all ingredients. Place in an airtight container or in a self-sealing plastic bag. Store in cool, dry place up to 1 year.

2 To prepare, in saucepan bring 6 cups water to boiling. Add dry mix; reduce heat. Simmer, covered, 35 to 40 minutes or until lentils are soft. To serve, ladle stew into bowls. If desired, garnish with *fresh thyme*. Makes 4 main-dish servings.

Nutrition Facts per serving: 231 cal., 1 g total fat (0 g sat. fat), 0 mg chol., 606 mg sodium, 40 g carbo., 20 g fiber, 18 g pro.
Daily Values: 5% vit. A, 118% vit. C, 6% calcium, 29% iron.

LOW FAT

Black Bean and Corn Soup

Soak: 1 hour **Prep:** 20 minutes
Cook: 4 hours

2¼ cups dry black beans (1 lb.)
1 10-oz. pkg. frozen whole kernel corn
1 cup chopped onion

4 cloves garlic, minced
1 Tbsp. ground cumin
1 tsp. salt
1 tsp. ground coriander
¼ to ½ tsp. bottled hot pepper sauce
4 cups boiling water
1 14½-oz. can Mexican-style stewed tomatoes
1 recipe Pepper Salsa (see below)

1 Rinse beans; place in a large saucepan. Add enough *water* to cover beans by 2 inches. Bring to boiling; reduce heat. Simmer, uncovered, for 10 minutes. Remove from heat. Cover and let stand for 1 hour. (Or, place beans in water in a large saucepan. Cover and let beans soak in a cool place overnight.) Drain and rinse beans.

2 In a 3½-, 4-, or 5-quart crockery cooker combine the beans, corn, onion, garlic, cumin, salt, coriander, and hot pepper sauce. Pour boiling water over all. Cover; cook on low-heat setting for 8 to 10 hours or on high-heat setting for 4 to 5 hours.

3 To serve, mash beans slightly to thicken. Stir in tomatoes. Serve with Pepper Salsa. Makes 6 main-dish servings.

Pepper Salsa

In a bowl combine 1½ cups finely chopped yellow and/or green sweet pepper; 1 finely chopped small jalapeño pepper; ⅓ cup chopped, seeded tomato; and 1 tablespoon snipped fresh cilantro. Cover and chill up to 24 hours.

Nutrition Facts per serving: 321 cal., 2 g total fat (0 g sat. fat), 0 mg chol., 604 mg sodium, 62 g carbo., 4 g fiber, 18 g pro.
Daily Values: 25% vit. A, 104% vit. C, 8% calcium, 38% iron.

CLEVER COOK

Thicken Soup Instantly

If you accidentally make your soup too thin, you can easily thicken it. Stir in a few tablespoons of instant mashed potato flakes. Give them a couple of minutes to work, then stir in more, if needed, until your soup is the desired consistency.

Teresa Jacobs
Traverse City, Michigan

30 MINUTE, LOW FAT

Italian Wedding Soup

Orzo pasta, sometimes called "rosamarina," is small, rice-shaped pasta. If orzo is not available, you can substitute spaghetti or linguini that has been broken into ¼- to ½-inch-long pieces. (See the photograph on page 244.)

Prep: 5 minutes **Cook:** 25 minutes

- 12 oz. lean ground beef or lean ground lamb
- 1 small fennel bulb, chopped (about ⅔ cup)
- ½ cup chopped onion
- 2 cloves garlic, minced
- 4 cups beef broth
- 2 cups water
- 1 tsp. dried oregano, crushed
- 2 bay leaves
- ¼ tsp. cracked black pepper
- ½ cup orzo pasta
- 4 cups shredded escarole, curly endive, and/or fresh spinach
- 3 oz. Parmigiano-Reggiano or domestic Parmesan cheese with rind, cut into 4 wedges (optional)

1 In a large saucepan cook beef or lamb, fennel, onion, and garlic, uncovered, over medium-high heat for 5 minutes or until meat is brown and vegetables are nearly tender, stirring occasionally. Drain fat, if necessary.

2 Add beef broth, water, oregano, bay leaves, and pepper. Bring to boiling; reduce heat. Simmer, covered, for 10 minutes. Remove bay leaves.* If desired, reserve for garnish.

3 Stir in orzo. Return to boiling; reduce heat to medium. Boil gently, uncovered, about 10 minutes or until pasta is just tender, stirring occasionally. Remove from heat; stir in escarole, curly endive, or spinach.

4 To serve, place a wedge of cheese in four soup bowls. Ladle hot soup into bowls. If desired, top with the reserved bay leaves. Makes 4 servings.

*Note: Bay leaves contribute a wonderful flavor and aroma to recipes. However, they should be removed before eating.

Nutrition Facts per serving: 262 cal., 10 g total fat (4 g sat. fat), 54 mg chol., 873 mg sodium, 22 g carbo., 7 g fiber, 21 g pro.
Daily Values: 11% vit. A, 11% vit. C, 5% calcium, 18% iron.

LOW FAT

Persian-Style Stew

In Persian stews like this one, yellow split peas are a classic ingredient. During cooking, the peas soften and fall apart, which gives the stew a thick consistency.

Prep: 25 minutes **Cook:** 4 hours

- 1½ to 2 lb. lamb or beef stew meat, cut into 1-inch cubes
- 1 Tbsp. cooking oil
- 3 leeks, cut into 1-inch pieces
- 1 large onion, chopped
- ½ cup dry yellow split peas
- 4 cloves garlic, sliced
- 2 bay leaves
- 1 Tbsp. snipped fresh oregano or 1 tsp. dried oregano, crushed
- 1½ tsp. ground cumin
- ¼ tsp. pepper
- 3 cups chicken broth
- ⅓ cup raisins
- 2 Tbsp. lemon juice
- 3 cups hot cooked bulgur or rice

1 In a large skillet brown meat, half at a time, in hot oil. Drain off fat. Transfer meat to a 3½-, 4-, or 5-quart crockery cooker. Stir in leeks, onion, split peas, garlic, bay leaves, dried oregano (if using), cumin, and pepper. Pour chicken broth over all.

2 Cover; cook on low-heat setting for 8 to 10 hours or on high-heat setting for 4 to 5 hours. If using low-heat setting, turn to high-heat setting. Stir raisins into stew. Cover; cook for 10 minutes more. Remove bay leaves and discard. Stir in lemon juice and, if using, the fresh oregano. Serve with hot bulgur or rice. Serves 6 to 8.

Nutrition Facts per serving: 357 cal., 9 g total fat (2 g sat. fat), 58 mg chol., 449 mg sodium, 42 g carbo., 7 g fiber, 29 g pro.
Daily Values: 12% vit. C, 6% calcium, 33% iron.

Sancocho Pork Stew

This hearty stew, with its origin attributed to Panama, is mildly spiced with chili powder and chili peppers. The yams or sweet potatoes lend a complementary sweetness.

Prep: 20 minutes **Cook:** 3½ hours

- 3 medium yams or sweet potatoes, peeled and cut into 2-inch pieces
- 1 large green sweet pepper, cut into strips
- 1 cup frozen whole kernel corn
- 1 medium onion, sliced and separated into rings
- 3 cloves garlic, minced
- 1½ lb. boneless pork shoulder, cut into ¾-inch cubes
- 1 tsp. chili powder
- ¾ tsp. ground coriander
- ½ tsp. salt
- 2 cups water
- 1 10-oz. can chopped tomatoes with green chili peppers, undrained
- 1 9-oz. pkg. frozen cut green beans

1 In a 3½-, 4-, or 5-quart crockery cooker place yams or sweet potatoes, sweet pepper, corn, onion, and garlic. Add pork, chili powder, coriander, and salt. Pour the water and the undrained tomatoes over all.

2 Cover; cook on low-heat setting for 7 to 8 hours or on high-heat setting for 3½ to 4 hours, adding the frozen green beans the last 15 minutes of cooking time. Makes 6 to 8 servings.

Nutrition Facts per serving: 299 cal., 12 g total fat (4 g sat. fat), 74 mg chol., 446 mg sodium, 26 g carbo., 3 g fiber, 23 g pro.
Daily Values: 135% vit. A, 54% vit. C, 5% calcium, 14% iron.

---

30 MINUTE

Thai-Style Shrimp Soup

The lemongrass for this simple soup can be found in Asian specialty markets or larger supermarkets. (See the photograph on page 244.)

Prep: 20 minutes **Cook:** 4 minutes

- 1 14½-oz. can chicken broth
- 1 small zucchini, cut into match-stick-size pieces (about 1½ cups)
- 1 green onion, bias-cut into 1¼-inch slices (2 Tbsp.)
- 2 Tbsp. minced fresh ginger
- 2 Tbsp. minced fresh lemongrass or 1½ tsp. finely shredded lemon peel
- ¼ tsp. crushed red pepper
- 12 oz. small shrimp, peeled and deveined
- 1 14-oz. can unsweetened coconut milk
- 2 Tbsp. shredded fresh basil
- 2 Tbsp. toasted shaved coconut Fresh basil sprigs (optional)

1 In a saucepan bring broth to boiling. Add zucchini, green onion, ginger, lemongrass, and crushed red pepper. Return to boiling; reduce heat. Simmer, uncovered, 3 minutes, stirring occasionally.

2 Add shrimp. Simmer, uncovered, 1 to 3 minutes or until shrimp turn opaque. Add coconut milk. Heat through (do not boil).

3 To serve, ladle into bowls. Top with shredded basil, coconut, and, if desired, basil sprig. Serves 3 or 4.

EDITOR'S TIP

Going Coconuts

Adding a touch of the exotic to home cooking is easy with ready-to-use coconut milk. This naturally sweet nondairy liquid is made from pressed coconuts. Fortunately, the popularity of Caribbean and Asian cuisines has made coconut milk readily available; you can purchase it in specialty stores as well as many supermarkets. (Don't confuse coconut milk with similar products made for mixed drinks—those usually contain extra sweeteners and other added ingredients and may not be suitable for main dishes.)

With 6 grams of fat and 60 calories per ounce, coconut milk is a rich ingredient. But the fat in coconut has been shown to have little impact on cholesterol levels. Use coconut milk in place of milk or cream in curries and other Asian dishes, or substitute it for part of the milk or cream in desserts. Here are a few ideas to get you started.

Fast Coconut Curry

Stir-fry strips of beef with broccoli florets and minced garlic, plus some curry powder (try 1 teaspoon per pound of meat). Simmer for 2 or 3 minutes in coconut milk and serve over cooked rice with cilantro sprigs for garnish.

Thai-Style Coconut Soup

Slowly heat together equal parts coconut milk and chicken broth, then stir in cooked chicken strips and whole fresh basil leaves for a different approach to chicken soup.

Coconut Rice Pudding

Switching coconut milk for half the milk in rice pudding and adding a little ginger gives an Eastern nuance to a classic dessert. Top with toasted almonds and serve warm.

Nutrition Facts per serving: 445 cal., 37 g total fat (31 g sat. fat), 115 mg chol., 708 mg sodium, 12 g carbo., 4 g fiber, 21 g pro.
Daily Values: 7% vit. A, 18% vit. C, 8% calcium, 25% iron.

Navy Beans and Pork

Amidst a robust assembly of diced veggies and plump navy beans stand tender barbecued pork spare ribs. (See the photograph on page 239.)

Prep: 10 minutes **Cook:** 1¼ hours
Bake: 50 minutes

- 2 lb. meaty pork spare ribs or loin-back ribs
- 1 Tbsp. cooking oil
- 1 cup chopped onion
- 1 cup chopped celery
- ¾ cup chopped carrot
- 2 tsp. dried sage, crushed
- ½ tsp. pepper
- 2 15-oz. cans navy beans, rinsed and drained
- 2 14½-oz. cans chicken broth
- ¼ cup bottled barbecue sauce

1 Trim separable fat from ribs. Cut meat into two-rib portions. In a Dutch oven heat oil over medium heat. Add ribs, onion, celery, carrot, dried sage, and pepper. Cook, uncovered, over medium heat for 5 minutes.

2 Add navy beans and chicken broth. Bring to boiling; reduce heat. Cook, covered, for 20 minutes, stirring often. Remove ribs. Cover and reduce heat. Cook for 50 minutes, stirring occasionally.

3 Meanwhile, preheat oven to 350°. Line a shallow roasting pan with a double thickness of foil. Place ribs, meaty side down, in pan. Brush with half of the barbecue sauce. Bake for 25 minutes. Turn and brush with remaining sauce. Bake about 25 minutes more or until tender.

EDITOR'S TIP

Super Soup Toppers and Stir-ins

Sometimes a simple ingredient, either stirred in or sprinkled over, is all it takes to make a bowl of soup beyond basic. Here are a few ideas to try:

● Snipped fresh herbs or purchased or homemade pesto are fragrant and lively when added to creamy soups, such as potato and other vegetable soups or thick stews and chowders.

● Crumbled crispy bacon or roasted garlic is just the right addition for hearty concoctions.

● Drop some dried tomatoes or a little crumbled Parmigiano-Reggiano cheese into simmering broth-based soups. The hot broth will soften the tomatoes and melt the cheese, while bringing out the flavor.

4 To serve, place one double-rib piece into each bowl. Slightly mash beans in soup. Ladle soup over ribs. Makes 6 servings.

Nutrition Facts per serving: 443 cal., 19 g total fat (7 g sat. fat), 65 mg chol., 1,199 mg sodium, 36 g carbo., 8 g fiber, 31 g pro.
Daily Values: 40% vit. A, 8% vit. C, 12% calcium, 21% iron.

Salmon Pan Chowder

For extra pepper pep, substitute a dark green poblano pepper and a red jalapeño pepper for the green sweet pepper and red sweet pepper. (See the photograph on page 243.)

Prep: 25 minutes **Cook:** 28 minutes

- Nonstick cooking spray
- 1¼ cups white and/or purple pearl onions, peeled
- 1 medium red sweet pepper, cut into ½-inch strips
- 1 medium yellow sweet pepper, cut into ½-inch strips
- 1 medium green sweet pepper, cut into ½-inch strips
- 1 large banana pepper, cut into ¼-inch rings
- 1 14½-oz. can vegetable broth or chicken broth
- 1 cup whipping cream
- ½ tsp. caraway seed, lightly crushed
- ¼ tsp. salt
- 4 2-oz. skinless, boneless salmon fillets
- Fresh dill sprigs

1 Coat a Dutch oven with nonstick cooking spray; heat pan. Add onions. Cook and stir, uncovered, over medium-high heat about 7 minutes or until tender. Add red pepper, yellow pepper, green pepper, and banana pepper. Cook and stir for 1 minute more. Carefully add broth. Bring just to boiling; reduce heat. Simmer, uncovered, for 10 minutes. Stir in whipping cream. Return to boiling; reduce heat. Simmer for 10 minutes.

2 Meanwhile, rub caraway seed and salt on both sides of fish. Coat a medium skillet with nonstick cooking spray; heat skillet. Cook fillets, uncovered, over medium-high heat for 3 to 4 minutes per side or until fish flakes easily with a fork.

3 To serve, place a salmon fillet in each of four shallow soup bowls. Ladle soup mixture over salmon fillets. Top with dill sprigs. Makes 4 servings.

Nutrition Facts per serving: 327 cal., 25 g total fat (14 g sat. fat), 112 mg chol., 647 mg sodium, 14 g carbo., 3 g fiber, 15 g pro.
Daily Values: 48% vit. A, 233% vit. C, 11% calcium, 6% iron.

LOW FAT

Turkey and Sweet Potato Chowder

Make-ahead pointer: Peel and cut up the potatoes, turkey, and parsley the day before. Refrigerate the potatoes, covered, in water. Refrigerate the turkey and parsley separately in airtight containers.

Start to finish: 35 minutes

- **1 large potato, peeled and chopped (about 1½ cups)**
- **1 14½ oz. can chicken broth**
- **2 small ears frozen corn on the cob, thawed**
- **12 oz. cooked turkey breast, cut into ½-inch cubes (2¼ cups)**
- **1½ cups milk**
- **1 large sweet potato, peeled and cut into ¾-inch cubes (about 1½ cups)**
- **¼ tsp. pepper**
- **¼ cup coarsely snipped fresh Italian parsley**

1 In a 3-quart saucepan combine chopped potato and chicken broth. Bring just to boiling; reduce heat. Simmer, uncovered, about 12 minutes or until potato is tender, stirring occasionally. Remove from heat. Using potato masher, mash potato until mixture is thickened and smooth.

2 Cut the kernels from one of the ears of corn. Carefully cut the second ear of corn crosswise into ½-inch circles.

3 Stir corn, turkey, milk, sweet potato, and pepper into potato mixture in saucepan. Bring to boiling; reduce heat. Cook, uncovered, for 12 to 15 minutes or until the sweet potato is tender.

4 To serve, ladle chowder into bowls. Sprinkle with parsley. Makes 4 servings.

Nutrition Facts per serving: 309 cal., 5 g total fat (2 g sat. fat), 66 mg chol., 381 mg sodium, 32 g carbo., 4 g fiber, 33 g pro.
Daily Values: 98% vit. A, 38% vit. C, 15% calcium, 13% iron.

LOW FAT

Split Pea and Smoked Turkey Soup

Numerous varieties of cooked smoked turkey are found in your supermarket deli. Also check out the selection of turkey sausage at the meat counter.

Prep: 20 minutes **Cook:** 3 hours

- **2 cups dry yellow split peas (1 lb.)**
- **2 cups chopped cooked smoked turkey or sliced cooked turkey sausage**
- **1½ cups coarsely shredded carrots**
- **1 cup chopped fresh chives**
- **1 clove garlic, minced**
- **1 Tbsp. snipped fresh basil or 1 tsp. dried basil, crushed**
- **1 Tbsp. snipped fresh oregano or 1 tsp. dried oregano, crushed**
- **5 cups chicken broth**
- **2 cups water**
- **½ cup snipped dried tomatoes (not oil-packed)**
- **Fresh chives (optional)**

WEEKDAY MENU

- **Split Pea and Smoked Turkey Soup (see left)**

- **Salad of fresh spinach or assorted greens, thin pear slices, and thin onion slices, drizzled with a sweet vinaigrette and sprinkled with honey-roasted nuts**

- **Crusty hard rolls with butter**

- **Crumb-topped fruit pie with ice cream**

1 Rinse split peas; drain. In a 3½- or 4-quart crockery cooker combine the split peas, smoked turkey or turkey sausage, carrots, chives, garlic, and dried basil and oregano (if using). Pour chicken broth and water over all.

2 Cover and cook on low-heat setting for 6 to 8 hours or on high-heat setting for 3 to 4 hours. Stir in dried tomatoes; cover and let stand for 10 minutes. If using, stir in fresh basil and oregano.

3 To serve, ladle soup into bowls. If desired, garnish with fresh chives. Makes 6 to 8 servings.

Nutrition Facts per serving: 204 cal., 2 g total fat (1 g sat. fat), 22 mg chol., 1,313 mg sodium, 26 g carbo., 5 g fiber, 22 g pro.
Daily Values: 141% vit. A, 13% vit. C, 4% calcium, 15% iron.

LOW FAT

Tex-Mex Chicken Soup

An attractive serving style is to bias-cut each chicken breast half into ¼-inch slices. Assemble the sliced chicken in the bottom of the bowl before ladling the soup on top. (See the photograph on page 242.)

Start to finish: 45 minutes

- 3 14½-oz. cans reduced-sodium chicken broth
- 1 canned chipotle pepper in adobo sauce, cut into 4 pieces*
- 1 7- or 8-inch spinach, tomato, and/or plain flour tortilla, quartered
- 2 tsp. olive oil
- 4 small skinless, boneless chicken breast halves (about 12 oz. total)
- ½ tsp. ground cumin
- 2 tsp. olive oil
- 1 small avocado, halved, seeded, peeled, and sliced
- ½ of a 14½-oz. can white or yellow hominy, drained and rinsed (about ¾ cup)
  Dairy sour cream
  Cilantro sprigs (optional)

1 Preheat oven to 375°. In a 2-quart saucepan combine the chicken broth and chipotle pepper. Bring to boiling; reduce heat. Simmer, uncovered, for 20 minutes. Discard the pepper.

2 Meanwhile, for tortilla cones, place tortilla quarters on a clean white microwave-safe paper towel; microcook on 100% power (high) 15 to 20 seconds or until just softened. Brush tortilla quarters with the 2 teaspoons olive oil. Shape each into a cone; secure with a wooden toothpick. Place on a baking sheet.

3 Bake for 8 minutes or until cones are lightly browned and slightly crisp. Cool slightly.

4 Rub both sides of chicken breasts with ground cumin. In a large skillet cook chicken breasts in 2 teaspoons hot olive oil for 10 to 12 minutes or until chicken is tender and no longer pink, turning once.

5 To serve, place one cooked chicken breast half in each of four warmed soup bowls. Add avocado and hominy to each bowl. Pour simmering broth into each bowl. Spoon a small amount of sour cream into each tortilla cone. If desired, add cilantro sprig. Serve cones with soup. Makes 4 servings.

*Note: Hot peppers contain oils that can burn eyes, lips, and sensitive skin, so wear plastic gloves while preparing them and wash your hands thoroughly afterward.

Nutrition Facts per serving: 227 cal., 9 g total fat (2 g sat. fat), 52 mg chol., 895 mg sodium, 10 g carbo., 2 g fiber, 25 g pro.
Daily Values: 6% vit. A, 5% vit. C, 6% calcium, 10% iron.

EDITOR'S TIP

Turn on the Heat

A veritable heat wave of sauces and condiments radiates on supermarket shelves these days. Add fire to your penchant for spicy cooking with one of these sizzling products:

● **Jalapeño sauce:** This green sauce, made from ripe jalapeño peppers and found in a small slim bottle, is not as intensely hot as the more familiar bottled red pepper sauce. Stir it into pizza sauce before spreading the sauce on the crust, use it in omelet fillings, or shake it on nachos.

● **Harissa sauce:** Originating from North Africa, this fiery sauce is a blend of dried red peppers, spices, and garlic packed into jars with olive oil (drain off before using the harissa). Stir small amounts into a marinara sauce, brush it on barbecued shrimp, or stir it into your favorite salsa or bean dip, tasting and adding more as desired.

● **Pickapeppa sauce:** This is the brand name for a Jamaican specialty that combines peppers and mangoes for a sweet-hot, chutneylike seasoning. Aged for one year in oak casks and then bottled, Pickapeppa sauce delivers sizzle to many foods. Stir a few teaspoonfuls into rice or couscous, add it to your favorite poultry marinade, or brush directly on tuna steaks while grilling. If you're unable to find Pickapeppa sauce in your stores, substitute Worcestershire sauce for use in recipes.

● **Spicy oils:** Savvy cooks fuse flavor and function by using vegetable oils infused with the flavor of chile peppers. These products vary in hotness by brand (with the Asian ones usually being the spiciest). Substitute ¼ to ½ teaspoon spicy oil for the cooking oil called for in stir-fries, salad dressings, or marinades.

● **Pepper jelly:** This Southern treat is a blend of sweet green peppers and jalapeños, so the heat factor can range from mild to hot. Spread the jelly on cornmeal biscuits, tuck one or two teaspoons inside quesadillas, or melt it to glaze grilled chicken.

Chicken & Garbanzo Bean Soup

Fennel has a creamy white bulblike base, pale green stalks, and feathery green leaves. It has a light, licorice flavor and a texture that is similar to celery.

Prep: 20 minutes **Soak:** 1 hour
Cook: 4 hours

- 1   cup dry garbanzo beans (chickpeas)
- 1   lb. skinless, boneless chicken breasts or thighs
- 2½ cups sliced carrots
- 1   medium fennel bulb, trimmed and cut into ¼-inch slices, or 1½ cups sliced celery
- 1   large onion, chopped
- 1   Tbsp. snipped fresh marjoram or 1 tsp. dried marjoram, crushed
- 1   Tbsp. snipped fresh thyme or 1 tsp. dried thyme, crushed
- 1   Tbsp. instant chicken bouillon granules
- ¼   tsp. salt
- ¼   tsp. pepper
- 4   cups water
- 1   cup shredded fresh spinach or escarole
     Fresh thyme sprigs (optional)

1 Rinse the garbanzo beans; place in a large saucepan. Add enough water to cover the beans by 2 inches. Bring to boiling; reduce heat. Simmer, uncovered, for 10 minutes. Remove from heat. Cover and let stand for 1 hour. (Or place beans in water in a large saucepan. Cover and let soak in a cool place overnight.) Drain and rinse the beans.

2 Place chicken and beans in a 3½-, 4-, or 5-quart crockery cooker. Add carrots, fennel or celery, onion, dried marjoram and thyme (if using), bouillon granules, salt, and pepper. Pour 4 cups water over all.

3 Cover; cook on low-heat setting for 8 to 10 hours or on high-heat setting for 4 to 5 hours. Remove the chicken; cool slightly. Cut the meat into bite-size pieces. Return to cooker. Add the spinach or escarole and, if using, the fresh marjoram and thyme. Let stand 5 minutes before serving.

4 To serve, ladle soup into bowls. If desired, garnish with fresh thyme sprigs. Makes 6 servings.

Nutrition Facts per serving: 205 cal., 4 g total fat (1 g sat. fat), 40 mg chol., 625 mg sodium, 23 g carbo., 9 g fiber, 20 g pro.
Daily Values: 149% vit. A, 12% vit. C, 6% calcium, 18% iron.

Chicken and Sausage Paella

The flavor of paella comes from saffron, the dried threads or stigmas of the purple crocus. Saffron lends a yellow color, bittersweet flavor, and wonderful aroma.

Prep: 30 minutes **Cook:** 3½ hours

- 2½ to 3 lb. meaty chicken pieces (breasts, thighs, and drumsticks)
- 1   Tbsp. cooking oil
- 8   oz. cooked smoked turkey sausage, halved lengthwise and sliced
- 1   large onion, sliced
- 3   cloves garlic, minced

- 2   Tbsp. snipped fresh thyme or 2 tsp. dried thyme, crushed
- ¼   tsp. black pepper
- ⅛   tsp. thread saffron or ¼ tsp. ground turmeric
- 1   14½-oz. can reduced-sodium chicken broth
- ½   cup water
- 2   cups chopped tomatoes
- 2   yellow or green sweet peppers, cut into very thin bite-size strips
- 1   cup frozen green peas
- 3   cups hot cooked rice

1 Skin chicken. In a large skillet brown chicken pieces, half at a time, in hot oil. Drain off fat. In a 3½-, 4-, or 5-quart crockery cooker place chicken pieces, turkey sausage, and onion. Sprinkle with garlic, dried thyme (if using), black pepper, and saffron or turmeric. Pour chicken broth and water over all.

2 Cover; cook on low-heat setting for 7 to 8 hours or on high-heat setting for 3½ to 4 hours. Add the tomatoes, sweet peppers, peas, and, if using, the fresh thyme to the cooker. Cover; let stand for 5 minutes.

3 To serve, in each of six shallow bowls, spoon chicken and vegetable mixture over the hot cooked rice. Makes 6 servings.

Nutrition Facts per serving: 397 cal, 12 g total fat (3 g sat. fat), 101 mg chol., 608 mg sodium, 35 g carbo., 2 g fiber, 36 g pro.
Daily Values: 8% vit. A, 109% vit C, 6% calcium, 22% iron.

LOW FAT

Fennel Cheese Bread

Enhance the flavor of a loaf of bread with fennel and hazelnuts. Ricotta cheese produces the light, airy texture in this much-loved loaf. It's so good, you may want to eat it straight from the bread machine.

Prep: 15 minutes

1½-POUND LOAF* (16 slices)

- ¾ cup part-skim ricotta cheese
- ⅔ cup milk
- 1 egg
- 2 Tbsp. margarine or butter, cut up
- 3 cups bread flour
- 2 Tbsp. brown sugar
- 1½ tsp. fennel seed, crushed
- ¾ tsp. salt
- 1 tsp. active dry yeast or bread machine yeast
- ⅓ cup finely chopped hazelnuts (filberts), toasted

2-POUND LOAF* (22 slices)

- 1 cup part-skim ricotta cheese
- ¾ cup milk
- 2 eggs
- 3 Tbsp. margarine or butter, cut up
- 4 cups bread flour
- 3 Tbsp. brown sugar
- 2 tsp. fennel seed, crushed
- 1 tsp. salt
- 1¼ tsp. active dry yeast or bread machine yeast
- ½ cup finely chopped hazelnuts (filberts), toasted

1 Select the loaf size. Add the ingredients to the bread machine according to the manufacturer's directions. Select the basic white bread cycle.

*Note: For the 1½-pound loaf, the bread machine pan must have a capacity of 10 cups or more. For the 2-pound loaf, the bread machine pan must have a capacity of 12 cups or more.

Nutrition Facts per slice: 153 cal., 5 g total fat (1 g sat. fat), 18 mg chol., 141 mg sodium, 22 g carbo., 1 g fiber, 6 g pro.
Daily Values: 4% vit A, 4% calcium, 8% iron.

Black Walnut Bread

Black walnuts, native to America, are particularly tasty in baked goods. This tender loaf, abundant with nutty nuggets, showcases them perfectly.

Prep: 15 minutes

1½-POUND LOAF* (16 slices)

- ⅔ cup milk
- 1 egg**
- 3 Tbsp. water
- 2 Tbsp. walnut oil or cooking oil
- 3 cups bread flour
- 2 Tbsp. sugar
- ¾ tsp. salt
- 1 tsp. active dry yeast or bread machine yeast
- ⅔ cup chopped black walnuts or English walnuts

2-POUND LOAF* (22 slices)

- ¾ cup milk
- 1 egg**
- ¼ cup water
- 3 Tbsp. walnut oil or cooking oil
- 4 cups bread flour
- 3 Tbsp. sugar
- 1 tsp. salt
- 1¼ tsp. active dry yeast or bread machine yeast
- ¾ cup chopped black walnuts or English walnuts

1 Select the loaf size. Add the ingredients to the machine according to the manufacturer's directions. Select the basic white bread cycle.

*Note: For the 1½-pound loaf, the bread machine pan must have a capacity of 10 cups or more. For the 2-pound loaf, the bread machine pan must have a capacity of 12 cups or more.

**Note: The Better Homes and Gardens® Test Kitchen recommends 1 egg for either size recipe.

Nutrition Facts per slice: 156 cal., 6 g total fat (1 g sat. fat), 14 mg chol., 110 mg sodium, 21 g carbo, 1 g fiber, 5 g pro.
Daily Values: 1% vit A, 1% calcium, 8% iron.

TEST KITCHEN TIP
Walnut Oil

In French villages, fresh walnuts are cold-pressed following time-honored methods to extract their aromatic oils—a traditional culinary specialty. Just a splash of this nutty elixir elevates a simple salad dressing into something special or intensifies the flavor of a nut bread. Store this delicate oil away from light and heat.

TEACH YOUR CHILDREN HEALTHY

One out of every 5 kids is obese in this country, and the number of overweight children has more than doubled in the past 20 years. Doctors are beginning to notice a disturbingly high incidence of obese children with diabetes, high blood pressure, and high cholesterol—ailments that once mostly affected adults. We talked with doctors and nutritionists to find out how to help children slim down and get a healthier start in life.

How do kids get heavy?

For statistical purposes, doctors consider a child obese when he or she is at or above the 95th weight percentile. However, some kids who are in the upper reaches of the weight chart are more muscular and, therefore, weigh more than their smaller peers. It's best to check with your pediatrician. Most of the time, if you think your child has a weight problem, he probably does.

"The best way to tell if a child is obese is to look at the child," says Dr. Laura Nathanson, a pediatrician at the University of California Medical School at San Diego. "After age four, normal-weight children don't have 'pudge.' Their bellies don't stick out and there aren't any creases in their upper arms or thighs. The problem is that we have gotten so used to seeing chubby children that chubby looks normal and normal looks thin."

Where does that pudge come from? Genetics may determine general body type and size, but genes don't determine what is eaten for dinner. "We can't attribute the increase in childhood obesity to genes, because the gene pool hasn't changed in millennia," says Dr. Dennis Bier, a professor of pediatrics and director of the Children's Nutrition Research Center at Baylor College of Medicine.

Most overweight children are heavy because, for months or years, they take in more daily calories than their bodies need. Over time, these unused calories add up. Dr. Nathanson says that even 50 extra calories a day can lead to weight gain. Keep in mind that 50 calories translates to a couple ounces of juice or one cookie. A child who eats 50 extra calories a day for a year will double her normal weight gain.

Because our bodies aren't designed to carry lots of excess weight, some obese children develop medical problems. Dr. Nathanson has seen a host of health problems in her patients—high blood pressure, high cholesterol, joint pain, and even sleep apnea. Others have skin problems caused by chafing.

One of the most serious medical problems in overweight children is Type 2 diabetes, which happens when organs become resistant to insulin. Small studies have found that Type 2 diabetes in children has more than tripled in the past five years.

Now what do you do?

If you suspect that your child is overweight, talk to your pediatrician and, possibly, a nutritionist. "The longer a child remains overweight, the higher his or her risk of becoming an obese adult," says Dr. William Cochran, a pediatric gastroenterologist and nutritionist at the Geisinger Clinic in Danville, Pennsylvania.

Pediatricians agree that, in most cases, the goal should not be to lose weight. Rather, focus on maintaining weight and letting the child grow into her weight. A child should also be ready and willing to make changes unless parents relish every-night battles at the dinner table.

Before you put your child on a diet, find out what and why he is eating. There is usually a reason why your child eats more than he needs, says Ellyn Satter, a registered dietitian,

nutritionist, and author of *Child of Mine: Feeding with Love and Good Sense.* Satter says that some parents who become concerned with their child's weight restrict food intake. When this happens, some kids become preoccupied with food and overindulge when left alone. Ironically, Satter has found that restricting food tends to make children fatter, not thinner.

Take control

One of the most important things a parent can do is establish a division of responsibility for food, Satter says. Parents should decide what, when, and where children eat, and kids can decide how much and whether to eat. Although this may sound a bit militaristic, the idea is to give kids choices, but not free reign.

The easiest way to eat healthier is to buy healthy foods. If mass quantities of chips and cookies aren't in the house, a child won't be tempted to eat them. Obviously, moderation is the key. For little kids, it's sometimes helpful to explain the concept of moderation with phrases "sometimes" and "everyday" foods.

It's also important to establish a routine for meals and snacks. You can limit food panhandling by feeding kids on a schedule, such as three meals a day plus an after-school snack. Snacks should have a "stick-to-your-ribs" quality to them, Satter says. Try a small bowl of cereal and milk or an apple with peanut butter.

If you can, it's best to sit down together at the table for dinner. Eating as a family means that you'll be talking, which will probably cause your child to eat more slowly. Dr. Cochran says that many overweight kids inhale their food and eat too much because they don't recognize they're full. It takes 20 minutes for your body to give you the signal that you've had enough to eat, so chatting at the table serves a dual purpose—family bonding and buying time between bites for your child to realize she's full.

A recent study in the *Archives of Family Medicine* looked at the nutritional quality of the diets of 16,000 kids ages 9 to 14. It found kids who ate more often with their families ate less fried foods, drank less soda, and ate more fruits and vegetables than the kids who didn't.

Now to the kids' part of the bargain. Satter says that each child inherently knows how much to eat, but that doesn't mean you're off the hook. A parent's job is to provide healthy options on a schedule. Living in a society where restaurant portions that should be the size of your fist are closer to the size of your head, kids get confused about how much their bodies need.

To prevent gargantuan portions and the temptation to eat food just because it's there, nutritionist Patti Chulock suggests parents serve from the stove, rather than family-style. Immediately putting leftovers away also can discourage grazing.

For the plan to really work, enlist everyone's help. It's important that your child receives consistent messages about food from both parents, siblings, grandparents, and even babysitters. You set yourself up for failure if you allow three meals a day and a small after-school snack, and grandma lets him eat whatever he wants.

As you modify your family's diet, begin to work more activity into your lives. "Children sit a lot today," says Dr. Nathanson. "They sit in cars. They sit in school." To make matters worse, the daily dose of physical education in public schools has dropped dramatically—from 42 percent in 1991 to 27 percent by 1997.

Do something active for 20 minutes a day. As you walk or bike, let your child know you love and care for her, no matter her size.

LOW FAT

Sesame Bâton

For fun variations, shape the bread dough into a large ring or separate rolls before baking. The instructions for both variations follow this recipe. (See the photographs on pages 237 and 240.)

Prep: 30 minutes **Rise:** 1 hour 35 minutes
Bake: 30 minutes

- 2½ to 3 cups all-purpose flour
- 1 pkg. active dry yeast
- 1 tsp. salt
- 1 cup warm water (120° to 130°)
- 1 tsp. toasted sesame seed oil
- ¼ cup toasted sesame seed
- 1 egg white, beaten

1 In a large mixing bowl stir together 1 cup of the flour, yeast, and salt. Add the warm water and toasted sesame oil to flour mixture. Beat with an electric mixer on low to medium speed for 30 seconds, scraping bottom and sides of bowl. Beat on high speed for 3 minutes. Using a wooden spoon, stir in half of the sesame seed and as much of the remaining flour as you can.

2 Turn the dough out onto a lightly floured surface. Knead in enough of the remaining flour to make a stiff dough that is smooth and elastic (8 to 10 minutes). Shape the dough into a ball. Place dough in a lightly greased bowl, turning once to grease surface of the dough. Cover and let rise in a warm place until double (about 1 hour).

1. Use your fingertips to roll the flattened dough into a tight spiral.

2. Draw the ends of the rolled dough together. Pinch the ends softly to seal.

3 Punch dough down. Turn dough out onto a floured surface. Cover and let rest for 10 minutes. Lightly grease a large baking sheet; set aside.

4 On a lightly floured surface roll dough into a 15×10-inch rectangle. Roll up into a spiral, starting from a long side; seal well (see photo 1, above). Pinch ends and pull slightly to taper. Place, seam side down, on the prepared baking sheet. Brush with egg white. Sprinkle with remaining sesame seeds. Cover and let rise until nearly double (35 to 45 minutes).

CLEVER COOK

Shake, Rattle, and Pour

I keep a diner-style sugar pourer filled with flour. If I need only a spoon or two for baking or cooking, I don't have to drag out the large flour canister.

Susan Maloney
Safety Harbor, Florida

5 Preheat oven to 375°. Bake for 30 to 35 minutes or until bread sounds hollow when lightly tapped. Immediately transfer to a wire rack. Cool completely. Makes 15 servings.

Nutrition Facts per serving: 89 cal., 2 g total fat (0 g sat. fat), 0 mg chol., 160 mg sodium, 15 g carbo., 1 g fiber, 3 g pro.
Daily Values: 3% calcium, 7% iron.

Sesame Ring

Prepare dough as directed, following Steps 1 through 4 to sealing. Pull ends to form a nearly complete circle (see photo 2, left). Place, seam side down, on a lightly greased baking sheet. Brush with egg white. Sprinkle with remaining sesame seeds. Cover and let rise until nearly double in size (35 to 45 minutes). Bake as directed.

Sesame Rolls

Prepare dough as directed, following Steps 1 through 4 to sealing. Cut crosswise into 4 to 6 equal pieces. Place each piece, seam side down, on a greased baking sheet. Brush with egg white. Sprinkle with remaining sesame seed. Cover and let rise until nearly double in size (35 to 45 minutes). Bake as directed.

Top: Farmer's Vegetable Broth (page 226)

Above: Toasted Caraway & Rye Skillet Bread (page 245), Olive Flatbreads (page 245), Sesame Bâton (page 236), Sourdough Breadsticks (page 246)

Top: Sheetpan Focaccia (page 246)
Above: Navy Beans and Pork (page 230)
Page 238: Beet Borscht (page 225)

Above: Butternut Squash Soup with Ravioli (page 224) and Sesame Rolls (page 236)
Right: Sheetpan Focaccia and Sourdough Breadsticks (page 246)
Page 241: Two-Tomato Soup (page 223)

Top: Tortilla Cones (served with Tex-Mex Chicken Soup, page 232)
Above: Tex-Mex Chicken Soup (page 232)
Page 243: Salmon Pan Chowder (page 230)

Right: Italian Wedding
Soup (page 228)
Below left: Thai-Style
Shrimp Soup (page 229)
Below right: Herb and
Pepper Lentil Stew
(page 226)

Olive Flatbreads

Prepare the Olive Spread up to a week ahead and refrigerate, tightly covered. You may substitute with a purchased olive spread called "tapenade." (See the photograph on page 237.)

Prep: 30 minutes
Bake: 16 minutes per batch

  2 **cups all-purpose flour**
  ½ **cup semolina**
  ½ **tsp. baking soda**
  ¼ **tsp. coarse salt**
  2 **Tbsp. cold butter**
  1 **cup buttermilk**
      Coarse salt (optional)
  1 **to 2 Tbsp. olive oil**
  1 **recipe Olive Spread (see right)**

1 Preheat oven to 375°. Grease baking sheets; set aside.

2 In a large bowl stir together flour, semolina, baking soda, and the ¼ teaspoon salt. Using a pastry blender, cut in butter until mixture resembles coarse crumbs. Make a well in center of flour mixture. Add buttermilk. Using a fork, stir until mixture can be formed into a ball.

3 Turn dough out onto a lightly floured surface. Knead dough 8 to 10 times or until smooth. Divide dough into 4 portions. On floured surface, roll each portion into a 9-inch square, about ⅛ inch thick. Cut each square into three 9×3-inch rectangles.

4 Place rectangles 1 inch apart on prepared baking sheets. Sprinkle with additional coarse salt, if desired. Using a fork, prick rectangles (see photo, right). Brush with olive oil; spread 2 tablespoons Olive Spread on each rectangle.

5 Bake 16 to 20 minutes or until edges and bottoms are browned and flatbreads are crisp. Transfer from baking sheet to racks; cool. Makes 12.

Olive Spread

In a small bowl stir together ¾ cup very finely chopped pitted ripe olives; ⅓ cup chopped, drained capers; ⅓ cup very finely chopped almonds; and 1 tablespoon olive oil.

Nutrition Facts per flatbread: 163 cal., 6 g total fat (2 g sat. fat), 6 mg chol., 322 mg sodium, 22 g carbo., 2 g fiber, 5 g pro.
Daily Values: 2% vit. A, 1% vit. C, 5% calcium, 9% iron.

Prick flatbread dough with fork before baking. This lets steam escape and keeps bread from puffing and coming out too soft.

LOW FAT

Toasted Caraway & Rye Skillet Bread

See the photograph on page 237.

Prep: 20 minutes **Cook:** 20 minutes

  1 **tsp. caraway seed**
  1⅓ **cups all-purpose flour**
  ⅔ **cup rye flour**
  1½ **tsp. baking powder**
  ½ **tsp. salt**
  ¼ **tsp. baking soda**
  2 **Tbsp. cold butter**
  1 **cup buttermilk**
      Nonstick cooking spray

1 In a heavy, large skillet heat caraway seed over medium-low heat for 3 to 5 minutes or until toasted, shaking skillet occasionally to prevent seeds from burning. Remove seeds from skillet; set skillet aside to cool. In a large bowl combine toasted seeds, all-purpose flour, rye flour, baking powder, salt, and baking soda. Using a pastry blender, cut butter into flour mixture until mixture resembles coarse crumbs. Make a well in the center of dry mixture. Using a fork, stir in buttermilk just until moistened.

2 Turn the dough out onto a well-floured surface. Quickly knead for 10 to 12 strokes until dough is nearly smooth. Roll or pat dough into a circle about 7 inches in diameter and ¾ inch thick. Cut into 8 wedges.

3 Coat the cool skillet with nonstick cooking spray. Heat skillet over medium-low heat for 1 to 3 minutes or until a drop of water sizzles. Carefully place the dough wedges in the pan.

4 Cover and cook about 20 minutes or until golden brown and a wooden toothpick inserted into the side of a wedge comes out clean, turning wedges several times to brown both sides. Sides may still look moist. Check bottoms occasionally and decrease heat, if necessary, to prevent overbrowning. Serve bread warm or at room temperature. Makes 8 servings.

Nutrition Facts per serving: 140 cal., 4 g total fat (2 g sat. fat), 9 mg chol., 323 mg sodium, 23 g carbo., 2 g fiber, 4 g pro.
Daily Values: 3% vit. A, 1% vit. C, 9% calcium, 6% iron.

LOW FAT

Sheetpan Focaccia

Use the same recipe minus the onion and sage to make crispy breadsticks (see variation, below). (See the photographs on pages 237, 239 and 240.)

Initial prep: 1 hour **Chill:** overnight
Final prep: 1 hour **Bake:** 19 minutes

2¼	to 2½ cups all-purpose flour
1	pkg. active dry yeast
2	tsp. dried Italian seasoning, crushed
1¼	cups warm water (120° to 130°)
2	Tbsp. olive oil
½	cup semolina
	Nonstick cooking spray
2	Tbsp. olive oil
2	cups coarsely chopped onion
1	tsp. brown sugar
	Fresh sage leaves

1 In a large mixing bowl combine 1½ cups of the flour, yeast, Italian seasoning, and 1 teaspoon *salt*. Add water and 2 tablespoons olive oil. Beat with an electric mixer on low to medium speed 30 seconds, scraping bowl. Beat on high speed 3 minutes. Stir in semolina and as much of the remaining flour as you can.

2 Turn dough onto a floured surface. Knead in enough of the remaining flour to make a moderately soft dough that is smooth and elastic (3 to 5 minutes total). Shape into a ball. Place dough in greased bowl, turning once. Cover. Let rise in a warm place until double (45 to 60 minutes).

3 Punch dough down. Coat inside of a large, self-sealing plastic bag with nonstick cooking spray. Place dough inside; close bag, allowing room for dough to rise. Refrigerate 16 to 24 hours.

4 Remove dough from bag. Place dough onto a greased large baking sheet. Gently pull and stretch dough into a 15×8-inch rectangle, being careful not to overwork dough. Spray dough lightly with cooking spray. Cover loosely with plastic wrap; let rise in a warm place until nearly double (about 45 minutes).

5 Meanwhile, in a medium skillet heat 2 tablespoons olive oil. Cook onion, covered, in hot oil over medium-low heat 10 minutes, stirring often. Uncover; add brown sugar and ¼ teaspoon *salt*. Cook and stir over medium-high heat 4 to 5 minutes. Remove from heat; set aside. Preheat oven to 450°.

6 Using the tips of your fingers, press deep indentations into the surface of the dough every 1½ to 2 inches (see photo 2, right). Cover and let dough rest for 10 minutes.

7 Bake about 15 minutes or until light golden brown. Remove from oven; spread onion mixture over surface. Dot sage leaves randomly on top, pressing gently. Bake 4 to 5 minutes more or until golden brown. Cut into wedges or rectangles. Serve warm. Makes 16 to 24 servings.

Nutrition Facts per serving: 118 cal., 4 g total fat (1 g sat. fat), 0 mg chol., 184 mg sodium, 18 g carbo., 1 g fiber, 3 g pro.
Daily Values: 2% vit. C, 1% calcium, 7% iron.

Sourdough Breadsticks

1. Prepare dough as directed in Steps 1 through 3. Punch dough down and remove from bag. Form dough into a ball; place on a work surface lightly dusted with additional flour or semolina. Cover; let rest 10 minutes.

2. Roll dough to a 15×8-inch rectangle. Using a sharp knife, cut dough into 30 strips, 8 inches long and ½ inch wide. Using hands, roll each strip to a 12- to 15-inch length.
3. Place strips on two large greased baking sheets. Cover with plastic wrap or a towel. Let rise in a warm place until doubled, about 30 minutes. Meanwhile, preheat oven to 450°.
4. Uncover dough. Bake 12 to 15 minutes. Cool on a wire rack. Makes 30 breadsticks.

1. Use the heel of your hands to knead the dough.

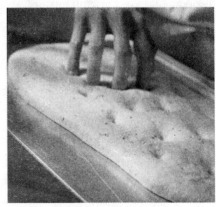

2. Use your fingertips to press indentations in the dough. This will keep the focaccia flat during baking, plus add extra chewiness to the finished bread.

Spicy Pumpkin Loaf

A cinnamon- and nutmeg-flavored glaze adds zest to this pumpkin loaf.

Prep: 25 minutes **Bake:** 60 minutes

2	cups all-purpose flour
1	cup sugar
2½	tsp. baking powder
1	tsp. ground cinnamon
½	tsp. baking soda
½	tsp. ground nutmeg
⅛	tsp. ground cloves
1	cup canned pumpkin
½	cup cream sherry or milk
2	eggs
⅓	cup shortening
1	cup raisins
	Spiced Glaze

1 Preheat oven to 350°. Grease a 7-cup fluted tube mold or two 7½×3½×2-inch loaf pans. Set the mold or loaf pans aside.

2 In a large mixing bowl stir together 1 cup of the flour, sugar, baking powder, cinnamon, baking soda, nutmeg, cloves, and ¼ *teaspoon salt.* Add pumpkin, cream sherry or milk, eggs, and shortening. Beat with an electric mixer on low to medium speed about 30 seconds or until combined. Beat on high speed for 2 minutes more, scraping the sides of the bowl occasionally. Add remaining flour; beat until well mixed. Stir in raisins.

3 Pour batter into the prepared mold or pans. Bake for 60 to 65 minutes for mold or 45 to 50 minutes for loaves or until a wooden toothpick inserted in center comes out clean. Cool in mold or pans on a wire rack for 10 minutes. Remove bread; cool on rack. Wrap and store overnight. Before serving, drizzle with glaze. Makes 1 bread ring or 2 loaves (16 servings).

Spiced Glaze

In a bowl stir together ½ cup sifted powdered sugar, ⅛ teaspoon ground cinnamon, ⅛ teaspoon ground nutmeg, and 2 to 3 teaspoons cream sherry or water to make an icing of drizzling consistency. Makes about ¼ cup.

Nutrition Facts per serving: 203 cal., 5 g total fat (1 g sat. fat), 27 mg chol., 112 mg sodium, 35 g carbo., 1 g fiber, 3 g pro.
Daily Values: 68% vit. A, 2% vit. C, 5% calcium, 7% iron.

Double Chocolate-Almond Cheesecake

For an extra boost of flavor, toast the almonds before grinding them.

Prep: 35 minutes **Bake:** 45 minutes
Cool: 1 hour **Chill:** 4 hours

2	tsp. butter or margarine
¾	cup ground almonds
16	ounces white baking bar with cocoa butter, chopped
4	8-ounce packages cream cheese, softened
½	cup butter or margarine, softened
3	Tbsp. milk
1	Tbsp. vanilla
	Dash salt
4	eggs
1	egg yolk
4	1.45-ounce bars milk chocolate with almonds, chopped
	Chocolate curls (optional)

1 Preheat oven to 375°. Use the 2 teaspoons butter or margarine to grease the bottom and sides of a 10-inch springform pan. Press ground almonds onto the bottom of the springform pan. Set pan aside.

2 For filling, in a heavy medium saucepan heat and stir the white baking bar over low heat just until melted. In a large mixing bowl beat melted baking bar, cream cheese, the ½ cup butter or margarine, milk, vanilla, and salt with an electric mixer on medium to high speed until combined. Add whole eggs and egg yolk all at once. Beat on low speed just until combined. Stir in chopped milk chocolate.

3 Pour filling into the prepared springform pan. Bake cheesecake on a shallow baking pan for 45 to 50 minutes or until center appears nearly set when gently shaken.

4 Cool cheesecake in springform pan on a wire rack for 10 minutes. Using a small metal spatula, loosen cheesecake from the sides of the springform pan. Cool for 30 minutes more. Remove sides of the springform pan. Cool completely, then chill at least 4 hours. If desired, garnish with chocolate curls. Makes 16 servings.

Nutrition Facts per serving: 537 cal., 44 g total fat (25 g sat. fat), 153 mg chol., 299 mg sodium, 24 g carbo., 1 g fiber, 11 g pro.
Daily Values: 23% vit. A, 14% calcium, 7% iron.

Apple Cake with Caramel-Raisin Sauce

Prep: 25 minutes **Bake:** 45 minutes

- 2   cups all-purpose flour
- ¾   cup granulated sugar
- ½   cup packed brown sugar
- 2   tsp. baking powder
- 1   tsp. ground cinnamon
- ½   tsp. baking soda
- ½   tsp. salt
- ½   tsp. ground ginger
- ¼   tsp. ground cloves
- 2   eggs, slightly beaten
- 1   8-oz. carton dairy sour cream
- ¼   cup butter or margarine, melted
- 3   Tbsp. milk
- 1   tsp. vanilla
- 1   medium apple, peeled and coarsely shredded (1 cup)
- ⅔   cup chopped walnuts
- 1   recipe Caramel-Raisin Sauce (see right)

1 Preheat oven to 350°. Grease and lightly flour an 8-inch springform pan or a 9×9×2-inch baking pan; set aside. In a large bowl stir together the flour, sugars, baking powder, cinnamon, soda, salt, ginger, and cloves. Make a well in the center of the dry ingredients.

2 In a medium bowl combine eggs, sour cream, melted butter or margarine, milk, and vanilla. Add egg mixture all at once to dry ingredients. Stir just until moistened. Fold in shredded apple and walnuts. Spread batter into the prepared pan.

3 Bake 50 minutes for springform pan or 45 minutes for 9×9×2-inch pan, or until a wooden toothpick inserted near center comes out clean. Cool in pan on a wire rack 20 minutes. Remove sides of springform pan (or leave cake in the

9×9×2-inch pan). Serve warm or cool with Caramel-Raisin Sauce. Makes 12 servings.

Caramel-Raisin Sauce

In a medium saucepan melt ½ cup butter or margarine. Stir in 1 cup packed brown sugar and 2 tablespoons light corn syrup. Cook and stir over medium heat until mixture comes to a full boil. Stir in ½ cup whipping cream. Return to a full boil. Remove from heat; stir in ¼ cup raisins. Serve warm.

Nutrition Facts per serving: 480 cal., 24 g total fat (7 g sat. fat), 58 mg chol., 391 mg sodium, 63 g carbo., 1 g fiber, 5 g pro.
Daily Values: 17% vit. A, 2% vit. C, 12% calcium, 10% iron.

Buttermilk Carrot Cake

The carrots need to be finely shredded or they may sink to the bottom of the pan during baking.

Prep: 30 minutes **Bake:** 40 minutes
Cool: 1 hour

- 2   cups all-purpose flour
- 2   cups granulated sugar
- 2   tsp. baking soda
- 1½   tsp. ground cinnamon
- 1   tsp. baking powder
- 2   cups finely shredded carrots
- ¼   cup buttermilk or sour milk
- ¼   cup cooking oil
- 1   8¼-oz. can crushed pineapple, drained
- 1   cup chopped walnuts
- 3   eggs
- ½   cup coconut
- 1   tsp. vanilla
- 1   recipe Buttermilk Glaze (see right)
- 1   recipe Cream Cheese Frosting (see right)
- ½   cup chopped walnuts

1 Preheat oven to 350°. Grease a 13×9×2-inch baking pan or grease and lightly flour two 9×1½-inch round baking pans; set aside. In a large bowl combine flour, granulated sugar, baking soda, cinnamon, baking powder, and ¼ teaspoon *salt*. Add shredded carrots, buttermilk or sour milk, cooking oil, drained pineapple, walnuts, eggs, coconut, and vanilla. Stir until combined. Spread batter into prepared pan(s).

2 Bake for 40 to 45 minutes or until cake(s) spring back when touched lightly. Pour Buttermilk Glaze evenly over top(s) of cake(s). Cool layer cakes in pans on wire racks for 15 minutes. Remove from pans. Cool thoroughly on wire racks. Or, place 13×9-inch pan on wire rack. Cool completely. Frost with Cream Cheese Frosting. Sprinkle with nuts. Store in refrigerator. Makes 16 servings.

Buttermilk Glaze

In a medium saucepan combine ½ cup granulated sugar, ¼ cup buttermilk or sour milk, ¼ cup margarine or butter, and 2 teaspoons light corn syrup. Bring to boiling; reduce heat. Cook and stir for 4 minutes. Remove from heat and stir in ½ teaspoon vanilla.

Cream Cheese Frosting

In a large mixing bowl beat two 3-ounce packages cream cheese, ½ cup softened margarine or butter, and 2 teaspoons vanilla with an electric mixer on medium to high speed until light and fluffy. Gradually add 4½ to 4¾ cups sifted powdered sugar, beating to spreading consistency.

Nutrition Facts per serving: 544 cal., 25 g total fat (10 g sat. fat), 75 mg chol., 360 mg sodium, 79 g carbo., 2 g fiber, 6 g pro.
Daily Values: 53% vit. A, 4% vit. C, 5% calcium, 10% iron.

november

IN THIS CHAPTER

30-minute recipes indicated in COLOR.
Low-fat and no-fat recipes indicated
with a ♥.
Photographs indicated in italics.
*Bonus recipe

Squash-Barley Stuffing

Simply terrific: This moist and flavorful saucepan recipe eliminates the work and mess of stuffing and trussing the turkey. (See the photograph on page 279.)

Prep: 20 minutes **Cook:** 20 minutes

- 1 cup chopped onion
- 2 Tbsp. margarine or butter
- 2¾ cups chicken broth
- 1 cup pear nectar
- 1 cup bulgur
- ½ tsp. ground cardamom
- 1 cup quick-cooking barley
- 3 cups baby zucchini, halved lengthwise, or 2 cups coarsely chopped zucchini
- ¾ cup toasted sliced almonds
- 2 Tbsp. snipped fresh thyme

1 In a large saucepan cook onion in margarine or butter for 3 to 4 minutes or until tender. Carefully add chicken broth, pear nectar, bulgur, and cardamom. Bring to boiling; add barley. Return to boiling; reduce heat. Simmer, covered, about 12 minutes or until grains are almost tender and most of the liquid is absorbed.

2 Add zucchini to mixture in saucepan. Cook, covered, for 3 to 4 minutes more or until zucchini is crisp-tender. Stir in almonds and thyme. Makes 10 to 12 servings.

Nutrition Facts per serving: 239 cal., 9 g total fat (1 g sat. fat), 1 mg chol., 306 mg sodium, 35 g carbo., 8 g fiber, 7 g pro.
Daily Values: 4% vit. A, 18% vit. C, 5% calcium, 8% iron.

30 MINUTE, LOW FAT

Orange-Balsamic Cabbage

Use either a halogen or microwave oven for a holiday-special side dish that goes together fast and easy. (See the photograph on page 279.)

Prep: 15 minutes **Cook:** 10 minutes

- ½ cup orange marmalade
- 3 Tbsp. balsamic vinegar
- 3 Tbsp. margarine or butter, melted
- 1 2- to 2½-lb. cabbage, cored and cut into coarse chunks
- 1 large onion, coarsely chopped (about 1 cup)
- 2 Tbsp. water
  Finely shredded orange peel (optional)

1 For sauce, stir together orange marmalade, balsamic vinegar, and melted margarine or butter; set aside.

2 Place cabbage and onion in a 3-quart glass casserole with glass cover. Sprinkle with the water. Place cover on casserole.

3 Place casserole on turntable of the Advantium™ oven. Cook, covered, for 10 to 12 minutes at U=0, L=0, M=10 or until cabbage is crisp-tender, stirring once halfway through cooking.

4 Lift cabbage and onion to a serving platter with a slotted spoon. Drizzle with some of the sauce. Pass the remaining sauce. If desired, sprinkle with shredded orange peel. Makes 12 servings.

Microwave Method:
Using a microwave-safe casserole, prepare the recipe as directed through Step 2. Micro-cook, covered, on 100% power (high) for 10 to 12 minutes or until cabbage is crisp-tender, stirring once halfway through the cooking. Continue at Step 4.

Nutrition Facts per serving: 85 cal., 3 g total fat (1 g sat. fat), 0 mg chol., 53 mg sodium, 14 g carbo., 3 g fiber, 1 g pro.
Daily Values: 3% vit. A, 55% vit. C, 4% calcium, 2% iron.

30 MINUTE, NO FAT

Kumquat Cranberry Sauce

Tiny tart kumquats brighten a favorite Thanksgiving condiment. (See the photograph on page 279.)

Start to finish: 20 minutes

- 12 oz. fresh kumquats, halved crosswise and seeded (2 cups)
- 1 cup packed brown sugar
- 1 cup cranberry juice
- 2 inches stick cinnamon
- 8 oz. fresh cranberries (2 cups)

1 In a large saucepan combine kumquats, brown sugar, cranberry juice, and stick cinnamon. Bring to boiling; reduce heat. Simmer, uncovered, about 3 minutes or until kumquats are slightly softened.

2 Stir in cranberries. Bring to boiling; reduce heat. Simmer, uncovered, for 5 to 6 minutes more or until syrup begins to thicken. Remove stick cinnamon; serve sauce warm or at room temperature. Makes 3⅓ cups.

Nutrition Facts per ¼ cup: 96 cal., 0 g total fat, 0 mg chol., 13 mg sodium, 26 g carbo., 3 g fiber, 0 g pro.
Daily Values: 3% vit. A, 32% vit. C, 3% calcium, 4% iron.

Walnut-Sage Potatoes au Gratin

This creamy casserole totes well. (See the photograph on page 279.)

Prep: 30 minutes **Bake:** Advantium™ oven, 23 minutes; standard oven, 70 minutes
Stand: 10 minutes

6	medium potatoes (2 lb.)
½	cup chopped onion
2	cloves garlic, minced
3	Tbsp. walnut oil
3	Tbsp. all-purpose flour
½	tsp. salt
¼	tsp. pepper
2½	cups milk
3	Tbsp. snipped fresh sage
1	cup shredded Gruyère cheese (4 oz.)
⅓	cup broken walnut pieces
	Fresh sage leaves (optional)

1 Peel potatoes, if desired, and thinly slice (should have 6 cups). Place slices in a colander. Rinse with cool water; set aside to drain.

2 For sauce, in a medium saucepan over medium heat cook onion and garlic in walnut oil until tender but not brown. Stir in flour, salt, and pepper. Add milk all at once. Cook and stir over medium heat until thickened and bubbly. Remove from heat; stir in snipped sage.

3 Grease a 2-quart round glass casserole with glass cover. Layer half of the potatoes in casserole. Cover with half the sauce. Sprinkle with half the cheese. Repeat layering with the potatoes and sauce. (Cover and chill remaining cheese until needed.)

Advantium™ Oven Method:
Place assembled casserole on turntable of the Advantium oven. Cook, covered, for 20 minutes at U=6, L=5, M=4 or until potatoes are just tender. Uncover; sprinkle remaining cheese and the walnuts over top. Bake 3 to 5 minutes more. Remove from oven. Let stand 10 minutes before serving. If desired, garnish with the sage leaves. Makes 10 to 12 servings.

Standard Oven Method:
Bake casserole, covered, in a conventional oven at 350° for 40 minutes. Uncover; bake 25 minutes more or until potatoes are just tender. Sprinkle remaining cheese and walnuts over top. Bake, uncovered, 5 minutes more. Let stand 10 minutes before serving. If desired, garnish with the sage leaves.

Microwave Method:
Using a microwave-safe casserole, assemble ingredients through Step 3. Cover with plastic wrap, turning back an edge of wrap to allow steam to escape. Micro-cook on 70% power (medium-high) for 25 to 30 minutes or until potatoes are tender. Uncover; sprinkle remaining cheese and walnuts over top. Cover and let stand 5 minutes. If desired, garnish with the sage leaves.

Nutrition Facts per serving: 217 cal., 12 g total fat (3 g sat. fat), 17 mg chol., 187 mg sodium, 20 g carbo., 2 g fiber, 9 g pro.
Daily Values: 7% vit. A, 23% vit. C, 20% calcium, 6% iron.

EDITOR'S TIP

What's a Mandoline?

The mandoline (MAHN-duh-lihn), appreciated by cooking professionals as well as home cooks, is a small, manually operated slicing tool. Its adjustable blades enable a cook to slice, shred, julienne, and waffle-cut hard-to-cut vegetables and fruits, such as potatoes, carrots, and apples, with uniformity and precision.

● Resembling a washboard, a mandoline's long, rectangular body is made of plastic, wood, or stainless steel. This tool is available in a range of qualities and prices. Simple models have a single blade; more expensive models have two blades of different thicknesses or the capacity to adjust the blades for a range of thicknesses. A lid with a knob on a metal carriage glides on tracks, protecting your hand from the blades.

● Because each one has slight variations, follow the manufacturer's directions for using and cleaning your mandoline. Keep in mind that mandoline blades are extremely sharp. Care must be taken at all times to avoid touching the blades.

● Because a mandoline can cut foods as thin as paper, it is the perfect tool to thinly slice the potato for the Walnut-Sage Potatoes au Gratin (see left).

STUFFED WHOLE TURKEY ROASTING GUIDE

Ready-to-cook turkey weight	Oven temperature	Roasting time
8 to 12 lb.	325°	3 to 3¾ hours
12 to 14 lb.	325°	3¼ to 4½ hours
14 to 18 lb.	325°	4 to 5 hours
18 to 20 lb.	325°	4½ to 5¼ hours
20 to 24 lb.	325°	4¾ to 5¾ hours

For unstuffed turkeys of the same weight, reduce the total cooking time by 15 to 45 minutes.

Herb-Crusted Turkey

A coating of seasoned bread crumbs puts a golden spin on the holiday bird. (See the photograph on page 279.)

Prep: 30 minutes **Roast:** convection oven, 1¾ hours; standard oven, 2¾ hours
Stand: 15 minutes

  1 **10- to 12-lb. turkey**
  1 **medium onion, cut into wedges**
  3 **sprigs fresh oregano**
  3 **sprigs fresh sage**
  ⅔ **cup fine dry bread crumbs**
  3 **Tbsp. snipped fresh sage**
  3 **Tbsp. snipped fresh oregano**
  ½ **tsp. pepper**
  ¼ **tsp. salt**
  3 **Tbsp. margarine or butter, melted**
  ¼ **cup honey**
  4 **firm, ripe medium pears, halved and cored**
  2 **Tbsp. olive oil**

1 Preheat convection oven to 300°. To prepare turkey for roasting, see Turkey Roasting Guide, page 253. Season turkey cavity with *salt* and *pepper*. Place onion, oregano, and sage sprigs in cavity of bird.

2 If a band of skin crosses the tail, tuck the drumsticks under the band. If there is no band, tie drumsticks securely to tail using kitchen string. Pull turkey neck skin to back; fasten with a skewer. Twist wing tips under back.

3 In a small bowl combine bread crumbs, snipped sage, snipped oregano, the ½ teaspoon pepper, and the ¼ teaspoon salt. Stir in the melted margarine or butter; cover and set aside.

4 Place bird, breast side up, on a broiler pan. Roast turkey until a thermometer inserted into the center of one of the inside thigh muscles registers 150° (about 1½ hours).

5 Brush turkey with honey. Using a wide metal spatula, pat the bread crumb mixture evenly onto bird. Cut

band of skin or string between the drumsticks so thighs will cook evenly. Arrange pears around turkey on broiler pan. Brush pears with olive oil. Continue to roast until a thermometer registers 180° in center of one of the inside thigh muscles (about 15 to 30 minutes more).

6 Remove turkey from oven. Remove onion and herbs from cavity. Cover and let stand for 15 to 20 minutes before carving. Serve with pears. Makes 10 to 12 servings.

Standard Oven Method:

1. Preheat oven to 325°. Prepare recipe through Step 3. Roast turkey until thermometer registers 150° (about 2¼ hours).

2. Brush turkey with honey. Using a wide metal spatula, pat the bread crumb mixture evenly onto bird. Cut band of skin or string between the drumsticks so thighs will cook evenly.

3. Arrange pears in bottom of pan around turkey; brush pears with olive oil. Continue to roast until thermometer registers 180° in the center of one of the inside thigh muscles (about 30 to 45 minutes more). Remove turkey from oven. Remove onion and herbs from cavity. Cover and let stand 15 to 20 minutes before carving.

Nutrition Facts per serving: 471 cal., 22 g total fat (35 g sat. fat), 124 mg chol., 211 mg sodium, 20 g carbo., 2 g fiber, 44 g pro.
Daily Values: 4% vit. A, 5% vit. C, 6% calcium, 19% iron.

Turkey Roasting Guide

Here's a slice of Thanksgiving wisdom for you to pass down: For the best turkey, keep the oven shut. Baste if you wish, but remember that slow, steady heat will coax maximum flavor out of the bird and produce the golden, crackly skin that's the hallmark of great cooking.

Buying the turkey

With birds that weigh 12 pounds or less, allow 1 pound per person. With birds over 12 pounds, which are meatier, count on ¾ pound per serving. For boneless turkey breast, you should figure ½ pound per person. If you want leftovers, buy a bird 2 to 4 pounds larger.

Look for the "sell by" date on the label of fresh turkeys. This date is the last day it should be sold. The unopened turkey should maintain its optimal quality and be safe to use for 1 or 2 days after the "sell by" date. For frozen turkeys, the package should be clean, undamaged, and free of frost.

Thawing safely

For a whole frozen turkey, leave the bird in its wrapping; place on a tray in the refrigerator for 2 to 5 days. Plan on 24 hours for every 5 pounds; don't count the day you'll be roasting. For instance, a 15-pound bird for Thanksgiving should start thawing Sunday night. Thawed birds will keep 1 or 2 days if refrigerated.

The bird is thawed and ready for roasting when the giblets can be removed easily and there are no ice crystals in the body or neck cavities. (If the center is still frozen, the bird will cook unevenly.) If your turkey is not completely thawed on the day you plan to roast it, place the bird still wrapped, if possible, in a clean sink full of cold water. Change the water every 30 minutes. Do not thaw at room temperature, in the microwave, or in warm water; those methods will allow harmful bacteria to grow quickly to dangerous food-poisoning levels. After thawing, remove giblets and neck from the interior. Rinsing is not necessary and can spread bacteria. Pat dry with paper towels.

Safe stuffing

Because stuffing comes in contact with the raw bird, it must be cooked to 165°. If you don't have a meat thermometer, consider cooking the stuffing in a covered casserole alongside the turkey rather than in the bird. To stuff, first measure out the amount of stuffing that will go into the bird, allowing ¾ cup per pound of bird. (That's 11 cups for a 15-pound bird.) Release drumsticks from band of skin, unhooking the tail or leg clamp if one is provided. The clamp may be removed if you prefer not to use it. Spoon some stuffing loosely into neck cavity. Pull the neck skin over stuffing; fasten to turkey's back with a short skewer.

Loosely spoon stuffing into the body cavity; do not pack, or stuffing may not be cooked by the time the turkey is done. Spoon remaining stuffing into a casserole; cover and chill until ready to bake. (If you prefer not to stuff the bird, place quartered onions and celery in the body cavity to add flavor to the drippings for gravy. Pull the neck skin to back; fasten with a short skewer.)

Tuck the drumsticks under the band of skin that crosses the tail, or reset into leg clamp. If there isn't a band or if you've removed the clamp, tie drumsticks to tail using kitchen string. Twist wing tips under the back.

Oven roasting

Place oven rack in lowest position; preheat oven to 325°. Place turkey, breast side up, on a rack in a shallow pan. To enhance browning, brush with cooking oil. Push a meat thermometer into the center of an inside thigh muscle, not touching bone. Cover turkey loosely with foil, pressing it over drumsticks and neck. Roast, using timings in the chart on page 252 as a guide. Since many turkeys are self-basting, it is not necessary to baste, but it will add flavor.

When the bird has been in the oven for two-thirds of the time shown on the chart, cut skin or string between drumsticks. Remove foil the last 30 to 45 minutes. When done, the thigh meat should be 180° and the stuffing should be at least 165°. Check with a meat thermometer. The temperature of the meat will rise about 5° after the bird comes out of the oven.

If you don't have a thermometer, use these tests: The drumsticks should move very easily in their sockets, and their thickest parts should feel soft when pressed. In addition, juices from the thigh should run clear when pierced deeply with a long-tined fork. Remove from the oven and cover loosely with foil. Let stand 20 minutes. Release legs from leg clamp, if present. To avoid burn, do not remove clamp until bird has cooled slightly. Remove stuffing before carving.

Leftovers

Refrigerate turkey within 2 hours after it comes out of the oven. Turkey and stuffing may be covered and refrigerated separately for up to 2 days.

Chestnut-Carrot Sipping Soup

This soup can be made ahead through Step 2. Refrigerate, covered; then reheat. Prepare the foamy cream topping just before serving.

Prep: 30 minutes **Cook:** 35 minutes

4½ cups coarsely chopped carrots
2 14½-oz. cans reduced-sodium chicken broth
1 10-oz. can whole, peeled chestnuts packed in water, drained
1 cup chopped onion
¾ tsp. ground ginger
¼ tsp. pepper
2 cups half-and-half, light cream, or fat-free milk
2 Tbsp. dry sherry (optional)
Chive stems (optional)

1 In a large saucepan or Dutch oven combine carrots, chicken broth, chestnuts, onion, ginger, and pepper. Bring to boiling; reduce heat. Simmer, covered, about 30 minutes or until chestnuts and carrots are very tender. Cool slightly.

2 In a blender container or food processor bowl blend or process mixture, one-third at a time, until nearly smooth. Return all to saucepan. Stir in 1 cup of the half-and-half, light cream, or fat-free milk and, if desired, sherry; heat through.

3 Meanwhile, in a small saucepan over medium heat warm the remaining half-and-half until small bubbles form around edge of pan.

Remove from heat. Using a rotary beater, carefully beat the half-and-half until foamy.

4 To serve, divide soup among ten to twelve 6-ounce heat-proof cups; top with the foamed cream. If desired, add chives. Makes 10 to 12 side-dish servings.

Nutrition Facts per serving: 152 cal., 6 g total fat (4 g sat. fat), 18 mg chol., 252 mg sodium, 21 g carbo., 2 g fiber, 4 g pro.
Daily Values: 143% vit. A, 23% vit. C, 7% calcium, 4% iron.

LOW FAT

Two-Bite Veggie Wraps

Italian parsley leaves and carrot and green onion strips accent each pastry appetizer.

Prep: 45 minutes **Bake:** Advantium™ oven, 7 minutes per batch; standard oven, 11 minutes per batch

6 sheets frozen phyllo dough (17×12-inch rectangles), thawed
⅓ cup butter, melted
½ cup loosely packed fresh Italian parsley leaves
4 carrots, cut into matchstick-size strips (about 2 cups)
6 green onions, coarsely chopped

1 Unroll phyllo dough; cover with plastic wrap. Remove one sheet and place on cutting board or flat surface; brush lightly with melted butter. (Keep remaining phyllo covered while working.) Arrange one-third of parsley leaves in a single layer over phyllo. Place another phyllo sheet on top of the first; brush

with some of the melted butter. Cut phyllo in half crosswise (making 8½×12-inch rectangles).

2 Lay one-sixth of the carrot strips, end to end, across one 12-inch side of phyllo; sprinkle with one-sixth of the onion. Starting with the 12-inch side, roll phyllo up into a spiral. Cut the phyllo roll into 4 diagonal pieces, each about 3 inches long. Repeat with other half of phyllo.

3 Repeat the process with remaining four sheets of phyllo, butter, parsley, green onion, and carrot, making a total of 24 wraps. Brush any remaining butter on top of appetizers.

Advantium™ Oven Method:
Arrange half the appetizers on the black metal tray (cover remaining appetizers with plastic wrap; set aside). Bake in Advantium oven at U=5, L=1, M=2 for 7 to 8 minutes or until golden. Transfer to clean white paper towels; let stand 1 minute. Serve warm, or cool on wire rack. Repeat with remaining appetizers. Makes 24.

Standard Oven Method:
Place appetizers on baking sheet. Bake in a 375° oven for 11 to 13 minutes or until golden brown. Transfer to clean white paper towels; let stand 1 minute. Serve warm, or cool on a wire rack.

Nutrition Facts per appetizer: 44 cal., 3 g total fat (2 g sat. fat), 7 mg chol., 55 mg sodium, 4 g carbo., 1 g fiber, 1 g pro.
Daily Values: 29% vit. A, 5% vit. C, 1% calcium, 2% iron.

Seed Rolls with Dipping Oils

Serving all three of the oils creates a fall harvest of color and flavor.

Prep: 30 minutes Bake: convection oven, 5 minutes; standard oven, 8 minutes

- ¼ cup flax seed, poppy seed, sesame seed, fennel seed, and/or caraway seed
- 2 8-oz. pkg. brown-and-serve hearth rolls
- 1 egg white, slightly beaten
- ½ cup purchased roasted garlic-flavored oil, 1 recipe Roasted Red Pepper Oil (see below), and/or 1 recipe Cilantro Oil (see right)

1 Preheat convection oven to 350° or standard oven to 375°. In a small bowl stir together desired seeds. Place rolls on a cookie sheet. Brush tops of rolls with egg white. Sprinkle seed mixture over rolls.

2 Bake for 5 to 7 minutes in convection oven or 8 to 10 minutes in standard oven. If desired, keep rolls warm in warming drawer. Serve with desired dipping oils. Makes 24 rolls.

Nutrition Facts per 2 rolls plus garlic-flavored oil: 205 cal., 13 g total fat (2 g sat. fat), 0 mg chol., 202 mg sodium, 20 g carbo., 2 g fiber, 4 g pro.
Daily Values: 7% calcium, 8% iron.

Roasted Red Pepper Oil

In the bowl of a small food processor place ½ cup olive oil and ½ cup drained, bottled roasted red sweet pepper. Cover and process until nearly smooth. Strain through a fine mesh strainer lined with a double thickness of 100-percent cotton cheesecloth. Cover; chill up to 24 hours. Makes ½ cup.

Cilantro Oil

Place 1½ cups firmly packed fresh cilantro leaves and stems (about 2 ounces) in a small bowl. Cover with boiling water. Let stand 30 seconds. Drain. Place the cilantro in the bowl of a small food processor. Add ½ cup olive oil and a dash salt. Cover and process until nearly smooth. Place mixture in a small saucepan; bring mixture to simmering. Simmer for 1 minute. Strain through a fine mesh strainer lined with a double thickness of 100-percent cotton cheesecloth. Cover; chill up to 24 hours. Makes ½ cup.

Warm Sweet Potato And Spinach Salad

The vegetables and hot dressing cook just as well in a very large skillet should you not have a wok. (See the photograph on page 279.)

Prep: 20 minutes Cook: 14 minutes

- 2 Tbsp. olive oil
- 2 oz. Genoa salami, finely chopped
- 5 cups cubed, peeled sweet potatoes (1¾ lb.)
- 2 cloves garlic, minced
- 1 medium tart apple, peeled, cored, and coarsely shredded
- ⅔ cup apple juice
- 3 Tbsp. cider vinegar
- 1 Tbsp. olive oil
- ¼ tsp. ground allspice
- ¼ tsp. coarsely ground pepper
- ⅛ tsp. ground cloves
- 8 cups fresh baby spinach
  Thinly sliced red onion

1 In a wok or a very large skillet heat the 2 tablespoons olive oil. Cook and stir salami in hot oil about 1 minute or until crisp and brown. Using a slotted spoon, remove salami from wok; drain on paper towels.

TEST KITCHEN TIP

Tasty, Toasty Nuts

Nuts are naturally rich and tasty right from the shell, but their flavor can be enhanced by a simple toasting step. Here's how to do it:

Spread the nuts in a single layer in a shallow baking pan. Bake them in a 350° oven for 5 to 10 minutes or until the nuts are light golden brown, watching them carefully and stirring once or twice so they don't burn.

Nuts also can be "toasted" in the microwave. Place nuts in a 2-cup measure. Cook, uncovered, on 100% power (high) until they are light golden brown, stirring after 2 minutes, then stirring every 30 seconds. Allow 2 to 3 minutes for ½ cup almonds or pecans; 2 to 3 minutes for 1 cup almonds; 3 to 4 minutes for 1 cup pecans; 3 to 4 minutes for ½ cup raw peanuts or walnuts; and 3½ to 5 minutes for 1 cup raw peanuts or walnuts. Allow the nuts to cool on paper towels. Nuts will continue to toast as they stand.

2 Add sweet potatoes, garlic, and ½ teaspoon *salt* to wok. Cook and stir constantly over medium to medium-high heat 12 to 14 minutes or until potatoes are tender. Transfer to a large bowl; add apple to potatoes. Toss gently to combine; spoon into a heatproof bowl. Keep warm.

3 Combine apple juice, vinegar, the 1 tablespoon olive oil, allspice, pepper, and cloves. Carefully add to wok; bring to boiling. Divide spinach among ten to twelve salad plates. Spoon potato mixture over spinach. Drizzle hot dressing over salads. Top with red onion slices. Sprinkle salami over all. Makes 10 to 12 servings.

Nutrition Facts per serving: 151 cal., 6 g total fat (1 g sat. fat), 4 mg chol., 260 mg sodium, 21 g carbo., 5 g fiber, 3 g pro.
Daily Values: 133% vit. A, 26% vit. C, 4% calcium, 12% iron.

Caramelized Oranges

The citrus slices glisten from the ginger-flavored poaching syrup. (See the photograph on page 278.)

Prep: 50 minutes **Cook:** 10 minutes
Chill: up to 24 hours

- 10 to 12 medium oranges or blood oranges
- 1½ cups sugar
- 1 cup freshly brewed hot tea
- 2 Tbsp. finely snipped crystallized ginger
- ½ tsp. vanilla
- 1 recipe Meringue Cookies (see right) (optional)

1 Finely shred 1 teaspoon of orange peel; set aside. Using a sharp knife, remove and discard the peel and white membrane from the oranges. Place the peeled oranges in a large bowl and set aside.

2 In a large heavy skillet heat the 1½ cups sugar over medium-high heat until sugar begins to melt, shaking skillet occasionally to heat sugar evenly. Do not stir. Once sugar starts to melt, reduce heat to medium-low; cook for 5 to 6 minutes or until sugar is melted and turns a deep golden brown, stirring as needed with a wooden spoon. Do not overcook. Remove from heat.

3 Very slowly, carefully stir the hot tea into caramelized sugar. If necessary, return to heat; cook until any hard sugar particles dissolve. Cool. Stir in shredded orange peel, crystallized ginger, and vanilla. Spoon mixture over oranges in the bowl. Toss to coat. Cover and chill up to 24 hours. Stir again before serving.

4 To serve, slice each orange crosswise, then reassemble in individual dessert dishes. Divide syrup evenly among dishes. If desired, serve with Meringue Cookies. Makes 10 to 12 servings.

Nutrition Facts per serving: 149 cal., 0 g total fat, 0 mg chol., 2 mg sodium, 38 g carbo., 2 g fiber, 1 g pro.
Daily Values: 1% vit. A, 54% vit. C, 2% calcium, 10% iron.

Meringue Cookies

To get a head start on these sweet treats, bake them up to three days ahead and store undipped cookies in a tightly covered container. Dip each one in the melted chocolate an hour or two before serving. (See the photograph on page 278.)

Prep: 20 minutes **Bake:** convection oven, 10 minutes; standard oven, 20 minutes
Dry: 30 minutes

- 2 egg whites
- ¼ tsp. cream of tartar
- 1⅓ cups sifted powdered sugar
- ½ cup semisweet chocolate pieces
- ½ tsp. shortening

1 Let egg whites stand in a large mixing bowl at room temperature for 30 minutes. Line a very large cookie sheet with parchment paper or foil; set aside.

2 Add cream of tartar to egg whites. Beat with an electric mixer on medium speed until soft peaks form (tips curl). Add powdered sugar, 1 tablespoon at a time, beating well after each addition. Beat for 6 to 7 minutes on high speed until stiff peaks form (tips stand straight) and sugar is almost dissolved.

3 Preheat convection or standard oven to 300°. Spoon meringue mixture into a self-sealing plastic bag. Snip off one corner. Pipe 20 to 24 designs about 1½ to 2 inches long and 1½ inches apart onto prepared cookie sheet. Bake in a convection oven for 10 minutes or in a standard oven for 20 minutes. Turn off oven. Let shells dry in oven, with door closed, for 30 minutes.

4 Transfer cookies to a wire rack and let cool. Place in a covered container and store at room temperature up to 3 days.

5 To dip cookies, in a small saucepan combine chocolate pieces and shortening. Stir over low heat until chocolate is melted. Dip one edge or tip of each meringue cookie into melted chocolate. Place on waxed paper until chocolate is set. Makes 20 to 24 cookies.

Nutrition Facts per cookie: 100 cal., 2 g total fat (1 g sat. fat), 0 mg chol., 11 mg sodium, 16 g carbo., 1 g fiber, 1 g pro.
Daily Values: 5% iron.

Celebration Cake

A combination of cream, sour cream, and sugar whips into a wonderfully rich and fluffy frosting. (See the photograph on page 281.)

Prep: 45 minutes **Bake:** convection oven, 25 minutes; standard oven, 30 minutes
Cool: 1 hour

- 2 cups all-purpose flour
- 2 cups granulated sugar
- 1 tsp. baking powder
- 1 tsp. baking soda
- 1½ tsp. apple pie spice

¼ tsp. salt
2 cups coarsely shredded carrots
1 cup coarsely shredded apple
¾ cup cooking oil
4 eggs
½ cup chopped nuts
1 cup whipping cream
1 8-oz. carton dairy sour cream
2 Tbsp. brown sugar
1 tsp. vanilla
¼ cup coarsely crushed purchased apple chips
Whole purchased apple chips (optional)
3 5- to 6-inch-long cinnamon sticks (optional)

1 Preheat convection oven to 325° or standard oven to 350°. Grease and lightly flour two 9×1½-inch round baking pans; set aside.

2 In a large mixing bowl combine flour, granulated sugar, baking powder, baking soda, apple pie spice, and salt. Add shredded carrots, shredded apple, cooking oil, and eggs. Beat with an electric mixer on low speed until combined. Beat for 1 minute on medium speed. Stir in nuts. Pour batter into prepared pans, spreading evenly.

3 Bake cake layers in a convection oven about 25 minutes, or bake in a standard oven about 30 minutes or until a wooden toothpick inserted near the center comes out clean. Let cool in pans on wire racks for 10 minutes. Remove cakes from pans and cool completely on wire racks.

4 For frosting, in a large food processor bowl place the whipping cream, sour cream, brown sugar, and vanilla. Cover and process for 2 to

2½ minutes or until stiff peaks form (tips stand straight), stopping to scrape down sides every 30 seconds. (Or, place ingredients in a large mixing bowl. Beat with an electric mixer on medium speed until stiff peaks form.)

5 To assemble cake, place one cake layer on a serving plate. Spread about ¾ cup of the frosting on top of the first cake layer. Sprinkle on the crushed apple chips. Top with second cake layer; frost top and sides of cake

with remaining frosting. If desired, decorate cake with whole apple chips and cinnamon sticks. Store in the refrigerator. Makes 12 servings.

Nutrition Facts per serving: 510 cal., 31 g total fat (10 g sat. fat), 107 mg chol., 235 mg sodium, 56 g carbo., 2 g fiber, 6 g pro.
Daily Values: 62% vit. A, 4% vit. C, 8% calcium, 9% iron.

TEST KITCHEN TIP

High Altitude Cooking

Adapting recipes for high altitudes is challenging. There are no magic formulas, but these tips can help minimize the guesswork. Because air pressure is low at high altitudes, baked goods tend to stick in the pans, be drier and dry out quickly, and rise too fast. Liquids boil at lower temperatures at high altitudes, so foods take longer to cook on the stove top.

Baking
Grease and flour baking pans well to minimize sticking. Take care not to overbake, promptly unmold baked goods from pans after 5 minutes of cooling, and wrap baked goods airtight when barely cool to prevent them from drying out.

For cakes and muffins leavened with baking powder or baking soda, adjust the leavening, liquid, and sugar amounts according to the following chart.

ALTITUDE	3,000 ft.	5,000 ft.	7,000 ft.
LIQUID Add for each cup	1 to 2 Tbsp.	2 to 4 Tbsp.	3 to 4 Tbsp.
SUGAR Decrease for each cup	up to 1 Tbsp.	up to 2 Tbsp.	1 to 3 Tbsp.
BAKING POWDER Decrease for each teaspoon	⅛ Tbsp.	⅛ to ¼ Tbsp.	¼ Tbsp.

To slow the leavening action, use eggs and liquids cold. Don't overbeat eggs. Angel food cakes overexpand if whites are beaten according to sea-level directions. For best results, beat whites to soft rather than stiff peaks.

Increasing the oven temperature by 25° may help.

RANGE-TOP COOKING
Increase the cooking time rather than the temperature, as foods may scorch easily. Add water as necessary.

For deep-fat fried foods, lower the temperature of the fat 3° for each 2,000 feet above sea level.

For candies, frostings, and jellies, decrease the temperature 2° for each 1,000 feet above sea level.

Browned Butter Bread Pudding

To make dry bread cubes, spread the cubes out on a large baking sheet. Let them stand, uncovered, on a kitchen counter overnight, stirring occasionally. (See the photograph on page 278.)

Prep: 40 minutes **Cook:** steamer, 45 minutes; standard oven, 40 minutes

       Nonstick cooking spray
  8 cups 1-inch cubes dry, sweet egg bread (such as challah or Hawaiian)
  1 cup chopped pitted dates
  ¾ cup butter
  6 eggs, beaten
  3 cups milk
  ⅓ cup granulated sugar
  1 Tbsp. vanilla
  ¼ tsp. ground nutmeg
  ¼ tsp. ground cinnamon
  2 Tbsp. coarsely chopped toasted hazelnuts (filberts)
  1 recipe Browned Butter Sauce (see right)

1 Coat steamer pan or a 2-quart rectangular baking dish with nonstick cooking spray; set aside. In a very large bowl combine the bread cubes and dates; set aside.

2 In a small skillet heat and stir butter until browned. Remove from heat. Place ¼ cup of the melted butter in a large mixing bowl (set remaining butter aside for sauce). Beat in eggs, milk, granulated sugar, vanilla, nutmeg, and cinnamon until combined. Pour egg mixture over bread mixture, tossing to coat well.

3 Turn the bread mixture into prepared steamer pan or baking dish. If using the steamer, cover tightly with foil. Cook using steamer or oven method below.

4 Remove steamer pan from steamer unit or baking dish from oven; cool slightly. Sprinkle bread pudding with hazelnuts. Pass Browned Butter Sauce. Makes 8 to 10 servings.

Steamer Method:

Fill steamer to first water mark and insert pan of pudding. Cover with lid and set to steam setting. Cook about 45 minutes or until a knife inserted near the center comes out clean.

Standard Oven Method:

Preheat oven to 350°. Place baking dish on a baking sheet. Bake, uncovered, for 40 to 45 minutes or until a knife inserted near the center comes out clean.

Browned Butter Sauce

In a small bowl stir together the reserved browned butter (approximately ½ cup) 2 cups sifted powdered sugar, 2 tablespoons milk, and ¼ teaspoon vanilla until smooth. (Sauce will be thick but will melt on the warm pudding.)

Nutrition Facts per serving: 627 cal., 28 g total fat (15 g sat. fat), 243 mg chol., 544 mg sodium, 81 g carbo., 3 g fiber, 14 g pro.
Daily Values: 31% vit. A, 2% vit. C, 20% calcium, 15% iron.

PRIZE WINNER

Salmon Croustades

Meredith Kornfeld
San Rafael, California
$200—Holiday Appetizers

Prep: 20 minutes **Broil:** 2 minutes

  24 slices light party rye or ½-inch-thick baguette slices

APPETIZER MENU

- **Salmon Croustades (see below, left)**

- **Prosciutto-Arugula Roll-Ups (see page 259)**

- **Assorted cheeses with pear and apple slices and grapes**

- **White wine or champagne**

  1 large ripe avocado, halved, seeded, and peeled
  3 Tbsp. capers, drained
  1 Tbsp. lemon juice
  4 to 6 oz. thinly sliced smoked salmon (lox-style)
  1 cup loosely packed arugula leaves
  ½ cup thinly sliced quartered red onion
       Freshly ground pepper

1 Preheat broiler. Arrange bread slices in a single layer on a 17×14-inch ungreased baking sheet. Broil 3 to 4 inches from heat for 1 to 2 minutes per side or until lightly toasted.

2 In a small bowl mash avocado. Stir in capers and lemon juice. Spread avocado mixture on one side of each bread slice (about 1 rounded teaspoon per slice). Layer salmon, arugula, and onion slices over avocado mixture. Sprinkle with pepper. Serve at once. Makes 24 appetizers.

Nutrition Facts per appetizer: 44 cal., 2 g total fat (0 g sat. fat), 1 mg chol., 190 mg sodium, 5 g carbo., 1 g fiber, 2 g pro.
Daily Values: 1% vit. A, 2% vit. C, 1% calcium, 2% iron.

Italian-Style Wontons

Each crispy little triangle oozes with a mozzarella cheese filling.

Prep: 30 minutes
Cook: 1 minute per batch

- ½ cup finely shredded mozzarella cheese (2 oz.)
- ¼ cup snipped fresh basil
- ¼ cup finely chopped walnuts
- 3 Tbsp. oil-packed dried tomatoes, drained and finely chopped
- 2 Tbsp. finely chopped pitted ripe olives
- 1 green onion, thinly sliced
- 24 wonton wrappers
  Cooking oil or shortening for deep-fat frying
- ¾ cup bottled marinara sauce (optional)

1 Preheat oven to 300°. In a small bowl stir together mozzarella cheese, basil, walnuts, dried tomatoes, ripe olives, and green onion.

2 For each wonton, place one wonton wrapper on a flat surface with one corner toward you. Spoon a rounded teaspoon of filling just below the center of the wonton wrapper. Fold the bottom point over the filling and tuck it under the filling. Roll the wonton wrapper once to cover filling, leaving about 1 inch unrolled at the top of the wrapper. Moisten the right corner with water. Grasp right and left corners and bring them toward you below the filling. Overlap the left corner over the right corner. Press firmly to seal.

3 In a heavy saucepan or deep-fat fryer heat 2 inches of oil to 365°. Fry wontons, a few at a time, for 1 to 2½ minutes or until golden brown. Drain on paper towels. Keep warm in oven while frying the remainder. If desired, serve with warmed marinara sauce. Makes 24.

Nutrition Facts per wonton: 81 cal., 6 g total fat (1 g sat. fat), 3 mg chol., 63 mg sodium, 5 g carbo., 0 g fiber, 1 g pro.
Daily Values: 1% vit. A, 2% vit. C, 2% calcium, 2% iron.

LOW FAT

Prosciutto-Arugula Roll-Ups

The prosciutto must be sliced thin enough to roll up easily but not so thin that it tears or shreds when separating the slices. Ask your butcher to cut 8 slices that measure 9×3 inches and are about 1⁄16 of an inch thick.

Prep: 30 minutes **Chill:** up to 6 hours

- 1 5-oz. container semi-soft cheese with garlic and herb
- 2 oz. soft goat cheese (chèvre)
- ⅓ cup toasted pine nuts or chopped toasted almonds
- 4 oz. thinly sliced prosciutto (8 slices)
- 1½ cups arugula or spinach leaves, stems removed (about 2½ oz.)

1 Stir together semi-soft cheese, goat cheese, and pine nuts or almonds. Spread about 2 tablespoons cheese mixture over each prosciutto slice. Top each with arugula or spinach leaves. Roll up each slice from a short side. Cut into ½-inch-thick slices. Serve immediately or cover and chill up to 6 hours. Makes about 48 slices.

Nutrition Facts per slice: 33 cal., 3 g total fat (1 g sat. fat), 4 mg chol., 55 mg sodium, 0 g carbo., 0 g fiber, 2 g pro.
Daily Values: 1% vit. A, 1% calcium, 1% iron.

LOW FAT

Greek Salad Bites

For ultimate impact, serve these cucumber stacks just as soon as you're done assembling.

Prep: 15 minutes **Chill:** 2 hours

- 1 cup crumbled feta cheese (4 oz.)
- ½ cup dairy sour cream
- ¼ cup snipped fresh parsley
- 2 Tbsp. oil-packed dried tomatoes, drained and finely chopped
- 2 cloves garlic, minced
- ½ tsp. cracked black pepper
- 1½ medium cucumbers
- ¼ cup finely shredded fresh basil
- ¼ cup chopped pitted kalamata olives

1 In a small bowl stir together feta cheese, sour cream, parsley, dried tomatoes, garlic, and pepper. Cover and chill at least 2 hours.

2 Using a sharp knife, trim the ends from cucumbers; discard ends. Bias-slice the cucumbers into ¼-inch-thick slices. Spoon 1½ teaspoons cheese mixture onto each cucumber slice. Arrange cucumber slices on a serving platter.

3 In a small bowl combine basil and olives. Spoon some of the mixture over each cucumber slice. Serve immediately. Makes 30 appetizers.

Nutrition Facts per appetizer: 22 cal., 2 g total fat (1 g sat. fat), 5 mg chol., 57 mg sodium, 1 g carbo., 0 g fiber, 1 g pro.
Daily Values: 2% vit. A, 2% vit. C, 3% calcium, 1% iron.

- **Salad of mixed greens, fresh pear slices, chopped shallots, and a fruit vinaigrette**

- **Roasted pork loin**

- **Stuffing with Root Vegetables (see below, right)**

- **Steamed green beans drizzled with butter and sprinkled with toasted almonds and finely shredded lemon peel**

- **Cranberry Tarts (see page 268)**

PRIZE WINNER

Mushroom Stuffing

Marnie Jubelirer Green
Martinez, California
$200—Stuffings and Dressings

Prep: 25 minutes **Bake:** 35 minutes

¼	cup margarine or butter
6	cups sliced fresh shiitake and/or button mushrooms
¼	cup sliced green onions
2	tsp. soy sauce
2	tsp. Worcestershire sauce
½	tsp. dried rosemary, crushed
¼	tsp. pepper
5	cups herb-seasoned stuffing mix (about 8 oz.)
3	cups coarsely shredded carrots (6 medium)
1	to 1¼ cups water

1 In a large skillet melt the margarine or butter over medium heat. Add mushrooms. Cook about 5 minutes or until just tender, stirring occasionally. Add green onions during the last 1 minute of cooking. Remove from heat. Stir in soy sauce, Worcestershire sauce, rosemary, and pepper.

2 In a large bowl combine herb-seasoned stuffing mix, carrots, and mushroom mixture. Drizzle with enough of the 1 to 1¼ cups water to moisten.

3 Use to stuff one 11- to 12-pound turkey (see tip, page 261). Or, place in a 3-quart casserole. Bake, covered, in a 325° oven for 50 to 60 minutes or until heated through or in a 375° oven for 35 to 45 minutes or until heated through. (Internal temperature should register 165° with an instant-read thermometer.) Makes 10 to 12 servings.

Nutrition Facts per serving: 192 cal., 7 g total fat (3 g sat. fat), 13 mg chol., 541 mg sodium, 28 g carbo., 4 g fiber, 6 g pro.
Daily Values: 120% vit. A, 6% vit. C, 5% calcium, 10% iron.

Stuffing with Root Vegetables

Break away from traditional stuffing with this savory dish that's full of fresh vegetables—carrots, parsnips, celery, and onion.

Prep: 40 minutes **Bake:** 35 minutes

⅓	cup margarine or butter
1½	cups chopped carrots
1	cup chopped parsnips
1	cup chopped celery
1	cup chopped onion
¼	tsp. salt
¼	tsp. pepper
8	cups dry bread cubes (see tip, page 261)
½	cup snipped fresh parsley
½	to ¾ cup chicken broth
1	egg, beaten

1 Preheat oven to 325°. In a large skillet melt margarine or butter over medium heat. Add carrots, parsnips, celery, and onion. Cook, covered, for 15 to 20 minutes or until tender and lightly golden, stirring occasionally. Stir in salt and pepper.

2 In a large bowl combine bread cubes and parsley; add carrot mixture. In a small bowl combine ½ cup chicken broth and egg. Drizzle bread mixture with the broth mixture, tossing lightly. Drizzle with additional broth, if necessary, to desired moistness.

3 Transfer stuffing to a 2-quart casserole. Bake, covered, for 35 to 40 minutes or until heated through. (Internal temperature should register 165° with an instant-read thermometer.) Makes 8 to 10 servings.

Nutrition Facts per serving: 216 cal., 10 g total fat (5 g sat. fat), 49 mg chol., 433 mg sodium, 26 g carbo., 3 g fiber, 5 g pro.
Daily Values: 75% vit. A, 20% vit. C, 7% calcium, 10% iron.

Mushroom and Wild Rice Stuffing

You can also opt to stuff a 10- to 12-pound turkey with this stuffing. If you do, follow the roasting directions on the turkey packaging or see the tips on pages 252 and 253.

Prep: 55 minutes **Bake:** 25 minutes

½	cup wild rice, rinsed
1	14½-oz. can reduced-sodium chicken broth

2 cups sliced fresh mushrooms
½ cup chopped onion
2 Tbsp. margarine or butter
1½ cups herb-seasoned stuffing mix
½ cup chopped toasted walnuts
½ cup dried cranberries

1 In a medium saucepan combine uncooked wild rice and chicken broth. Bring to boiling; reduce heat. Simmer, covered, for 50 to 60 minutes or until rice is just tender. Remove from heat; do not drain.

2 Preheat oven to 325°. Meanwhile, in a large skillet cook mushrooms and onion in margarine or butter until tender; remove from heat. Stir in stuffing mix and undrained rice. Add toasted walnuts and cranberries. If mixture seems dry, stir in 1 to 2 tablespoons *water*.

3 Transfer stuffing to a 2-quart casserole. Bake, covered, for 25 to 30 minutes or until heated through. Makes 8 to 10 servings.

Nutrition Facts per serving: 187 cal., 8 g total fat (1 g sat. fat), 0 mg chol., 305 mg sodium, 25 g carbo., 3 g fiber, 5 g pro.
Daily Values: 3% vit. A, 3% vit. C, 3% calcium, 7% iron.

Fennel and Pine Nut Dressing

With its hint of lemon and rosemary, this tangy dressing is perfect paired with roasted leg of lamb or pan-fried lamb chops.

Prep: 30 minutes **Bake:** 55 minutes

1 1-lb. loaf sourdough bread, cut into ½-inch cubes (12 cups)

3 cups sliced fresh mushrooms
1 8-ounce fennel bulb, chopped (1 cup)
½ cup chopped onion
4 cloves garlic, minced
½ cup margarine or butter
½ cup pine nuts, toasted
1 tsp. dried rosemary, crushed
1 tsp. finely shredded lemon peel
¼ tsp. pepper
1 to 1½ cups reduced-sodium chicken broth
½ cup finely shredded Parmesan cheese

1 Preheat oven to 350°. Spread bread cubes in a large shallow baking pan. Bake, uncovered, about 20 minutes or until crisp, stirring once or twice. (You should have about 10 cups of dry cubes.)

2 Meanwhile, in a large skillet cook the mushrooms, fennel, onion, and garlic in margarine or butter over medium heat about 5 minutes or until tender. Transfer cooked vegetables to a very large bowl.

3 Stir pine nuts, rosemary, lemon peel, and pepper into vegetables in bowl. Add bread cubes, tossing to combine. Add enough chicken broth to moisten, tossing gently.

4 Transfer stuffing to a 3-quart casserole. Bake, covered, for 50 minutes. Sprinkle with Parmesan cheese. Bake, uncovered, about 5 minutes more or until heated through. Makes 12 to 16 servings.

Nutrition Facts per serving: 245 cal., 13 g total fat (6 g sat. fat), 26 mg chol., 413 mg sodium, 25 g carbo., 2 g fiber, 8 g pro.
Daily Values: 7% vit. A, 3% vit. C, 6% calcium, 10% iron.

TEST KITCHEN TIP
Stuffing Tips

● To make dry bread cubes for stuffing, cut bread into ½-inch-square pieces. (You'll need 12 to 14 slices of bread for 8 cups of dry cubes.) Spread in a single layer in a 15½×10½×2-inch baking pan. Bake in a 300° oven for 10 to 15 minutes or until dry, stirring twice; cool. (Bread will continue to dry and crisp as it cools.) Or, let stand, loosely covered, at room temperature for 8 to 12 hours.

● Never stuff a turkey or other poultry until just before you roast it.

● You'll need no more than ¾ cup stuffing for each pound of ready-to-cook turkey.

● Spoon the stuffing into the turkey loosely so that there will be room for it to expand during roasting. If the stuffing is too tightly packed, it will not reach a safe temperature by the time the turkey is done. Put remaining stuffing in a casserole and heat thoroughly.

● Stuffing temperatures should reach at least 165°. Since there is no visual doneness test, use a meat thermometer. Insert it through the body cavity into the thickest part of the stuffing and let it stand for 5 minutes. Or, after removing from the oven, use an instant-read or rapid-response thermometer to check the temperature of center of the stuffing.

● If desired, you can bake an entire recipe of stuffing in a casserole instead of using it to stuff a bird. Bake the casserole, covered, in a 325° oven for 40 to 45 minutes or in a 375° oven about 30 minutes. (These times may vary, depending on the specific recipe used. To be safe, always use an instant-read thermometer, as directed above.)

Food by Mail

Mail order is the convenient way to shop for everyone on your gift list, and food gifts avoid problems of color or fit. When it comes to ordering perishable food, though, an extra measure of care is in order.

Whether you are shopping from a mail-order catalog or a website, patronize only reputable companies. A complete address and phone number should be available. Call and talk directly to a customer service representative with any questions before placing your order.

You'll want to ask: How will the food be packaged and shipped? Will perishables be kept chilled in transit and arrive frozen or ready to cook? Will good-quality packaging be used so the food will arrive undamaged? What are the shipping and packaging costs? Will storage and preparation instructions be included with an order?

Insist on an exact delivery date so that the recipient can arrange to refrigerate the box that day. Companies may only ship on certain days, ship directly from the producer, or use a central warehouse. Have a street for your recipient because most companies will not deliver to post office boxes, and include a telephone number in case of delivery problems.

Write down the name of the customer service representative and your order number in case problems arise.

Price shop. There can be significant cost differences. You may save money by calling some food companies directly rather than going through gift catalog companies.

PRIZE WINNER

Apricot-Pecan Stuffing

Susan Runkle
Walton, Kentucky
$400—Stuffings and Dressings

Prep: 25 minutes **Bake:** 30 minutes

1　cup sliced leeks
½　cup chopped onion
¼　cup margarine or butter
2　medium apples, peeled (if desired), cored, and chopped
1　cup chopped pecans
¾　cup snipped dried apricots
½　tsp. ground nutmeg
4　cups dry whole wheat or white bread cubes (see tip, page 261)
1　Tbsp. snipped fresh rosemary or ½ tsp. dried rosemary, crushed
1　Tbsp. snipped fresh thyme or ½ tsp. dried thyme, crushed
1　Tbsp. snipped fresh parsley
½　to ¾ cup half-and-half or light cream
1　egg, beaten
1　tsp. salt
½　tsp. pepper

1 In a large skillet cook the leeks and onion over medium heat in hot margarine or butter until tender but not brown. Stir in apples, pecans, apricots, and nutmeg. Cook and stir for 3 minutes more.

2 In a large bowl toss together bread cubes, rosemary, thyme, parsley, and cooked onion mixture. In a small bowl combine ½ cup of the half-and-half, the egg, salt, and pepper. Add to bread mixture and stir gently to coat. Add enough additional cream, if necessary, to make of desired consistency.

3 Use to stuff an 8- to 10-pound turkey. Or, place in a greased 1½-quart casserole. Bake, covered, in a 325° oven for 25 minutes or in a 375° oven for 20 minutes. Uncover and bake an additional 10 to 15 minutes or until heated through. (Internal temperature should register 165° with an instant-read thermometer.) Makes 8 to 10 servings.

Nutrition Facts per serving: 299 cal., 20 g total fat (6 g sat. fat), 49 mg chol., 502 mg sodium, 30 g carbo., 6 g fiber, 6 g pro.
Daily Values: 18% vit. A, 9% vit. C, 7% calcium, 13% iron.

Southwestern Corn Bread Dressing

Prep: 40 minutes **Bake:** 1 hour
Stand: 20 minutes (to cool corn bread)

1　cup all-purpose flour
1　cup cornmeal
3　Tbsp. sugar
1　Tbsp. baking powder
½　tsp. salt
2　eggs, beaten
1　cup milk
¼　cup cooking oil
5　cups chopped yellow summer squash
1　cup chopped celery
¾　cup chopped green sweet pepper
½　cup chopped onion
⅓　cup margarine or butter
½　cup sliced pitted ripe olives
1　4-oz. can diced green chili peppers
1　10¾-oz. can condensed cream of mushroom soup
1　egg, beaten
½　to ¾ cup milk
¾　cup shredded Monterey Jack cheese with jalapeño peppers

1 Preheat oven to 425°. Grease the bottom and ½ inch up the sides of a 9×9×2-inch baking pan; set aside. In a medium bowl stir together the flour, cornmeal, sugar, baking powder, and salt. Make a well in the center of the dry mixture; set aside. Combine the 2 eggs, 1 cup milk, and cooking oil. Add egg mixture all at once to dry mixture. Stir just until moistened (batter should be lumpy). Spread batter in prepared pan. Bake about 20 minutes or until a toothpick inserted near center comes out clean. Cool completely in pan on a wire rack. Reduce oven temperature to 350°.

2 In a large saucepan cook the squash in a small amount of boiling water about 5 minutes or until just tender. Drain well and transfer to a very large bowl.

3 In a large skillet cook celery, sweet pepper, and onion in margarine or butter until tender. Add to squash in bowl along with olives and chili peppers. Stir together condensed soup, the 1 egg, and ½ cup of the milk. Add to squash mixture and mix well. Coarsely crumble corn bread. Add to squash mixture; stir gently to combine. If necessary add enough of the remaining milk to moisten.

4 Transfer mixture to a lightly greased 3-quart rectangular baking dish. Bake, covered, for 35 minutes. Uncover; sprinkle with cheese. Bake about 5 minutes more or until cheese melts. (Internal temperature should register 165° with an instant-read thermometer.) Serves 16 to 20.

Nutrition Facts per serving: 247 cal., 15 g total fat (7 g sat. fat), 65 mg chol., 517 mg sodium, 21 g carbo., 2 g fiber, 6 g pro.
Daily Values: 13% vit. A, 18% vit. C, 17% calcium, 7% iron.

Yam and Raisin Bread Stuffing

Prep: 30 minutes **Bake:** 40 minutes

- 2 medium sweet potatoes, peeled and cut into ½-inch pieces
- 1 cup chopped celery
- ½ cup chopped onion
- ¼ cup margarine or butter
- 2 tsp. poultry seasoning
- ⅛ tsp. ground cinnamon
- 6 cups dry raisin bread cubes (see tip, page 261)
- 2 to 4 Tbsp. water
- ¼ cup chopped pecans
- 1 Tbsp. sugar

1 Preheat oven to 375°. In a Dutch oven cook sweet potatoes, celery, and onion in hot margarine or butter for 3 to 4 minutes or until vegetables are crisp-tender. Stir in poultry seasoning, ¾ teaspoon *salt*, ¼ teaspoon *pepper*, and cinnamon. Add bread cubes, tossing to mix. Add 2 to 4 tablespoons water to reach desired moistness.

2 Transfer to a greased 2-quart casserole. Bake, covered, for 30 minutes. Meanwhile, combine pecans, sugar, and 2 teaspoons *water*; sprinkle over stuffing. Bake, uncovered, for 10 minutes more. Serve with roast chicken or pork. Makes 10 servings.

Nutrition Facts per serving: 154 cal., 8 g total fat (1 g sat. fat), 0 mg chol., 319 mg sodium, 20 g carbo., 2 g fiber, 3 g pro.
Daily Values: 52% vit. A, 9% vit. C, 3% calcium, 6% iron.

30 MINUTE, LOW FAT
Curried Cherry Pilaf

Start to finish: 25 minutes

- 1 8-oz. fennel bulb with top leaves
- ½ cup chopped onion
- 1 Tbsp. margarine or butter
- 1 14½-oz. can reduced-sodium chicken broth
- 1 cup long grain rice
- ½ cup water
- ½ tsp. curry powder
- ½ cup dried tart red cherries, halved

1 Cut off upper stalks of fennel, reserving the top feathery leaves. Remove wilted outer layer of stalks; cut off a thin layer from base. Wash fennel bulb and chop (should have about 1 cup).

2 In a medium saucepan cook chopped fennel and onion in margarine or butter about 3 minutes or until crisp-tender. Carefully stir in chicken broth, uncooked rice, water, and curry powder. Bring to boiling; reduce heat. Simmer, covered, about 15 minutes or until the rice is tender.

3 Stir in dried cherries and 1 tablespoon snipped feathery leaves of the fennel. Remove from heat. Cover and let stand 5 minutes. Makes 6 to 8 servings.

Nutrition Facts per serving: 177 cal., 2 g total fat (0 g sat. fat), 0 mg chol., 209 mg sodium, 35 g carbo., 5 g fiber, 4 g pro.
Daily Values: 8% vit. A, 4% vit. C, 2% calcium, 7% iron.

Breakfast Wraps

In keeping with the freshness that the spinach leaves and tomato give to this meal, choose a fresh tomato salsa—one from the refrigerated section of your grocery store or supermarket.

Start to finish: 20 minutes

- 4 6- to 8-inch flour tortillas
- 4 eggs
- ¼ cup milk
- ⅛ tsp. pepper
- 1 8-oz. pkg. brown-and-serve sausage patties, chopped
- ¼ cup chopped onion
- 1 Tbsp. margarine or butter
   Fresh spinach leaves
- 1 cup chopped tomato
   Salsa (optional)

1 Preheat oven to 350°. Wrap tortillas tightly in foil. Heat in oven for 10 minutes to soften.

2 Meanwhile, in a medium mixing bowl beat together the eggs, milk, and pepper; set aside. In a large skillet cook the sausage and onion in margarine or butter until onion is tender and sausage is brown. Add the egg mixture. Cook, without stirring, until the mixture begins to set on the bottom and around the edge. Using a spatula or large spoon, lift and fold the partially cooked eggs so the uncooked portion flows underneath. Continue cooking over medium heat for 2 to 3 minutes or until the eggs are cooked through but are still glossy and moist. Remove from heat.

3 Line warm tortillas with spinach leaves. Divide egg mixture among tortillas. Top egg mixture with tomatoes. Fold in one side of the tortilla to partially cover the filling.

Starting from an adjacent side, roll up. Serve immediately with salsa, if desired. Makes 4 servings.

Nutrition Facts per serving: 421 cal., 29 g total fat (10 g sat. fat), 269 mg chol., 963 mg sodium, 20 g carbo., 1 g fiber, 21 g pro.
Daily Values: 19% vit. A, 19% vit. C, 10% calcium, 15% iron.

Chorizo & Egg Stacks

Break out of the mold of thinking that eggs are just for breakfast. This Mexican-style entrée makes a great one-dish supper.

Start to finish: 30 minutes

- 6 oz. chorizo or bulk Italian sausage
- 6 eggs, beaten
- ¼ cup milk
- ½ tsp. salt
- ½ tsp. pepper
- 2 to 3 tsp. cooking oil (optional)
- ¾ cup milk
- 4 tsp. all-purpose flour
- ½ cup shredded Monterey Jack cheese or Monterey Jack cheese with jalapeño peppers (2 oz.)
- 4 5½-inch tostada shells
- 2 cups finely shredded lettuce
- 2 plum tomatoes, thinly sliced
- 1 small ripe avocado, halved, seeded, peeled, and sliced

1 In a large skillet cook chorizo or Italian sausage over medium heat until brown. Remove and drain on clean white paper towels.

2 In a medium bowl stir together the eggs, ¼ cup milk, salt, and pepper. If necessary, add 2 to 3 teaspoons cooking oil to skillet

to prevent sticking. Add egg mixture to skillet. Cook over medium heat, without stirring, until mixture begins to set on the bottom and around the edge. Using a spatula or large spoon, lift and fold partially cooked eggs so uncooked portion flows underneath. Continue cooking until eggs are just set. Remove from skillet.

3 Combine the ¾ cup milk, flour, and Monterey Jack cheese. Add to skillet. Cook and stir until thickened and cheese is melted. Gently stir in sausage and eggs; heat through.

4 To serve, place tostada shells on a large serving platter. Top each with the shredded lettuce, egg mixture, tomato slices, and avocado slices. Makes 4 servings.

Nutrition Facts per serving: 538 cal., 39 g total fat (13 g sat. fat), 374 mg chol., 1,120 mg sodium, 20 g carbo., 3 g fiber, 28 g pro.
Daily Values: 26% vit. A, 16% vit. C, 25% calcium, 17% iron.

TEST KITCHEN TIP

How to Cook a Pumpkin

If you would like to cook a fresh pumpkin for use in your holiday baking, here's how:

Cut a medium fresh pumpkin (about 6 pounds) into 5-inch-square pieces. Remove the seeds and fibrous strings. Arrange the pieces in a single layer, skin side up, in a large, shallow baking pan. Cover with foil. Bake in a 375° oven 1 to 1½ hours or until tender.

Scoop the pulp from the rind. Working with part of the pulp at a time, place pulp in a blender container or food processor bowl. Cover and blend or process until smooth. Place pumpkin in a cheesecloth-lined strainer, and press out liquid. Makes about 2 cups.

Pumpkin Crunch Coffee Cake

See the photograph on page 277.

Prep: 30 minutes **Bake:** 45 minutes
Cool: 45 minutes

- 1 **cup packed brown sugar**
- 1 **cup chopped walnuts**
- ¼ **cup all-purpose flour**
- ½ **tsp. ground nutmeg**
- ⅓ **cup butter, chilled**
- 1 **cup canned pumpkin**
- 1 **egg**
- ¼ **cup granulated sugar**
- ½ **tsp. ground nutmeg**
- ½ **cup butter, softened**
- ¾ **cup granulated sugar**
- 3 **eggs**
- 2 **cups all-purpose flour**
- 1½ **tsp. baking powder**
- ½ **tsp. baking soda**
- 1 **cup buttermilk or sour milk**

1 Preheat oven to 350°. Grease a 13×9×2-inch baking pan; set aside. For streusel, in a medium bowl combine brown sugar, walnuts, ¼ cup flour, and ½ teaspoon nutmeg. Using a pastry blender, cut in ⅓ cup chilled butter until crumbly; set aside.

2 For filling, in a medium bowl stir together pumpkin, 1 egg, ¼ cup granulated sugar, and ½ teaspoon nutmeg. Set aside.

3 In a large mixing bowl beat ½ cup butter for 30 seconds; gradually beat in ¾ cup granulated sugar until fluffy. Add 3 eggs, one at a time, beating well after each. Stir together the 2 cups flour, baking powder, baking soda, and ¼ teaspoon *salt*. Add flour mixture alternately with buttermilk to beaten pumpkin mixture. Spread half of the batter into the prepared baking pan. Sprinkle with half of the streusel. Add remaining batter, spreading evenly. Spoon on pumpkin mixture and sprinkle with remaining streusel.

4 Bake about 45 minutes or until a wooden toothpick inserted near center comes out clean. Cool on a wire rack at least 45 minutes. Serve warm or cool. Makes 12 servings.

Nutrition Facts per serving: 438 cal., 22 g total fat (10 g sat. fat), 109 mg chol., 288 mg sodium, 55 g carbo., 2 g fiber, 7 g pro.
Daily Values: 61% vit. A, 2% vit. C, 8% calcium, 12% iron.

LOW FAT

Quaker Bonnet Biscuits

Updated from a 1915 recipe in *Mary at the Farm* and *Book of Recipes,* these hat-shaped biscuits will remind you of tender yeast rolls. Don't worry that the tops of these biscuits are slightly off-center. It just adds to their old-fashioned charm. (See the photograph on page 283.)

Prep: 20 minutes **Rise:** 1½ hours
Bake: 13 minutes

- 1⅓ **cups warm milk (105° to 115°)**
- 1 **pkg. active dry yeast**
- 4 **cups all-purpose flour**
- ⅓ **cup butter, shortening, or lard**
- 2 **eggs, beaten**
- 1 **Tbsp. butter, melted**
- 1 **egg yolk**
- 1 **tsp. milk**

1 In a bowl combine warm milk and yeast; let stand about 5 minutes for yeast to soften.

2 In a large bowl combine flour and 1 teaspoon *salt.* Using a pastry blender, cut in the ⅓ cup butter,

Stack the smaller biscuit rounds slightly off-center on top of the larger rounds for a "bonnet" effect.

shortening, or lard until pieces are the size of small peas. Make a well in center; add yeast mixture and eggs. Stir until all the dough is moistened. Transfer the dough to a lightly greased bowl. Cover and let rise in a warm place until double in size (1 to 1¼ hours).

3 Lightly grease baking sheets; set aside. Turn dough out onto a well-floured surface. Knead 10 to 12 times. Roll dough to ¼-inch thickness. Cut dough with floured round cutters, making twenty-four 2½-inch rounds and twenty-four 2-inch rounds. Place the larger rounds on prepared baking sheets. Brush tops with melted butter. Top each with a smaller round (see photo, above), stacking slightly off-center. Cover and let rise in a warm place 30 minutes.

4 Preheat oven to 400°. Brush tops of biscuits with a mixture of egg yolk and 1 teaspoon milk. Bake for 13 to 15 minutes or until tops are golden. Serve warm. Makes 24.

Nutrition Facts per biscuit: 115 cal., 4 g total fat (2 g sat. fat), 36 mg chol., 142 mg sodium, 16 g carbo., 1 g fiber, 3 g pro.
Daily Values: 5% vit. A, 2% calcium, 6% iron.

Maple Sugar Biscuits

Imagine the sweetness of sugar infused with the flavor of natural maple syrup. Maple sugar is worth the effort to track down in specialty food stores or by mail order. (See the photograph on page 280.)

Prep: 15 minutes **Bake:** 12 minutes

  1 **8-oz. carton dairy sour cream**
  1 **egg, beaten**
  1 **cup granulated maple sugar or**
        ¾ cup granulated sugar and
        ¼ tsp. maple flavoring
  ½ **tsp. ground allspice**
  2¼ **cups all-purpose flour**
  ¾ **tsp. baking soda**
  ⅛ **tsp. salt**

1 Preheat oven to 375°. Grease a very large baking sheet; set aside.

2 In a large bowl combine sour cream, egg, maple sugar, and allspice. In a medium bowl stir together flour, baking soda, and salt. Add the flour mixture all at once to the sour cream mixture. Stir just until combined.

3 Turn dough out onto a well-floured surface. Knead 10 to 12 strokes. Pat or lightly roll dough to a ½-inch thickness. Cut dough with a floured 2½-inch round cutter. Place biscuits on prepared baking sheet.

4 Bake for 12 to 15 minutes or until bottoms are brown. Transfer to a wire rack to cool slightly. Serve warm. Makes 14 biscuits.

Nutrition Facts per biscuit: 148 cal., 4 g total fat (2 g sat. fat), 22 mg chol., 102 mg sodium, 25 g carbo., 1 g fiber, 3 g pro.
Daily Values: 4% vit. A, 2% calcium, 5% iron.

Dried Apple Cider Pie

You get a double-the-fruit flavor in this labor-saving dessert piled with apples that require no peeling. (See the photograph on page 1.)

Prep: 45 minutes **Bake:** 48 minutes

  2 **5-oz. pkg. dried apples (4 cups)**
  3½ **cups apple cider or apple juice**
  ¼ **cup sugar**
  ½ **tsp. ground cinnamon**
  ¼ **tsp. freshly grated nutmeg**
  1 **recipe Apple Pie Pastry**
        (see below, right)
  1 **Tbsp. butter**

1 Preheat oven to 400°. In a large saucepan combine dried apples and cider or juice. Bring to boiling; reduce heat. Simmer, covered, 15 minutes. Stir in sugar, cinnamon, and nutmeg. Simmer, uncovered, for 15 minutes (juices will be slightly thickened).

2 Meanwhile, prepare Apple Pie Pastry. Roll two-thirds of the pastry to a 12-inch circle. Transfer to a 9-inch pie plate. Trim pastry to ½ inch beyond edge of pie plate. Fold under extra pastry. Crimp edge as desired. Add prepared apple filling, spreading evenly. Dot with butter.

3 Cover edge of pie with foil. Bake for 20 minutes. Remove foil; bake 20 to 25 minutes more or until pastry is golden brown and apple edges begin to brown. Cool on a wire rack.

4 Roll remaining pastry into an oval about 6×4 inches. Cut into ½-inch-wide slivers (see Photo 1, top right). Place on a baking sheet; bake 8 to 10 minutes. Scatter slivers over pie before serving (see Photo 2, above right). Makes 8 servings.

1. Cut free-form shapes with a pastry wheel or a pizza cutter.

2. Artfully scatter the baked pastry pieces on top of the finished pie.

Apple Pie Pastry

In a medium bowl combine 1¾ cups all-purpose flour and ½ teaspoon salt. Using a pastry blender, cut in ½ cup shortening until pieces are the size of small peas. Using a total of 5 to 6 tablespoons cold water, sprinkle 1 tablespoon water over part of the mixture; gently toss with a fork. Push moistened dough to side of bowl. Repeat until all is moistened. Form into a ball.

Nutrition Facts per serving: 388 cal., 15 g total fat (4 g sat. fat), 4 mg chol., 199 mg sodium, 55 g carbo., 5 g fiber, 3 g pro.
Daily Values: 1% vit. A, 4% vit. C, 2% calcium, 12% iron.

Lemon Stack Pie

This make-ahead pie keeps well overnight. When you're ready to cut the stack, use a serrated knife to carefully cut through the layers using a sawing motion.

Prep: 90 minutes **Bake:** 20 minutes

3	cups all-purpose flour
¾	tsp. salt
¾	tsp. cream of tartar
¼	tsp. baking soda
1	cup shortening
8	to 10 Tbsp. cold water
1	cup butter, softened
1¾	cups granulated sugar
10	egg yolks
2	Tbsp. lemon juice
1	Tbsp. finely shredded lemon peel
1	cup packed brown sugar
½	cup whipping cream

1 Preheat oven to 450°. Line three 9-inch pie plates with foil, allowing foil to extend over the edges of each pie plate.* Set aside.

2 In a large bowl stir together the flour, salt, cream of tartar, and baking soda. Using a pastry blender, cut in the shortening until pieces are the size of small peas. Sprinkle 1 tablespoon of the water over part of the mixture; gently toss with a fork. Push moistened dough to one side of bowl. Repeat, using 1 tablespoon water at a time, until all the dough is moistened. Form dough into a ball. Divide dough into three equal portions.

3 On a lightly floured surface, roll one portion of dough to a 12-inch circle. Ease into a prepared 9-inch pie plate. Trim pastry to ½ inch beyond edge of pie plate. Fold under extra pastry. Crimp edge and prick pastry all over with the tines of a fork. Line pastry-lined pie plate with a double thickness of foil. Bake for 8 minutes. Remove foil. Bake 4 to 5 minutes more or until golden. Cool on a wire rack.

4 Roll out the remaining portions of dough to 10-inch circles. Ease each pastry circle into a prepared pie plate. Trim so that dough goes only ¾ inch up the sides of the pie plate. Prick pastry all over. Line pastry-lined pie plates with a double thickness of foil. Bake for 8 to 10 minutes or until golden. Cool on wire racks. Reduce oven temperature to 350°.

5 For filling, in a large mixing bowl beat butter with an electric mixer on medium to high speed for 30 seconds. Add granulated sugar and beat until fluffy. Add egg yolks, a few at a time, beating well after each addition. Beat in lemon juice. Stir in the lemon peel.

6 Divide mixture among the three baked crusts, spreading evenly. Bake about 20 minutes or until set and lightly browned on top. Cool on wire racks. When cool, use foil edges to carefully lift and remove pies from pie plates. Carefully peel away foil. Place larger pie on a serving plate. Carefully stack the remaining pies on top.

7 For frosting, in a medium saucepan stir together the brown sugar and whipping cream. Bring to boiling over medium-high heat, stirring constantly to dissolve sugar. Reduce heat to medium-low. Continue boiling at a moderate, steady rate, stirring occasionally, for 10 minutes. Remove pan from heat. Let cool for 5 minutes. Stir vigorously about 5 minutes or until mixture thickens and lightens in color.

TEST KITCHEN TIP

A Shred of Peel

Just a tiny bit of shredded lime, lemon, or orange peel delivers a burst of flavor to baked goods. If a recipe calls for shredded citrus peel, use only the colored surface of the peel, not the bitter-tasting, spongy, white pith. Hand graters and zesters are convenient, but you can also use a vegetable peeler to remove layers of peel. Finely mince the peel with a sharp kitchen knife. Prepare extra peel to keep on hand and freeze it in a resealable plastic bag.

8 Pour frosting over stacked pies, spreading to allow some of the frosting to flow down the sides. Cool. Serve at room temperature. Or, cover and chill up to 24 hours before serving. Makes 16 servings.

*Note: If you only have one pie plate, work with one portion of pastry dough at a time; cover remaining portions of dough. Roll out and bake fluted pastry shell in foil-lined pie plate as directed in Step 3. Cool thoroughly on a wire rack. Carefully remove baked shell from pie plate. Carefully peel away foil. Transfer pie shell to a large foil-lined baking sheet. Roll out and bake remaining two pastry shells, one at a time, lining the pie plate with foil each time. Place shells on foil-lined baking sheet. Fill and bake shells as directed.

Nutrition Facts per serving: 496 cal., 31 g total fat (14 g sat. fat), 176 mg chol., 266 mg sodium, 52 g carbo., 1 g fiber, 4 g pro.
Daily Values: 21% vit. A, 2% vit. C, 4% calcium, 9% iron.

TEST KITCHEN TIP

Alcohol-Free Cooking and Baking

Although the alcohol content of one serving of most foods is a fraction of that found in a typical beverage serving of alcohol, those wishing to avoid all alcohol can easily make substitutions in most recipes.

When making substitutions, keep the amount of liquid the same as what the recipe specifies. Do not increase the amount of eggs or fats for added moisture because that will adversely affect the outcome of the recipe.

For savory dishes and sauces, use a broth or an appropriate juice, such as tomato or orange. For sweet dishes, use extra milk, cream, yogurt, sour cream, or fruit juices.

Instead of sweet-flavor liqueurs, add a small amount of extract (¼ teaspoon of extract for every 2 tablespoons of liqueur) for flavoring and light-color corn syrup (1 tablespoon for every ¼ cup liquid) for sweetness; then make up the remaining liquid.

Here are a few specific substitution ideas:

Dry red wine
- beef, chicken, or vegetable broth or cooking liquid
- tomato juice
- grape or cranberry juice with a splash of lemon juice (1 tablespoon per ½ cup juice)
- diluted cider vinegar or red wine vinegar to taste

Dry white wine
- chicken or vegetable broth or cooking liquid
- ginger ale
- white grape juice
- diluted cider vinegar or white wine vinegar

Beer or ale
- chicken broth
- white grape juice
- ginger ale

Brandy, Cognac, or bourbon
- apple juice, white grape juice, peach juice, apricot juice, or pear juice with, if desired, vanilla or brandy extract
- apple cider

Rum
- white grape juice, pineapple juice, apple juice, or apple cider with, if desired, rum extract

Champagne
- ginger ale or sparkling apple juice

Amaretto
- apple juice with, if desired, almond extract

Kirsch
- cherry, raspberry, currant, grape, or boysenberry juice or syrup
- cherry cider

Cointreau, Grand Marnier, or orange liqueur
- frozen orange juice concentrate
- orange juice with, if desired, orange extract

Port, sweet sherry, Madeira, or Marsala
- orange, apple, or pineapple juice or cherry cider with, if desired, vanilla extract

Kahlua or coffee- or chocolate-flavor liqueur
- water or coffee with chocolate extract

Cranberry Tarts

Cranberries plus a handful of other ingredients make this filling amazingly simple. Your only challenge will be deciding whether to make individual tarts or one large tart. (See the photograph on page 2.)

Prep: 30 minutes **Bake:** 30 minutes

2	cups all-purpose flour
¼	tsp. salt
⅓	cup shortening
⅓	cup butter
6	to 7 Tbsp. cold water
⅓	cup water
2½	cups cranberries
2	Tbsp. dry red wine or orange juice
1	cup sugar
2	Tbsp. all-purpose flour
1	Tbsp. butter, cut up

1 Preheat oven to 375°. In a large bowl stir together the 2 cups flour and the salt. Cut in shortening and butter until pieces are the size of small peas. Sprinkle 1 tablespoon of the cold water over part of the mixture; gently toss with a fork. Push moistened dough to one side of bowl. Repeat, using 1 tablespoon water at a time, until all the dough is moistened.

2 Form dough into a ball. Divide dough into 8 portions. Roll each portion into a 5-inch circle. Line a 4-inch tart pan with removable bottom with one dough circle. Trim dough even with rim of tart pan. Repeat with remaining dough circles. (Or, if desired, roll dough to a 12-inch circle. Place in a 9½- to 10-inch tart pan with removable bottom. Trim dough even with the rim.)

3 For filling, in a large saucepan combine cranberries, ⅓ cup *water*, and the wine or juice. Bring to boiling.

Cook, stirring frequently, for 2 to 3 minutes or until berries pop. In a small bowl stir together the sugar and the 2 tablespoons flour. Add to hot cranberry mixture. Cook and stir until thickened and bubbly. Stir in butter until melted.

4 Spoon about ¼ cup filling into each individual tart. (Or spoon all of the filling into large tart.) Place tart(s) on a large baking sheet. Bake until filling is bubbly and edges of tart(s) are golden. Allow 30 minutes for individual tarts or 35 to 40 minutes for large tart. Place tart(s) on a wire rack to cool. Remove tart(s) from pans. Makes 8 servings.

Nutrition Facts per serving: 376 cal., 18 g total fat (8 g sat. fat), 26 mg chol., 180 mg sodium, 51 g carbo., 3 g fiber, 4 g pro.
Daily Values: 12% vit. A, 8% vit. C, 1% calcium, 9% iron.

Puffets

The original version of this recipe called for "butter the size of an egg" and other methods of measuring you might not recognize today. We've added dried cherries to give these treats a touch of tartness. (See the photograph on page 283.)

Prep: 20 minutes **Bake:** 20 minutes

   2 **cups all-purpose flour**
   1 **Tbsp. baking powder**
   1 **Tbsp. sugar**
   1 **egg, slightly beaten**
   1 **cup milk**
   3 **Tbsp. butter, melted**
   ¾ **cup snipped dried tart red cherries**
   2 **Tbsp. butter, melted**
   2 **Tbsp. sugar**
   ¼ **tsp. ground cinnamon**

1 Preheat oven to 400°. Grease twelve 2½-inch muffin cups; set aside. In a bowl combine flour, baking powder, 1 tablespoon sugar, and ¼ teaspoon *salt*. Make a well in center of flour mixture; set aside.

2 In a small bowl combine egg, milk, and the 3 tablespoons melted butter. Add to flour mixture along with cherries. Stir just until dry ingredients are moistened.

3 Divide batter among prepared muffin cups. Bake about 20 minutes or until tops are golden brown. Remove from pans. Brush tops of warm puffets with the 2 tablespoons melted butter. Dip tops in a mixture of 2 tablespoons sugar and cinnamon. Serve warm. Makes 12.

Nutrition Facts per puffet: 168 cal., 6 g total fat (4 g sat. fat), 33 mg chol., 216 mg sodium, 25 g carbo., 1 g fiber, 4 g pro.
Daily Values: 11% vit. A, 9% calcium, 5% iron.

Sweet Indian Pudding

A warm scoop of this cinnamon-molasses dessert is bound to banish all signs of holiday stress. Spoon up every last bit of flavor in the sweet syrup you'll find at the bottom of the baking dish. (See the photograph on page 280.)

Prep: 15 minutes **Bake:** 1¼ hours
Cool: 1 hour

   1 **cup milk**
   ⅓ **cup yellow cornmeal**
   2 **Tbsp. margarine or butter, cut up**
   ⅓ **cup molasses**
   ¼ **cup granulated sugar**
   ½ **tsp. ground ginger**
   ½ **tsp. ground cinnamon**
   2 **eggs, beaten**

EDITOR'S TIP

Old-Time Sweeteners

The gingerbread made in Europe in medieval times contained the familiar spices used in today's gingerbread but was sweetened with honey. The first gingerbread made in this country also was honey-sweetened, and the early settlers raided bee trees to harvest the valuable sweet.

After England acquired Jamaica, molasses produced from sugarcane was shipped to the American colonies in great quantities and became cheaper than honey. Only then did molasses become the most popular sweetener for gingerbread and other baked goods.

Because of its cost, refined sugar was reserved for fancy baking. Housewives purchased it in solid cones and crushed it at home as it was needed.

   1½ **cups milk**
      Whipped cream (optional)
      Raw sugar crystals (optional)

1 Preheat oven to 350°. In a medium saucepan combine the 1 cup milk, cornmeal, and margarine or butter. Bring to boiling, stirring constantly; reduce heat. Cover and cook over low heat for 5 minutes. Remove from heat. Stir in molasses, granulated sugar, ginger, cinnamon, and ¼ teaspoon *salt;* mix well. Combine eggs and 1½ cups milk; stir into cornmeal mixture.

2 Turn mixture into an ungreased 1-quart casserole. Bake 1¼ hours. Cool on a wire rack for 1 to 1½ hours. Serve warm. If desired, top with whipped cream and sprinkle lightly with raw sugar crystals. Serves 6.

Nutrition Facts per serving: 218 cal., 8 g total fat (4 g sat. fat), 89 mg chol., 217 mg sodium, 32 g carbo., 1 g fiber, 6 g pro.
Daily Values: 13% vit. A, 2% vit. C, 17% calcium, 9% iron.

- Egg casserole or scrambled eggs

- Thick-cut ham slices and/or assorted breakfast sausages

- Fruit bowl with assorted fall fruits

- Snail's House Cake (see below)

Snail's House Cake

It's amazing what a little kitchen science will do to make a yummy recipe even better. The 1886 recipe contained very little liquid, although it did have more eggs. This updated version captures the original flavor of candied citrus and crunchy almonds in a swirl of tender texture. (See the photograph on page 4.)

Prep: 45 minutes **Rise:** 2 hours
Bake: 20 minutes

1	pkg. active dry yeast
½	cup warm water (105° to 115°)
3¼	to 3¾ cups all-purpose flour
3	eggs
½	cup sugar
⅓	cup butter, melted and cooled
1	cup coarsely chopped almonds
¾	cup chopped candied orange peel
½	cup sugar
¼	cup butter, melted

1 In a large mixing bowl combine yeast and warm water; let stand 5 minutes for yeast to soften. Stir in 1 cup of the flour, the eggs, ½ cup sugar, ⅓ cup melted butter, and ½ teaspoon *salt*. Beat with an electric mixer on medium speed 30 seconds. Beat on high speed 3 minutes. Using a wooden spoon, stir in as much of the remaining flour as you can.

2 Turn the dough out onto a floured surface. Knead in enough of the remaining flour to make a moderately soft dough that is smooth and elastic (3 to 5 minutes). Shape dough into a ball. Place dough in a lightly greased bowl, turning once to grease surface of the dough. Cover and let rise in a warm place until double in size (about 1½ hours).

3 Punch dough down. Turn dough out onto a lightly floured surface. Cover and let rest for 10 minutes.

4 Lightly grease a 13×9×2-inch baking pan; set aside. For filling, in a small bowl combine almonds, candied orange peel, the ½ cup sugar, and ¼ cup melted butter; set aside.

5 Roll dough into an 18×10-inch rectangle. Brush with water. Spread filling over dough rectangle and gently press. Roll up rectangle into a spiral, starting from a long side. Seal seam. Slice roll into twelve equal pieces. Place, cut sides down, in prepared pan. Cover and let rise in a warm place until nearly double in size (about 30 to 45 minutes).

6 Preheat oven to 350°. Bake rolls for 20 to 25 minutes or until golden. If necessary, cover rolls loosely with foil for the last 5 to 10 minutes of baking to prevent overbrowning. Cool slightly on a wire rack; remove from pan. Serve warm. Makes 12 rolls.

Nutrition Facts per roll: 385 cal., 17 g total fat (7 g sat. fat), 79 mg chol., 210 mg sodium, 51 g carbo., 3 g fiber, 8 g pro.
Daily Values: 11% vit. A, 5% calcium, 12% iron.

Thanksgiving Cake

To toast coconut chips, spread in a single layer in a shallow baking pan. Bake in a 350° oven for 3 to 5 minutes or until light golden brown. (See the photograph on page 282.)

Prep: 1 hour **Bake:** 12 minutes
Cool: 1 hour **Stand:** 2 hours

1¼	cups all-purpose flour
¾	tsp. cream of tartar
¼	tsp. baking soda
⅓	cup butter, softened
1	cup granulated sugar
¾	cup milk
4	egg whites
	Sifted powdered sugar
1	cup chopped hickory nuts, black walnuts, or pecans
¼	cup honey
2	tsp. finely shredded lemon peel
1	cup snipped dried Calimyrna figs
1	recipe Snow-White Frosting (see page 271)
½	cup coconut chips, toasted

1 Preheat oven to 350°. Grease a 15×10×1-inch baking pan; line pan with waxed paper. Grease and lightly flour paper; set aside. Stir together flour, cream of tartar, and baking soda; set aside.

2 In a medium mixing bowl beat butter with an electric mixer on medium speed for 30 seconds. Gradually beat in granulated sugar until well combined. Add dry mixture and milk alternately to butter mixture, beating on low speed after each addition just until combined.

3 Wash and dry beaters thoroughly. In a large mixing bowl beat egg whites with an electric mixer on medium speed until stiff peaks form (tips stand straight). Stir a small amount of egg whites into cake batter to lighten; fold batter into remaining egg whites.

4 Spread batter evenly into prepared pan. Bake for 12 to 15 minutes or until a wooden toothpick inserted near the center comes out clean. Loosen sides. Immediately invert onto a clean kitchen towel sprinkled with powdered sugar; remove pan and waxed paper. Cool cake completely. Cut cake crosswise into three 10×5 inch rectangles.

5 Meanwhile, in a small bowl combine nuts with 2 tablespoons of the honey and 1 teaspoon of the lemon peel. Set aside.

6 In another small bowl combine figs, remaining 2 tablespoons honey, and remaining 1 teaspoon lemon peel.

7 To assemble, place one cake rectangle on platter. Spread nut mixture over cake layer. Carefully top with one-third of the frosting, allowing frosting to flow over edges. Top with second cake layer. Spread fig mixture over cake. Carefully top with another third of the frosting. Top with third cake layer. Spread with remaining frosting, allowing it to flow over edges. Sprinkle top with toasted coconut chips. Let stand 2 hours before serving. Or, cover and chill overnight. Makes 12 servings.

Snow-White Frosting

In a large mixing bowl combine ⅓ cup pasteurized liquid egg whites or refrigerated or frozen egg product, thawed; 2 tablespoons lemon juice; 1 tablespoon honey; and 1 teaspoon

vanilla. Gradually beat in 5 to 5½ cups sifted powdered sugar until frosting is a slightly flowing consistency.

Nutrition Facts per serving: 484 cal., 14 g total fat (5 g sat. fat), 16 mg chol., 122 mg sodium, 89 g carbo., 3 g fiber, 6 g pro.
Daily Values: 7% vit. A, 4% vit. C, 6% calcium, 8% iron.

Mary's Sorghum Cake

Sorghum, a dark syrup with an old-fashioned flavor, is similar to molasses. Look for it in most major grocery stores. This cake can be made as a small three-tiered tower or as a single-layer 8×8-inch square. (See the photograph on page 280.)

Prep: 30 minutes **Bake:** 20 minutes for round cakes, 30 minutes for square cake

> 1¾ **cups all-purpose flour**
> ¾ **tsp. baking soda**
> 3 **Tbsp. butter, softened**
> ½ **cup packed brown sugar**
> 1 **egg**
> ½ **cup sorghum or molasses**
> ½ **cup milk**
> 1 **recipe Chocolate-Sorghum Glaze (see right)**

1 Preheat oven to 350°. Grease and lightly flour one 3×2-inch, one 5×2-inch, and one 7×2-inch round cake pan. Or, grease and lightly flour an 8×8×2-inch square baking pan. Set aside. Stir together flour and baking soda; set aside.

2 In a medium mixing bowl beat butter with an electric mixer on medium speed for 30 seconds. Add brown sugar; beat until well combined. Beat in egg until fluffy. Beat in sorghum or molasses on low speed. Add dry mixture and milk

alternately to beaten mixture, beating on low speed after each addition just until combined. Pour ⅓ cup batter into the 3-inch pan, 1 cup batter into the 5-inch pan, and remaining batter into the 7-inch pan, or spread all of the batter into the 8×8×2-inch pan.

3 Bake for 20 to 30 minutes for round pans and 30 to 35 minutes for square pan or until a wooden toothpick inserted near the center comes out clean. (Baked cake layers may dip slightly in center.) Cool in pan(s) on wire rack for 10 minutes. Remove from pan(s); cool completely on rack.

4 To assemble three-layer cake, place the 7-inch layer, top side down, on a serving plate. Spoon about one-third of the glaze over this layer, allowing it to flow down the sides. Top with the 5-inch layer, top side down, spooning another one-third of glaze over as directed above. Top with the 3-inch layer, top side down, spooning on remaining glaze. (If making square cake, spoon all of the glaze over the top.) Serves 8 to 10.

Chocolate-Sorghum Glaze

In a small saucepan melt together 2 ounces bittersweet or semisweet chocolate and 1 tablespoon butter over low heat. Remove from heat; stir in ⅔ cup sifted powdered sugar, 1 tablespoon sorghum or molasses, and ½ teaspoon vanilla. Gradually add 1 to 2 tablespoons hot water, beating with a wire whisk until glaze is smooth and of thin spreading consistency.

Nutrition Facts per serving: 327 cal., 10 g total fat (6 g sat. fat), 44 mg chol., 201 mg sodium, 56 g carbo., 1 g fiber, 6 g pro.
Daily Values: 8% vit. A, 4% calcium, 13% iron.

Caraway Cookies

Taken from *Early American Recipes: Traditional Recipes from New England Kitchens,* this cookie stands up to the book's promise of being "smackin' good." (See the photograph on page 1.)

Prep: 25 minutes **Chill:** 3 hours
Bake: 7 minutes per batch

  2   cups all-purpose flour
  1   Tbsp. caraway seed
  1   tsp. baking powder
  ¼   tsp. baking soda
  ¼   tsp. salt
  ½   cup butter, softened
  1   cup sugar
  2   eggs

1 In a medium bowl stir together flour, caraway seed, baking powder, baking soda, and salt; set aside.

2 In a large mixing bowl beat butter with an electric mixer on medium to high speed for 30 seconds. Add sugar. Beat until combined, scraping sides of bowl occasionally. Beat in eggs, one at a time, beating well after each addition. Beat in as much of the dry ingredients as you can with the mixer. Using a wooden spoon, stir in remaining dry ingredients. Divide dough in half. Cover and chill dough about 3 hours or until dough is easy to handle.

3 Preheat oven to 375°. Lightly grease cookie sheets. On a lightly floured surface roll dough, half at a time, to ⅛-inch thickness. Using a 2½-inch cookie cutter, cut into desired shapes. Place 2 inches apart on prepared cookie sheet.

4 Bake for 7 to 8 minutes or until edges are lightly browned. Transfer cookies to a wire rack; let cool. Makes about 54 cookies.

Nutrition Facts per cookie: 48 cal., 2 g total fat (1 g sat. fat), 13 mg chol., 45 mg sodium, 7 g carbo., 0 g fiber, 1 g pro.
Daily Values: 2% vit. A, 1% calcium, 1% iron.

Apricot-Sage Cookies

These jam-filled sandwich cookies— made crunchy with cornmeal—are an elegant holiday treat. For a different flavor, substitute rosemary or lemon thyme for the baked-in fresh sage.

Prep: 25 minutes
Bake: 7 minutes per batch

  1¾   cups all-purpose flour
  ⅓   cup sugar
  ¼   cup yellow cornmeal
  ½   cup butter
  2   Tbsp. snipped fresh sage, lemon
       thyme, or rosemary, or 2 tsp.
       dried sage or rosemary,
       crushed
  3   Tbsp. milk
  1   egg white
  1   Tbsp. water
       Fresh sage leaves (optional)
       Sugar
  2   Tbsp. apricot preserves

1 Preheat oven to 375°. In a medium bowl stir together flour, sugar, and cornmeal. Using a pastry blender, cut in butter until mixture resembles fine crumbs and starts to cling. Stir in herb. Add milk and stir with a fork to combine. Form mixture into a ball; then knead dough until smooth. Divide dough in half.

2 On a lightly floured surface, roll half of the dough at a time to ⅛-inch thickness. Using a 2½-inch round cookie cutter, cut out cookies.

3 In a small bowl combine the egg white and water. Brush half of the cookies with the egg white mixture. If desired, place a small sage leaf or two on each cookie that has been brushed with the egg white mixture. Brush leaves with egg white mixture. Sprinkle with sugar. Place all cookies on an ungreased cookie sheet.

4 Bake about 7 minutes or until edges are firm and bottoms are very lightly browned. Transfer cookies to a wire rack; let cool.

5 Snip any large pieces of fruit in preserves. Spread apricot preserves on the bottom of each cookie without a sage leaf. Top preserves layer with a sage-leaf-topped cookie, bottom side down. Makes 16 (2½-inch) sandwich cookies.

Nutrition Facts per cookie: 130 cal., 6 g total fat (4 g sat. fat), 16 mg chol., 64 mg sodium, 18 g carbo., 0 g fiber, 2 g pro.
Daily Values: 5% vit. A, 1% calcium, 5% iron.

Cashew-Filled Sandwich Cookies

Look for cashew butter at a natural foods store. Chocolate-hazelnut spread, available at most grocery stores, can be substituted, if you like.

Prep: 1¼ hours
Bake: 5 to 7 minutes per batch

  ½   cup shortening
  ⅓   cup granulated sugar
  ⅓   cup packed brown sugar
  ½   tsp. baking powder

- ¼ tsp. baking soda
- 1 egg
- 1 tsp. vanilla
- 1½ cups all-purpose flour
- ¾ cup quick-cooking rolled oats
- 1 recipe Cashew-Butter Filling (see below) or ½ cup chocolate-hazelnut spread
- 1 recipe Chocolate Glaze (see right) (optional)
- Finely chopped cashews (optional)

1 In a large mixing bowl beat shortening with an electric mixer on medium to high speed for 30 seconds. Add sugars, baking powder, baking soda, and ⅛ teaspoon *salt*. Beat until combined. Beat in egg and vanilla until combined. Beat in as much flour as you can. Using a wooden spoon, stir in any remaining flour and the oats.

2 Preheat oven to 375°. Shape dough into ½-inch balls. Place balls 2 inches apart on an ungreased cookie sheet. Flatten balls to 1 inch.

3 Bake for 5 to 7 minutes or until edges are firm and bottoms are lightly browned. Transfer cookies to a wire rack; let cool.

4 Spread bottom of half the cookies with a scant ½ teaspoon Cashew-Butter Filling. Place another cookie, top side up, on filling. If desired, spoon a little Chocolate Glaze on top and sprinkle nuts over glaze. Let stand until set. Cover and store in refrigerator up to 3 days or freeze for longer storage. Makes about 78 sandwich cookies.

Cashew-Butter Filling

In a mixing bowl beat ⅓ cup cashew butter and 2 tablespoons softened butter until fluffy. Slowly beat in ½ cup sifted powdered sugar and 1 tablespoon milk. Beat in additional milk, if needed, for spreading consistency.

Chocolate Glaze

In a heavy small saucepan melt 1 cup semisweet chocolate pieces and 1 tablespoon shortening over low heat, stirring mixture frequently.

Nutrition Facts per cookie: 35 cal., 2 g total fat (1 g sat. fat), 4 mg chol., 14 mg sodium, 4 g carbo., 0 g fiber, 0 g pro.
Daily Values: 1% iron.

Butterscotch Shortbread Bars

The only thing better than buttery shortbread is buttery shortbread crowned with a topping of butterscotch and nuts. Half confection, half cookie, these sweet treats are 100-percent delicious.

Prep: 25 minutes **Bake:** 37 minutes

- 1¼ cups all-purpose flour
- 3 Tbsp. brown sugar
- ¼ tsp. baking powder
- ½ cup butter
- ¼ cup butter
- ⅓ cup granulated sugar
- ⅓ cup packed brown sugar
- ⅓ cup light-color corn syrup
- 1 Tbsp. water
- ¼ tsp. salt
- ½ cup coarsely chopped walnuts
- ½ cup coarsely chopped cashews
- ¾ cup whipping cream
- 1 tsp. vanilla

1 Preheat oven to 350°. Line a 9×9×2-inch baking pan with foil; extend foil over pan edges. Butter foil; set aside.

TEST KITCHEN TIP

Foiled!

If your bar cookies play tricks on you by sticking to the baking pan, try lining the pan with foil. It may save you a tad on cleanup, too.

Tear off a piece of foil bigger than the pan. Press it into the pan, extending it over the pan's edges slightly. If a recipe calls for a greased pan, grease the foil. Spread the dough evenly in the pan. Bake and cool the bars in the pan; then pull the foil edges down to the counter and lift the bars out. Cut into bars, squares, triangles, or diamonds.

2 For crust, in a medium bowl combine flour, the 3 tablespoons brown sugar, and the baking powder. Cut in the ½ cup butter until mixture resembles coarse crumbs. Press into prepared pan. Bake 25 minutes or until golden brown.

3 Meanwhile, for butterscotch sauce, in a heavy medium saucepan melt the ¼ cup butter. Stir in granulated sugar, the ⅓ cup brown sugar, corn syrup, water, and ¼ teaspoon salt; stir in the chopped nuts. Bring to boiling over medium-high heat, stirring constantly. Boil, uncovered, for 5 minutes, stirring often. Remove from heat. Stir in whipping cream and vanilla.

4 Spread butterscotch mixture evenly over the baked crust. Bake for 12 to 15 minutes more or until most of the surface is bubbly. Cool in pan on a wire rack. Lift foil out of pan; cut into bars. Makes 24 bars.

Nutrition Facts per bar: 152 cal., 10 g total fat (5 g sat. fat), 19 mg chol., 108 mg sodium, 16 g carbo., 0 g fiber, 2 g pro.
Daily Values: 6% vit. A, 1% calcium, 5% iron.

Handle with Care

Even the Scrooge on your holiday gift list will rejoice in a parcel of homemade cookies. For faraway friends and family, a tin of homemade goodies makes a charming gift. Here are some hints for sending cookies by mail:

● Choose sturdy cookies that can travel well. Most bars or soft, moist cookies are good choices. Frosting or fillings may soften, causing cookies to stick together or to the wrapping.

● Wrap cookies back-to-back in pairs or individually with plastic wrap.

● Choose a heavy box and line it with plastic wrap or foil. Place a generous layer of filler, such as plastic bubble wrap, foam packing pieces, crumpled waxed paper, or paper towels, on the bottom of the box.

● Layer the cookies and filler. Top the last cookie layer with plenty of filler to prevent the contents from shifting during shipping.

Honey and Poppy Seed Hearts

The addition of honey to these cinnamon-spiced cookies gives them great flavor and a slightly soft texture.

Prep: 40 minutes **Chill:** 2 hours
Bake: 8 to 10 minutes per batch

¾ cup butter, softened
⅔ cup sugar
3 Tbsp. honey
2 tsp. finely shredded lemon or orange peel
1 tsp. baking powder
1 tsp. ground cinnamon
¼ tsp. baking soda
1 egg
2¼ cups all-purpose flour
1 egg white
1 Tbsp. water
2 Tbsp. poppy seed

1 Lightly grease a cookie sheet; set aside. In a large mixing bowl beat butter with electric mixer on medium to high speed about 30 seconds. Add the sugar, honey, lemon or orange peel, baking powder, cinnamon, and baking soda. Beat until combined, scraping sides of bowl occasionally. Beat in the egg until combined. Beat in as much of the flour as you can with the mixer. Using a wooden spoon, stir in any remaining flour.

2 Divide dough in half. Cover and chill about 2 hours or until dough is easy to handle.

3 Preheat oven to 375°. On a lightly floured surface, roll half of the dough at a time to ¼-inch thickness. Using a 2½- to 3-inch heart-shaped cookie cutter, cut out dough. Place 2 inches apart on prepared cookie sheet.

4 In a small mixing bowl beat egg white with water. Brush tops of the cookies with egg white mixture and sprinkle with poppy seed.

5 Bake for 8 to 10 minutes or until edges are golden. Transfer cookies to a wire rack; cool. Makes about 36 (2½-inch) cookies.

Nutrition Facts per cookie: 85 cal., 4 g total fat (2 g sat. fat), 16 mg chol., 61 mg sodium, 11 g carbo., 0 g fiber, 1 g pro.
Daily Values: 3% vit. A, 1% calcium, 3% iron.

Hickory Nut Sandwich Cookies

The rich, pecanlike hickory nut lends a touch of down-home exotica to these cream-filled, double-decker cookies.

Prep: 20 minutes **Chill:** 3 hours
Bake: 12 minutes per batch

1 cup butter, softened
¾ cup sugar
1½ tsp. vanilla
1¾ cups all-purpose flour
¾ cup finely ground hickory nuts, pecans, or black walnuts
½ cup finely chopped hickory nuts, pecans, or black walnuts
3 oz. bittersweet chocolate, chopped (optional)
1 tsp. shortening (optional)
1 recipe Buttercream (see page 275)

1 In a large mixing bowl beat butter with an electric mixer on medium to high speed for 30 seconds. Add sugar and vanilla. Beat until combined. Beat in as much flour as you can with the mixer. Stir in any remaining flour and the ¾ cup ground nuts.

2 Divide dough in half. Shape each half into a 6-inch-long roll. On waxed paper, roll one dough half in ¼ cup finely chopped nuts. Repeat with remaining nuts and dough. Wrap each roll in plastic wrap or waxed paper. Chill for 3 to 24 hours.

3 Preheat oven to 325°. Cut dough into slightly less than ¼-inch-thick slices. Place 1 inch apart on an ungreased cookie sheet.

4 Bake for 12 to 15 minutes or until bottoms of cookies are very lightly browned. Transfer cookies to a wire rack; let cool.

5 If desired, in a heavy small saucepan cook and stir chocolate and shortening over low heat until melted. With a small clean pastry brush, paint bottoms of half of the cookies with chocolate. Place cookies, chocolate side up, on a rack; let dry.

6 To assemble, spread bottoms of the plain cookies with a rounded teaspoon of Buttercream. Top with chocolate-coated cookies, chocolate side down. Chill cookies to store. Makes about 30 sandwich cookies.

Buttercream

In a small bowl beat together 2 egg yolks; set aside. In a heavy small saucepan combine ⅓ cup sugar and 2 tablespoons water. Bring to boiling; remove from heat. Gradually stir about half of the sugar mixture into the egg yolks. Return entire egg yolk mixture to saucepan. Bring to a gentle boil; reduce heat. Cook and stir for 2 minutes more. Remove from heat. Stir in ½ teaspoon vanilla. Cool to room temperature. In a large mixing bowl beat ½ cup softened butter on medium speed 30 seconds. Add cooled sugar mixture; beat until combined. If necessary, chill until easy to spread.

Nutrition Facts per cookie: 169 cal., 13 g total fat (6 g sat. fat), 39 mg chol., 63 mg sodium, 13 g carbo., 1 g fiber, 2 g pro.
Daily Values: 10% vit. A, 3% iron.

LOW FAT

Acorn Squash Bread

See the photograph on page 280.

Prep: 25 minutes **Rise:** 1¼ hours
Bake: 35 minutes

- **1** large acorn squash (1¼ to 1½ lb.)
- **1½** cups milk
- **2** Tbsp. sugar
- **2** Tbsp. butter
- **1** tsp. salt
- **5¾** to 6¼ cups all-purpose flour
- **1** pkg. active dry yeast
- **½** tsp. dried sage, crushed
    Milk
- **1** Tbsp. butter, melted

1 Preheat oven to 350°. Wash, halve, and remove seeds from squash. Cut a 1-inch-thick slice off one of the squash halves; set aside. Place squash halves, cut sides down, in a baking dish. Bake for 50 to 55 minutes or until tender. Remove pulp from squash; discard shells. Measure 1 cup.

2 Place the 1 cup of squash in a medium saucepan. Add the 1½ cups milk, the sugar, 2 tablespoons butter, and salt. Heat and stir just until warm (120° to 130°). Set aside.

3 In a large mixing bowl combine 2 cups of the flour, the yeast, and sage. Add the squash mixture. Beat with an electric mixer on low to medium speed for 30 seconds, scraping sides of the bowl. Beat on high speed for 3 minutes. Using a wooden spoon, stir in as much of the remaining flour as you can.

4 Turn the dough out onto a lightly floured surface. Knead in enough of the remaining flour to make a moderately stiff dough that is smooth and elastic (6 to 8 minutes). Shape dough into a ball. Place dough in a lightly greased bowl, turning once to grease surface of the dough. Cover and let rise in a warm place until double in size (45 to 60 minutes).

5 Punch dough down. Turn dough out onto a lightly floured surface. Divide dough in half. Cover and let rest for 10 minutes. Lightly grease two 8×4×2-inch loaf pans.

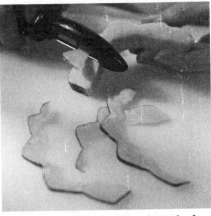

A vegetable peeler simplifies the task of making thin strips of acorn squash to place on top of the bread.

6 Gently shape each portion of dough into a loaf, tucking edges under. Place the shaped dough in the prepared loaf pans. Cover and let rise in a warm place until nearly double in size (about 30 minutes).

7 Preheat oven to 375°. Use a vegetable peeler to make several thin strips from the 1-inch slice of squash (see photo, above). Brush surface of bread dough with milk. Place squash strips on top of loaf. Brush squash strips with the melted butter.

8 Bake about 35 minutes or until bread sounds hollow when lightly tapped. (If necessary, cover loosely with foil the last 15 minutes of baking to prevent overbrowning.) Immediately remove bread from pans. Cool on wire racks. Makes 2 loaves (32 servings).

Nutrition Facts per serving: 102 cal., 2 g total fat (1 g sat. fat), 4 mg chol., 91 mg sodium, 19 g carbo., 1 g fiber, 3 g pro.
Daily Values: 2% vit. A, 3% vit. C, 2% calcium, 6% iron.

LOW FAT

Pear-Fennel Bread

This holiday bread found its way to America from Germany where it is known as *hutzelbrot,* meaning "wrinkled" fruit bread. Letting the yeast mixture sit overnight allows it to develop a wonderful tangy flavor. You'll have two loaves of fragrant, sweet bread when you're finished. (See the photograph on page 277.)

Prep: 30 minutes **Rise:** 2 hours
Bake: 40 minutes

4	cups water
2	cups dried pears (about 7 oz.)
1	pkg. active dry yeast
¼	cup warm water (105° to 115°)
5	to 5¼ cups all-purpose flour
½	tsp. salt
⅛	tsp. baking soda
2	Tbsp. warm water (105° to 115°)
⅓	cup butter, softened
½	cup packed brown sugar
1	egg
1½	tsp. fennel seed, crushed
1	tsp. ground cinnamon
1½	cups raisins
1	Tbsp. butter, melted

1 In a large saucepan combine the 4 cups water and the dried pears. Bring to boiling; reduce heat. Simmer, covered, about 20 minutes or until pears are very tender. Drain pears, reserving 1 cup of the cooking liquid. Chop the pears; cover and refrigerate. Cool the reserved liquid to lukewarm (105° to 115°).

2 In a large bowl combine the yeast and the ¼ cup warm water. Let stand about 5 minutes for yeast to soften. Stir in the reserved pear liquid. Stir in 1½ cups of the flour. Cover and let stand overnight at room temperature.

3 Stir together salt, baking soda, and the 2 tablespoons warm water. Stir into yeast mixture; set aside.

4 In a large mixing bowl beat butter with an electric mixer on medium speed for 30 seconds. Beat in brown sugar until well combined. Beat in egg, fennel seed, and cinnamon. Add the yeast mixture and beat just until combined. Using a wooden spoon, stir in pears, raisins, and as much of the remaining flour as you can.

5 Turn the dough out onto a lightly floured surface. Knead in enough of the remaining flour to make a moderately stiff dough that is smooth and elastic (6 to 8 minutes). Shape dough into a ball. Place dough in a lightly greased bowl, turning once to grease surface of the dough. Cover and let rise in a warm place until double in size (1¼ to 1½ hours).

6 Punch dough down. Turn dough out onto a lightly floured surface. Divide dough in half. Cover and let rest 10 minutes. Lightly grease two 8×4×2-inch loaf pans.

7 Gently shape each dough half into a loaf, tucking edges under. Place the shaped dough in the prepared loaf pans. Brush loaves with the melted butter. Cover and let rise in a warm

place until nearly doubled in size (45 to 60 minutes).

8 Preheat oven to 375°. Bake about 40 minutes or until bread sounds hollow when lightly tapped. (If necessary, cover loosely with foil the last 10 minutes of baking to prevent overbrowning.) Immediately remove bread from pans. Cool on wire racks. Makes 2 loaves (32 servings).

Nutrition Facts per serving: 153 cal., 3 g total fat (2 g sat. fat), 13 mg chol., 72 mg sodium, 31 g carbo., 2 g fiber, 3 g pro.
Daily Values: 3% vit. A, 1% vit. C, 2% calcium, 8% iron.

TEST KITCHEN TIP

Assuring Yeast Bread Success

Remember that yeast is a living organism. Too much heat will kill it. Too cold a temperature keeps the yeast from making the bread rise.

Always start by adding the smallest amount of flour listed. Then, knead in as much additional flour as you can. Don't go over the maximum amount listed; too much flour will make your bread heavy, dry, and compact.

The best place for a yeast dough to proof (or rise) is a draft-free spot that's between 80° and 85°. An unheated oven is an ideal spot.

Let doughs rise only until they are doubled in size. You can tell if the dough has risen enough by pressing two fingers about ½ inch into the dough. If the indentation remains, the dough is ready to shape.

For soft, shiny crusts, brush your bread loaves with margarine or butter. Use milk, water, or beaten egg for glossy, crisp crusts.

Left: Pumpkin Crunch Coffee Cake (page 265)
Below: Pear-Fennel Bread (page 276)

Left: Herb-Crusted Turkey (page 252) with Squash-Barley Stuffing (page 250), Orange-Balsamic Cabbage (page 250), and Kumquat Cranberry Sauce (page 250)
Below left: Warm Sweet Potato and Spinach Salad (page 255)
Below right: Walnut-Sage Potatoes au Gratin (page 251)
Page 278: Browned Butter Bread Pudding (page 258) and Caramelized Oranges (page 256) with Meringue Cookies (page 256)

Top left: Sweet Indian Pudding (page 269)
Above left: Acorn Squash Bread (page 275)

Top right: Mary's Sorghum Cake (page 271)
Above right: Maple Sugar Biscuits (page 266)
Page 281: Celebration Cake (page 256)

Above: Quaker Bonnet Biscuits (page 265)
Right: Puffets (page 269)
Page 282: Thanksgiving Cake (page 270)

Left: Pepperoni Biscotti (page 285)
Below: Cheese Triangles (page 285)

Cheese Triangles

These puffy, crisp appetizers probably got their start as a variation of early Southern cheese straws, which were slim, cylinder-shaped crackers. A good hostess would always include the treats when entertaining. (See the photograph on page 284.)

Prep: 25 minutes **Bake:** 12 minutes

- 2 cups all-purpose flour
- 2 tsp. baking powder
- ¾ tsp. ground red pepper (optional)
- ½ tsp. salt
- 3 Tbsp. shortening
- ½ cup finely shredded sharp cheddar cheese (2 oz.)
- ¾ cup milk
- 1 Tbsp. milk
- ½ cup finely shredded sharp cheddar cheese (2 oz.)

1 Preheat oven to 400°. Lightly grease baking sheets; set aside. In a large bowl stir together flour, baking powder, red pepper (if using), and salt. Using a pastry blender, cut in shortening until the size of coarse crumbs. Stir in ½ cup finely shredded cheese. Add the ¾ cup milk, stirring just until dry ingredients are moistened. Form into a ball.

2 On a lightly floured surface, roll dough to a 10-inch square, ¼ inch thick. Brush with the 1 tablespoon milk and sprinkle with ½ cup finely shredded cheese; press lightly. Cut into sixteen 2½-inch squares. Cut each square in half diagonally to make 32 triangles. Place on the prepared baking sheets.

3 Bake about 12 to 15 minutes or until golden brown. Serve warm. Makes 32 triangles.

Nutrition Facts per triangle: 54 cal., 3 g total fat (1 g sat. fat), 4 mg chol., 86 mg sodium, 6 g carbo., 0 g fiber, 2 g pro.
Daily Values: 1% vit. A, 5% calcium, 2% iron.

Pepperoni Biscotti

Kathy Specht
Cambria, California
$400—Holiday Appetizers
(See the photograph on page 284.)

Prep: 30 minutes **Cool:** 1 hour
Bake: 40 minutes

- ⅓ cup butter, softened
- ¼ cup grated Parmesan cheese
- 4 cloves garlic, minced
- 1 Tbsp. sugar
- 1 tsp. baking powder
- 1 tsp. Italian seasoning
- 1 egg
- 1 Tbsp. milk
- 1½ cups all-purpose flour
- ½ cup chopped pepperoni
- ¼ cup finely chopped red sweet pepper
- 2 Tbsp. finely chopped onion
- 2 Tbsp. snipped fresh parsley
- 2 Tbsp. grated Parmesan cheese

1 Preheat oven to 350°. Lightly grease a cookie sheet; set aside. In a large mixing bowl beat butter with an electric mixer on medium to high speed for 30 seconds. Add the ¼ cup Parmesan cheese, garlic, sugar, baking powder, and Italian seasoning. Beat until combined. Beat in egg and milk. Beat in as much flour as you can with the mixer. Using a wooden spoon, stir in remaining flour, pepperoni, red sweet pepper, onion, and parsley.

CLEVER COOK

Better Buttermilk

I've discovered powdered buttermilk, and it's great because it saves time, money, and fat calories. Time, because it's on hand when I need it in recipes. Money, because it's more economical and there's no waste. And, the best part of all, because it contains zero fat calories.

Desiree Evers
Centralia, Washington

2 Knead dough gently until it clings together. Shape dough into two 9×1½-inch rolls. Roll dough rolls in the 2 tablespoons Parmesan cheese to coat. Place rolls on prepared cookie sheet; flatten slightly.

3 Bake for 20 to 25 minutes or until a wooden toothpick inserted near the center comes out clean. Cool on cookie sheet for 1 hour.

4 Preheat oven to 325°. Cut each roll crosswise into ¾-inch-thick slices. Place slices, cut side down, on an ungreased cookie sheet. Bake for 10 minutes. Turn and bake for 10 to 12 minutes more or until biscotti are dry and crisp. (Do not overbake.) Transfer biscotti to a wire rack; let cool. Makes about 24 biscotti.

Nutrition Facts per biscotti: 80 cal., 5 g total fat (3 g sat. fat), 20 mg chol., 140 mg sodium, 7 g carbo., 0 g fiber, 2 g pro.
Daily Values: 4% vit. A, 6% vit. C, 4% calcium, 3% iron.

Gruyère-Pecan Biscuits

Gruyère cheese has a slightly sweet, nutlike flavor.

Prep: 20 minutes **Bake:** 10 minutes

- 2   cups all-purpose flour
- 1   Tbsp. baking powder
- ½   tsp. cream of tartar
- ½   cup butter or margarine
- ½   shredded Gruyère or
       Swiss cheese (2 ounces)
- ½   cup finely chopped pecans
- ⅔   cup milk

1 Preheat oven to 450°. In a medium bowl stir together flour, baking powder, and cream of tartar. Using a pastry blender, cut in butter or margarine until mixture resembles coarse crumbs. Stir in cheese and pecans. Make a well in the center of the dry mixture; add milk all at once. Using a fork, stir just until moistened.

2 Turn the dough out onto a lightly floured surface. Quickly knead dough by gently folding and pressing dough for 10 to 12 strokes or until dough is nearly smooth. Pat or lightly roll dough to ½-inch thickness. Cut the dough with a floured 2½-inch biscuit cutter, dipping the cutter into flour between cuts.

3 Place biscuits on an ungreased baking sheet. Bake for 10 to 12 minutes or until biscuits are golden. Remove biscuits from the baking sheet and serve hot. Makes 10 to 12.

Nutrition Facts per biscuit: 239 cal., 16 g total fat (8 g sat. fat), 34 mg chol., 247 mg sodium, 19 g carbo., 1 g fiber, 5 g pro.
Daily Values: 9% vit. A, 16% calcium, 7% iron.

South-of-the-Border Cornmeal Biscuits

Prep: 20 minutes **Bake:** 12 minutes

- 1½   cups all-purpose flour
- ½   cup yellow cornmeal
- 2   tsp. baking powder
- ¼   tsp. baking soda
- ¼   tsp. salt
- ½   cup butter or margarine
- ½   cup shredded cheddar cheese
       (2 ounces)
- ½   cup buttermilk or sour milk
- 1   4-oz. can diced green chili
       peppers

1 Preheat oven to 450°. In a medium bowl stir together flour, cornmeal, baking powder, baking soda, and salt. Using a pastry blender, cut in butter or margarine until mixture resembles coarse crumbs. Stir in cheese. Make a well in the center of the dry mixture; set aside.

2 In a small bowl stir together buttermilk and undrained chili peppers. Add buttermilk mixture all at once to the dry mixture. Using a fork, stir just until moistened.

3 Turn the dough out onto a lightly floured surface. Quickly knead dough by gently folding and pressing dough for 10 to 12 strokes or until dough is nearly smooth. Pat or lightly roll dough to ½-inch thickness. Cut the dough with a floured 2½-inch biscuit cutter, dipping the cutter into flour between cuts.

4 Place biscuits on an ungreased baking sheet. Bake for 12 to 15 minutes or until golden. Remove biscuits. Serve hot. Makes 10 to 12.

Nutrition Facts per biscuit: 204 cal., 12 g total fat (7 g sat. fat), 33 mg chol., 359 mg sodium, 20 g carbo., 1 g fiber, 4 g pro.
Daily Values: 9% vit. A, 4% vit. C, 12% calcium, 6% iron.

Cream Cheese Savory Muffins

Prep: 15 minutes **Bake:** 20 minutes

- 2   cups all-purpose flour
- 1   Tbsp. sugar
- 2½   tsp. baking powder
- ¼   tsp. salt
- 1   3-oz. package cream cheese
- ¼   cup finely chopped onion
- ¼   cup snipped fresh parsley
- 1   beaten egg
- ¾   cup milk
- ¼   cup butter or margarine, melted

1 Preheat oven to 400°. Grease twelve 2½-inch muffin cups or line with paper bake cups. Set muffin cups aside.

2 In a large bowl stir together flour, sugar, baking powder, and salt. Using a pastry blender, cut in cream cheese until mixture resembles coarse crumbs. Stir in onion and parsley. Stir together egg, milk, and melted butter or margarine. Add all at once to flour mixture. Stir just until moistened (batter should be lumpy).

3 Spoon batter into the prepared muffin cups, filling each ⅔ full. Bake for 20 to 25 minutes or until done. Remove from muffin cups and cool slightly on a wire rack. Serve warm. Makes 12.

Nutrition Facts per muffin: 150 cal., 7 g total fat (4 g sat. fat), 38 mg chol., 208 mg sodium, 17 g carbo., 1 g fiber, 4 g pro.
Daily Values: 8% vit. A, 3% vit. C, 8% calcium, 6% iron.

december

IN THIS CHAPTER

30-minute recipes indicated in COLOR.
Low-fat and no-fat recipes indicated
with a ♥.
Photographs indicated in italics.
*Bonus recipe

Creamy Goat Cheese Ornaments

Like charming little ornaments that adorn the tree, each bite-size appetizer is unique. Red sweet pepper, green cilantro, and toasty brown pumpkin seeds create the designs.

Prep: 30 minutes **Chill:** 3 hours

- 1 8-oz. pkg. cream cheese, softened
- 6 oz. semi-soft goat cheese (chèvre) or crumbled feta cheese
- 24 pickled jalapeño pepper slices* or small pimiento-stuffed green olives, well drained
- ½ cup dried red sweet pepper, finely chopped
- ½ cup snipped fresh cilantro
- ⅓ cup chopped toasted pumpkin seeds

1 In a medium bowl stir together the cream cheese and the goat or feta cheese until smooth. Cover and chill for 1 hour.

2 Using a rounded tablespoon of the cheese mixture, form it around a jalapeño slice or green olive, completely enclosing the pepper or olive.** Mixture will be sticky; moisten hands as necessary. (Chill mixture if it becomes too soft to handle.) Place shaped balls on a shallow pan. Cover with plastic wrap; chill for 1 hour.

3 Roll one-third of the balls in the red sweet peppers, one-third in the cilantro, and one-third in the pumpkin seeds to coat, leaving some white showing. Cover and chill at least 1 hour or up to 6 hours. Serve with picks. Makes 24 appetizers.

*Note: Hot peppers contain oils that can burn eyes, lips, and sensitive skin, so wear plastic gloves while preparing them and wash your hands thoroughly afterward.

**Note: For smaller balls, use a rounded teaspoon of the cheese mixture and omit the jalapeno slices or pimiento-stuffed green olives. Shape into balls.

Nutrition Facts per appetizer: 78 cal., 7 g total fat (4 g sat. fat), 16 mg chol., 155 mg sodium, 2 g carbo., 0 g fiber, 3 g pro.
Daily Values: 8% vit. A, 6% vit. C, 4% calcium, 4% iron.

LOW FAT

Shrimp and Vegetable Flowers

If you like, leave the tails on the shrimp to use as "handles," and add a few chive blossoms to the serving platter for extra color.

Prep: 1 hour **Marinate:** 10 minutes

- 24 wonton wrappers (½ of a 12-oz. pkg.)
- 2 Tbsp. cooking oil
- ¼ cup rice wine vinegar
- 2 Tbsp. cooking oil
- 2 Tbsp. toasted sesame oil
- 1 Tbsp. soy sauce
- 1 Tbsp. fish sauce
- 1 tsp. finely chopped lemongrass or finely shredded lemon peel
- 1 tsp. lemon juice
- 24 fresh snow pea pods (about 1 cup)
- 24 medium fresh or frozen peeled, deveined, cooked shrimp (12 oz. cooked and peeled; thaw, if frozen)
- 24 thin radish slices (4 to 6 radishes)
- 24 2-inch lengths of green portion of green onions (4 to 6 green onions)
- ½ of a 3.2-oz. pkg. fresh enoki mushrooms

1 Preheat oven to 400°. Lightly brush both sides of the wonton wrappers with 2 tablespoons cooking oil. Press wrappers into twenty-four 1¾-inch muffin cups, with tips pointing up to resemble a flower petal. Bake for 7 to 8 minutes or until golden brown and crisp. Remove from pans and cool on a wire rack.

2 For marinade, in a small bowl whisk together vinegar, 2 tablespoons cooking oil, the sesame oil, soy sauce, fish sauce, lemongrass, and lemon juice; set aside.

3 In a small saucepan cook snow peas in boiling water for 30 to 60 seconds or until just crisp-tender. Drain; plunge into ice water to cool quickly. Drain thoroughly.

4 Add snow peas, shrimp, radish slices, green onions, and mushrooms to marinade mixture. Marinate for 10 to 30 minutes. Drain shrimp mixture, reserving marinade. Divide shrimp mixture evenly among the wonton shells. Drizzle each filled "flower" with a few drops of the marinade; discard remaining marinade. Serve within 1 hour of filling. Serve with decorative picks. Makes 24 appetizers.

To Make Ahead:

Prepare and bake wonton "flowers" as directed. Cool completely. Place in an airtight container and store at room temperature up to 1 day. Prepare as directed from Step 2.

Nutrition Facts per appetizer: 53 cal., 2 g total fat (0 g sat. fat), 28 mg chol., 89 mg sodium, 5 g carbo., 0 g fiber, 4 g pro.
Daily Values: 1% vit. A, 4% vit. C, 1% calcium, 4% iron.

30 MINUTE, LOW FAT

Orange-Beet Dip

Serve this brightly colored dip with melba toast rectangles or rounds or cut-up vegetable dippers.

Start to finish: 15 minutes

- 1 15-oz. can beets, drained
- ½ cup dairy sour cream
- 2 Tbsp. chopped crystallized ginger
- 1 Tbsp. frozen orange juice concentrate, thawed
- ¼ tsp. salt
  Dash pepper

1 Place drained beets in a food processor bowl or blender container. Cover and process or blend until beets are coarsely chopped. Add sour cream, ginger, orange juice concentrate, salt, and pepper; cover and process or blend until nearly smooth. Makes about 1⅓ cups.

Nutrition Facts per tablespoon: 25 cal., 1 g total fat (1 g sat. fat), 2 mg chol., 82 mg sodium, 4 g carbo., 0 g fiber, 0 g pro.
Daily Values: 1% vit. A, 3% vit. C, 1% calcium, 1% iron.

30 MINUTE, LOW FAT

Toasted Cumin-Lime Avocado Dip

For a variation on the guacamole theme, try this cumin-flavored dip. Serve with fresh-cut jicama sticks or crispy tortilla chips.

Start to finish: 15 minutes

- 2 tsp. cumin seed
- 2 very ripe avocados, halved, seeded, peeled, and cut up
- 1 tsp. finely shredded lime peel
- 1 Tbsp. lime juice
- ¼ tsp. salt
- ⅛ tsp. ground red pepper

1 In a small skillet heat cumin seed over medium-high heat for 1 to 2 minutes or until lightly toasted. Remove seeds from pan; cool. Coarsely crush the cumin seed; set aside.

2 In a medium bowl coarsely mash the avocado with a fork. (If avocado is too firm to mash with a fork, use a food processor to coarsely mash the avocado.) Add lime peel, lime juice, salt, and red pepper. Stir in cumin seed. Serve immediately or cover and refrigerate up to 24 hours.* Makes about 1¼ cups.

*Note: The color of the dip may darken upon chilling.

Nutrition Facts per tablespoon: 6 cal., 1 g total fat (0 g sat. fat), 0 mg chol., 30 mg sodium, 0 g carbo., 1 g fiber, 0 g pro.
Daily Values: 1% vit. C, 1% iron.

30 MINUTE, LOW FAT

Broccoli Rabe and White Bean Dip

Stop by the bakery and pick up some rustic-style breads to serve with this garlicky green dip.

Start to finish: 20 minutes

- 1 oz. prosciutto, diced
- 1 Tbsp. olive oil
- 4 cloves garlic, chopped
- 6 to 10 oz. broccoli rabe, trimmed and coarsely chopped (4 cups)
- 1 15-oz. can white kidney beans (cannellini), drained but not rinsed
- ⅛ tsp. salt
- 2 Tbsp. lemon juice
- 1 Tbsp. olive oil (optional)

1 In a medium skillet cook and stir prosciutto over medium heat about 3 minutes or until golden and slightly

PARTY MENU

- ■ **Creamy Goat Cheese Ornaments (see page 288)**

- ■ **Thinly sliced roast beef, corned beef, and/or ham rolled up and served with a variety of mustards**

- ■ **Orange-Beet Dip served with melba toast rectangles or rounds and vegetable crudites (see left)**

- ■ **Broccoli Rabe and White Bean Dip (see left)**

- ■ **Assorted bite-size cookies, candies, and/or pastries**

- ■ **Champagne, white wine, or punch**

crisp. Remove from skillet. Carefully add the 1 tablespoon olive oil to the skillet. Cook the garlic and broccoli rabe over medium heat, stirring often, for 3 to 5 minutes or until broccoli rabe is wilted. Remove from heat.

2 In a food processor bowl place the beans and salt. Cover and process until nearly smooth. With motor running, add lemon juice through the feed tube. Process until smooth. Add the broccoli rabe mixture and process with 2 or 3 on-off turns just to mix.

3 Spoon dip into a serving container and sprinkle with the prosciutto. If desired, drizzle with the 1 tablespoon olive oil. Serve at room temperature. Makes about 2½ cups.

Nutrition Facts per tablespoon: 15 cal., 1 g total fat (0 g sat. fat), 0 mg chol., 42 mg sodium, 2 g carbo., 1 g fiber, 1 g pro.
Daily Values: 1% vit. A, 8% vit. C, 1% calcium, 1% iron.

Fragrant Ginger Cashews

Garam masala, a traditional Indian mix of cumin, cardamom, cinnamon, and other spices, is available in many supermarket spice sections and at specialty food stores.

Prep: 10 minutes **Roast:** 20 minutes

- 2 cups lightly salted cashews
- 1 Tbsp. butter, melted
- 1 Tbsp. minced or grated fresh ginger
- 2 tsp. garam masala

1 Preheat oven to 300°. Line a shallow baking pan with foil or parchment paper. In a bowl toss together the cashews, melted butter, ginger, and garam masala. Spread nuts in foil-lined pan.

2 Roast the nuts about 20 minutes, stirring occasionally, until golden brown and very fragrant. Serve warm or at room temperature. Store nuts in a tightly covered container at room temperature for 24 hours or in the refrigerator for 2 days. If desired, rewarm nuts on a baking sheet in a 300° oven about 5 minutes. Makes 2 cups.

Nutrition Facts per 2-tablespoon serving: 114 cal., 10 g total fat (2 g sat. fat), 2 mg chol., 42 mg sodium, 5 g carbo., 1 g fiber, 4 g pro.
Daily Values: 1% vit. A, 7% iron.

Latke "Macaroons"

Prep: 20 minutes **Bake:** 45 minutes

- 4 large potatoes* (about 2 lb.)
- 1 egg
- 1 Tbsp. olive oil
- ¾ tsp. salt

1 Preheat oven to 350°. Peel potatoes. Shred lengthwise into fine, long strands (see Photo 1, right). Place shredded potatoes in a colander. Rinse well with cold water. Press to remove as much liquid as possible.

2 In a medium mixing bowl beat egg with olive oil and salt. Add the shredded potatoes to egg mixture. Using your hands, gently form 1 to 2 tablespoons of the potato mixture into 1½-inch "haystacks," squeezing out slightly more than half of liquid as you shape (see Photo 2, right). Place latkes on a greased, shallow baking pan.

3 Bake for 45 minutes or until golden brown. Serve with lamb and roasted vegetables, if desired. Makes 12 macaroons.

*Note: Use russet or long white potatoes. They're lower in moisture than other varieties. Using higher-moisture potatoes may make the macaroons gummy.

Nutrition Facts per macaroon: 61 cal., 1 g total fat (0 g sat. fat), 13 mg chol., 107 mg sodium, 11 g carbo., 1 g fiber, 1 g pro.
Daily Values: 1% vit. A, 6% vit. C, 1% iron.

1. Using a smooth motion that follows the potato's natural curve, shred the potato along the surface of the grater. Turn the potato often to make it easier to grip.

2. Take 1 to 2 tablespoons of the potato mixture in the center of your palm. Squeeze out slightly more than half of the liquid. Gently fluff the potato mixture; then shape loosely into a "haystack" about 1½ inches high.

Stuffed Belgian Endives

Prep: 30 minutes **Cook:** 5 minutes

- 4 cups water
- 6 medium Belgian endives
- ¼ cup semi-soft goat cheese (chèvre) or cream cheese
- 1 tsp. snipped fresh thyme or ¼ tsp. dried thyme, crushed
- ⅛ to ¼ tsp. ground white pepper
- 1 egg, beaten
- 2 Tbsp. milk

Use a paring knife with a sharp tip to carefully cut away the center core of the endive. Discard the core or save for later use in salads or mixed vegetable dishes.

¼ **cup all-purpose flour**
½ **cup seasoned fine dry bread crumbs**
¼ **cup cooking oil**

1 In a large saucepan bring the water to boiling; add endives. Simmer, covered, for 2 to 3 minutes or until just tender. Drain; rinse with cold water. Drain rinsed endives well, gently squeezing out any excess water. Set aside on paper towels.

2 In a bowl combine cheese, thyme, and pepper. Spread outer endive leaves and carefully cut away center core (see photo, above). Spoon about 2 teaspoons of the cheese mixture into each endive; gently squeeze closed. In a small bowl beat together egg and milk. Dip each stuffed endive into egg mixture. Roll dipped endives in flour. Dip again in egg mixture and roll in bread crumbs.

3 In a large skillet heat oil over medium heat. Cook endives, uncovered, about 5 minutes or until browned, turning twice. Remove

endives from skillet. Drain on paper towels. Serve immediately. Makes 6 side-dish servings.

Nutrition Facts per stuffed endive: 140 cal., 9 g total fat (1 g sat. fat), 40 mg chol., 96 mg sodium, 13 g carbo., 0 g fiber, 4 g pro.
Daily Values: 2% vit. A, 14% vit. C, 2% calcium, 8% iron.

Mashed Potatoes With Shiitake Gravy

When plain mashed potatoes just won't do, make these dressed-up potatoes. Use shiitakes, another mushroom variety, or a combination of mushrooms for the gravy. (See the photograph on page 318.)

Start to finish: 40 minutes

2 **lb. russet potatoes, peeled and cut into 2-inch pieces**
¼ **cup butter**
⅓ **to ⅔ cup half-and-half or whole milk**
¼ **cup plain yogurt**
½ **tsp. salt**
¼ **tsp. pepper**
¾ **cup thinly sliced green onions or ⅓ cup snipped chives**
3 **Tbsp. butter**
¼ **cup finely chopped onion**
2 **cloves garlic, minced**
1 **lb. shiitake mushrooms, trimmed and sliced**
⅓ **cup beef broth**
⅓ **cup Madeira or beef broth**
2 **Tbsp. snipped fresh tarragon**
¼ **tsp. salt**
¼ **tsp. pepper**
2 **Tbsp. whipping cream**

1 Cook potatoes, covered, in lightly salted boiling water for 20 to 25 minutes or until fork-tender. Drain. Partially mash the potatoes

with a ricer or beat with an electric mixer on low speed. Add the ¼ cup butter and ⅓ cup of the half-and-half, mashing until nearly smooth. Add yogurt, ½ teaspoon salt, and ¼ teaspoon pepper, continuing to mash until smooth and fluffy. If desired, add additional pepper to taste. If necessary, add enough remaining half-and-half to make desired consistency. Stir in the green onions. Spoon into an ovenproof dish, cover tightly, and keep warm in a 300° oven for up to 30 minutes. Additional half-and-half may be needed if potatoes become too stiff.

2 Meanwhile, in a medium saucepan melt 3 tablespoons butter. Add onion and garlic; cook and stir over medium heat for 1 minute. Add mushrooms and cook over medium heat until mushrooms are just tender, stirring occasionally. Stir in the broth, Madeira, tarragon, ¼ teaspoon salt, and ¼ teaspoon pepper. Cook about 3 minutes more or until mushrooms are very tender, stirring occasionally. Stir in whipping cream and simmer 2 minutes more. Use immediately or cool, transfer to a storage container, cover, and refrigerate up to 12 hours. Reheat, adding additional broth or Madeira, if necessary.

3 To serve, spoon potato mixture into a serving bowl. Make a depression in the center, and spoon mushroom gravy over potatoes. Or, pass potatoes and mushroom gravy separately. Makes 8 servings.

Nutrition Facts per serving: 256 cal., 14 g total fat (8 g sat. fat), 38 mg chol., 379 mg sodium, 40 g carbo., 1 g fiber, 37 g pro.
Daily Values: 9% vit. A, 12% vit. C, 3% calcium, 3% iron.

Colorful Caraway Veggie Relish

Marinating the vegetables in plastic bags saves on clean-up and makes it easy to distribute the marinade flavors throughout the vegetables.

Prep: 50 minutes **Chill:** 4 hours

- 1½ lb. small carrots with tops, trimmed and peeled*
- 1 head cauliflower (1¾ to 2 lb.), cut into florets (about 6 cups)
- 2 medium red sweet peppers, seeded and cut up
- ¾ cup salad oil
- 1 Tbsp. caraway seed, crushed
- 1 cup white wine vinegar
- ½ tsp. salt
- ½ tsp. crushed red pepper

1 Cook carrots, covered, in a small amount of boiling water for 3 to 5 minutes or until crisp-tender. Drain; rinse with cold water. Cook cauliflower, covered, in a small amount of boiling water for 3 minutes. Drain; rinse with cold water. Place carrots, cauliflower, and sweet peppers in separate self-sealing plastic bags.

2 For dressing, in a small saucepan heat oil and crushed caraway seed over low heat for 4 to 5 minutes or until oil is warm and slightly fragrant; cool slightly. In a large measuring cup whisk together the oil-caraway seed mixture, wine vinegar, salt, and crushed red pepper. Pour about half of the dressing over cauliflower. Pour one-fourth of the dressing over carrots, and the remaining one-fourth of the dressing over sweet peppers; seal bags and turn to coat. Chill at least 4 hours or up to 3 days, turning bags occasionally.

3 To serve, in a deep 2-quart glass bowl or jar layer half of each vegetable; repeat layers. Pour dressing over all. Serve with a slotted spoon. Makes 12 servings.

*Note: If desired, substitute 12 ounces packaged peeled baby carrots (halved lengthwise, if large) for the small carrots with tops.

Nutrition Facts per serving: 159 cal., 14 g total fat (2 g sat. fat), 0 mg chol., 124 mg sodium, 7 g carbo., 3 g fiber, 2 g pro.
Daily Values: 82% vit. A, 87% vit. C, 3% calcium, 4% iron.

Herbed Leek Gratin

Line up the slender, tender leek halves in an au gratin dish; then add a creamy marjoram sauce and cheesy crumb topping. (See the photograph on page 319.)

Prep: 15 minutes **Bake:** 25 minutes

- 3 lb. slender leeks
- ½ cup whipping cream
- ½ cup chicken broth
- ½ tsp. salt
- ½ tsp. freshly ground black pepper
- 3 Tbsp. snipped fresh marjoram
- 1½ cups fresh French or Italian seasoned bread crumbs
- 3 Tbsp. grated Parmesan cheese
- 3 Tbsp. butter, melted
  Fresh marjoram sprigs (optional)

1 Preheat oven to 425°. Generously butter a 2-quart au gratin dish or rectangular baking dish. Trim roots off leeks, leaving pieces 4 to 5 inches long with white and pale green parts. Cut the leeks in half lengthwise and rinse thoroughly under running cold water; pat dry. Arrange leeks, cut side down, in the baking dish, overlapping as necessary to fit. (Leeks should all be facing in the same direction.)

2 Combine the whipping cream and chicken broth; pour over the leeks. Sprinkle with salt, pepper, and half of the snipped marjoram. Cover the dish tightly with foil and bake 15 minutes.

3 Meanwhile, in a small bowl combine the bread crumbs, Parmesan cheese, melted butter, and remaining snipped marjoram. Uncover leeks and sprinkle with bread crumb mixture. Bake, uncovered, about 10 to 15 minutes more or until leeks are tender and crumbs are golden brown. If desired, garnish with fresh marjoram sprigs. Makes 6 servings.

Nutrition Facts per serving: 237 cal., 15 g total fat (9 g sat. fat), 46 mg chol., 476 mg sodium, 23 g carbo., 2 g fiber, 4 g pro.
Daily Values: 16% vit. A, 20% vit. C, 13% calcium, 16% iron.

30 MINUTE

Pink Grapefruit Stacked Salad

If pomegranate seeds are not available, sprinkle the salad with snipped dried cranberries or cherries. (See the photograph on page 318.)

Start to finish: 30 minutes

- 6 medium pink grapefruit
- 3 medium white grapefruit
- ½ cup apricot nectar
- 2 Tbsp. hazelnut oil or walnut oil
- 1 Tbsp. snipped fresh mint or ½ tsp. dried mint, crushed
- ⅛ tsp. salt
- ⅛ tsp. cracked black pepper
- 4 cups fresh baby spinach leaves or shredded spinach leaves
- ½ cup chopped toasted walnuts
- ¼ cup pomegranate seeds (optional)

1 Peel the grapefruit, removing all of the white pith. Cut sides from the flesh of each grapefruit to form a square piece (reserve extra grapefruit trimmings for another use). Slice each square crosswise to form four slices. Set slices aside.

2 For dressing, in a small bowl whisk together apricot nectar, hazelnut or walnut oil, mint, salt, and pepper until combined.

3 Line a serving plate with spinach. Stack three slices of grapefruit, alternating colors, on top of spinach leaves. Drizzle with dressing. Sprinkle with walnuts and, if desired, pomegranate seeds. Makes 8 servings.

Nutrition Facts per serving: 128 cal., 8 g total fat (1 g sat. fat), 0 mg chol., 56 mg sodium, 13 g carbo., 3 g fiber, 2 g pro.
Daily Values: 12% vit. A, 79% vit. C, 4% calcium, 9% iron.

30 MINUTE

Beans and Hot Ham Dressing

Use a combination of green and wax beans for extra color. Or, if both varieties aren't available in your market, use all fresh green beans and top them with the chunky chickpea topping.

Start to finish: 15 minutes

- 1 **lb. whole green and/or yellow wax beans, ends trimmed**
- ½ **cup diced (or cubed) cooked smoked ham or Canadian-style bacon**
- 2 **Tbsp. olive oil**
- 1 **cup cooked or canned chickpeas (garbanzo beans), rinsed and drained**
- 2 **Tbsp. finely chopped shallots**
- 3 **Tbsp. red wine vinegar**

1 In a large saucepan cook green and/or yellow beans, covered, in a small amount of boiling salted water about 3 minutes or until crisp-tender. Drain well. Transfer to a serving bowl; keep warm.

2 Meanwhile, in a medium skillet cook ham or Canadian-style bacon in 1 tablespoon of the olive oil over medium heat for 3 minutes, stirring occasionally. Add the chickpeas and shallots. Cook and stir 2 to 3 minutes more or until pieces of ham are crisp and golden brown. Reduce heat to medium-low. Push mixture to one side of skillet.

3 Carefully add vinegar to skillet. Heat just until bubbly, scraping up the browned bits in bottom of skillet. Stir in the remaining olive oil. Stir together chickpea-ham mixture and the vinegar mixture. Pour over beans; toss gently to coat. Makes 6 to 8 servings.

Nutrition Facts per serving: 120 cal., 6 g total fat (1 g sat. fat), 7 mg chol., 303 mg sodium, 11 g carbo., 4 g fiber, 7 g pro.
Daily Values: 5% vit. A, 16% vit. C, 4% calcium, 7% iron.

30 MINUTE, LOW FAT

Triple-Decker Tortilla

Build a healthful family entrée with this towering hot tortilla pie. Add a salad to make an abundant, fun meal.

Prep: 15 minutes **Bake:** 15 minutes

  Nonstick cooking spray
- 1 **cup canned pinto beans, rinsed and drained**
- 2 **Tbsp. bottled sliced jalapeño peppers (optional)**
- 1 **cup bottled salsa**
- 4 **6-inch corn tortillas**
- ½ **cup frozen whole kernel corn**
- ½ **cup shredded reduced-fat Monterey Jack cheese (2 oz.)**
- ½ **of an avocado, seeded, peeled, and chopped**
- 1 **Tbsp. fresh cilantro leaves**

1 Preheat oven to 450°. Lightly coat a 9-inch pie plate with nonstick cooking spray. Lightly mash the pinto beans. In a skillet cook and stir beans and, if using, jalapeño pepper slices over medium heat for 2 to 3 minutes. Set aside.

2 To assemble, spoon ¼ cup of the salsa into bottom of prepared pie plate, spreading evenly. Layer with a corn tortilla, half of the warm mashed beans, another corn tortilla, the corn, ¼ cup of the Monterey Jack cheese, ¼ cup salsa, another corn tortilla, the remaining bean mixture, remaining corn tortilla, and remaining ½ cup salsa.

3 Cover with foil and bake for 12 minutes. Uncover and sprinkle with the remaining ¼ cup cheese. Bake, uncovered, 3 minutes more or until cheese is melted. Sprinkle with avocado and cilantro. Makes 4 main-dish servings.

Nutrition Facts per serving: 221 calories, 7 g total fat (2 g sat. fat), 12 mg chol., 876 mg sodium, 30 g carbo., 9 g fiber, 11 g pro.
Daily Values: 12% vit. A, 39% vit. C, 15% calcium, 19% iron.

Pearl-of-an-Oyster Stew

Be sure to rinse the drained oysters to remove any bits of sand or shell. For a richer stew, substitute two additional cups of half-and-half or light cream for the milk.

Start to finish: 35 minutes

- ⅔ cup sliced leeks (2 medium)
- 2 Tbsp. margarine or butter
- 3 Tbsp. all-purpose flour
- 1 tsp. anchovy paste
- 2 cups half-and-half or light cream
- 2 cups milk
- 6 cups shucked oysters (3 pints)
  Several dashes bottled hot pepper sauce (optional)

1 In a 4-quart saucepan cook leeks in margarine or butter until tender. Stir in flour and anchovy paste until combined. Add half-and-half or light cream and milk. Cook and stir until slightly thickened and bubbly. Cook and stir 1 minute more. Meanwhile drain oysters, reserving 3 cups liquid. Strain liquid.

2 In a large saucepan combine reserved oyster liquid and oysters. Bring just to simmering over medium heat; reduce heat. Cook, covered, about 1 to 2 minutes or until oysters curl around the edges. Skim surface of cooking liquid. Stir oyster mixture into cream mixture. If desired, add hot pepper sauce. Makes 8 servings.

Nutrition Facts per serving: 242 cal., 14 g total fat (7 g sat. fat), 97 mg chol., 248 mg sodium, 15 g carbo., 1 g fiber, 14 g pro.
Daily Values: 27% vit. A, 14% vit. C, 17% calcium, 61% iron.

Mustard-Coated Beef Tenderloin

This elegant roast with its flavorful coating deserves a special mixture of full-flavored salad greens. Toss the greens with a generous amount of fresh tarragon leaves, the herb with aniselike flavor overtones.

Prep: 25 minutes **Stand:** 30 minutes
Roast: 30 minutes

- 3 Tbsp. coarse-grain brown mustard
- 2 tsp. olive oil
- 2 tsp. cracked black peppercorns
- 2 tsp. snipped fresh tarragon
- 1 tsp. coarse salt
- 1 2- to 3-lb. beef tenderloin
- ¼ cup balsamic vinegar
- 8 cups mixed baby greens, mesclun, or torn romaine and radicchio
- ¼ cup fresh tarragon leaves

1 In a small bowl stir together 1 tablespoon of the mustard, the olive oil, peppercorns, snipped tarragon, and salt. Spread mixture over top and sides of meat. Let stand 15 minutes at room temperature or refrigerate up to 4 hours.

2 Preheat oven to 425°. Place meat on a rack in a shallow roasting pan. Roast, uncovered, for 30 to 45 minutes or until a meat thermometer registers 145° for medium-rare. Remove meat from pan, cover meat with foil, and let stand 15 minutes before slicing.

3 While meat is standing, place roasting pan over low heat. Add balsamic vinegar to pan and cook, scraping up browned bits from bottom of pan. Stir in remaining brown mustard and any juices that have

HOLIDAY MENU

- Mustard-Coated Beef Tenderloin (see left)

- Herbed Leek Gratin (see page 292)

- Roasted whole new potatoes with butter and fresh thyme

- Panna Cotta with Cranberry Port Sauce (see page 302)

accumulated from the roast during standing. (If mixture seems thick, stir in 2 to 3 tablespoons of water to thin it to drizzling consistency.)

4 Toss together greens and tarragon leaves. Line a platter with greens. Drizzle greens with about three-fourths of the pan juices. Slice meat and overlap slices on the greens. Drizzle with remaining pan juices. Makes 6 to 8 servings.

Nutrition Facts per serving: 432 cal., 32 g total fat (12 g sat. fat), 102 mg chol., 640 mg sodium, 5 g carbo., 1 g fiber, 28 g pro.
Daily Values: 3% vit. A, 5% vit. C, 3% calcium, 23% iron.

Pork with Apple and Onion Compote

It's generally known that pork and applesauce go together like bread and butter. Here the accompanying apple and onion compote roasts right alongside the meat.

Prep: 30 minutes **Roast:** 1 hour, 25 minutes
Stand: 15 minutes

- 1 3½- to 4-lb. pork loin center rib roast, backbone loosened
- 2 tsp. snipped fresh sage

1½ tsp. coarsely ground black pepper
3 slices bacon
6 medium cooking apples, cored and cut into bite-size chunks
1 large red onion, cut into thin wedges
3 large cloves garlic, peeled and thinly sliced
8 whole sage leaves
¼ tsp. salt
⅓ cup apple juice
Fresh sage sprigs (optional)

1 Preheat oven to 325°. Rub the meat with the snipped sage and 1 teaspoon of the pepper. Place roast, rib side down, in a shallow roasting pan. Place bacon slices across top of roast. Insert a meat thermometer. Roast 1 to 1¼ hours or until meat thermometer registers 130°.

2 Remove pan from oven. Add apples, onion, garlic, and the whole sage leaves to roasting pan. Sprinkle with salt and remaining ½ teaspoon pepper. Stir fruit and vegetables to coat with pan juices. Return to oven and roast for 25 to 30 minutes more or until apples and onion are golden and tender and meat thermometer registers 155°; stir apple and onion mixture several times.

3 Transfer the pork to a serving platter. Cover with foil; let stand for 15 minutes before carving. (The temperature of the meat will rise 5° during standing.)

4 Using a slotted spoon, transfer the apple and onion mixture to a large bowl; cover and keep warm. Pour drippings from the roasting pan into a small saucepan, scraping out, and including, the crusty browned bits. Stir in apple juice. Bring mixture just to boiling over medium heat. Pour over the apple mixture, tossing to coat.

5 To serve, spoon the apple mixture around the pork roast. If desired, garnish with additional sage sprigs. Makes 6 to 8 servings.

Nutrition Facts per serving: 341 cal., 11 g total fat (4 g sat. fat), 82 mg chol., 202 mg sodium, 27 g carbo., 5 g fiber, 34 g pro.
Daily Values: 1% vit. A, 16% vit. C, 3% calcium, 10% iron.

Crimson Cherry-Glazed Holiday Hens

During the holiday season, presentation of a spectacular entrée may be what you're looking for. If so, serve a whole game hen for that special occasion. Or, you may choose to make smaller, yet still hearty servings by splitting the hens before roasting. Either way, your guests will love the flavor of the cherry glaze.

Prep: 30 minutes **Roast:** 40 minutes

4 1¼- to 1½- lb. Cornish game hens*
6 cloves elephant garlic, peeled and halved
3 Tbsp. butter, melted
½ tsp. salt
¼ tsp. pepper
⅓ cup sliced or chopped shallots
2 Tbsp. butter
1 cup red cherry preserves (with whole cherries)
¼ cup red wine vinegar
½ tsp. ground allspice
¼ tsp. ground cloves

1 Preheat oven to 425°. Rub the skin of each hen with cut side of garlic cloves; reserve garlic. Tie drumsticks to tail. Brush hens with the 3 tablespoons melted butter and sprinkle with the salt and pepper. Place hens on a rack in a shallow roasting pan; twist wingtips under the back of each hen. Place halved garlic cloves around the hens. Roast for 40 to 45 minutes or until juices run clear. (Garlic may turn green during roasting, but that's OK.)

2 Meanwhile, in a small saucepan cook shallots in 2 tablespoons butter over medium heat until tender, about 3 minutes, stirring often. Stir in preserves, vinegar, allspice, and cloves. Bring to boiling; reduce heat. Boil gently, uncovered, about 20 minutes or until desired glazing consistency. Remove one of the pieces of garlic from the roasting pan; cool slightly. Finely chop garlic; stir into sauce.

3 To serve, transfer hens and garlic to a serving platter. Spoon glaze over hens. Makes 4 or 8 servings.

*Note: For smaller portions, split hens in half lengthwise. Ask the butcher to cut the hens in half for you and remove the backbone. Or, use a long heavy knife or kitchen shears to split the hens lengthwise. Cut through the breast bone, just off-center, and cut through the backbone; then discard the backbone. Place hen halves, skin side up, on a rack in a shallow roasting pan. Add the garlic to the pan and roast for 40 to 45 minutes or until juices run clear.

Nutrition Facts per serving (one-half hen): 478 cal., 26 g total fat (9 g sat. fat), 120 mg chol., 312 mg sodium, 30 g carbo., 1 g fiber, 31 g pro.
Daily Values: 7% vit. A, 9% vit. C, 2% calcium, 2% iron.

- Salad of mixed greens, shredded carrots, very thinly sliced onions, and a sweet vinaigrette

- Tangy Stir-Fried Pork (see below, right)

- Gingery Apple Sundaes (see page 303)

LOW FAT

Moroccan Lamb Roast

Prep: 15 minutes **Marinate:** 2 hours
Roast: 1¾ hours **Stand:** 10 minutes

  1 5-lb. bone-in leg of lamb
  4 to 8 cloves garlic, peeled and cut into slivers
  2 Tbsp. coriander seed, crushed
  2 Tbsp. finely shredded lemon peel
  1 Tbsp. olive oil
  1 tsp. cumin seed, crushed
  ½ tsp. salt
  ½ tsp. whole black peppercorns, crushed
    Assorted peeled and cut-up vegetables, such as carrots, turnips, and sweet peppers (optional)

1 Trim excess fat from lamb. Cut several ½-inch-wide slits randomly into top and sides of roast. Insert garlic slivers into slits. In a small bowl stir together coriander seed, lemon peel, olive oil, cumin seed, salt, and pepper. Rub lamb surface with spice mixture. Cover and chill for several hours or overnight, if desired.

2 Preheat oven to 350°. Place lamb on a rack in a shallow roasting pan. Roast lamb for 1¾ to 2¼ hours or until a meat thermometer inserted in the thickest portion of the meat registers 140° for medium-rare doneness or registers 155° for medium doneness. If desired, add assorted cut-up vegetables during last 45 minutes of cooking.

3 Remove lamb from oven. Loosely cover with foil. Let stand for 10 minutes (the temperature of the meat will rise about 5° during standing time). Slice and serve lamb with the roasted vegetables, if desired. Makes 10 servings.

Nutrition Facts per serving: 235 cal., 10 g total fat (3 g sat. fat), 101 mg chol., 185 mg sodium, 1 g carbo., 0 g fiber, 32 g pro.
Daily Values: 3% vit. C, 1% calcium, 18% iron.

30 MINUTE, LOW FAT

Tangy Stir-Fried Pork

A little stir-fry flash in the pan makes pork jump with flavor. It's time to wok and roll!

Start to finish: 20 minutes

  1 tsp. cooking oil
 12 oz. lean pork tenderloin, cut into ½-inch-thick slices
  ¼ cup dry white wine or low-sodium chicken broth
  6 unpeeled kumquats, thinly sliced, or ¼ of an orange, thinly sliced
  2 Tbsp. bottled hoisin sauce
  1 green onion, bias-cut into ¼-inch slices
  1 tsp. toasted sesame seed
  2 cups hot, cooked quick-cooking brown rice

1 Pour cooking oil into a wok or large skillet. (Add more oil as necessary during cooking.) Preheat over medium-high heat. Stir-fry pork for 6 to 8 minutes or until no pink remains. Remove pork from wok.

2 Add the white wine or chicken broth to the hot wok. Reduce heat. Stir in the kumquats or orange slices and the hoisin sauce. Cook and stir for 1 minute. Return pork to wok. Heat through. Stir in the green onion and toasted sesame seed.

3 To serve, divide cooked brown rice among four shallow bowls or plates. Serve pork mixture over top. Makes 4 servings.

Nutrition Facts per serving: 292 cal., 5 g total fat (1 g sat. fat), 60 mg chol., 205 mg sodium, 33 g carbo., 4 g fiber, 21 g pro.
Daily Values: 1% vit. A, 19% vit. C, 3% calcium, 12% iron.

PRIZE WINNER

Dinner Rolls

Janette Miller
Smith River, California
$400—Savory Breads and Rolls

Prep: 40 minutes **Rise:** 1½ hours
Bake: 12 minutes

  1 pkg. active dry yeast
  1 cup warm water (105° to 115°)
 2¾ to 3¼ cups all-purpose flour
  ¼ cup finely shredded Parmesan cheese
  2 Tbsp. snipped fresh basil
  2 Tbsp. sugar
  1 tsp. salt
  1 Tbsp. milk
  2 Tbsp. finely shredded Parmesan cheese

1. In a small bowl stir yeast into warm water to soften. Let stand 5 minutes or until bubbly.

2. Meanwhile, in a large bowl combine 2¾ cups of the flour, the ¼ cup Parmesan cheese, the basil, sugar, and salt. Add the yeast mixture to the flour mixture. Using a wooden spoon, stir until combined.

3. Turn dough out onto a lightly floured surface. Knead in enough remaining flour to make a moderately stiff dough that is smooth and elastic (6 to 8 minutes total). Shape the dough into a ball. Place dough in a lightly greased bowl, turning once to grease the surface of the dough. Cover and let rise in a warm place until double in size (about 1 hour).

4. Punch dough down. Turn dough out onto a lightly floured surface. Divide dough in half. Cover and let rest for 10 minutes. Meanwhile, lightly grease twenty-four 1¼-inch muffin cups.

5. Divide each half of dough into twelve portions (24 portions total). Gently pull each portion of dough into a ball, tucking edges beneath. Arrange balls, smooth side up, in the prepared muffin cups. Cover and let rise in a warm place until nearly double in size (about 30 minutes).

6. Preheat oven to 400°. Brush roll tops with milk and sprinkle with the 2 tablespoons Parmesan cheese. Bake 12 to 15 minutes or until tops are golden brown. Remove rolls from muffin cups. Serve warm. Makes 24.

Nutrition Facts per roll: 60 cal., 1 g total fat (0 g sat. fat), 1 mg chol., 125 mg sodium, 11 g carbo., 0 g fiber, 2 g pro.
Daily Values: 2% calcium, 4% iron.

Cheddar Cheese Spirals

Tender and rich, these cheesy spirals are a great accompaniment for a hearty bowl of stew, chili, or chowder.

Prep: 35 minutes **Rise:** 1 hour 5 minutes
Bake: 15 minutes

2	pkg. active dry yeast
1	Tbsp. sugar
¾	cup warm water (105° to 115°)
1	cup milk
½	cup butter
1	tsp. salt
5¼	to 5¾ cups all-purpose flour
6	egg yolks
2	cups shredded cheddar cheese (8 oz.)

1. In a small mixing bowl stir yeast and sugar into warm water to soften yeast. Let mixture stand at room temperature for 15 minutes.

2. Meanwhile, in a medium saucepan heat and stir milk, ⅓ cup of the butter, and the salt just until warm (120° to 130°) and butter almost melts.

3. In a large mixing bowl combine 2 cups of the flour, egg yolks, the milk mixture, and yeast mixture. Beat with an electric mixer on low to medium speed for 30 seconds, scraping sides of the bowl constantly. Beat on high speed for 3 minutes. Using a wooden spoon, stir in 1 cup of the cheddar cheese and as much of the remaining flour as you can.

4. Turn dough out onto a lightly floured surface. Knead in enough of the remaining flour to make a moderately stiff dough that is smooth and elastic (6 to 8 minutes). Shape the dough into a ball. Place in a lightly greased bowl, turning once to grease surface of the dough. Cover and let rise in a warm place until double in size (45 to 60 minutes).

5. Punch dough down. Turn dough out onto a lightly floured surface; divide dough in half. Cover and let rest for 10 minutes. Grease two large baking sheets; set aside.

6. On a lightly floured surface, roll half of the dough to a 12×10-inch rectangle. Cut into ten 1-inch-wide strips (12 inches long). Gently roll each strip into a spiral; pinch ends to seal. Place on the prepared baking sheets. Repeat with remaining half of dough. Cover and let rise until nearly double (20 to 30 minutes).

7. Preheat oven to 350°. Melt remaining butter. Brush spirals with butter and sprinkle with remaining cheese. Bake about 15 minutes or until bottoms are golden. Serve warm. Makes 20 rolls.

To Make Ahead:
Prepare and bake rolls as directed; cool completely. Place rolls in a single layer in a freezer container or bag and freeze for up to 3 months. Before serving, thaw rolls at room temperature for 2 hours. Or, to reheat, wrap the frozen rolls in foil and bake in a 300° oven 15 minutes or until warm.

Nutrition Facts per roll: 227 cal., 11 g total fat (6 g sat. fat), 90 mg chol., 245 mg sodium, 25 g carbo., 1 g fiber, 8 g pro.
Daily Values: 11% vit. A, 11% calcium, 10% iron.

PRIZE WINNER

Ham and Cheese On Rye

Jenny Maguire
Poquoson, Virginia
$200—Savory Breads and Rolls

Prep: 20 minutes **Rise:** 1 hour 5 minutes
Bake: 30 minutes **Stand:** 30 minutes

1¾ to 2⅓ cups bread flour or
    all-purpose flour
1 pkg. active dry yeast
1 Tbsp. brown sugar
1 Tbsp. caraway seed
1 Tbsp. finely chopped onion
1½ tsp. salt
1 cup warm water (120° to 130°)
1 Tbsp. cooking oil
1 cup rye flour
1 2½-oz. pkg. very thinly sliced
    cooked ham
3 Tbsp. sweet-hot mustard
½ cup shredded cheddar
    cheese (2 oz.)
1 egg yolk
1 Tbsp. water
    Caraway seed

1 In a medium mixing bowl stir together 1¼ cups of the bread or all-purpose flour, the yeast, brown sugar, caraway seed, onion, and salt. Add the 1 cup water and the oil to the dry mixture. Beat with an electric mixer on low to medium speed for 30 seconds, scraping sides of bowl constantly. Beat on high speed for 3 minutes.

2 Using a wooden spoon, stir the rye flour into the beaten mixture. Stir in as much of the remaining bread or all-purpose flour as you can with a wooden spoon. Turn the dough out onto a floured surface. Knead in enough of the remaining flour to make a moderately stiff dough that is smooth and elastic (6 to 8 minutes total). Shape dough into a ball. Place dough in a lightly greased bowl, turning once to grease surface of the dough. Cover; let rise in a warm place until double in size (45 to 60 minutes).

3 Punch dough down. Turn out onto a lightly floured surface. Cover; let rest 10 minutes. Meanwhile, lightly grease a cookie sheet.

4 Roll dough into a 12-inch circle. Place ham slices over the dough, overlapping as necessary, leaving a 1-inch border around the edge of the dough. Spread mustard over the ham. Sprinkle with cheese. Roll up; moisten edge with water and seal seams and ends. Place loaf, seam side down, on prepared cookie sheet. Cut several shallow diagonal slashes across top of loaf. Cover and let rise in a warm place until nearly double (about 20 minutes). Preheat oven to 375°.

5 In a small bowl stir together egg yolk and 1 tablespoon water; brush over loaf. Sprinkle with additional caraway seed. Bake for 30 minutes or until golden brown and loaf sounds hollow when tapped. Cool on a wire rack for 30 minutes. Serve warm. Makes 1 loaf (12 appetizer servings).

To Make Ahead:

Prepare, shape, and roll up as directed; transfer loaf to a greased cookie sheet. Cover with plastic wrap. Chill for 2 to 24 hours. Let stand at room temperature for 20 minutes. Remove plastic wrap and bake as directed.

Nutrition Facts per serving: 143 cal., 4 g total fat (1 g sat. fat), 25 mg chol., 421 mg sodium, 21 g carbo., 2 g fiber, 5 g pro.
Daily Values: 2% vit. A, 5% calcium, 8% iron.

Panforte

Prep: 1 hour **Bake:** 30 minutes

⅔ cup walnut halves
½ cup whole almonds
½ cup hazelnuts (filberts)
2 Tbsp. pine nuts
½ cup chopped mixed candied fruit
    and peels (with citron)
⅓ cup raisins
1½ tsp. grated orange peel
⅔ cup all-purpose flour
3 Tbsp. unsweetened cocoa
    powder
2 oz. bittersweet or semisweet
    chocolate, grated
1½ tsp. ground cinnamon
¼ tsp. ground black pepper
¼ tsp. ground cloves
¼ tsp. grated nutmeg
⅛ tsp. salt
⅛ tsp. ground cardamom
⅔ cup honey
½ cup sugar
2 Tbsp. white grape juice or water

1 Preheat oven to 325°. In a 15×10×1-inch baking pan combine walnuts, almonds, and hazelnuts. Bake, uncovered, for 5 minutes. Add pine nuts to the baking pan and bake about 8 minutes more or until all the nuts are toasted. Let the nuts cool. Reserve 1 cup whole nuts. By hand, coarsely chop remaining nuts.

2 In a large bowl combine the whole and chopped nuts, candied fruit, raisins, and orange peel. In another bowl stir together the flour, cocoa powder, grated chocolate, cinnamon, pepper, cloves, nutmeg, salt, and cardamom. Add the dry ingredients to the fruits and nuts, tossing to coat well.

3 In a medium saucepan bring the honey and sugar to boiling, stirring to dissolve the sugar. Boil gently for 3 minutes. Stir in the grape juice or water. Pour the hot syrup over the fruit and nut mixture, stirring to coat (batter will be thick).

4 Press the mixture into a greased 10-inch springform pan. Bake about 30 minutes or until just firm in the center. Cool in pan on a wire rack for 15 minutes. Loosen from sides of pan. Cool completely in pan.

5 To serve, use a sharp knife to cut the panforte into thin wedges. Serve when cool or wrap and store several days before slicing. Serves 24.

Nutrition Facts per serving: 153 cal., 7 g total fat (1 g sat. fat), 0 mg chol., 15 mg sodium, 23 g carbo., 1 g fiber, 3 g pro.
Daily Values: 2% vit. C, 3% calcium, 5% iron.

Pumpkin and Banana Bread

Prep: 20 minutes **Bake:** 50 minutes

- 2¾ cups all-purpose flour
- 1½ cups granulated sugar
- ½ cup packed brown sugar
- 1 Tbsp. baking powder
- 2 tsp. pumpkin pie spice
- ½ tsp. baking soda
- 4 eggs, beaten
- 1 cup canned pumpkin
- 1 cup mashed ripe banana
- ½ cup cooking oil
- 2 Tbsp. lemon juice
- 1 cup chopped walnuts or pecans

1 Preheat oven to 350°. Grease the bottom and ½ inch up the sides of two 8×4×2-inch or 9×5×3-inch baking pans; set aside. In a very large bowl stir together flour, granulated sugar, brown sugar, baking powder, pumpkin pie spice, baking soda, and ¼ teaspoon *salt*. Make a well in the center of the

dry mixture. In a medium bowl combine eggs, pumpkin, banana, cooking oil, and lemon juice. Add to flour mixture. Stir just until moistened. Fold in nuts.

2 Divide batter evenly between prepared pans. Bake about 50 minutes or until a wooden toothpick inserted near the center comes out clean. Cool in pans on a wire rack for 10 minutes. Remove from pans and cool on a wire rack. Wrap and let store overnight for easier slicing. Makes 2 loaves (32 servings).

Nutrition Facts per serving: 157 cal., 7 g total fat (1 g sat. fat), 27 mg chol., 85 mg sodium, 23 g carbo., 1 g fiber, 0 g pro.
Daily Values: 18% vit. A, 3% vit. C, 4% calcium, 5% iron.

Squash Apple Bread

Prep: 20 minutes **Bake:** 55 minutes

- 2 cups all-purpose flour
- 1 cup whole wheat flour
- 1 Tbsp. baking powder
- 1 tsp. ground cinnamon
- ½ tsp. baking soda
- ¼ tsp. ground cloves
- 4 eggs, beaten
- 1 12-oz. pkg. frozen cooked winter squash, thawed, or 1⅓ cups mashed cooked winter squash
- 1½ cups packed brown sugar
- 1 cup applesauce
- ⅔ cup cooking oil
- 2 tsp. vanilla
- ⅔ cup raisins
- ½ cup slivered almonds, toasted

1 Preheat oven to 350°. Grease and flour two 8×4×2-inch loaf pans. In a large bowl combine flours, baking powder, cinnamon, soda, cloves, and ¼ teaspoon *salt*. Make a well in the center of dry mixture.

TEST KITCHEN TIP

Pick a Pan for Quick Breads

One recipe of quick-bread batter can be divided many ways, depending on your needs. Sometimes you want one big loaf for dinner; other times, you need several small loaves to give as gifts. Use this chart to convert the recipe to the size pans you like. Fill the pans about two-thirds full, and if any batter remains, use it to make muffins. A quick note: The baking times in this chart are approximate and may vary with the recipe.

Pan Size	Baking Time
One 9×5×3-inch loaf pan	1 to 1¼ hours
One 8×4×2-inch loaf pan	50 to 60 minutes
Two 7½×3½×2-inch loaf pans	40 to 45 minutes
Two 5¾×3×2-inch loaf pans	30 to 35 minutes
Six 4½×2½×1½-inch loaf pans	30 to 35 minutes
Twelve 2½-inch muffin cups	15 to 20 minutes

2 In a medium bowl combine eggs, squash, brown sugar, applesauce, oil, and vanilla. Add to flour mixture. Stir just until moistened. Fold in raisins and nuts.

3 Divide batter evenly between prepared pans. Bake for 55 to 60 minutes or until a wooden toothpick inserted in the center comes out clean. Cool in pans on a wire rack for 10 minutes. Remove from pans and cool completely on wire rack. Wrap and store overnight for easier slicing. Makes 2 loaves (32 servings).

Nutrition Facts per serving: 159 cal., 6 g total fat (1 g sat. fat), 27 mg chol., 89 mg sodium, 24 g carbo., 1 g fiber, 3 g pro.
Daily Values: 11% vit. A, 1% vit. C, 5% calcium, 6% iron.

LOW FAT

Oatmeal 'n' Honey Bread

Long in shape, this crispy-crusted loaf has a tender, moist inside. If there's any leftover, try slicing it up and using it to make French toast.

Prep: 25 minutes **Rise:** 1½ hours
Bake: 30 minutes

  2½ to 3 cups all-purpose flour
   1 pkg. active dry yeast
   1 tsp. salt
   1 cup warm water (120° to 130°)
   ⅔ cup quick-cooking rolled oats
   3 Tbsp. honey
   2 Tbsp. cooking oil
      Yellow cornmeal

1 In a large mixing bowl stir together 1 cup of the flour, the yeast, and salt. In a small bowl stir together the water and rolled oats; let stand 3 minutes. Add to flour mixture along with honey and cooking oil. Beat with an electric mixer on low to medium speed for 30 seconds, scraping sides of bowl constantly. Beat on high speed for 3 minutes. Using a wooden spoon, stir in as much of the remaining flour as you can.

2 Turn the dough out onto a lightly floured surface. Knead in enough remaining flour to make a moderately stiff dough that is smooth and elastic (6 to 8 minutes total). Shape the dough into a ball. Place the dough in a lightly greased bowl, turning once to grease the surface of the dough. Cover and let rise in a warm place until double (about 1 hour).

3 Punch dough down. Turn the dough out onto a lightly floured surface. Cover and let rest for 10 minutes. Meanwhile, lightly grease a baking sheet. Sprinkle baking sheet with cornmeal.

4 Roll dough to a 15×10-inch rectangle. Roll up, starting from a long side. Seal well. Pinch ends and pull slightly to taper. Place loaf, seam side down, on prepared baking sheet. Cover and let rise until nearly double (30 to 45 minutes).

5 Preheat oven to 375°. Bake for 30 to 35 minutes or until bread sounds hollow when tapped. Immediately remove bread from baking sheet and cool on a wire rack. Makes 1 loaf (16 servings).

Nutrition Facts per serving: 111 cal., 2 g total fat (0 g sat. fat), 0 mg chol., 147 mg sodium, 20 g carbo., 1 g fiber, 3 g pro.
Daily Values: 1% calcium, 6% iron.

Spiced Pears and Camembert

Forelle and Seckel pears are two varieties that are perfect for this dessert. Choose 4-ounce pears, and leave the stems and cores intact so they'll hold their shape during poaching. Don't forget to serve some of the spicy liquid with each pear. (See the photograph on page 317.)

Prep: 20 minutes **Cook:** 6 minutes
Cool: 30 minutes

   3 cups dry white wine
   1 cup sugar
   ¼ cup coarsely chopped
      crystallized ginger
  12 inches stick cinnamon, broken
   8 whole allspice
   8 whole cloves
   8 cardamom pods, slightly crushed
   8 small firm ripe pears, peeled
      Cranberries (optional)
   1 8-oz. round Camembert cheese,
      cut into wedges

1 In a saucepan large enough to hold the pears, combine the wine, sugar, ginger, cinnamon, allspice, cloves, and cardamom. Cook, uncovered,* over medium heat to a gentle boil. Add the peeled pears. Return liquid just to boiling; reduce heat. Simmer, uncovered,* for 6 to 7 minutes or until pears are just fork-tender. Let the pears cool in the poaching liquid, turning, if necessary, to be sure all sides are moistened.

2 Using a slotted spoon, transfer pears to a serving dish. Strain poaching liquid. Serve the pears slightly warm, at room temperature, or chilled, with the poaching liquid spooned over. If desired, surround the serving dish with cranberries. Accompany with cheese wedges. Makes 8 servings.

*Note: Be sure to cook the wine mixture uncovered to avoid the wine's vapors bursting into flames.

Nutrition Facts per serving: 309 cal., 7 g total fat (4 g sat. fat), 20 mg chol., 245 mg sodium, 43 g carbo., 2 g fiber, 6 g pro.
Daily Values: 7% vit. A, 6% vit. C, 13% calcium, 4% iron.

Fresh Spice

The flavors in spices come from their volatile oils, which deteriorate in time. Old spices may give baked goods a bitter taste. Buy spices in small amounts and throw out any spices that have been in your pantry more than 6 months.

Pumpkin-Pear Trifle

Ripe, juicy pears; soft, silky custard with a hint of nutmeg; and sturdy squares of spicy pumpkin bread all combine to make an English-style trifle that takes the cake at any winter gathering.

Prep: 55 minutes **Chill:** 4 to 6 hours

- 1   14-oz. pkg. pumpkin quick-bread mix or 1 loaf purchased pumpkin bread, cut into 1-inch cubes (8 cups)
- 1   recipe Custard Sauce
- 1¼ cups sweet white wine, such as Sauternes or Riesling
- ⅓   cup sugar
- 1½ tsp. finely shredded lemon peel
- ½   tsp. ground nutmeg
- ¼   tsp. ground cinnamon
- 4   large ripe pears, peeled, cored, and cut into ½-inch slices
  Lemon peel curls (optional)

1 Prepare and cool pumpkin bread, if using a mix. Prepare and chill Custard Sauce.

2 In a large skillet stir together wine, sugar, lemon peel, nutmeg, and cinnamon. Cook and stir over low heat until sugar is dissolved. Bring mixture to boiling; reduce heat. Simmer, uncovered, about 10 minutes or until reduced by half. Carefully add pear slices into wine mixture, stirring to coat. Bring to boiling; reduce heat. Simmer, covered, for 3 to 5 minutes

or until pears are tender, stirring occasionally. Using a slotted spoon, remove pears from skillet; discard any cooking liquid. Cover and chill pears up to 24 hours.

3 In a 2-quart serving bowl alternate layers of half the pumpkin bread cubes, Custard Sauce, and pear slices. Repeat with remaining bread, sauce, and pears. Cover and chill for 4 to 6 hours. If desired, garnish with lemon peel curls. Makes 10 to 12 servings.

Custard Sauce

In a heavy medium saucepan stir together ¾ cup sugar, ¼ cup all-purpose flour, ¼ teaspoon salt, and ¼ teaspoon ground nutmeg. Gradually stir in 2¾ cups milk, 4 beaten egg yolks, and 1 teaspoon vanilla. Cook and stir custard mixture over medium heat until thickened and bubbly. Cook and stir for 2 minutes more. Remove from heat. Cover surface with plastic wrap. Chill in the refrigerator for 4 to 6 hours.

Nutrition Facts per serving: 446 cal., 11 g total fat (2 g sat. fat), 133 mg chol., 334 mg sodium, 72 g carbo., 3 g fiber, 8 g pro.
Daily Values: 22% vit. A, 6% vit. C, 10% calcium, 10% iron.

Pumpkin Bread Pudding

When the winter winds are whipping, cozy in for a bowl of this comforting dessert that's replete with moist chunks of roasted pumpkin and drizzled with warm Caramel Sauce.

Prep: 20 minutes **Roast:** 30 minutes
Bake: 50 minutes

- 1   1- to 1¼- lb. pumpkin
- 3¼ cups milk
- 1½ cups dairy eggnog
- 5   eggs, beaten
- ¾   cup packed brown sugar
- 2   tsp. vanilla
- 1½ tsp. pumpkin pie spice
- ⅓   cup golden raisins
- 8   to 10 oz. French bread, cut into 1-inch cubes (8 cups)
- 1   recipe Caramel Sauce

1 Preheat oven to 350°. Cut pumpkin into quarters; remove seeds. Discard seeds or save for roasting. Place pumpkin, cut-side down, on a lightly greased baking pan. Roast, uncovered, about 30 minutes or until almost tender. Remove peel; cut baked pumpkin into ¾-inch pieces.

2 In a large bowl stir together milk, eggnog, eggs, brown sugar, vanilla, and pumpkin pie spice. Sprinkle raisins on bottom of an ungreased 3-quart rectangular baking dish. Spread bread cubes over raisins. Pour egg mixture evenly over bread. Carefully stir in cubed pumpkin.

3 Bake about 50 minutes or until the pudding is puffy and a knife inserted near the center comes out clean. Cool pudding slightly (pudding will fall in center). Drizzle with warm Caramel Sauce. Makes 12 servings.

Caramel Sauce

In a heavy saucepan melt 10 vanilla caramel squares with ½ cup whipping cream over low heat, stirring constantly until smooth. Stir in ¼ teaspoon anise seed, crushed, and, if desired, ¼ teaspoon rum flavoring. Cool slightly before serving.

Nutrition Facts per serving: 289 cal., 11 g total fat (4 g sat. fat), 107 mg chol., 222 mg sodium, 40 g carbo., 1 g fiber, 8 g pro.
Daily Values: 81% vit. A, 3% vit. C, 13% calcium, 1% iron.

LOW FAT

Winter Fruit Shortcake

Save that leftover eggnog from your holiday get-together to spice up some of your favorite holiday dessert recipes. In this creamy shortcake topping, we replaced the traditional milk with thick and creamy eggnog.

Prep: 10 minutes **Chill:** 2 hours

- ½ of an 8-oz. pkg. cream cheese, softened
- 1 Tbsp. powdered sugar
- ⅓ cup dairy eggnog
- 2 medium bananas, cut into bite-size chunks
- 1 medium apple, cut into bite-size chunks
- 1 cup seedless green grapes, halved
- 1 10¾-oz. reduced-calorie or regular frozen loaf pound cake
- Ground nutmeg

1 In a small mixing bowl beat cream cheese and sugar with an electric mixer on medium speed until fluffy. Gradually beat in eggnog until just combined. Cover and chill for 2 hours or until ready to serve.

2 In a medium bowl toss together bananas, apples, and grapes; set aside. To serve, cut cake into nine ¾-inch slices. Place a cake slice in each of nine shallow dessert bowls. Top each with some of the fruit mixture. Spoon eggnog mixture over fruit. Sprinkle with ground nutmeg. Makes 9 servings.

Nutrition Facts per serving: 187 cal., 5 g total fat (3 g sat. fat), 14 mg chol., 171 mg sodium, 34 g carbo., 1 g fiber, 3 g pro.
Daily Values: 8% vit. A, 7% vit. C, 5% calcium, 5% iron.

Panna Cotta with Cranberry Port Sauce

If you don't have eight molds of the same kind, use an assortment of small molds or divide the creamy mixture into small teacups, demitasse cups, or small bowls.

Prep: 25 minutes **Chill:** 4 hours

- Nonstick cooking spray
- 2 Tbsp. cold water
- 2 Tbsp. orange liqueur or orange juice
- 1 envelope unflavored gelatin
- 1 8-oz. carton mascarpone cheese or one 8-oz. pkg. cream cheese, softened
- 1 8-oz. carton dairy sour cream
- ⅔ cup sugar
- 1 tsp. vanilla
- 1 cup whipping cream
- 1¾ cups cranberries
- ½ cup port wine or orange juice
- ⅓ cup sugar
- 2 tsp. finely shredded orange peel
- Miniature scented geranium sprigs (optional)

1 Lightly coat eight ½-cup molds or small cups with nonstick cooking spray; set aside. For the panna cotta, in a microwave-safe glass cup or measure combine water and orange liqueur or juice. Sprinkle gelatin over the top. Let stand 1 minute or until gelatin is softened. Micro-cook on 100% power (high) for 30 to 45 seconds or until gelatin is dissolved.*

2 In a medium mixing bowl beat mascarpone or cream cheese with an electric mixer on medium speed until light and fluffy. Beat in the sour cream, ⅔ cup sugar, gelatin mixture, and vanilla on low speed until smooth. Stir in whipping cream. Pour into prepared molds or cups. Cover and

chill in the refrigerator until firm, at least 4 hours or up to 2 days.

3 For sauce, in a small saucepan combine the cranberries, port, and the ⅓ cup sugar. Bring to boiling, stirring to dissolve sugar; reduce heat. Simmer, uncovered, stirring often, about 5 minutes or until berries have popped and sauce is slightly thickened. Stir in orange peel. Let cool slightly. Serve at room temperature or chill up to 2 days. (Stir in additional orange juice if sauce has thickened too much.)

4 To remove panna cotta from molds, wrap a warm cloth around mold just to loosen. Or, if using cups, do not unmold. Transfer sauce to a serving bowl; pass with panna cotta. If desired, add geranium sprigs. Serves 8.

*Note: Or, omit the microwave. In a small saucepan combine gelatin with water and orange liqueur; let stand 5 minutes. Heat over low heat until gelatin is dissolved, stirring constantly.

Nutrition Facts per serving: 426 cal., 30 g total fat (18 g sat. fat), 90 mg chol., 51 mg sodium, 34 g carbo., 1 g fiber, 8 g pro.
Daily Values: 20% vit. A, 7% vit. C, 6% calcium, 3% iron.

Eggnog Pecan Caramel Custard

Fluted aluminum molds give each custard a pretty edge. However, simple custard cups work well, too.

Prep: 20 minutes **Bake:** 45 minutes
Chill: 4 hours

- ⅔ cup sugar
- 1¾ cups dairy eggnog
- 3 eggs, beaten
- ⅛ tsp. pumpkin pie spice
- ¼ cup chopped toasted pecans

1 Preheat oven to 325°. In a heavy 8-inch skillet cook half of the sugar over medium-high heat until sugar begins to melt, gently shaking skillet occasionally to heat sugar evenly. Do not stir. Reduce heat to low. Cook for 2 minutes or until sugar is melted and golden brown, stirring often with a wooden spoon. Immediately and carefully pour caramelized sugar syrup into five 6-ounce custard cups or fluted aluminum molds. Tilt the cups to coat bottoms evenly.

2 In a medium mixing bowl combine eggnog, eggs, remaining sugar, and pumpkin pie spice. Using a rotary beater or wire whisk, beat until combined but not foamy.

3 Divide egg mixture evenly among custard cups. Arrange the syrup-filled custard cups in a 13×9×2-inch baking pan. Carefully transfer pan with cups to oven rack. Pour boiling water into the baking pan around the cups to a depth of 1 inch. Bake for 45 to 55 minutes or until a knife inserted near centers comes out clean. Carefully remove the baked custards from the baking pan. Cool slightly on a wire rack. Cover and chill for 4 hours.

4 To unmold the custards, loosen edges gently with a knife. Invert a dessert plate over each custard. Carefully turn custard cup and plate over together. Sprinkle toasted pecans on top of each custard. Makes 5 servings.

Nutrition Facts per serving: 297 cal., 13 g total fat (1 g sat. fat), 128 mg chol., 94 mg sodium, 39 g carbo., 0 g fiber, 6 g pro.
Daily Values: 9% vit. A, 6% calcium, 3% iron.

30 MINUTE

Gingery Apple Sundaes

True to decadent sundaes served in ice cream parlors—from the bottom up, you'll find sweet ginger cookie crumbles, mellow cinnamon ice cream, warm spicy apples, bellows of whipped cream, and crunchy candied ginger.

Start to finish: 20 minutes

- 2 medium cooking apples, peeled, cored, and sliced
- 1 tsp. grated fresh ginger or
  ¼ tsp. ground ginger
- 2 Tbsp. butter or margarine
- 3 Tbsp. packed brown sugar
- ⅓ cup apple juice
- ½ tsp. cornstarch
- ¼ cup whipping cream
- 2 tsp. granulated sugar
- 4 3-inch purchased ginger or molasses cookies
- 2 cups cinnamon ice cream or vanilla ice cream
- 2 tsp. finely chopped candied ginger

1 In a large skillet cook apples and fresh or ground ginger in butter, uncovered, about 5 minutes or until apples are just tender. Stir in brown sugar. Combine apple juice and cornstarch; add to skillet. Cook and stir until thickened and bubbly. Cook and stir for 2 minutes more.

2 Meanwhile, in a small mixing bowl beat whipping cream and 2 teaspoons granulated sugar to soft peaks (tips curl). Set aside.

3 Crumble a ginger or molasses cookie into the bottom of each of four dessert dishes. Add a scoop of ice cream. Divide warm apple mixture

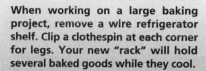

CLEVER COOK

Rack and Roll

When working on a large baking project, remove a wire refrigerator shelf. Clip a clothespin at each corner for legs. Your new "rack" will hold several baked goods while they cool.

C. E. Thomas
Jonesboro, Alabama

among the sundaes. Top with whipped cream and sprinkle with candied ginger. Makes 4 servings.

Nutrition Facts per serving: 446 cal., 26 g total fat (16 g sat. fat), 90 mg chol., 194 mg sodium, 52 g carbo., 2 g fiber, 4 g pro.
Daily Values: 27% vit. A, 5% vit. C, 12% calcium, 4% iron.

LOW FAT

Chilly Peach Sundaes

Prep: 5 minutes **Stand:** 30 minutes

- 1 16-oz. pkg. frozen unsweetened peach slices
- ½ cup milk
- ⅓ cup amaretto-flavored liquid non-dairy creamer
- 3 Tbsp. sugar
- ½ cup granola

1 Let peaches stand at room temperature 30 minutes. Do not drain. In a food processor or blender combine peaches, milk, creamer, and sugar. Cover and process until smooth and slushy. Spoon mixture into dessert dishes. Sprinkle with granola. Serve immediately. Makes 6 to 8 servings.

Nutrition Facts per serving: 128 cal., 4 g total fat (1 g sat. fat), 2 mg chol., 1 mg sodium, 21 g carbo., 2 g fiber, 2 g pro.
Daily Values: 5% vit. A, 9% vit. C, 4% calcium, 3% iron.

Apricot-Pistachio Pound Cake

Simplify the task of snipping the dried apricots by coating the scissor blades with nonstick cooking spray so that the fruit doesn't stick to them.

Prep: 45 minutes **Bake:** 40 minutes
Cool: 1 hour

- 1¼ cups chopped pistachio nuts
- 1¼ cups snipped dried apricots (one 7-oz. pkg.)
- 2½ cups all-purpose flour
- ½ tsp. salt
- ½ tsp. baking powder
- ½ tsp. ground ginger
- ¼ tsp. baking soda
- 1 cup butter, softened
- 2 cups sugar
- 6 eggs
- ¼ cup dairy sour cream
- ¼ cup apricot nectar or apricot brandy
- 2 tsp. vanilla extract
- ¼ cup apricot jam or preserves
- 1 Tbsp. apricot nectar or apricot brandy
  Pistachio nuts (optional)
  Fresh apricot halves (optional)
  Glacé apricots (optional)

1 Preheat oven to 325°. Grease and lightly flour one 10-inch square tube pan or two 8×8×2-inch square baking pans. In a medium bowl toss the 1¼ cups nuts and dried apricots with ¼ cup of the flour. Set aside. In a bowl combine the remaining flour, salt, baking powder, ginger, and baking soda.

2 In a large mixing bowl beat the butter with an electric mixer on medium to high speed for 30 seconds. Gradually add sugar, beating until fluffy (this should take about 10 minutes). Beat in the eggs, one at a time, beating about 1 minute after each addition. With mixer on low speed, beat in sour cream, the ¼ cup nectar or brandy, and the vanilla. Add the flour mixture, beating just until blended. Stir in nut mixture by hand.

3 Pour batter into prepared tube pan or divide batter between the square pans, smoothing the tops. Bake 50 to 55 minutes for tube pan or 40 to 45 minutes for square pans or until a wooden toothpick inserted near the center comes out clean. Let cool in pan(s) on a wire rack for 10 minutes. Remove from pan(s) and cool completely on a wire rack.

4 For glaze, snip any large fruit pieces in jam. In a small saucepan or microwave-safe bowl combine jam and the 1 tablespoon nectar or brandy. Heat until melted or micro-cook on on 100% power (high) for 20 to 40 seconds or until melted.

5 Brush warm glaze over top of cake(s). Let stand until firm. If desired, garnish cake with pistachio nuts, fresh apricot halves, and glacé apricots. Makes 24 servings.

To Make Ahead:

Prepare and glaze cake(s) as directed. Cover and store at room temperature for up to 2 days. Or, prepare, bake, and cool cake(s). Place the unglazed cake(s) in a freezer container or bag(s) and freeze up to 2 weeks. Before serving, thaw cake(s) at room temperature. Glaze before serving.

Nutrition Facts per serving: 266 cal., 13 g total fat (6 g sat. fat), 76 mg chol., 172 mg sodium, 34 g carbo., 2 g fiber, 5 g pro.
Daily Values: 16% vit. A, 1% vit. C, 3% calcium, 8% iron.

PRIZE WINNER

Apple Bistro Tart

Debbie Vanni
Libertyville, Illinois
$400—Easy Desserts

Prep: 30 minutes **Bake:** 20 minutes

- ½ of a 15-oz. pkg. folded refrigerated unbaked piecrust (1 crust)
- 1 Tbsp. granulated sugar
- 1 tsp. ground cinnamon
- 1 tsp. finely shredded lemon peel
- 2 medium tart green apples, peeled, cored, and cut into ½-inch-thick slices
- ½ cup caramel apple dip
- ½ cup chopped pecans
- ¼ cup apple jelly
  Powdered sugar

1 Preheat oven to 425°. Let the piecrust stand according to package directions. In a bowl combine granulated sugar, cinnamon, and lemon peel. Add apple slices, tossing to coat.

2 Place unfolded piecrust on a large baking sheet. Spread caramel apple dip over crust to within 2 inches of edges. Place apple mixture over caramel. Sprinkle with nuts. Fold edges of crust 2 inches up and over apples, folding edges as necessary.

3 Bake 20 minutes or until crust is golden brown and apples are just tender. In a small saucepan melt apple jelly over low heat. Brush melted jelly over entire tart and edges. Sprinkle with powdered sugar. Serve warm. Makes 8 servings.

Nutrition Facts per serving: 273 cal., 12 g total fat (3 g sat. fat), 5 mg chol., 174 mg sodium, 41 g carbo., 2 g fiber, 2 g pro.
Daily Values: 1% vit. A, 4% vit. C, 2% calcium, 2% iron.

Chunky Mincemeat Pie

This fruity, meatless dessert pie is a tasty example of holiday eating at its best. Breaking tradition of round pie, you can bake it in one or two ovals.

Prep: 1 hour **Bake:** 20 minutes

> 1 medium orange
> 3 medium tart cooking apples, peeled, cored, and coarsely chopped
> ⅔ cup granulated sugar
> ½ cup golden raisins
> ½ cup dried cranberries
> ½ cup lemon- or orange-flavored pitted prunes, snipped
> ½ cup snipped dried apples
> ¾ cup apple cider or orange juice
> 1 tsp. finely shredded lemon peel
> 2 Tbsp. lemon juice
> 2 tsp. apple pie spice
> ¾ cup chopped walnuts
> 1 recipe Double-Crust Pastry
> 2 Tbsp. butter
> 1 Tbsp. half-and-half, light cream, or milk
> 1 Tbsp. granulated sugar
> 1 tsp. finely shredded orange peel (optional)
>   Crème fraîche or whipped cream (optional)

1 Cut up orange, removing any seeds, and place unpeeled orange pieces in the bowl of a food processor. Cover and process until chopped.

2 In a large saucepan combine the chopped unpeeled orange, fresh apples, ⅔ cup granulated sugar, raisins, cranberries, prunes, dried apples, cider or orange juice, lemon peel, lemon juice, and apple pie spice. Bring to boiling; reduce heat. Simmer, uncovered, for 10 to 15 minutes or until slightly thickened, stirring occasionally. Remove from heat; cool. Stir in nuts; set aside.*

3 Preheat oven to 425°. Grease two baking sheets or one very large baking sheet; set aside. On a lightly floured surface, roll each half of the pastry to a 12×10-inch oval. Or, do not halve dough and roll the entire portion of pastry to an 18×12-inch oval. Wrap pastry around rolling pin. Transfer to prepared baking sheet(s). Spoon half of the filling into the center of each small oval or all of the filling into the center of large oval, spreading to within 2 inches of the edges. Dot filling with butter. Fold edges of pastry up and over the filling, leaving filling in center exposed, pleating pastry as necessary. Brush folded edges of tart with half-and-half; sprinkle with 1 tablespoon sugar and, if desired, 1 teaspoon orange peel.

4 Bake one sheet at a time for 20 to 25 minutes or until pastry is golden brown and filling is bubbly. Cool on a wire rack. If desired, serve with crème fraîche. Makes 16 servings.

*Note: Mincemeat can be prepared up to 2 days ahead, omitting the nuts. Cover and refrigerate. Stir in nuts before using mincemeat.

Double-Crust Pastry

In a large bowl combine 2 cups all-purpose flour and ½ teaspoon salt. Using a pastry blender, cut in ⅔ cup shortening until pieces are pea-size. Sprinkle 1 tablespoon cold water over part of the mixture; gently toss with a fork. Push moistened dough to side of bowl. Repeat, using 5 to 6 more tablespoons cold water, 1 tablespoon at a time, until all of the dough is moistened. Divide dough in half. Form each half into a ball.

TEST KITCHEN TIP
Troubleshooting Pastry

If your pastry didn't turn out perfectly, look for one of the following problems (and its solution, too!):

If your pastry is crumbly and hard to roll:

● Add more water, 1 teaspoon at a time.

● Toss the flour mixture and water together just a little more, or until evenly moistened.

If your pastry is tough:

● Use a pastry blender to cut in the shortening or lard until well mixed and the entire mixture resembles small peas.

● Use less water to moisten the flour mixture.

● Toss the flour mixture and water together only until all of the flour mixture is moistened.

● Use less flour when rolling out your pastry.

If your crust shrinks excessively:

● Mix in the water only until the mixture is evenly moistened.

● Let pastry rest for 5 minutes if it is hard to roll.

● Don't stretch the pastry when transferring it.

If the bottom crust is soggy:

● Use either a dull metal or glass pie plate rather than a shiny metal pan.

● Patch any cracks in the pastry with a scrap of pastry before adding the filling.

● Make sure your oven temperature is accurate. If the temperature is too low, the bottom crust won't bake properly.

Nutrition Facts per serving: 286 cal., 14 g total fat (4 g sat. fat), 4 mg chol., 87 mg sodium, 38 g carbo., 3 g fiber, 3 g pro.
Daily Values: 3% vit. A, 12% vit. C, 3% calcium, 7% iron.

EDITOR'S TIP

Simple Gifts

Sweet holiday treats deserve outstanding packaging. Share a sample in a box that has been wrapped in a striking gift wrap, lid and all. Or, have the kids decorate a box with stickers, buttons, and snippets of lace and ribbon for interest. Be sure to line the box with colored tissue paper, waxed paper, or heavy cellophane before filling it with goodies.

PRIZE WINNER

Spiced Rum Cake

Denise Perez
Bristol, Indiana
$200—Easy Desserts

Prep: 20 minutes **Bake:** 35 minutes

- 1 pkg. 2-layer-size spice cake mix
- 1 cup milk
- ⅓ cup cooking oil
- ¼ cup dairy sour cream
- ¼ cup rum
- 4 eggs
- 1 tsp. pumpkin pie spice
- 1 recipe Rum Glaze
    (see above, right)

1 Preheat oven to 350°. Grease and lightly flour a 10-inch fluted tube pan; set aside. In a large mixing bowl combine cake mix, milk, cooking oil, sour cream, rum, eggs, and pumpkin pie spice. Beat with an electric mixer on low speed until just moistened. Beat on medium speed for 2 minutes, scraping sides of bowl occasionally. Pour batter into prepared pan.

2 Bake for 35 to 40 minutes or until a wooden toothpick inserted near the center comes out clean. Cool in pan on a wire rack for 10 minutes.

Remove cake from pan and cool completely on wire rack. Spoon Rum Glaze over cake. Makes 12 servings.

Rum Glaze

In a small bowl combine 1 cup sifted powdered sugar, 1 teaspoon melted butter, and 1 tablespoon rum. Stir in additional water (1 to 2 teaspoons), one teaspoon at a time, until glaze is a thin consistency.

Nutrition Facts per serving: 317 cal., 12 g total fat (3 g sat. fat), 75 mg chol., 307 mg sodium, 45 g carbo., 0 g fiber, 4 g pro.
Daily Values: 5% vit. A, 12% calcium, 6% iron.

30 MINUTE, LOW FAT

Peppermint Bark

Before sprinkling on the peppermint candies, sift the crushed candies through a fine strainer to remove very fine, dustlike particles.

Start to finish: 25 minutes

- 10 to 12 oz. white baking pieces
- 8 to 10 drops liquid red or green food coloring
- ½ cup crushed striped round peppermint candies or candy canes

1 Line a large baking sheet with foil. In a small saucepan melt the baking pieces over medium-low heat, or place in a microwave-safe bowl and micro-cook on 100% power (high) for 1½ to 2 minutes, stirring every 30 seconds. When baking pieces are nearly melted, remove from heat (or microwave) and stir gently to melt.

2 Spread the melted baking pieces on the prepared baking sheet, smoothing with an offset thin metal spatula until about ¼ inch thick. Add the food coloring, drop by drop, over the melted baking pieces. Use a toothpick to swirl the color to form desired design. Sprinkle with candies, pressing them in lightly with spatula.

3 Place baking sheet in refrigerator about 10 minutes to set the baking pieces. When ready to serve, break into irregular pieces. The bark can be stored, covered, at cool room temperature or in the refrigerator for up to 5 days. Makes about 32 pieces.

Nutrition Facts per piece: 55 cal., 3 g total fat (2 g sat. fat), 2 mg chol., 9 mg sodium, 6 g carbo., 0 g fiber, 1 g pro.
Daily Values: 2% calcium.

LOW FAT

White Chocolate Dessert Mix

Serve this tumbled mixture with after-dinner coffee or package individual bags and give as a holiday sweet gift to friends and family.

Prep: 45 minutes **Stand:** 1 hour

- 2 cups bite-size wheat or rice square cereal or bite-size shredded wheat biscuits or bite-size shredded wheat biscuits with raisin filling
- 2 cups broken graham crackers, graham crackers with cinnamon-sugar topping, or chocolate graham crackers
- 2 cups pretzel sticks

- 2 cups broken rice cakes
- 1 cup tiny marshmallows
- 1 cup raisins or mixed dried fruit bits
- 1 cup whole or slivered almonds or cashews
- 1 lb. white chocolate baking squares or baking bars, chopped
- ⅓ cup whipping cream
- 1 Tbsp. light-color corn syrup
- ½ tsp. almond extract

1 Line a very large baking sheet with waxed or parchment paper; set aside. In a very large bowl mix together the cereal, graham crackers, pretzels, rice cakes, marshmallows, raisins or fruit bits, and nuts; set aside.

2 In a medium saucepan place the white chocolate, whipping cream, and corn syrup. Cook and stir over low heat until nearly melted; remove from heat and stir gently until smooth. Stir in almond extract.

3 Pour warm chocolate mixture over cereal mixture. Using a large spoon, toss until all the cereal mixture is coated. Immediately spread the mixture onto the prepared baking sheet. Let cool about 1 hour or until chocolate is set. Let stand up to 12 hours. Seal in plastic bags for longer storage. Makes 14 to 16 cups.

Nutrition Facts per ¼-cup serving: 105 cal., 5 g total fat (2 g sat. fat), 4 mg chol., 75 mg sodium, 14 g carbo., 1 g fiber, 2 g pro.
Daily Values: 1% vit. A, 1% vit. C, 3% calcium, 6% iron.

Hazelnut Cereal Treats

To firmly and evenly press the mixture into the pan, place a piece of plastic wrap on the surface of the cereal mixture and press down with your hands or the back of a large spoon.

Prep: 15 minutes Stand: 2 hours

- 3 cups crisp rice cereal
- ½ cup snipped pitted dates
- ½ cup chopped hazelnuts (filberts)
- ½ cup packed light brown sugar
- ½ cup light-color corn syrup
- 1 Tbsp. butter
- ½ cup chocolate-hazelnut spread

1 Line an 8×8×2-inch pan with foil. Grease the foil; set aside. In a large bowl combine the cereal, dates, and hazelnuts; set aside.

2 In a small saucepan bring the brown sugar, corn syrup, and butter just to boiling, stirring constantly. Remove from heat and stir in chocolate-hazelnut spread.

3 Pour the brown sugar mixture over the cereal mixture, stirring until coated. Firmly press the mixture into the prepared pan. Let stand at room temperature at least 2 hours or chill several minutes in the refrigerator before cutting into bars. Store tightly covered at cool room temperature or in the refrigerator up to 2 days. These do not freeze well. Makes 16 to 20 bars.

Nutrition Facts per bar: 161 cal., 6 g total fat (1 g sat. fat), 2 mg chol., 83 mg sodium, 28 g carbo., 1 g fiber, 2 g pro.
Daily Values: 3% vit. A, 4% vit. C, 1% calcium, 4% iron.

LOW FAT
Molasses Chews

Gather all family members together to help wrap these individual gingery-molasses candies.

Prep: 25 minutes Chill: 1 hour
Wrap: 45 minutes

- 2 oz. unsweetened chocolate, cut up
- 1 Tbsp. butter
- ¼ cup mild-flavored molasses
- 1 tsp. vanilla
- ½ tsp. ground ginger
- 2 cups sifted powdered sugar

1 In a medium saucepan melt the chocolate and butter over low heat, stirring until smooth. Remove from heat. Stir in molasses, vanilla, and ginger. Gradually add powdered sugar, stirring with a wooden spoon until mixture is stiff. Cover and chill for 1 hour.

2 Divide mixture in fourths. Roll each portion to a 16-inch log (about ½ inch in diameter). Cut each log crosswise into 1-inch pieces. Wrap each piece of candy individually in waxed paper, twisting ends to seal. Makes about 64 pieces of candy.

Nutrition Facts per piece: 22 cal., 1 g total fat (0 g sat. fat), 1 mg chol., 1 mg sodium, 4 g carbo., 0 g fiber, 0 g pro.
Daily Values: 1% iron.

Organize a Cookie Exchange

Imagine starting the day with a plate piled high with gingerbread cookies and ending it with a collection of springerle, chocolate chippers, sugar cutouts, shortbread, and fruit-filled spirals. That's just what happens when you participate in a cookie exchange. A cookie exchange can be a large organized affair with dozens of participants, perhaps held to raise funds for a church or school. Or, you can plan a small gathering with a handful of friends in your home.

The Concept
The concept is simple. Maybe you have a group of friends who want a variety of cookies but don't have a lot of time to spend baking. A small cookie exchange in someone's home can satisfy their cookie wish lists. For an informal cookie exchange, each person brings one or two dozen cookies to share. (For a fund-raiser or larger event, ask participants to supply two to three dozen cookies.) Everyone goes home with the same number of cookies as they brought. The benefit: More varieties to enjoy!

Holding a Fund-Raiser
As with any endeavor, the success of a cookie exchange fund-raiser requires careful planning.
● Plan the Objective. A cookie exchange for a larger group requires more organizing. Consider charging admission or holding a bake sale. Ask everyone to bring an extra dozen cookies to sell.
● Find a Location. You'll need a large room with plenty of tables. Access to a kitchen area is helpful, especially if you plan to serve refreshments.
● Set the Date. Be sure to give plenty of notice. Evenings and weekend afternoons book up quickly between Thanksgiving and Christmas, so for maximum participation, spread the word as early as the first of November. People will want plenty of time to bake their specialties.

● Spread the Word. Create a flier and news release to promote the cookie exchange. Include details about the event such as the date, time, place, and what people need to bring—a few dozen cookies and a container to transport their cookies home, a phone number in case people want recipes or additional directions, and the name of the recipe written on a notecard, for example. Include information on how the proceeds will be used. Send your news release to the local media.
● Enlist Help. Organize a committee of volunteers to carry out necessary responsibilities. You'll need helpers to set up tables, serve refreshments, and clean up.

Exchange Day
The set-up committee should arrive an hour or two before the cookie exchange. This will allow ample time for them to set up and decorate the room. Cover the tables with inexpensive paper tablecloths. Bring plenty of paper plates, aluminum foil or plastic wrap for everyone to wrap their goodies, and paper towels and garbage bags for cleanup. As people arrive with their cookies, place their platters or tins of cookies on the tables, allowing enough room to move from one platter to the next.

Stay on schedule. Start the exchange no more than 15 minutes after the designated time.

When it's time to begin, choose someone from your committee with a good speaking voice to explain the process. Remind everyone they are to take home the same number of cookies they brought. You might want to set a limit on the number of cookies people may take from any one selection (four to six is a good number).

Be sure someone is available throughout the cookie exchange to answer questions and direct any latecomers. After the cookie exchange, the cleanup committee should make sure the room is left as it was found, with all garbage placed in the trash cans.

Black and White Twists

These sophisticated sweets have real eye and mouth appeal. They're easy to make, too. Mix them up and shape them one day; then chill them overnight and bake them the next.

Prep: 45 minutes **Chill:** 2 to 24 hours
Bake: 12 to 15 minutes per batch

1½	cups butter, softened
2½	cups sifted powdered sugar
¼	tsp. salt
1	egg
1	tsp. vanilla
4¼	cups all-purpose flour
2	oz. unsweetened chocolate, melted and cooled
1	Tbsp. milk
1	egg white, slightly beaten
1	cup finely chopped hazelnuts (filberts) or pecans

1 In a large mixing bowl beat the butter with an electric mixer on medium to high speed for 30 seconds. Add the powdered sugar and salt. Beat until combined, scraping sides of bowl occasionally. Beat in the egg and vanilla until combined. Beat in as much of the flour as you can with the mixer. Using a wooden spoon, stir in the remaining flour.

2 Divide dough in half. Add the melted chocolate and milk to half of the dough.* Using your hands, knead dough until well combined.

3 On a lightly floured surface, shape each dough half into a 12-inch-long log. Cut each log into 12 equal pieces. Roll each dough piece into a 12-inch-long rope about ½-inch-thick. Place a chocolate rope and a vanilla rope side by side; gently twist together 8 to 10 times. Press lightly to seal ends and transfer to a cookie sheet. Repeat with the remaining dough. Cover and chill for 2 to 24 hours or until firm.

4 Preheat oven to 350°. Lightly grease a cookie sheet; set aside. Cut each twisted log into 2½-inch-long pieces. Dip one end of each piece into beaten egg white, then into the chopped hazelnuts or pecans. Place the cookies about 2 inches apart on the prepared cookie sheet.

5 Bake for 12 to 15 minutes or until vanilla dough is lightly golden. Transfer cookies to a wire rack; let cool. Makes 48 cookies.

***Note:** If desired, add several drops of food coloring to the vanilla dough half.

To Make Ahead:

Prepare and bake cookies as directed. Place in a freezer container or bag and freeze for up to 1 month. Before serving, thaw for 15 minutes.

Nutrition Facts per cookie: 131 cal., 8 g total fat (4 g sat. fat), 20 mg chol., 26 mg sodium, 14 g carbo., 1 g fiber, 2 g pro.
Daily Values: 5% vit. A, 4% iron.

Marbled Magic Wands

Dub yourself the royal baker and the kids your loyal helpers with these treats. A little kitchen magic—food coloring, a cookie press, and colored sugars and candies—gives them the wow! factor kids love.

Prep: 40 minutes **Bake:** 10 minutes

- 1 **cup butter, softened**
- 1 **cup granulated sugar**
- 1 **tsp. baking powder**
- 1 **egg**
- 2 **tsp. vanilla**
- 3½ **cups all-purpose flour**
  Paste food coloring
- 1½ **cups white baking pieces**
- 1 **Tbsp. butter-flavor or regular shortening**
  Colored sugars or small multicolored decorative candies

1 In a large mixing bowl beat the butter with an electric mixer on medium to high speed for 30 seconds. Add the granulated sugar and baking powder. Beat until combined, scraping sides of bowl occasionally. Beat in the egg and vanilla. Beat in as much of the flour as you can with the mixer. Using a wooden spoon, stir in any remaining flour.

2 Divide dough in half. Tint half of the dough as desired with paste food coloring. Leave the remaining half of dough plain or tint with another color.

3 Preheat oven to 375°. Pack unchilled dough in both colors into a cookie press fitted with a large star plate, keeping the doughs separate by placing them side by side in the press. Force dough through press onto an ungreased cookie sheet to form wands about 5 inches long.

4 Bake about 10 minutes or until edges are firm but not brown. Cool on cookie sheet for 1 minute. Transfer cookies to a wire rack; let cool.

5 In a heavy small saucepan heat and stir white baking pieces and shortening over low heat until melted.

6 Dip an end of each cookie into melted white baking pieces, allowing excess to drip off. Sprinkle with colored sugar or multicolored candies. Place on waxed paper and allow coating to set. Makes about 36 cookies.

To Make Ahead:

Prepare and bake cookies as directed. Do not dip in melted baking pieces. Place cookies in a freezer container or bag and freeze for up to 1 month. Before serving, thaw for 15 minutes. Dip and decorate cookies as directed.

Nutrition Facts per cookie: 153 cal., 8 g total fat (5 g sat. fat), 22 mg chol., 71 mg sodium, 18 g carbo., 0 g fiber, 2 g pro.
Daily Values: 4% vit. A, 1% calcium, 3% iron.

LOW FAT

Snickerdoodle Pinwheels

A whirl of cinnamon is at the center of this crisp cookie inspired by the homey flavor of one of America's favorite native treats.

Prep: 25 minutes **Chill:** 4 hours
Bake: 8 to 10 minutes per batch

- ⅓ cup sugar
- 1 Tbsp. ground cinnamon
- ½ cup butter, softened
- 1 3-oz. pkg. cream cheese, softened
- 1 cup sugar
- ½ tsp. baking powder
- 1 egg
- 1 tsp. vanilla
- 2⅔ cups all-purpose flour
- 1 Tbsp. butter, melted

1 For cinnamon-sugar mixture, in a small bowl combine the ⅓ cup sugar and the cinnamon; set aside.

2 In a large mixing bowl beat the ½ cup butter and the cream cheese with an electric mixer on medium to high speed for 30 seconds. Add the 1 cup sugar and baking powder. Beat until combined, scraping sides of bowl occasionally. Beat in egg and vanilla until combined. Beat in as much of the flour as you can with the mixer. Using a wooden spoon, stir in remaining flour.

3 Divide dough in half. Roll half of dough between two sheets of waxed paper into a 12×8-inch rectangle. Remove top sheet of waxed paper. Brush dough with half of the melted butter. Sprinkle with 2 tablespoons of the cinnamon-sugar mixture.

4 Roll up, starting from one of the short sides, removing waxed paper as you roll. Seal edges. Repeat with remaining dough, butter, and 2 tablespoons of the cinnamon-sugar mixture. Roll each log in remaining cinnamon-sugar mixture. Wrap each log in plastic wrap or waxed paper. Chill in the refrigerator 4 hours or until firm.

5 Preheat oven to 375°. Using a sharp knife, cut dough into ¼-inch-thick slices. Place slices 1 inch apart on an ungreased cookie sheet. Bake for 8 to 10 minutes or until edges are firm. Cool on cookie sheet for 1 minute. Transfer to a wire rack; let cool. Makes about 64 cookies.

Nutrition Facts per cookie: 57 cal., 2 g total fat (1 g sat. fat), 10 mg chol., 26 mg sodium, 8 g carbo., 0 g fiber, 1 g pro.
Daily Values: 2% vit. A, 1% iron.

LOW FAT

Gossamer Spice Cookies

Prep: 35 minutes **Chill:** 1 hour
Bake: 5 to 6 minutes per batch

- ⅓ cup butter
- ⅓ cup molasses
- ¼ cup packed dark brown sugar
- 1⅓ cups all-purpose flour
- ½ tsp. ground ginger
- ½ tsp. apple pie spice
- ¼ tsp. ground cloves
- ¼ tsp. ground cardamom
- ⅛ tsp. ground red pepper

1 In a large mixing bowl beat the butter with an electric mixer on medium speed for 30 seconds. Add molasses and brown sugar. Beat until combined. In a second bowl stir together flour, ginger, apple pie spice, cloves, cardamom, and red pepper.

Add to molasses mixture. Beat until just combined. Divide dough in half; shape each half into a ball. Wrap in plastic wrap and chill for 1 hour.

2 Preheat oven to 375°. On a lightly floured surface, roll one portion of dough to ¹⁄₁₆-inch thickness. Cut with a 2-inch round scalloped cutter. Place on ungreased cookie sheets. Bake 5 to 6 minutes or until edges are browned. Transfer cookies to wire racks; let cool. Repeat with remaining dough. Store cookies in an airtight container for up to 3 days. Makes about 66 cookies.

Nutrition Facts per cookie: 25 cal. 1 g total fat (0 g sat. fat), 1 mg chol., 9 mg sodium, 4 g carbo., 0 g fiber, 0 g pro.
Daily Values: 1% iron.

LOW FAT

Jeweled Cookie Sandwiches

Squish thick jams, preserves, and melted chocolates between tiny cutout cookies for colorful, ornament-looking cookies. For make-ahead convenience, freeze chocolate-filled sandwiches or plain cutouts up to 1 month, but fill with jam or preserves before serving. (See the photograph on page 320.)

Prep: 35 minutes **Chill:** 2 hours
Bake: 7 to 8 minutes per batch, or 5 to 6 minutes per batch

- ½ cup butter, softened
- ¾ cup sugar
- ½ tsp. baking powder
- ¼ tsp. baking soda
- ¼ tsp. salt
- ¼ tsp. ground mace
- 1 egg yolk
- ¼ cup dairy sour cream
- 1 tsp. vanilla
- 2 cups all-purpose flour

About ½ cup jam, preserves, or marmalade, and/or melted white, milk, or semisweet chocolate

1 In a large mixing bowl beat the butter with an electric mixer on medium to high speed for 30 seconds. Add the sugar, baking powder, baking soda, salt, and mace. Beat until combined, scraping bowl. Beat in egg yolk, sour cream, and vanilla. Beat in as much of the flour as you can with the mixer. Stir in remaining flour. Divide dough in half. Cover and chill for 2 hours or until easy to handle.

2 Preheat oven to 375°. Lightly grease a cookie sheet. On a lightly floured surface, roll half of dough at a time to ¼- to ⅛-inch thickness. Cover and chill remaining half of dough. Using a 1- to 2-inch cookie cutter, cut into desired shapes. Place 1 inch apart on prepared cookie sheet. Repeat with second half of dough.

3 Bake for 7 to 8 minutes for 2-inch cookies or 5 to 6 minutes for 1-inch cookies or until edges are firm and bottoms are very lightly browned. Transfer cookies to a wire rack; cool.

4 Frost the bottom surface of half of the cooled cookies with ¼ teaspoon (for 1-inch cookies) of desired filling or ¾ teaspoon (for 2-inch cookies) of desired filling. Place another cookie, top side up, on top of filling. Makes about 40 (1-inch) sandwich cookies or 20 (2-inch) sandwich cookies.

Nutrition Facts per 1-inch cookie sandwich: 72 cal., 3 g total fat (2 g sat. fat), 12 mg chol., 54 mg sodium, 11 g carbo., 0 g fiber, 1 g pro.
Daily Values: 3% vit. A, 1% vit. C, 1% calcium, 2% iron.

EDITOR'S TIP

Get Rolling: Cookie Dough Is a Breeze to Freeze

Having freshly baked holiday cookies ready in a jiffy is a simple task when you've got a batch of homemade dough in the deep freeze. Consider these tips to avoid last-minute cookie-making chaos.

Most cookie doughs can be frozen up to six months. (Bar cookie batters, meringues, and macaroons don't freeze well.)

For cookie cutouts, roll out and cut the dough into shapes; freeze in a single layer. It's important that the cookies be frozen in a single layer before placing in the container or bag to prevent cookies from sticking together. Once frozen, the cutouts can be carefully stacked with waxed paper between each layer, and placed in a sealed container. Do not thaw dough before baking, although you may need to add a minute or two of baking time to recipe instructions.

For pinwheels or other refrigerator cookies that are sliced from rolls, make the dough, shape into rolls as directed in your recipe, wrap tightly in foil, and freeze. Slice and bake as needed. The Better Homes and Gardens® Test Kitchen has discovered these cookies are easier to slice when frozen. So don't bother thawing them before you slice and bake.

For drop cookies, freeze dough in cookie-size mounds to save work later. Place the frozen mounds in a sealed container or freezer bag. When ready to bake, place cookies on cooking sheet, thaw in the refrigerator, then pop them in the oven as directed in your recipe. Bake as few or as many cookies as you want.

Most drop, sliced, bar, and shaped cookies also freeze well after they are baked. Be sure to place them in a sealed container or freezer bag.

For bar cookies, line baking pan with foil, leaving an extra 2 inches of foil at each end. Add batter and bake as directed. Cool in pan. Lift foil to remove entire batch in one piece. Wrap tightly in foil; freeze. Frost and cut bar cookies after thawing.

LOW FAT

Cherry-Coconut Drops

Looking like colorful Christmas lights encased in freshly fallen snow, these moist cookies are as festive and fun to look at as they are to eat.

Prep: 20 minutes
Bake: 12 to 15 minutes per batch

- 1 7-oz. pkg. (2⅔ cups) flaked coconut
- 2 Tbsp. cornstarch
- ½ cup sweetened condensed milk
- 1 tsp. vanilla
- ½ cup chopped red and/or green candied cherries

1 Preheat oven to 325°. Grease and flour a cookie sheet; set aside.

2 In a medium bowl combine coconut and cornstarch. Stir in sweetened condensed milk and vanilla until mixture is combined. Stir in the chopped candied cherries.

3 Drop by small rounded teaspoonfuls about 1 inch apart on the prepared cookie sheet.

4 Bake for 12 to 15 minutes or until lightly browned on bottoms. Cool on cookie sheet for 1 minute. Transfer cookies to a wire rack; let cool. Makes about 24 cookies.

Nutrition Facts per cookie: 71 cal., 3 g total fat (3 g sat. fat), 2 mg chol., 10 mg sodium, 10 g carbo., 1 g fiber, 1 g pro.
Daily Values: 1% calcium, 1% iron.

CASUAL WEEKEND BREAKFAST

Savor a weekend morning when you have time to sit back and enjoy a real breakfast.

- **Banana French Toast (page 26)**

- **Breakfast sausages**

- **Fruit bowl**

- **Coffee and/or Fruit Blast Refresher (page 189)**

The day before:
- Assemble French toast; cover and chill

35 minutes before:
- Bake French toast
- Prepare fruit bowl
- Cook sausages
- Make coffee and/or fruit drink

Just before serving:
- Pour coffee into cups or fruit drink into glasses

BISTRO-STYLE LUNCH

Simple yet elegant, and you don't have to dine out to get this outstanding meal.

- **Salad of fresh arugula or baby spinach, sliced red pears, sliced sweet onions, and hot bacon dressing**

- **Salmon Pan Chowder (page 230)**

- **Ciabatta, focaccia, or other breads**

- **Triple Fruit Pie (page 185)**

The day before:
- Prepare pastry for pie; cover and chill

5 hours before (or up to 8 hours before):
- Assemble and bake pie; cool

1 hour before:
- Prepare chowder
- Make salad (except for dressing); cover and chill

Just before serving:
- Slice bread
- Dress salad
- Ladle chowder into bowls

Between courses:
- Cut pie and place on dessert plates

SPRINGTIME CELEBRATION

Once the fresh spring produce makes its debut at the farmer's market, gather your goods for this spectacular meal.

- **Walnut-Crusted Chicken Breasts (page 56)**

- **Cooked asparagus drizzled with butter and served with lemon wedges**

- **Herb or tomato bread with butter**

- **Rhubarb Surprise Crisp (page 166)**

45 minutes before:
- Make and bake chicken

30 minutes before:
- Prepare crisp; bake while dinner is being served
- Slice bread
- Cook asparagus and drizzle with butter

Between courses:
- Spoon crisp into dessert bowls

BIRTHDAY DINNER

Tried and true, this homespun meal is just right for celebrations for kids of all ages.

- **Salad of mixed greens, thinly sliced cucumbers, thinly sliced onions, thinly sliced oranges, and citrus vinaigrette**

- **French-Style Short Ribs (page 75)**

- **Crusty seed or multigrain bread with butter**

- **Burnt Sugar Candy Bar Cake (page 15)**

The day before:
- Make and bake cake layers; cool, cover, and store
- Prepare Candied Pralines; cover and store

Up to 6 hours before:
- Prepare frosting for cake
- Assemble, frost, and decorate cake

2 hours before:
- Prepare ribs

30 minutes before:
- Assemble salad (except vinaigrette)

Just before serving:
- Slice bread
- Dress salad

Between courses:
- Slice cake

TAILGATE PARTY

Whether at the stadium or in your backyard, this all-star lineup of food will score a victory.

- **Picnic Hot Dog Platter (page 150)**

- **Skillet Roasted Potato Salad (page 144)**

- **Three-Bean Salad (page 143)**

- **Sliced watermelon**

- **Brownies, bars, and/or cookies**

- **Assorted cold beverages**

The day before:
- Make any of the mustards that accompany the Picnic Hot Dog Platter
- Prepare potato salad and bean salad; cover and chill

30 minutes before:
- Prepare grill and cook assorted frankfurters, bratwursts, and sausages
- Slice watermelon

Just before serving:
- Stir salads
- Place frankfurters, bratwursts, and sausages on buns and arrange on a platter or in a basket

*Note: Pack the meats, mustards, salads, watermelon, and beverages on ice if transporting to a stadium location

EAST-MEETS-WEST HANUKKAH

Flavors from around the globe unite in this delectable tapestry of a meal.

- **Moroccan Lamb Roast (page 296)**

- **Mixed roasted vegetables**

- **Latke "Macaroons" (page 290)**

- **Assorted kosher chocolates**

The day before:
- Rub the leg of lamb with spice mixture; cover and chill

2½ hours before:
- Roast the leg of lamb

1 hour before:
- Add vegetables for roasting to lamb; roast
- Prepare and bake Latke "Macaroons"

Just before serving:
- Slice lamb and arrange with roasted vegetables and latkes on a serving platter

SUMMERTIME LUNCH

Take advantage of sunshiny days when kids are home with a lunch they'll request again and again.

- **Taco Turkey Sandwiches (page 180)**

- **Corn chips or tortilla chips**

- **Fresh fruit kabobs including fresh strawberries, peach slices, and pineapple chunks**

- **No-Drip Chocolate Dip (page 215)**

3 weeks before:
- Prepare dip; cover and chill
- Bake cookies; cool, cover, and freeze

1 hour before:
Thaw cookies

30 minutes before:
- Make and bake sandwiches
- Prepare fruit kabobs

Just before serving:
- Reheat dip

BACKYARD PICNIC

Pack this picnic only as far as the backyard—the sandwiches are best when served right away.

- **Chicken and Pesto Focaccia Wedges (page 181)**

- **Cooked corn-on-the-cob with butter**

- **Thinly sliced tomatoes, sprinkled with garlic and fresh basil leaves and drizzled lightly with olive oil**

- **Apricot Shortbread Squares (page 183)**

Up to 3 days before:
- Make and bake shortbread squares; cool, cut, cover, and chill

Up to 1 hour before:
- Prepare tomatoes; cover and let stand at room temperature

30 minutes before:
- Prepare sandwiches
- Cook corn

SIMPLE PASTA SUPPER

Be sure the whole family has time to sit down for this meal—the kids will love it.

- Salad of mixed greens, halved grape or cherry tomatoes, shredded mozzarella cheese, and Italian vinaigrette

- Skillet Pasta Supper (page 205)

- Seed Rolls with Dipping Oils (page 255)

- Upside-Down Chip Cake (page 88)

The day before:
- Prepare desired dipping oil(s); cover and chill

1½ hours before:
- Make and bake cake

1 hour before:
- Make Skillet Pasta Supper
- Prepare salad (except vinaigrette)
- Let dipping oil(s) stand at room temperature

Just before serving:
- Prepare and bake rolls
- Dress salad

Between courses:
- Slice cake

FALL HARVEST DINNER

Autumn days are just right for reminiscing. This traditional-style meal is sure to stir delicious memories.

- Salad of mixed greens, chopped apple, raisins, toasted walnuts, and sweet vinaigrette

- Roasted pork

- Stuffing with Root Vegetables (page 260)

- Cooked tiny carrots

- Quaker Bonnet Biscuits (page 265)

- Dried Apple Cider Pie (page 266)

Up to 8 hours before:
- Prepare and bake pie

2 hours before:
- Prepare and roast a 2- to 3-pound boneless top loin pork roast (single loin); let stand and slice
- Prepare biscuit dough, rise, and shape

1¼ hours before:
- Prepare and bake stuffing

30 minutes before:
- Prepare salad (except for vinaigrette)
- Prepare carrots

Just before serving:
- Bake biscuits
- Arrange pork on a platter
- Transfer stuffing to a serving bowl
- Dress salad

Between courses:
- Cut pie and place on dessert plates

COUNTRY-STYLE CHRISTMAS DINNER

After the carols are sung and the gifts are opened, gather around the table for this treasured collection of recipes.

- **Crimson Cherry-Glazed Holiday Hens (page 295)**

- **Mashed potatoes topped with butter and snipped fresh herbs**

- **Steamed green beans**

- **Pink Grapefruit Stacked Salad (page 292)**

- **Dinner Rolls (page 296)**

- **Chunky Mincemeat Pie (page 305)**

Up to 2 days before:
- Prepare mincemeat; cover and chill

Up to 8 hours before:
- Make and bake pie

2½ hours before:
- Start rolls

1½ hours before:
- Prepare and roast Cornish game hens

1 hour before:
- Make salad
- Prepare mashed potatoes
- Steam green beans
- Bake rolls

Between courses:
- Cut pie, place on dessert plates, and garnish with crème fraîche or whipped cream

HOLIDAY OPEN HOUSE

While the house is adorned with decorations and holiday excitement is in the air, invite a crowd of friends for an evening of good cheer.

- **Fresh Onion Dip (page 142)**

- **Greek Salad Bites (page 259)**

- **Cheese Triangles (page 285)**

- **Prosciutto-Arugula Roll-Ups (page 259)**

- **Chicken Liver and Mushroom Pâté (page 168)**

- **Holiday cookies and candies**

- **Assorted beverages**

Up to 3 days ahead:
- Prepare pâté; cover and chill

The day before:
- Make dip; cover and chill
- Stir together cheese mixture for Greek Salad Bites; cover and chill

Up to 6 hours before:
- Prepare roll-ups; cover and chill

40 minutes before:
- Prepare and bake Cheese Triangles

Just before serving:
- Assemble Greek Salad Bites
- Arrange appetizers, cookies, and candies on platters

Spiced Pears and Camembert (page 300)

Above: Pink Grapefruit Stacked
Salad (page 292)
Right: Mashed Potatoes with
Shitake Gravy (see page 291),
Page 319: Herbed Leek Gratin
(see page 292),

Jeweled Cookie Sandwiches (page 310)

BONUS RECIPE INDEX

New recipes previously unpublished in **Better Homes and Gardens®** *magazine. (Main index follows.)*

30-minute recipes indicated in **COLOR**.
Low-fat and no-fat recipes indicated with a ♥.
Photographs indicated in italics.

MAIN INDEX

30-minute recipes indicated in
COLOR.
Low-fat and no-fat recipes
indicated with a ♥.
Photographs indicated in italics.

A

Almonds
and blood cholesterol, 182
Toasted Almond Pastry, 188
Amazon Bars, 20
Appetizers (see also Dips; Spreads)
Artichoke & Olive Boboli Bites, 35
Blue Cheese-Walnut Bites, 29 ♥
Cheese Triangles, *284, 285* ♥
Chicken Liver and Mushroom
Pâté, 168 ♥
Crab and Vegetable Roll-Ups,
111, *124* ♥
Creamy Goat Cheese Ornaments, 288
Date-Maple Drop Scones, 92 ♥
Fragrant Ginger Cashews, 290
Greek Salad Bites, 259 ♥
Incredible Quesadillas, 105 ♥
Italian-Style Wontons, 259
Pepperoni Biscotti, *284, 285* ♥
Prosciutto-Arugula Roll-Ups, 259 ♥
Salmon Croustades, 258 ♥
Sausage Calzone Bites, 169 ♥
Shrimp and Vegetable Flowers, 288 ♥
Two-Bite Veggie Wraps, 254 ♥
Apples
Apple and Cranberry Maple
Crisp, 154
Apple Bistro Tart, 304
Apple Breakfast Bars, 192
Apple Cake with Caramel Sauce, 248
Apricot-Pecan Stuffing, 262
Caramel-Apple Pudding Cake, 49
Cranberry-Apple Dumplings, *199,* 214
Dried Apple Cider Pie, *1,* 286
Fruit-Filled Oven Pancake, 91 ♥
PB&A Sandwich, 59 ♥
Polenta-Pecan Apple Cobbler, 47
Snappy Apple Brunch Cake, 27
Squash Apple Bread, 299
Taffy Apple Doughnuts, 26, *39*
Tart Apple Mustard, 151 ♥

Apricots
Apricot-Corn Pudding, 178
Apricot Cornucopias, *44,* 45
Apricot-Pecan Stuffing, 262
Apricot-Pistachio Pound Cake, 304
Apricot-Sage Cookies, 272
Apricot Shortbread Squares, 183
Spinach-Apricot Salad, 218
Strawberry and Apricot Shake, 213
Triple Fruit Pie, 185
Artichokes
Artichoke & Olive Boboli Bites, 35
Chicken and Artichoke Pizza, 222 ♥
Italian Bean and Artichoke Salad, 98
Kalamata Artichokes, 53, *78*
Asparagus
Asparagus Quiche, 67
**Asparagus with Fresh
Mozzarella, 97**
Tossed Crisp Vegetable Salad, 96
**Avocado Dip, Toasted Cumin-
Lime, 289** ♥
Avocado Rings with Radish
"Fireworks," 96, *118*

B

Baked goods, cooling rack for, 303
Bananas
Banana and Caramel Cocoa, 24 ♥
Banana French Toast, 26
Bananas Foster Crème Brûlée, 46
Bananas Foster Oatmeal, 193 ♥
Banana Split Ice Cream Tart, 154
Go-Bananas Caramel Shake, 133
Beans (see also Beans, green)
Beans and Hot Ham Dressing, 293
Black Bean and Corn Soup, 227 ♥
**Lamb Chops and Lima Beans,
103, *119***
Navy Beans and Pork, 230, *239*
Spiced Pot Roast with Garbanzo
Beans, 60
Summer Herbed Beans, 173
Three-Bean Salad, 143, *160*
Two-Bean Salad, 173
White Bean and Cumin Chili, 54, *78*
Beans, green
Italian Bean and Artichoke Salad, 98
Minted French Green Beans, 97 ♥

Summer Herbed Beans, 173
Two-Bean Salad, 173
Beaujolais Sauce, 85 ♥
Beef (see also Beef, ground)
Dilled Pot Roast, 33
Easy Pot Roast, *201,* 210
French-Style Short Ribs, *75*
Jamaican Jerk Beef Roast, 33
Mustard-Coated Beef
Tenderloin, 294
Persian-Style Stew, 228
Polenta Beef Stew, 36, *37*
Spiced Pot Roast with Garbanzo
Beans, 60
steak grades, 209
Steak Salad with Cilantro Oil, 138
Top Sirloin with Onions and
Carrots, *203,* 209 ♥
Beef, ground
Italian Wedding Soup, 228, *244* ♥
Meat Loaf Supper Salad, 210
Thai Peanut Meatballs, 34
Beets
Beet Biscuits, 169
Beet Borscht, 225, *238* ♥
Orange-Beet Dip, 289 ♥
Red Flannel Corned Beef, 57, *82*
Belgian Endives, Stuffed, 290
Betties, facts about, 47
**Beverages (see also Cocoa, hot;
Shakes)**
Chocolate Chai, 24
Fruit Blast Refresher, 189 ♥
Fizzy Mint Chocolate Soda,
122, 133
Fuzzy Kiwi Lemonade, 110 ♥
glasses, frosty, 133
Hot Gingered Cider, 23 ♥
iced tea, tips for making, 152
Kiwi Ice Cubes, 110
mugs, warming, 23
Mulled Raspberry Tea, 23 ♥
Piña Colada Plus, 195 ♥
Sangria for Kids, 50 ♥
Super Mango Smoothie, 131 ♥
Sweet Zinfandel Granita, 110 ♥
Biscotti, Chocolate-Dipped Orange,
204, 216
Biscotti, Pepperoni, *284, 285* ♥

EMERGENCY SUBSTITUTIONS

IF YOU DON'T HAVE:	SUBSTITUTE:
1 teaspoon baking powder	½ teaspoon cream of tartar plus ¼ teaspoon baking soda
1 tablespoon cornstarch (for thickening)	2 tablespoons all-purpose flour
1 package active dry yeast	1 cake compressed yeast
1 cup buttermilk	1 tablespoon lemon juice or vinegar plus enough milk to make 1 cup (let stand 5 minutes before using); or 1 cup plain yogurt
1 cup whole milk	½ cup evaporated milk plus ½ cup water; or 1 cup water plus ⅓ cup nonfat dry milk powder
1 cup light cream	1 tablespoon melted butter or margarine plus enough whole milk to make 1 cup
1 cup dairy sour cream	1 cup plain yogurt
1 whole egg	2 egg whites, 2 egg yolks, or 3 tablespoons frozen egg product, thawed
1 cup margarine	1 cup butter; or 1 cup shortening plus ¼ teaspoon salt, if desired
1 ounce semisweet chocolate	3 tablespoons semisweet chocolate pieces; or 1 ounce unsweetened chocolate plus 1 tablespoon granulated sugar
1 ounce unsweetened chocolate	3 tablespoons unsweetened cocoa powder plus 1 tablespoon cooking oil or shortening, melted
1 cup corn syrup	1 cup granulated sugar plus ¼ cup liquid
1 cup honey	1¼ cups granulated sugar plus ¼ cup liquid
1 cup molasses	1 cup honey
1 cup granulated sugar	1 cup packed brown sugar or 2 cups sifted powdered sugar
1 cup beef broth or chicken broth	1 teaspoon or 1 cube instant beef or chicken bouillon plus 1 cup hot water
2 cups tomato sauce	¾ cup tomato paste plus 1 cup water
1 cup tomato juice	½ cup tomato sauce plus ½ cup water
¼ cup fine dry bread crumbs	¾ cup soft bread crumbs, ¼ cup cracker crumbs, or ¼ cup cornflake crumbs
1 small onion, chopped (⅓ cup)	1 teaspoon onion powder or 1 tablespoon dried minced onion
1 clove garlic	½ teaspoon bottled minced garlic or ⅛ teaspoon garlic powder
1 teaspoon lemon juice	½ teaspoon vinegar
1 teaspoon poultry seasoning	¾ teaspoon dried sage, crushed, plus ¼ teaspoon dried thyme or marjoram, crushed
1 teaspoon dry mustard (in cooked mixtures)	1 tablespoon prepared mustard
1 tablespoon snipped fresh herb	½ to 1 teaspoon dried herb, crushed
1 teaspoon dried herb	½ teaspoon ground herb
1 teaspoon grated fresh ginger	¼ teaspoon ground ginger
1 teaspoon apple pie spice	½ teaspoon ground cinnamon plus ¼ teaspoon ground nutmeg, ⅛ teaspoon ground allspice, and dash ground cloves or ginger
1 teaspoon pumpkin pie spice	½ teaspoon ground cinnamon plus ¼ teaspoon ground ginger, ¼ teaspoon ground allspice, and ⅛ teaspoon ground nutmeg

Better Homes and Gardens